PACIFIC NORTHWEST CAMPING DESTINATIONS

A Guide to Great RV and Car Camping Destinations in Oregon, Washington, and British Columbia

MIKE *and* TERRI CHURCH

ROLLING HOMES PRESS

Published by
Rolling Homes Press
161 Rainbow Dr., #6157
Livingston, TX 77399-1061

www.rollinghomes.com

Printed in the United States of America
First Printing 2006

Publisher's Cataloging in Publication

Church, Mike, 1951-
Pacific Northwest Camping Destinations : a guide to great RV and car camping destinations in Oregon, Washington, and British Columbia / Mike and Terri Church
p.cm.
Includes index.
Library of Congress Control Number: 2006903053
ISBN 0-97494-713-X

1. Camping–Northwest, Pacific–Guidebooks. 2. Recreational vehicle living–Northwest, Pacific–Guidebooks. 3. Camp sites, facilities, etc–Northwest, Pacific–Guidebooks. 4. Northwest, Pacific–Guidebooks. I. Church, Terri. II. Title.

GV191.42.N75C48 2006
796.54'09795–dc21   2006 903053

This book is dedicated to the next generation of Northwest campers -

Giovanni, Chiyo, Sophie, Emily, Miye, Ellen, Perry, Matt,
Ben, Jace, Natalya, Kelsey, Julie,
Jeremy, Tiffany, and Jon.

Warning, Disclosure, and Communication With The Authors and Publishers

Half the fun of travel is the unexpected, and self-guided camping travel can produce much in the way of unexpected pleasures, and also complications and problems. This book is designed to increase the pleasures of Pacific Northwest camping and reduce the number of unexpected problems you may encounter. You can help ensure a smooth trip by doing additional advance research, planning ahead, and exercising caution when appropriate. There can be no guarantee that your trip will be trouble free.

Although the authors and publisher have done their best to ensure that the information presented in this book was correct at the time of publication they do not assume and hereby disclaim any liability to any party for any loss or damage caused by errors, omissions, or any other cause.

In a book like this it is inevitable that there will be omissions or mistakes, especially as things do change over time. If you find inaccuracies we would like to hear about them so that they can be corrected in future editions. We would also like to hear about your enjoyable experiences. If you come upon an outstanding campground or destination please let us know, those kinds of things may also find their way to future versions of the guide or to our internet site. You can reach us by mail at:

Rolling Homes Press
161 Rainbow Dr., #6157
Livingston, TX 77399-1061

You can also communicate with us by sending an email through our web site at:

www.rollinghomes.com

Other Books by Mike and Terri Church
and
Rolling Homes Press

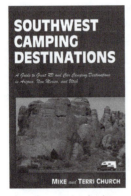
Southwest Camping
Destinations

Traveler's Guide To
Mexican Camping

Traveler's Guide To
Camping Mexico's Baja

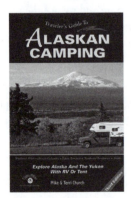
Traveler's Guide To
Alaskan Camping

Traveler's Guide To
European Camping

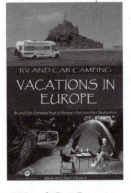
RV and Car Camping
Vacations in Europe

A brief summary of the above books is provided on pages 414 and 415

www.rollinghomes.com Rollinghomes.com has updated information for each of our books which comes from information submitted by others and also from our travels between editions. This information is updated until we begin the process of researching and writing a new edition. Once we start the research process there is just no time to update the website and the new information goes in the next edition. Just go to our Website at www.rollinghomes.com and click on the *Book Updates Online* button to review updates.

TABLE OF CONTENTS

CHAPTER 5
WASHINGTON 183

CHAPTER 6

8

Preface

Pacific Northwest Camping Destinations is the first book in our new Camping Destinations Series. Even as this book goes to press we are hard at work on another titled *Southwest Camping Destinations*. The new series will join our original Traveler's Guide Series that is made up of five books: *Traveler's Guide to European Camping, Traveler's Guide to Mexican Camping, Traveler's Guide to Alaskan Camping, Traveler's Guide to Camping Mexico's Baja*.

The new series is designed for both RV and car camping travelers in the Continental U.S. and adjoining Canada and Mexico. These books are travel guides aimed at a large part of the traveling public that has been virtually ignored by traditional travel book publishers – camping travelers. There are lots of travel guides available, but very few include the information that the camping traveler needs for a fun-filled and comfortable trip.

We have not attempted to include all of the campgrounds in the Pacific Northwest in this book, the large catalog-style guides take care of that. Instead, we've selected destinations and campgrounds that stand out. You'll find a brief description of what each area has to offer in the way of attractions, then a listing of some of the better campgrounds in the area.

Our campground entries deserve a little explanation. You'll note that we've made heavy use of icons or pictograms to convey information in a compact format. We think you'll find them very useful. By using the pictograms we've allowed ourselves room to use text to try to give you a better feel for what the campground offers and to give useful driving instructions for finding it. You'll also find latitude and longitude so that you can easily use a GPS-based mapping program for navigation and we've included maps showing approximate locations for each campground.

Writing this book has been a lot of fun. We had a chance to visit our family members and friends in the area and to visit or revisit some great camping destinations. We'll continue to visit the Pacific Northwest most years as we travel between Alaska and Mexico and we hope to meet you somewhere along the way.

PACIFIC NORTHWEST

MOUNT RAINIER IN WASHINGTON STATE

Chapter 1 - Introduction

The Pacific Northwest is a wonderful camping destination. It is hard to think of another place in the world with such a diverse range of natural attractions and with such good highway access to them. While it is a temptation to think of the Northwest as just two regions, the rainy west of the mountains and the dry east of the mountains, the Northwest is really much more complex. Here's a quick rundown on the geographical layout.

Much of the Pacific Ocean coastline is easily accessible because there are highways running along almost the entire length. In the south, in Oregon, there are charming small towns and larger regional centers. Farther north, in Washington, there are fewer people and wilder beaches. In the far north Vancouver Island is really wild, the only way to visit the coast is along remote highways that stretch westward to isolated small towns. If you want to explore the coastline north and south from the towns you'll have to walk or use a boat.

Inland from the coast are a range of coastal mountains. In Washington some of this range is the Olympic National Park. In Oregon the coastal range isn't quite as spectacular, but much of it is partially protected as national forest. Geologically speaking, Vancouver Island in British Columbia is really part of this coastal range too.

Between the coastal range and the Cascade Mountains is a flat region with most of the Northwest's people. Here you'll find the big cities: Vancouver, Seattle, and Portland. But this region isn't all cities, there's also the Willamette Valley, Puget Sound, Vancouver Island's east coast, and B.C.'s Sunshine Coast.

Moving eastward, the next range of mountains are the Cascades. Geologically the Cascade Mountains are a young range. They're much higher than the coastal range, and have steep slopes and deep valleys. They form a barrier to moisture that creates one of the most memorable features of the Northwest – while the western part of the region is wet and lush the eastern part is dry, much is actual desert. The Cascades are full of interesting destinations. There are national parks and monuments: the North Cascades, Rainier, St Helens, and Crater Lake. The mountains are cut by transportation routes that are destinations themselves including but not limited to the Fraser Canyon, the Columbia Gorge, and the North Cascades Highway.

In British Columbia the Cascades get confused. Almost the entire southern part of the province is mountainous, to the traveler there's really no well-defined separation between the Cascade Range and the Rocky Mountains. But the Columbia River starts in B.C., and farther south its valley widens to form the Columbia Basin that occupies much of the dry eastern part of the state of Washington. Eastern Oregon is dry too, but here the topography is a high, dry, rugged plateau. Ranges like the Blue Mountains provide pine-covered relief from parched lower elevations.

Camping Travel

We realize that not everyone who uses this book will be an experienced camper. Certainly not everyone has or even wants to travel in their own personal RV. Camping is becoming more and more popular each year as more people recognize the unique benefits of this type of travel. Traveling in your own car or RV, sleeping in your own mobile bed, visiting the great outdoors but having the comforts of home, and saving lots of money doing it – that's camping travel.

You don't need an RV to travel this way. During the summer months you can comfortably camp out of the back of your car. For just a small investment you can equip yourself with everything you need to stay in a campground. Today's camping equipment is inexpensive and usually pretty well designed. You don't need expedition-quality gear for car camping, and there is no reason to spend extra money to get something that is ultra-light weight. You're not going to be carrying this equipment on your back. It is much more important to get equipment that will be comfortable. Get a big tent, they're not really expensive. You don't have to sleep on the ground, there are foam and air mattresses, not to mention cots, that are almost as comfortable as your bed at home

If sleeping in a tent seems a little more like roughing it than you are willing to accept you still can camp. Rental RVs are readily available. Later in this chapter you'll find information about renting RVs in Portland, Seattle, and Vancouver. When you check prices remember that the RV provides both transportation and lodging, you'll also spend less on food because you can easily cook in the RV and won't have to eat every meal in a restaurant. It won't take long to feel at home at the wheel of your rental RV, most roads aren't crowded, and you'll be surprised at the great views that you'll have from that high RV seat. When renting we recommend that you don't get a RV that is larger than you need. Big is not necessarily better with RV's, especially when you are traveling most of the time. If you have kids along consider having them sleep in a tent, they'll probably like it better anyway.

This is a good place to mention RV maneuverability. When you are parked comfortably in a campsite you want the biggest RV possible, but when you are on the road you want the smallest one possible. We've all seen the huge RVs traveling the interstate, usually pulling a tow car (often called a "toad" by RVers). Those RVs are fine when you are in an RV park but they're not really very convenient when on the road. For the type of travel outlined in this book you'll be much happier in a smaller RV. It will be easier to park when shopping, easier to fill with gas at a station, and be more economical. Most importantly, smaller RVs have much more choice when it come to picking a campsite.

Once you reach the destinations you're going to want to be able drive around to see the sights, go shopping, and conveniently get around. Fortunately, most of the destinations in this book aren't crowded urban areas so you can use an RV for local access. Those with really big RVs will want to have a "toad" or (in the case of those pulling trailers) use their towing vehicle. Rental motorhomes in the 18 to 22 foot range are not too difficult to maneuver and park so you won't need a "toad" if you have one of those. In urban areas it is probably best to just rely on public transportation. Portland, Seattle, and Vancouver all have good systems and decent service from most RV parks.

Tour Routes

In Chapter 2 of this book we outline several tours that you can follow to enjoy much of what the Northwest has to offer. They all start at one of what we call the gateway cities: Portland, Seattle, and Vancouver, B.C. Each includes six or seven destinations that offer good RV facilities and things to see and do. The idea is that you can spend a week traveling and know that you will enjoy each of the stops you make. Actually, it would be easy to spend two or three weeks on each route, but that is up to you. These routes are just ideas. You can take it from there.

Campgrounds

Campgrounds in the Northwest can be classified in many ways, but we think of them as described below. When they are available we've tried to provide a range of campground types to choose from at each destination. The type you like will depend upon how much you value hookups, amenities, natural settings, convenience and cost.

Commercial campgrounds provide the widest range of amenities. They are owned by companies or individuals and must make at least a small profit to stay open. This does not necessarily mean that they are always the most expensive campground choice since the government-owned campgrounds have been raising their rates in recent years. Commercial campgrounds almost always offer hookups, dump stations, and hot showers, they also often have swimming pools and other amenities. A big advantage of commercial campgrounds is that they usually will accept reservations over the phone with no additional charge. They are usually the only type of campground that is located near or inside a town. Parking sites in commercial campgrounds are usually closer to each other than those in government campgrounds, land is a big cost to a commercial campground but is pretty much free to the government. Commercial campgrounds have been forced to enlarge sites to remain viable so most can deal fairly well with large RVs.

Washington and Oregon state campgrounds are similar to each other. Most are located in scenic or historical locations. Government campgrounds tend to have lots of land so parking sites are spread farther apart than in a commercial campground and landscaping is usually very nice. Sites themselves can be large enough for the largest RVs although this varies, older campgrounds were built when RVs were smaller and many have not been updated. State campgrounds in Washington and Oregon often have hookups, but not always. They also often provide showers, although there is usually a small charge in the form of a coin-operated timer. State campgrounds are much more likely to allow campfires than commercial campgrounds, usually wood can be purchased at the campground. During the summer most state campgrounds now have an on-site "host". Usually the host is an RVer who parks in one of the sites and helps run the campground by collecting fees, marking reserved sites, providing information, and helping state employees keep the facility clean, safe, and organized. Many state campgrounds in Washington and Oregon are now on a reservation system although the system is not nearly as convenient or inexpensive as the system provided by commercial campgrounds. State campgrounds at popular destinations are often crowded, particularly on weekends, to use them you must either reserve a space or arrive early in the day. The reservation system is described under the *Campground Reservations* heading below.

British Columbia provincial campgrounds are similar to Washington and Oregon state campgrounds. They are located in scenic areas, they tend to have lots of acreage, and sites are often plenty large enough for big RVs. Provincial campgrounds, on the other hand, do not have utility hookups, and they often do not have showers. There is a reservation system, it is described under the *Campground Reservations* heading below. Provincial campgrounds often lower fees in early October because fewer amenities are available in the winter.

U.S. Forest Service campgrounds are the least developed type of campground listed in this book. These are located in the national forests, they are usually fairly small and usually do not have hookups or showers. Many have pit toilets instead of flush ones. Sites are usually separated by vegetation but can be small, particularly in old campgrounds built before the advent of big RVs. On the other hand, these are the least expensive campgrounds and often the least crowded with the best natural setting. They're particularly good for tent campers and those with small maneuverable RVs.

Other federal campgrounds are a mixed bag. The ones in this book are mostly national park campgrounds. They range from the beautiful and highly-developed sites in Canada's Banff National Park to the basic sites at most U.S. national parks. See the individual entries in this book for more details.

For many RVers camping is just not camping without a campfire. European visitors seem to particularly enjoy them, maybe because they don't find campfires in European campgrounds. Many commercial campgrounds do not allow campfires, probably due to burning restrictions in urban areas and the supervision and clean-up that fires require. Most state, provincial, and federal campgrounds do allow campfires although burning restrictions are often in effect in dryer areas.

You will not be able to find sufficient firewood on the ground in any of the campgrounds listed in this book. That means that you must either bring your own or purchase it at the campgrounds. Most campgrounds that allow fires do sell firewood (at a steep price).

Campground Reservations

The destinations in this book are popular. If you are traveling during the period from Memorial Day (end of May) to Labor Day (beginning of September), as most RV travelers do, you will find that campgrounds are sometimes full when you arrive. To avoid a late-in-the-day search for a place to stay all you have to do is take the time to reserve a space. We have indicated whether campgrounds accept reservations in the individual campground listings in this book.

It is easy to make reservations at virtually all commercial campgrounds. Almost all accept MasterCard or Visa charges and some even have toll-free numbers. Best of all, there is almost always no additional charge for making a reservation.

Federal, state, and provincial campgrounds are another story. The good news is that many do now accept reservations. The bad news is that most charge a substantial fee to make reservations and most use a sub-contractor for the reservation-taking process. Unfortunately, often the sub-contractor has limited information about the campground. Also, it is usually necessary to make reservations several days in advance. Information about how to make state and provincial campground reservations is listed at the beginning of the *Oregon*, *Washington*, and *British Columbia* chapters. You'll find much more about reservation systems in the introductory material to these campground chapters.

Renting an RV

It is not necessary to own your own RV to enjoy the destinations and campgrounds described in this book. You can easily rent an RV in Portland, Seattle, or Vancouver. Here are a few of the firms in that business. Give them a call or drop them a line for information about RVs and rates. Don't forget to ask if they will pick you up at the airport if that is important to you.

Portland Area

Cruise America, Mt Scott Motors, 8400 SE 82nd Ave, Portland, OR 97266; (503) 777-9833

RV Gold, 1570 SE Paloma Ct, Gresham, OR 97080; (503) 491-1592 or (888) 481-0592; arnellro@comcast.net

RV Northwest, 4350 SW 142 Avenue, Beaverton, OR 97005; (503) 641- 9140 or (877) 641-9140; becky@rv-northest.com

RVs To Go Portland, PO Box 733, Wilsonville, OR 97070; Reservations@portland-rvrentals.com

Seattle Area

Cruise America – Seattle, 12201 Hwy 99 South, Everett, WA 98204; (425) 355-8935

Cruise America, Ja-merica Motors, 4111 NE Sunset Blvd, Renton, WA 98059; (425) 204-8735

Cruise America, B&M Enterprises, Inc, 10600 18th Ave E, Tacoma, WA 98445; (253) 538-2710

LEARNING THE ROPES (HOSES) OF A RENTAL RV

Five Corners RV, 16068 Ambaum Blvd S, Seattle, WA 98148; (206) 241-6111 or (800) 249-6860

Western RV, 19303 Highway 99, Lynwood, WA 98036; (800) 800-1181

Vancouver Area

Alldrive Canada, 4053 – 208th Street, Langley, BC V3A 2H3; (604) 514-2668 or (888) 489-9777 or (888) 736-8787

Candan RV Center, 20257 Langley Bypass, Langley, BC V3A 6K9; (604) 530-3645

Cruise America – Cruise Canada, 7731 Vantage Way, Vancouver, BC V4G 1A6; (604) 946-5775

Cruise America – Gammon Motor Cars, 2397 W Railway, Abbotsford, BC V2S 2E3; (604) 850-0321

Go West Campers International Ltd, 1577 Lloyd Avenue, Vancouver, BC; (800) 661-8813

El Monte RV – Vancouver, 5242 Pacific Hwy, Ferndale, WA 98248; (360) 380-3300

Fraserway RV Centre Ltd, 747 Cliveden Place, Delta BC V3M 6C7; (604) 527-1102 or (800) 661-2441

Border Crossing

It is very possible that you will wish to cross the U.S.-Canada border during a Northwest camping trip. Crossing the border is nothing to fear, even in an RV the process is relatively painless.

Until December 31, 2007 no visa or passport is required for U.S. or Canadian citizens crossing either way but proof of citizenship must be carried. This means a passport, certified birth certificate, or voters registration card, along with a photo I.D. like your driver's license. A driver's license alone is not enough. If you have children along it is very important to have certified copies of their birth certificates and permission letters from parents if they are not yours. Beginning December 31, 2007 all persons entering the U.S. including U.S. citizens, will be required to use a passport.

For your vehicle you'll want the following: registration, up-to-date license tags and proof of insurance. Make sure you have your vehicle registration with you and if you are not the registered owner a signed statement that it is OK to take it out of the country. Check to make sure your automobile insurance is good in Canada. You can get a Canadian Non-Resident Interprovincial Motor Vehicle Liability Insurance Card from your insurance company. It is likely that you will not have to show any of these documents but having them on hand is definitely nice if you are asked for them.

Guns are a problem in Canada, don't try to take one in from the U.S. unless yours is a hunting trip. If it is a hunting trip check with Canadian officials before you leave home about regulations. Never fib about weapons at the border, vehicles are often searched and penalties are steep.

Many people like to carry pepper spray for defense against bears. This can be a problem at the border going into Canada. Several different laws are involved, if your spray wasn't manufactured in Canada it probably isn't legal. Sprays designed for defense against people definitely aren't allowed. If you must have pepper spray buy it in Canada once you are there.

For more information about border crossings you can use these addresses: Canadian Customs, Connaught Building, Sussex Drive, Ottawa, Ontario, Canada K1A 0L5 or Customs Office, 333 Dunsmuir Street, Suite 503, Vancouver, B.C., Canada V6B 5R4 (604 666-0545 or 888 732-6222); United States Customs, P.O. Box 7407, Washington, D.C. 20044, U.S.A. (202 566-8195 or 877 CBP-5511). There are also internet sites with lots of information, check our web site at www.rollinghomes.com for links to these sites.

Ferries

Washington State Ferries operate in Puget Sound. For schedules and information call 206 464-6400. Reservations are not taken for most runs. One special route is of interest. There is a Washington State ferry route from Anacortes (north of Seattle) to Victoria. This can be used to travel between the U.S. and Vancouver Island without visiting the Vancouver area. For schedules and information call 206 464-6400.

The British Columbia Ferry Corporation operates ferries between Vancouver Island and the Mainland. Ferries also connect the Sunshine Coast with the road system. For schedules and information from Victoria call 250 386-3431, from elsewhere in B.C. call toll-free 888 223-3779, from outside B.C. call 250 386-3431. The B.C. Ferry Corporation has a web site with lots of information, check our web site at www.rollinghomes.com for a link to the site.

A ferry also operates across the Straight of Juan de Fuca between Victoria and Port Angeles Washington. This ferry is run by a private company, Black Ball Transport. For schedules, information, and reservations call 360 457-4491 in Port Angeles, 250 386-2202 in Victoria.

Visitor Information

We're strong believers in the usefulness of local traveler's information offices. British Columbia, Washington, and Oregon all have fine offices in virtually every town. We've given their mailing addresses at the end of each chapter so that you can send for information before you leave home. When you are on the road you will find that the offices are well signed from most town approaches, just follow the signs to the office. They can provide you with maps, a listing of sights to see, opening times, and locations for any service you may require. Most towns also maintain a web site with useful information, you can find links to them at www.rollinghomes.com.

Internet Resources

Every day there are more and more Websites devoted to information about destinations, campgrounds, interesting sites, parks, and transportation. New sites appear and old ones disappear or change addresses. We've found that the only way to maintain a current listing is to set up

A WASHINGTON STATE FERRY ARRIVING IN ANACORTES

our own Internet site. The address is **www.rollinghomes.com** and has current links to a large variety of sites that will be of interest to readers of this guide. Don't ignore this resource, it can make your trip much more rewarding.

When to Go

Camping in the Northwest is pretty much a spring, summer, and fall activity. We give dates for the period that each listed campground is open in the individual chapters. While it may be possible to visit most areas during the winter and stay at campgrounds most people would probably not find the experience enjoyable. Winter in the Northwest, at least on the west side of the Cascade Mountains, is wet and cool. Temperatures seldom fall below freezing but there are few sunny days and daytime temperatures are often in the low forty's (Fahrenheit). On the east side of the Cascades winter weather is generally much cooler, often below freezing, but the skies tend to be clearer.

The camping season generally runs from the last half of April to the end of September with the most popular period between Memorial Day (end of May) and Labor Day (beginning of September).

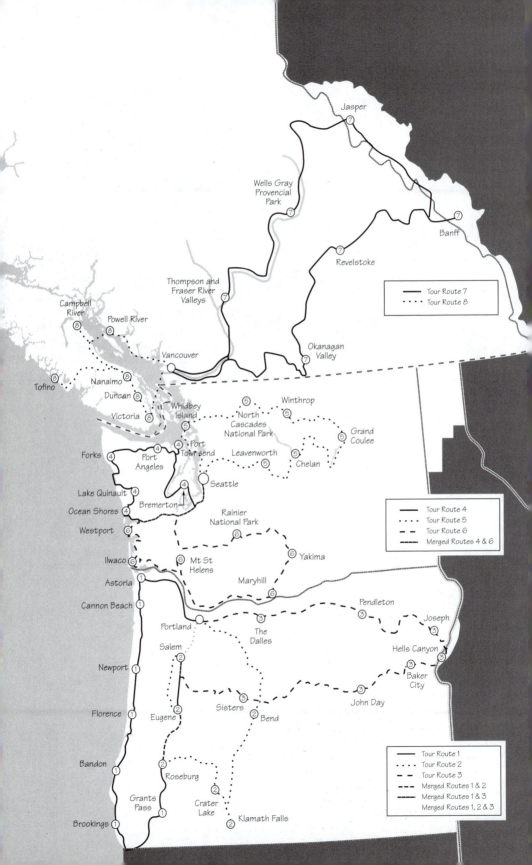

Chapter 2 - Suggested Touring Routes

This chapter contains eight tours of the Pacific Northwest. There are three tours from Portland, three from Seattle, and two from Vancouver. We've included these tours because the Northwest has so much to offer that it can be tough to decide where to go and what to see. You can use the suggested tours as a starting point and cut them or expand them as you like.

Each suggested tour has either seven or eight driving days. That means you can do them in a long week, but that would be a hard week of driving. If you only have a week consider cutting out some of the destinations, most of the tours have suggestions for doing this.

TOUR 1 – THE OREGON COAST

Summary: This tour starts in Portland, Oregon. You'll travel quickly south to reach the extreme south end of Oregon's Pacific coast, then leisurely wander north on US-101 to return to Portland. Please note that coaches over 40 feet long are restricted from traveling a section of this route, see the *Big Coaches* section below.

High Points

- » The Oregon Caves
- » Oregon Coast lighthouses and jetties
- » Rogue River from a jet-powered mail boat
- » Oregon Dunes National Recreation Area
- » Sea Lion Caves
- » Yaquina Head near Newport
- » Cannon Beach
- » Seaside
- » Historic Astoria and Lewis and Clarks' Fort Clatsop

General Description

This tour makes a quick dash south from Portland but then makes a leisurely return north along the full length of Oregon's Pacific coast. As you drive south on Interstate Highway 5 through the Willamette Valley you may feel that you are missing lots of interesting stops, and you are. But save that until later. After one day on the interstate things start to get interesting. You'll cross the coastal mountains and by the afternoon of the second day you are on the coast. There is so much to see and do that you may want to spend a month returning north to Portland. The total distance of this tour is 861 miles (1,388 km), driving time about 23 hours over 8 days.

The Roads

During the first day you'll be traveling down Interstate 5 (I-5), the major north-south highway on the west coast of the United States. On day two you'll leave the interstate at Grant's Pass and head southwest through the Siskiyou Mountains along winding US-199. Note that coaches over 40 feet long are not allowed on the California section of this road, see the *Big Coaches* section below. At the coast you'll join the coastal US-101. This road has been designated as the **Pacific Coast National Scenic Byway**, and it lives up to its name, it is really scenic. The standard of the road varies, but it is mostly good two-lane highway allowing vehicles of any size to easily and safely maintain the speed limit.

US-101 is well marked with mileage posts. These start in Astoria in the north and reach mile 363 at the Oregon-California border. They make a great way to locate campgrounds and interesting sights, we'll use them extensively in describing this tour.

Practical Tips

You will quickly notice that our favored campgrounds on this loop are in Oregon state parks. This is generally true throughout Oregon but particularly along the coast. Any private campground owner will tell you that government campgrounds have an unfair advantage – lots of prime real estate. Many other states do not take advantage of this, but Oregon and Washington do. The state campgrounds offer full hookups (in at least two cases even cable TV), beautiful settings and landscaping, lots of room, and a reservation system.

The reservation system is key. From Memorial Day to Labor Day the coast is very popular and reservations are usually necessary, especially on weekends. Make them as soon as you can, particularly if you are traveling on weekends or holidays. We describe the reservation system under *Campground Reservations* in the *Oregon* chapter of this book.

The Oregon Coast changes with the seasons. It's a great destination all year long and many campgrounds remain open during the entire year, but it's a completely different place in the winter than in the middle of the summer. This is one of the few tours in this book that is fine for winter travel although you may have to deal with snow during the drive from Grants Pass to Brookings. When snow is a problem you can use a different route to reach the coast, perhaps US-20 from south of Salem to Newport would be the best choice but there are several choices. During wet winter weather the coastal US-101 is sometimes closed by landslides, regional news programs will have reports if this happens. The road usually reopens within a day or two. In the winter you don't really need to worry about making reservations at the campgrounds.

Whale watching is a very popular pastime on the coast. Gray whales winter in Baja California and summer in the far north, therefore they pass the Oregon coast twice. During December, January, and early February they are going south, in March, April and May they are headed north. A small population also summers in Oregon waters. You can see the whales from high points on shore and also take whale-watching boat trips from several ports.

Fishing is another popular activity along the coast. You can fish from charter boats from many ports, fish in salt water along the beaches, or fish the estuaries and rivers along the coast.

Big Coaches

The State of California restricts coaches over 40 feet long from traveling many roads. One of these is US-199 between the California border and its intersection with US-101 near Cres-

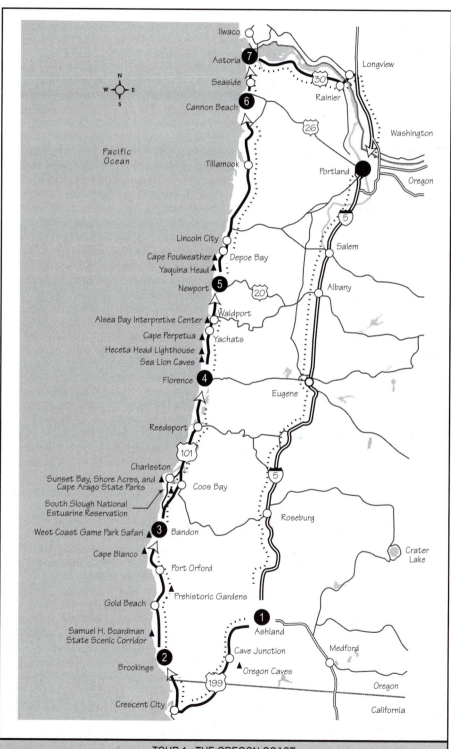

TOUR 1 - THE OREGON COAST

cent City. Coaches over 40' long will need to modify this touring route. One idea would be to travel south on I-5 to Redding and then west on US-299 to the coast at Arcata. From there you would follow US-101 north to Brookings. From Ashland this is a total driving distance of 375 miles (605 km), so you'd probably want to overnight somewhere in California, perhaps Arcata. Alternately you could travel west on SR-20 from Albany to Newport, overnight there or in Florence, and then continue on to Brookings the next day. Since both Florence and Newport are already overnight stops on this tour route when heading north you could bypass one of them northbound and shorten the tour by one day. See the *California Links* page on rollinghomes.com for more about the large coach restrictions.

🚐 Day 1 – Destination Ashland – 285 miles (460 km), 5 hours

From Portland we'll head south on Interstate 5 (I-5). This is a major four-lane highway that actually runs the length of the westernmost states from Blaine on the Canadian border to Tijuana on the Mexican border. It's almost never within sight of the ocean, only between Los Angeles and San Diego.

From Portland the highway runs straight down the length of the Willamette Valley. There are coastal mountains on the right and the Cascades on the left. After leaving the Portland metropolitan area you'll drive through farming country and pass the towns of Salem, Albany, and Eugene. After Eugene the highway begins to climb to pass across the Middle Range before dipping into the Umpqua River Valley where Roseburg is located and then climbing again over a pass to reach the Rogue River Valley with Grants Pass and Ashland.

You'll stop for the night near the town of *Ashland*, see page 64 for a description of the area and the available campgrounds. If you want to make a shorter day of it we also describe the following places that you'll be passing through: *Salem* (page 159), *Eugene* (page 103) and *Roseburg and the Umpqua Valley* (page 156).

🚐 Day 2 – Destination Brookings – 140 miles (226 km), 4 hours

Retrace your tracks a few miles northward and take Exit 55 from I-5 just east of Grant's Pass. This is the most convenient exit for US-199 and is clearly marked. US-199 is a mostly two-lane road but it's OK for RVs to 40 feet. Coaches over 40 feet are not legal on this road on the California side of the border, see the *Big Coaches* section above. Portions of US-199 are winding and somewhat narrow, so take it easy on those sections. Drivers with large coaches or trailers or who have less experience might want to consider taking one of the alternate routes described in the *Big Coaches* section above.

About twenty-eight miles (45 km) from Grants Pass you'll reach **Cave Junction**, from here a small paved road leads east 20 miles (32 km) to the **Oregon Caves**. This side trip is well worth your while, the caves are unique in the Northwest. They have marble formations from mineral-laden water flows. Unfortunately the road is not recommended for large RVs. If you have a smaller vehicle available (tow vehicle or towed car) you can leave your larger RV or trailer in the parking lot at the visitor center in Cave Junction and make the side trip in it. There are also a few campgrounds near the junction if you choose to stay overnight in the area.

Some 15 miles (24 km) beyond Cave Junction you reach the California border. During some seasons you'll be stopped and asked if you have any fruits on board, then you're on your way. You're in California, but not for long. After 35 miles (56 km), much of it along highway bordered by tall redwoods (this portion of the road is named the Redwood Highway), you'll see the sign for US-101 north to the Oregon border and, six miles (10 km) beyond, Brookings. See page 80 for information about *Brookings* and the campgrounds there. If you are interested in a jet boat ride up the Rogue River you might consider traveling on another 28 miles (45 km) to *Gold Beach* (page 106) to overnight there.

🚐 Day 3 – Destination Bandon – 84 miles (135 km), 3 hours

The 29-mile (47 km) section of coastline from Brookings north to Gold Beach is very scenic. The road closely follows the coastline which is alternately rocky cliffs and sandy beaches.

From Mile 353 to Mile 343 you are in the **Samuel H. Boardman State Scenic Corridor**. There are many pull-offs giving you the opportunity to make short walks and take some photos from scenic viewpoints.

The town of **Gold Beach** is located at Mile 328. It sits at the mouth of the Rogue River. Jet boat trips from here are very popular. See the *Gold Beach* destination description at page 106.

You might find a visit to the **Prehistoric Gardens** at Mile 313.1 interesting, particularly if you have some youngsters along. There are full-sized dinosaur replicas in a rain forest setting.

Farther north **Port Orford** is the western-most incorporated city in the contiguous U.S. See *Port Orford* (page 135) for more information. Don't miss **Cape Blanco**, just to the north and accessed via the road from Mile 296.6.

Just south of Bandon you'll pass by an interesting stop, the **West Coast Game Park Safari**. It's at Mile 281.5 and features 75 different species.

Finally, at Mile 270 you'll reach your destination for the day, the town of *Bandon*. See page 74 for information and campgrounds. If you choose to stop before reaching Bandon you might take a look at the description of things to do and campgrounds in the sections of this book covering *Gold Beach* (page 106), or *Port Orford* (page 135).

🚐 DAY 4 – DESTINATION OREGON DUNES NEAR FLORENCE – 72 MILES (116 KM), 2 HOURS (TO FLORENCE)

Coos Bay lies north of Bandon. The route below bypasses much of the town by passing through Charleston and then rejoining US-101 north of the city.

Drive north from Bandon and take the left turn at Mile 256.9 marked Charleston. The Seven Devils Road soon passes **South Slough National Estuarine Reservation**. You'll find a visitor's center and paths down to and around the estuary. Continuing on you'll enter Charleston and see signs pointing left for **Sunset Bay State Park**, **Shore Acres State Park**, and **Cape Arago State Park**. See *Charleston* (page 92) for more about this area. If you wanted to add a day to this tour this might be a nice place to do it.

THE LIGHTHOUSE AT YAQUINA HEAD

Follow the highway across the bridge from Charleston and northeast through suburbs of Coos Bay. You'll eventually hit Hwy 101 again. Turn north and you'll soon be entering Oregon's dune country. For about 40 miles (65 km) between Coos Bay and Florence the highway passes inland of a large dune field. See *Reedsport and the Oregon Dunes* (page 148) for more about his area. You can overnight in one of the many campgrounds serving the dunes area or continue north to Florence. See our *Waldport and Florence* section (page 166) for more about that area.

DAY 5 – DESTINATION NEWPORT – 50 MILES (81 KM), 2 HOURS

From Florence continue north on US-101.

The twenty miles (32 km) or so between Mile 186 and Yachats at Mile 165 are within the Siuslaw National Forest and are very scenic. The *Waldport and Florence* destination description (page 166) describes the section north to Waldport at Mile 156. Along the way you'll pass **Sea Lion Caves** (Mile 179.3), **Heceta Head Lighthouse** (Mile 178.3), and the **Cape Perpetua Interpretive Center** (Mile 167.3).

At Mile 165 you'll pass through little **Yachats**, and then at Mile 156 reach **Waldport**. Just south of the big bridge is the **Alsea Bay Interpretive Center**. To the north the flat coastline is less scenic, at Mile 143 you'll find that you are approaching Newport. See *Lincoln to Newport* (page 122) for information about the area and its campgrounds.

DAY 6 – DESTINATION CANNON BEACH – 110 MILES (177 KM), 4 HOURS

Driving north from Newport you'll pass the **Yaquina Head** entrance at Mile 137.6 and pass around **Cape Foulweather** at about Mile 131. Little **Depoe Bay** (Mile 128.0) is so scenic that almost everyone stops for a look. You'll reach Lincoln City at about Mile 120. This entire section of road is described under *Lincoln City to Newport* (page 122).

At Mile 90.4 turn off US-101 and follow the **Three Capes Loop** toward Pacific City. This scenic loop and Tillamook at the other end are described under *Tillamook and the Three Capes Loop* (page 162).

After a stop in Tillamook at the **Tillamook Cheese Visitor's Center** you can continue north. From Tillamook US-101 winds its way north through a series of towns along the Tillamook Bay, Nehalem Bay, and the coast. These are **Bay City** (Mile 60.8), **Garibaldi** (Mile 55.6), **Barview** (Mile 53.7), **Rockaway Beach** (Mile 50.8), **Wheeler** (Mile 47.0), **Nehalem** (Mile 44.7), **Manzanita** (Mile 43.0), and finally, Cannon Beach. You can spend the night in Cannon Beach which is described in our section titled *Astoria, Seaside and Cannon Beach* (page 67) or stop sooner at a campground farther south. These are described in our section titled *Nehalem Bay and Manzanita* (page 130).

DAY 7 – DESTINATION ASTORIA – 25 MILES (40 KM), 1 HOUR

Today's drive is a short one, but en route you'll pass through **Seaside**, one of the most-visited cities on the coast, and end the day near **Astoria** which is one of the coast's most historical sites. There's lots to see so don't spend too much time eating a leisurely breakfast in Cannon Beach.

Just 3 miles (5 km) north of Cannon Beach at Mile 25 you'll begin to pass through the road-side outskirts of Seaside. Seaside is described in our section titled *Astoria, Seaside and Cannon Beach* (page 67).

Continuing north you will spot the southern access road to Fort Stevens and Warrenton at Mile 7.5. There's another access road at Mile 6.5, all three of the Astoria area campgrounds are along this road. Astoria is northeast across the long bridge across the mouth of the Youngs River. Again, see the *Astoria, Seaside and Cannon Beach* section (page 67) for information about things to do and campgrounds in Astoria.

DAY 8 – DESTINATION PORTLAND – 95 MILES (153 KM), 2 HOURS

From Astoria it is an easy drive back to Portland along US-30. This highway generally follows the south bank of the Columbia but is seldom within view of the river. For most of the distance it is a decent two-lane road. It is possible to cross the river at a bridge from Rainier in Oregon to Longview in Washington. There you can pick up the I-5 interstate, the same highway we followed south from Portland on this trip. I-5 follows the north bank of the Columbia to Portland and is quicker than US-30. It also offers easier access to Portland campgrounds.

TOUR 2 – CENTRAL OREGON LOOP

Summary: This tour starts in Portland, Oregon. It crosses the Cascade Mountains near Portland and then travels down the east side of the range as far as the California border. Then you return north through Crater Lake National Park and the length of the Willamette Valley.

High Points

- » Mt Hood
- » Mt Bachelor
- » Cascade Lakes Highway
- » Newberry National Volcanic Monument
- » High Desert Museum
- » Klamath Basin National Wildlife Refuges
- » Lava Beds National Monument
- » Crater Lake National Park
- » Umpqua River Valley
- » McKenzie River Valley
- » Robert Aufderheide Memorial Drive
- » Willamette Valley

General Description

On this tour you will have a chance to explore Oregon's section of the Cascade Mountains. First you'll cross the mountains from Portland and drive south along the eastern slopes. You'll visit Bend and Klamath Falls. Then you'll drive northwest to spend some time at Crater Lake National Park before descending to the western slopes. There, in Oregon's historical heartland, you'll visit the towns of Roseburg, Eugene, and Salem. Each has its own access to the wild Cascades to the east, as well as covered bridges, wineries, and historical sites in the fertile farming country nearby. Total driving distance is 659 miles (1,063 km), time on the road about 17 hours.

Oregon's Cascades are much more accessible than Washington's. While Washington has only six east-west highways, Oregon has 10 of them. Rather than zigzag our way back and forth across the mountain range we'll only cross twice, once in the north and again toward the south. Both of the routes you will follow are very suitable for big RVs of all kinds with easily handled two-lane highways and medium grades.

On the east side of the mountains and headed south the tour follows US-97 which is mostly two lanes and fairly flat. There is quite a lot of traffic on US-97 but it moves right along.

On the west side of the mountains headed north you'll travel on either the I-5 interstate or good rural roads.

Even though the tour only crosses the Cascades twice it still gives you the opportunity to drive in the mountains. It's also easy to drive into the mountains on day trips from Bend, Eugene and Springfield. If you are driving an unwieldy larger RV you can leave it parked in the campground and do the exploring in your tow car.

Practical Tips

This would generally be considered a summer tour. Some of the destinations, however, do offer possibilities in the winter. On the east side of the Cascades the weather is usually decent, and you'll see that the campgrounds at lower elevations around Bend are open all year. This is a very popular winter sports area with Mt Bachelor's skiing nearby. The Klamath Falls area also

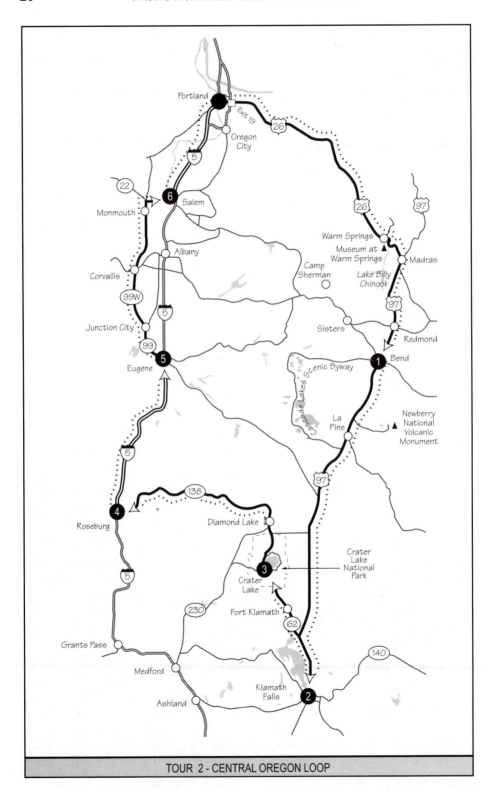

has its winter attractions, during the months of December through February the area attracts the Lower 48's largest concentration of bald eagles.

A problem with a winter visit is the higher elevations, of course. Crater Lake National Park is snowed in until June most years so in winter you'll probably be better off to cross westward to I-5 using US-97 to Weed. Once you make it north to Roseburg you'll again find the valley campgrounds to be open, although winter days are short and the weather generally wet.

DAY 1 – DESTINATION BEND – 165 MILES (266 KM), 4 HOURS

From the ring road around the east side of Portland (I-205) take Exit 19 and follow the signs for Hwy 26. Once you leave the populated areas around Gresham the highway will take you up across the south slopes of Mt Hood and down the far side into the dry country on the eastern slopes of the Cascade Mountains. As you start to descend you'll be amazed at how fast the evergreens disappear and the temperatures rise.

The town of Warm Springs is in the 600,000-acre Warm Springs Indian Reservation. Attractions in this area include the **Museum at Warm Springs** as well as **Lake Billy Chinook** to the south. See our section titled *Warm Springs and Madras* (page 174) for more about the region as well as a wealth of interesting places to stay.

South from Madras on US-97 you'll pass through Redmond and in just a few more miles reach the northern outskirts of Bend. The Bend area is full of attractions. See the following sections of this book for information: *Bend and La Pine* (page 77), *Camp Sherman and the Metolius River* (page 83), *Cascade Lakes Scenic Byway Loop* (page 86), *Newberry National Volcanic Monument* (page 131), and *Redmond and Sisters* (page 145).

DAY 2 – DESTINATION KLAMATH FALLS – 138 MILES (223 KM), 3 HOURS

The drive from Bend to Klamath Falls couldn't be simpler. You just follow US-97 south. The road is mostly two-lane although there are many places where it has been widened to three or four lanes for passing, there is quite a bit of traffic along this highway since it is the main

ONE OF OREGON'S COVERED BRIDGES NEAR EUGENE

north-south corridor on the east side of Oregon's Cascades. See our *Klamath Falls* section (page 118) for things to do and places to stay in Klamath Falls.

⛺ DAY 3 – DESTINATION CRATER LAKE NATIONAL PARK – 54 MILES (87 KM), 2 HOURS (TO CRATER LAKE LODGE)

From Klamath Falls drive north on Hwy 97 toward Bend. The intersection with Hwy 62 is 20 miles (32 km) north, turn on to Hwy 62 and follow it 30 miles (48 km) through Fort Klamath to the south entrance of the park.

If you plan to camp in the park you have arrived. However, camping opportunities in the park are limited. If you plan to go on to a campground outside the park you should have plenty of time to drive the road around the crater, stop and take in some of the sights, and then drive on out to those campgrounds. See our section titled *Crater Lake National Park* (page 99) for information about things to do and places to stay in the area.

⛺ DAY 4 – DESTINATION ROSEBURG – 107 MILES (173 KM), 3.5 HOURS

When you are ready to depart Crater Lake make your way out the north entrance. Soon after you pass the entrance station the road intersects SR-138. Head westward toward Roseburg. Four miles (6 km) after that intersection you'll come to another, this one with SR-230 toward Medford and Grants Pass. At this point you are very near Diamond Lake.

From Crater Lake SR-138 leads down the canyons of the Clearwater and North Fork of the Umpqua River to Roseburg. This is a very scenic route with many places to pull off and enjoy views of the river and surrounding mountains. See our section titled *Roseburg and the Umpqua Valley* (page 156) for information about this area and places to stay.

⛺ DAY 5 – DESTINATION EUGENE – 70 MILES (113 KM), 1.25 HOURS

The route from Roseburg to Eugene is an easy one, just follow the I-5 freeway north. See our section titled *Eugene* (page 103) for information about things to do and places to stay.

⛺ DAY 6 – DESTINATION SALEM – 80 MILES (129 KM), 2.5 HOURS

While it is possible to drive right up I-5 from Eugene to Salem, a distance of 59 miles (95 km), there is a better alternate route. This is the old US-99.

Follow US-99 out of Eugene toward Junction City. At first the highway is lined with commercial activities of various kinds with quite a few stoplights, but soon you'll be driving through flat quiet farming country.

At Junction City the highway splits into US-99 West and US-99 East. Much of the old US-99 East is parallel to or covered by the I-5 Interstate but US-99 West remains a good countryside route.

Forty-three miles (69 km) north of Junction City is **Corvallis**. Corvallis is a pleasant city with a population of about 50,000. It is home to Oregon State University.

From Corvallis continue north on US-99. You'll pass through little Monmouth and then catch SR-22, the Willamina-Salem Highway, east to Salem. See our section titled *Salem* (page 159) for things to do and places to see in the Salem area.

⛺ DAY 7 – DESTINATION PORTLAND – 45 MILES (73 KM), 1 HOUR

The drive north to Portland goes by pretty quickly. You're barely on the road before you start to arrive in the suburbs. Portland is described in our section titled *Portland* (page 138).

TOUR 3 – EASTERN OREGON LOOP

Summary: This tour starts in Portland, Oregon. It heads eastward through the Columbia Gorge and then across the Blue Mountains as far as Hells Canyon, then returns westward through the John Day country and crosses the Cascades near Sisters, Oregon.

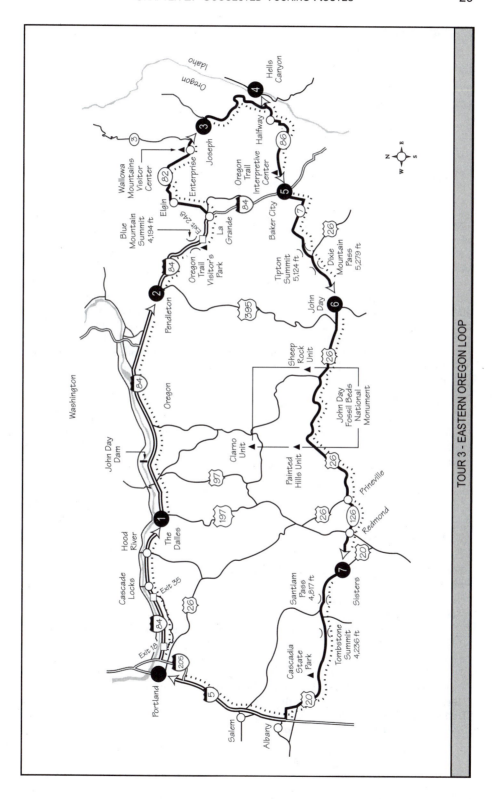

TOUR 3 - EASTERN OREGON LOOP

High Points

» Columbia River Scenic Highway
» Bonneville and The Dalles Dams
» Wallowa Lake
» Hells Canyon
» Oregon Trail
» John Day Fossil Beds
» Metolius Meadows
» McKenzie Pass

General Description

This tour crosses northern Oregon to the Idaho border, then returns along a more southerly route. Along the way it stops for the night at a variety of interesting places. Most nights are spent in or near popular outdoor destinations although, surprisingly, the route does not pass through or near any national parks. It, however, does visit a national scenic area, a national recreation area and a national monument. The total driving distance of this tour is 853 miles (1,376 km), driving time will be about 24.5 hours.

The first day is spent near Portland as you tour the southern shore of the Columbia Gorge. The following day the route travels east to Pendleton where you can spend the night at an Indian-owned resort offering a golf course and a casino. Day 3 heads into the wild northeast corner of the state for a night at beautiful Wallowa Lake. The next day's route follows small (but paved) roads through the Wallowa National Forest to the spectacular Hells Canyon. Heading westward finally you can visit the Oregon Trail in Baker City. Day 6 offers a visit to the John Day Fossil Beds National Monument and then you'll spend the final evening in scenic Sisters near the famous Metolius River.

The Roads

You'll find lots of variety in this chapter. The first day you'll visit one of the most famous roads in the country - the **Columbia River Scenic Highway**. This is a very scenic but narrow road so larger RVs may want to drive directly to Cascade Locks via I-84, park the RV in a campground, and then explore the highway in a smaller tow car or truck.

The following two days will find you on I-84, a major east-west freeway route, for most of the time. When you do leave I-84, however, you'll be on paved two-lane highways for most of the remainder of the trip. Only on the last day will you again drive on a freeway when you join I-5 south of Albany to drive north to Portland.

Practical Tips

For RVers this is a summer or fall trip. The road between Joseph and Hells Canyon is not open in the winter and many campgrounds throughout the route are also not open in the winter.

For the most part this route is not as heavily traveled as the Oregon Coast route but reservations are still a good idea, particularly in the state park campgrounds.

You can easily combine this tour with the Central Oregon Tour to make a two or three week trip. The last night on this tour is spent at Sisters which is just a few miles from Bend, the first night's stop on that tour.

The theme of this tour could easily be the **Oregon Trail**. Locations with Oregon trail exhibits along the way are the **Columbia Gorge Discovery Center and Waasco County Historical Museum** in The Dalles, the **Tamástslikt Cultural Institute** just outside Pendleton, **Oregon Trail Visitor's Park** near the Blue Mountains summit east of Pendleton, and the **Oregon Trail Interpretive Center** near Baker, Oregon.

🚐 DAY 1 – DESTINATION THE COLUMBIA GORGE – 93 MILES (150 KM), 3 HOURS (TO THE DALLES)

From Portland follow I-84 eastward. The Dalles is 85 miles (137 km) from Portland. See our section titled *Columbia Gorge* (page 94) for information about the area and its campgrounds.

Smaller RVs (to about 25 feet) will want to leave I-5 at Exit 18 and follow the **Columbia River Scenic Highway** (US-30) eastward to Exit 35. It's very scenic and passes a number of spectacular waterfalls. If you're in a big RV and want to drive the highway in a tow car consider overnighting in Cascade Locks and driving back to see the highway. Cascade Locks campgrounds are covered in the *Columbia Gorge* section (page 94).

🚐 DAY 2 – DESTINATION PENDLETON – 119 MILES (192 KM), 2 HOURS

The route from the Columbia Gorge to Pendleton follows I-84. The distance from Cascade Locks to Pendleton is 162 miles (261 km), from The Dalles to Pendleton the distance is 119 miles (192 km).

From The Dalles eastward the highway continues to follow the Columbia River. At first you will be following the shore of **Celilo Lake** behind The Dalles Dam but soon you will spot **John Day Dam**. Above it the Columbia is called Lake Umatilla. About 50 miles (81 km) east of John Day Dam you will reach Boardman and the highway leaves the river and cuts inland for 54 miles (87 km) to Pendleton through a rolling landscape filled with irrigation circles. See the *Pendleton* section (page 133) for information about Pendleton attractions and campgrounds.

🚐 DAY 3 – DESTINATION JOSEPH AND LAKE WALLOWA – 121 MILES (195 KM), 3 HOURS (TO JOSEPH)

Wallowa Lake and the adjoining town of Joseph lie about 50 miles (81 km) northeast, as the crow flies, of Baker City Oregon. The drive from Pendleton is very scenic, first on I-84 through the Blue Mountains and then from La Grande on back roads through farming country and then through wooded canyons.

FLY FISHERMEN ON THE METOLIUS RIVER

From Pendleton take I-84 eastward. Almost immediately you'll reach the long grade up into the Blue Mountains. The scenery changes quickly from dry grasslands to pine forests. Emigrant Springs State Park, an alternate campground for Pendleton, is just off the freeway at Exit 234.

You'll pass the Blue Mountains Summit (elevation 4,194 feet) and reach an interesting stop, the **Oregon Trail Visitor's Park**. To reach it take Exit 248 and follow a winding road for 3 miles (5 km) to the park. You'll find a short trail that leads up the hill to a section of the **Oregon Trail**, ruts are visible and an interpretive trail and volunteers help you make sense of what you see.

Back on the freeway you'll soon descend into the Grand Ronde Valley. There are several exits for the town of La Grande, take Exit 261 which is marked for Elgin. You will want to go left toward the northeast, but you might want to make a brief detour to the right to take a look at La Grande.

Head out of La Grande on SR-82, this highway takes a few unexpected turns but you will have no problem following it if you just watch for signs for Elgin and then Enterprise. If you zero your odometer when you leave the freeway you'll reach Elgin at 19 miles (31 km), Enterprise at 63 miles (102 km) , and Joseph at 70 miles (113 km).

You may want to make two stops in Enterprise before going on to Joseph. Just before you arrive in town you'll pass the **Wallowa Mountains Visitor Center**. A stop here will bring you up to speed on the area's attractions. Then, in Enterprise you'll find the last large supermarket in this neck of the woods, you might stop and pick up groceries for the next few nights.

See the *Wallowa Lake Region* (page 171) for information about things to do and places to see in this area.

DAY 4 – DESTINATION HELLS CANYON – 68 MILES (110 KM), 3 HOURS (TO COPPERFIELD)

The drive from Wallowa Lake to Hells Canyon is described in our section titled *Hells Canyon Scenic Byway* (page 112). There are a number of national forest campgrounds along the route. When you reach Hells Canyon take a look at the section titled *Hells Canyon* (page 109) for information about things to do and campgrounds in the area.

DAY 5 – DESTINATION BAKER CITY – 70 MILES (113 KM), 2 HOURS

From Hells Canyon SR-86 leads west to Baker City. For the most part this road runs through open range and irrigated farmland with one decent summit with a good climb just past the town of Halfway, the top is at 3,653 feet.

As you approach Baker City you will spot the **Oregon Trail Interpretive Center** on top of Flagstaff Hill to your right. This is a must-see attraction. See the *Baker City and Sumpter* section (page *71*) for more about the Baker City area and places to stay.

DAY 6 – DESTINATION JOHN DAY – 79 MILES (127 KM), 2.5 HOURS (TO JOHN DAY)

From Baker City and Sumpter travel eastward on SR-7. East of Sumpter you'll climb over 5,124 foot Tipton Summit and then link up with US-26 and travel westward. The highway soon crosses another summit, this one the 5,279-foot Dixie Mountain Pass, and finally reaches the town of John Day.

See the *John Day Country* section (page 114) for things to do and campgrounds in the area.

DAY 7 – DESTINATION SISTERS – 155 MILES (250 KM), 5 HOURS

The drive from John Day to Sisters follows US-26 eastward to Prineville, then branches south on SR-126 to pass through Redmond and on to Sisters. Until the highway reaches the Prineville area this is a very sparsely populated area of Oregon, and also extremely scenic with miles and miles of open pine forest.

Along the way you'll have the opportunity to visit two of the sections of the **John Day Fossil Beds National Monument**. They are described in the *John Day Country* section (page 114) and include the Sheep Rock section near Mile 38 of this day's drive and the Painted Hills section near Mile 66 of the drive.

Prineville, a possible place to overnight if you're running late, is covered in our *Prineville* section (page 144). See the *Redmond and Sisters* section (page 145) for places to stay and things to do in the the Sisters area. *Camp Sherman and the Metolius River* (page 83) are nearby and make a good alternate with their many national forest campgrounds.

⏏ DAY 8 – DESTINATION PORTLAND – 148 MILES (239 KM), 4 HOURS

From Sisters the easiest route back to Portland for big RVs is US-20 across Santiam Pass (4,817 feet) and Tombstone Summit (4,236 feet) to Interstate I-5 just south of Albany.

Cascadia State Park, 59 miles (95 km) from Sisters, makes a good place to take a break. The park is located along the South Santiam River at the site of a spring long famous for its healthful soda water. There's an historic covered bridge nearby. Once you reach I-5 it's about 55 freeway miles (89 km) north to Portland. See our *Portland* section (page 138) for things to do and places to stay in the Portland area.

TOUR 4 – WASHINGTON'S OLYMPIC PENINSULA LOOP

Summary: This tour starts in Seattle, Washington. After crossing Puget Sound near Tacoma you circle the Olympic Peninsula with visits to mountains, a hot spring, ocean beaches, and resorts.

High Points

- » Hood Canal
- » Kitsap Peninsula
- » Port Townsend
- » Olympic National Park
- » Hurricane Ridge
- » Olympic Mountains
- » Dungeness Spit
- » Sol Duc Hot Springs
- » Rialto Beach
- » Hoh Valley Rain Forest
- » The North Beaches
- » Grays Harbor

General Description

This is the shortest of the Washington tours. Northwest residents often drive the Olympic loop over a weekend. That's pretty fast, it wouldn't give you time to enjoy an area that is filled with natural wonders. Total distance driven on this tour is 511 miles (824 km), driving time should be about 13 hours.

The tour follows Interstate 5 south from Seattle to Tacoma. In Tacoma you leave I-5 and cross the Tacoma Narrows to the Kitsap Peninsula. The campgrounds along Hood Canal make a good place to stop for the night.

During the following days the tour leads you north to Port Townsend and then Port Angeles along the Strait of Juan de Fuca and then circles on around the Olympic Peninsula. This is a sparsely populated region famed for natural attractions and dominated by Olympic National Park.

Finally, on the last day of the tour you reach the ocean-side resort of Ocean Shores. You'll find a lot to do here and in the small towns stretched along the beaches to the north as well as in Hoquiam and Aberdeen to the east.

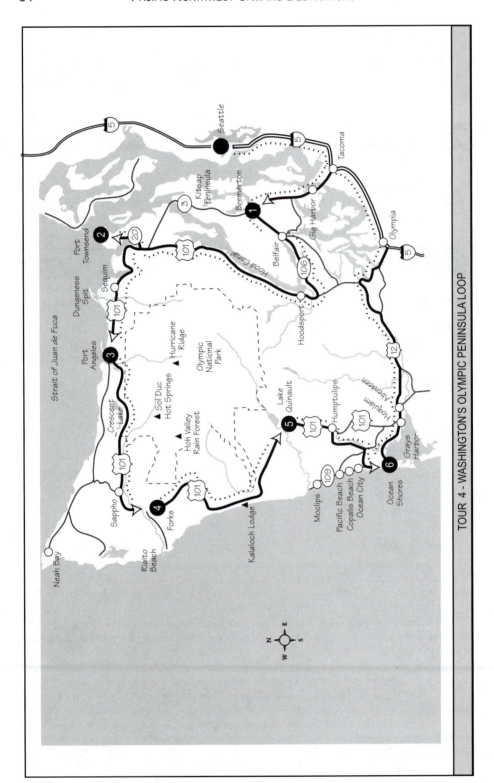

TOUR 4 - WASHINGTON'S OLYMPIC PENINSULA LOOP

The Roads

The greater part of this tour follows US-101 in a loop around the Olympic Peninsula. You will be driving this two-lane paved highway from a point near Hoodsport on the Hood Canal until you reach Aberdeen, a distance of 252 miles (406 km). This is a uniformly good road, no problem at all for RVs.

Practical Tips

Like the Oregon Coast Tour from Portland this is a tour that can be fun at any time of the year. During the winter you must expect a lot of rain, but temperatures rarely descend below about 40 degrees Fahrenheit. Coastal storms actually attract visitors during the winter.

You could easily combine this tour with our Southern Washington tour in either of two ways. From Aberdeen you could head south to Westport and then do the entire Southern Washington tour in a counter-clockwise direction. Alternately, instead of returning to Seattle you could drive to Packwood and start the tour in a clockwise direction.

It is also easy to connect with the Vancouver Island tour by taking a ferry north from Port Angeles to Victoria.

🚐 DAY 1 – DESTINATION THE KITSAP PENINSULA – 69 MILES (111 KM), 2 HOURS (TO BREMERTON)

Rather than deal with the crowded and somewhat expensive (especially for RVs) ferries that ply the waters of Puget Sound we'll do an end run and drive around the south end of the sound.

From Seattle head south on I-5. You'll pass through Tacoma and take Exit 132 (marked for Gig Harbor) and US-16 to drive across the **Tacoma Narrows Suspension Bridge**. Don't give it a thought, but this is the bridge that replaced the infamous "Galloping Gertie", that bridge collapsed in 1940. If you want to investigate Tacoma you could spent the evening here, see our *Tacoma* section (page 275) for things to do and places to stay including campgrounds near Gig Harbor.

Stay on US-16 as it leads north to Bremerton. See the *Kitsap Peninsula and Bainbridge Island* section (page 216) for things to do and places to stay on the Kitsap Peninsula.

🚐 DAY 2 – DESTINATION PORT TOWNSEND – 102 MILES (165 KM), 3 HOURS

From the Kitsap Peninsula you have a choice. You can travel directly to Port Townsend using SR-3 and the Hood Canal Floating Bridge. From Bremerton to Port Townsend using this route the distance is 48 miles (77 km).

Alternately, you can follow the south and west shores of Hood Canal using SR-106 and US-101. From Bremerton to Port Townsend using this route is a distance of 102 miles (165 km). This is by far the most scenic route, much of it is described in our *Hood Canal* section (page 208). There are many campgrounds along the canal so this is a good place to add an extra day to the tour.

Eventually the highway leaves the shore of the canal and approaches the north shore of the Olympic Peninsula. Just before you get there you will see a sign for Port Townsend (SR-20). Take the right turn and in 13 miles (21 km) you will find yourself entering one of the most interesting towns on the peninsula. See the *Port Townsend* section (page 255) for information about Port Townsend.

🚐 DAY 3 – DESTINATION THE PORT ANGELES AREA – 46 MILES (74 KM), 1.5 HOURS (TO PORT ANGELES)

The direct route to Port Angeles doesn't take long, the distance is very short. You'll retrace your steps back to US-101, then follow that highway for 35 miles (56 km) west to Port Angeles. Between Port Townsend and Port Angeles you'll pass through Sequim. See our *Sequim* section (page 267) for more about this town. Port Angeles is just beyond, see our *Port Angeles and the*

North Olympic Park section (page 248) for details about what to do and where to stay. Sequim and Port Angeles are so close to each other that you can spend the night in either one.

DAY 4 – DESTINATION FORKS, HOH VALLEY AND RIALTO BEACH – 56 MILES (90 KM), 1.5 HOURS (TO FORKS)

As you head west from Port Angeles you'll pass north of the **Olympic National Park** past extremely scenic **Crescent Lake**. This region is described in our *Port Angeles and the North Olympic Park* section (page 248).

After 44 miles (71 km) you'll reach a town, really a populated intersection, called Sappho. SR-113, which joins the highway here, will take you north to join SR-112 as it connects Port Angeles with **Neah Bay**. This can be an interesting side trip if you have the time, plan on at least 3 hours even if you only drive out to Neah Bay and back. Neah Bay is describe in our *Forks and the Western Sections of Olympic National Park* section (page 197). So is Forks, just 11 miles (18 km) beyond the intersection.

DAY 5 – DESTINATION LAKE QUINAULT AND THE KALALOCH COAST – 67 MILES (108 KM), 1.5 HOURS (TO LAKE QUINAULT)

From Forks US-101 travels south. After 13 miles (21 km) you'll see the Upper Hoh Road going east to the **Hoh Rain Forest Visitor Center** in Olympic National Park. It's well worth the 32 mile (52 km) roundtrip drive to visit the place. Then the highway curves back out to the coast and passes **Ruby Beach** and **Kalaloch Lodge** before again passing inland toward **Lake Quinault**. This entire section is covered in our *Forks and the Western Sections of Olympic National Park* section (page 197). You could overnight in the Hoh Valley, at Kalaloch Lodge, or at Lake Quinault. Take your pick.

DAY 6 – DESTINATION OCEAN SHORES AND THE NORTH BEACHES – 41 MILES (66 KM), 1 HOUR (TO OCEAN SHORES)

Back on US-101 and headed south you have a choice of routes. The main highway will take you directly to Hoquiam with little delay. From there you can cut west to the North Beaches area. This is the route to take if you are in need of supplies, there is a better choice of stores in Hoquiam than you will find in the little towns along the coast.

A more direct route, all on paved roads, takes you west on back roads to Moclips at the north end of the North Beaches coastal strip. From there you can follow the coast road south. This back road leaves US-101 at Humptulips near Mile 109 of US-101. Drive west 12 miles (19 km) to Copalis Crossing, then at the T intersection turn right and follow signs for Moclips north 10 miles (16 km) to a point on the coastal SR-109 just south of Pacific Beach. From there you can drive south on SR-109 to Copalis (8 miles (13 km)), Ocean City (11 miles (18 km)) or Ocean Shores (16 miles (26 km)).

See our *Ocean Shores and the North Beaches Area* section (page 243) for information about the area and places to camp.

DAY 7 – DESTINATION SEATTLE – 130 MILES (210 KM), 2.5 HOURS

The drive back to Seattle is quick and easy. Follow SR-109, US-101 and US-12 eastward through Hoquiam and Aberdeen. You'll hit 4-lane highway on the far side of Aberdeen and never really have to slow down much, except during rush hours, as you travel east to an intersection with I- 5 just south of Olympia, then north through Tacoma to Seattle.

TOUR 5 – WASHINGTON'S NORTH CASCADE LOOP

Summary: This tour starts in Seattle, Washington. You'll drive north and cross the North Cascades Highway to the Methow Valley. In eastern Washington you'll visit the sunny Grand Coulee area, then return through apple country and Stevens Pass.

High Points

» Ferry to Whidbey Island
» Deception Pass
» North Cascades National Park
» Winthrop and the Methow Valley
» Grand Coulee Dam
» Lake Chelan
» Leavenworth Alpine Village

General Description

The well-known Cascade Loop is one of the most heavily promoted tourist routes in the state of Washington. Deservedly so, this tour is definitely a great way to spend a week or two. You'll have a chance to enjoy a variety of landscapes: islands and seashores, rugged evergreen-clad mountains, piney ranchland, and the dry coulee country of eastern Washington. The total distance is 587 miles (947 km), total driving time about 17 hours.

You'll start your journey with a short ferry ride to Whidbey Island. The ferry runs from Mukilteo, which is just north of Seattle, to Clinton. The drive up the island offers several interesting side trips and stops. You don't have to use a ferry to get off Whidbey Island, the bridge at **Deception Pass** at the north end of the island not only brings you back to the mainland, it offers you one of the most scenic views in the state. Actually, this bridge doesn't really take you to the mainland, it takes you to Fidalgo Island. From there it is easy to travel onward since this so-called island is really only separated from the mainland by what is little more than a wide canal.

From Fidalgo Island you'll travel on SR-20 up the Skagit Valley to the North Cascades National Park. After spending a night in or near the park you drive on eastward descending into the Methow Valley. Winthrop is the center of activity in the Methow, it's a friendly little town with a western theme.

HIKING IN THE CASCADES

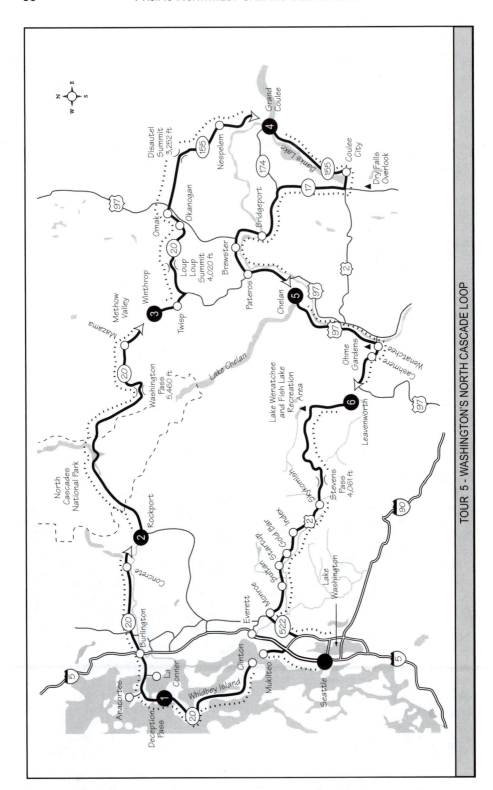

TOUR 5 - WASHINGTON'S NORTH CASCADE LOOP

Your route continues eastward the next day, you cross Loup Loup Pass, drive through the Colville Indian Reservation, and stop for the night at one of the world's manmade wonders, Grand Coulee Dam. The Grand Coulee area has more than just the dam, the surrounding area is a water-sports paradise.

If you liked Grand Coulee you'll probably also like Lake Chelan. It too offers a lot for water-oriented RVers, but there's more. The apple orchards on the surrounding hills give its own unique flavor.

From Chelan you'll start back through the mountains toward Seattle. Your route takes you down the Columbia River and then up the Wenatchee River Valley through fruit orchards and past fruit stands. You'll spend the night in Leavenworth, an unabashedly tourist-oriented town with a Bavarian motif.

Finally, to return to Seattle you'll follow US-2 across Stevens Pass. At 4,061 feet this pass is about 1,400 feet lower than Washington Pass on the North Cascades Highway, it stays open all winter long.

The Roads

This tour almost exclusively follows two-lane highways. All are suitable for any RV.

SR-20, the North Cascades Highway, is only open in the summer. Crews do not clear it of snow so when the snow starts falling in November the road is closed from Mile 134 near Diablo to Mile 171. It doesn't open again until about mid-April, the date depends upon how much snow fell the preceding winter.

Highway 2, which you will follow to return back across the Cascades from the east side is also a two-lane road. This is a well-traveled highway, you'll share the road with lots of others because many people like to drive this scenic route as an alternative to the massive freeway that crosses Snoqualmie Pass to the south.

Practical Tips

Like almost all the tours in this book this one is long if you really only have a week to do it. Fortunately you can easily bypass some of the stops and spend time in the ones that have the most appeal to you. A quick look at our route map will show you that it is particularly easy to bypass the stops at Whidbey Island and Grand Coulee, and thereby save yourself some driving miles too.

If you decide that the ferry ride to Whidbey Island isn't particularly appealing because of the expense or time involved you can easily bypass it by driving north on Interstate 5 to Mount Vernon and then driving westward a relatively short distance on SR-20 to the tour's first-night campgrounds. You'll retrace only a short part of this route the following day on your way to the North Cascades National Park.

As we mentioned above this is definitely a summer- and fall-only route since the North Cascades Highway (SR-20) is not open during the winter. Let the opening dates for the highway define proper season for this tour, all of the other destinations on this tour have excellent weather for the entire time that the North Cascades Highway is open.

🚐 DAY 1 – DESTINATION WHIDBEY ISLAND OR THE SKAGIT VALLEY – 60 MILES (97 KM), 3 HOURS (TO DECEPTION PASS VIA FERRY)

For the first day's drive of this tour you have a choice of routes. If you have the time and feel like taking a ferry ride you can take the ferry from Mukilteo to Whidbey Island and then drive up the island to the evening's destination. If you want to save the ferry toll you can drive farther north and then cut west to the same destination. We'll describe both routes.

For the leisurely ferry route drive north on I-5 for about 12 miles (19 km) to Exit 182 and follow the signs northwest to Mukilteo. A ferry from there provides frequent service to the town of Clinton on the south end of Whidbey Island. Our *Whidbey Island* section (page 281) describes the island and the campgrounds there.

If you don't want to take the ferry just drive north on I-5 for about 60 miles (97 km) to Exit

230. Drive west on US-20 to reach **Deception Pass** at the north end of Whidbey Island. Our section titled *Skagit Valley* (page 269) describes the area and campgrounds.

🚐 DAY 2 – DESTINATION NORTH CASCADES NATIONAL PARK – 57 MILES (92 KM), 2 HOURS (TO ROCKPORT)

From Deception Pass continue following SR-20 northeast. After a few winding miles there's a stop sign where our SR-20 meets what appears to be a major highway. Here a spur of SR-20 (known as 20W) goes left to Anacortes, we go right following what is still the same SR-20 we have been following up Whidbey Island. The road passes over the Swinomish Channel as a four-lane road, crosses farming country for a few miles, narrows to two lanes, and passes under I-5 and into the strip mall area on the outskirts of Burlington. You'll soon see a sign for SR-20 that jogs you north for about a mile before you are directed east on Avon Ave.

You are now established on the **North Cascades Highway**, still called SR-20. For the next 143 miles (231 km), until you reach a junction just south of Twisp, you won't have to make many route choices. The highway is well supplied with mile markers, you'll soon see Milepost 61 and then a sign telling you that Winthrop, on the far side of the Cascade Mountains, is 131 miles (211 km) ahead. The section titled *North Cascades National Park* (page 240) describes the road across the mountains, the park area, and the available campgrounds.

🚐 DAY 3 – DESTINATION WINTHROP – 94 MILES (152 KM), 3 HOURS

Continue east on SR-20. From Washington Pass the road descends steeply for a few miles, then follows the Methow Valley on in to Winthrop. See our section titled *Winthrop and the Methow Valley* (page 284) for information about this area.

🚐 DAY 4 – DESTINATION GRAND COULEE – 99 MILES (160 KM), 2.5 HOURS

From Winthrop head south on SR-20. You'll pass through Twisp and about 2 miles (3 km) south find the intersection where US-20 heads east over Loup Loup Summit. Watch carefully so that you do not miss the turn, although you would expect that US-20 would be the main road it really appears to be a minor side road.

It is 29 miles (47 km) from the intersection near Twisp to the twin towns of Okanogan and Omak. Loup Loup Summit at 4,020 feet presents no real problems even for large RVs, there are two forest service campgrounds near the summit. While it is possible to bypass Okanogan and Omak by jogging south to US- 97 near the western edge of Okanogan it is really not worth the bother, just head straight ahead through the towns, it is more interesting.

In Omak you will see the direction signs pointing right for SR-155. You'll pass across a fairly narrow bridge and then enter the Colville Indian Reservation. As you follow the highway the 50 miles (81 km) across the reservation to Grand Coulee Dam you'll pass across one more pine-clad summit, Disautel Summit at 3,252 feet, and also pass through Nespelem. This is the burial place of Chief Joseph, famous chief of the Nez Perce. Visits to his grave are discouraged. Just south of Nespelem you can stop at the Coleville Indian Agency for information about the reservation. You may also want to visit the **Coleville Tribal Museum** in the town of Grand Coulee if you have an interest in the native American connection here.

The section titled *Grand Coulee* (page 203) outlines things to do and places to stay in the area.

🚐 DAY 5 – DESTINATION CHELAN – 110 MILES (177 KM), 2.5 HOURS

Today's route is rather convoluted, but it passes by and through some interesting sites and country.

From the Grand Coulee Dam area head south on SR-155 along the eastern shore of Banks Lake. Basalt-topped cliffs dominate the landscape along most of the length of the lake. **Steamboat Rock**, almost an island, is impressive and hard to miss. At the south end of the lake you will join US-2 and pass through Coulee City and across the top the low Dry Falls Dam which forms the south end of Banks Lake. A few miles beyond the dam take the side trip south for 2 miles (3 km) to the **Dry Falls Overlook**. There is a small but interesting visitor center there describing the unusual geological history of the area.

Back on US-2 watch for the intersection with SR-17 in about 2 miles (3 km). You want to turn north here. SR-17 goes north through farm land studded with scattered rocks. Eventually, after 21 miles (34 km) you will join SR-174 and drive west to the Columbia at Bridgeport. **Chief Joseph Dam**, second largest electricity-producing dam in the U.S., is located here. The section titled *Lake Pateros Region* (page 221) describes the region and lists the available campgrounds.

Continuing west along the north shore of Lake Pateros you'll pass through Brewster and Pateros, and pass little Wells Dam. Finally you'll spot US-97 Alt branching right to climb the hill to Chelan.

The section titled *Chelan* (page 188) describes the area and the campgrounds there.

DAY 6 – DESTINATION LEAVENWORTH – 53 MILES (85 KM), 1.25 HOURS

From Chelan follow US-97 Alt west along the south shore of the lake and then south through scenic Knapp Coulee and down to the Columbia. The highway follows the river south past Rocky Reach Dam toward Wenatchee.

As you approach the northern outskirts of Wenatchee watch for signs for US-2. Just before you reach the intersection you will see a sign pointing right for **Ohme Gardens**. These hillside gardens are well worth a stop. The Wenatchee area is described in the section titled *Wenatchee* (page 277).

Once established on US-2 you will follow the Wenatchee River Valley westward through fruit tree orchards. After passing Cashmere the valley narrows and the evergreens take over, before long you'll find yourself approaching Leavenworth.

The Leavenworth area is described in our section titled *Leavenworth* (page 225). Just beyond is another interesting area, see *Lake Wenatchee and Fish Lake Recreation Area* (page 224).

DAY 7 – RETURN TO SEATTLE – 114 MILES (184 KM), 3 HOURS

From Leavenworth US-2 leads westward and over Stevens Pass. The pass is 4,061 feet and located 33 miles (53 km) from Leavenworth. Stevens Pass Ski Area at the top of the pass is a popular destination during the winter for Seattle-area skiers.

Once past the summit the road descends steeply to the Skykomish River Valley and passes through a string of little towns: Skykomish, Index, Gold Bar, Startup, Sultan, and finally, Monroe. In Monroe watch for signs for SR-522 on the west side of town. SR-522 will take you southeast to I-405, the Seattle ring road on the east side of Lake Washington.

TOUR 6 – WASHINGTON'S SOUTHERN LOOP

Summary: Starts in Seattle, Washington. On this tour you'll visit Rainier National Park, tour the Yakima Valley wine district, see the north side of the Columbia Gorge, travel up the Spirit Lake Memorial Highway to view Mt St Helens, then circle west to visit Washington State's southern Pacific Coast.

High Points

>> Mt Rainier National Park
>> Yakima Wine Country
>> Columbia Gorge
>> Mt St Helens National Monument
>> Long Beach Peninsula and Willapa Bay
>> Grays Harbor

General Description

This one-week tour will take you to a large variety of landscapes and climates. In seven days

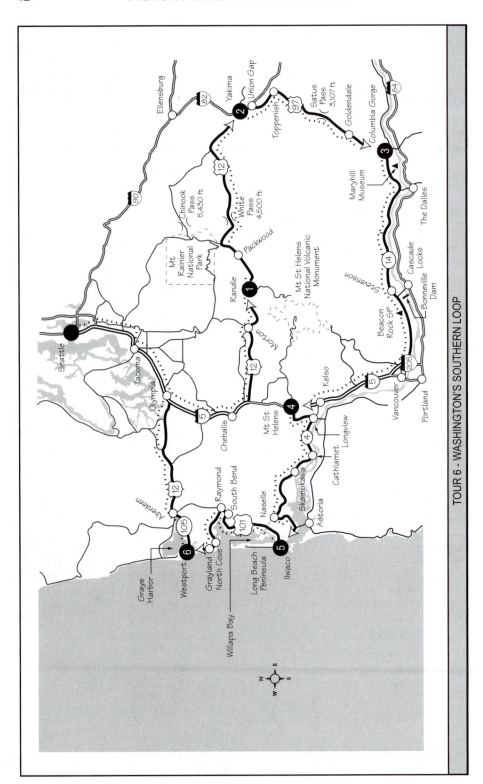

you'll visit mountains, productive farmlands, dry grasslands, an active river corridor, and even the Pacific Coast. Of the three Washington State tours in this book this one visits areas that are probably a little less well-known than the others, yet in many ways it is the best of the three. You'll visit a national park, a national scenic area, and a national volcanic monument. The total distance covered is 766 miles (1,236 km) or an average of about 110 miles (177 km) each day, not at all an uncomfortable distance. Total driving time should be about 20 hours.

From Seattle you'll drive south on I-5 and then east to spend the night near (or in) Mt Rainier National Park. The next day you cross the Cascades through White Pass to the Yakima Valley. From there you head southward to spend the night on the shores of the Columbia River. Traveling westward you will visit Mt St Helens National Monument and then continue westward along the lower Columbia River to the river mouth at Ilwaco and the Long Beach Peninsula. Finally, you'll circle north around Willapa Bay to Westport and then return to Seattle.

The Roads

All of the roads that you will travel on this tour are paved and fairly heavily traveled, big RVs will find no particular obstacles. Almost all of the roads are two-lane although about 200 miles (323 km) of the trip are on the I-5 Interstate or four-lane roads between Aberdeen and Olympia.

About the only places you might have some concern if you are driving a big RV would be the side-trips up the mountain in Mt Rainier National Park and again up the mountain at Mt St Helens National Park. Tow cars are handy at these destinations.

Practical Tips

There is a lot to see and do on this trip. Although the tour is laid out as a 7-day trip you will probably find that you could use more time in the schedule to enjoy the various destinations. It is very easy to cut two or three days from the itinerary by traveling I-5 back to Seattle from Mt St Helens rather than making a visit to the coast. It would also be possible to spend an enjoyable week just visiting the beaches and not even crossing the Cascades.

If you have a lot of time it is also easy to combine this tour with several of the others. When

THE PACIFIC NORTHWEST STONEHENGE

you examine the maps you will see that a combination with the Olympic Peninsula tour makes a lot of sense. You could also combine with Tour 1 of the Oregon coast or Tour 3 of northern Oregon.

DAY 1 – DESTINATION RANDLE AND MT RAINIER NATIONAL PARK – 140 MILES (226 KM), 3.5 HOURS (TO RANDLE)

From Seattle head south on I-5. Avoid the rush hour, traffic between Seattle and Tacoma can be bad. Take Exit 68 south of Chehalis and follow US-12 eastward through Morton and Randle. This area and its campgrounds are described in our Mt *Rainier National Park* section (page 232).

DAY 2 – DESTINATION YAKIMA – 89 MILES (144 KM), 2.5 HOURS

SR-123 into the park branches off US-12 about 7 miles (11 km) northeast of Packwood. US-12 continues east over 4,500 foot White Pass. This road is open year round and presents no problems for larger RVs. The crest of the pass is occupied by the White Pass ski area which is probably best known for the Mahre brothers. These two Olympic skiers grew up skiing here. The climb from the intersection to the pass is 13 miles (21 km), have someone keep an eye on the back window for views of Mt Rainier. Watch for The Palisades turnout, a good place to stop for the view and to see the interesting basalt cliff-side columns.

After the pass the road descends through dryer country, pines begin to appear. You pass Rimrock Lake behind Tieton Dam and follow the Tieton River through canyons rimmed by basalt cliffs. There are several small Forest Service campgrounds along the way. Thirty-four miles (55 km) from the pass US-12 meets SR-410, a summer-only route over 5,430-foot Chinook Pass, and together they soon become a 4-lane highway and continue the 17 miles (27 km) east to Yakima. US-12 meets the I-82 freeway just north of Yakima.

The Yakima area is described in our section titled *Yakima and the Yakima Valley* (page 287).

DAY 3 – DESTINATION MARYHILL – 79 MILES (127 KM), 2 HOURS

US-97 branches off I- 82 just south of Union Gap on the south side of Yakima. For the first 15 miles (24 km) it is a four-lane highway with some side road access.

Just outside **Toppenish** after passing the **Yakama Nation Heritage Center,** the road branches to the right and becomes a two lane highway. This part of the drive, from Union Gap until crossing Satus Pass about 34 miles (55 km) south of Toppenish, is on the Yakama Indian Reservation. It is mostly grasslands with the occasional wooded drainage. As the road climbs you will encounter more trees.

After crossing Satus Pass (3,107 feet) and entering Klickitat County don't be surprised if you encounter a good cross-wind. The Columbia Gorge is famous for its winds, and they often extend far inland from the river.

Sixteen miles (26 km) south of the pass you'll pass the town of Goldendale, a good place to gas up. Goldendale is home of the **Goldendale Observatory**. In the evening visitors are allowed to use the telescope here to view the planets and stars. The observatory is located in Goldendale Observatory State Park just north of town, a good spot for views of mounts Hood, St Helens, Adams, and Rainier.

After passing Goldendale you'll soon start descending into the Columbia Gorge. US-97 meets SR-14 which follows the river's north shore. Follow the signs for US-97 as it jogs down the steep hillside to the river. This area is described in the section titled *Maryhill Region* (page 128 in the *Oregon* chapter).

DAY 4 – DESTINATION MT ST HELENS NATIONAL VOLCANIC MONUMENT – 160 MILES (258 KM), 4 HOURS (TO SILVER LAKE)

From the eastern end of the Columbia Gorge drive along the Washington shore on SR-14. This is a two-lane highway and not nearly as busy as I-84 on the Oregon shore of the river.

The distance from Maryhill to the I-205 freeway at Vancouver, Washington is 95 miles (153 km). Along the way you'll have excellent views of the far side, the river traffic and the windsurfers.

This is a long day's drive and there are several good place to stop and stretch your legs.

About 55 miles (89 km) west of the Maryhill Museum, about a mile west of the town of Stevenson, you might enjoy a visit to the new **Columbia Gorge Interpretive Center**. It is architecturally impressive and houses a variety of objects from the area including a fish wheel, a steam engine, and the largest collection of rosaries in the world.

A few miles farther west you reach **Bonneville Dam.** You can either cross the river on the Bridge of the Gods to the Cascade Locks area and visit the main visitor center (described in the *Oregon* chapter under *Columbia Gorge*, page 94) or visit the newer Second Powerhouse on the Washington side.

Back on the road you won't get far before you reach **Beacon Rock State Park**. The huge Beacon Rock is 848 feet high. It's the core of an ancient volcano and has a path (with railings) all the way to the top, a distance of about a mile and pretty steep.

When you reach I-205 head north toward Seattle, you'll soon merge onto I-5 and after driving a little less than an hour reach Exit 49, your turnoff for Mt St Helens.

This area and its campgrounds are described in our *Mt St Helens National Volcanic Monument* section (page 237).

DAY 5 – DESTINATION ILWACO AND LONG BEACH – 90 MILES (145 KM), 2.5 HOURS

To reach the Long Beach Peninsula from Mt St Helens National Monument you will follow SR-4, the Ocean Beach Hwy, which runs westward on the north shore of the Columbia River. This is not as fast a route as US-30 on the south side of the river. If you are in a hurry you can cross the river into Oregon at Longview and then return when you reach Astoria.

From the Mt St Helens campgrounds near Castle Rock drive south on I-5 a few miles to Exit 39. This is marked as the exit for SR-4. Follow the signs through Longview and soon you'll be leaving town and spot the river off to the left. The highway follows the river until it reaches Cathlamet, then it jogs inland for a short distance, returns to the river at Skamokawa, and then goes inland to climb over a range of hills. Near Naselle take the left onto SR-401 which will take you back to the river. You'll pass the Astoria-Megler Bridge and spot Astoria on the far shore of the river. Ilwaco is just 11 miles (18 km) ahead.

This area is described in the section titled *Ilwaco and Long Beach* (page 213).

DAY 6 – DESTINATION WESTPORT – 80 MILES (129 KM), 2.5 HOURS

To reach Westport you follow US-101 east and then north around the eastern shore of Willapa Bay. At Raymond, just past South Bend and 45 miles (73 km) from the Long Beach area, turn westward toward the coast again and follow the highway through North Cove and Grayland. You'll reach an intersection where the stub road to Westport meets SR-105 and, continuing north three miles (5 km), soon find yourself in Westport.

This area is described in the section titled *Westport* (page 279)

DAY 7 – DESTINATION SEATTLE – 128 MILES (206 KM), 3 HOURS

The drive back to Seattle is an easy one, most roads are limited access highways. Follow SR-105 east to Aberdeen. Turn eastward on US-12. You'll soon hit 4-lane highway and never really have to slow down much, except during rush hours, as you travel east to an intersection with Interstate 5 just south of Olympia, then north on I-5 through Tacoma to Seattle

TOUR 7 – BRITISH COLUMBIA MAINLAND LOOP

Summary: This tour starts in Vancouver, British Columbia. It travels eastward to the Okanagan Valley, then even farther east to the Rocky Mountain national parks: Yoho, Banff, and Jasper. As you turn back toward Vancouver you'll visit two more parks, Mt Robson and

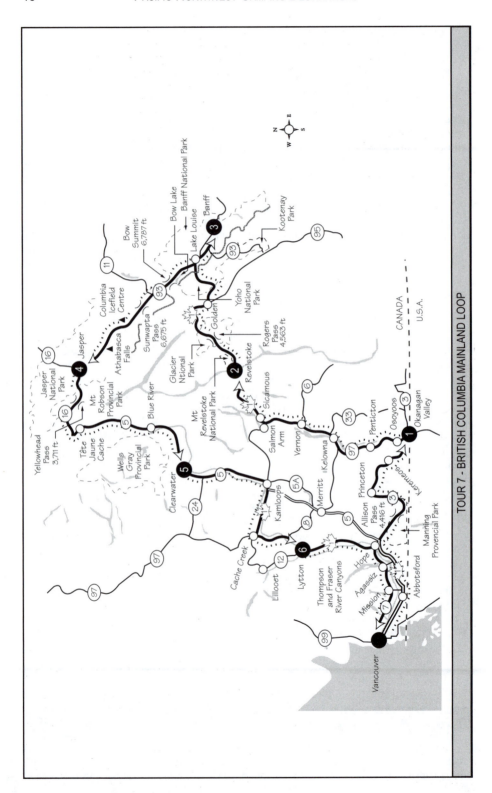

Wells Gray, before descending through the Fraser Canyon to the coast.

High Points

- » Okanagan Valley
- » Canadian Rockies including Yoho, Banff, and Jasper National Parks
- » Lake Louise
- » Icefields Parkway and the Columbia Icefield
- » Mt Robson
- » Wells Gray Provincial Park and Helmcken Falls
- » Fraser River Canyon

General Description

Inland British Columbia represent one of the premier RVing destinations in North America. This is a spectacularly beautiful region, you'll see more impressive mountain scenery here than anywhere else you are likely to ever take an RV.

This is a huge area. While it would theoretically be possible to make this entire tour in one week we definitely would not recommend that you try to do so. At the end of your trip you would be exhausted. You would also feel like you had missed more than you had seen. The distances are long and the miles are packed with things to see while several individual destinations offer plenty to keep you busy for several days. Our advice: plan on at least two weeks if you want to do this entire trip. Driving distance for the tour is 2,018 km (1,251 miles), approximate driving time is 32 hours.

The route starts at the coast in the province's largest city, Vancouver. As you drive up the Fraser River Valley you will be crossing a very civilized area of farms and small towns. However, when you reach Hope you leave all this and immediately begin climbing into a much more sparsely populated region. Highway 3 crosses both the Hozameen and Okanagan Ranges and passes through Manning Provincial Park before descending into irrigated fruit-growing country in the Okanagan Valley.

After spending some time in the valley this tour heads north to Salmon Arm where it joins the transcontinental Highway 1 and turns eastward. After stopping for a night near Revelstoke in the Columbia River Valley you'll climb to cross through Glacier National Park and the Dogtooth Range, descend to cross over the Columbia River once again, and then ascend into the Canadian Rockies through Yoho National Park to Banff National Park.

When you've had a chance to see all there is to see in Banff you can head north along the Icefields Parkway past the Columbia Icefield to Jasper National Park. Jasper too has a lot to offer, but after a couple of days it is time to begin the drive back toward Vancouver. During the day you'll pass through Mt Robson Provincial Park and then spend the night either in or near Wells Gray Provincial Park.

Continuing southward you'll follow a slightly out-of-the-way route to thread your way down the impressively scenic Thompson and Fraser River Valleys. You'll spend the night in the canyons and then continue south to meet the expressway near Hope and retrace your way down the Fraser Valley to Vancouver.

The Roads

Virtually all of the roads on this tour are of the two-lane variety. On the other hand, although they are two-lane roads they are in excellent condition with good shoulders and frequent passing lanes and rest areas. This is a mountainous route, it starts at sea level and travels over may passes reaching its highest altitude on the Icefields Parkway in Banff National Park, 2,067 meters (6,787 feet). If you have toured Colorado this may not seem high but rest assured that you will be more than satisfied by the mountains you find along this route.

Practical Tips

Since this tour traverses fairly high mountain country, particularly in Banff and Jasper National Parks, it is a summer trip. Plan to start no earlier than May and to be out of the mountains before the end of September. Even within these boundaries it is very possible that you might receive a dusting of snow during the night.

In this section you'll find lots of ways to make a one-week tour into a two or three-week one. Here's one way to shorten things a bit. One way to make more time is to use the new Highway 5, also known as the Coquihalla Highway. Using the Coquihalla from Hope to Merritt and then the Okanagan Connector from Merritt to Kelowna you can cut the first day's 7 hour drive down to only 4 to 5 hours. On your way home, if you've overstayed along the way, you can drive directly from Clearwater to Vancouver and cut an entire day from your itinerary by following the Coquihalla Highway from Kamloops to Hope.

▣ DAY 1 – DESTINATION THE OKANAGAN VALLEY – 371 KILOMETERS (230 MILES), 6.5 HOURS (TO OSOYOOS)

From Vancouver point your RV's nose east and follow the Trans-Canada Highway to the town of Hope. The entire 188 kilometer (117 mile) distance is along a multi-lane limited access freeway.

Hope forms a kind of transportation crossroads. In or near the town three major routes intersect. Highway 1 heads north from town up the Fraser Canyon. Highway 5, also called the Coquihalla Highway, provides a quick and direct toll route north to Kamloops. And finally, Highway 3 , the Crowsnest Highway, winds its scenic way east. You'll be following Highway 3 but first you might want to stop and take a look at Hope. The section titled *Hope* (page 325) describes the area and campgrounds.

Highway 3 is a fine two-lane highway, but it does cross some healthy mountains. From Hope to Osoyoos at the south end of Canada's section of the Okanagan Valley is a distance of 246 kilometers (153 miles). The highest point along the route is Allison Pass in Manning Provincial Park with an altitude of 1,352 meters (4,416 feet).

Deep in the Cascades the highway enters **Manning Provincial Park**. There are four campgrounds in the park, all are suitable for RVs. The campgrounds, a visitor center, and the Manning Park Resort with a restaurant and other services are all located near each other about 42 kilometers (26 miles) east of Hope. You'll note signs for several hiking trails as you drive through the park, some have decent parking areas for big RVs.

Continuing east you'll begin to notice that the countryside is becoming much dryer. You'll pass through the ranch and lumber town of Princeton and then, 198 kilometers (123 miles) from Hope enter Keremeos. You can't miss the huge number of fruit stands along the highway in this town, you're entering British Columbia's fruit country. A combination of warm sunny weather and abundant water from irrigation make this the country's fruit basket. Expect to find cherries by the end of June, apricots in July, peaches just a little later, pears toward the end of August, and apples in September. Fruit ripens first in the southern Okanagan and later in the north because the south is warmer.

Just 48 more kilometers (30 miles) along Hwy 3 and you will arrive in Osoyoos, the south end of Canada's Okanagan Valley, almost on the U.S. border.

The *Okanagan Valley* section (page 342) describes the area and some of its campgrounds.

▣ DAY 2 – DESTINATION REVELSTOKE – 321 KILOMETERS (199 MILES), 4.5 HOURS

From the Okanagan Valley follow Hwy 97 north to intersect the Trans-Canada highway (Hwy 1) near Salmon Arm and Sicamous. Both of these towns are on the shore of **Shuswap Lake**. See the *Shuswap* section (page 361) for more about this region.

The distance from Salmon Arm to Revelstoke through the Monashee Mountains is only 104 kilometers (64 miles) so you'll soon find yourself approaching Revelstoke. The *Revelstoke* section (page 354) describes the attractions and campgrounds of this area.

▣ DAY 3 – DESTINATION BANFF NATIONAL PARK – 233 KILOMETERS (145 MILES), 3 HOURS (TO LAKE LOUISE)

From Revelstoke to Banff National Park Highway 1 follows the original route of the Ca-

SHEEP ARE COMMON IN THE BRITISH COLUMBIA NATIONAL PARKS

nadian Pacific Railway. This portion of the railroad was one of the most problematic when it was being built in the 1880s because of the terrain it crosses. Today, for highway travelers, that translates into a scenic and interesting day of driving.

East of Revelstoke just 72 kilometers (45 miles) the highway crosses **Rogers Pass** (1,387 meters, 4,563 feet) in the middle of Glacier National Park. See the *Glacier National Park* section (page 321) for more about this area.

Continuing westward the highway descends to the Columbia River at the town of Golden. Here the river is flowing north, not south. From Golden the road ascends the valley of the Kicking Horse River and soon enters Yoho National Park. See the section titled *Yoho National Park and Golden* (page 395) for more about this area.

You'll enter Banff National Park at the eastern border of Yoho National Park. See the section titled *Banff National Park* (page 300) for information about this area and its campgrounds.

⛟ DAY 4 – DESTINATION JASPER NATIONAL PARK – 232 KILOMETERS (144 MILES), 5 HOURS (TO JASPER TOWNSITE)

The route to be followed today is entirely along the 230 kilometer (143 mile) Icefields Parkway stretching from an intersection on the Trans-Canada Highway near Lake Louise north through the mountains to Jasper. Don't hurry along this highway, there is plenty of magnificent scenery and many places to stop, enjoy the view, and even take some hikes.

Like most Canadian national parks there is a day fee for the use of Banff and Jasper National Parks. It is possible to drive through Banff Park on Highway 1 without paying the fee, but not the Icefield Parkway. There are kiosks on both ends of the Icefields Parkway to collect the fee.

Some 35 kilometers (21 miles) from the start of the Parkway you'll come to **Bow Lake**. From here you'll see no more of the Bow River. There's a viewpoint where you can look across the turquoise-colored lake and see Num-Ti-Jah Lodge and the Bow Glacier beyond.

Six kilometers (4 miles) beyond Bow lake the highway crests Bow Summit at 2,067 meters (6,787 feet). This is the highest point on the Parkway.

Seventy-five kilometers (47 miles) north of the intersection with Highway 1 the Parkway crosses the North Saskatchewan River. To the west is the Howse Valley. The North Saskatchewan River and the Howse Valley were one of the early passes used by explorers and fur traders to cross the Rocky Mountains. Highway 11 heads east from here to Rocky Mountain House and Red Deer.

Sunwapta Pass (2,035 meters, 6,675 feet) marks the boundary between Banff National Park and Jasper National park. A few kilometers north of the pass is the huge **Columbia Icefield Center**. This is an observatory with great views across the valley to the Athabasca Glacier and the Columbia Icefield. It also serves as the embarkation point for bus tours onto the glacier. Busses leave the Center and drive to edge of the glacier, there passengers change to special vehicles with huge tires called snocoaches to actually drive out onto the glacier. As an alternative you can drive to the foot of the glacier yourself and take a short hike for a close look. The Icefield Center also houses a Parks Canada Visitor Centre.

It is well worth a short side trip off the highway to take a look at **Athabasca Falls**. The access road is actually a short section of Highway 93A which was an older version of today's highway that runs north along the western side of the valley parallel to today's road for about 25 kilometers. The turn for Athabasca Falls is well marked, it is 73 kilometers (45 miles) north of the Columbia Icefield Center. The Athabasca River drops over a ledge and tumbles through a narrow canyon. Overlooks and a pedestrian bridge offer excellent views, a great place for pictures.

Thirty kilometers (19 miles) beyond the falls the Icefield Parkway intersects Highway 16 which crosses the Rockies through Yellowhead Pass. If you continue straight on across the highway you will find yourself in Jasper townsite. See the section titled *Jasper National Park* (page 327) for more about this area.

▦ DAY 5 – DESTINATION WELLS GRAY PROVINCIAL PARK – 318 KILOMETERS (197 MILES), 5.5 HOURS (TO CLEARWATER)

From the Jasper townsite area we'll follow Hwy 16 westward across Yellowhead Pass (1,131 meters, 3,711 feet), and into **Mt Robson Provincial Park**. You'll be driving along the upper Fraser River Valley and pass Yellowhead and Moose Lakes. **Mt Robson** is the highest mountain in the Canadian Rockies (3,954 meters, 12,972 feet). You can stop at the visitor center near the western border of the park some 62 kilometers (38 miles) west of Yellowhead Pass. From the visitor center you have a spectacular view of the mountain. The reason it is so impressive is that the visitor center sits at an altitude of only about 850 meters (2,800 feet) and is only 11 kilometers from the mountain, you definitely get the full effect.

From Mt Robson Provincial Park the highway continues westward until it meets Highway 5 near Tête Jaune Cache. Turn south here toward Kamloops. The highway climbs over a low pass and then follows the North Thompson River Valley through the small town of Blue River and eventually reaches Clearwater. See the section titled *Wells Gray Provincial Park (Clearwater River Corridor Section) and Clearwater* (page 387) for information about this area and its camping possibilities.

▦ DAY 6 – DESTINATION THOMPSON AND FRASER RIVER VALLEYS – 286 KILOMETERS (177 MILES), 4 HOURS (TO LYTTON)

From Clearwater we follow Highway 5 and the North Thompson River for 115 kilometers (71 miles) south to Kamloops. See the section titled *Kamloops* (page 332) for more about the region and its campgrounds. Here you have a choice. If you want to get back to Vancouver a day early you can continue on Highway 5, known as the Coquihalla Highway, from here to Hope. This is a high speed toll highway that will cut several driving hours from the trip back to Vancouver.

On the other hand, if you have another day and wish to see one of the most impressive river canyons and railroad/road engineering projects in the world, head westward from Kamloops on Highway 1. This is our old friend, the Trans-Canada Highway, last seen in Banff National Park.

From Kamloops the road travels along Kamloops Lake and then parallel to the Thompson River. When it reaches Cache Creek the highway turns south and soon you are in the Thompson River Canyon. See the section titled *Thompson and Fraser River Canyons* (page 369) for information about the area and its camping possibilities.

DAY 7 – DESTINATION VANCOUVER – 256 KILOMETERS (159 MILES), 3.5 HOURS

Once Highway 1 crosses to the west bank of the Fraser River you have reached the lower reaches of the canyon. The road remains on the west side for 42 kilometers (26 miles) until it crosses again at Hope.

Just before reaching Hope you have a route choice. If you are in a hurry you can continue on to Hope and then follow Highway 1 back to Vancouver, this is the same highway that you drove when you were heading east on the first day of this tour.

If you have more time you can follow Highway 7 along the north side of the Fraser River. This is a much smaller two-lane highway. You can follow it all the way to Vancouver or cross over the Fraser River to intersect Highway 1 near Agassiz (near Bridal Falls on Hwy 1) or Mission (near Abbotsford on Hwy 1).

TOUR 8 – BRITISH COLUMBIA'S SUNSHINE COAST AND VANCOUVER ISLAND LOOP

Summary: This tour starts in Vancouver, British Columbia. Hop up the Sunshine Coast to Powell River using a combination of ferries and roads, then cross to Vancouver Island. Visit the west coast of the Island at Tofino, then head southward to Victoria before returning to Vancouver, again by ferry.

Top Attractions

- » The Sunshine Coast
- » Ferry rides up the Sunshine Coast and through the Gulf Islands
- » Campbell River and great salmon fishing
- » Pacific Rim National Park
- » First Nations Culture
- » Victoria

General Description

One of the most popular destinations in the Pacific Northwest is Vancouver Island. This large island is easily accessible using frequent ferries from near Vancouver on the mainland. On the island you'll find British Columbia's capital, Victoria, as well as remote beaches, northwest Indian culture (called First Nations in Canada), some of the best salmon fishing in the world, and pristine evergreen forests. An added bonus of this tour is the Sunshine Coast which stretches over 100 kilometers (62 miles) north from the city of Vancouver along the mainland and offers surprisingly good weather and warm water because it is in the rain shadow of Vancouver Island's mountains.

The tour starts at the Horseshoe Bay ferry terminal just north of Vancouver. On the first day you take two ferry rides and do some driving on scenic two-lane roads as you travel up the Sunshine Coast to Powell River. Later, when you are ready, you take another ferry across to Vancouver Island. On the Island you visit Campbell River, and then work your way down the island with visits to Tofino, Nanaimo, Duncan, and finally the Victoria area in the south. This circular route ends with another ferry trip through the Gulf Islands to Tsawwassen which is located on the mainland just south of the city of Vancouver.

This is a relaxed tour with relatively short distances between most of your stops. Many days you will have time for a significant amount of sightseeing or just plain enjoying the outdoors. There are also plenty of reasons to expand this tour into a two or three week trip.

The Roads and Ferries

The ferries used in this circular tour are all operated by the British Columbia Ferry Cor-

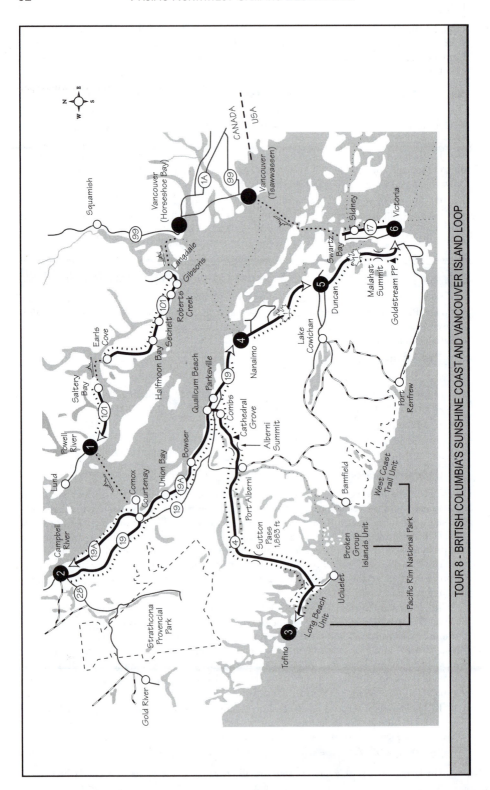

TOUR 8 - BRITISH COLUMBIA'S SUNSHINE COAST AND VANCOUVER ISLAND LOOP

poration, also known as BC Ferries. It is not possible to make reservations for these crossings. Reservations are not usually necessary anyway. However, it is best to avoid travel on weekends during the high season: late May, June, July, August and early September, to avoid long lines. There is a special fare plan for this circle route which is known as the Circlepac and which will net you a discount of about 15%. If your RV is over 7 feet high or 20 feet long you will be paying more than the normal passenger vehicle rate for ferry travel. See the individual route sections for other information about the ferries. You will find additional information about the ferries in Chapter 1.

For the most part the roads traveled on this tour are very good. Few are more than two-lane highways, but they are adequate for all types of RVs and there are no high passes. You will find much more information about the roads in the individual sections of this chapter. Total driving distance on this tour is 815 kilometers (505 miles) with 23 hours on the road (including ferries).

Practical Tips

It is best to make this tour during the summer, say from May to September. The months of April and October are acceptable if you don't mind some rain and have a good warm RV in which to spend the night. You will find that some campgrounds are open year-round, some folks love to visit the wild western coast around Tofino just for the winter storms.

It is pretty easy to shorten this loop if you don't have time for the whole thing. One way would be to cut out the Sunshine Coast and Campbell River by taking a ferry directly from Horseshoe Bay to Nanaimo. You could still make the drive out to Tofino (day three's destination) or skip that too.

🚐 DAY 1 – DESTINATION POWELL RIVER – 127 KILOMETERS (79 MILES) (DOES NOT INCLUDE FERRY), 5 HOURS (DOES INCLUDE FERRY)

The first segment of today's drive is a 45-minute ferry ride from Horseshoe Bay across Howe Sound to Langdale. There are frequent ferries from Horseshoe Bay (approximately every two hours) so you don't have to worry much about your schedule there, but you should check when you buy your ticket to see when the Earls Cove to Saltery Bay ferry runs. Otherwise you might find yourself waiting for quite a long period at the dock in Earls Cove, particularly if you arrive there in the early afternoon. The travel time given above for this day's drive includes a half-hour for loading and unloading at each of the ferry landings.

When you leave the boat in Langdale you are on the Sunshine Coast proper. Some folks call this area the Lower Coast. Highway 101 runs north near the coast for 79 kilometers (49 miles) through the communities of Gibsons, Roberts Creek, Sechelt, Halfmoon Bay, Madeira Park, and Pender Harbor to Earls Cove. See the section titled *Sunshine Coast (Lower)* (page 364) for information about the attractions and campgrounds in this area.

The ferry from Earls Cover to Saltery Bay also runs approximately every two hours, but there is a 4-hour gap in the schedule in the afternoon. This run takes about 50 minutes and crosses Jervis Inlet. The coast north from Saltery Bay to Powell River could properly be called the Upper Sunshine Coast but it is so dominated by the town of Powell River that most folks just call it Powell River. The distance from Saltery Bay to Powell River is 27 kilometers (17 miles). See the section titled *Sunshine Coast (Upper)* (page 366) for more about this area and its campgrounds.

🚐 DAY 2 – DESTINATION CAMPBELL RIVER – 48 KILOMETERS (30 MILES) (DOES NOT INCLUDE FERRY), 3.5 HOURS (INCLUDING FERRY)

The ferry from Powell River to Little River near Comox on Vancouver Island makes the trip only a few times each day. Make sure to check the schedule so that you don't oversleep. The crossing takes about an hour and a half.

From Comox follow Highway 19A north to Campbell River. By selecting Hwy 19A as you near Campbell River you'll come into town along the coast.

See the section titled *Campbell River* (page 308) for information about the area and its campgrounds.

🚐 DAY 3 – DESTINATION TOFINO – 268 KILOMETERS (166 MILES), 5 HOURS

The drive from Campbell River to Tofino takes you south through the Comox Valley region to Qualicum Beach and then all the way across the island to the west coast. While the drive sounds ambitious it really is no problem.

From Campbell River follow Highway 19 south. After 45 kilometers (28 miles) you'll reach Courtenay and drive through an area of strip malls and giant supermarkets. Watch for signs for Highway 19A, it is the road that follows the coast south. A new section of Hwy 19 passes farther inland and is not as scenic. You'll pass several small seaside towns including Union Bay, Fanny Bay, Bowser, and finally reach Qualicum Beach. This is an attractive stretch of ocean-side country, it is one of the places you could spend the night on Day 4 after returning from the west coast.

At Qualicum Beach you will spot Highway 4 heading up the hill to the west toward Port Alberni and eventually Tofino. Turn here and you'll pass through the business district, cross under the inland Highway 19, and then pass the little town of Coombs. Pull over and take a look around. You'll probably enjoy visiting the old Coombs General Store, Frontier Town, antique shops, and the Old Country Market. Don't miss the goats on the roof! Heading west from Coombs toward Port Alberni watch for the sign for **Butterfly World**, it's a tropical garden filled with butterflies and birds. Farther west you'll see the signs for Qualicum Falls Provincial Park. There's a good campground here as well as hiking paths to see the falls. A little farther west you'll find yourself passing through an area of huge trees, mostly Douglas Firs. There's a pull-off parking area here and you can follow trails through **Cathedral Grove** in MacMillan Provincial Park.

The road soon rises and passes over low Alberni Summit (375 meters, 1230 feet) and then descends to pass through the northern edge of the town of Port Alberni. See the section titled *Port Alberni* (page 345) for more about this area.

About 48 kilometers (30 miles) beyond Port Alberni you'll reach 574-meter (1,883 foot) Sutton Pass and then the road descends steeply and in another 10 kilometers (6 miles) you will reach a T intersection. Ucluelet is to the left (6 kilometers, 4 miles) and Tofino to the right (33 kilometers, 20 miles). Most of the Long Beach section of Pacific Rim National Park is also to the right. For now turn to the right, you can come back and explore Ucluelet later if you desire.

See the section titled *Tofino, Ucluelet, and the Pacific Rim National Park* (page 371) for more about this area and its campgrounds.

🚐 DAY 4 – DESTINATION NANAIMO – 215 KILOMETERS (133 MILES), 4 HOURS (TO NANAIMO)

To drive to Nanaimo you must retrace your trip westward on Highway 4 as far as Qualicum Beach. You might stop and take a look at Ucluelet which we bypassed on the outbound trip.

When you have backtracked across the island and again reached the east coast in Qualicum Beach, turn south. Just south of Qualicum Beach is Parksville, which, like Qualicum Beach, has many campgrounds. You can overnight here or farther south near Nanaimo. See the section titled *Oceanside* (page 339) for more about this area and its campgrounds.

Highways 19 and 19A merge just south of Parksville, then 16 kilometers (10 miles) south, they split again with the new Highway 19 Nanaimo Parkway (bypass route) being the preferred route to the Nanaimo campgrounds. See the section titled *Nanaimo* (page 336) for more about the area and its campgrounds.

🚐 DAY 5 – DESTINATION DUNCAN AND COWICHAN LAKE – 52 KILOMETERS (32 MILES), 1 HOUR (TO DUNCAN)

Duncan lies only an hour's drive south of Nanaimo along what is designated as Highway 1. It's really the same highway that you have been following south along the east side of Vancouver

MURAL PAINTED ON A CHEMAINUS BUILDNG

Island, but here it is considered to be the final kilometers of the Trans-Canada Highway that begins in Newfoundland and ends in Victoria.

For information about the area and campgrounds surrounding Duncan see *Cowichan Valley: Chemainus, Duncan, and Cowichan Lake* (page 315).

⬛ Day 6 – Destination Victoria – 56 kilometers (35 miles), 1 hour

From Duncan it is only a short drive south to Victoria. Twenty-nine kilometers (18 miles) south of Duncan the highway climbs to the **Malahat Summit**, there is a great viewpoint but access from the southbound lanes is limited, you may have to drive another kilometer or so to a good turnaround if you want to stop and enjoy the view.

A few kilometers after the summit viewpoint you pass through Goldstream Provincial Park. This park has an excellent campground and is convenient to Victoria. It also has a number of hiking trails through first-growth forest of Douglas Fir and cedar as well as waterfalls and lookout points.

Once you pass Goldstream Park you're only a short distance from Victoria and it is time to start watching for the city campgrounds. See the section titled *Victoria* (page 383) for information about the area and its campgrounds.

⬛ Day 7 – Destination Vancouver – 48 kilometers (30 miles) (does not include ferry), 3.5 hours (including ferry)

The ferry back to Vancouver departs from Swartz Bay at the north end of the Saanich Peninsula. To get there just drive north on Hwy 17 from Victoria for 32 kilometers (20 miles). Ferries run frequently. They dock at Tsawwassen which is only a half hour drive south of Vancouver.

Chapter 3 - How to use the Destination Chapters

The chapters titled Oregon, Washington, and British Columbia are the meat of this book. Each starts with an index map, it's the easiest way to find the information you need. The chapters begin with general descriptions of the landforms and regions of each state or province. Then there's information about the government campgrounds and their reservations systems (if any).

Finally you'll come to the ***Destinations and Their Campgrounds*** section. Each destination section includes a map to give you the lay of the land and to pinpoint campground locations. The maps are for the most part pretty easy to interpret, here is a symbol key.

MAP LEGEND

84 Major Freeway	**97** Secondary Road No.	State Border
Other Paved Roads	**20** Other Road No.	Country Border
Unpaved Roads	Canadian National Hwy	Campground with Text Write-up
Freeway Off-ramp	Railroad	Campground - no Text Write-up
Exit 2 Off-ramp - Name Indicated	Ferry Route	) (Mountain Pass
5 Freeway Number	○ City, Town, or Village	▲ Area of Interest
City Center	◉ Roundabout	Major Airport
		Other Airport

We have selected destinations that are great places to visit in an RV. These are places with convenient campgrounds as well as lots to see and do. Some of these are cities and towns, others are general recreational areas that may cover quite a bit of territory. We give you some background information about the place and also describe some of the attractions that you might want to visit.

Campground Information

Immediately after the name of the campground we give the opening and closing dates. Then there is contact information for making reservations or making inquiries by phone or email.

A location line gives the campground location with respect to some nearby landmark. The latitude and longitude data can be used if you have an electronic mapping program, a dashboard navigation system, or handheld GPS. At the end of the line is the approximate elevation of the campground.

Next is a line of pictograms or symbols. These are designed to convey important information about the campground at a glance. For your convenience abbreviated keys to these symbols are located on the back inside cover to this book.

FREE	Free	$ $$$	Over $15 and up to $20
$	Up To $5	$$ $$$	Over $20 and up to $25
$$	Over $5 and up to $10	$$$ $$$	Over $25 and up to $30
$$$	Over $10 and up to $15	Over $$$ $$$	Over $30

The first symbols are for price. Since campground prices do change frequently this is really an approximation, but it is the price that was in effect when the book was issued. It is the price for a standard full-hookup site with 30-amp power (if available) for a 30-foot RV. If you are tent camping you may find that no-hookup tent sites are often available for considerably less. If you are in a larger RV requiring a pull-thru site, 50-amp power, or yours is a premium or view site you will probably find that the price is higher.

The remaining symbols are as follows:

 Tents – The campground does allow tent campers.

 Rentals – The campground has rental cottages of some kind for those who do not want to sleep in a tent or RV. They may be yurts, motel rooms, cabins, or even tepees.

 20 Amp Electric – Low amp electrical hookups are available. High-amp hookups are not as important in the Northwest as they are in some other places since air conditioning is usually not necessary. In the hot desert country on the eastern side of the mountains it may be. Most low amp electrical hookups have 20 amp breakers but occasionally you'll find a 15 or even 10 amp circuit.

 30 Amp Electric – 30 amp electrical outlets are available.

 50 Amp Electric – 50 amp electrical outlets are available.

 Water – There is water at some or all of the sites. If there is no symbol then water is at faucets or a pump not at the sites. If there is no water we indicate so in the text section.

 Sewer – The sewer symbol means that there are sewer drains available at some or all sites.

 Dump – Indicates that there is a dump station (sani-station) available.

 Flush Toilets – All of the campgrounds listed in this book have toilets, the toilet symbol in our descriptions shows which ones are flush toilets. You may also run into pit or vault (outhouse-style) toilets, particularly in provincial or federal campgrounds.

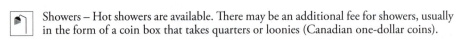

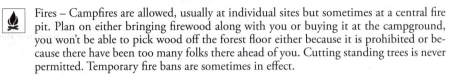

Showers – Hot showers are available. There may be an additional fee for showers, usually in the form of a coin box that takes quarters or loonies (Canadian one-dollar coins).

Fires – Campfires are allowed, usually at individual sites but sometimes at a central fire pit. Plan on either bringing firewood along with you or buying it at the campground, you won't be able to pick wood off the forest floor either because it is prohibited or because there have been too many folks there ahead of you. Cutting standing trees is never permitted. Temporary fire bans are sometimes in effect.

Swimming – Swimming is available either on-site or very nearby. It may be a swimming pool, lake, river, or even the ocean if folks customarily swim there. There are almost never lifeguards, you swim at your own risk. If the swimming is outdoors (not an inside pool) it will be seasonal.

Playground – There is a playground for children with swings, slides and the equivalent or there are horseshoes, a play field, or provisions for some other type of sports.

Telephone – There is a pay phone or courtesy phone available.

TV – TV hookups are available at some or all sites.

Internet – Internet access of some kind is available. It may be an outlet (dataport) for you to plug in your computer modem cable or it may be a computer with internet access that you will be allowed to use.

WI-Fi – Indicates that Wi-Fi (wireless internet) is available in the campground. Wi-Fi access is the fastest changing amenity offered by campgrounds today. Campgrounds are adding Wi-Fi access at a pretty good clip. If this is important to you don't hesitate to ask before making a reservation or perhaps call ahead as you approach your destination to determine the current offerings of the campgrounds you are considering.

Free Wi-Fi – Wi-Fi is not only available – it's free. Since Wi-Fi is such a new thing many campground owners are feeling their way on this. We're finding that many that charged at first are now offering it for free, but also that some that originally didn't charge now are. If you like free Wi-Fi you should let campgrounds owners know it.

Groceries – Many campgrounds have small stores. We've included this symbol if the store appears to have enough stock to be useful, or if there is an off-site store within easy walking distance.

Restaurants – Few campgrounds in the U.S. or Canada have restaurants, but if they do, or if there is one within easy walking distance, we include the restaurant symbol.

Laundry – The campground has self-operated washers.

Propane – The campground offers either bottled propane or a propane fill station.

Ice – Either block or cubed ice is available for ice chests or drinks.

Handicap – The wheelchair symbol indicates that at least partial handicapped access is provided. These provisions vary considerably, you should call the information number listed for the campground to get more details if this is a consideration for you.

No Pets – No dogs or cats are allowed. Virtually all campgrounds require leashes and the majority restrict number, size, and breed. Call the information number to inquire if this might apply to you.

Reservations – Reservations are taken. Please refer to the *Campground Reservations* sections at the beginning of the Destinations chapters for information about making reservations at government campgrounds. Commercial campgrounds are easier, just call the listed telephone number.

 Credit Cards – Either Master Card or Visa is accepted.

 Good Sam – Many campgrounds give a discount to members of the Good Sam Club. We include the symbol if they are official Good Sam campgrounds. We find that the standards required for listing by Good Sam mean that in general these campgrounds stand out as having decent facilities, good management, and relatively fair prices. For club information call (800) 234-3450 or see their website at www.goodsamclub.com.

 Escapees – The Escapee symbol means that discounts are offered to members of the Escapees RV Club. Call (888) 757-2582 or (936) 327-8873 for more information or see their website – www.escapees.com.

 FMCA – Discounts are available to FMCA members. Call (800) 543-3622 or (513) 474-3622 for more information if you own a qualifying motorhome, or check the website at www.fmca.com.

 Passport America – Passport America discount cards are accepted. Most campgrounds offering this discount also will sell you the card.

 Coast to Coast – This is a Coast to Coast park.

 40 Foot RVs – Coaches to 40 feet will fit in the park. See *RV Size* below for more about this.

In the text portion of the campground listing we try to give you some feeling for the campground as well as detailed instructions for how to find it. We've included a count of the number of sites in a campground so that you'll have some idea of the size of the campground. These are our count and may vary from the owner's count, particularly if there are tent sites at the campground since the separation in these is often difficult to distinguish.

RV Size

Our Big Rig symbol means that there is room for coaches to 40 feet to enter the campground, maneuver, and park. Usually this means we've seen them do it. The driver we saw may have been a better driver than most so exercise caution. If you pull a fifth-wheel you'll have to use your own judgment of how your RV handles compared with a coach. If you drive an even larger 45-foot coach you can at least use our symbol as a starting point in making your campground decisions. There's often more in the write-up itself about this, and we also usually mention pull-thrus if available. Always evaluate the campground and assigned space yourself before attempting to maneuver and park, the final decision is yours. A properly trained outside spotter is essential, most RV accidents occur during the parking phase.

Units of Measurement

The region covered by this guide uses two different sets of measurements. Canada is on the metric system while the U.S. uses miles and gallons.

We've given mileages in both kilometers and miles. In the U.S. the miles come first, in British Columbian the kilometers do.

Here are some handy conversion factors:

1 km = .62 mile	1 liter = .26 U.S. gallon
1 mile = 1.61 km	1 U.S. gallon = 3.79 liters
1 meter = 3.28 feet	1 kilogram = 2.21 pounds
1 foot = .3 meters	1 pound = .45 kilogram

Convert from °F to °C by subtracting 32 and multiplying by 5/9
Convert from °C to °F by multiplying by 1.8 and adding 32

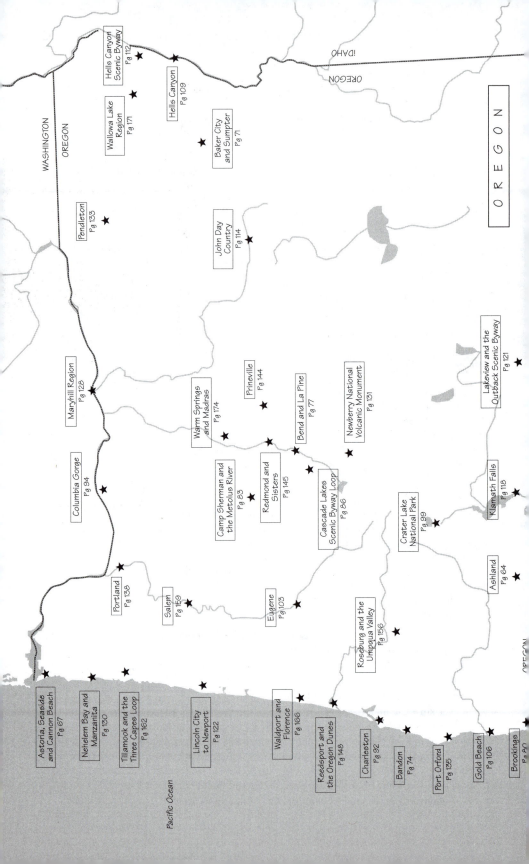

WASHINGTON
OREGON

IDAHO
OREGON

OREGON

Pacific Ocean

O R E G O N

Hells Canyon Scenic Byway
Pg 112

Wallowa Lake Region
Pg 171

Hells Canyon
Pg 109

Baker City and Sumpter
Pg 71

Pendleton
Pg 133

John Day Country
Pg 114

Maryhill Region
Pg 128

Columbia Gorge
Pg 94

Warm Springs and Madras
Pg 174

Prineville
Pg 144

Bend and La Pine
Pg 77

Newberry National Volcanic Monument
Pg 131

Lakeview and the Outback Scenic Byway
Pg 121

Camp Sherman and the Metolus River
Pg 83

Redmond and Sisters
Pg 145

Cascade Lakes Scenic Byway Loop
Pg 86

Klamath Falls
Pg 118

Crater Lake National Park
Pg 99

Portland
Pg 138

Salem
Pg 159

Eugene
Pg 103

Roseburg and the Umpqua Valley
Pg 156

Ashland
Pg 64

Astoria, Seaside and Cannon Beach
Pg 67

Nehalem Bay and Manzanita
Pg 130

Tillamook and the Three Capes Loop
Pg 162

Lincoln City to Newport
Pg 122

Waldport and Florence
Pg 166

Reedsport and the Oregon Dunes
Pg 148

Charleston
Pg 92

Bandon
Pg 74

Port Orford
Pg 135

Gold Beach
Pg 106

Brookings
Pg 80

Chapter 4 - Oregon

Oregon is a varied and beautiful state. The people who live here, as in Washington and British Columbia, are very outdoors oriented, and that means that there are lots of camping opportunities.

Like Washington the state of Oregon is cut from north to south by a mountain range, the Cascades. This causes a dramatic division of the state. These mountains isolate the eastern part of the state from the marine climate of the west. That means that eastern Oregon is hot and dry in the summer and cold and dry in the winter. The western part of the state has a much wetter and more moderate climate. The summers are pleasantly warm but don't offer as many clear days as in the east, the winters almost never see snow, but they do see a lot of rain.

It's an amazing fact that although Oregon is full of natural wonders it is only home to one national park. Crater Lake is one of the more remote National Parks in the country, but also one of the easiest to explore in your own vehicle. The drive around the crater rim makes it a snap.

REGIONS AND THEIR CAMPGROUND RESOURCES

Oregon Coast

One of the top camping destinations in the entire country is the Oregon Coast. The region changes with the seasons. It's a great destination all year long and many campgrounds remain open during the entire year, but it's a completely different place in the winter than in the middle of the summer. This is one of the few destination areas in Oregon that is fine for winter camping travel. During wet winter weather the coastal highway US-101 is sometimes closed by landslides. Regional news programs will have reports if this happens. The road generally opens within a day or two. In the winter you don't really need to worry about making reservations at the campgrounds.

Whale watching is a very popular pastime on the coast. Gray whales winter in Baja California and summer in the far north, therefore they pass the Oregon coast twice. During December, January, and early February they are going south, in March, April and May they are headed north. A small population also summers in Oregon waters. You can see the whales from high points on shore and also take whale-watching voyages from several ports.

Fishing is another popular activity along the coast. You can fish from the charter boats that are based at many ports, fish in salt water along the beaches, or fish the estuaries and rivers along the coast. Every destination described in this region offers fishing possibilities.

In this book you will find a full selection of Oregon Coast campgrounds. There are 114 of them here including 61 commercial campgrounds, 18 state campgrounds, 20 federal Forest Service or BLM campgrounds and 15 municipal or county campgrounds. The following sections list almost all campgrounds along the Oregon coast from north to south: • *Astoria*, • *Seaside and Cannon Beach*, • *Manzanita and Nehalem Bay*, • *Tillamook and The Three Capes Loop*, • *Lincoln City and Newport*, • *Waldport and Florence*, • *Reedsport and the Oregon Dunes*, • *Charleston*, • *Bandon*, • *Port Orford*, • *Gold Beach*, • *Brookings*.

Willamette Valley and Portland

A low range of mountains, the Coastal Range, separates the Oregon coast from the Willamette Valley which stretches south from Portland. The valley is both the population center of Oregon and an important farming and recreational area. I-5 crosses the Willamette Valley from north to south, and then continues on to the California border. The following is a listing of the destinations in this book along the I-5 corridor from north to south: • *Portland*, • *Salem*, • *Eugene*, • *Roseburg*, • *Ashland*.

Cascade Mountains

The Cascade Mountains cover an average of about 80 miles (130 km) from west to east. This is a young range geologically and it shows. Hillsides are steep and valleys are narrow. There are some major volcanic peaks in Oregon's Cascades including Mt. Hood (11,235 ft.), the Three Sisters (all a little over 10,000 ft.), Mt. Bachelor (9,065 ft.), Broken Top (9,173 ft.) and Mount Mazama, home to Crater Lake (with the south rim to near 8,000 ft.), Mt. Scott (8,926 ft.), and Mt. McLoughlin (9,295 ft.). Crater Lake National Park is the only national park in Oregon. Our Cascade Mountains destinations are • *Crater Lake State Park* and • *Camp Sherman and the Metolius River*. Other destinations which include some Cascade Mountain campgrounds border the range to west and east, they are: • *Bend and La Pine*, • *Cascade Lakes Scenic Byway Loop*, • *Redmond and Sisters*, • *Eugene*, and • *Roseburg and the Umpqua Valley*.

Columbia River

The northern border of Oregon is the Columbia River. The Columbia has always been an important transportation corridor so it offers quite a bit of history. It also is very scenic with waterfalls as well as huge lakes behind massive dams. Two destination sections in this book cover the area: • *Columbia Gorge* and • *Maryhill Region*.

Bend Area

East of the Cascades Oregon is composed of high plateau country with smaller dry mountain ranges. Just east of the Cascades the area around Bend stands out as a really great camping destination. It's so good that in this book a total of seven different destination sections describe the area: • *Bend and La Pine*, • *Camp Sherman and the Metolius River*, • *Cascade Lakes Highway*, • *Madras*, • *Newberry National Monument*, • *Redmond and Sisters*, • *Prineville*.

The East

There are other destinations east of the Cascades. They tend to be widely scattered in this almost-empty landscape. In this book you'll find: • *Pendleton*, • *Wallowa Lake Region*, • *Hells Canyon Scenic Byway*, • *Hells Canyon*, • *Baker City*, • *Upper John Day Country*, • *Klamath Falls*, • *Lakeview*.

GOVERNMENT LANDS AND THEIR CAMPGROUNDS

Oregon State Campgrounds

Oregon has one of the best state campgrounds systems in the country. There are 55 State of Oregon parks that have campgrounds. Thirty-nine of the most interesting and accessible are listed in this book.

We think that these campgrounds are the cream of the crop in Oregon. Given a choice most campers choose to stay in a state campground if one is convenient. Any private campground owner will tell you that government campgrounds have an unfair advantage – lots of prime real estate. Many other states do not take advantage of this, but Oregon does. The state campgrounds offer hookups, beautiful settings and landscaping, lots of room, and even an excellent reservation system.

These campgrounds cater to all types of campers. Tenters will find hiker/biker walk-in sites as well as vehicle accessible sites. RVers will find long, wide sites suitable for big RVs, often with full hookups, sometimes even with cable TV or Wi-Fi. Restrooms often offer good showers as part of the package, not an extra cost add-on. If you are looking for even more in the way of sleeping quarters, there are often cabins, yurts, or teepees that will get you out of the weather. Finally, Oregon state park campgrounds all accept credit cards at the park, even if there is only a self-registration kiosk.

The reservation system is key. From Memorial Day to Labor Day state campgrounds are very popular and reservations are often necessary, especially on weekends. Make them as soon as you can, particularly if you happen to have a large RV since sites for big RVs with slide-outs are at a premium in the state park campgrounds. About half of the Oregon state parks accept reservations, the others are first-come, first served.

Reservations for State of Oregon campgrounds are easy to make. For a telephone reservation call (800) 452-5687. The internet address for reservations is www.reserveamerica.com. Both of these systems have information about site size, so if you have a big RV they can assign you an appropriate location. You can also check site availability on the website and then call the telephone number to make your reservation. Reservations can be made from 9 months to two days in advance, they cost $6 per reservation. The fee applies to each site reserved, no matter for how long, it's not a per-day fee. Note however, that there is a 14 day limit on stays in most Oregon state campgrounds

Oregon state parks cost less in the winter. From October 1 to April 30 it's Discovery Season and rates are about 20% lower. Summer rates for no-hookup vehicle campsites are from $14 to $17, winter rates from $10 to $13. Summer rates for hookup campsites are from $16 to $21, winter rates from $12 to $17. There are also inexpensive hiker/biker (no parking pad) tent sites, the charge is generally $4 per person for these sites.

Federal Campgrounds

In this chapter you'll find a variety of federal campground types. These include National Forest Campgrounds in 8 different national forests: Siuslaw, Rogue River, Umpqua, Willamette, Deschutes, Ochoco, Freemont-Winema, and Wallowa-Whitman. They also include other campgrounds also administered by the National Forest Service including those in the Crooked River National Grasslands, Newberry National Monument, Columbia Gorge National Scenic Area, and Oregon Dunes National Recreation Area. There are also national park campgrounds in Crater Lake National Park, and BLM and Corps of Engineers campgrounds in a variety of other federal lands areas. In all there are 83 federal campgrounds in the Oregon chapter.

Most RVers think of federal lands campgrounds as best for tent campers and small RVs. Many are, but you'll also find some big-rig campgrounds including a few with utility hookups. Look in our *Baker City and Sumpter, Crater Lake National Park*, and *Waldport and Florence* sections for federal campgrounds offering hookups. It is possible to use a big RV in some Federal campgrounds and we've included a lot of information in this chapter that will help you decide which ones are right for you and your camping vehicle.

Seniors can get a discount on most federal government campgrounds. If you're a U.S. citizen or permanent resident and 62 years old you can buy a Golden Access passport. The cost is $10 for life, it gets you half off on most federal campground fees as well as free access to National Parks and other federal lands.

OREGON

THE CORPS OF ENGINEERS LE PAGE CAMPGROUND ON THE COLUMBIA RIVER

Many campgrounds on Federal lands can be reserved. Most use the National Recreation Reservation Service. Access is via the www.reserveusa.com website or telephone number – (877) 444-6777. Individual campground write-ups below tell which federal campgrounds can be reserved. Most campsites have a $9 fee per reservation and they can be reserved up to 240 days in advance.

DESTINATIONS AND THEIR CAMPGROUNDS

ASHLAND

Ashland (population 16,200) is probably best known for the **Oregon Shakespeare Festival**. It runs from late February to October in three different venues, including an outdoor theater. Performances each year include many different productions, both Shakespeare and modern. It is best to get your tickets before you arrive in town. The nearby town of Jacksonville offers the **Britt Pavilion** with many music performances of all genres during the year.

Several towns and interesting destinations line I-5 to the north of Ashland, several of the campgrounds listed for Ashland are actually along I-5 to the north.

Medford (population 47,000) is the big town of the area. It is located about 12 miles (19 km) north of Ashland. As the big city Medford acts as the business center for a region known for its fruit. A popular stop in Medford is **Harry and David's Country Village**. You probably know them for their mail-order gift baskets. They're located in the Southgate Mall. There are signs on I-5 directing you to the store. Medford has a **Pear Blossom Festival** in mid-April and hosts the **Jackson County Fair** on the third weekend of July.

The town of **Grants Pass** (population 17,500) is a pleasant and quiet town located about 40 miles (65 km) north of Ashland. It occupies the banks of the Rogue River, you may decide to take a ride on the river from this inland base. You can also take a jet boat ride from the mouth of the river in Gold Beach, take a look at that section for more information. From Grants Pass the river flows into the coastal mountains and becomes a designated Wild and Scenic River. You can ride a jet boat from downtown Grants Pass and through **Hellgate Canyon**, the jet boats are not permitted to run all the way down the river to the coast. The Rogue is popular for fishing and river raft trips, Grants Pass is a center for companies that specialize in guiding these activities. It is also possible to take a scenic drive to Hellgate Canyon. To do so take Exit 61 from I-5 about 3 miles (5 km) north of Grants Pass. Drive west through Merlin and you'll soon be in the canyon. You probably won't want to drive much past the town of Galice which serves as civilization in this part of the valley. It is actually possible to drive all the way across the Coast Range on small roads but these are not suitable for most larger RVs. Grants Pass annual events include the **Boatnik Festival** on Memorial Day, and the **Josephine County Fair** in mid-August.

Twenty miles (32 km) north of Grants Pass at Exit 76 you might enjoy a stop at **Wolf Creek Inn State Heritage Site.** Now a state park, this may be the oldest hotel in the state, it dates to the early 1880s when it was a stage-coach stop. It has eight rooms, but RV travelers will be more interested in the meals served in the dining room which is decorated as it was in the early days. Just south, at Exit 71, is the **Applegate Trail Interpretive Center**. The Applegate Trail was a southern route of the Oregon Trail, there's also a covered bridge nearby.

Tent campers visiting Ashland will enjoy the Emigrant Lake Campground when it is open. Otherwise the Glenyan Campground is an excellent choice. If you don't mind the long drive the Valley of the Rogue State Park is also good. For really big RVs the easiest choices are along the freeway and include Valley of the Rogue State Park, Holiday RV Park, and Pear Tree Resort. The Glenyan is our favorite and any RV can fit with careful driving.

⊞ VALLEY OF THE ROGUE STATE PARK *(Open All Year)*

Reservations:	(800) 452-5687, www.reserveamerica.com
Information:	(541) 582-1118, (800) 551- 6949, www.oregonstateparks.org,
Location:	32 Miles (52 Km) N of Ashland Along I-5, *N 42° 24' 38", W 123° 07' 50"*, 1,000 Ft

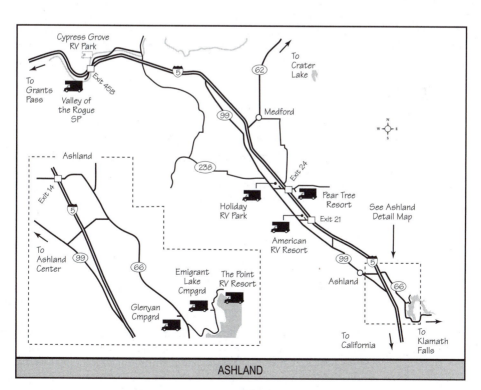

ASHLAND

167 Sites – This is a popular state park with a very convenient location. It's located right next to I-5 between Grants Pass and Medford. The sites here are off loops with both pull-thru and back-in sites, many over 50 feet long, some as long as 83 feet. The grounds are grass-covered and have many attractive shade trees. This park is unusual for a state campground because it has both Wi-Fi (from a commercial vendor, there is a fee) and a laundry room and machines. There's also a boat launch on the Rogue River and an interpretive hiking trail along the river. Other activities are fishing and fish-watching (salmon) in the river and river swimming in the summer. To reach the park take Exit 45B from I-5. This is 10 miles (16 km) south of Grants Pass and 13 miles (21 km) north of Medford.

HOLIDAY RV PARK *(Open All Year)*

Reservations:	(800) 452-7970
Information:	(541) 535-2183, kprv@aol.com
Location:	10 Miles (16 Km) N of Ashland, *N 42° 16' 59", W 122° 49' 07"*, 1,500 Ft

110 Sites – This is a modern big-rig park with pull-thrus to 70 feet. Amenities include an outdoor heated pool. There's a McDonalds nearby. It's conveniently located just west of I-5 at Exit 24. This is 10 miles (16 km) north of Ashland's Exit 14.

PEAR TREE RESORT *(Open All Year)*

Reservations:	(800) 645-7332
Information:	(541) 535-4445
Location:	10 Miles (16 Km) N of Ashland, *N 42° 16' 43", W 122° 48' 40"*, 1,500 Ft

31 Sites – The Pear Tree is a much smaller resort than the Holiday and is located off the same freeway exit. This is a campground behind a motel. There are sizeable back-in sites and pull-thrus to 75 feet. Amenities include a seasonal outdoor swimming pool and hot tub. You can pick up Wi-Fi (fee) from the truck stop next door, you can also walk next door to a restaurant. Take Exit 24 from I-5 and travel south on the access road on the east side of the freeway for .1 mile (.2 km) to the campground.

AMERICAN RV RESORT *(Open All Year)*

Res. and Info.:	(541) 535-6632
Location:	7 Miles (11 Km) N of Ashland Along I-5, *N 42° 14' 48", W 122° 46' 36"*, 1,600 Ft

63 Sites – The American is an older resort. Sites are back-ins. Although some are as long as 50 feet the park prefers RVs no longer than 40 feet. A paved bike trail runs next to the park along Bear Creek and there is a seasonal swimming pool. The resort is located just west of I-5 at Exit 21. This is 7 miles (11 km) north of Ashland at Exit 14.

GLENYAN CAMPGROUND *(Open All Year)*

Reservations:	(877) 453-6926, www.glenyancampground.com
Information:	(541) 488-1785, info@glenyancampground.com
Location:	5 Miles (8 Km) E of Ashland on SR-66, *N 42° 09' 19", W 122° 37' 46"*, 2,100 Ft

68 Sites – The Glenyan is the closest and most convenient campground for a visit to Ashland and has long been a popular choice for visitors. It's a very friendly campground. Sites here are set in trees and no two are alike. There are back-ins and pull-thrus to 70 feet. There's a sea-

sonal outdoor swimming pool as well as Wi-Fi in the office, it does reach a few of the sites. To reach the campground drive east from Ashland or Exit 14 of I-5 on SR-66. The campground entrance is on the right 3.0 miles (4.8 km) from I-5.

EMIGRANT LAKE CAMPGROUND *(Open March 16 to Oct 15 - Varies)*

Information:	(541) 774-8183, parksinfo@jacksoncounty.org, www.jacksoncountyparks.com
Location:	6 Miles (10 Km) E of Ashland on SR-66, *N 42° 09' 24", W 122° 37' 06"*, 2,100 Ft

42 Sites – This is one of two campgrounds overlooking Emigrant Lake Reservoir in the Emigrant Lake Jackson County Park. The other is The Point RV Park which has hookups, see below. Emigrant Lake Campground does not have hookups. It is located across the park road from the lake and day-use area. Farther along the road are a dump station and the RV park. There is also a water park and boat launch in the park. Sites in the campground are as long as 45 feet, but they are narrow although there are few shrubs or trees that would get in the way of slide-outs for RVs using the park. To reach the campground drive east from Ashland at Exit 14 of I-5 on SR-66. The entrance road to the park is on the left 3.2 miles (5.2 km) from I-5. When you follow the access road the campground is on the left in .9 mile (1.5 km).

THE POINT RV PARK *(Open March 16 to Oct 15 - Varies)*

Reservations:	(541) 774-8183, benchml@jacksoncounty.org
Information:	(541) 774-8183, parksinfo@jacksoncounty.org, http://www.jacksoncountyparks.com
Location:	6 Miles (10 Km) E of Ashland on SR-66, *N 42° 09' 40", W 122° 36' 59"*, 2,300 Ft

32 Sites – This county RV park has nice paved sites overlooking the Emigrant Lake Reservoir. Some stretch to 50 feet, most are long back-ins with only three pull-thrus. Reservations are very important here, this is a popular place. To reach the campground drive east from Ashland at Exit 14 of I-5 on SR-66. The entrance road to the park is on the left 3.2 miles (5.2 km) from I-5. When you follow the access road the campground is at the end in 1.3 mile (2.1 km).

ASTORIA, SEASIDE, AND CANNON BEACH

Some folks claim **Astoria** (population 10,100) is the oldest town in this part of the country, but that can be disputed since it has not been continually occupied since the early days of Fort Astoria. Astoria was founded in 1811 as a fur-trading post, but later abandoned. Only since the 1840s was the town site permanently occupied, and by that time Oregon City on the outskirts of today's Portland had begun to grow.

The Columbia River is the town's reason for existence. Even today the river pilots that guide the huge ships across the bar are based here. There's an excellent museum, the **Columbia River Maritime Museum**, that gives the whole fascinating story on Columbia River shipping.

Another river-oriented site here is the huge Astoria Bridge. You can't miss it because it towers over the little town and stretches 4.1 miles (6.6 km) north across the Columbia to Washington State. On a nice day the drive across is well worth the time it takes for the great views. Once across you might look around. The **Lewis and Clark Campsite Heritage Area** just 2.4 miles (3.9 km) to the west occupies the spot where Lewis and Clark first saw the Pacific Ocean. At 3.0 miles (4.8 km) is **Fort Columbia State Park**. This was a second fort (of three) guarding the entrance to the Columbia, Fort Stevens was on the south bank and Fort Canby was farther west on the north shore.

Back in Astoria there are at least two more must-see attractions. The **Astoria Column**, erected by the Northern Pacific Railroad in 1926, offers great views after a 164-step climb up the interior spiral stairway. The **Flavel House Museum** is a Victorian-style mansion built by Oregon's first steamship captain, it has the original furnishings and was built in 1883.

Finally, one of the campgrounds just to the south, Fort Stevens State Park, has a great deal of historical interest. Fort Stevens was built during the Civil War. It was also shelled by a Japanese submarine during World War II. You can find out more at the **Museum** in the park. At the far north end of the park is a huge **jetty** jutting out into the Pacific. It was designed to help protect the entrance to the Columbia and to help control the sand bars that want to close the shipping channels. It is not entirely successful, extensive dredging is still required and the entrance to the Columbia is one of the world's more dangerous shipping routes, particularly during winter storms.

The area near the mouth of the Columbia River is well-known for its fishing, and also as a fairly treacherous piece of water. Fishing charters from both Astoria and Warrenton/Hammond are available.

Astoria celebrates the **Astoria Warrenton Crab and Seafood Festival** on the last weekend in April and the **Scandinavian Midsummer Festival** about the middle of June.

South of Astoria, at Mile 7, old Highway 101 leads 3 miles (5 km) east to **Fort Clatsop National Memorial**. This is where the Louis and Clark Expedition spent the winter of 1805-1806. Unfortunately a reconstruction of their fort here recently burned, but the memorial is still open and interesting.

Fourteen miles (23 km) south of Astoria is **Seaside**. The center of town is between the highway and the ocean. The town is about 100 years old, and the main business here has always been tourism. The main drag leading from US-101 to the beach is Broadway, there's a turnaround at the end of it. With a large RV a better bet is the public parking lot at Columbia Avenue and First Street which is just north of Broadway and near the beach. Seaside has a variety of attractions. There's the two-mile paved **Promenade** along the beach, shopping and restaurants along **Broadway**, and the **Seaside Aquarium**. If you are interested in the town's history visit the **Seaside Museum**. There almost always seems to be something going on in Seaside, particularly in the summer, check at the Seaside Chamber of Commerce for information.

Cannon Beach (population 1,300), 6 miles (10 km) south of Seaside, is cute and upscale. There's an excellent beach, big rocks called sea stacks just offshore, and lots of little restaurants,

SEA STACKS ON THE BEACH NEAR CANNON BEACH

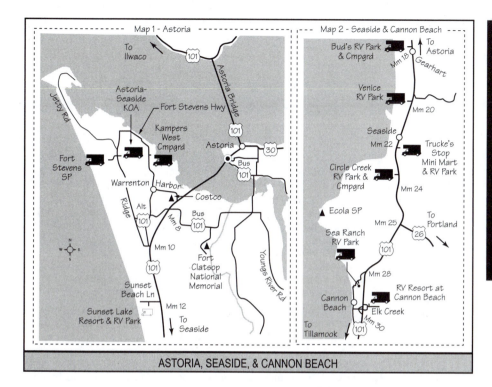

ASTORIA, SEASIDE, & CANNON BEACH

shops and galleries. Cannon Beach hosts a **Sandcastle Day** about the middle of June as well as the **Stormy Weather Arts Festival** near the beginning of November. One of Cannon Beach's big advantages in the way of ambiance is that the highway bypasses the town.

Adjoining Cannon Beach to the north is **Ecola State Park**. It encompasses **Tillamook Head**, there is a hiking trail through the park from Cannon Beach to Seaside. Captain William Clark of the Lewis and Clark expedition is thought to have viewed the Cannon Beach area from a vantage point in the park, it was probably the farthest point south along the coast reached by the expedition.

The campgrounds below are listed from north to south. We've done this all along the Oregon coast. If you're traveling from north to south this book covers virtually all campgrounds along the coast. The destinations after this one fall in this order: *Nehalem Bay and Manzanita,* • *Tillamook and the Three Capes Loop,* • *Lincoln City to Newport,* • *Waldport and Florence,* • *Reedsport and the Oregon Dunes,* • *Charleston,* • *Bandon,* • *Port Orford,* • *Gold Beach,* • *Brookings.* See the index map at the beginning of this chapter for easy orientation.

FORT STEVENS STATE PARK *(Open All Year)*

Reservations:	(800) 452-5687, www.reserveamerica.com
Information:	(503) 861-1671, (800) 551- 6949, www.oregonstateparks.org
Location:	6 Miles (10 Km) SW of Astoria, *N 46° 10' 56", W 123° 57' 45",* Near Sea Level

496 Sites – This is the largest state campground in Oregon. The parking area for checking in is larger than some of the other campgrounds. Sites have large paved parking pads, many suitable for the largest RVs. There are also yurt rentals, a hiker/biker area, 14 miles (23 km) of bicycle and hiking trails, and a very long beach. This large state park is a former military fort. You can tour the old batteries and a museum, there's even a brochure with a self-guided tour. You can drive to the campground by heading northwest from either Mile 6.5 or Mile 7.5 of US-101.

Signs will guide you along back roads to the campground.

ASTORIA-SEASIDE KOA *(Open All Year)*

Reservations:	(800) 562-8506, www.koa.com
Information:	(503) 861-2606, astoriakoa@aol.com, www.astoriakoa.com
Location:	6 Miles (10 Km) SW of Astoria, *N 46° 11' 04", W 123° 57' 22"*, Near Sea Level

255 Sites – This large KOA is located right across from the entrance to Fort Stevens State Park and offers a commercial alternative with virtually the same location. This too is a huge campground with facilities to match and excellent management. Sites include pull-thrus to 60 feet and longer. Amenities include a very large indoor year-round swimming pool. There are also bicycle rentals, very handy for those bike trails at Fort Stevens State Park across the street. Follow the directions given for the state park above to reach the campground.

KAMPERS WEST KAMPGROUND *(Open All Year)*

Reservations:	(800) 880-5267
Information:	(503) 861-1814, kamperswest@charterinternet.com, www.kamperswest.com
Location:	5 Miles (8 Km) SW of Astoria, *N 46° 11' 05", W 123° 55' 42"*, Near Sea Level

157 Sites – This is a large big-rig campground near the Columbia River. It caters to fishermen with boat trailer parking, fish-cleaning tables and seafood cooking areas. Sites are back-ins to 50 feet on gravel and grass. The grass sites are also used by tent campers. The campground is located near Warrenton. From US-101 about 2 miles (3 km) south of Astoria follow E. Harbor Drive west to Warenton where it curves north and becomes Fort Stevens Highway. Some 2.8 miles (4.5 km) from US-101 you will see the campground on the right.

BUD'S RV PARK AND CAMPGROUND *(Open All Year)*

Reservations:	(800) 730-6855
Information:	(503) 738-6855
Location:	2 Miles (3 Km) N of Seaside, *N 46° 02' 17", W 123° 54' 48"*, Near Sea Level

39 Sites – This campground is located behind a convenience store. There is a large area with grass for tent camping and also back-in RV sites. Each of these has a patio and picnic table. Most sites are about 25 feet long but a few can take large RVs to 40 feet. The campground is located on the west side of US-101 at the north end of Gearhart, which is just outside Seaside to the north.

VENICE RV PARK *(Open All Year)*

Res. and Info.:	(503) 738-8851
Location:	Northern Edge of Seaside, *N 46° 00' 39", W 123° 54' 43"*, Near Sea Level

20 Sites – This local RV park has many full-time resident trailers, but about 20 spaces are set aside for travelers too. It's an old RV park with simple facilities and RVs are really packed in. Traveler sites are back-ins and pull-thrus to 70 feet. Maneuvering room is tight and spaces are narrow. Slide-outs are not recommended. The Neawanna River runs along the side of the park. The RV park is located just off US-101 on the west side near the northern edge of Seaside.

TRUCKE'S STOP MINI MART AND RV PARK *(Open All Year)*

Information: (503) 738-8863
Location: Seaside, *N 45° 58' 50", W 123° 55' 34"*, Near Sea Level

13 Sites – Trucke's is a very simple RV park. It's a lot behind a gas station and convenience store. There are 13 back-in sites on grass to 30 feet in length. Only electric hookups are available, there are restrooms but no showers at the store out front. Tent campers can stay here too. Watch for Truck's on the east side of US-101 toward the southern end of the strip of business that line the highway as it passes through Seaside.

CIRCLE CREEK RV PARK AND CAMPGROUND *(Open March 15 to Nov 1)*

Res. and Info.: (503) 738-6070, circlecreek101@hotmail.com
Location: 1 Mile (1.6 Km) S of Seaside, *N 45° 57' 55", W 123° 55' 29"*, Near Sea Level

64 Sites – Circle Creek is Seaside's premier campground. In fact it's the only large full-service traveler's campground servicing Seaside. The sites here are widely spaced back-in and pull-thru sites to 60 feet. Extensive areas of clipped grass separate the sites and also cover a large tent-camping area. Reservations are recommended all summer long, even during the week. The campground is located about 1 mile (1.6 km) south of Seaside on the west side of US-101.

SEA RANCH RV PARK *(Open All Year)*

Res. and Info.: (503) 436-2815, searanch@seasurf.net, searanch@ssurt.net,
www.searanchrv.com, www.campingfriends.com/searanchrvpark
Location: Cannon Beach, *N 45° 54' 07", W 123° 57' 23"*, Near Sea Level

94 Sites – Many people think this is the most ideally located campground on the Oregon coast, it's within walking distance of central Cannon Beach. Sites here are irregularly laid out in an area of trees. There are tent sites, small vehicle camping sites, and back-in sites to 55 feet. Maneuvering room for big RVs is limited but parking is definitely possible. If you take the northern exit (near Mile 28) to Cannon Beach you'll see the campground on the left in just .3 mile (.5 km).

RV RESORT AT CANNON BEACH *(Open All Year)*

Res. and Info.: (503) 436-2231, (800) 847-2231, info@cbrvresort.com, www.cbrvresort.com
Location: 1 Mile (2 Km) E of Cannon Beach, *N 45° 53' 20", W 123° 57' 20"*, Near Sea Level

100 Sites – This resort is Cannon Beach's upscale big RV resort. There are back-in and pull-thru sites to 60 feet. Amenities include an indoor swimming pool and an hourly shuttle to Cannon Beach and Seaside. If you want to walk you can be at the beach in a half mile, central Cannon Beach is just under a mile on foot. The campground is located just east of US-101 at the middle Cannon Beach exit at Mile 29.5.

BAKER CITY AND SUMPTER

Although the **Oregon Trail** passes near Baker City (population 10,100) the town really dates from the gold mining period of the 1860s. Located on I-84 Baker City is more than a spot to stop for gas and a quick bite, the town has a surprising number of interesting nearby tourist attractions.

First on the list must be the **Oregon Trail Interpretive Center**. Completed in 1992 this modern museum presents a fascinating look at the Oregon Trail. The trail itself passes below, you can see the ruts from the center but there are walking trails leading down for a closer look. In the center itself you pass along a winding path past dioramas, slide shows, and exhibits - plan on at least an hour to take it all in. We RVers should especially appreciate this monument to some of the first of our tribe. If you look close you'll see that many of the large mural-type pictures are attributed to well known RVing author Bill Moeller. There is quite a bit of RV parking at the center.

In Baker City itself there are a number of worthwhile sites. The **Central Oregon Regional Museum** is a huge building with a large variety of exhibits. The **Geiser Grand Hotel**, dating from 1889, has recently been restored and is designated as a National Historic Landmark.

Baker's annual celebration is the **Miner's Jubilee**, held during the third week of July.

From Baker follow SR-7 westward out of town. The road follows the Powder River toward the old dredge tailing piles near Sumpter. Twenty miles (32 km) after leaving town you'll pass the entrance road for Union Creek Campground. Four and eight-tenths miles (7.7 km) farther along take a left to visit **Railroad Park**. From here, on weekends and holidays from Memorial Day to the end of September, you can ride to the dredge at Sumpter behind a historic steam locomotive, the **Stump Dodger**. Driving on, in just 2.3 miles (3.7 km), you'll reach a junction, take a right and visit the historic gold mining town of Sumpter.

Sumpter offers a number of attractions. The main street is lined with several restaurants, small stores, and other tourist-oriented establishments. The most interesting attraction, however, is the **Sumpter Gold Dredge**. Neglected for many years the dredge had sunk in its pond, but has been raised and is being restored. You can wander through it now, it is already a well-done exhibit that will only get better.

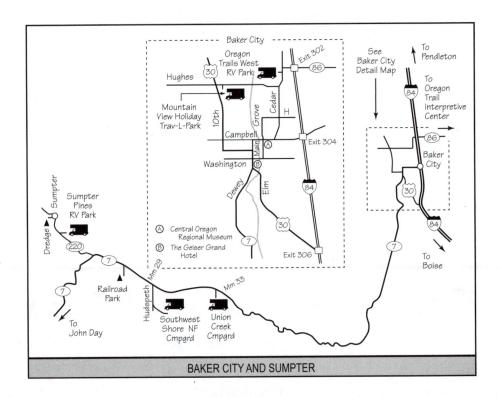

BAKER CITY AND SUMPTER

⛺ MOUNTAIN VIEW HOLIDAY TRAV-L-PARK *(Open All Year)*

Reservations: (800) 806-4824
Information: (541) 523-4824, mtviewrv@oregontrail.net, www.mtviewrv.com
Location: Baker City, *N 44° 47' 40", W 117° 50' 29"*, 3,400 Ft

97 Sites – The campground for travelers is located behind a mobile home park and is very clean and well-managed. This is a big-rig park with pull-thru sites to 70 feet. The buildings have a western theme and amenities include a swimming pool and hot tub. Easiest access to the campground is from I-84 at Exit 302. Go west from the intersection and follow the highway as it immediately turns to the south. In .5 miles (8 km) take the right onto Hughes Lane. One mile (1.6 km) after the turn you'll see the campground entrance on your left.

⛺ OREGON TRAILS WEST RV PARK *(Open All Year)*

Reservations: (888) 523-3236
Information: (541) 523-3236
Location: Baker City, *N 44° 48' 10", W 117° 49' 05"*, 3,400 Ft

57 Sites – This is an older commercial park but it is very convenient to the freeway and has long pull-thrus to about 60 feet. The tent sites here are very large grassy areas with fences outlining each one and they're located toward the front of the park away from the RVs. The campground has a gas station and small convenience store out front. Take Exit 302 from I-84, you'll see the campground on the west side of the highway. This exit is also the one where SR-86 from Hells Canyon reaches the interstate.

⛺ UNION CREEK CAMPGROUND *(Open Memorial Day to Sept 30 - Varies)*

Information: (541) 523-4476
Location: 17 Miles (27 Km) SW of Baker City, *N 44° 41' 29", W 118° 01' 47"*, 4,100 Ft

71 Sites – This large Wallowa-Whitman National Forest campground is unusual, it has electrical and water hookups. The park covers a very large area on the shore of Phillips Reservoir. Access roads are wide, paved loops and sites are large enough to handle RVs to 45 feet. It's actually a good big-rig park. The campground is located 17 miles (7 km) from Baker City and 10 miles (6 km) from Sumpter on SR-7.

⛺ SOUTHWEST SHORE FOREST CAMPGROUND *(Open Memorial Day to Sept 30 - Varies)*

Information: (541) 523-4476
Location: 23 Miles (37 Km) SW of Baker City, *N 44° 40' 33", W 118° 05' 02"*, 4,100 Ft

16 Sites – This smaller Wallowa-Whitman National Forest campground occupies the southwest shore of Phillips Reservoir. Actually, with the water down as it was when we last visited, the campground is about a half-mile from the reservoir. There is no drinking water at this campground but the sites are large, many to 60 feet, and the internal roads are wide enough to allow big RVs to maneuver. To reach the campground drive south on Hudspeth Road from an intersection on SR-7 that is 22 miles (35 km) west of Baker City and 7 miles (11 km) east of Sumpter. Some 1.1 miles (1.8 km) south of the intersection turn left on Lake Road, you'll soon see the campground entrance on your left.

SUMPTER PINES RV PARK *(Open April 1 to Oct 31 - Varies)*

Res. and Info.: (541) 894-2328, sumpterpines@qwest.net, www.sumpterpinesrvpark.com
Location: .6 Miles (1 Km) S of Sumpter, *N 44° 44' 01", W 118° 11' 45"*, 3,700 Ft

28 Sites – This is a small and very pleasant commercial RV park located just outside Sumpter. It makes an excellent base for exploring the area and has full-hookup back-in and pull-thru sites to 60 feet set in trees. There is also a separate tent camping area with vehicle parking next to the tent sites. The campground is located just .6 miles (1 km) south of Sumpter on the road into town, SR-220.

BANDON

For such a small town Bandon (population 2,900) has lots to offer. Today's visitors know the town as an artist's colony and laid-back tourist town with interesting attractions including cranberry farms. The cute little Old Town sits just south of the harbor. Bandon is located near the mouth of the Coquille River and has its own jetties and lighthouse. It has been a port attracting visitors since the 1800s.

Once you have set yourself up in a campground take a stroll around the **Old Town,** also called Bandon By The Sea. The **Chamber of Commerce** is located along the highway at the entrance to the area. You'll find shops and good restaurants. Don't miss the stores selling cranberry sweets and products. There's even a museum - **The Bandon Historical Society Museum**, located in the old Coast Guard Station.

If you approached Bandon from the south you may have noticed fields that are surrounded by dikes and flooded with water. Those aren't rice paddies, they're **cranberries**. Bandon calls itself the **cranberry capital of the world**. Check with the Chamber of Commerce visitor center

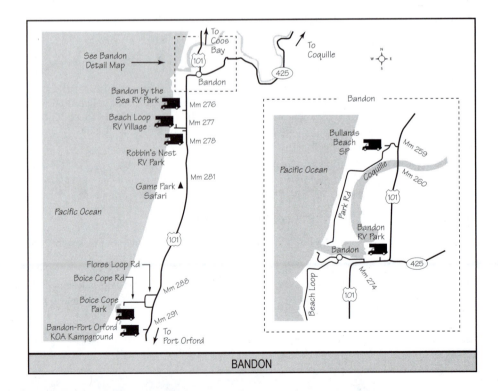

BANDON

THE CUTE LITTLE OLD TOWN OF BANDON

for the location of these fields, they may be able to set you up with a visit or tour during the fall harvest activities.

Bandon has good beaches and also a good selection of sea stacks - big rocks offshore. You can best see them from **Beach Loop Drive** which follows the coast on the south side of the Coquille River. The **Bandon State Natural Area** and **Face Rock Scenic Viewpoint** provide several beach access points, necessary since this stretch of coast is fairly built up with private residences and motels.

Bandon is also a fishing town. Charter boats are available at the boat basin next to the old town. The Coquille River offers salmon, and in the lower section it is possible to catch crabs. Surf fishing is popular from the beach north and south of the river mouth.

Bandon's lighthouse, the **Coquille River Lighthouse**, is located on the north bank of the river near the mouth. It makes a good photograph from town but to reach it you must follow US-101 north to Bullards Beach State Park. The same road provides access to the campground, the lighthouse, and long sandy Bullards Beach. This lighthouse is not operational but serves as an interpretive center. The state park also offers hiking trails and the river mouth area of the park is popular with windsurfers.

The big event of the year is the **Cranberry Festival** in the first half of September.

About six miles (10 km) south of Bandon you'll find the **West Coast Game Park Safari** at Mile 281.5. This is a large private zoo with a reported 75 different species. Some of the animals are free-roaming while others are in exhibit areas.

BULLARDS BEACH STATE PARK *(Open All Year)*

Reservations:	(800) 452-5687, www.reserveamerica.com
Information:	(541) 347-2209, (800) 551- 6949, www.oregonstateparks.org
Location:	1.5 Miles (2.4 Km) N of Bandon, *N 43° 09' 08", W 124° 23' 54"*, Near Sea Level

185 Sites – This large state park campground is on the north side of the Coquille River. The

campground is away from the beach and set in a large grove of shore pines. A mile-long paved trail leads to the beach and the Coquille River Lighthouse. Tours of the lighthouse are available in the summer. The campground offers a hiker-biker camp as well as dry, full-hookup, and partial-hookup back-in vehicle camping sites. Some of the hookup sites are as long as 64 feet, many are over 50 feet long. The campground entrance road goes west to the campground and day-use area about a mile north of Bandon, just north of the bridge over the Coquille.

BANDON RV PARK *(Open All Year)*

Reservations: (800) 393-4122　　　　　**Information:** (541) 347-4122
Location: Bandon, *N 43° 07' 09", W 124° 24' 09"*, Near Sea Level

44 Sites – This small RV park doesn't have a lot of extra amenities but has full hookups and an excellent location, you can easily stroll in to Bandon's Old Town. There are gravel sites, both back-ins and pull-thrus, to 55 feet. The campground is located right in Bandon about a half-mile east of the downtown harbor and right on Highway 101. Reservations are recommended year-round.

BANDON BY THE SEA RV PARK *(Open All Year)*

Res. and Info.: (541) 347-5155
Location: 2 Miles (3 Km) S of Bandon, *N 43° 05' 03", W 124° 24' 57"*, 100 Ft

42 Sites – Despite the name this campground is not by the sea. Instead, it is located along US-101 south of Bandon. This is an older park that is being expanded. Plans are for about 80 sites, most suitable for big RVs with some pull-thrus to 70 feet. Amenities include a hot tub, meeting room, and kitchen in the clubhouse. The campground is on the west side of US-101, 2.3 miles (3.7 km) south of where the highway makes its 90° turn in Bandon to head south.

ROBBIN'S NEST RV PARK *(Open All Year)*

Res. and Info.: (541) 347-7400, bandonbluesky@aol.com
Location: 3 Miles (5 Km) S of Bandon, *N 43° 04' 04", W 124° 24' 55"*, 100 Ft

20 Sites – Robbin's Nest is a brand-new big-rig RV park located on US-101 south of Bandon. There are back-in and pull-thru sites to 70 feet. There's a small grocery store across the street and a rock shop out front. The campground is on the west side of US-101, 3.4 miles (5.5 km) south of where the highway makes its 90° turn in Bandon to head south.

BEACH LOOP RV VILLAGE *(Open All Year)*

Res. and Info.: (541) 347-2100, beachlooprvvillage@highstream.net, www.beachlooprv.com
Location: 4 Miles SW of Bandon, *N 43° 04' 09", W 124° 25' 42"*, 100 Ft

38 Sites – This older campground has new ownership and is being refurbished. The new owners are also installing park units for sale and rental. There is a grass tent-camping area and RV sites are back-ins and pull-thrus to 60 feet. From the point where US-101 make its 90° turn in Bandon drive south for 3.4 miles (5.5 km). Turn right on Beach Loop Dr and the campground will be on your right in .6 miles (1 km).

BOICE COPE PARK *(Open All Year)*

Location: 17 Miles (27 Km) S of Bandon, *N 42° 54' 06", W 124° 30' 07"*, Near Sea Level

34 Sites – This Curry County park is a little off the beaten path and is not well known but it's definitely worth a visit. The campground overlooks Floras Lake and the beach with trails leading out to the beach. The lake is popular with wind surfers and the campground fills up on good windy weekends. A reader board explains that at one time in the early 1900s there were plans to dredge an outlet to the lake and turn this into a lucrative port along this otherwise shelterless coast. Unfortunately, it turned out that the lake was higher that the ocean so if an outlet was dug it would drain itself empty into the ocean. All of the disappointed settlers of the new town that had formed in anticipation of the port then moved away. Sites here are back-ins to 45 feet arranged around a large lawn area. There are also tent sites. From US-101 near Mile 288.5, 14 miles (23 km) south of Bandon, turn seaward on Flores Loop Road. In 1.1 miles (1.7 km) turn right onto Flores Lake Road. In another 1.4 miles (2.3 km), make a 90° left, then turn right onto Boice Cope Road and you'll reach the park in another .3 mile (.5 km).

⊞ BANDON – PORT ORFORD KOA KAMPGROUND *(Open March 1 to Nov 30)*

Reservations:	(800) 562-3298, www.koa.com
Information:	(541) 348-2358, koacamp@harborside.com
Location:	17 Miles (27 Km) S of Bandon, *N 42° 52' 39", W 124° 28' 07"*, 100 Ft

66 Sites – This KOA serves both Bandon and Port Orford. It is also handy for visiting the popular Game Park Safari, 9.4 miles (15 km) to the north. Sites here are set in a native forest for a woodsy setting. There are long pull-thrus to 100 feet as well as a variety of other sites. There's also a seasonal swimming pool. The campground is near Mile 291.5. That's 17 miles (27 km) south of Bandon and 9 miles (15 km) north of Port Orford.

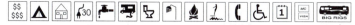

BEND AND LA PINE

The Bend area (population about 52,000) offers a wealth of outdoor recreational opportunities. The town is large enough to offer pretty much anything you would need, it makes a great base.

The **Deschutes National Forest** is to the west and south. It has miles of trails and back roads. There are dozens of Forest Service campgrounds in the forest, at least 25 are convenient to the Bend area. The Deschutes River is very popular for white-water rafting.

Just south of Bend (about 3 miles) you'll find the **High Desert Museum.** With live animals, western art, and historical dioramas this is a nationally-acclaimed do-not-miss attraction.

Bend area has at least 24 **golf courses** nearby, it would be hard to find a better place to get out on the fairways.

The events that Bend celebrates include the **Cascade Festival of Music** in late summer and the **Bend Summer Fest** on the second weekend in July.

Six other listings in this chapter are near Bend and can easily be reached on day trips. These are *Camp Sherman and the Metolius River,* • *Cascade Lakes Scenic Byway Loop,* • *Warm Springs and Madras,* • *Newberry National Volcanic Monument,* • *Redmond and Sisters* • and *Prineville.*

⊞ TUMALO STATE PARK *(Open All Year)*

Reservations:	(800) 452-5687, www.reserveamerica.com
Information:	(541) 382-3586, (800) 551- 6949, www.oregonstateparks.org
Location:	4 Miles W of Bend, *N 44° 07' 43", W 121° 19' 50"*, 3,200 Ft

60 Sites – Tumalo State Park is located not far west of Bend along the Deschutes River. Sites here are all back-ins and a few reach 50 feet, several exceed 40 feet. There are also hiker/biker

OREGON

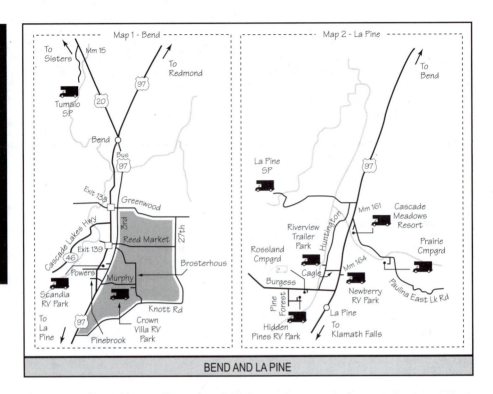

tent sites. Swimming and fishing are both possible in the river and there are nice hiking trails. The park is located south of US-20 some 4 miles (6 km) west of Bend.

SCANDIA RV PARK *(Open All Year)*

Res. and Info.: (541) 382-6206, scandiarv@hwy97.net
Location: Bend, N 44° 01' 49", W 121° 18' 43", 3,800 Ft

60 Sites – Although this is an older campground with quite a few permanent residents it has a separate new section for big RVs. Pull-thru sites vary in size but reach 70 feet and are well-spaced in this section. There are also tent-camping sites in this park. The Scandia is in southern Bend off the business US-97 loop. If you are driving south on the main US-97 highway exit to the east on SE Powers Rd. which is about 2 miles (3 km) south of the center of town. Drive east one block to business US-97, also called SE 3rd Street. Turn left and the campground will be on the left almost immediately.

CROWN VILLA RV PARK *(Open All Year)*

Res. and Info.: (541) 388-1131, (866) 500-5300, info@crownvillarvresort.com,
www.crownvillarvresort.com
Location: Bend, *N 44° 01' 00", W 121° 17' 43"*, 3,700 Ft

119 Sites – This is a really first-class RV resort catering to big RVs. Most sites are back-ins but they're 90 feet long and separated by well-groomed lawns and shaded by large trees. There is no swimming pool but there is a hot tub, tennis courts, and a chipping green. The campground

is located in southeast Bend. From central Bend drive south on US-97 about 2.5 miles (4 km) to SW Pinebrook. Turn east and drive a block to SE 3rd Street (also called Bus US-97), then jog south a short distance and turn east again on SE Murphy Road. In 1.2 mile (1.9 km) turn right on SE Brosterhous Rd and the campground entrance in on the right in just a short distance.

HIDDEN PINES RV PARK *(Open All Year)*
Res. and Info.:   (541) 536-2265, hprvrsw@netzero.com
Location: 26 Miles (42 Km) S of Bend, *N 43° 41' 41", W 121° 31' 17"*, 4,200 Ft

24 Sites – Hidden Pines is a small family-run park located away from the main highways in a residential neighborhood. It's a clean and well-managed park. Some pull-thru sites extend to 65 feet and there are grassy tent sites. From US-97 24 miles (39 km) south of Bend or 2 miles (3 km) north of La Pine turn west on Burgess Rd. In 2.4 miles (3.9 km) turn south on Pine Forest Road and drive 3 blocks. Turn left on Wright Ave, drive a block, and the campground is on the left.

RIVERVIEW TRAILER PARK *(Open All Year)*
Res. and Info.:   (541) 536-2265
Location: 24 Miles (39 Km) S of Bend, *N 43° 42' 57", W 121° 29' 20"*, 4,200 Ft

20 Sites – This is another campground located away from the highway near La Pine. It has long back-in sites to 70 feet with lots of maneuvering room as well as a grassy tenting area. From US-97 some 23 miles (37 km) south of Bend or 3 miles (4.8 km) north of La Pine turn west on Cagle Road. In .8 miles (1.3 km), at the T, turn north on Huntington Road. The campground entrance will be on the left almost immediately.

PRAIRIE CAMPGROUND *(Open May 15 to Oct 15 - Varies)*
Information: (541) 383-4000
Location: 23 Miles (37 Km) S of Bend, *N 43° 43' 30", W 121° 25' 24"*, 4,300 Ft

17 Sites – This small Deschutes National Forest campground is located near the intersection of US-97 and the road up to Newberry National Monument. Sites here are large pull-thrus that will take coaches to 45 feet. The campground is off the access road to the Newberry Volcanic National Monument (Paulina-East Lake Rd.). From US-97, 20 miles (32 km) south of Bend and 6 miles (10 km) north of La Pine, drive east on Paulina-East Lake Rd for 2.8 miles (4.5 km), the campground entrance is on your right.

CASCADE MEADOWS RESORT *(Open All Year)*
Res. and Info.:   (541) 536-2244, thepinedrop@hotmail.com
Location: 20 Miles (32 Km) S of Bend, *N 43° 45' 01", W 121° 27' 32"*, 4,200 Ft

117 Sites – Cascade Meadows is a large big-rig park conveniently located at the junction of US-97 and the highway up to Newberry Volcanic National Monument. Amenities include a swimming pool, hot tub, and free Wi-Fi in the office/reception area. The campground has full-hookup pull-thru sites to 70 feet and also tent camping. The junction is located 20 miles (32 km) south of Bend and 6 miles (10 km) north of La Pine. The access to the park is off the Paulina-East Lake Rd which is the access road to the monument.

OREGON

⊟ LaPine State Park *(Open All Year)*

Reservations: (800) 452-5687, www.reserveamerica.com
Information: (541) 536-2071, (800) 551- 6949, www.oregonstateparks.org,
Location: 19 Miles (31 Km) S of Bend, *N 43° 46' 28", W 121° 32' 15"*, 4,200 Ft

128 Sites – This large state park straddles the Deschutes River. There is room for big RVs with many pull-thru and back-in full-hookup sites over 50 feet long. The park is also home to the "Big Tree". It's the largest ponderosa pine in Oregon. Nice hiking trails follow both sides of the river and the fishing is good. The campground entrance is off US-97 some 19 miles (31 km) south of Bend and 7 miles (11 km) north of La Pine.

⊟ Newberry RV Park *(Open All Year)*

Res. and Info.:   (541) 536-7596
Location: 23 Miles (37 Km) S of Bend, *N 43° 42' 45", W 121° 28' 25"*, 4,200 Ft

38 Sites – The Newberry is a brand-new big-rig RV park. It's a large flat park with gravel-surfaced pull-thru sites to 75 feet as well as back-ins. The campground is on the east side of US-97 about 3 miles (5 km) north of the town of La Pine.

BROOKINGS

Brookings (population 6,300) is the most southerly town on the Oregon coast. The town is increasingly popular and growing, largely because it has better weather than most towns along the coast. Warm air descending from the Rogue Valley mixes with marine air to produce comfortable temperatures year round. Unfortunately, as is common along the entire coast, there is still lots of rain, particularly in the winter.

About 75% of the **Easter lilies** produced in the U.S. come from near Brookings. Early July is the time to see large fields of blooming flowers.

There are three business centers in Brookings with a downtown area on high ground north of the Chetco River and smaller unincorporated Harbor along the south shore of the Chetco River outlet. There are also many stores and other businesses strung out along the highway south of town.

A **State Welcome Center** (open May through October, 8 a.m. to 6 p.m. on Monday-Saturday and 9 a.m. to 5 p.m. on Sunday) is located at a rest area near Mile 355.6. It has Wi-Fi, there is a charge. This is just across the highway from the Harris Beach State Park and about a half-mile north of Brookings. The welcome center has pamphlets covering the whole state and is designed to provide information for folks driving north from California. There is parking for RVs.

While you are in Brookings you may want to visit **Brookings Harbor** for a meal at one of the seafood restaurants and perhaps even book a fishing charter. Brookings Harbor is said to be the safest port on the Oregon coast. Many coastal ports have dangerous entrances due to waves coming across the sandbars at river and estuary entrances. Fishing excursions are available for salmon and rockfish in the summer.

There's river fishing at Brookings too, the Chetco for steelhead (winter) and salmon (fall) and the Winchuck River a little to the south for rainbows and cutthroat.

The town is proud of **Azalea Park**, a small park just north of the river with many Azaleas, they bloom from April to June. It's a pleasant place for a picnic. **Harris State Park** is located just north of town. It's a great place to camp but also has a day-use area with picnic tables overlooking huge rocks and a beach that is large enough to allow you to indulge in some beachcombing. Inland from Brookings along the Chetco River near Loeb State Park is the **Redwood Nature**

Trail which runs through some of the world's northernmost redwoods. Drive eight miles (13 km) east on North Bank Road to reach the trail.

The 29-mile (47 km) section of coastline from Brookings north to Gold Beach is very scenic. The road closely follows the coastline which is alternately rocky cliffs and sandy beaches. From Mile 343 to Mile 353 you are in the **Samuel H. Boardman State Scenic Corridor**. There are many pull-offs giving you the opportunity to make short walks and take some photos from scenic viewpoints.

WHALESHEAD RV PARK *(Open All Year)*

Reservations: (800) 943-4325
Information: (541) 469-7446, whaleshead@charter.net, www.whalesheadresort.com
Location: 6 Miles (10 Km) N of Brookings, *N 42° 08' 50", W 124° 21' 12"*, 200 Ft

36 Sites – This park perches above the highway and the ocean north of Brookings. At one time there were over 140 RV sites here but only 36 remain, the remainder are occupied by park units. Sites are back-ins occupying terraces, the terrain here is steep. Some are as long as 60 feet, most have cedar decks with picnic tables. When you drive in to register a circular drive leads you around the main registration and restaurant building. It looks like it will be tight but it's not bad. The entrance of the park is on the east side of US-101 at Mile 349.2.

BROOKINGS RV PARK *(Open All Year)*

Res. and Info.: (541) 469-6849
Location: 1 Mile (2 Km) N of Brookings, *N 42° 04' 24", W 124° 18' 21"*, 200 Ft

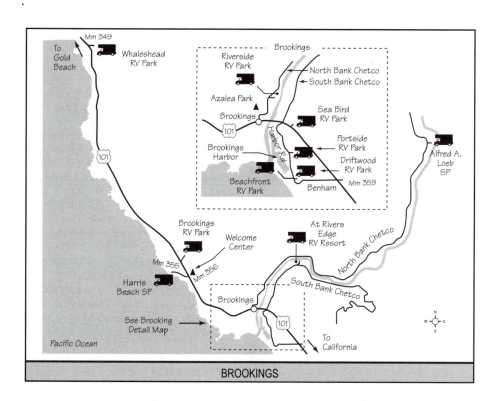

BROOKINGS

38 Sites – This is the only campground located at the northern approaches to Brookings other than Harris Beach State Park. It occupies a site on the hillside above US-101 and is popular with long-term residents. Because it sits on a hillside it often has sunshine when the other campgrounds in the area still have fog. The campground has back-in and pull-thru sites to about 50 feet, most are shorter. The entrance road is near Mile 355.3. Stay left at the Y and climb the hill for .3 miles (.5 km) to the campground entrance.

🚐 HARRIS BEACH STATE PARK *(Open All Year)*

Reservations: (800) 452-5687, www.reserveamerica.com
Information: (541) 469-2021, (800) 551-6949, www.oregonstateparks.org,
Location: ½ Mile (1 Km) N of Brookings, *N 42° 04' 05", W 124° 18' 41"*, 100 Ft

140 Sites – Yes, this state campground does have TV hookups at many of the sites, it also offers Wi-Fi and a laundry room. It is conveniently located at the northern edge of Brookings and has a beautiful beach area bordered by very photogenic rocks as well as the largest offshore island along the coast. The campground is above the beach in trees with most sites having no views, but the day area below on the beach is just a nice stroll down the hill. Sites are back-ins with many to 50 feet and even a bit larger. The entrance road is near Mile 355.9.

🚐 ALFRED A. LOEB STATE PARK *(Open All Year)*

Information: (541) 469-2021, (800) 551-6949, www.oregonstateparks.org
Location: 7 Miles E of Brookings, *N 42° 06' 46", W 124° 11' 17"*, 100 Ft

48 Sites – Alfred A. Loeb is located inland from Brookings along the Chetco River. Sites here are all back-ins, many exceed 40 feet and many of these exceed 50 feet. The campground is set in a myrtle forest. There is a riverside trail to a nearby redwood forest (the trees are at the northernmost point in their range here) and also fishing in the Chetco. From Brookings follow North Bank Chetco River Road eastward for 7.3 miles (11.8 km) to the campground.

🚐 RIVERSIDE RV PARK *(Open All Year)*

Res. and Info.: (541) 469-4799, (888) 201-9506, carolyn@riverside-rv.com, www.riverside-rv.com
Location: .5 Miles (1 Km) E of Brookings, *N 42° 03' 35", W 124° 16' 06"*, Near Sea Level

30 Sites – A very pleasant small RV park along the bank of the Chetco River near Brookings. It's popular with long-term residents, reservations are a must. It has tent sites that are good for bicycle and motorcycle campers. For RVers there are a few pull-thrus but most sites are back-ins, several reach 55 feet and a few are longer. From Brookings follow North Bank Chetco River Road .4 mile (.6 km) east to the campground entrance.

🚐 AT RIVERS EDGE RV RESORT *(Open All Year)*

Res. and Info.: (541) 469-3356, (888) 295-1441, stay@riversedge.com, www.atriversedge.com
Location: 2 Miles (3 Km) E of Brookings, *N 42° 04' 15", W 124° 15' 09"*, Near Sea Level

128 Sites – The park occupies a large cleared area on the south bank of the Chetco. Facilities are modern. There are many back-in spaces with cement patios and 10 new long pull-thrus to 60 feet. Amenities include a small boat ramp and a clubhouse with an exercise and game room. Follow the South Bank Chetco Road eastward for 1.3 miles (2.1 km) to the park.

BEACHFRONT RV PARK *(Open All Year)*

Res. and Info.: (541) 469-5867, (800) 441-0856, pat@port-brookings-harbor.or,
www.port-brookings.harbor.org
Location: Brookings Harbor, *N 42° 02' 35", W 124° 15' 57"*, Near Sea Level

133 Sites – The Beachfront is operated by the Port of Brookings. It has sites not 50 feet from the water between the marina and the ocean. Access is not controlled, there is a stream of automobile traffic in front of the RVs, and also public parking. The restrooms are grim cement block units and access is not limited to campground residents. Sites are both back-ins and pull-thrus to 60 feet. There are tent sites here behind the row of RVs, the surface for these is grass. There's a restaurant and the harbor and boat ramp is nearby. To reach the park follow the Harbor Road toward the water from the south end of the bridge over the Chetco. The park will be on your right in 1 mile (2 km).

PORTSIDE RV PARK *(Open All Year)*

Res. and Info.: (541) 469-6616, (877) 787-2752, rvpark@destinationbrookings.com,
www.destinationbrookings.com
Location: Brookings Harbor, *N 42° 02' 54", W 124° 15' 50"*, Near Sea Level

45 Sites – The Portside actually has about 90 sites, but close to half of them are taken up by nice park model homes. This definitely changes the character of an RV park. Some people will like it and some won't. Across the road is the Portside Suites hotel with a restaurant. Most sites are back-ins to 50 feet long but there are some longer pull-thrus. To reach the park follow the Harbor Road toward the water from the south end of the bridge over the Chetco. The park will be on your left in .5 mile (.8 km).

DRIFTWOOD RV PARK *(Open All Year)*

Res. and Info.: (541) 469-9089, rsvp@driftwoodrvpark.com, www.driftwoodrvpark.com
Location: Brookings Harbor, *N 42° 02' 34", W 124° 15 '46"*, Near Sea Level

106 Sites – The Driftwood is a friendly and pleasant park located near the boat harbor. It's not right on the edge of the bay but it's nearby. Most sites in this park are 40 to 45 feet long although there are some pull-thrus to 70 feet. Some sites have instant-on telephone and the park has free Wi-fi. To reach the park follow the Harbor Road toward the water from the south end of the bridge over the Chetco. The park will be on your left in .9 mile (1.4 km).

SEA BIRD RV PARK *(Open All Year)*

Res. and Info: (541) 469-3512, www.seabirdrv.com
Location: Brookings, *N 42° 03' 15", W 124° 15' 48"*, 100 Ft

60 Sites – The Seabird is probably the most popular campground in Brookings. The low price has a lot to do with that. It's a simple well-run park with both back-in and pull-thru sites to 50 feet. The park is located on the east side of US-101 just south of the Chetco bridge.

CAMP SHERMAN AND THE METOLIUS RIVER

The **Metolius River** springs from the ground as a good-sized clear mountain river. It is thought to pass underground from the nearby mountains. After emerging the river flows through a beautiful area of ponderosa pine and grasslands. The Metolius is a famous fishing spot (fly fish-

OREGON

ing only), the area extremely scenic with many hiking trails. The commercial center of the region is called Camp Sherman, it amounts to little more than a store and post office. There are quite a few homes and resorts set in seclusion among the pines in the surrounding area. To get there just follow US-20 some 9 miles (15 km) toward Salem and then take the Camp Sherman road (Rd. 14) to the right. After 2.7 miles (4.4 km) there is a fork, take the right (Rd. 14) to visit the source of the Metolius River and the National Forest Service Campgrounds downstream. A left at the fork puts you on Rd. 1419 and a drive through an area of lodges and other facilities. You can take a right after another 2.2 miles (3.5 km) to reach the Camp Sherman Store which has groceries, gas, a deli, and a post office.

The Camp Sherman area has a dump station. It is located across from the entrance to the Allingham Campground and services all eleven of the national forest campgrounds in the area.

▣ BLACK BUTTE RESORT MOTEL AND RV PARK *(Open All Year)*

Reservations: reservations@blackbutterv.com, www.hoodoo.com
Information: (541) 595-6514, (541) 822-3799, manager@blackbutterv.com,
                  www.campshermanrv.com
Location: Camp Sherman, *N 44° 27' 36", W 121° 38' 50"*, 2,900 Ft

23 Sites – The Black Butte Resort is probably the best stop for travelers who want full hookups in the Camp Sherman area. Some sites will take RVs to 45 feet. Parking is on grass or gravel in a mowed lawn area. Restrooms and showers here are available for a fee to folks staying at the other campgrounds nearby. To reach this campground take the SW Camp Sherman Road from US-20 some 10 miles (16 km) northwest of Sisters. Follow the road north taking the left fork at 2.6 miles (4.2 km). Four and eight tenths miles (7.7 km) from where you left US-20 follow SW Camp Sherman Road to the right, the campground is on the right .4 mile (.6 km) from the corner.

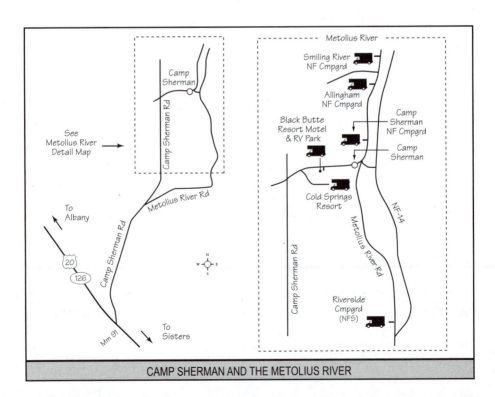

CAMP SHERMAN AND THE METOLIUS RIVER

COLD SPRINGS RESORT *(Open All Year)*

Res. and Info.: (541) 595-6271, lodging@coldsprings-resort.com, www.coldsprings-resort.com
Location: Camp Sherman, *N 44° 27' 28", W 121° 38' 46"*, 2,900 Ft

41 Sites – This campground is primarily for long-term campers but maintains about 10 sites for travelers. These back-in sites are used by coaches to 40 feet but careful maneuvering is required and the sites are really most suitable for RVs to 35 feet. The office and restroom building is located at the manager's unit which is located at the back of the park, there is a free Wi-Fi connection back there too but it doesn't reach the parking sites. A nice grassy area fronts the Metolius River. To reach the campground take the SW Camp Sherman Road from US-20 some 10 miles (16 km) northwest of Sisters. Follow the road north taking the left fork at 2.6 miles (4.2 km). Four and eight tenths miles (7.7 km) from where you left US-20 follow SW Camp Sherman Road to the right, the campground entrance road is on the right .2 mile (.3 km) from the corner.

RIVERSIDE CAMPGROUND *(Open May 13 to Oct 25 - Varies)*

Information: www.hoodoo.com
Location: Stretches North of Camp Sherman, *N 44° 26' 21", W 121° 38' 01"*, 2,900 Ft

16 Sites – The Riverside is a Deschutes National Forest walk-in tent campground that stretches along the Metolius River Road between Camp Sherman and the Head of the Metolius. There are parking pull-offs along the dirt road, the campsites are scattered near the Metolius River about 75 yards from the parking sites. There are picnic tables and fire pits as well as vault toilets and hand-operated water pumps. To reach the campground take the SW Camp Sherman Road from US-20 some 10 miles (16 km) northwest of Sisters. Follow the road north taking the right fork at 2.6 miles (4.2 km). Four and three tenths miles (6.9 km) from where you left US-20 you'll see the campground sign on the left.

CAMP SHERMAN CAMPGROUND *(Open All Year)*

Information: www.hoodoo.com
Location: Camp Sherman, *N 44° 27' 48", W 121° 38' 20"*, 2,900 Ft

15 Sites – This is the first of the riverside Deschutes National Forest vehicle campgrounds you reach as you travel north (downstream) along the Metolius. It has sites to 40 feet and is next to the river. Exercise care entering this campground in larger RVs. To reach the campground take the SW Camp Sherman Road from US-20 some 10 miles (16 km) northwest of Sisters. Follow the road north taking the left fork at 2.6 miles (4.2 km). Four and eight tenths miles (7.7 km) from where you left US-20 follow SW Camp Sherman Road to the right. You'll pass the entrance to Black Butte Resort, pass the Camp Sherman store, and cross a bridge over the Metolius. Just after crossing the bridge follow SW Metolius River Rd. to the left and you'll see the campground entrance on the left.

ALLINGHAM CAMPGROUND *(Open May 13 to Sept 25 - Varies)*

Information: www.hoodoo.com
Location: .5 Mile (.8 Km) N of Camp Sherman, *N 44° 28' 19", W 121° 38' 16"*, 2,900 Ft

10 Sites – Allingham is the next Deschutes National Forest campground to the north of the Camp Sherman Campground along the Metolius. It's small but coaches approaching 40 feet use it with careful driving. If you have a big RV you'll have to park and walk in to see if

you can make it. To reach the campground follow the instructions in the previous write-up, the entrance to Allingham is .5 miles (.8 km) beyond that for the Camp Sherman National Forest Campground.

SMILING RIVER CAMPGROUND *(Open May 13 to Sept 25 - Varies)*

Information: www.hoodoo.com
Location: .8 Mile (1.3 Km) N of Camp Sherman, *N 44° 28' 30", W 121° 38' 11"*, 2,900 Ft

36 Sites – This is the next Deschutes National Forest campground north along the Metolius. Although this is considered an RV campground it has huge ponderosa pines closely bordering the road and making access with anything larger than a 30 foot coach pretty difficult. Yet we see 40 foot RVs in the campground and a few sites could accommodate even larger RVs if they were just accessible. It would be best to walk the driveway before attempting entry in a big RV. To reach the campground follow the directions given for the Camp Sherman National Forest Campground. Then drive another .8 miles (1.3 km) north to reach the entrance for Smiling River.

CASCADE LAKES SCENIC BYWAY LOOP

An interesting drive southwest from Bend is known as the **Cascade Lakes Scenic Byway**. This spectacularly scenic two-lane paved road heads west from Bend to **Mt. Bachelor**, a very popular winter ski area. In the summer you can ride the lift up the mountain for the view. The highway passes around the north side of the mountain and then south along a chain of lakes. The highway in this section is called the Cascade Lakes Highway (NF-46).

After passing the mountain you will find that a maze of Forest Service roads - some paved, some not - offer the opportunity to do lots of exploring, fishing, and camping. The road beyond Mt. Bachelor is closed by snow in winter.

A VIEW OF MT BACHELOR FROM THE THE CRAINE PRAIRIE RESORT

For the campgrounds shown below we've shortened the loop. Forty-nine miles (79 km) from Bend turn east on South Century Drive (NF-42). Then, 9 miles (15 km) from that intersection, the route turns right on Burgess Road and continues 11 miles (18 km) to US-97 at a point 22 miles (35 km) south of Bend and 2 miles (3 km) north of La Pine. The entire loop as outlined here is paved although side roads to campgrounds are often gravel.

The many lakes in the area vary in size and usage. Some are reservoirs and others are not. Most lakes are carefully managed and stocked to maximize the fishing possibilities. Here's a brief roundup of the lakes bordered by campgrounds we've listed below.

Sparks Lake is a very shallow natural lake with a surface area of about 800 acres. Much of the lake is surrounded by lava flows making access difficult for fishermen without boats. This is fly-fishing-only water and the lake has a 10 mph speed limit. Brook and cutthroat trout are present.

Elk Lake is a deep natural lake with a surface area of about 300 acres. It's a fairly deep lake and very clear. There are small kokanee and the lake is heavily stocked with brook trout. Boat speed is limited to 10 mph.

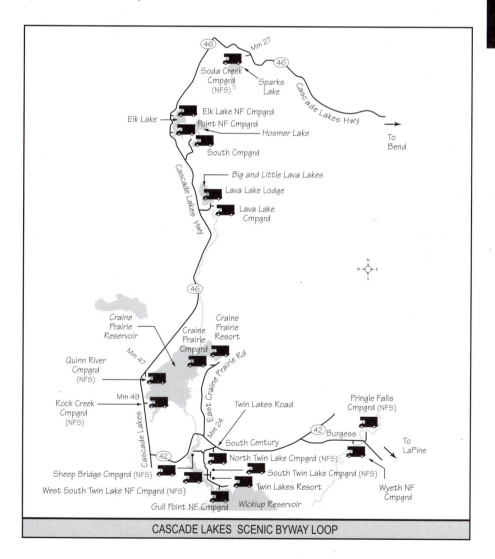

CASCADE LAKES SCENIC BYWAY LOOP

Hosmer Lake is a shallow clear 160-acre lake offering great views of the mountains to the northeast. It's a fly-fishing-only lake with populations of Atlantic salmon, brook trout, and rainbows. This is also a great canoeing lake. There are actually two lakes here connected by a long channel. No engines are allowed, but electric motors are OK.

Big and Little Lava Lakes are actually only connected during unusually high water levels during the spring. Little Lava Lake is the source of the Deschutes River which flows south through Craine Prairie Reservoir and Wickiup Reservoir before turning north to flow into the Columbia. These are old spring-fed natural lakes with a combined surface area of about 500 acres. Fishermen will find rainbows and brook trout.

Craine Prairie Reservoir is a large shallow lake with a surface area of about five square miles. It was first created in 1922 by damming the Deschutes River. This is an extremely productive fishing lake. It's most famous for its "crainebows". These, of course, are large rainbow trout, said to grow in this friendly environment at a rate of two inches per month during the summer. Whitefish, brook trout, kokanee, and largemouth bass are also present.

North Twin Lake is a small, fairly deep circular lake with a surface are of about 130 acres. The lake is heavily stocked with rainbows. Motors are not allowed.

South Twin Lake is another small, fairly deep circular lake. It has a surface area of about 100 acres and, like North Twin, is heavily stocked with rainbows. No motors are allowed on the lake.

Wickiup Reservoir is another reservoir formed by damming the Deschutes River. Wickiup is deeper than Crane Reservoir but water levels vary greatly. Surface area of the lake when full is 10,300 acres. Wickiup is know for its very large brown trout. Fishing is usually excellent in the lake with rainbows, brook trout, kokanee, coho salmon and whitefish also present.

The campgrounds below are arranged along a route that follows the Cascade Lake Highway (FR-46) west and then south for 49 miles (79 km). Then it turns east on FR-42 and Burgess Road to return to US-97 just north of La Pine. The distance from Bend that is listed assumes you travel this route. From Rock Creek campground eastward it's actually shorter to travel south from Bend on US-97 and then eastward on FR-42 or Burgess Road to the campgrounds.

SODA CREEK CAMPGROUND *(Open June 15 to Oct 15 - Varies)*

Information:	(541) 383-4000, www.fs.fed.us/r6/centraloregon/recreation/campgrounds/
Location:	26 Miles (42 Km) W of Bend, *N 44° 01' 30", W 121° 43' 41"*, 5,400 Ft

10 Sites – Soda Creek is a Deschutes National Forest campground. It is one of the closest of the national forest campgrounds to Bend but it is only suitable for tent camping or RVs to about 30 feet. The campground has no water other than the nearby creek but there is a vault toilet, tables, and fire pits. A trail leads to Sparks Lake. The campground has no identifying sign. Watch for the sign for Sparks Lake on the Cascade Lakes Highway 23 miles (37 km) west of Bend. Turn south onto the lake road and then almost immediately turn right into the campground.

ELK LAKE CAMPGROUND *(Open June 10 to Sept 30 - Varies)*

Information:	(541) 383-4700, www.fs.fed.us/r6/centraloregon/recreation/campgrounds/
Location:	33 Miles (53 Km) SW of Bend, *N 43° 58' 48", W 121° 48' 33"*, 4,900 Ft

23 Sites – Elk Lake is a Deschutes National Forest Campground. The entrance for this campground is right off the paved Cascade Lakes Highway. It is a lakeside campground with a resort next door where you can find rental boats and a restaurant. The campground has a beach area and a boat ramp and some of the sites are suitable for RVs to 26 feet. There is a good sign at the entrance, it's 30 miles (48 km) west of Bend.

POINT CAMPGROUND *(Open June 10 to Oct 31 - Varies)*

Information:	(541) 383-4700, www.fs.fed.us/r6/centraloregon/recreation/campgrounds/
Location:	31 Miles (50 Km) SW of Bend, *N 43° 58' 00", W 121° 48' 31"*, 4,900 Ft

10 Sites – Just south of the Elk Lake Campground is the smaller but very similar Point Campground (Deschutes National Forest). It too will take RVs to 26 feet and has a boat ramp and beach. Some sites are along the lake. Watch for the entrance road 31 miles (50 km) west of Bend on the Cascade Lakes Highway.

SOUTH CAMPGROUND *(Open June 10 to Oct 31 - Varies)*

Information:	(541) 383-4700, www.fs.fed.us/r6/centraloregon/recreation/campgrounds/
Location:	34 Miles (55 km) SW of Bend, *N 43° 57' 41", W 121° 47' 24"*, 5,000 Ft

23 Sites – This Deschutes National Forest campground along Hosmer Lake has pull-thru sites suitable for RVs to 26 feet with the limiting factor being maneuvering room. There is no drinking water at this campground but there are picnic tables, fire pits, outhouses and a boat ramp. To reach the campground drive 32.5 miles (52 km) west from Bend on the Cascade Lakes Highway. Turn east on the access road at the sign and drive 1.2 miles (1.9 km) to the campground.

LAVA LAKE CAMPGROUND *(Open April 20 to Oct 31 - Varies)*

Information:	(541) 383-4700, www.fs.fed.us/r6/centraloregon/recreation/campgrounds/
Location:	36 Miles (58 Km) SW of Bend, *N 43° 54' 48", W 121° 46' 01"*, 4,800 Ft

44 Sites – This is a large national forest campground suitable for larger RVs than most. The forest service says the campground is good for RVs to 30 feet but you'll see coaches to 35 feet in here. The Lava Lake Lodge, right next door, has a dump station and showers. There is also a boat ramp at the campground. To reach the campground drive west on the Cascade Lakes Highway for 35 miles (56 km). Turn east on Lava Lake Road and follow it .8 miles (1.3 km) to the campground.

LAVA LAKE LODGE *(Open April 20 to Oct 31 - Varies)*

Res. and Info.:	(541) 382-9443
Location:	36 Miles (58 Km) SW of Bend, *N 43° 54' 52", W 121° 46' 05"*, 4,800 Ft

24 Sites – This lodge, sitting next to Lava Lake, has full hookup back-in sites for RVs to 45 feet. To reach the campground drive west on the Cascade Lakes Highway for 35 miles (56 km). Turn east on Lava Lake Road and follow it .8 miles (1.3 km) to the campground.

QUINN RIVER CAMPGROUND *(Open April 20 to Oct 31 - Varies)*

Information:	(541) 383-4700, www.fs.fed.us/r6/centraloregon/recreation/campgrounds/
Location:	45 Miles (73 Km) SW of Bend, *N 43° 47' 14", W 121° 50' 08"*, 4,400 Ft

41 Sites – Quinn River Campground is a Deschutes National Forest campground that is located on the shore of Crane Prairie Reservoir. Sites here will take RVs to 35 feet, there is also a boat ramp. The access road to the campground is on the Cascade Lakes Highway 45 miles (73 km) from Bend.

ROCK CREEK CAMPGROUND *(Open April 20 to Oct 31 - Varies)*

| Information: | (541) 383-4700, www.fs.fed.us/r6/centraloregon/recreation/campgrounds/ |
| Location: | 47 Miles (76 Km) SW of Bend, *N 43° 45' 57", W 121° 50' 11"*, 4,400 Ft |

32 Sites – This is another Deschutes National Forest campground along the western shore of Crane Prairie Reservoir. The back-in sites are located off two loop drives and measure to 50 feet but limited maneuvering room makes 35 feet the practical maximum for RV size here. There is a boat ramp at the campground. The access road to the campground is on the Cascade Lakes Highway 47 miles (76 km) from Bend.

CRANE PRAIRIE CAMPGROUND *(Open April 20 to Oct 31 - Varies)*

Reservations:	(877) 444-6777, www.reserveusa.com
Information:	(541) 383-4700, www.fs.fed.us/r6/centraloregon/recreation/campgrounds/
Location:	57 Miles (92 Km) SW of Bend, *N 43° 47' 50", W 121° 45' 30"*, 4,400 Ft

152 Sites – This is the largest of the Deschutes National Forest campgrounds on the Crane Prairie Reservoir. The sites here are off five different loops, most are back-ins. There are some sites to at least 45 feet in length but limited maneuvering room makes 35 feet the largest practical RV size. There is a boat ramp, of course. The campground is adjacent to the Crane Prairie Resort which provides coin-operated showers and a laundry which are available to people staying at the national forest campground. To reach the campground from Bend drive west on the Cascade Lakes Highway for 49 miles (79 km), then turn left on Forest Road 42, also called South Century Drive. Drive for 3.8 miles (6.2 km) and then turn left onto East Crane Prairie Road (also called NF-4270). The campground will be on your left in another 4.4 miles (7.1 km).

CRANE PRAIRIE RESORT *(Open May 1 to Oct 15 - Varies)*

| Res. and Info.: | (503) 383-3939, (541) 383-3939, www.crane-prairie-resort-guides.com |
| Location: | 57 Miles (92 Km) SW of Bend, *N 43° 47' 53", W 121° 45' 29"*, 4,400 Ft |

36 Sites – This is a commercial campground with full-hookup sites. Some sites are 75 feet long, the campground is suitable for any size RV. The resort has canoe and boat rentals and a small store with fishing tackle and some groceries. Note that there is not a dump site or any dumping available for folks from outside the campground but that campsites do have sewer hookups. The view of the mountains to the north over the docks and lake is fantastic. To reach the campground from Bend drive southwest on the Cascade Lakes Highway for 49 miles (79 km), then turn left on Forest Road 42, also called South Century Drive. Drive for 3.8 miles (6.1 km) and then turn left onto East Crane Prairie Road (also called NF-4270). The campground will be at the end of the road in 4.5 miles (7.3 km).

NORTH TWIN LAKE CAMPGROUND *(Open April 20 to Oct 31 - Varies)*

| Information: | (541) 383-4700, www.fs.fed.us/r6/centraloregon/recreation/campgrounds/ |
| Location: | 54 Miles (87 Km) SW of Bend, *N 43° 44' 02", W 121° 45' 51"*, 4,300 Ft |

19 Sites – This Deschutes National Forest campground on North Twin Lake has sites to about 40 feet but limited maneuvering room means that 35 feet is the practical maximum RV size. There is no drinking water but there is a boat ramp The Twin Lakes service area (see *Twin Lakes Resort* listing below) is about 2.5 miles (4 km) distant. To reach the campground from Bend drive west on the Cascade Lakes Highway for 49 miles (79 km), then turn left on Forest Road 42, also called South Century Drive. Drive for 4.5 miles (7.3 km) and turn right onto

Twin Lake Road. The campground is on the left in another .2 miles (.3 km).

🚐 SHEEP BRIDGE CAMPGROUND *(Open April 20 to Oct 31 - Varies)*

Information: (541) 383-4700, www.fs.fed.us/r6/centraloregon/recreation/campgrounds/
Location: 54 Miles (87 Km) SW of Bend, *N 43° 43' 56", W0 121° 47' 02"*, 4,400 Ft

23 Sites – The sites in this Deschutes National Forest campground are not clearly marked off but there is lots of room to park. This is a campground where parking big RVs of any size is possible if they are carefully driven. The access road is .5 mile (.8 km) of gravel. The Twin Lakes service area (see *Twin Lakes Resort* listing below) is about 2 miles (3 km) distant. The campground is located on the Deschutes channel of Wickiup Reservoir which is known for its brown trout. To reach the campground from Bend drive west on the Cascade Lakes Highway for 49 miles (79 km), then turn left on Forest Road 42, also called South Century Drive. Drive for 4.5 miles (7.3 km) and turn right onto Twin Lake Road. The campground entrance road is on the right in another .7 miles (1.3 km).

🚐 TWIN LAKES RESORT *(Open April 20 to Oct 15 - Varies)*

Res. and Info.: (541) 593-6526, www.twinlakesresortoregon.com
Location: 55 Miles (89 Km) SW of Bend, *N 43° 42' 52", W 121° 46' 16"*, 4,300 Ft

22 Sites – This resort serves as a service center of sorts for the campgrounds in the Twin Lakes and Wikiup Reservoir area. The store and restaurant overlook South Twin Lake and there is a shower building and laundry nearby. The resort has a campground too, although it is .2 miles (3 km) farther south on the west side of Twin Lake Road and overlooks the reservoir rather than South Twin Lake. Just a little further south along Twin Lakes Road is a Forest Service dump station that serves the area. The Twin Lakes Resort camping area has many back-in sites to 50 feet with full hookups. There are showers and flush toilets at the campground in addition to those at the resort. To reach the campground from Bend drive west on the Cascade Lakes Highway for 49 miles (79 km), then turn left on Forest Road 42, also called South Century Drive. Drive for 4.5 miles (7.3 km) and turn right onto Twin Lakes Road. The resort entrance road is on the left in 1.9 miles (3.1 km), the campground is on the right in another .2 miles (.3 km).

🚐 SOUTH TWIN LAKE CAMPGROUND *(Open April 20 to Oct 31 - Varies)*

Information: (541) 383-4700, www.fs.fed.us/r6/centraloregon/recreation/campgrounds/
Location: 55 Miles (89 Km) SW of Bend, *N 43° 42' 59", W 121° 46' 16"*, 4,300 Ft

21 Sites – This Deschutes National Forest campground sits just to the north of the Twin Lakes Resort on the shore of South Twin Lake. There is a boat ramp. A few of the sites reach 40 feet and carefully driven 40-foot coaches do camp here. The South Twin Lake store, restaurant, showers and laundry are conveniently located just across a parking lot. To reach the campground from Bend drive west on the Cascade Lakes Highway for 49 miles (79 km), then turn left on Forest Road 42, also called South Century Drive. Drive for 4.5 miles (7.3 km) and turn right onto Twin Lakes Road. The campground entrance road is on the left in 1.9 miles (3.1 km).

🚐 WEST SOUTH TWIN LAKE CAMPGROUND *(Open April 20 to Oct 15 - Varies)*

Information: (541) 383-4700, www.fs.fed.us/r6/centraloregon/recreation/campgrounds/
Location: 55 Miles (89 Km) SW of Bend, *N 43° 42' 53", W 121° 46' 22"*, 4,300 Ft

24 Sites – This is another Deschutes National Forest campground in the cluster around Twin Lakes Resort. This one is just across the road and overlooks the inlet arm of Wickiup Reser-

voir. There is a boat ramp for Wickiup Reservoir here too. It's an easy stroll to the resort and the facilities there. The sites in this campground are off a paved loop road. Some reach 40 feet but because of limited maneuvering room we recommend that coaches no longer than 35 feet use this campground. To reach the campground from Bend drive west on the Cascade Lakes Highway for 49 miles (79 km), then turn left on Forest Road 42, also called South Century Drive. Drive for 4.5 miles (7.3 km) and turn right onto Twin Lakes Road. The campground entrance road is on the right in 1.9 miles (3.1 km).

GULL POINT CAMPGROUND *(Open April 20 to Oct 31 - Varies)*

Information:	(541) 383-4700, www.fs.fed.us/r6/centraloregon/recreation/campgrounds/
Location:	55 Miles (89 Km) SW of Bend, *N 43° 42' 19", W 121° 45' 28"*, 4,300 Ft

81 Sites – This is a large Deschutes National Forest campground located on the north shore of Wickiup Reservoir. While some sites reach 45 feet, maneuvering room limits recommended RV size to 35 feet. There is a dump station just to the north of the campground and the Twin Lake Resort is about 1.1 miles (1.8 km) distant. To reach the campground from Bend drive west on the Cascade Lakes Highway for 49 miles (79 km), then turn left on Forest Road 42, also called South Century Drive. Drive for 4.5 miles (7.3 km) and turn right onto Twin Lakes Road. The campground entrance road is on the right in 3 miles (4.8 km).

WYETH CAMPGROUND *(Open April 20 to Oct 31)*

Information:	(541) 383-4700, www.fs.fed.us/r6/centraloregon/recreation/campgrounds/
Location:	61 Miles (98 Km) SW of Bend, *N 43° 44' 16", W 121° 36' 58"*, 4,200 Ft

3 Sites – Wyeth is a tiny Deschutes National Forest campground located on the shore of the Deschutes River. It is a take-out point for floaters since it is just above Pringle Falls. The few sites are small and uneven, they limit use to tent campers and RVs to about 25 feet. There is no potable water at this campground, just the river. To reach the campground from Bend drive west on the Cascade Lakes Highway for 49 miles (79 km), then turn left on Forest Road 42, also called South Century Drive. Drive for 9 miles (15 km) and turn right on Burgess Road. After another 3 miles (5 km) follow the access road right for a short distance to the campground.

PRINGLE FALLS CAMPGROUND *(Open April 20 to Oct 31 - Varies)*

Information:	(541) 383-4700, www.fs.fed.us/r6/centraloregon/recreation/campgrounds/
Location:	61 Miles (98 Km) SW of Bend, *N 43° 44' 54", W 121° 36' 13"* 4,200 Ft

6 Sites – Pringle falls is a very small Deschutes National Forest campground with a narrow and rough access road, it is only suitable for RVs to about 25 feet. Sites are back-ins arranged off a sandy central clearing. There are vault toilets but no water other than what is in the Deschutes River which runs past the campground. To reach the campground from Bend drive west on the Cascade Lakes Highway for 49 miles (79 km), then turn left on Forest Road 42, also called South Century Drive. Drive for 9 miles (15 km) and turn right on Burgess Road. After another 3.5 miles (5.6 km) follow the access road left to the campground.

CHARLESTON

Between Reedsport and Gold Beach is Coos Bay, center of commercial life on the southern Oregon coast. Rather than concentrating on Coos Bay we'll focus instead on **Charleston**, the most attractive of the Coos Bay-area towns. It is a fishing village, with more convenient access to the ocean for fishing boats than Coos Bay and North Bend which are located farther from the estuary mouth. In Charleston you'll find, a fishing pier, fishing charter companies, restaurants, and shops.

From Charleston you'll see signs pointing toward the coast for **Sunset Bay State Park**, **Shore Acres State Park**, and **Cape Arago State Park**. These three small state parks along the shore offer a variety of options. **Shore Acres State Park** is the former estate of a timber magnate: Louis J. Simpson. There are formal gardens with roses, azaleas, and rhododendrons, and also a Japanese garden. There's a bluff-top lookout with views along the rocky coast. **Cape Arago State Park**, at the end of the road, also offers a coastal lookout, often with views of sea lions and seals, not to mention the occasional whale. The park also has excellent tide pools. **Sunset Bay State Park,** the first park you come to, has a small bay where the water gets warm enough for the hardy to swim. It also has a campground.

⭐ CHARLESTON MARINA RV PARK *(Open All Year)*

Res. and Info: (541) 888-9512, www.charlestonmarina.com
Location: Charleston, *N 43° 20' 36", W 124° 19' 32"*, Near Sea Level

115 Sites – Charleston Marina RV Park is very popular with fishermen, it bills itself as a working fishing village. It's also a good place to base yourself even if you have no interest in the area's fishing at all. Unlike some marina campgrounds this one doesn't overlook the marina, it's a block or so from the water. The campgrounds has a few tent sites, also two rental yurts. The RV sites here occupy a large lot. They are back-ins and pull-thrus to 50 feet. Most are wide sites designed to let you park your boat trailer next to the RV. In Charleston go north on Boat Basin Road from the corner in Charleston on the Cape Arago Highway that is just west of the bridge. Drive north about .2 mile (.3 km) to Kingfisher Dr., turn right, and you'll soon see the campground entrance on your left.

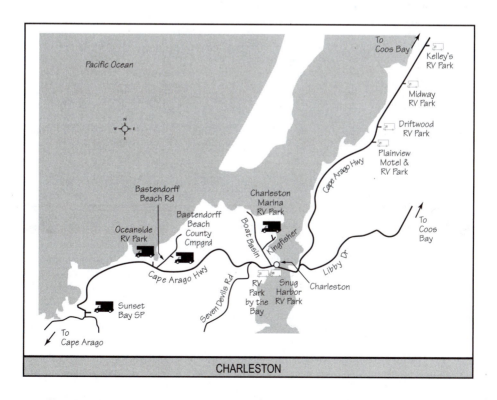

CHARLESTON

🚐 BASTENDORFF BEACH COUNTY CAMPGROUND *(Open All Year)*

Reservations: (cabins only) (541) 396-3121, ext 354
Information: (541) 888-5353, www.co.coos.or.us/ccpark/bastendorff/
Location: 2 Miles W of Charleston, *N 43° 20' 27", W 124° 20' 57"*, 100 Ft

100 Sites – Bastendorff Beach County Campground sits on a hillside overlooking the Pacific just west of Charleston. The sites are off four loops. There are tents sites (including hiker/bicyclist sites) as well as RV sites. Almost all of the RV sites are back-ins, but some extend to 45 feet. To reach the campground travel west from Charleston on the Cape Arago Highway. In 1.7 miles (2.7 km) you'll see the Bastendorff Beach Road going right. The campground is a short distance up this road on the right.

🚐 OCEANSIDE RV PARK *(Open All Year)*

Res. and Info.: (541) 888-2598, (800) 570-2598, oceanside@harborside.com,
www.harborside.com/~oceanside
Location: 2 Miles (3.2 Km) W of Charleston, *N 43° 20' 22", W 124° 21' 16"*, Near Sea Level

83 Sites – The Oceanside is a real find. It's a full-hookup park suitable for larger RVs, and it's just a short stroll from a good beach. There are few commercial campgrounds offering this amenity within a hundred miles north or south. Sites here are in two parts. An older section is near the entrance, but a nicer new section is nearer the beach with full-hookup back-ins and pull-thrus to 60 feet. Maneuvering room is good and there are no obstructions to your slides. The campground is located 1.8 miles (2.9 km) east of Charleston on the Cape Arago Highway, the entrance is on the right just after you pass Bastendorff Beach Road.

🚐 SUNSET BAY STATE PARK *(Open All Year)*

Reservations: (800) 452-5687, www.reserveamerica.com
Information: (541) 888-4902, (800) 551-6949, www.oregonstateparks.org
Location: 5 Miles (8 Km) W of Charleston, *N 43° 19' 50", W 124° 22' 15"*, Near Sea Level

130 Sites – Sunset Bay is a pleasant state park campground. The campsites are in a small valley, across from the entrance road is the day use area on a beautiful little half-moon of beach. Trails from the park lead along the cliffs to Shore Acres State Park and Cape Arago to the south. There are vehicle tenting sites as well as a hiker/biker camping area. RV sites here include both partial and full hook-up parking as well as yurts and dry sites. The RV sites here aren't as long as at some Oregon State Park campgrounds, but there are 30 sites from 40 to 51 feet. Some have electricity and water, other are full hookups. The entrance to the campground is 5.1 miles (8.2 km) from Charleston on the Cape Arago Highway.

COLUMBIA GORGE

The section of the Columbia Gorge covered in this section stretches from the eastern suburbs of Portland to The Dalles. The first miles, as far as Cascade Locks, are the most impressive with most of the interesting stops. The Columbia River Scenic Highway is one of the prime attractions of the Gorge, but it is narrow with limited parking and not suitable for RVs over about 25 feet. A tow car or smaller RV are essential for visiting this attraction. If you have a larger RV you might drive directly from Portland to Cascade Locks on Interstate 84, a distance of 35 miles (56 km), and park your RV. Use your smaller vehicle to tour the western section of the Scenic Highway.

The **Historic Columbia River Scenic Highway** was completed in 1915. It was considered an engineering triumph and was built as much as a scenic attraction as a transportation route.

I-84 obliterated much of the highway but two good sections remain. The first is about 23 miles (37 km) long and runs between Exit 18 of I-84 to Exit 35. This section of road has famous scenic viewpoints and many waterfalls. The second section leaves I-84 at Exit 69 and climbs the bluffs to Rowena Crest Viewpoint before descending to meet I-84 at Exit 76, just west of The Dalles.

To follow the scenic highway from west to east (again, in a vehicle no longer than 25 feet) leave I-84 at Exit 18. You will follow the quiet Sandy River for several miles before starting to climb. Make a stop at the **Portland Women's Forum State Scenic Viewpoint** for an excellent view of the Crown Point Vista House ahead and slightly lower against the backdrop of the Gorge. This is a very popular photographic viewpoint. In just over a mile you will arrive at the **Vista House**, the views here are outstanding and there's also a gift shop and some exhibits about the highway and local wildflowers.

After the Vista House the highway descends and the waterfalls start. They're all different and all worth a stop. In order they are **Latourell Falls, Shepperds Dell, Bridal Veil, Wahkeena Falls, Multnomah Falls, Oneonta Gorge**, and **Horsetail Falls**. Multnomah Falls is the best known and has the best facilities. There is a lodge with restaurant and information office as well as good paved trails up to a scenic walking bridge just below the falls. The falls themselves have a drop of 620 feet and are clearly viewable from the lodge below.

You'll reach I-84 at Exit 35 after passing Ainsworth State Park Campground. In just 5 miles (8 km) you'll reach the **Bonneville Dam** exit. This dam offers one of the best of the many dam touring opportunities on the Columbia, if you want to see a dam close up this is a good one. There is plenty of room for parking big RVs here. Take a look at the visitor's center which has exhibits and a fish-viewing room. Just a short walk from the center you can view the generator room. This dam also has huge locks, you may be lucky enough to watch a tug with barges passing through. Finally, the dam has a fish hatchery with a unique sturgeon-viewing pond.

Exit 44 for Cascade Locks (for traffic from the west) is four miles (6 km) beyond Bonneville Dam. **Cascade Locks** (population 1,100) is a small town and a good base for a visit to the western end of the gorge. Before the Bonneville Dam was built there was a set of locks here

TAKE A RIDE ON THE COLUMBIA GORGE STERN-WHEELER AT CASCADE LOCKS

to let boats on the river bypass the **Cascades of the Columbia**, a treacherous series of rapids. Bonneville Dam flooded the locks, but there is a pleasant waterfront park, and the top of the drowned locks are still above lake level. You can take a cruise on the **Columbia Gorge stern-wheeler** which is based here during the summer. There is a bridge across the river at Cascade Locks, it is called the **Bridge of the Gods**. The name comes from an Indian legend, probably based upon the fact that a huge landslide once stopped up the Columbia at this point. The **Cascades Crest Trail**, a long-distance hiking trail following the entire crest of the Cascades, crosses the Columbia on the bridge.

Eastward from Cascade Locks you continue to follow I-84. You'll want to make a stop at **Hood River** (population 5,200). This little town has become the windsurfing capital of the U.S. Drive down the hill and across the railroad and park next to the river, if there's wind there will be lots of **windsurfers**. Watching them can be very entertaining.

Also in Hood River is the terminal for the **Mount Hood Railroad**. They offer scenic and dinner train trips up the Hood River Valley to the south.

East of Hood River is another chance to leave I-84 and follow the original US-30 (Historic Columbia River Scenic Highway). Take Exit 69. The road climbs onto the cliffs above the river. There is an excellent overlook with lots of parking room some 12 miles (19 km) along, it's called **Rowena Crest Viewpoint** and offers great views up and down the river. From there the road once again descends and rejoins I-84 at Exit 76.

Next stop is The Dalles (population 11,800). There's a new attraction here, the **Columbia Gorge Discovery Center and Waasco County Historical Museum**. It is a very well-done facility, particularly the Waasco County section. Take Exit 82 and follow the signs. They have lots of parking for big RVs.

Just past The Dalles is the second dam on the river. Take Exit 88 for **The Dalles Dam**. It is much the same as Bonneville Dam, but is unique in that you make a short train trip to reach the visitor facilities.

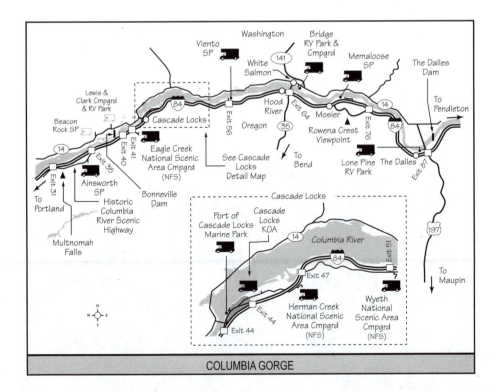

COLUMBIA GORGE

AINSWORTH STATE PARK *(Open March 15 to Oct 31 - Varies)*

Information: (503) 695-2301, (800) 551-6949, www.oregonstateparks.org
Location: 9 Miles (15 Km) W of Hood River, *N 45° 35' 46", W 122° 03' 01"*, 900 Ft

50 Sites – Ainsworth is located toward the eastern end of the most scenic section of the Historic Columbia River Highway. Large RVs shouldn't drive the highway because it is narrow and crowded but it is OK to access this campground as described below. The campground is a jewel. The park area is small but it has large pull-thru sites to 60 feet and good restrooms. It's also the most convenient place for RVers to leave their RVs while they take a smaller vehicle to visit the highway and falls to the west. The Gorge 400 trail leads west from the campground to Multnomah Falls and beyond. From I-84 take Exit 35. Then drive west on the Historic Columbia River Highway for .3 mile (.5 km) to the campground.

PORT OF CASCADE LOCKS MARINE PARK *(Open All Year)*

Information: (541) 374-8619, www.sternwheeler.com
Location: Cascade Locks, *N 45° 40' 03", W 121° 53' 44"*, 100 Ft

16 Sites – This is a small beautifully-located campground in a municipal riverside park in Cascade Locks. The Columbia Gorge sternwheeler docks nearby. Sites are back-ins to 50 feet. Restrooms at the campground are only port-a-potties but there are flush toilets and showers at the visitor center about a quarter-mile distant through the park. The fly in the ointment at this park is that you must use a railroad underpass to enter the park and it only allows RVs to 12 feet high. To reach the campground follow entrance signs from the center of Cascade Locks which is most easily reached by taking Exit 44 from I-84.

CASCADE LOCKS KOA *(Open Feb 1 to Nov 30)*

Reservations: (800) 562-8698, www.koa.com
Information: (541) 374-8668, cascadelockskoa@clbb.net
Location: Cascade Locks, *N 45° 40' 43", W 121° 52' 06"*, 100 Ft

80 Sites – This KOA is up to the normal KOA standards making it a good base for both tenters and big RVs, particularly for those with children along. Some sites are very long pull-thrus and there is a swimming pool. To reach the campground from the west take Exit 44 from I-84. Follow the main road through town, Wa-na-pa Street, and then turn north on Forest Lane Road. You'll see the campground on the left 1 mile (1.6 km) from the turn.

WYETH NATIONAL SCENIC AREA CAMPGROUND *(Open May 1 to Sept 30)*

Information: (541) 386-2333, www.fs.fed.us/r6/columbia/forest/
Location: 6 Miles E of Cascade Locks, *N 45° 41' 22", W 121° 46' 19"*, 400 Ft

13 Sites – This is one of three Columbia River Gorge National Scenic Area campgrounds run by the Forest Service. These are great little parks, reasonably priced. Wyeth is limited to RVs to 30 feet, largely because the drives are lined with bricks which shred tires. The campground is most easily reached by taking Exit 51 from I-84. Then follow Herman Creek Road eastward on the south side of the highway for a short distance. The campground entrance is on the right.

HERMAN CREEK NATIONAL SCENIC AREA CAMPGROUND *(Open May 1 to Sept 30)*

Information: (541) 386-2333, www.fs.fed.us/r6/columbia/forest/
Location: 2 Miles (2 Km) E of Cascade Locks, *N 45° 40' 57", W 121° 50' 39",* 100 Ft

7 Sites – Herman Creek sits on a ridge above the highway. It's one of the few campgrounds in the region that is set up for horses, several of the sites have tie rails for them. It will take tents and RVs to 30 feet although the steep narrow entrance drive may give RVers a few bad moments. Access is a little convoluted. From the east on I-84 take Exit 47, then follow Forest Lane southwest on the south side of the highway for .5 mile (.8 km) to the entrance on your left. From the west take Exit 44 from I-84. Drive through Cascade Locks and in 1 mile (1.6 km) turn left on Forest Lane. Follow Forest Lane for 1.9 miles (3.1 km) until it passes under I-84. Then follow the frontage road to the left for .4 mile (.6 km) to the campground.

EAGLE CREEK NATIONAL SCENIC AREA CAMPGROUND *(Open May 1 to Sept 30)*

Information: (541) 386-2333, www.fs.fed.us/r6/columbia/forest/
Location: 6 Miles (10 Km) W of Cascade Locks, *N 45° 38' 27", W 121° 55' 35",* 400 Ft

18 Sites – Constructed in 1915, this is the first National Forest Service campground constructed in the US. It is also the first one with flush toilets. This campground sits on a ridge above the Eagle Creek fish hatchery. Sites in the park would take some RVs to 35 feet but there is a sharp hairpin on the access road and tight interior roads that put a practical limitation of about 30 feet on the campground. Even in an RV that short it is important to be careful. Westbound on I-84 take Exit 41 and follow the access road to the hatchery and around back to the campground. There is no access eastbound so continue to Exit 40, reverse course, and use Exit 41.

VIENTO STATE PARK *(Open May 15 to Oct 31 - Varies)*

Information: (503) 695-2301, (800) 551-6949, www.oregonstateparks.org
Location: 6 Miles (10 Km) W of Hood River, *N 45° 41' 52", W 121° 40' 03",* 100 Ft

73 Sites – This is a beautiful state park with one big problem. The railroad runs right next to the park and there is a level crossing to provide access to the lower part of the park along the river. That means that every train going by blows its horn, and that goes on all day and night, approximately every 15 minutes. Otherwise it's a very enjoyable place with good facilities, back-in sites to 50 feet, and access to the river for windsurfing. It's seldom full, for good reason. There are some very small vehicle access sites on the south side of the freeway farther from the highway that provide a quieter location for tent campers. Access is from Exit 56 of I-84. The main campground is on the north side of the highway beyond the day use area.

BRIDGE RV PARK AND CAMPGROUND *(Open All Year)*

Res. and Info.: (509) 493-1111, (888) 550-7275, bridgerv@bridgerv.com, www.bridgerv.com
Location: White Salmon, WA, *N 45° 43' 21", W 121° 29' 16",* 100 Ft

50 Sites – An almost-new park with both a grassy tent area and back-in and pull-thru sites to 65 feet. The campground is actually on the Washington side even though we talk about this area in the Oregon chapter in this book. It's easy to reach the campground from Oregon. Just cross the Hood River Bridge from Hood River, Oregon to White Salmon, Washington. On the north side turn right on SR-14 and you'll see the entrance to the RV park in .1 mile (1.6 km), just beyond the Union 76 station.

MEMALOOSE STATE PARK CAMPGROUND *(Open March 18 to Oct 31 - Varies)*

Reservations: (800) 452-5687, www.reserveamerica.com
Information: (503) 695-2301, (800) 551-6949, www.oregonstateparks.org
Location: 6 Miles (10 Km) W of Hood River, *N 45° 41' 45", W 121° 20' 39"*, 200 Ft

110 Sites – This is the largest of the state campgrounds in the Gorge area. It's also reportedly located in the hottest part of the Gorge. Fortunately it has nice shade trees. This campground has large back-in sites (to 55 feet) in an open park-like setting overlooking the river, it's popular with big-rig owners. Access is from the rest area near Mile 73 of I-84 westbound. There is no access eastbound.

LONE PINE RV PARK *(Open All Year)*

Res. and Info.: (541) 506-3755
Location: The Dalles, *N 45° 36' 21", W 121° 08' 18"*, 100 Ft

39 Sites – Lone Pine is a no-nonsense big-rig camping area located at the south end of the bridge over the Columbia at The Dalles. There is no access to the river from the campground, it's used primarily by overnighters passing through the area because it's so handy to the interstate. Many sites are full-hookup pull-thrus to 60 feet. We seldom find a manager on-site, there's a self-registration board that makes it easy to check in. Pull off I-84 at Exit 87, the campground is located behind the McDonalds on the north side of the highway.

CRATER LAKE NATIONAL PARK

Crater Lake was designated a national park in 1902. The primary attraction here is the deep blue lake in the volcanic caldera of Mount Mazama. The caldera and lake are a fairly recent geologic occurrence, the mountain blew off its top about 7,500 years ago, well within the time that this region was populated by Native Americans. The explosion is calculated by geologists to have been 42 times as powerful as the recent eruption of Mt. St. Helens. The lake in the caldera is definitely one of the scenic wonders of the world. It is the deepest lake in the U.S. at 1,932 feet.

A 37-mile (60 km) road circles the rim of the caldera offering many viewpoints. While some folks follow the rim drive in their RVs it is best to use a smaller vehicle if you have one available. The road is narrow in many places and parking at viewpoints is sometimes tight, particularly on weekends and during August.

Facilities in the park are limited. There are two visitor centers. **Steele Visitor Center** is open all year, the **Rim Visitor Center** is only open during the summer when melting snow allows the opening of the rim drive. This varies from year to year, usually the road is open from early July to about the end of October.

One popular activity in the park is the narrated **boat tour** of the lake. It takes about an hour and forty-five minutes and circles the lake with a stop at Wizard Island. To take the tour you must walk the 1-mile **Cleetwood Cove Trail** down to the lake, not too difficult on the way down but another story climbing the 700 vertical feet back out. Remember, you are at an altitude of 6,176 feet at the lake's surface, Don't try this unless you are in reasonably good shape. At the peak of the season there are 9 trips each day, tickets are sold at the parking lot.

Camping sites inside the park are limited, that's OK because there are lots of possibilities within easy driving distance but outside the park boundaries. Mazama Village Campground is the only possibility inside the park for RVs. There's also a tent-only campground called Lost Creek Campground. North of the park is the Umpqua National Forest's Diamond Lake Recreation Area. Three of the campgrounds listed below are near this lake. It has swimming beaches, 11 miles (18 km) of paved hiker/biker trails circling the lake, boat ramps, and is a popular

OREGON

CRATER LAKE

rainbow trout fishery. One of the campgrounds at the lake is a commercial big-rig RV park with full hookups. There is also a commercial lodge offering a restaurant, pizza joint, service station, grocery stores, laundromat, fishing charters and bike rentals. Two other areas with campgrounds offering good access to the park are east and west of the southern park entrance. Crater Lake Resort and Jo's Motel and Campground are east of the southern park entrance in the Klamath Lake region. The last three campgrounds listed below are national forest campgrounds in the Rogue River Valley to the west of the southern entrance to the park.

MAZAMA VILLAGE CAMPGROUND *(Open June 15 to Oct 3 - Varies)*

Information: (541) 594-3100, www.nps.gov/crla/
Location: Crater Lake National Park, *N 42° 52' 02", W 122° 09' 57"*, 6,000 Ft

200 Sites – Mazama is the largest campground in the park and the only one that will take RVs. Although the campground does not take reservations and is often full at night you can usually get in if you arrive in the early afternoon. There are only 15 electrical hookup sites so be prepared to do without electricity if you're in an RV. Quite a few of the sites here are pull-thrus and some can accommodate RVs to 45 feet although slide-outs can often not be extended. This campground is carefully managed and each site is specifically assigned when you check in, the managers know which sites will fit which RVs. The campground is located at the newly renovated Mazama Village which is just inside the south (Annie Springs) entrance to the park. It's about 7 miles (11 km) from Rim Village at the lake.

LOST CREEK CAMPGROUND *(Open June 15 to Sept 15- Varies)*

Information: (541) 594-3100, www.nps.gov/crla/
Location: Crater Lake National Park, *N 42° 52' 46", W 122° 02' 20"*, 6,300 Ft

16 Sites – Lost lake is a vehicle-accessible tent camping area. RVs are not allowed. There is water at the campground. To reach Lost Creek follow Rim Drive 11 miles (18 km) counterclockwise from Rim Village. Turn right away from the lake on Pinnacles Road and you'll see the campground entrance road in 3.1 miles (5 km).

BROKEN ARROW CAMPGROUND *(Open May 15 to Oct 1 - Varies)*

Information: (541) 793-3310, (541) 498-2531, http://www.fs.fed.us/r6/umpqua/
Location: 4 Miles (6 Km) N of Crater Lake National Park,
N 43° 07' 57", W 122° 08' 48", 5,200 Ft

147 Sites – Broken Arrow is one of two large Umpqua National Forest campgrounds near Diamond Lake. This one is on flat ground away from the lake, and as a result the sites tend to be easier to access and more suitable for larger RVs. There are back-ins and pull-thrus for coaches to 35 feet. It is south of the lake. From the Diamond Lake entrance off SR-230 near the junction of SR-230 and SR-138 drive north for .7 mile (1.1 km). Turn left and the entrance to the campground is on the left in .6 mile (1 km).

DIAMOND LAKE RV PARK *(Open May 15 to Oct 1 - Varies)*

Res. and Info.: (541) 793-3318, dlrvp@chatlink.com, diamondlakervpark.com
Location: 4 Miles (6 Km) N of Crater Lake National Park,
N 43° 08' 20", W 122° 08' 02", 5,300 Ft

120 Sites – This is the closest full-hookup big-rig campground to Crater Lake. It sits away from Diamond Lake but does offer back-in and pull-thru sites to 60 feet. Only pets to 35 pounds are allowed. From the Diamond Lake entrance off SR-230 near the junction of SR-230

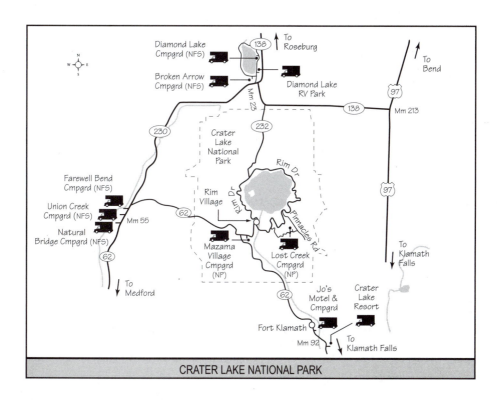

CRATER LAKE NATIONAL PARK

and SR-138 drive north for 1 mile (1.6 km). The campground is on the right.

DIAMOND LAKE CAMPGROUND *(Open May 15 to Oct 31 - Varies)*

Reservations:	(877) 444-6777, www.reserveusa.com
Information:	(541) 793-3310, (541) 498-2531, http://www.fs.fed.us/r6/umpqua/
Location:	5 Miles (8 Km) N of Crater Lake National Park,
	N 43° 09' 33", W 122° 08' 00", 5,200 Ft

238 Sites – This huge Umpqua National Forest campground occupies a sloping site on the east shore of Diamond Lake. Some sites will take coaches to 35 feet but maneuvering room isn't as good as at Broken Arrow due to the sloping terrain. From the Diamond Lake entrance off SR-230 near the junction of SR-230 and SR-138 drive north for 2.7 miles (4.4 km). The entrance is on the left.

CRATER LAKE RESORT *(Open May 1 to Oct 31 - Varies)*

Res. and Info.:	(541) 381-2349, crtrlkrst@aol.com, www.craterlakeresort.com
Location:	18 Miles (29 Km) SE of Crater Lake National Park,
	N 42° 41' 04", W 121° 58' 21", 4,200 Ft

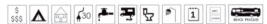

21 Sites – This little motel and campground along Fort Creek is a very pleasant place to stay. It's 18 miles (29 km) from the southern entrance to the park so it's convenient to the park but away from the congestion. The full-hookup RV sites back up to the little river and some will take RVs to 40 feet. Partial hookup sites that back up to the front fence will take even larger RVs on a grass surface and there is tenting on several pleasant lawn areas. You can fish or canoe on the crystal-clear creek. The campground is located on the east side of SR-62 two miles (3 km) south of Fort Klamath.

JO'S MOTEL & CAMPGROUND (FORMERLY FORT KLAMATH RV PARK) *(Open May 1 to Oct 31 - Varies)*

Res. and Info.:	(541) 381-2234
Location:	16 Miles (26 Km) SE of Crater Lake National Park,
	N 42° 42' 13", W 121° 59' 42", 4,100 Ft

11 Sites – This small campground behind a motel is located in the little town of Fort Klamath. It's 16 miles (26 km) from the south entrance of the park. The campground has two sites that will accommodate RVs to 40 feet, the others are pretty short, 25 to 30 feet long. There is also a separate tent-camping area nearer the river. Watch for the sign on the east side of the road as you pass through Fort Klamath.

NATURAL BRIDGE CAMPGROUND *(Open May 15 to Oct 30 - Varies)*

Information:	(541) 560-3400, www.fs.fed.us/r6/rogue
Location:	19 Miles (31 Km) W of Crater Lake National Park,
	N 42° 53' 33", W 122° 27' 46", 3,300 Ft

17 Sites – Natural Bridge is the smallest of the three Rogue River National Forest campgrounds in a stretch along the Rogue River here. Trails lead along the river letting you view the lava tubes where the river passes underground. There is no drinking water in this campground. Some site are 50 feet long but limited narrow roads and lack of maneuvering room means that coach size should be limited to about 35 feet. From the intersection of SR-62 and SR-230 travel southwest for 2.6 miles (4.2 km) to the campground entrance. This is 19 miles (31 km) from the south entrance to the park.

UNION CREEK CAMPGROUND *(Open May 15 to Oct 30 - Varies)*

Information: (541) 560-3400, www.fs.fed.us/r6/rogue, www.roguerec.com
Location: 17 Miles (27 Km) W of Crater Lake National Park,
N 42° 54' 23", W 122° 26' 54", 3,200 Ft

78 Sites – This large Rogue River National Forest campground is situated on both sides of Union Creek where it empties into the Rogue and is best for RVs to about 30 feet. There are a few sites to 40 feet but narrow roads and big trees limit maneuvering room. Check with the host or walk the road before attempting to take a big RV in here. There are also three nearby full-hookup sites for big RVs associated with this campground, check with the host for more information. From the intersection of SR-62 and SR-230 travel southwest for 1.4 miles (2.3 km) to the campground entrance. This is 17 miles (27 km) from the south entrance of the park.

FAREWELL BEND CAMPGROUND *(Open May 15 to Oct 20 - Varies)*

Information: (541) 560-3400, www.fs.fed.us/r6/rogue, www.roguerec.com
Location: 16 Miles (26 Km) W of Crater Lake National Park,
N 42° 54' 57", W 122° 26' 04", 3,100 Ft

61 Sites – Farewell Bend Rogue River National Forest campground is the best of the three campgrounds along here for RVs. There are sites from 46 to 65 feet long and they are angled making entry possible for larger RVs. Still, remember that this is a national forest campground and exercise caution. A trail leads from the campground to the Rogue Gorge Viewpoint. From the intersection of SR-62 and SR-230 travel southwest for .5 mile (.8 km) to the campground entrance. This is 16 miles (26 km) from the south entrance to the park.

EUGENE

Eugene (population 134,000), home to the University of Oregon, has a lot to offer. Actually, this is a twin city, Springfield (population 52,000) is just to the east. Often considered one of the most livable middle-sized towns in the U.S., Eugene has the cultural attractions of a university town and the outdoor attractions of the nearby McKenzie River Valley climbing east into the Cascades.

Eugene is laced with **bike paths**, particularly along the Willamette River. If you are a biker rider, jogger, or walker you should take advantage of them.

The **University of Oregon** campus covers 250 acres near downtown Eugene. It is very attractive and a good place for a stroll. It has two good museums: the **Museum of Art** and the **Museum of Natural History**.

Eugene occupies the south end of the fertile Willamette Valley. There are several small **wineries** in the area that deserve a visit.

State Route 126 leads east toward Bend up the **McKenzie River Valley**. While Sisters is 90 miles (145 km) away, you can find a lot to enjoy by just making a side trip as far as McKenzie Bridge, 50 miles (81 km) up the valley. Watch for the **Goodpasture** covered bridge at about Mile 22 just west of Vida. You can make an excellent loop trip out of the drive by following the paved **Robert Aufderheide Memorial Drive** (a National Forest Service Byway), from a point five miles (8 km) short of McKenzie bridge, south 57 miles (92 km) to meet SR-58 and then return 41 miles (66 km) to Eugene on that highway. As you near Eugene on SR-58 you'll have a chance to visit 5 more covered bridges. You'll also find a wealth of Forest Service campgrounds along the route since the eastern portion is within the Willamette National Forest.

The Eugene area campgrounds below are described from south to north.

🚐 PASS CREEK DOUGLAS COUNTY PARK *(Open All Year)*

Information: (541) 942-3281, www.co.douglas.or.us/parks.asp
Location: 25 Miles (40 Km) S of Eugene, *N 43° 43' 21", W 123° 12' 31"*, 300 Ft

30 Sites – This is one of those simple but good campgrounds near the freeway that make great overnight stops. This one has long back-in sites to 60 feet with full hookups. Sites are separated by expanses of lawn and there are shade trees. Leave I-5 at Exit 163 and then follow signs north along the west side of the freeway to the park. Exit 163 is 25 miles (40 km) south of Eugene and 35 miles (56 km) north of Roseburg.

🚐 CASCARA CAMPGROUND *(Open May 1 to Sept 30)*

Information: (541) 937-1173, (800) 551-6949, www.oregonstateparks.org
Location: 26 Miles (42 Km) E of Eugene, *N 43° 58' 20", W 122° 40' 01"*, 900 Ft

47 Sites – This campground is in Fall Creek State Recreation Area on Fall Creek Reservoir. Cascara is a popular swimming and water sports park (including personal watercraft and water skiing) in the summer. Water levels in the reservoir are low in the fall and the park tends to be pretty much empty then. There are good tent sites and back-ins to 40 feet although there are no hookups here. There are also walk-in tent sites along the shoreline of the reservoir. If you follow the route below to reach the park you'll see two of the region's covered bridges. Travel east from Exit 188 of I-5 on SR-58, the Willamette Highway, for 12.7 miles (20.5 km). Turn left toward Lowell just past the Lowell covered bridge and pass through Lowell (the road make a two-block jog to the left in Lowell) and drive 2.8 miles (4.5 km) until you see the Unity covered bridge ahead. Don't cross it, instead turn right and follow Big Fall Creek Road 8 miles (13 km) to the park.

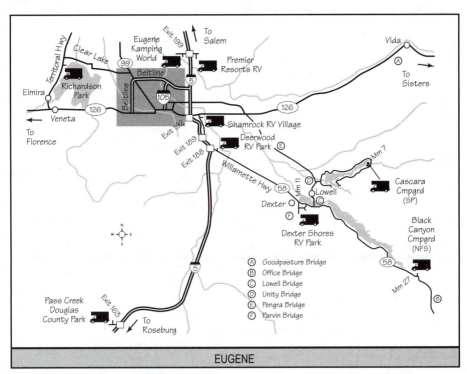

DEXTER SHORES RV PARK *(Open All Year)*

Reservations: (866) 558-9777
Information: (541) 937-3711, www.dextershoresrvpark.com
Location: 14 Miles (23 Km) E of Eugene, *N 43° 54' 48", W 122° 48' 35"*, 600 Ft

56 Sites – This is a popular local RV park with good access to a day-use park on nearby Dexter Reservoir. There are some resident units here, but also a separate large area for travelers. These traveler sites are back-ins and pull-thrus to 65 feet. There are also tent sites. Travel east from Exit 188 of I-5 on SR-58, the Willamette Highway, for 11.1 miles(17.9 km). The campground entrance is signed on the right.

BLACK CANYON CAMPGROUND *(Open April 22 to Sept 25 - Varies)*

Reservations: (877) 444-6777, www.reserveusa.com
Information: (541) 822-3799, http://www.hoodoo.com/blackcanyon.htm
Location: 28 Miles (45 Km) E of Eugene, *N 43° 48' 20", W 122° 33' 53"*, 1,000 Ft

74 Sites – This large Willamette National Forest campground is set in a dense forest of cedars and hemlocks. The access roads inside the park are paved but very narrow and winding making it suitable only for tent campers and coaches to about 30 feet. Black Canyon is located at the upper end of Lookout Point Reservoir. It's really on the Middle Fork of the Willamette River before it flows into the lake but at high water levels the lake does reach the campground. There is a boat ramp. Travel east from Exit 188 of I-5 on SR-58, the Willamette Highway, for 27 miles (44 km). The campground entrance is signed on the left.

DEERWOOD RV PARK *(Open All Year)*

Reservations: (877) 988-1139, info@deerwoodrvpark.com
Information: (541) 988-1139, www.deerwoodrvpark.com
Location: 3 Miles (5 Km) S of Eugene, *N 43° 59' 45", W 123° 00' 04"*, 400 Ft

75 Sites – This new big-rig park is certainly a convenient and popular stop in a town that has plenty of big-rig spaces. It's south of the town, however, while most of the other big-rig sites are north of town near the RV manufacturing plants there. Sites are back-ins and pull-thrus to 75 feet. Instant-on telephone hookups are available and so is Wi-Fi. To reach the park take Exit 188 from I-5 south of Eugene. Follow the access road north on the east side of the highway to the park entrance.

SHAMROCK RV VILLAGE *(Open All Year)*

Reservations: (877) 877-1004
Information: (541) 747-7473, shamrockrv@televar.com
Location: Eugene, *N 44° 02' 27", W 123° 01' 41"*, 400 Ft

38 Sites – This is the only RV park we list that is actually in town. It's a popular spot when the Ducks have an at-home game. This older campground has a lot of long-term resident RVs but there are traveler sites in two areas. One has full-hookup pull-thrus to 50 feet that require careful driving if you're RV is at all large. The others are partial hookup 30-amp parallel parking sites along the river. To most easily reach the campground from I-5 take Exit 189 at the southern edge of town. Then travel north on Franklin Blvd. on the east side of the freeway for 1.9 miles (3.1 km) to the campground entrance. It's on the right.

OREGON

RICHARDSON PARK *(Open April 15 to Oct 15)*

Reservations: (541) 935-2005
Information: (541) 682-2000, www.lanecounty.org/parks
Location: 13 Miles (21 Km) W of Eugene, *N 44° 07' 10", W 123° 19' 15"*, 300 Ft

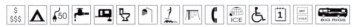

97 Sites – This large county park is on the shore of Fern Ridge Lake to the west of Eugene. The campground is a little out of the way but sites are large and surrounded by grassy lawns, it's a very pleasant campground. Sites here are back-ins and pull-thrus and reach 70 feet or more, good for big RVs. The park has many water-related amenities including docks, boat launch, and a swimming area. The lake is popular with sailboarders. To reach the campground follow SR-126 west from Eugene. You'll pass south of Fern Ridge Lake and after about 13 miles (21 km) near Veneta turn north on Territorial Highway. In another 4.6 miles (7.4 km) the road to the park goes east and the campground entrance is .2 mile (.3 km) from that turn.

PREMIER RESORTS RV *(Open All Year)*

Reservations: (888) 710-8451, www.premierrvresorts.com
Information: (541) 686-3152, terrypremiereugene@msn.com
Location: 4 Miles (6 Km) N of Eugene, *N 44° 08' 02", W 123° 02' 54"*, 400 Ft

150 Sites – This is the most upscale of the RV parks just north of Eugene. The same company also has nice resorts in Salem and Redding. Most of the sites are pull-thrus to 110 feet and there is free Wi-Fi (although there is an annual five dollar fee which covers use in all of the Premier parks). Amenities include a swimming pool. Take Exit 199 from I-5 and head east, the campground will be on your right next to the freeway.

EUGENE KAMPING WORLD *(Open All Year)*

Reservations: (800) 343-3008
Information: (541) 343-4832
Location: 4 Miles (6 Km) N of Eugene, *N 44° 08' 03", W 123° 03' 23"*, 400 Ft

132 Sites – Kamping World is the closest campground to the large RV manufacturing plants in Coburg. The campground offers tent camping sites as well as a variety of RV sites including many pull-thrus to 70 feet. Amenities include mini golf and a game room, there's a Country Pride Restaurant nearby. This campground is on the opposite side of the freeway from the Premier Resorts park. Take Exit 199 from I-5 and head west. Just past the big Travel America truck stop turn into the entrance road. Be careful here, it's easy to make a mistake and turn into the truck stop.

GOLD BEACH

Gold Beach is 27 miles (44 km) north of Brookings and 26 miles (42 km) south of Port Orford at the mouth of the Rogue River. A jet-boat trip up the river is one of the most popular day trips along the entire Oregon Coast, most people thoroughly enjoy it. Until a road was built to reach the small town of Agnes, some 32 miles (52 km) up the Rogue, mail was delivered by mail boat. Today you can drive to Agnes, but the boats are more fun! Two outfits in Gold Beach offer rides, they are Jerry's Rogue Jets and Mail Boat Hydro-Jets. A variety of trips are offered.

Fishing is also good in the area. The Rogue is a famous fishing river, and offshore fishing is also popular.

The campgrounds below are listed from north to south.

HONEY BEAR CAMPGROUND AND RV RESORT *(Open All Year)*

Reservations: (800) 822-4444
Information: (541) 247-2765, www.honeybearrv.com
Location: 17 Miles (27 Km) N of Gold Beach, *N 42° 32' 12", W 124° 23' 50"*, 100 Ft

85 Sites – This is an unusual campground, great for an overnight stop or an extended stay. The owners run a German restaurant and specialty food shop (Black Forest Sausage Kitchen) on the property. People stop here for the German food specialties like sausages, honey-cured hams, and rye breads that are sold out of the little store. The camping area is nicely landscaped and occupies a hillside away from the beach. There's easy walking access to the ocean and also stocked fish ponds on the property. Sites line several loops, many are pull-thrus to 60 feet. There is also excellent tent camping. The park is located just a short distance off US-101, the route is well signed. The turn off US-101 is at Mile 318.3. This is 17 miles (27 km) south of Port Orford and 9 miles (15 km) north of Gold Beach.

NESIKA BEACH RV PARK *(Open All Year)*

Res. and Info.: (541) 247-6077
Location: 6 Miles (10 Km) N of Gold Beach, *N 42° 30' 05", W 124° 24' 49"*, Near Sea Level

32 Sites – This small RV park along a quiet road back from the beach is popular with longer-term tenants but also has a few spaces for travelers including tent campers. Most sites are back-ins to 40 feet although there are just a couple of longer pull-thrus. Maneuvering space is

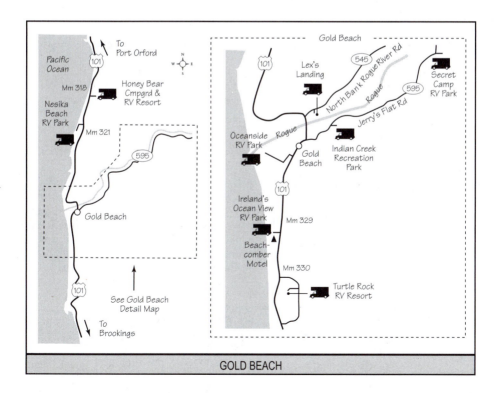

GOLD BEACH

tight for larger RVs. The campground is located on Nesika Beach Road which leaves US-101 near Mile 321. The campground is signed from the intersection.

▄ LEX'S LANDING *(Open All Year)*

Res. and Info.: (541) 247-0909, (800) 290-6208, Info@lexslanding.com, www.lexslanding.com
Location: 1 Mile (2 Km) NE of Gold Beach, *N 42° 25' 50", W 124° 24' 37"*, Near Sea Level

30 Sites – Lex's has just installed a long line of big-rig, back-in and pull-thru RV sites to 50 feet overlooking the river from the north bank. There's a new restroom and laundry building too, it overlooks the RV sites. Other amenities include a grocery store, boat ramp, and dock. This campground is on North Bank Rogue River Road which goes eastward on the north bank of the Rogue, it's about .2 mile (.3 km) from the intersection with US-101.

▄ INDIAN CREEK RECREATION PARK *(Open All Year)*

Reservations: (877) 537-7704
Information: (541) 247-7704, indiancreek@harborside.com, www.indiancreekrv.com
Location: 1 Mile (2 Km) E of Gold Beach, *N 42° 25' 39", W 124° 24' 13"*, 100 Ft

114 Sites – This campground is on the south side of the Rogue River east of Gold Beach. Sites are on the opposite side of the road from the river and behind a small store and restaurant. Most sites are back-ins to 45 feet, there are also some smaller pull-thrus. The campground also has nice tent-camping sites on grass. From Gold Beach follow Jerry's Flat Road east along the south shore of the Rogue for .7 mile (1.2 km) to the campground.

▄ SECRET CAMP RV PARK *(Open All Year)*

Reservations: (888) 308-8338
Information: (541) 247-2665, www.secretcamprvpark.com
Location: 3 Miles E of Gold Beach, *N 42° 26' 40", W 124° 22' 07"*, 100 Ft

16 Sites – This tiny campground is excellent for tent campers and smaller RVs. It has a couple of long pull-thrus but most sites are back-ins to about 35 feet. The campground is located off Jerry's Flat Road on the south side of the Rogue about 3 miles (5 km) from the intersection with US-101.

▄ OCEANSIDE RV PARK *(Open All Year)*

Information: (541) 247-2301
Location: Gold Beach, *N 42° 25' 13", W 124° 25' 35"*, Near Sea Level

80 Sites – If you like the ocean this will be your pick in Oceanside. It's located on the south bank of the mouth of the Rogue River. The campground has both back-in and pull-thru sites but they're not really large. Full-hookup sites will only allow one slide-out, the back-ins are wide enough for two slides. Management prefers RVs only to 35 feet. From US-101 in Gold Beach about .6 mile (1 km) south of the bridge over the Rogue follow signs west for the RV park.

▄ IRELAND'S OCEAN VIEW RV PARK *(Open All Year)*

Res. and Info.: (541) 247-0148, www.irelandsrvpark.com
Location: Gold Beach, *N 42° 24' 08", W 124° 25' 21"*, Near Sea Level

32 Sites – Ireland's is the most attractive of the Gold Beach RV parks. Sites are paved and

separated by lawn. The pull-thrus are 50 feet long, the back-ins about 35 feet. The campground isn't visible from the road, the entrance is just north of the Beachcomber Motel on the west side of US-101. That's toward the south end of Gold Beach, about 1.8 miles (2.9 km) south of the Rogue River bridge.

🚐 TURTLE ROCK RV RESORT *(Open All Year)*

Reservations:	(800) 353-9754, turtlereserverations@earthlink.net
Information:	(541) 247-9203, www.turtlerockresorts.com
Location:	2 Miles (3 Km) S of Gold Beach, *N 42° 23' 20", W 124° 25' 01"*, Near Sea Level

109 Sites – Turtle Rock is located along an unpopulated section of the coast just south of Gold Beach. The campground itself is located in a very large parcel of land on the east side of the highway, there is a trail that leads under the highway to the beach. Sites here are back-ins to about 40 feet and pull-thrus to 55+ feet. There are also luxury rental cottages. To reach the campground leave US-101 at Mile 330.2. Head east on County 637 for .4 mile (6 km) and you'll see the campground entrance on the right.

HELLS CANYON

Hells Canyon stretches along the Oregon-Idaho border for 110 miles (177 km) from Oxbow Dam to the Oregon-Washington border in the north. The canyon is sometimes called the deepest in the U.S. with a depth of about 8,900 feet. This is measured from the top of nearby He Devil Mountain so purists might be right is saying that the Grand Canyon is actually a deeper canyon. Irregardless, Hells Canyon is impressive, particularly from the bottom. The bordering ridges average 5,500 feet above the river.

The portion of the canyon that we are concerned with here is the top part, a 30-mile (48 km) stretch actually beginning above the canyon with road access along the entire length. There

MANY SITES AT THE WOODHEAD PARK CAMPGROUND HAVE GREAT VIEWS

are three dams in this area operated by the Idaho Power Company: Brownlee, Oxbow, and Hells Canyon. These dams are very controversial in ecological circles since they do not have fish ladders and act as a barrier to the migration of salmon up the Snake River. Some people would like to see the dams removed entirely.

As with most of this type of controversy there are arguments for keeping the dams. In addition to economic and flood control arguments there is the one about the recreational potential of the lakes behind the dams. In this case the recreational opportunities are outstanding. The three lakes offer flat-water water sports opportunities, vehicle-accessible camping along the shores, sightseeing, and excellent fishing.

State Route 86 reaches the river from the direction of Baker, OR at Copperfield, a few miles below Oxbow Dam. The river here is actually a narrow lake, Hells Canyon Reservoir. You can cross the lake into Idaho and follow an excellent paved road to the left or down river for 23 miles (37 km) to a point just beyond Hells Canyon Dam. The scenery along this section of road is spectacular with barren cliffs rising thousands of feet from the river. The drive has been designated a Scenic Drive by the state of Idaho. When you reach **Hells Canyon Dam** you can drive across it and then descend a steep road to a National Forest information center. This center is at a put-in point for popular float trips of the lower canyon which is designated as a wild river for 31.5 miles (50.8 km) and then as a scenic river for another 36 miles (58 km). Large RVs (over about 26 feet or towing a trailer) will not want to make this final crossing of the dam and descent to the information center because there is a sharp switchback and limited maneuvering room at the information center. Drivers of large RVs should watch carefully for the appearance of the dam ahead, about the time they see it they will reach a large flat turn-around area, the last place to do so before the dam. Unfortunately there are no warning signs so you are on your own.

From Copperfield the road also extends upriver on the Oregon side of the river. It soon passes **Oxbow Dam**, which is barely visible off to the left and not accessible by road, and runs along the shore of Oxbow Reservoir. This section of road is not as impressive as the section

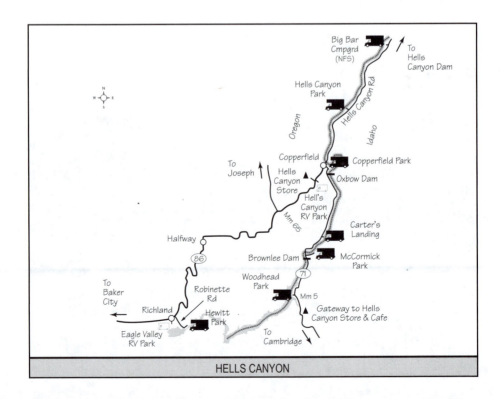

HELLS CANYON

downstream but it's still outstanding. After 11 miles (18 km) the road crosses the river just below hulking **Brownlee Dam** and then climbs the cliff face to reach huge Brownlee Reservoir. After following the shore of the reservoir for a few miles the road heads east into Idaho and away from the river toward Cambridge, ID.

COPPERFIELD PARK *(Open All Year)*

Information:	(800) 422-3143, (541) 785-3323,
	www.idahopower.com/riversrec/parksrec/copperfield.htm
Location:	Hells Canyon, *N 44° 58' 26", W 116° 51' 28"*, 1,700 Ft

72 Sites – This campground, run by Idaho Power, is extremely nice. Sites are separated and surrounded by clipped grass and shade trees. Facilities are excellent with paved sites and full hookups. Most sites are back-ins but there are also a few pull-thrus, some will take RVs to 45 feet. There are also dedicated tent sites. The park sits on the bank of Hells Canyon Reservoir. It's the first campground you'll see as you arrive on SR-86 from the west.

BIG BAR CAMPGROUND *(Open All Year)*

Location:	Hells Canyon, *N 45° 07' 44", W 116° 44' 18"*, 1,700 Ft

Approx. 50 Sites – Big Bar Payette National Forest Recreation Site is a former orchard site located on the east shore of Hells Canyon Reservoir. There is a boat ramp here and a large gravel parking lot. RVs of any size can camp in the lot. There are also some beautiful lakeside locations to the south but they can only be accessed on very uneven rough roads so access to them is limited to small RVs to about 25 feet. The only facilities here are a scattering of vault toilets. To reach the campground cross the bridge near Copperfield Park and follow the road north along the lakeshore for another 13 miles (21 km).

HELLS CANYON PARK *(Open All Year)*

Information:	(800) 422-3143, (541) 785-3323,
	www.idahopower.com/riversrec/parksrec/hellscanyon.htm
Location:	Hells Canyon, *N 45° 02' 47", W 116° 48' 51"*, 1,700 Ft

38 Sites – This is an Idaho Power campground located on the east shore of Hells Canyon Reservoir. There is a tent camping area where you pitch on grass away from your vehicle. There are also 22 power and water RV sites that are parallel parking along a wide driveway. Some of the sites are right next to the lake. There are also four back-in overflow sites with only power hookups in a gravel lot next to the boat ramp. RV sites will take RVs to 40 feet, some longer depending upon the other RVs parked on both sides. To reach the campground cross the bridge near Copperfield Park and follow the road north along the lakeshore for 6 miles (10 km).

CARTER'S LANDING *(Open All Year)*

Information:	(800) 422-3143, (541) 785-3323
Location:	Hells Canyon, *N 44° 52' 42", W 116° 51' 42"*, 1,800 Ft

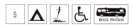

10 Sites – This is another Idaho Power camping area. Carter's Landing is a small basic camping area along the shore of Oxbow Reservoir with no hookups. There are some picnic tables and barbeques, there's also a compost toilet. RVs of any size can park here and there's lots of maneuvering room. From Copperfield Park go south. You'll see the campground on the left in 7 miles (11 km).

McCORMICK PARK *(Open All Year)*

Information: (800) 422-3143, (541) 785-3323,
www.idahopower.com/riversrec/parksrec/mccormick.htm
Location: Hells Canyon, *N 44° 51' 03", W 116° 53' 43"*, 1,800 Ft

37 Sites – McCormick Park is an Idaho Power campground. It is on the shore of Oxbow Reservoir with Brownlee Dam looming over it in the south. This campground isn't as polished as Copperfield, Hells Canyon or Woodland Park. There are 8 tent sites with nice sand tent pads and vehicle parking at each site. RV sites are back-ins around a very large open circle, they will take RVs of any size. These sites have power hookups but no water. There are, however, water faucets for filling with water and also a dump station. The park also has a large overflow area for RVs, the charge here is $4.00 per night. There is also a boat ramp. From Copperfield drive south along the shore of Oxbow Lake. In 11 miles (18 km) you'll cross the bridge below Brownlee Dam, the campground entrance is immediately beyond on the left.

WOODHEAD PARK *(Open All Year)*

Information: (800) 422-3143, (541) 785-3323,
www.idahopower.com/riversrec/parksrec/woodhead.htm
Location: Hells Canyon, *N 44° 48' 17", W 116° 55' 10"*, 2,100 Ft

139 Sites – This is the largest and the nicest of the Idaho Power campgrounds in the canyon. It sits on rocky outcrops above Brownlee Reservoir. Most sites have great views. The sites have water and electric hookup and are of various sizes with some to 55 feet. Most sites are back-ins but there are a few pull-thrus. There's a large boat ramp area dividing the campground into two sections but both are accessed from the same entry road. The campground is the farthest to the south in the Canyon. From the direction of Baker zero your odometer when you reach Copperfield. Turn right and follow Oxbow Reservoir and then Brownlee Reservoir for 15 miles (24 km) to the campground.

HEWITT PARK *(Open All Year)*

Res. and Info.: (541) 893-6147, hewittpark@pinetel.com, www.bakercounty.net/parks&recreation
Location: Near Richland, 28 Miles (45 Km) W of Hells Canyon,
N 44° 45' 29", W 117° 07' 27", 2,100 Ft

40 Sites – This campground is located on the far western arm of Oxbow Reservoir where it backs up into the Powder River Valley. This is much closer to Baker City than the rest of the Hells Canyon campgrounds listed above. It's not actually in the canyon at all, but if you have a boat it gives access to the same lake. This is a municipal park with a boat ramp. The spaces are back-ins around the edge of the asphalt parking lot. The spaces will take RVs to 40 feet without getting in the way of traffic circulation in the lot. There are also separate tent sites with camping on grass. The park is southeast of Richland. This town is 39 miles (63 km) east of Baker City on SR-86 and about 28 miles (45 km) west of Hells Canyon. To reach the campground travel east from town on SR-86. In .7 mile (1.1 km) turn south on Robinette Road, you'll reach the campground in 1.4 miles (2.3 km).

HELLS CANYON SCENIC BYWAY

The drive from Wallowa Lake to Hells Canyon runs through the Wallowa-Whitman National Forest. It is the most scenic section of the Hells Canyon Scenic Byway which actually runs from La Grande to Baker. This is an extremely pleasant drive on paved forest service roads. It has

OREGON

been designated an Oregon State Scenic Byway and an All American Road and a National Forest Byway by the federal government.

In spring and fall it is a good idea to contact the Forest Service at (541) 426-5546 for information about the condition of the road, it is not cleared in winter.

From near the center of Joseph follow Highway 350 east toward Imnaha and Furguson Ridge. After 8.1 miles (13.1 km) take the right turn marked Highway 39 and Wallowa Mountain Road. Signs will tell you it is now 64 miles (103 km) to Halfway and 37 Miles (60 km) to the Hells Canyon Scenic Overlook.

You soon enter the Wallowa-Whitman National Forest. The road climbs to Salt Creek Summit which is 8 miles (13 km) from the junction. Five miles (8 km) after the summit the road enters **Hells Canyon Recreation Area**.

Twenty-four miles (39 km) from the summit you'll see a sign directing you left to **Hells Canyon Overlook**. This three-mile (5 km) spur road is paved, follow it to a nice overlook area with great views of Hells Canyon. You can't actually see the river from here, but it will give you a much different view of the canyon that the one you see from the bottom.

Back at the main road continue south. The road descends in 19 miles (31 km) to meet US-86. Turn left and follow US-86 down to the river, a distance of 8 miles (13 km). Two miles (3 km) before reaching the river you'll pass through Pine Creek which has gasoline and a small grocery store.

LICK CREEK CAMPGROUND *(Open June 15 to Oct 15 - Varies)*

Information: (541) 426-5546
Location: 24 Miles (39 Km) SE of Joseph, *N 45° 09' 26", W 117° 02' 02"*, 5,400 Ft

9 Sites – This Wallowa-Whitman National Forest camping area next to Lick Creek has big

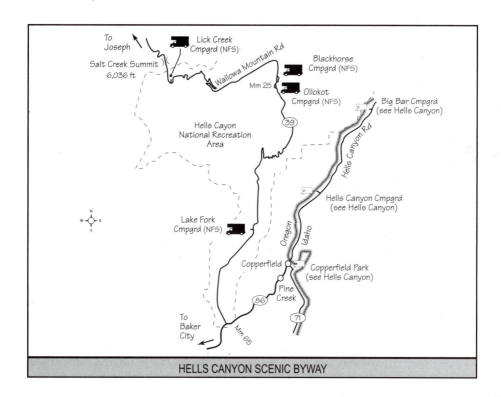

HELLS CANYON SCENIC BYWAY

sites to 60 feet, both back-in and pull-thru. There's lots of room to maneuver. The only water availability is from the creek. The campground is 24 miles (39 km) from Joseph and 36 miles (58 km) from the junction with SR-86.

BLACKHORSE CAMPGROUND *(Open June 15 to Oct 15 - Varies)*

Information:	(541) 426-5546
Location:	36 Miles (58 km) SE of Joseph, *N 45° 09' 23", W 116° 52' 30"*, 4,000 Ft

16 Sites – Sites in this Wallowa-Whitman National Forest campground are off a loop road that has two entrances on the highway. A few sites will take RVs to 35 feet, most sites are smaller. The access road is narrow and makes entering the sites difficult for larger RVs so this campground is best for RVs to 30 feet. The campground is 36 miles (58 km) from Joseph and 24 miles (39 km) from the junction with SR-86.

OLLOKOT CAMPGROUND *(Open April 15 to Oct 15 - Varies)*

Information:	(541) 426-5546
Location:	37 Miles (60 Km) SE of Joseph, *N 45° 09' 06", W 116° 52' 37"*, 4,000 Ft

12 Sites – This Wallowa-Whitman National Forest campground is located in a light, open forest and is near the highway with a good paved access road. It's on the Imnaha River. There's a turn-around circle at the end of the access road but it's small and doesn't allow enough room for turning if you're towing. There are sites to 50 feet here but due to access difficulties the campground is best for RVs to 40 feet. The campground is 37 miles (60 km) from Joseph and 23 miles (37 km) from the junction with SR-86.

LAKE FORK CAMPGROUND *(Open April 15 to Oct 15 - Varies)*

Information:	(541) 426-5546
Location:	51 Miles (82 Km) SE of Joseph, *N 45° 00' 34", W 116° 54' 45"*, 3,300 Ft

10 Sites – Sites in this Wallowa-Whitman National Forest campground are off two narrow loop roads, sites will take RVs to about 30 feet. The only water in the campground is from the Lake Fork Creek. The campground is 51 miles (82 km) from Joseph and 9 miles (15 km) from the junction with SR-86.

JOHN DAY COUNTRY

John Day is a town of 2,075 souls. Today it is the largest town in Grant County, although Canyon City (population 725), two miles (3 km) south, is the county seat. In the 1860s these towns served the nearby **Strawberry Mountain gold fields**. You can visit the fields near Canyon City, the **Grant County Historical Museum** has exhibits describing this period.

During the 1800s large numbers of Chinese came to the west from southern China. They worked the railroads and fish canneries, and they also worked the mines. John Day had one of the largest Chinese populations in the western mining areas, and the tiny **Kim Wah Chung and Co. Museum** in John Day offers a fascinating look back at this period. It occupies the rickety building that served as home, store, opium den, card room, and Chinese herbal pharmacy for a pair of Chinese entrepreneurs. The building was locked up and remained undisturbed for years following the owner's deaths. When reopened it was a treasure house of interesting things including Chinese herbs and groceries from the early part of the century.

The **Grant County Fair** is held in John Day during the second week of August.

To the west of John Day are the three units of the **John Day Fossil Beds National Monu-**

ment. There is a brand-new visitor center located on SR-19 some 2 miles (3 km) north of its intersection with US-26 and 40 miles (65 km) from John Day.

The visitor center is located in the **Sheep Rock section** of the monument. Other interesting attractions in this section are **Picture Gorge** (which you pass through just before reaching the visitor center), **Sheep Rock** to the east of the visitor center, **Blue Basin** with hiking trails 3 miles (5 km) north of the visitor center, and the **Forsee Area**, also with hiking trails, about 7 miles (11 km) north of the visitor center.

There are two other sections of this monument. Far to the north, off SR-218 near the town of Fossil, is the **Clarno Unit**. The prime attraction here is the **Palisades**, a rugged cliff rising from the flatlands. There are several trails here offering you a look at plant fossils.

The other section of the monument is known as the **Painted Hills**. Just west of Mitchell, 66 miles (106 km) west of John Day along US-26, a small paved road leads north into the section. You'll find an overlook offering you the opportunity to take photos of smoothly rounded hills with bands of colored minerals. The area also offers hiking trails and a small rest area with picnic tables and restrooms.

OREGON CAMPGROUND *(Open May 15 to Sept 15 - Varies)*

Information: (541) 446-3351
Location: 37 Miles (60 Km) E of John Day, *N 44° 32' 47", W 118° 20' 33"*, 4,900 Ft

6 Sites – This tiny Wallowa-Whitman National Forest campground is right off US-26 in the Blue Mountains. It's just east of 5,109 ft. Blue Mountain Pass and serves as the entrance to an Oregon Off Highway Vehicle Area. There's parking for the off-highway area in the campground. Although one site is over 60 feet long maneuvering room is limited and the campground is best

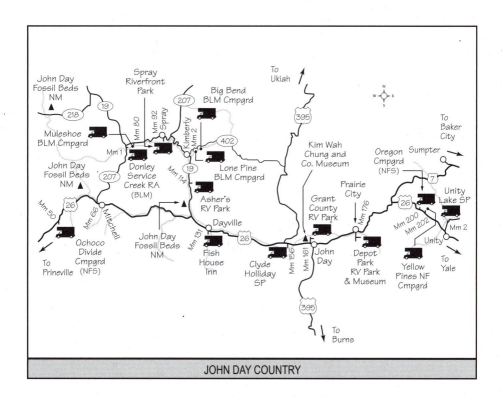

JOHN DAY COUNTRY

for RVs to 30 feet. The campground is located 9 miles (15 km) southeast of Austin Junction and 12 miles (19 km) northwest of Unity.

YELLOW PINE CAMPGROUND *(Open May 15 to Sept 15 - Varies)*

Information: (541) 446-3351
Location: 40 Miles E of John Day, *N 44° 31' 45", W 118° 18' 45"*, 4,500 Ft

21 Sites – This is a larger Wallowa-Whitman National Forest campground. It's a very pretty place set in an open grove of towering pines. There are sites here to 40 feet but limited maneuvering room means that 35 foot RVs are the practical maximum. The campground is located 11 miles (18 km) southeast of Austin Junction and 10 miles (16 km) northwest of Unity.

UNITY LAKE STATE PARK *(Open April 1 to Oct 31)*

Information: (541) 932-4453, (800) 551-6949, www.oregonstateparks.org,
Location: 48 Miles (77 Km) E of John Day, *N 44° 30' 06", W 118° 11' 04"*, 4,100 Ft

35 Sites – Unity Lake State Campground is located on the shore of Unity Lake, a reservoir, in open grasslands east of the Blue Mountains along US-26. There is a hiker-biker tent camping area in this park as well as very large RV sites including some pull-thrus to 100 feet long. There are also rental teepees and a boat ramp. The showers here are solar-heated, but that works pretty well in this sunny location. There is a swimming area and a boat dock, a well as a launching area. To reach the campground follow US-26 19 miles (31 km) southeast from Austin Junction or 2 miles (3 km) northwest from Unity. Turn north on Dooley Mountain Highway, the campground entrance is on the left in 2.4 miles (3.9 km).

DEPOT PARK RV PARK AND MUSEUM *(Open May 1 to Oct 31 - Varies)*

Information: (541) 820-3605
Location: 13 Miles (21 Km) E of John Day, *N 44° 27' 28", W 118° 42' 25"*, 3,500 Ft

20 Sites – Depot Park is a Prairie City municipal campground located on the grounds of the city museum. There are tent camping sites on grass as well as 20 RV sites including several pull-thrus to 60 feet long. The campground is just a few blocks from the center of this little town. To find the campground turn south on Main Street from Front Street (SR-26) in the center of town. The campground will be on your left in about 3 blocks, a distance of .3 miles (.5 km).

GRANT COUNTY RV PARK *(Open All Year)*

Information: (541) 575-0110, (541) 575-0946 after hours
Location: John Day, *N 44° 25' 16", W 118° 57' 14"*, 3,000 Ft

25 Sites – The Grant County RV Park is located on the Grant County Fairgrounds in John Day. The famous Kim Wah Chung Museum is nearby. This campground has long pull-thru sites to 70 feet with full hookups as well as back-in sites and a grassy area for tents. Swimming for park residents is possible at the city pool. To reach the campground drive north on NW Bridge Street from an intersection in the middle of town a block west of the intersection of US-26 and US-395. In four blocks you'll see the fairground entrance used by campers signed on the right. There is a self-registration sign and lockbox near the entrance gate.

CLYDE HOLLIDAY STATE PARK *(Open March 1 to Nov 31)*

Information: (541) 932-4453, (800) 551-6949, www.oregonstateparks.org
Location: 7 Miles (11 Km) W of John Day, *N 44° 24' 58", W 119° 05' 22"*, 3,200 Ft

31 Sites – State parks are scarce in this part of the state. This is one of the nicest. It's a small shady oasis in a fairly parched area. The park borders the John Day River which is pretty small at this point. Sites are back-ins with electricity and water, most longer than 50 feet. There is also a separate hiker-biker tent-camping area tucked away in a corner of the park and also some teepees for rent. The campground is on the south side of US-26 some 7 miles (11 km) west of John Day.

FISH HOUSE INN *(Open All Year)*

Information: fishinn@highdesertnet.com, www.fishhouseinn.com,
Location: In Dayville, 31 Miles (50 Km) W of John Day, *N 44° 28' 02", W 119° 32' 06"*, 2,400 Ft

7 Sites – This is a great little commercial campground in a small town. It's brand new and exceptionally neat and tidy. The seven sites are all back-ins with full hookup and are about 70 feet long. Watch for the Fish House Inn sign on the south side of US-26 as it passes through Dayville. This is about 31 miles (50 km) west of John Day and about 8 miles (13 km) east of the new John Day Fossil Beds National Monument visitor center at Sheep Rock.

ASHER'S RV PARK *(Open All Year)*

Location: 47 Miles (76 Km) W of John Day, *N 44° 38' 44", W 119° 38' 50"*, 2,000 Ft

20 Sites – This is a large open piece of ground next to the highway. There's no shade but there are 20 RV sites. These are back-in sites about 60 feet long. There is no water or dump facility, there are vault toilets. The campground is 7 miles (11 km) north of the new visitor center at the Sheep Rock Unit of John Day Fossil Beds National Monument.

LONE PINE CAMPGROUND *(Open As Weather Allows)*

Information: (541) 416-6700
Location: 58 Miles (94 Km) NW of John Day, *N 44° 46' 40", W 119° 37' 29"*, 1,800 Ft

8 Sites – This small BLM campground is just a small cleared lot next to the north fork of the John Day River. There are picnic tables and fire pits next to the river as well as a vault toilet. Some sites will take any size RV although you'll have to exercise care entering and leaving. The river provides the only water. The campground is located 2.8 miles (4.5 km) east of Kimberly on the Kimberly – Long Creek Highway. This is 19 miles (31 km) north of the Sheep Rock Visitor Center of John Day Fossil Beds National Monument.

BIG BEND CAMPGROUND *(Open As Weather Allows)*

Information: (541) 416-6700
Location: 59 Miles (95 Km) NW of John Day, *N 44° 46' 51", W 119° 36' 37"*, 1,900 Ft

4 Sites – Another small BLM campground set along the north fork of the John Day River. Sites here are down a short grade and next to the river. It's good for tents or RVs. Big RVs can get in here but will have to drop their tows in order to maneuver. The only water is in the river. The campground is located 1.9 miles (3.1 km) east of Kimberly on the Kimberly – Long Creek

OREGON

Highway. This is 20 miles (32 km) north of the Sheep Rock Visitor Center of John Day Fossil Beds National Monument.

SPRAY RIVERFRONT PARK *(Open As Weather Allows)*

Information:	(541) 468-2069
Location:	In Spray, 69 Miles (111 Km) NW of John Day, *N 44° 49' 37", W 119° 47' 38"*, 1,700 Ft

6 Sites – The town of Spray has a riverfront park campground located just south of the village. The park has five long pull-thru parking sites with no hookups. The river runs next to the park, there are some shade trees, and vault toilets are provided. This campground has water. To reach the campground turn south on Parish Creek Road (1st Ave.) in the town of Spray. Spray is on SR-19 some 21 miles (34 km) north and west of the Sheep Rock Visitor Center of John Day Fossil Beds National Monument and 32 miles (52 km) south and east of the town of Fossil.

MULESHOE RECREATION SITE *(Open All Year)*

Information:	(541) 468-2069
Location:	80 Miles (129 Km) NW of John Day, *N 44° 48' 27", W 119° 57' 59"*, 1,600 Ft

10 Sites – This is a good BLM campground for both tents and big RVs. There are five 70-foot back-in sites overlooking the river as well as smaller vehicle accessible tent or small RV sites. This campground also has a boat launch, but no water other than the river. The campground is located 11 miles (18 km) west of Spray on the south side of SR-19.

DONLEY SERVICE CREEK RECREATION AREA *(Open All Year)*

Information:	(541) 468-2069
Location:	82 Miles (132 Km) NW of John Day, *N 44° 47' 35", W 120° 00' 03"*, 1,600 Ft

10 Sites – This BLM recreation area has 4 walk-in campsites for tent campers. There is also a large gravel lot suitable for any size RV but this RV area has no fire pits or picnic tables. This campground has no water except from the river, there is a boat launch. The recreation area is on the east side of SR-207 some .3 miles (.5 km) south of the intersection with SR-19 which is 13 miles (21 km) west of Spray.

OCHOCO DIVIDE CAMPGROUND

Information:	(541) 416-6500
Location:	85 Miles (137 Km) W of John Day, *N 44° 30' 00", W 120° 23' 12"*, 4,600 Ft

30 Sites – Ochoco Divide is a large Ochoco National Forest campground located in ponderosa pines high in the mountains at the top of Ochoco Pass. The campground has walk-in tent sites as well as vehicle accessible tent and RV sites to 60 feet, some are pull-thrus. This campground is a popular overnight stop with many one-nighters but there is also a good hiking trail system with trailheads just west of the campground. This easily accessible campground is just off US-26 some 31 miles (50 km) east of Prineville.

KLAMATH FALLS

Founded in 1876 and originally called Linkville, the town of Klamath Falls (population 19,000) occupies the Klamath Basin. It is surrounded by national wildlife refuges set aside for migrating birds. The refuges extend south across the California border. At one time there were even more wetlands in the area, many were drained to create farmland early in the century.

Many visitors to the town come for the bird-watching. There's something to see all year long. A good place to start is with a visit to the **Refuge Headquarters and Visitors Center** about 5 miles (8 km) west of Tulelake which is across the border in California, about 14 miles (23 km) south of Klamath Falls. There are actually six different refuges in the area. They offer auto tour routes, canoe trails, walking trails, and photography blinds.

In Klamath Falls you will probably enjoy a visit to the **Favell Museum of Western Art and Indian Artifacts**. This is an outstanding museum with exhibits including a huge arrowhead collection, Indian artifacts from all the western states, a miniature firearm collection, and western art created by over 300 artists including Charles Russell.

The **Kla-Mo-Ya Casino** is located in the small town of Chiloquin about 22 miles (35 km) north of Klamath Falls on US-97.

Lava Beds National Monument is in California, but not far from Klamath Falls. The monument actually adjoins the wildlife refuges to the south. The monument is a large area covered by shield volcano lava beds. Hundreds of lava tube caves make this a popular and easy place to explore underground. It's as dry as the wildlife refuges are wet. There is a visitors center and also a campground in the monument. The visitor center sells inexpensive protective helmets, highly recommended if you plan to do any spelunking. The area was the scene of the Modoc Indian War, several sites in the monument are related to that 1872 conflict. To get there drive south on SR-39 (which becomes SR-139 in California) to Tulelake, about 4 miles (6 km) beyond Tulelake you'll see the entrance to the monument. From there a paved road circles around the south end of Tule Lake Wildlife Refuge and then south through the monument to the visitor center and campground.

KLAMATH FALLS KOA *(Open All Year)*

Reservations:	(800) 562-9036, www.koa.com
Information:	(541) 884-4644, kfallskoa@charterinternet.com
Location:	Klamath Falls, *N 42° 12' 50", W 121° 44' 47"*, 4,100 Ft

78 Sites – This KOA is the only campground listed in this guide that is actually inside the city of Klamath Falls. It is a full-service KOA with all that that means. There are a variety of sites including a grassy tent camping area and pull-thrus to 90 feet. Amenities include a swimming pool and also gasoline sales out front. The campground is located on the east side of Klamath Falls about 2 miles (3 km) from the central area. Easiest access is from the East Side Bypass (SR-39) which becomes SR-140 to Lakeview. Turn west on Shasta and the campground is on the right just .1 mile (.2 km) from the corner.

OREGON 8 MOTEL AND RV PARK *(Open All Year)*

Res. and Info.:	(541) 883-3431
Location:	2 Miles (3 Km) N of Klamath Falls, *N 42° 16' 30", W 121° 48' 40"*, 4,100 Ft

31 Sites – The RV park here is a large gravel lot behind an older hotel. The RV park is neat and clean and has large pull-thrus to 60 feet with parking on gravel. Some sites have grass separating them. The campground has a seasonal pool and a lounge area with TV. The Oregon 8 is located 2 miles (3 km) north of Klamath Falls on the east side of US-97.

WATERWHEEL CAMPGROUND *(Open All Year)*

Res. and Info.:	(541) 783-2738
Location:	21 Miles (34 Km) N of Klamath Falls, *N 42° 31' 29", W 121° 53' 13"*, 4,100 Ft

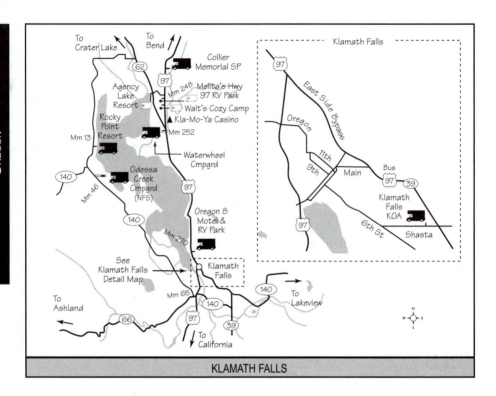

KLAMATH FALLS

34 Sites – The Waterwheel has a pleasant streamside location along the Williamson River north of Klamath Falls near the Kla-Mo-Ya Casino. Tent camping is possible on a small island in the river reached by a footbridge. Some of the RV parking is on grass next to the river and there are also pull-thrus to 70 feet just back from the river. This is a popular fishing location and the campground has a small boat launch area and also a dock. The campground is located about 21 miles (34 km) north of Klamath Falls on the west side of US-97.

COLLIER MEMORIAL STATE PARK *(Open April 15 to Oct 31 - Varies)*

Information: (541) 783-2471, (800) 551-6949, www.oregonstateparks.org
Location: 30 Miles (48 Km) N of Klamath Falls, N *42° 38' 35", W 121° 52' 30"*, 4,200 Ft

68 Sites – A large campground with full hookups and big sites (both back-ins and pull-thrus over 45 feet long) along the Williamson River. This river is a well-known trout fishery. Nearby is a state-run outdoor logging museum and pioneer village. The campground is located about 30 miles (48 km) north of Klamath Falls on the east side of US-97.

ROCKY POINT RESORT *(Open April 1 to Nov 1)*

Res. and Info.: (541) 356-2287, rvoregon@aol.com, www.rockypointoregon.com
Location: 32 Miles (52 Km) NW of Klamath Falls, *N 42° 28' 46", W 122° 05' 12"*, 4,300 Ft

34 Sites – The resort sits along the shore of Upper Klamath Lake on the Upper Klamath Wildlife Refuge & Canoe Trail. This is on the opposite side of the lake from Klamath Falls, a distance of about 32 miles (51 km) by road. The resort has 18 full-hookup sites with some pull-thrus to 50 feet. The resort rents canoes, kayaks, pedal boats, and motorboats and sells fishing supplies. From SR-140 25 miles (40 km) north of its intersection with SR-66 near Klamath Falls

drive north on West Side Road for 3 miles (5 km). You'll see signs leading you to the lakeshore and resort.

🚐 ODESSA CREEK CAMPGROUND *(Open All Year)*

Information: (541) 885-3400
Location: 25 Miles NW of Klamath Falls, *N 42° 25' 48", W 122° 03' 40"*, 4,200 Ft

5 Sites – This is a very small Freemont-Winema National Forest campground that is best for very small RVs and tent campers. It is located at the point where Odess Creek enters Upper Klamath Lake and is considered something of a birding hotspot, particularly for woodpeckers. A canoe is useful for accessing the nearby marsh. One site near the entrance will take RVs to 30 feet, the rest are very small sites. There is no potable water at the campground. Follow SR-140 north along the west side of Klamath Lake for 23 miles (37 km) from the intersection of SR-140 and SR-66 near Klamath Falls. Near Mile 46 turn on the marked gravel road and drive .9 miles (1.5 km) east to the campground.

LAKEVIEW AND THE OUTBACK SCENIC BYWAY

There is another highway route from Bend to Klamath Falls. This is **The Outback Scenic Byway** which follows SR-31 south from La Pine (29 miles (47 km) south of Bend on US-97) to Valley Falls, then US-395 south to Lakeview, and then SR-140 west to Klamath Falls. The drive is probably named as it is because the country it traverses resembles the remote Australian outback. Along the way you can visit **Fort Rock**, a formation that stands in for Australia's Ayers rock to make the comparison even more realistic. If you take this route plan on a long day, the distance from Bend to Klamath Falls is 270 miles (435 km). You could make it a two-day trip by

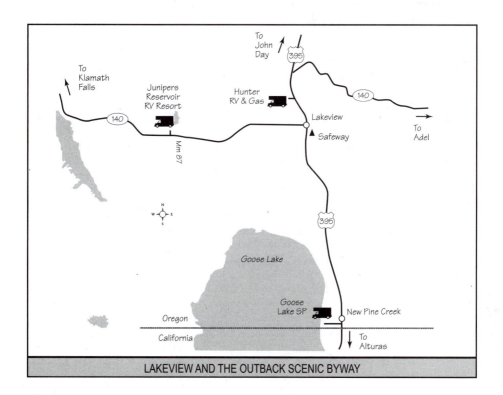

LAKEVIEW AND THE OUTBACK SCENIC BYWAY

spending the night at the **Goose Lake State Recreation Area** campground south of Lakeview and right on the California border.

The following campgrounds are all near Lakeview.

Goose Lake State Park *(Open April 15 to Oct 22 - Varies)*

Information: (541) 947-3111, (800) 551-6949, www.oregonstateparks.org
Location: 13 Miles (21 Km) S of Lakeview, *N 41° 59' 36", W 120° 19' 06"*, 4,700 Ft

48 Sites – Goose Lake State Park is right on the border between California and Oregon. The park offers lake swimming, boating, and fishing – it's also a great place for waterfowl viewing. Sites are back-ins to 45 feet with electric and water hookups. There's also a dump station. From Lakeview drive 12 miles (19 km) south on US-395. Then, at the state line, drive 1 mile (2 km) west on State Line Road to the campground.

Hunter's RV and Gas *(Open All Year)*

Res. and Info.:   (541) 947-4968, huntersrvpark@gooselake.com
Location: 1 Mile (2 Km) N of Lakeview, *N 42° 13' 02", W 120° 21' 53"*, 4,800 Ft

33 Sites – Hunter's RV is the only choice here for year-round campsites. It's nothing fancy, just RV sites behind a gas station, small convenience store, and café. Parking is on gravel with sites to at least 55 feet. There are quite a few long-term residents here but also space for travelers. The campground is on the west side of US-395 about a mile (.2 km) north of Lakeview.

Junipers Reservoir RV Resort *(Open May 1 to Oct 15)*

Res. and Info.:   (541) 947-2050, junipers@junipersrv.com, www.junipersrv.com
Location: 9 Miles W of Lakeview, *N 42° 10' 59", W 120° 31' 58"*, 4,900 Ft

45 Sites – This campground is located near Junipers Reservoir to the west of Lakeview. There are grassy tent sites and RV sites including full-hookup pull-thrus to 80 feet. The reservoir has good fishing and birding. The resort is located north of SR-140 some 9 miles (15 km) west of Lakeview.

LINCOLN CITY TO NEWPORT

As you drive down the Oregon coast **Lincoln City** appears at about Mile 113. It continues for about 7 miles (11 km). With a population of over 7,000 people this is one of the largest cities on the coast and it draws many tourists. The attraction is the beach. You will find access at **Roads End State Recreation Site** at Mile 112.8, the **D River Wayside** at Mile 115, and at **Siletz Bay** at Mile 118. Inland at Lincoln City is **Devil's Lake**, several of the campgrounds listed below are near the lake. It's a shallow lake with a large winter population of ducks. Fishing for rainbow trout, perch, and bass is possible in the lake too. Finally, the **Chinook Winds Casino** is located in Lincoln City, and so is **the Tanger Outlet Centers** shopping mall.

At Mile 128.0 you'll find yourself in tiny **Depoe Bay**. As you cross the bridge look inland to see one of the smallest and snuggest harbors along the entire coast. Then stop and take a look at the very narrow entrance to the harbor. Depoe Bay was the site of the charter-fishing sequence in the movie *One Flew Over the Cuckoo's Nest*. You can catch a whale-watching cruise from the harbor or check out the many shops and restaurants.

When Captain Cook arrived in 1778 he must not have been enjoying the weather when he first spotted the continent at the cape he named **Cape Foulweather**. There is an excellent viewpoint and a small shop just down from the highway on a short access road from Mile 131.2.

A little over a mile south a road leads west to the small town of Otter Crest and a parking area and viewpoint for the **Devil's Punchbowl**. The Punchbowl is a bowl that has been worn in the rocks by the wave action. If waves and tide are right the vertical spray can be impressive. Watch for the turn at Mile 132.5. Turn-around room for big RVs is limited. It's also a good place for an impressive coastal picture to the south.

Just north of Newport, at Mile 137.6, a road leads to **Yaquina Head**. Formally designated the Yaquina Head Outstanding Natural Area it is run by the Bureau of Land Management and has seen improvements over the last few years that now make it one of the most interesting stops along the coast. The head is occupied by Yaquina Head lighthouse, tallest along the Oregon coast. Below the cliffs and easily accessible is an excellent area of tide pools. New is another tide pool area called Quarry Cove, created out of an old rock quarry and fully wheelchair accessible. Offshore is Colony Rock, a sea-bird rookery where you can sometimes see puffins. Yaquina Head has a new and very nice visitors center with excellent exhibits about the tide pools and nearby lighthouse.

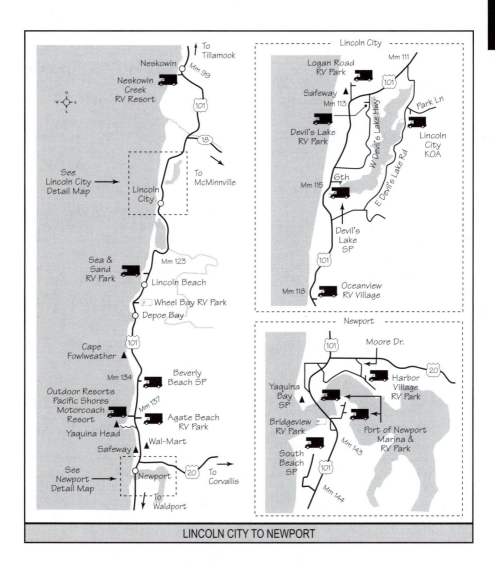

LINCOLN CITY TO NEWPORT

OREGON

Newport (population 8,800) is one of the two most popular tourist destination towns along the coast, the other is Seaside to the north. One reason is that Newport is only two highway hours from Portland.

In town the main attraction is probably the **Old Town** situated along the north shore of Yaquina Bay. Here you'll find a variety of tourist-trap-type attractions including restaurants, shops, Oregon Undersea Gardens and, believe it or not, a Ripley's Believe It or Not! The Old Town can be a lot of fun, and the presence of an actual working fish-processing plant or two is a nice touch. Large murals grace the walls of some buildings.

Seaward from the Old Town, west of the bridge, is **Yaquina Bay State Park**. There you'll find **Yaquina Bay Lighthouse**, views of the harbor entrance, and trails to the beach. A little farther north is **Nye Beach**, an old and established beachside neighborhood where most resort hotels are located.

South of the big bridge over the outlet of Yaquina Bay are two ocean-oriented attractions. These are the **Oregon Coast Aquarium** and the **Hatfield Marine Science Center**. The very impressive aquarium is probably best known as the former home of Keiko the killer whale, but don't let Keiko's absence stop you from visiting. The aquarium is modern and well thought out with great displays of the region's marine life including tide pools, a seabird aviary, jellyfish, seals, sea lions, and sea otters. The science center next door is a branch of Oregon State University and has a public wing with marine displays.

Newport has a big charter fishing fleet. Also offered are whale-watching tours and boat tours of local oyster beds and the harbor.

Newport's big event is in February, the **Newport Seafood and Wine Festival**, there's also **Loyalty Days and Sea Faire** in May.

⛺ NESKOWIN CREEK RV RESORT *(Open All Year)*

Information: (503) 392-3355, (888) 275-1491, www.neskowincreekrv.com
Location: 8 Miles (13 Km) N of Lincoln City, *N 45° 05' 35", W 123° 58' 31"*, Near Sea Level

300 Sites – This is a membership campground, it will accept non-members when space is available. There are a very large number of sites in a large open field with no trees. Sites are easy to access and are mostly pull-thrus of about 65 feet with parking on gravel and grass. Amenities include a large clubhouse and an indoor swimming pool. This RV park is not on the beach but it is near both the Neskowin Beach State Rec. Site for beach access and the Cascade Head trail and bike trails. It is on the west side of US-101 about 32 miles (52 km) south of Tillamook and 8 miles (13 km) north of Lincoln City.

⛺ LINCOLN CITY KOA *(Open All Year)*

Reservations: (800) 562-2791, www.koa.com
Information: (541) 994-2961, lincolnkoa@harborside.com
Location: 2.5 Miles (4 Km) E of Lincoln City, *N 44° 59' 31", W 123° 58' 42"*, Near Sea Level

67 Sites – This small KOA has a pleasant location in a country setting to the east of Devil's Lake. It's not on the water, you must walk about a quarter-mile to the community park if you want to enjoy the lake. There are sites here of all types including some for tents as well as full-hookup pull-thrus to 50 feet. To reach the campground follow East Devil's Lake Road southward from US-101 about .5 mile (.8 km) north of Lincoln City. In 1 mile (1.6 km) turn left into NE Park Lane and almost immediately you'll see the campground entrance on your right.

OREGON

DEVIL'S LAKE RV PARK *(Open All Year)*

Res. and Info.:   (541) 994-3400
Location: Lincoln City, *N 44° 59' 45", W 123° 59' 53"*, 100 Ft

80 Sites – This is a big-rig park occupying a sloping site that overlooks the north end of Devil's Lake. It's not on the lake, however. Sites are mostly pull-thrus on terraced sites to 80 feet long. It is located just southeast of US-101 at the north entrance to Lincoln City.

LOGAN ROAD RV PARK *(Open All Year)*

Res. and Info.:   (877) 564-2678, (541) 994-4261, www.loganroadrvpark.com
Location: Lincoln City, *N 44° 59' 58", W 124° 00' 14"*, 100 Ft

51 Sites – This RV park is an almost-new big-rig park. It occupies the upper end of a large parking lot near the Chinook Winds Casino, the main reason many people stay here. Sites and driveways are paved and separated by small grassy plots, there are back-in sites and also pull-thrus to 50 feet with plenty of room for slide-outs. There is a shuttle to the casino but it's really not much of a walk, only about 300 yards. In Lincoln City turn northwest on Logan Road which is .2 miles (.3 km) north of the Mile 113 marker. You'll pass a Safeway store (on your right) and come to the campground entrance in .2 miles (.3 km).

DEVIL'S LAKE STATE PARK *(Open All Year)*

Reservations: (800) 452-5687, www.reserveamerica.com
Information: (541) 947-3111, (800) 551-6949, www.oregonstateparks.org
Location: Lincoln City, *N 44° 58' 13", W 124° 00' 46"*, Near Sea Level

87 Sites – This state park campground is located away from the ocean near Devil's Lake. All sites here are back-ins but some reach 55 feet in length. The campground is one of the few state park campgrounds in Oregon that offer cable TV hookups. To enter the park turn east on NE 6th Dr from US-101, that's between Mile 115 and 116. The entrance is just a short distance down this road on the right. A day use area has a separate entrance off US-101 about a half-mile (1 km) south. The day use area has a boat ramp and connects with the campground via a nature trail.

OCEANVIEW RV VILLAGE *(Open All Year)*

Reservations: (877) 871-0663
Information: (541) 996-2778, village@harborside.com, www.oceanviewrvvillage.com
Location: Lincoln City, *N 44° 56' 05", W 124° 01' 17"*, Near Sea Level

92 Sites – This modern big-rig campground is located on the east side of US-101, some sites have views of the ocean. Sites are mostly back-ins although there are a few pull-thrus too. Most sites are between 40 and 50 feet although a few are longer. A nice amenity here is the instant-on telephone connections at the sites. Watch for the RV park on the east side of US-101 near Mile 118.3.

SEA AND SAND RV PARK *(Open All Year)*

Res. and Info.:   (541) 764-2313
Location: 5 Miles S of Lincoln City, *N 44° 51' 38", W 124° 02' 21"*, Near Sea Level

WALKING ON BEVERLY BEACH ON A FOGGY DAY

46 Sites – The Sea and Sand is an older park with two sections. Permanently located RVs are near the highway and a traveler section is near the ocean. The best sites are back-ins that overlook the ocean just below. Rules here limit RV size to 35 feet and two slides because site size and maneuvering room are limited. The campground is located near Mile 123.4 in Lincoln Beach, 4.5 miles (7.3 km) north of the Depoe Bay bridge.

BEVERLY BEACH STATE PARK *(Open All Year)*

Reservations:	(800) 452-5687, www.reserveamerica.com
Information:	(541) 265-9278, (800) 551-6949, www.oregonstateparks.org
Location:	6 Miles (10 Km) N of Newport, *N 44° 43' 44", W 124° 03' 18"*, Near Sea Level

255 Sites – Beverly Beach is a large state park occupying a wide ravine that opens out onto a beautiful beach. Access to the beach is under US-101 but the bridges are high above. The sites here are both back-ins and pull-thrus, many will take RVs over 45 feet. The campground is located at Mile 134 on the east side of US-101 about 6 miles (10 km) north of Newport and 5.9 miles (9.5 km) south of the Depoe Bay bridge.

AGATE BEACH RV PARK *(Open All Year)*

Res. and Info.:	(541) 265-7670
Location:	2 Miles (3 Km) N of Newport, *N 44° 40' 54", W 124° 03' 44"*, 100 Ft;

33 Sites – This is a small older RV park located on the east side of US-101 in the community of Agate Beach. It's a comfortable park in a convenient location, and reasonably priced. Sites are back-ins, many of the full-hookup sites will take RVs to 40 feet. Sites with just electricity and water hookups are better for shorter RVs. The campground is located near Mile 137.3 on the east side of US-101. It's 2 miles (3 km) north of Newport and 9.1 miles (14.7 km) south of the Depoe Bay bridge.

OUTDOOR RESORTS PACIFIC SHORES MOTORCOACH RESORT *(Open All Year)*

Res. and Info.: (541) 265-3750 , (800) 333-1583, stay@pacificshores.com, wwwpacificshoresrv.com
Location: 2 Miles (3 Km) N of Newport, N 44° 41' 00", W 124° 03' 50" 100 Ft

210 Sites – This is a first class big-rig park. Only motorcoaches and Class-C units at least 30 ft. long are allowed to stay here. It's a location overlooking the beach with two swimming pools, saunas, Jacuzzis, fitness center, and a convenience center. All sites are back-ins and they extend to 70 feet. The campground is on the ocean side of US-101 2 miles (3 km) north of Newport and 9.1 miles (14.7 km) south of the Depot Bay bridge.

HARBOR VILLAGE RV PARK *(Open All Year)*

Res. and Info.: (541) 265-5088, gocamping@harborvillagervpark.com, www.harborvillagervpark.com
Location: Newport, *N 44° 37' 51", W 124° 02' 19", Near Sea Level*

150 Sites – With limited facilities, not too many traveler sites, smallish parking spaces, and many permanent residents, this older RV park has one big advantage - location. You can easily walk a few blocks west along the edge of the harbor to Newport's old town. About 50 of the sites are available for travelers. Most of these are smaller sites but a few will take RVs to 40 feet. The Wi-fi here is only available in the office and at a few nearby sites. Reservations are definitely recommended in all seasons. From the junction of US-101 and SR-20 in town go .5 miles (.8 km) east on SR-20, turn south on SE Moore Dr and drive down to the waterfront, turn left and you'll see the campground entrance in about a block on the left.

PORT OF NEWPORT MARINA AND RV PARK *(Open All Year)*

Res and Info.: (541) 867-3321, www.portofnewport.com
Location: 1 Mile (2 Km) S of Newport, *N 44° 37' 15", W 124° 02' 58", Near Sea Level*

150 Sites – The marina campground in Newport is located on the south side of the bay. It's away from the Old Town but convenient to one of Newport's top attractions, the Oregon Coast Aquarium. The RV park and marina share a building with a small store and restaurant. There are two sections to this RV park. Near the marina office is a parking lot with RV connections. This area is slated to be completely revamped during the winter of 2005-2006. The new area will have nice big-rig sites laid out like an RV park, not a parking lot. A smaller area adjoins a motel to the south of the large marina parking lot. This area will remain unchanged. It has 46 back-in sites to 40 feet long and its own set of restrooms. The two RV camping areas are about 200 yards apart and both are managed out of the office in the marina building between them. The entry road for the marina leaves US-101 just south of the big bridge over the Yaquina Bay outlet.

SOUTH BEACH STATE PARK *(Open All Year)*

Reservations: (800) 452-5687, www.reserveamerica.com
Information: (541) 867-4715, (800) 551-6949, www.oregonstateparks.org
Location: 2 Miles (3 Km) S of Newport, *N 44° 36' 15", W 124° 03' 41", Near Sea Level*

227 Sites – This large state park campground is conveniently located not far south of Newport. Campsites are quite a distance back from the beach here, there are hiking trails to reach it. The sites are all back-ins with electricity and water hookups. They stretch to 59 feet but the largest number fall into the 40 to 50 foot range. There is also a hiker-biker camp area and a number of rental yurts. The campground entrance road goes west from US-101 about 1.5 miles (2.4 km) south of Newport's Yaquina River bridge.

OREGON

OREGON

MARYHILL REGION

This region forms the eastern gateway to the Columbia Gorge which extends from the Maryhill area west for about 90 miles (145 km). US-97, the major north-south route on the east side of the Cascades, crosses the Columbia here. There are several unusual sights nearby, it is a small fruit-growing region, and the river offers dams, fishing, and windsurfing. While this region is listed in this book as an Oregon destination (since the major east-west highway, I-84, is on the Oregon side) it actually occupies both sides of the river.

On the Washington side there are two sights connected with the eccentric railroad heir Sam Hill. Hill was the son-in-law of railroad baron James J. Hill, builder of the Great Northern Railway. Hill's story is too involved to relate here, but you'll become familiar with it as you take a look at the two structures he built nearby.

The first is a concrete replica of Stonehenge in England. This **northwest Stonehenge** sits on a site which might have been more appropriate to a replica of the Parthenon in Athens. It overlooks the gorge from a hilltop just above the campgrounds mentioned below. To reach it you just follow the small paved road through fruit-tree orchards and the historic village of Maryhill, then up the hillside, a distance of about two miles (3 km) from the campgrounds. During the season you will find fruit stands between the campgrounds and the village.

Another nearby Sam Hill edifice is the **Maryhill Museum of Art**. Hill built the place as a mansion but didn't live there, reportedly because his wife refused to live in such an remote and windy place. At first glance you may think that the curators are hard-pressed to find exhibits for the museum, the collection is very eclectic. However, you'll find the varied exhibits well worth the stop. This museum draws a lot of people, especially considering its very remote and out-of-the-way location. The exhibits include an excellent collection of American Indian artifacts, memorabilia related to Queen Marie of Romania (a family friend), French fashion from the 1940's, and photos of Sam's work with road building in the northwest during the early part of

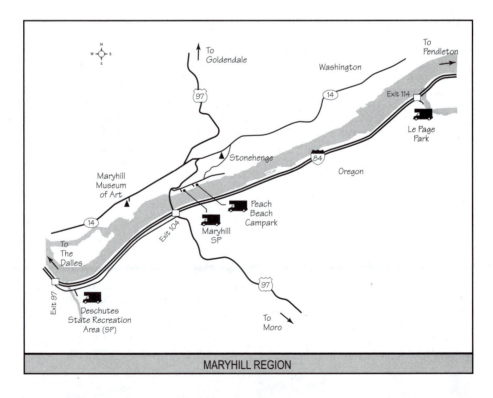

MARYHILL REGION

the last century. The museum is located a few miles west of the campgrounds along SR-14.

On the south side of the river the Deschutes and the John Day rivers empty into Lake Umatilla behind John Day Dam on the Columbia. Both have campgrounds at their mouths and are popular fishing destinations.

MARYHILL STATE PARK *(Open All Year)*

Reservations:	(888) 226-7688, www. camis.com/wa
Information:	(509) 773-5007, (360) 902-8844, www.parks,wa.gov
Location:	17 Miles E of The Dalles, *N 45° 40' 55", W 120° 50' 01"*, 100 Ft

71 Sites – This state campground is located right on the banks of the Columbia. It is very popular with windsurfers, expect it to fill up early on summer weekends. The terrain is very flat, large grassy areas separate the RVs and there is lots of shade. Many sites are long pull-thrus that can easily take RVs to 65 feet. Amenities include a swimming beach and a boat launch. You'll spot the campground next to the river as you descend the hill on US-97. It is just upriver from the Sam Hill Memorial Bridge where US-97 crosses the Columbia.

PEACH BEACH CAMPARK *(Open All Year)*

Res. and Info.:	(509) 773-4698
Location:	17 Miles (27 Km) E of The Dalles, *N 45° 41' 04", W 120° 49' 04"*, 100 Ft

82 Sites – Located just east of the state campground, this RV Park is so similar to the state park that it might be an extension. The major difference is that the campground isn't quite so structured and it's also less expensive. Sites are long back-ins or pull-thrus to 70 feet. Take the exit for the state campground off US-97. Drive past the state campground entrance and another .6 mile (1 km), then turn right into Peach Beach at the far end of the state campground.

DESCHUTES STATE RECREATION AREA *(Open All Year)*

Reservations:	(800) 452-5687, www.reserveamerica.com
Information:	(541) 739-2322, (800) 551-6949, www.oregonstateparks.org
Location:	13 Miles (21 Km) E of The Dalles, *N 45° 38' 02", W 120° 54' 29"*, 100 Ft

80 Sites – The Deschutes River empties into the Columbia about 4 miles (6 km) west of the US-97 bridge. This state campground is very popular with river-lovers, both those floating the river and those who launch their power boats at the ramp on the far side of the river at Heritage Landing. Fishing for salmon is good in the Columbia and trout fishing is good in the Deschutes. The first two miles of the Deschutes are reserved for bank fishermen. Several hiking trails are on the east bank of the Deschutes. There's also a mountain bike trail that stretches 17 miles up the river on an old railroad bed. There are separate non-hookup and hookup camping areas. Tent and non-hookup campers are on grass in open fields, all hookup sites are back-ins. There aren't many hookup sites that will take RVs over 35 feet, but the non-hookup sites in the "B" area will take any size RV. Note that this campground has no showers. To reach the campground take Exit 97 from I-84 and follow the frontage road on the south side of the highway east for 3 miles (5 km) to the campground entrance.

LE PAGE PARK *(Open April 1 to Oct 30 - Varies)*

Reservations:	(877) 444-6777, www.reserveusa.com
Information:	(541) 739-2713
Location:	27 Miles (44 Km) E of The Dalles, *N 45° 43' 40", W 120° 39' 11"*, 200 Ft

22 Sites – This is a small Corps of Engineers park located where the John Day River flows into Lake Umatilla behind John Day dam on the Columbia River. It's a very nice little campground with large back in and pull-thru sites including waterfront hookup sites to 50 feet. The campground has a manned entrance booth, a boat ramp and a swimming beach. To reach the campground take Exit 114 from I-84, the campground is located right at the exit.

NEHALEM BAY AND MANZANITA

Nehalem Bay offers easy to access crabbing and fishing opportunities. The spit of land that forms the bay is occupied by a large and very popular state park. There is a great beach. Cannon beach is near to the north and Tillamook to the south. What more could you want.

OSWALD WEST STATE PARK *(Open March 1 to Oct 31)*

Information:	(800) 551-6949, www.oregonstateparks.org
Location:	4 Miles (6 Km) N of Manzanita, *N 45° 45' 34", W 123° 57' 32"*, 100 Ft

30 Sites – Oswald West is a walk-in tent campground. Wheelbarrows are provided for carrying your gear down the hill a quarter-mile to the campground. There are flush toilets and firewood can be purchased. Beyond the campground the trail continues to descend to Short Sand Beach, popular with surfers and other beach-goers. There's a large parking lot along US-101 that is 10 miles (16 km) south of Cannon Beach and 3.7 miles (6 km) north of Manzanita.

NEHALEM BAY STATE PARK *(Open All Year)*

Reservations:	(800) 452-5687, www.reserveamerica.com
Information:	(503) 368-5154, (800) 551-6949, www.oregonstateparks.org
Location:	1 Mile (2 Km) S of Manzanita, *N 45° 42' 11", W 123° 56' 05"*, Near Sea Level

290 Sites – Nehalem Bay campground occupies a spit between Nehalem Bay and the ocean. It's just south of the village of Nehalem and shares a long, wide beach with the town. Campsites are sheltered behind dunes but the beach is extremely accessible. There's a boat launch at the park, not to mention an airstrip. RV sites are all back-ins. Many are over 50 feet long, over half are 40 feet or longer. In addition to the 265 RV sites with electricity there is a hiker/biker area, a horse camp with 17 sites, an airport camp with six sites for fly-in campers, and 18 yurts. To reach the campground watch for the sign just south of Manzanita, other signs will take you 2 miles (3 km) on back roads to the campground.

BRIGHTON MARINA AND RV PARK *(Open All Year)*

Res. and Info.:	(503) 368-5745
Location:	Brighton, *N 45° 40' 09", W 123° 55' 29"*, Near Sea Level

26 Sites – This marina on Nehalem Bay has back-in sites overlooking the marina. Camping is on gravel in a lot shared by parked cars. RVs to 45 feet can park here without getting in the way. A small restroom building services the RV sites. There is also a very small grassy area with no nearby vehicle parking north of the buildings and boat launch for tenters. Fishermen love this place because it has the facilities they need – boat launch, moorage, rental boats, and guided fishing trips. The campground is located right off US-101 as it runs along the bay 6 miles (10 km) south of Nehalem and 3.6 miles (5.8 km) north of Rockaway Beach.

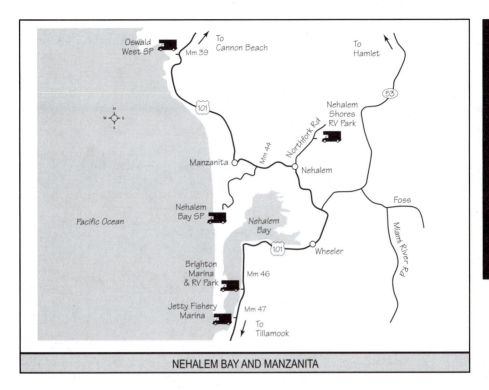

NEHALEM BAY AND MANZANITA

🚐 **JETTY FISHERY MARINA** *(Open All Year)*
   Res. and Info.: (503) 368-5746, (800) 821-7697, jettyfishery@coastwifi.com
   Location: 1 Mile (2 Km) S of Brighton, *N 45° 39' 35", W 123° 55' 45"*, Near Sea Level

30 Sites – Like the Brighton Marina mentioned above this place is also a fisherman's destination. They too have docks, marina, and boat launch. RV sites are back-ins near the entrance and there is a separate large tent area on grass to the north. Most RV sites will take RVs to 45 feet with no problem. The campground is located right off US-101 as it runs along the bay 6.7 miles (10.8 km) south of Nehalem and 2.9 miles (4.7 km) north of Rockaway Beach.

NEWBERRY NATIONAL VOLCANIC MONUMENT

South of Bend is the **Newberry National Volcanic Monument**. This national monument is a little unusual in that it is managed by the Forest Service rather than the National Park Service. That's largely because it's more efficient that way since the monument is surrounded by the Deschutes National Forest. The monument preserves a large section of interesting volcanic terrain.

There are two important destinations in the monument: **Lava Lands Visitor Center** and the **Newberry Volcano**. The visitor center is located 12 miles (19 km) south of Bend, just to the east of US-97. It has newly updated exhibits, and a bookstore. There's also a road up to the Lava Butte Lookout at the top of a small volcano.

The larger **Newberry Volcano** also has a road into the caldera. There are two lakes in the caldera: Paulina Lake and East Lake. All of the campgrounds listed below are located in the Newberry Volcano caldera and near the lakes.

There is a dump station as you enter the Newberry Caldera between Mile 12 and 13. The campgrounds below are beyond that point, none have their own dump station. The campgrounds are listed from end of the road back toward the west.

CINDER HILL CAMPGROUND *(Open May 15 to Oct 20 - Varies)*

Information: (541) 383-4000
Location: Newberry Caldera, *N 43° 43' 45", W 121° 11' 41"*, 6,400 Ft

110 Sites – This is the campground at the end of the paved road. It sits on the east side of East Lake and stretches for a long distance along the shoreline. There is a boat launch here. Sites reach 30 feet and maneuvering room is good. From US-97 some 20 miles (32 km) south of Bend and 6 miles (10 km) north of La Pine follow the Paulina-East Lake Rd east as it climbs to the monument. The campground is 18.3 miles (30 km) from the junction with US-97.

EAST LAKE RESORT AND RV PARK *(Open May 15 to Oct 20 - Varies)*

Res. and Info.:   (541) 536-2230, www.EastLakeResort.com
Location: Newberry Caldera, *N 43° 43' 22", W 121° 11' 35"*, 6,400 Ft

40 Sites – This resort serves as a place to get supplies, showers, and do laundry for the campers in the monument. The main resort buildings are on the lakeshore and amenities here include a boat ramp, restaurant, rooms, and small grocery store. On the upper side of the highway there is a campground with both back-in and long (75 foot) pull-thru sites with water and electricity. There is a shower building and laundry at the campground, they are also available (for a fee) to campers in the other campgrounds along the lakes. From US-97 some 20 miles (32 km) south of Bend and 6 miles (10 km) north of La Pine follow the Paulina-East Lake Rd east as it climbs

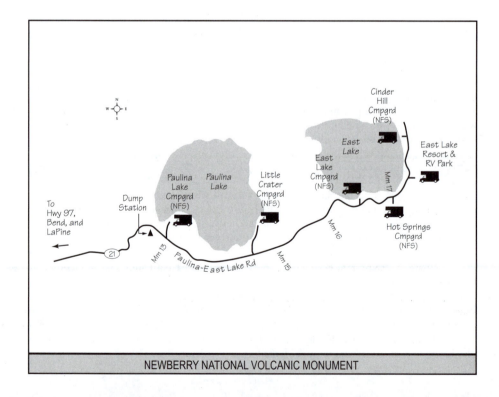

NEWBERRY NATIONAL VOLCANIC MONUMENT

to the monument. The campground is 18 miles (29 km) from the junction with US-97.

OREGON

HOT SPRINGS CAMPGROUND *(Open July 1 to Sept 30 - Varies)*
Information: (541) 383-4000
Location: Newberry Caldera, *N 43° 43' 07", W 121° 11' 57",* 6,400 Ft

52 Sites – Despite the name there is no hot springs in this campground. However, there is an interesting spill of lava, mostly obsidian, forming one border to the site. This campground is the only one in the monument that is not on a lakeshore. Sites are half of a pull-thru (in other words – back-ins) suitable only for RVs to 26 feet due to uneven terrain. From US-97 some 20 miles (32 km) south of Bend and 6 miles (10 km) north of La Pine follow the Paulina-East Lake Rd east as it climbs to the monument. The campground is 17.5 miles (28 km) from the junction with US-97.

EAST LAKE CAMPGROUND *(Open May 15 to Oct 20 - Varies)*
Information: (541) 383-4000
Location: Newberry Caldera, *N 43° 43' 04", W 121° 12' 36",* 6,400 Ft

29 Sites – This campground occupies the south shore of East Lake. Sites vary in size but some reach 40 feet including some pull-thrus right on the lakeshore. There is a boat ramp at the campground. From US-97 some 20 miles (32 km) south of Bend and 6 miles (10 km) north of La Pine follow the Paulina-East Lake Rd east as it climbs to the monument. The campground is 16.9 miles (27km) from the junction with US-97.

LITTLE CRATER CAMPGROUND *(Open May 15 to Oct 20 - Varies)*
Information: (541) 383-4000
Location: Newberry Caldera, *N 43° 42' 38", W 121° 14' 37",* 6,400 Ft

50 Sites – This waterfront campground is on the east shore of Paulina Lake. Many sites are pull-thrus and there are also long back-ins, some to 70 feet. There is a boat ramp at the campground. From US-97 some 20 miles (32 km) south of Bend and 6 miles (10 km) north of La Pine follow the Paulina-East Lake Rd east as it climbs to the monument. The campground is 14.9 miles (24 km) from the junction with US-97.

PAULINA LAKE CAMPGROUND *(Open May 20 to Oct 20 - Varies)*
Information: (541) 383-4000
Location: Newberry Caldera, *N 43° 42' 35", W 121° 16' 21",* 6,400 Ft

69 Sites – Pauline Lake Campground is the first you reach as you enter the monument. It occupies the south shore of Paulina Lake and has two entrances and two boat ramps. Many of the sites here are 60-foot pull-thrus but they tend to be difficult for really big RVs because they are sharply curved. From US-97 some 20 miles south (32 km) of Bend and 6 miles (10 km) north of La Pine follow the Paulina-East Lake Rd east as it climbs to the monument. The campground is 13.3 miles (21 km) from the junction with US-97.

PENDLETON

Pendleton (population 17,000) bills itself as "The real west". The little town does indeed have a western flavor. It is very well known for its **Pendleton Round-Up**, a 4-day rodeo held during mid-September. Make sure you have reservations if you visit during the round-up, you'll have lots of company. You should alsobuy your tickets to the rodeo early to avoid being disappointed.

The name Pendleton may make you think of wool blankets. This is the home of the **Pendleton Woolen Mills**. The company began operations in 1909 when it started making woolen Indian blankets, today they have 14 mills scattered around the country. The one in Pendleton has a store and gives tours of the factory.

Four miles (6 km) east of Pendleton is the **Wildhorse Resort**. This entertainment complex, run by the Confederated Tribes of the Umatilla Indian Reservation, has a casino, an 18-hole golf course, an RV park, and a museum. The museum is known as the **Tamástslikt Cultural Institute** and describes the Cayuse, Umatilla and Walla Walla tribes and cultures and their interaction with the travelers on the Oregon Trail. The easiest way to enjoy the resort is to stay at the convenient RV park.

If you take I-84 eastward almost immediately you'll reach the long grade up into the Blue Mountains. The scenery changes quickly from dry grasslands to pine forests. Emigrant Springs State Park, an alternate campground for Pendleton, is just off the freeway at Exit 234.

Heading even farther eastward you'll pass the Blue Mountains Summit (elevation 4,194 feet) and reach an interesting stop, the **Oregon Trail Visitor's Park**. To reach it take Exit 248 and follow a winding road for 3 miles (5 km) to the park. You'll find a short trail that leads up the hill to a section of the Oregon Trail, ruts are visible and an interpretive trail and volunteers help you make sense of what you see.

MOUNTAIN VIEW RV PARK *(Open All Year)*

Reservations:	(866) 302-3311
Information:	(541) 276-1041, rvpdt@oregontrail.net, www.nwfamilyrvresorts.com
Location:	Pendleton, *N 45° 39' 36", W 118° 46' 49"*, 1,300 Ft

107 Sites – This is a modern big-rig park. It has pull-thru sites to 65 feet but also tent sites. Access from the freeway is easy, the campground is located just south of the Red Lion that is easy to spot from the highway. Take Exit 210 from I-84. Turn south and take the first right onto Southwest Nye Ave. Follow Nye for one block and then turn left onto SE 3rd St., the campground is a block ahead and to the right.

THE LOOKOUT RV PARK *(Open All Year)*

Reservations:	(877) 604-6014
Information:	(541) 276-6014
Location:	Pendleton, *N 45° 40' 36", W 118° 50' 26"*, 1,100 Ft

42 Sites – This new park on the west side of Pendleton is located on a hillside. Sites are all long pull-thrus to 60 feet, this is a good big-rig park. Everything here is paved. To find the park take Exit 207 from I-84, you'll see the park on the hillside on the north side of the exit.

WILDHORSE CASINO RV PARK *(Open All Year)*

Reservations:	(800) 654-9453
Information:	(541) 278-2274, www.wildhorseresort.com
Location:	4 Miles (6 Km) E of Pendleton, *N 45° 38' 54", W 118° 40' 32"*, 1,400 Ft

100 Sites – Just a short drive east of Pendleton is the entertainment complex of the Confederated Tribes of Umatilla. You'll find a good big-rig RV park and also, within walking distance, a casino, a golf course, and a museum. Some pull-thru sites are 60 feet in length, others are long

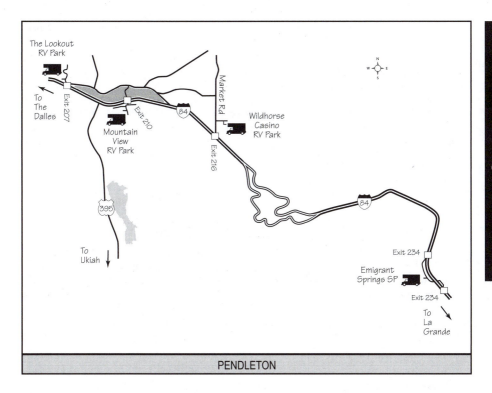

PENDLETON

back-ins. They are surrounded by clipped grass and have good separation but no shade. There is a swimming pool with spa and restrooms with hot showers. There's also a separate tent-camping area with a community fire ring. You can walk about a quarter-mile to the casino which has a restaurant, there is also a free shuttle bus for transportation to the casino, museum, or golf course. To reach the campground take Exit 216 from I-84 about 4 miles (6 km) east of Pendleton. Follow signs .3 mile (.5 km) north to the access road for the complex. The RV park entrance is .3 mile (.5 km) up the entrance boulevard, on the right.

![RV] EMIGRANT SPRINGS STATE PARK CAMPGROUND *(Open All Year)*

Reservations:	(800) 452-5687, www.reserveamerica.com
Information:	(541)983-2277, (800) 551-6949, www.oregonstateparks.org
Location:	20 Miles (32 Km) E of Pendleton, *N 45° 32' 24", W 118° 27' 43"*, 3,800 Ft

51 Sites – Emigrant Springs is one of the nicest Oregon State campgrounds but seems to get little use, perhaps due to its remote location. It is handy to the interstate, however, and makes a great overnight stop if you're traveling through the region. The campground is along the route of the Oregon Trail and has an information kiosk. It's set in pines, really a beautiful place. Sites include back-ins to 60 feet. To reach the campground take Exit 234 from I-84, the campground is on the south side of the highway. That's 20 miles (32 km) east of Pendleton.

PORT ORFORD

Port Orford is the western-most incorporated city in the contiguous U.S. You'll pass through this small town at Mile 301 of US-101 along the Oregon coast. Take the time to stop at **Battle Rock Wayside** at the south end of town for views and steep access to the beach. Those with small and easy to maneuver RVs can turn toward the ocean at the sign in town and drive out to the **Port Orford Heads Wayside**. There's a trail to a headland which can be an excellent whale-watching spot but turn-around room is limited.

Cape Blanco is the westernmost point in the contiguous U.S. You reach it by taking a five-mile (8 km) paved road from Mile 296.6 of US 101. That's just north of Port Orford. The lighthouse on the cape is the oldest on the Oregon coast, there's also a small state park campground with electrical hookups. There's plenty of room to turn big RVs just before the end of the road as the lighthouse comes into view in the distance, but very little maneuvering room at the lighthouse itself. RVers should use their tow car to visit the lighthouse. There are hiking trails all across Cape Blanco with magnificent views.

CAPE BLANCO STATE PARK *(Open All Year)*

Reservations:	800) 452-5687, www.reserveamerica.com
Information:	(541) 332-6774, (800) 551-6949, www.oregonstateparks.org
Location:	8 Miles (13 Km) N of Port Orford, *N 42° 49' 53", W 124° 32' 59"*, 200 Ft

53 Sites – The Cape Blanco State Park occupies Cape Blanco. On the end is the oldest remaining lighthouse on the Oregon Coast, the Cape Blanco Lighthouse, which dates from 1870. The campground sites are off a loop. They are all back-in sites, some to 65 feet with many longer than 40 feet. There are may trails on the cape, the lighthouse is .7 mile (1.1 km) west of the campground. The entrance road to Cape Blanco leaves US-101 near Mile 296.6. This is 3 miles (5 km) north of Port Orford. From the highway drive 4.7 miles (7.6 km) toward the cape and turn left to enter the campground.

ELK RIVER RV PARK *(Open All Year)*

Res. and Info.:	(541) 332-2255
Location:	4 Miles (6 Km) NE of Port Orford, *N 42° 46' 26", W 124° 28' 13"*, Near Sea Level

50 Sites – This commercial campground is a bit out of town. It's popular with salmon fishermen and has quite a few long-term residents. The campground is not on the Elk River but there's a private road to it so fishing is convenient. Sites here will take big RVs, many are pull-thrus to 60 feet. To reach the campground turn east on Elk River Road from US-101 near Mile 297.6. The campground entrance is 1.7 miles (2.7 km) from the highway.

PORT ORFORD RV VILLAGE *(Open All Year)*

Res. and Info.:	(541) 332-1041
Location:	1 Mile N of Port Orford, *N 42° 45' 40", W 124° 29' 39"*, 100 Ft

47 Sites – This is an older park with enthusiastic and friendly new owners, a popular place. Most sites here are back-ins to 50 feet but there are a few even longer pull-thrus. To reach the campground turn east on Madrona Ave at Mile 300 at the north end of Port Orford, the campground will be on your left in .5 miles (.8 km).

MADRONA 101 RV PARK *(Open All Year)*

Res. and Info.:	(541) 332-4025, (877) 7CALL-RV, madronacampers@msn.com
Location:	Port Orford, *N 42° 45' 21", W 124° 29' 49"*, 100 Ft

30 Sites – This is a small and somewhat run-down park. It has a new owner, however, and he seems intent on bringing it up to the standard of the other parks in Port Orford. Take a look when you visit the town. Maneuvering room is tight but there are a few back-in and pull-thru sites which will take 40-footers. To reach the campground turn east on Madrona Ave at Mile 300 at the north end of Port Orford, the campground is on the corner.

⊃ꝺ CAMP BLANCO RV PARK *(Open All Year)*

Res. and Info.: (541) 332-6175, www.campblanco.com
Location: Port Orford, *N 42° 45' 17", W 124° 29' 51"*, 200 Ft

25 Sites – This small RV park is neat as a pin and one of the best-run campgrounds we've ever seen. The owners, who live on-site, are very attentive to their customers needs. Sites are back-ins and pull-thrus to 60 feet. Although there's no laundry at the campground there's a laundromat across the street, even better. An unusual feature here is the "boatel", an old fishing boat that has been converted into a rental room – very cute. The RV park is located near the northern entrance to Port Orford, it's on the west side of US-101.

⊃ꝺ HUMBUG MOUNTAIN STATE PARK *(Open All Year)*

Information: (541) 332-6774, (800) 551-6949, www.oregonstateparks.org
Location: 6 Miles (10 Km) S of Port Orford, *N 42° 41' 18", W 124° 26' 01"*, Near Sea Level

95 Sites – This state park campground is located away from the coast and the sites are right next to the highway. There's a trail to the summit of Humbug Mountain from the campground and another to the beach. The campground has a hiker-biker camp as do most Oregon state campground on the Oregon coast, they're well-used by hikers traveling the coastal trail. Most of the vehicle sites here are back-ins. Only 32 have hookups, none have sewer drains. They reach 51 feet, 20 are over 40 feet. There is a dump station but it has been closed recently. The campground is on the east side of the highway near Mile 307.9. This is 6 miles (10 km) south of Port Orford and 21 miles (34 km) north of Gold Beach.

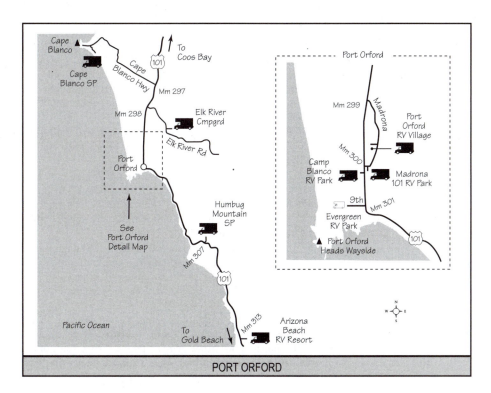

PORT ORFORD

OREGON

ARIZONA BEACH RV RESORT *(Open All Year)*
Res. and Info.:   (541) 332-6491, www.ArizonaBeachRV.com
Location: 12 Miles (19 Km) S of Port Orford, *N 42° 36' 49", W 124° 23' 36"*, Near Sea Level

135 Sites – The Arizona Beach Resort is a very large campground that occupies two sides of US-101 and has its own underpass. You get off on the east side of the highway. The office, store, and restrooms are located on that side of the highway. Then there's a road that passes under the highway (marked as having 13 feet, 6 inches of clearance) and leads to about 50 sites fronting the beach. You're just a few feet from the water. Sites are pull-ins and pull-thrus to 50 feet and longer, there's lots of maneuvering room. The entrance is at Mile 313.1. That's 12 miles (19 km) south of Port Orford and 14 miles (23 km) north of Gold Beach.

PORTLAND

The Portland region, with a population of about 1,000,000, is by far the largest concentration of people in Oregon. The area population depends, of course, upon how you define the region. The population is fairly dense as far south as Salem and also crosses the Columbia to Vancouver, Washington.

Portland is a young city by any standards, it was founded around 1844 when the first land claim was staked in what is now downtown Portland. Although the city is older than Seattle it is only older by a few years. The location is said to have been used for years as a seasonal campsite by Indians, there was a village nearby on Sauvie Island near the mouth of the Willamette.

Actually, by the time Portland was founded, Europeans had been in the neighborhood for quite a few years too. Fort Vancouver, across the Columbia River, was an important Hudson's Bay Company post beginning in 1825.

Like Seattle, much of Portland's early growth came as a timber port to fuel the demand for lumber in booming San Francisco down the west coast. Gold had been discovered in the Sacramento River Valley and San Francisco was growing rapidly. Portland served as a gateway to the Willamette River Valley which was attracting large numbers of settlers who traveled the Oregon Trail. It became much easier to reach Portland when the railroad arrived in 1883.

Lewis and Clark and passed near Portland in 1805 so Portland celebrated the fact 100 years later with the Lewis and Clark Centennial Exposition, actually a world's fair. Huge numbers of tourists attended the exposition and many decided to move to Portland. The population of the city leaped ahead during the next decade.

With the development of the Columbia River Valley's farming and industry during the 1900s Portland has become even more important as a transportation hub. Today, based on total tonnage, the city is the west coast's largest port.

Portland and its suburbs sprawl 25 miles (40 km) from east to west and 25 miles (40 km) from north to south. The northern border of the city is the Columbia River although Vancouver, Washington, on the north side of the river definitely qualifies as a suburb. The Willamette River runs right through the center of town with the downtown area on the west bank some 10 miles (16 km) from where the Willamette meets the Columbia.

Just west of the city center is a range of hills, much of them is covered by Washington Park and Forest Park. On the far side of the hills are the suburbs of Beaverton and Hillsboro. To the east rises Mt. Hood, on the lower slopes is the suburb of Greshem. South of Portland along the Willamette are many more suburbs, among them Milwaukee, Lake Oswego, West Linn, Oregon City, Tualatin, and Tigard.

Highway I-5 runs north and south through the center of Portland. Near downtown I-5 follows the east bank of the Willamette opposite the downtown business district. There is a short ring-road freeway, I-405, that leaves I-5 north of downtown, circles around the west side of the district, and then rejoins I-5 after less than four miles (6 km). There's a much longer ring-road

THE SKIDMORE DISTRICT'S SATURDAY STREET MARKET

freeway, I-205, around the east side of Portland. It leaves I-5 north of the Columbia River and makes a 36-mile (58-km) loop around the east side of the city before rejoining I-5 at the far southern border of the Portland suburbs. I-84 from the east also ends near the city center, it joins I-5 on the east bank of the Willamette River opposite downtown after having come in through eastern Portland.

Portland has an award-winning public transportation system. The crown jewel is the Max light rail system with extensions running far east to Gresham and west to Hillsboro. Extensions go north to the airport and Expo Center. Portland also has an excellent bus system.

Central Portland has a real parking problem, that means that you will probably want to visit using the public transportation system. Unfortunately the Max light rail system does not serve any of Portland's campgrounds, you'll have to use the bus at least part of the way. Once you reach downtown, however, there is free bus service in the central core and busses and the Max system provide easy access to the places you will probably want to visit.

Portland provides one bus route that is of particular interest to visitors. This is Bus 63, nicknamed **Art, The Cultural Bus**. It provides access to many of Portland's cultural attractions including the **Memorial Coliseum, Oregon Convention Center, Oregon History Center, Oregon Museum of Science and Industry (OMSI), Pacific Northwest College of Art, Portland Art Museum, Portland Center for the Performing Arts, Tom McCall Waterfront Park, RiverPlace shops and marina, Oregon Zoo, Japanese Garden, International Rose Test Garden, World Forestry Center and the Vietnam Memorial**.

Public transportation in central Portland is conveniently centered around the downtown Transit Mall. This is eleven-block-long area between 5th and 6th Avenues is closed to all traffic except public transportation. The Tri-Met (transit) main office is located at Pioneer Courthouse Square.

Once you have arrived in downtown Portland you might want start your tour by making your way to **Pioneer Courthouse Square**. It adjoins the transit mall and is bounded by Broadway, 6th Ave., Morrison, and Yamhill. Here you'll find the Tri-Met transit office and you'll also be in the center of downtown Portland's attractions. You are also in the center of Portland's upscale shopping district. Portland is a popular shopping destination with visitors because Oregon does not have a sales tax.

To find the **Greater Portland Convention and Visitor's Center** you can stroll east toward the river on Salmon St. to the three World Trade Center buildings. Across the street is **Governor Tom McCall Waterfront Park**. It stretches about a mile along the Willamette River and offers an excellent place for a promenade on a nice day. At the south end of the park is the **RiverPlace Marina** development with upscale shops and restaurants.

To really appreciate Portland you should know the names and locations of the various districts. Many are within easy walking distance of downtown, particularly since Portland's blocks are small, some downtown are only 200 feet square.

Four of the districts have their southern borders along W. Burnside Street, an east-west thoroughfare five blocks north of Pioneer Courthouse Square. The farthest west is called the **Northwest District**. Bounded on the west by NW 27th Ave. and on the east by NW 18th Ave. the district is just west of the I-405 ring road but still less than a mile from Pioneer Courthouse Square if you head northwest on Morrison. The whole district is filled with refurbished Victorian homes, many now serving as boutiques, coffee houses, book shops, theaters, pubs, and restaurants. The center of the action is known as **Nob Hill**, NW 21st through 23rd Ave.

The next district to the east and just east of the I-405 ring road is **The Pearl**, bounded on west by NW 15th Ave. and east by NW 8th Ave. It's an up-and-coming district of restored warehouses with art galleries and condominium conversions. Here you'll find one of Portland's best-known stores–**Powell's Books**. Covering a full block at 10th and Burnside this bookstore is the largest independent bookstore in the world.

The next district to the east is **Chinatown**. The Chinatown gates are at 4th and Burnside. Merging in from the east is **Old Town**. Many of the buildings here are from the 1880s, Portland had a fire in 1872 that razed much of this area and resulted in the building of these cast iron-fronted buildings typical of the period.

Now we've followed the districts eastward all the way to the river, there are two more just to the south. **Skidmore Historic District** and **Yamhill Historic District** adjoin the Riverfront Park from Burnside south to about Salmon St. Both are much like the **Old Town** district to the north. A popular attraction in the Skidmore District is the **Saturday Market**, a street crafts market held on Saturday and Sunday all year except in the dead of winter and located just south of Burnside near the Skidmore Fountain.

There are also a couple of interesting shopping districts on the east side of the Willamette. The **Hawthorne District** is along east-west Hawthorne Boulevard from about S.E. 17th to S.E. 55th Ave. It has kind of a counter-culture (or maybe 1960s) atmosphere and offers second-hand shops, book stores, cafes and galleries.

More mainstream is the huge **Lloyd Center** shopping mall. It is located about 10 blocks east of the river near the Memorial Coliseum and the Oregon Convention Center. The easiest way to get there is via the Gresham-bound Max.

Antique hunters will want to visit the **Sellwood District**. To reach it start at the Sellwood Bridge, Portland's southernmost. Drive east on Tacoma for 7 blocks to S.E. 13th and you are there. From Tacoma St. north to about Bybe St. you'll find many antique shops and also some good restaurants.

Portland is known for its city parks, but the best must be huge **Washington Park**. It is located in the hills west of downtown Portland and is easily accessible either by taking the Hillsboro-bound Max and getting off at the zoo stop or from US-26 west of downtown at the Zoo Exit. In the park are a number of Portland's most popular attractions including the **Washington Park Zoo**, **International Rose Test Garden**, **Japanese Gardens**, **Hoyt Arboretum**, and the **World Forestry Center**.

Science, and technology buffs will probably enjoy the **Oregon Museum of Science and Industry** (OMSI). Located on the east bank of the Willamette, OMSI covers 18 acres and offers a variety of hands-on technology-inspired exhibits including a decommissioned submarine, an

OREGON

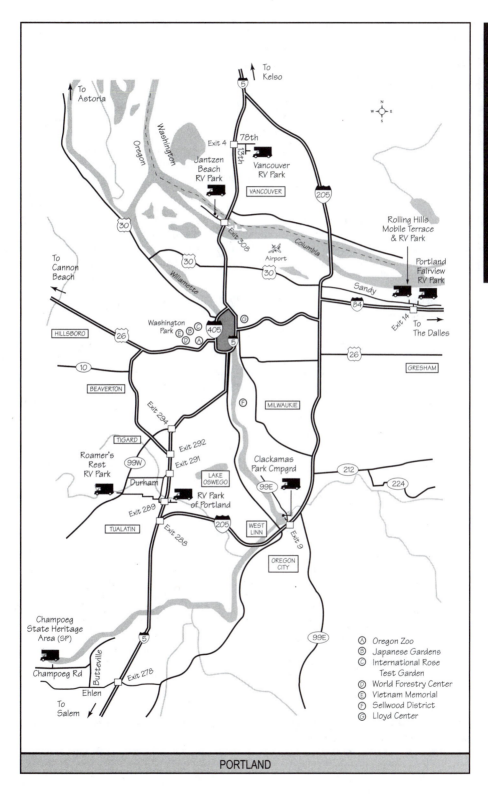

PORTLAND

OREGON

Omnimax theater, a giant walk-through heart, a shaking earthquake room, and even the bridge of the Starship Enterprise.

PORTLAND FAIRVIEW RV PARK *(Open All Year)*

Reservations:	(877) 777-1047
Information:	(503) 661-1047, info@portlandfairviewrv.com, www.portlandfairviewrv.com
Location:	Portland, *N 45° 32' 36", W 122° 26' 38"*, 100 Ft

407 Sites – This is a huge and fairly new big-rig RV park on the east side of Portland. If you are arriving on I-84 from the east access to the campground is very convenient. The park has over 400 sites, all have full hookups, most are large pull-thrus to 55 feet. Parking is on paved pads with patios separated by well-tended grass. Sites are arranged on several terraces sloping shallowly to the north toward the Columbia River. Amenities include nice restrooms, swimming pool, recreation room, exercise room playground, and laundry. A small market is nearby. To use public transportation to get to downtown Portland you take a bus from just outside the campground. To reach the campground take Exit 14 from I-84 east of Portland. Drive north one-quarter mile (.4 km) to Sandy Boulevard, turn right, and you'll see the campground on your left almost immediately.

ROLLING HILLS MOBILE TERRACE AND RV PARK *(Open All Year)*

Res. and Info.:	(503) 666-7282
Location:	Portland, *N 45° 32' 44", W 122° 27' 17"*, 100 Ft

137 Sites – This is a another choice for camping on the east side of Portland. This campground is just down the street from the Portland Fairview. It's an older campground with quite a few long-term residents but the services are adequate and the traveler sites are mostly pull-thrus to about 50 feet. There is a swimming pool here too. Take Exit 14 from I-84 east of Portland and travel north a quarter-mile to Sandy Boulevard. Turn left and you'll see the campground entrance on the right in .3 mile (.5 km).

CHAMPOEG STATE HERITAGE AREA *(Open All Year)*

Reservations:	(800) 452-5687, www.reserveamerica.com
Information:	(503) 678-1251, Ext. 225, (800) 551-6949, www.oregonstateparks.org
Location:	20 Miles (32 Km) S of Portland, *N 45° 14' 59", W 122° 52' 48"*, Near Sea Level

82 Sites – Champoeg is a historical park, it is set in one of the first locations settled in the Willamette Valley. It's about 6 miles (10 km) from I-5 but it's still a handy place to stop, particularly if you're approaching Portland from the south and just don't want to drive in to the city in the evening traffic. Sites here vary but many are back-ins exceeding 55 feet. From I-5 south of Portland take Exit 278. Drive west on Ehlen Rd. NE for 1.6 mile (2.6 km), then turn right on Butteville Rd NE. After another 1.7 mile (2.7 km) turn left on Champoeg Road NE and you'll see the campground entrance on the right in another 2.8 mile (4.5 km).

CLACKAMETTE PARK CAMPGROUND *(Open All Year)*

Location:	Portland, *N 45° 22' 12", W 122° 36' 11"*, Near Sea Level

38 Sites – This city park has RV camping sites along the Willamette River just north of where I-205 crosses near Oregon City. It's a gravel lot with back-in sites to 40 feet, there are pull-thrus too but they are shorter. Take Exit 9 from I-205. Drive north on SR-99E for only .3 mile (.5 km), the campground entrance is on the left.

■ **RV PARK OF PORTLAND** *(Open All Year)*

Reservations:	(800) 856-2066
Information:	(503) 692-0225, rvpkpdx@rvparkofportland.com
Location:	Portland, *N 45° 22' 59", W 122° 44' 42"*, 100 Ft

98 Sites – This is an older park, but it has large well-spaced sites in a park-like setting. It appears that the builders foresaw large RVs, very unusual. The park has quite a few long-term residents but it's well managed and maintained and seems like a traveler park. Sites are pull-thrus, most are 60 feet long. Take Exit 289 from I-5 in Tualatin, at the southern edge of Portland. Drive east on SW Nyberg Rd for .3 mile (.5 km), the campground is on the left.

■ **ROAMER'S REST RV PARK** *(Open All Year)*

Reservations:	(877) 4RV-PARK
Information:	(503) 692-6350, info@roamersrestrvpark.com, www.roamersrestrvpark.com
Location:	Portland, *N 45° 23' 33", W 122° 48' 02"*, 100 Ft

93 Sites – This small modern campground is a popular place to stay for folks spending some time in Portland. The stand-out feature is instant-on telephone at the sites, but it's a modern campground with good facilities. The compact site slopes steeply to the Tualatin River. Restrooms are nice, there are individual rooms with toilet, shower and sink. Sites here vary but there are quite a few pull-thrus to 60 feet and longer. Reach the campground most easily by taking Exit 291 from I-5. Drive southwest on Carman Dr. to join SW Upper Boones Ferry Rd heading south. At .5 mile (.8 km) from the freeway turn right on SW Durham Road and follow Durham west for 2.2 miles (3.5 km) to SR-99W (SW Pacific Hwy). Turn left and in .8 mile (1.3 km) you'll see the campground entrance on the right.

■ **JANTZEN BEACH RV PARK** *(Open All Year)*

Reservations:	(800) 443-7248
Information:	(503) 289-7626, www.jantzenbeachrv.com
Location:	Portland, *N 45° 36' 58", W 122° 41' 09"*, Near Sea Level

169 Sites – This campground is the closest to central Portland and it is an easy campground to reach if you are approaching from the north. It is located on Hayden Island which is an island in the Columbia River crossed by I-5 as it enters Portland. Sites here are back-ins and pull-thrus to 50 feet. Amenities include a swimming pool in the summer. Near the campground is a large shopping center but actually the area is a comparatively quiet retreat considering how close it is to central Portland. Bus transportation is available to downtown from near the campground. Take Exit 308 which is marked Jantzen Beach, then follow the campground signs 1/2 mile (.8 km) on Hayden Island Drive to the west of the freeway on the north bank of the island.

■ **VANCOUVER RV PARK** *(Open All Year)*

Reservations:	(877) 756-2972
Information:	(360) 695-1158, www.vancouverrvparks.com
Location:	Vancouver, WA, *N 45° 40' 38", W 122° 39' 31"*, 100 Ft

152 Sites – This new campground is north of the Columbia in Vancouver, Washington. It's just off the I-5 freeway and make a handy campground for visits to Portland. It's a modern big-rig park with back-in and pull-thru sites to 55 feet. Take Exit 4 from I-5. Drive east on NE 78th Street for two blocks and turn south on NE 13th Ave. The campground is on the left about halfway down the block.

OREGON

PRINEVILLE

Prineville (population 8,500) is located about 17 miles (27 km) east of Bend, an easy drive on SR-126. The main attraction for campers in the Prineville area is the Prineville Reservoir, about 16 miles (26 km) south of town. Here the Crooked River and Bowman Dam form a 3,030 acre lake that is popular for fishing, swimming, and boating of all kinds. Anglers will find rainbows as well as bass and crappie in the lake. Three of the RV parks listed below are on the shores of the reservoir, one is in town.

MAIN CAMPGROUND - PRINEVILLE RESERVOIR STATE PARK *(Open All Year)*

Reservations: (800) 452-5687, www.reserveamerica.com
Information: (541)447-4363, (800) 551-6949, www.oregonstateparks.org
Location: 14 Miles (23 Km) S of Prineville, *N 44° 07' 50", W 120° 43' 19"*, 3,200 Ft

68 Sites – This is one of two campgrounds at Prineville Reservoir State Park. This is the larger of the two and has sites with sewer, the other does not. Sites here aren't as long as at many Oregon state campgrounds but many are over 40 feet and a couple reach 50 feet. They're all back-in sites. The lakeside campground is popular for water sports and has a boat ramp and swimming area. From Prineville drive south on SR-380 (Combs Flat Rd.) for 1.3 miles (2.1 km). Then turn right on SE Juniper Canyon Road and follow the road to the campground entrance in another 13 miles (21 km).

JASPER CAMPGROUND - PRINEVILLE RESERVOIR STATE PARK *(Open April 15 to Sept 30)*

Information: (541)447-4363, (800) 551-6949, www.oregonstateparks.org
Location: 16 Miles (26 Km) S of Prineville, *N 44° 08' 06", W 120° 41' 41"*, 3,200 Ft

30 Sites – This is the second Prineville Reservoir State Park campground. It's the smaller of the two and has fewer facilities, but it has the only dump station in the park. It also has a boat launch. Sites here are smaller than at the main campground, but they're better separated and some overlook the water. They're suitable for RVs to about 35 feet, some present leveling problems since they're not quite flat. To reach the campground continue past the entrance to the main campground for another 2.1 miles (3.4 km).

PRINEVILLE RESERVOIR RESORT *(Open May 15 to Labor Day - Varies)*

Res. and Info.:   (541) 447-7468
Location: 17 Miles (27 Km) S of Prineville, *N 44° 07' 24", W 120° 41' 15"*, 3,200 Ft

71 Sites – This is a private resort located on the shore of Prineville Reservoir. Sites vary in size but 40-foot RVs can be accommodated. There's a marina here with a boat ramp and boat rentals as well as a store and cafe. To reach the resort continue on past the Jasper Campground for another 1.1 miles (1.8 km).

CROOK COUNTY RV PARK *(Open All Year)*

Reservations: (800) 609-2599
Information: (541) 447-2599, ccrvpark@crestviewcable.com, www.prineville-crookcounty.org
Location: Prineville, *N 44° 17' 35", W 120° 50' 44"*, 2,800 Ft

81 Sites – The town of Prineville hosts a very nice big-rig campground that is actually a county park. It is right next to the county fairgrounds. The managers live on site. Many sites are

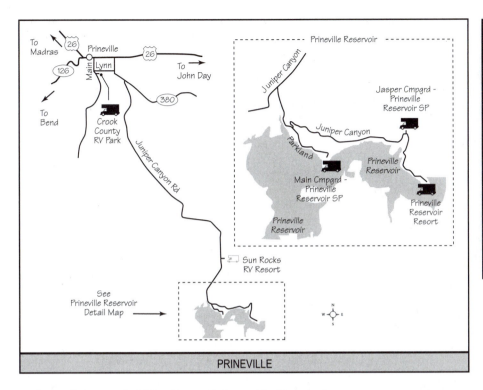

PRINEVILLE

70-foot pull-thrus with full hookups including cable. There is also a grassy tent-camping area. In central Prineville drive south on South Main. The campground is on your left in .7 mile (1.1 km).

REDMOND AND SISTERS

Redmond (population 45,000), is the northernmost of the big towns along US-97 as it passes along the east side of the Cascades through Oregon. Along with Bend the city forms the commercial nucleus of the region.

Sisters (population 900) is one of those theme towns, it may remind you of Leavenworth or Winthrop in Washington. It's located just 19 miles (31 km) east of Redmond. Sisters is a cute little place with a number of restaurants, shops, and art galleries. Plan to spend an hour or two wandering around.

These towns serve as a good base for exploring some beautiful countryside. The town of Bend is only 21 highway miles (34 km) south of Redmond so you might consider some of the same sights covered in the Bend section. The attractions listed in this book under *Camp Sherman and the Metolius River, the Cascade Lakes Highway,* and *Newberry National Volcanic Monument* are also near.

A popular drive from Sisters is the **McKenzie-Santiam Pass Loop**. This 82 mile (132 km) loop is a designated a National Forest Scenic Byway. The loop follows SR-242 westward from Sisters and across **McKenzie Pass**. There you'll find the **Dee Wright Observatory,** built of lava and offering an easy wheelchair-accessible trail through a lava flow. After the pass the road de-scends to the intersection with SR-126. Turn north and follow this highway up the McKenzie River Valley. There are a number of small National Forest Service campgrounds along this sec-tion of the road as well as the McKenzie River National Recreation Trail which offers access to the river and several waterfalls. Watch for signs for **Koosah and Sahalie Falls**, both are easily accessible. You'll come to another intersection, this time US-20. Turn east here and it will take you over **Santiam Pass** and past the Metolius River Recreation Area back to Sisters. The first portion of the route, SR-242, is narrow and steep and not suitable for large RVs, that's why it is listed here only as a day trip. Also, snow closes this portion of the loop from November until late June.

Sisters holds the **Sisters Rodeo** during the second week of June.

CROOKED RIVER RANCH RV PARK *(Open March 15 to Oct 31 - Varies)*

Reservations:	(800) 841-0563
Information:	(541) 923-1441, rvpark@crookedriverranch.com
Location:	13 Miles (21 Km) N of Bend, *N 44° 25' 25", W 121° 14' 18"*, 2,500 Ft

101 Sites – The Crooked River Ranch RV Park is operated by the homeowner's association of this large housing development. The campground sits in a wide canyon, next door is a nice golf course and there's a large swimming pool. Sites here include long pull-thrus as well as good tent sites. To reach the campground turn east on NW Lower Bridge Road from US–97 some 4 miles (6.5 km) north of Redmond and on the northern edge of the small town of Terrebonne. Drive west for 2.2 miles (3.5 km) and turn right on NW 43rd St. Follow this road north as it curves through the development and down into the canyon, you'll see the campground sign at 5.3 miles (8.5 km) from the turn onto NW 43rd.

RIVER RIM RV PARK *(Open All Year)*

Res. and Info.:	(541) 923-7239, riverrimrv@prodigy.net
Location:	13 Miles (21 Km) N of Bend, *N 44° 26' 02", W 121° 14' 41"*, 2,500 Ft

24 Sites – This is a smaller RV park located in the canyon not far from the Crooked River Ranch RV Park. This one is not owned by the homeowner's association and has few amenities, but it's still popular. Sites here will take larger RVs, many are back-ins to about 60 feet but there are also some pull-thrus. To reach this campground follow the directions for Crooked River Ranch RV Park above, the entrance for the River Rim is .4 miles (.6 km) beyond that for the Crooked River.

HIGHWAY 97 RV PARK *(Open All Year)*

Reservations:	(800) 243-7671
Information:	(541) 548-4157
Location:	Redmond, *N 44° 17' 312", W 121° 10' 19"*, 2,900 Ft

85 Sites – This modern commercial RV park in northern Redmond has lots of long-term residents but it is kept clean and tidy, a well-run park. There are a large number of traveler sites too. The entire park is paved, sites are pull-thrus from 45 to 55 feet long. The park is located off Maple Street just east of US–97 near the northern edge of Redmond. This is 1.5 miles (2.4 km) north of the intersection of SR-126 (the road west to Sisters) and US–97 in central Bend.

INDIAN FORD CAMPGROUND *(Open May 6 to Oct 9 - Varies)*

Information:	(541) 549-7700, www.hoodoo.com
Location:	5 Miles (8 Km) NW of Sisters, *N 44° 21' 30", W 121° 36' 40"*, 3,200 Ft

25 Sites – Indian Ford Deschutes National Forest Campground has a handy location just off SR-20 just 5 miles (8 km) northwest of Sisters. It's set in tall ponderosa pines, some sites reach 55 feet and there is plenty of room to maneuver.

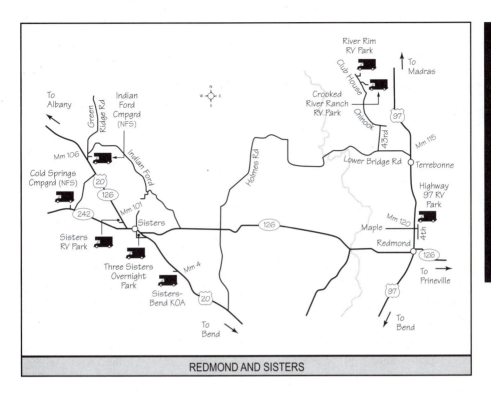

REDMOND AND SISTERS

COLD SPRINGS CAMPGROUND *(Open May 6 to Oct 9 - Varies)*
Information: (541) 549-7700, www.hoodoo.com
Location: 4 Miles (6.5 Km) W of Sisters, *N 44° 18' 36", W 121° 37' 48"*, 3,400 Ft

23 Sites – This campground sits 4 miles (6 km) west of Sisters just off SR-242. It is very popular with birders. Sites are located off a long loop road that winds through big trees. Some are pull-thrus, many of these and also many of the back-ins reach 45 feet.

SISTERS RV PARK *(Open All Year)*
Res. and Info.:   (541) 549-PARK, sistersinnandrvpark.com, dave@sistersinnandrvpark.com
Location: Sisters, *N 44° 17' 44", W 121° 33' 40"*, 3,000 Ft

106 Sites – Sisters RV Park is a newer big-rig park at the western edge of Sisters. The name has recently been changed, it was formerly the Mountain Shadow RV Park. If you want full hookups and easy access to Sisters this is the place. The pool is open all year long and there is free Wi-fi. Sites are paved, have patios, and are surrounded by lawns. They are back-ins and pull-thrus to 80 feet. You'll see the campground on the south side of US-20 (also called SR-126) at the western edge of Sisters.

THREE SISTERS OVERNIGHT PARK *(Open May 1 to Oct 31 - Varies)*
Information: (541) 549-6022, http://www.ci.sisters.or.us/parks.shtm
Location: Sisters, *N 44° 17' 15", W 121° 32' 31"*, 3,100 Ft

60 Sites – This municipal campground is located on the eastern approaches to Sisters just south of US-20. It has RV sites to 60 feet and longer (both back-in and pull-thru) but no hookups or showers. There is also a grass tent-camping area. There is a dump station. The campground is close enough for walking in to town, less than a half mile (.8 km) distant. Easiest access is off South Locust Street.

SISTERS-BEND KOA *(Open March 15 to Nov 15 - Varies)*

Reservations: (800) 562-0363, www.koa.com
Information: (541) 549-3021
Location: 4 Miles (6.5 Km) SE of Sisters, *N 44° 15' 01", W 121° 29' 19"*, 3,200 Ft

89 Sites – This is one of the nicer KOAs we've visited with all of the normal KOA amenities. It sits right where the junipers to the east and the ponderosa pines from the west meet so both species are scattered across the park. Pull-thru sites are sized to 85 feet long so it's a good big-rig park but also a decent tent-camping park. The KOA is on the south side of US-20 about 4 miles (6.5 km) southeast of Sisters.

REEDSPORT AND THE OREGON DUNES

For about 47 miles (76 km) between Coos Bay and Florence the highway passes inland of a large area of shifting sand dunes. Much of the area is incorporated into the **Oregon Dunes National Recreation Area**. Many visitors come here to roar across the dunes on sand buggies, it can be a lot of fun. Others enjoy hiking through sections closed to motorized vehicles or visit the beaches. If you didn't bring your own sand buggy they can easily be rented in the area. The Recreation Area charges a $3 daily fee, you must display a pass when parked at trailheads.

The official center of the dunes area is **Reedsport** at Mile 211.5 of U.S. 101, a town of

HIKING ON THE OREGON DUNES

about 5,000 near the mouth of the Umpqua River, the largest river between the Columbia and the Sacramento. Reedsport is the location of the **Oregon Dunes National Recreation Area Visitor Center**. SR-38 joins US-101 here, if you drive 3 miles (5 km) east you'll reach the **Dean Creek Elk Viewing Area**, a refuge where you can usually see and photograph elk.

About 10 miles (16 km) north of Reedsport is the **Oregon Dunes Overlook** at Mile 200.8. There's a special deal on the recreation area daily fee here, only $1. Boardwalks and ramps make it easy to see and understand the dunes. As you continue north on U.S. 101 you'll pass Jessie M Honeyman State Park (see camping below), and arrive at Florence at Mile 191.

One of the centers for RVing in this area is Winchester Bay about three miles (5 km) south of Reedsport. Both Reedsport and Winchester Bay are actually located on the Umpqua River but Winchester Bay is closer to the mouth. You'll find 8 campgrounds below that are located in this area. There is a very nice harbor here as well as access to ATV areas in the dunes to the south. Watch for the road west to **Umpqua Lighthouse State Park** south of Reedsport near Mile 217 and just south of Winchester Bay. There is also access directly from Winchester Bay. The lighthouse overlooks the south shore of the mouth of the Umpqua River. This is also the location of the **Umpqua River Whale Watching Station**, whales are often sighted in the estuary.

Sand dunes dominate this coast. Access and use is restricted and regulated by the Oregon Dunes Recreation Area, administered as part of the Siuslaw National Forest. Some areas allow all terrain vehicle (ATV) use, others are just for hikers.

The campgrounds below are listed from north to south.

JESSIE M. HONEYMAN MEMORIAL STATE PARK *(Open All Year)*

Reservations: (800) 452-5687, www.reserveamerica.com
Information: (541) 997-3641, (800) 551-6949, www.oregonstateparks.org
Location: 3 Miles (5 Km) S of Florence, *N 43° 55' 32", W 124° 06' 42"*, 200 Ft

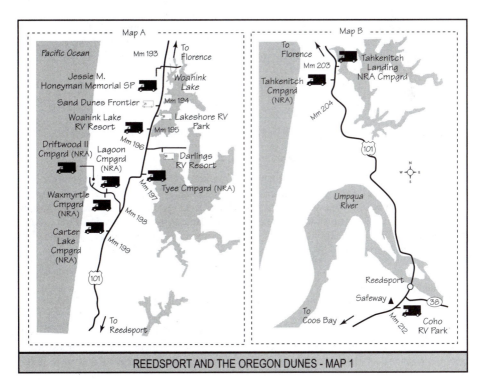

REEDSPORT AND THE OREGON DUNES - MAP 1

355 Sites – Honeyman is a beach campground but the beach here is on Cleawox Lake, not the ocean. Sand dunes separate the campground from the ocean and you can walk through them to the coast some two miles (3 km) distant. There's another day-use area on much larger Woahink Lake with is across the highway. It has a boat ramp. In summer Honeyman has no access for ATV riders to the dunes, but in winter from October 1 to April 30 access is allowed from one loop. This is Oregon's second largest state campground. Sites are back-ins to 55 feet, a large number of them are longer than 40 feet. The H loop is best for RVs with slide-outs. The entrance to Honeyman is directly off US-101 at Mile 193.5, about 2.6 miles (4.2 km) south of the Florence bridge.

WOAHINK LAKE RV RESORT *(Open All Year)*

Reservation:	(800) 659-6454
Information:	(541) 997-6454
Location:	4 Miles (7 Km) S of Florence, *N 43° 54' 12", W 124° 06' 58"*, Near Sea Level

75 Sites – This is a modern family-run commercial campground. The campground has access at the back to the dunes so it is a good place to stay if you have your own buggy. It also has it's own dock on Woahink Lake across the highway from the campground. Sites are back-ins and pull-thrus to 65 feet. The campground entrance is on the west side of US-101 near Mile 195.5, about 4.3 miles (6.9 km) south of the Florence bridge.

TYEE CAMPGROUND *(Open May 20 to Sept 30 - Varies)*

Reservations:	(877) 444-6777, www.reserveusa.com
Information:	(541) 271-3611
Location:	6 Miles (10 Km) S of Florence, *N 43° 53' 03", W 124° 07' 14"*, 100 Ft

15 Sites – Tyee is an old Oregon Dunes National Recreation Area campground with vehicle accessible sites suitable only for small rigs like cars and vans with lengths to 20 feet. The attraction at the campground is its boat launch onto little Siltcoos River, a popular canoe trail and fishing location. The entrance to the campground is at Mile 196.8, about 5.6 miles (9.0 km) south of the Florence bridge.

DRIFTWOOD II OFF HIGHWAY VEHICLE CAMPGROUND *(Open All Year)*

Reservations:	(877) 444-6777, www.reserveusa.com
Information:	(541) 271-3611
Location:	8 Miles (13 Km) S of Florence, *N 43° 52' 51", W 124° 08' 53"*, Near Sea Level

69 Sites – Driftwood II Oregon Dunes NRA Campground is primarily an ATV campground. Sites are back-ins to 35 feet in five large paved lots. ATVers have direct access to the dunes. Picnic tables and fire pits adjoin the lots. The modern restrooms here even have showers. To reach the campground turn west on the paved road marked Siltcoos Recreation Area. It leaves US-101 near Mile 198, about 6.8 miles (11.0 km) south of the Florence bridge. Driftwood II is the last of three campgrounds along the road, it is 1.2 mile (1.9 km) from US-101.

WAXMYRTLE CAMPGROUND *(Open May 1 to Sept 30 - Varies)*

Information:	(541) 271-3611
Location:	8 Miles (13 Km) S of Florence, *N 43° 52' 37", W 124° 08' 36"*, Near Sea Level

55 Sites – This Oregon Dunes NRA campground is extremely attractive, almost like a garden. Waxmyrtle Beach Trail leaves from the entrance of the campground and there is also

access to Stagecoach Trailhead. Sites are a little small here and maneuvering room limits access to RVs to about 35 feet. To reach the campground turn west on the paved road marked Siltcoos Recreation Area. It leaves US-101 near Mile 198, about 6.8 miles (11.0 km) south of the Florence bridge. Waxmyrtle is one of two campgrounds with entrances on opposite sides of the road about .8 mile (1.3 km) from the highway. It's the one on the left.

▣ LAGOON CAMPGROUND *(Open All Year)*

Information: (541) 271-3611
Location: 8 Miles (13 Km) S of Florence, *N 43° 52' 43", W 124° 08' 32"*, Near Sea Level

39 Sites – Located just across the road from Waxmyrtle Campground, this Oregon Dunes NRA campground is also very nice. There are quite a few back-in and pull-thru sites that can take RVs to 35 feet. To reach the campground turn west on the paved road marked Siltcoos Recreation Area. It leaves US-101 near Mile 198, about 6.8 miles (11.0 km) south of the Florence bridge. The campground entrance is on the right about .8 miles (1.3 km) from the highway.

▣ CARTER LAKE CAMPGROUND *(Open.May 20 to Sept 30 - Varies)*

Reservations: (877) 444-6777, www.reserveusa.com
Information: (541) 271-3611
Location: 8 Miles (13 Km) S of Florence, *N 43° 51' 39", W 124° 08' 30"*, Near Sea Level

23 Sites – This NRA campground has sites that are large enough for 30 foot RVs. The campground is located on the west side of the highway near Mile 199 at the north end of Carter Lake. This is 7.6 miles (12.3 km) south of the Florence Bridge.

▣ TAHKENITCH LANDING CAMPGROUND *(Open All Year)*

Reservations: (877) 444-6777, www.reserveusa.com,
Information: (541) 271-3611
Location: 8 Miles (13 Km) N of Reedsport, *N 43° 47' 59", W 124° 08' 48"*, Near Sea Level

27 Sites – This NRA campground has sites set off a loop overlooking the boat landing at Tahkenitch Lake. They are small sites with parking on grass, only suitable for tent campers and smaller rigs like vans and pickup campers. There is no potable water at this campground. A boat ramp is located .3 miles (.5 km) to the north. The campground is on the east side of the highway near Mile 203. This is 12.2 miles(19.7 km) south of the Florence bridge and 8.2 miles (13.2 km) north of Reedsport.

▣ TAHKENITCH CAMPGROUND *(Open May 20 to Sept 30)*

Reservations: (877) 444-6777, www.reserveusa.com
Information: (541) 271-3611
Location: 8 Miles (13 Km) N of Reedsport, *N 43° 47' 43", W 124° 08' 56"*, Near Sea Level

17 Sites – This is a small Oregon Dunes NRA campground with back-in sites to about 25 feet off one paved loop. Nearby Three Mile Lake Trail leads from a parking area to the lake and out to the ocean beach. Tahkenitch Lake is across the highway. The campground is on the west side of US-101 near Mile 204. This is 7.5 miles (12.1 km) north of Reedsport.

OREGON

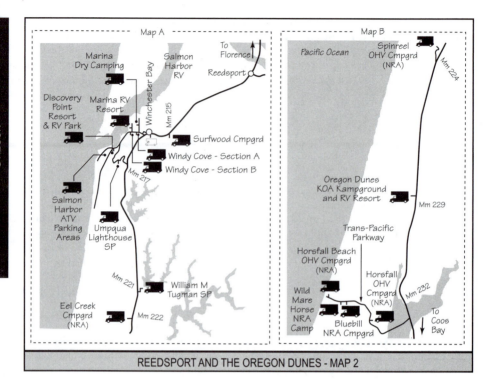

REEDSPORT AND THE OREGON DUNES - MAP 2

🚌 Coho RV Park *(Open All Year)*

Res. and Info.:   (541) 271-5411
Location: Reedsport, *N 43° 41' 50", W 124° 06' 43"*, Near Sea Level

49 Sites – The Coho is an older campground situated right in Reedsport. It's nothing fancy but the price is right and it's a popular place for fishing enthusiasts. There are back-in sites and pull-thrus to 60 feet with parking on gravel. Watch for the campground sign on the east side of the highway in Reedsport about .8 mile (1.3 km) south of the bridge.

🚌 Surfwood Campground *(Open All Year)*

Res. and Info.:   (541) 271-4020, www.surfwoodrvcampground.com
Location: 2 Miles (3 Km) S of Reedsport, *N 43° 40' 28", W 124° 09' 33"*, Near Sea Level

150 Sites – The Surfwood is a large older RV park located a few miles north of Winchester Bay. Sites are back-ins and pull-thrus to 50 feet, they are separated by lines of high shrubs so they're somewhat private. The park is popular with folks who like this coast but want to park away from the water and ATV activity. There is a seasonal swimming pool and ATVs can be rented, they must be trailered to the sand. The campground entrance road is at Mile 215. This is about .8 mile (1.3 km) northeast of the Winchester Bay cutoff.

🚌 Salmon Harbor ATV Parking Areas *(Open All Year)*

Information: (541) 440-4500
Location: Winchester Harbor, *N 43° 40' 04", W 124° 11' 53"*, Near Sea Level

Approx. 300 Sites – Plans are afoot to put in a new camping area that is set up for overnight parking for   ATVers. It will be located north of the South Jetty Beach Access Road and west of Salmon Harbor Road. It should have lots of room to park, permanent toilets of some kind, and picnic tables and fire pits. Until that camping area is built ATVers are allowed to park along Triangle Road and during heavy use time also at the South Staging Area. No campfires are allowed, port-a-potties are provided. There is a fee. From Mile 215.9 of US-101 drive west on Salmon Harbor Drive. Watch for a post with a box full of flyers opposite the entrance to the Windy Cove Section B campground in .6 mile (1 km). The flyers tell you where you can park. For more info or if you can't find the flyers check with the manager at Windy Cover Section B. About 1.4 miles (2.3 km) from US-101 Triangle Road continues straight ahead. The main road goes left and you'll soon spot the South Staging Area on the left.

DISCOVERY POINT RESORT AND RV PARK *(Open All Year)*

    Res. and Info.:   (541) 271-3443, www.discoverypointresort.com
    Location: Winchester Bay, *N 43° 40' 04", W 124° 11' 48",* Near Sea Level

50 Sites – Discovery point is the nearest commercial campground to the dunes in the Winchester Bay area. It caters to ATVers, often large parties of them. ATVs are available for rent. Tent campers are welcome. Some pull-thru RV sites reach 45 feet long. From Mile 215.9 of US-101 drive west on Salmon Harbor drive for 1.3 miles (2.1 km). The campground entrance is on the left.

MARINA RV RESORT *(Open All Year)*

    Reservations: (541) 271-0287
    Information: salmonh@codouglas.or.us, www.marinarvresort.com
    Location: Winchester Bay, *N 43° 40' 35", W 124° 11' 04",* Near Sea Level

138 Sites – The Marina RV Resort is a Douglas County campground. It's very upscale, one of the nicest places to stay, particularly in a big RV, along this section of the coast. Sites are all paved and landscaped. They are back-ins and pull-thrus to 60 feet. You have a choice of waterfront sites overlooking the marina or outer bay or interior sites where the views aren't quite so good. There's a nice paved walking trail around the exterior. Also, no ATV operation is allowed. From Mile 215.9 of US-101 drive west on Salmon Harbor drive for .5 miles (.8 km). The campground entrance is on the right.

UMPQUA LIGHTHOUSE STATE CAMPGROUND *(Open All Year)*

    Reservations: (800) 452-5687, www.reserveamerica.com
    Information: (541) 271-4118, (800) 551-6949, www.oregonstateparks.org
    Location: 1 Mile (2 Km) South of Winchester Bay, *N 43° 39' 43", W 124° 11' 37",* 100 Ft

44 Sites – This campground is along Maria Lake, just south of the Umpqua Lighthouse. Sites are arranged both off the entrance road and one loop. They are all back-ins, some around 50 feet and several over 40 feet. Although this campground is accessible from Salmon Harbor Drive it is easier to go east on an access road from Mile 216.7 of US-101, about .8 mile (1.3 km) south of the Salmon Harbor Drive junction with US-101 in Winchester Bay.

WINDY COVE SECTION A *(Open All Year)*

    Information: (541) 440-4500, www.co.douglas.or.us/parks.htm
    Location: Winchester Bay, *N 43° 40' 31", W 124° 10' 49",* Near Sea Level

OREGON

28 Sites – This is the first of two sections of the Windy Cove Douglas County campground. These are older campgrounds that preceded the Marina RV Resort across the street. The sites are back-ins from 32 to 60 feet long. From Mile 215.9 of US-101 drive west on Salmon Harbor drive for .2 miles (.3 km). The campground entrance is on the left.

🚐 WINDY COVE SECTION B *(Open All Year)*

Res. and Info.:	(541) 440-4500, www.co.douglas.or.us/parks.htm
Location:	· Winchester Bay, *N 43° 40' 30", W 124° 11' 08"*, Near Sea Level

69 Sites – This campground is the second of the Douglas County Windy Cove campgrounds. It is nearer to the dunes and popular with ATVers. The sites are located off two loops. One loop has back-in full-hookup sites to 60 feet. The second loop is much smaller back-in no-hookup sites. From Mile 215.9 of US-101 drive west on Salmon Harbor drive for .6 miles (1 Km). The campground entrance is on the left.

🚐 MARINA DRY CAMPING *(Open All Year)*

Location:	Winchester Bay, *N 43° 40' 41", W 124° 10' 50"*, Near Sea Level

171 Sites – In addition to all of the hook-up camping at Winchester Bay the marina provides five large parking areas for dry camping. Two of these are gravel lots that extend into the bay with back-in parking next to the water and picnic tables and grills. The daily fee for these areas is $12. Three others are paved parking lots a little back from the water but near the waterfront lots. These have no tables or barbecues and the daily fee is $10. Parking slots are from 50 to 60 feet long. There are restrooms nearby with flush toilets and showers. There is also a dump station. From Mile 215.9 of US-101 drive west on Salmon Harbor Drive for .1 mile (.2 km). Turn right into the large lot and look for the signs designating which areas are the camping sections of the lot.

🚐 WILLIAM M TUGMAN STATE PARK CAMPGROUND *(Open All Year)*

Reservations:	(800) 452-5687, www.reserveamerica.com
Information:	(541) 888-4902, (800) 551-6949, www.oregonstateparks.org
Location:	5 Miles (8 Km) S of Winchester Bay, *N 43° 36' 01", W 124° 10' 41"*, 100 Ft

102 Sites – This state park is located on the east side of the highway near Eel Lake. There is a day use area on the lake with a fishing dock. The campground sites are off three loops. All sites are back-ins from 30 to 60 feet, many exceed 40 feet in length so this is a decent big-rig park although there are no sewer connections, just a dump station. The campground entrance road is near Mile 221.3 of US-101. This is 8.1 miles (13.1 km) south of Reedsport and 12.3 miles (19.8 km) north of the Coos Bay suspension bridge.

🚐 EEL CREEK CAMPGROUND *(Open May 20 to Sept 30)*

Reservations:	(877) 444-6777, www.reserveusa.com
Information:	(541) 271-3611
Location:	6 Miles (10 Km) S of Winchester Bay, *N 43° 35' 18", W 124° 11' 11"*, Near Sea Level

52 Sites – Access to this Oregon Dunes NRA campground is directly off US-101. There is dune access for hikers but not ATVs from this park. The John Dellenbach trail leads through the dunes to the beach, a distance of about three miles (4.8 km) one way. A parking area for hikers not staying in the campground is located south of the park with a separate entrance. The sites here are back-ins and pull-thrus, they are suitable for RVs to about 35 feet. The campground

entrance is on the west side of US-101 at Mile 222.3. This is 9.1 miles (14.7 km) south of Reedsport and 11.3 miles (18.2 km) north of the Coos Bay suspension bridge.

SPINREEL OHV CAMPGROUND *(Open All Year)*

Reservations:	(877) 444-6777, www.reserveusa.com
Information:	(541) 271-3611
Location:	9 Miles (15 Km) N of the Coos Bay Bridge,
	N 43° 34' 09", W 124° 12' 13", Near Sea Level

36 Sites – Spinreel is an Oregon Dunes NRA campground that is primarily for ATV users. There is access to the dunes and ATVs can sometimes be rented near the entrance to the campground. There is also a large parking lot for day-use ATVers. Campsites are all back-ins here, they reach 40 feet but limited maneuvering room makes this campground best for RVs to 35 feet. These sites are separated sites, not parking-lot style. The campground entrance road is off US-101 at Mile 224.2. This is 11.1 miles (17.9 km) south of Reedsport and 9.3 miles (15 km) north of the Coos Bay suspension bridge.

OREGON DUNES KOA KAMPGROUND AND RV RESORT *(Open All Year)*

Reservations:	(800) KOA-4236, www.koa.com
Information:	(541) 756-4851, www.oregonduneskoa.com
Location:	4 Miles (6.5 Km) N of the Coos Bay Bridge,
	N 43° 30' 05", W 124° 13' 10", Near Sea Level

69 Sites – This KOA caters to the ATV crowd. Sites are set in a large open lot and many are long pull-thrus, some to 85 feet. The campground entrance road is off US-101 at Mile 228.8. This is 15.5 miles (25 km) south of Reedsport and 4.9 miles (7.9 km) north of the Coos Bay suspension bridge.

HORSFALL OHV CAMPGROUND *(Open All Year)*

Reservations:	(877) 444-6777, www.reserveusa.com
Information:	(541) 271-3611
Location:	2 Miles (3 Km) NW of the Coos Bay Bridge,
	N 43° 26' 33", W 124° 14' 47", Near Sea Level

70 Sites – This is another Oregon Dunes NRA campground with ATV access to the dunes. The sites are parking-lot style in paved lots with sites to 50 feet. There are picnic tables and fire pits along the edges, tenters can set up there off the asphalt. To reach the campground follow Trans-Pacific Parkway west from Mile 232.7. This is .7 mile (1.1 km) north of the Coos Bay suspension bridge. In 1 mile (1.6 km) take the right fork, the campground is on the right about 1.5 miles (2.4 km) from US-101.

BLUEBILL CAMPGROUND *(Open May 15 to Sept 15 - Varies)*

Information:	(541) 271-3611
Location:	4 Miles (6 Km) NW of the Coos Bay Bridge,
	N 43° 27' 04", W 124° 15' 46", Near Sea Level

18 Sites – Bluebill is a small campground. It is one of the four NRA campgrounds in the immediate area. Bluebill has back-in sites (and one pull-thru) for RVs to about 30 feet off a loop drive. The campground is located near the shore of Bluebill Lake, there is a one-mile trail around

the lake. To reach the campground follow Trans-Pacific Parkway west from Mile 232.7. This is .7 mile (1.1 km) north of the Coos Bay suspension bridge. In 1 mile (1.6 km) take the right fork, the campground is on the left about 2.8 miles (4.5 km) from US-101.

WILD MARE HORSE CAMP *(Open All Year)*

Reservations:	(877) 444-6777, www.reserveusa.com
Information:	(541) 271-3611
Location:	2 Miles (3.2 Km) NW of the Coos Bay Bridge,
	N 43° 26' 59", W 124° 16' 02", Near Sea Level

13 Sites – This NRA campground is designed for folks with horses. Twelve of the sites have room for parking a trailer and also small corrals and hitching posts. These are back-in sites to about 55 feet. The campground is about a half-mile from the beach. To reach the campground follow Trans-Pacific Parkway west from Mile 232.7. This is .7 mile (1.1 km) north of the Coos Bay suspension bridge. In 1 mile (1.6 km) take the right fork, the campground is on the left about 3.0 miles (4.8 km) from US-101.

HORSFALL BEACH OHV CAMPGROUND *(Open All Year)*

Reservations:	(877) 444-6777, www.reserveusa.com
Information:	(541) 271-3611
Location:	4 Miles (6 Km) NW of the Coos Bay Bridge,
	N 43° 27' 12", W 124° 16' 36", Near Sea Level

41 Sites – Horsfall Beach is an Oregon Dunes NRA campground that is really a large parking lot at the end of the road next to the beach. It serves as an overflow campground in this popular area. This camping parking lot has access to the beach and also ATV access to the dunes. Marked spaces take RVs to 50 feet. To reach the lot follow Trans-Pacific Parkway west from Mile 232.7. This is .7 mile (1.1 km) north of the Coos Bay suspension bridge. In 1 mile (1.6 km) take the right fork, the campground is about 3.5 miles (5.6 km) from US-101.

ROSEBURG AND THE UMPQUA VALLEY

Little Roseburg (population 20,200) is the main town of the Umpqua Valley. The Umpqua River, like the Rogue farther south, actually flows from the Cascades and then through the Coastal Mountains to the Pacific. At Roseburg the valley widens and becomes good farmland. Roseburg is an old town for Oregon, it was established by the Hudson Bay Company in 1836 as a fur-trading post.

Probably the best known of Roseburg's sights is the **Wildlife Safari**. It is located just north-west of Winston which is about 7 miles (11 km) south of Roseburg. At Wildlife Safari you drive your vehicle through fenced areas filled with wildlife from Africa, Asia, and North America on a 3-mile loop.

The Umpqua Valley is also a **wine-growing region**. Pick up a tour map at the visitor center that will lead you on a circuit of the valley's wineries and tasting rooms. You'll need the map to find these small wineries hidden on back roads.

Roseburg also has an excellent museum - The **Douglas County Museum of History and Natural History**. It is located right next to the RV park at the Douglas County Fairgrounds. Take Exit 123 from I-5 and follow the signs.

Roseburg hosts the **Douglas County Fair** the second week of August.

The North Fork of the Umpqua is a well-known fishing river. If you have a fly rod you may find the clear water flowing through gravel-bottom pools formed by basalt formations too attractive to pass by. This is said to be the best summer steelhead river in the U.S.

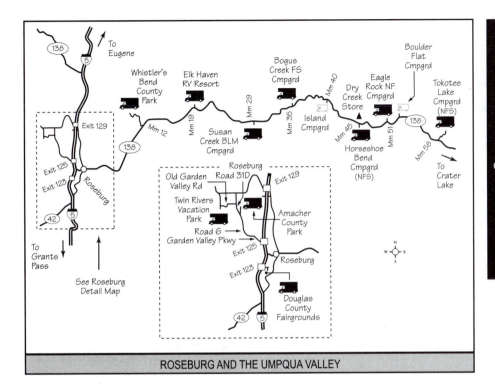

ROSEBURG AND THE UMPQUA VALLEY

The route along the North Fork of the Umpqua is well supplied with small Umpqua National Forest campgrounds, by our count there are at least 9 of them along the highway and several others up side roads. Four of them are included below.

 TOKETEE LAKE CAMPGROUND *(Open All Year)*

Information:	(541) 498-2531
Location:	57 Miles (92 Km) E of Roseburg, *N 43° 16' 21", W 122° 24' 19"*, 2,400 Ft

32 Sites – The campground is located off the main highway in the North Umpqua Valley above Toketee Dam and Lake. It's an Umpqua National Forest campground. No potable water is provided. Site size and maneuvering room limit access to coaches to 30 feet. There is a boat ramp at the campground. From SR-138 near mile marker 59, about 57 miles (92 km) from Roseburg, turn north on NF Road 34. At .3 mile (.5 km) take the left fork and climb for another 1.1 miles (1.8 km) passing the Toketee Dam and Lake to the campground entrance near the upper end of the lake.

 EAGLE ROCK CAMPGROUND *(Open May 20 to Sept 30 - Varies)*

Information:	(541) 496-3532
Location:	49 Miles (79 Km) E of Roseburg, *N 43° 17' 45", W 122° 33' 17"*, 1,600 Ft

28 Sites – Eagle Rock Umpqua National Forest campground has sites to 45 feet but limited maneuvering room limits coach size to about 30 feet. From SR-138 near Mile 51, about 49 miles (79 km) from Roseburg watch for the campground entrance on the north side of the road.

OREGON

⊞ HORSESHOE BEND CAMPGROUND *(Open May 20 to Sept 30)*

Information: (541) 496-3532
Location: 44 Miles (71 Km) E of Roseburg, *N 43° 17' 17", W 122° 37' 38"*, 1,400 Ft

26 Sites – This is one of the more upscale Umpqua National Forest campgrounds along the river. The restrooms have flush toilets and many of the campsites are right on the riverbank. There are sites exceeding 40 feet but limited maneuvering room means the campground is best for coaches to 35 feet. From SR-138 near Mile 46, about 44 miles (71 km) from Roseburg watch for the campground entrance on the south side of the road.

⊞ BOGUS CREEK CAMPGROUND *(Open May 20 to Oct 30)*

Information: (541) 496-3532
Location: 33 Miles (53 Km) East of Roseburg, *N 43° 19' 27", W 122° 48' 02"*, 1,100 Ft

15 Sites – The Umpqua National Forest Bogus Creek Campground has sites off two loops on the far side of the highway from the river. This campground has very narrow access roads limiting coach size to about 30 feet. From SR-138 near Mile 35, about 33 miles (53 km) from Roseburg, watch for the campground entrance on the north side of the road.

⊞ SUSAN CREEK CAMPGROUND *(Open May 1 to Oct 31)*

Information: (541) 440-4930, www.or.blm.gov/roseburg
Location: 27 Miles (44 Km) E of Roseburg, *N 43° 17' 52", W 122° 53' 42"*, 1,000 Ft

31 Sites – Sites in this BLM campground reach 40 feet but limited maneuvering room limits practical coach size to 35 feet. From the day-use area downstream there is a one-mile trail to Susan Falls. The campground is located near Mile 29 off SR-138, about 27 miles (44 km) from Roseburg.

⊞ ELK HAVEN RV PARK *(Open All Year)*

Res. and Info.:   (541) 496-3090, (888) 552-0166, vacation@elkhavenrv.com
Location: 18 Miles (29 Km) E of Roseburg, *N 43° 19' 27", W 123° 03' 07"*, 700 Ft

38 Sites – Elk Haven is a commercial big-rig park with pull-thrus and back-ins to 55 feet in a large open field near the highway. There are several fishing ponds on the property. The campground is off SR-138 near Mile 20 about 18 miles (29 km) east of Roseburg.

⊞ WHISTLER'S BEND COUNTRY PARK *(Open All Year)*

Information: (541) 673-4863, www.douglas.or.us/parks.asp
Location: 13 Miles (21 Km) E of Roseburg, *N 43° 18' 34", W 123° 12' 42"*, 600 Ft

28 Sites – Whistler's Bend is a Douglas County park located just outside Roseburg to the east. This is a large park, with a small campground located on the shore of the Umpqua River. There are shade trees and views across the river, a very pleasant place. Good restrooms are situated above the camping area near some rental yurts. There are tent sites as well as back-ins to 35 feet. To reach the campground turn north off SR-138 near Mile 12, about 10 miles (16 km) east of Roseburg. Follow the signs for 2.7 miles (4.4 km) to the park entrance and then up and over a low pass to the campground.

🛆 **DOUGLAS COUNTY FAIRGROUNDS** *(Open All Year)*

Information: (541) 957-7010
Location: Roseburg, *N 43° 11' 35", W 123° 21' 34"*, 400 Ft

50 Sites – This is a self registration campground right next to the freeway as you enter Roseburg from the south. It's a great place to stop if you're traveling I-5 and just want to stop and spend the night somewhere simple. The fair here is in August and it will be full then, but otherwise there's usually plenty of room. There are a few pull-thrus to 50 feet as well as long back-in sites. Restrooms are across the road. Take Exit 123 from I-5 and follow signs to the campground on the east side of the highway.

🛆 **TWIN RIVERS VACATION PARK** *(Open All Year)*

Res. and Info.: (541) 673-3811, twinr.v.@earthlink.net, www.twinriversrvpark.com
Location: 7 Miles (11 Km) W of Roseburg, *N 43° 16' 08", W 123° 26' 11"*, 300 Ft

85 Sites – This is a big-rig park that offers a lot more than just big spaces and good hookups. It's a little out of the way, about 6 miles (10 km) from the freeway west of town next to the Umpqua River, but if you plan to stay for more than a night in the area it's worth the drive. The sites are separated by lawns and trees and you are well away from any road noise. There are tent sites with camping on grass and also long pull-thrus to over 100 feet. Management here is excellent. To most easily reach the campground take Exit 125 from I-5. Drive west on NW Garden Valley Parkway for 2 miles (3 km), then turn north on County Road Six. In 3 miles (5 km) you'll come to a Y, turn left on County Road 31D. In another 1.4 miles (2.3 km) turn left on Old Garden Valley Road and you'll see the campground on the left in .9 mile (1.5 km).

🛆 **AMACHER COUNTY PARK** *(Open All Year)*

Information: (541) 957-7001, www.douglas.or.us/parks.asp
Location: 5 Miles (8 Km) N of Roseburg, *N 43° 16' 51", W 123° 21' 23"*, 400 Ft

30 Sites – Amacher is a small county park located almost under a freeway bridge and railway trestle north of Roseburg. Other than the freeway noise this is a nice place with paved back-in sites to 30 feet separated by lawn. The entryway has a height limitation marked as 12 foot, nine inches as it passes under a trestle. The park is on the bank of the North Umpqua River. On the other side of the river, a nice walk, is a fish ladder where you can watch salmon traveling up the river. Take Exit 129 from I-5. Drive south on SR-99 on the east side of the highway and cross the Umpqua River on a long and fairly narrow bridge. The campground entrance is on the west side of the highway on the south end of the bridge.

SALEM

Salem (population 127,000), Oregon's state capital, is an excellent base for exploring the upper Willamette Valley. This region was the goal of most of the trekkers of the Oregon Trail. Oregon City, 35 miles (56 km) north of Salem is considered the end of the Oregon Trail.

Since Salem is one of the older towns in the Willamette Valley you would expect the central area to have some sights of interest and you wouldn't be mistaken. Start at **Mission Mill Village** which is easy to find since it houses an information center for the city. There is also a wool museum set in the buildings of the old Thomas Kay Woolen Mill. Just follow the information signs posted near the entrances to town.

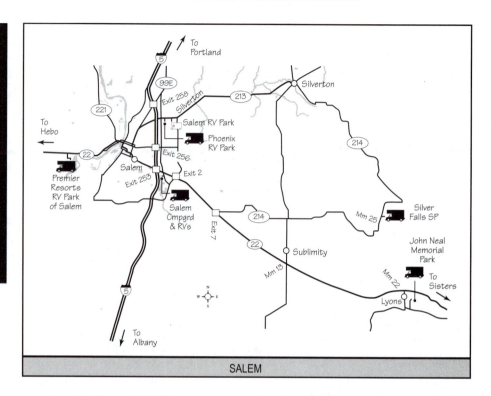

SALEM

From the Mission Mill Village you can visit the other sites of downtown Salem including **Willamette University**, the **State Capitol and grounds** and surrounding **historic area**, **Deepwood Estate and Gardens**, **Bush House Museum and Conservatory,** and the **Bush Barn Art Center**.

The Salem area is home to a large collection of **covered bridges** dating from the early 20th century. You can follow a loop visiting six of these bridges from Exit 253 off I-5 in Salem. The loop goes east on SR-22, then loops south to Albany on SR-226 from Mehama and Lyons. You'll need a guide pamphlet available from most area visitor's centers to find all of the bridges since they are tucked away on side roads.

Near Salem is the premier Oregon **wine growing area**. It is centered around McMinnville in Yamhill County to the west of Salem. The county has some 30 wineries, many offer tours. Pick up a guide to the wineries at the McMinnville tourist information center or other area information centers.

The area between Salem and Portland is full of interesting historical sites, particularly **Oregon City**, **Aurora**, and **Champoeg**. A driving tour from Salem north on I-5 to Oregon City, then south on 99E, west on country roads to Champoeg State Park, and then returning to Salem can make an interesting day trip. Once again, check with local information centers for more details.

If you have kids along they will probably be ready for something less historical after visiting all of the above. The answer is **Enchanted Forest**, a theme park located right along the I-5 freeway at Exit 248.

PREMIER RESORTS RV PARK OF SALEM *(Open All Year)*

Reservations: (503) 364-7714, (877) 364-9990, www.premierrvresorts.com
Location: 4 Miles (6 Km) W of Salem, *N 44° 55' 50", W 123° 07' 24"*, 100 Ft

180 Sites – This campground is on the western approaches to Salem. That's a little inconvenient if you're traveling I-5 and looking for a place to spend the night but even so many folks think it's worth the trouble to come out here. This is an upscale big-rig campground with pull-thru sites to 55 feet. Amenities include a swimming pool, nightly movies, a library/card room, a business center, meeting rooms, a game and exercise room, and free Wi-Fi (although there is an annual five dollar fee which covers use in all of the Premier parks). Watch for the resort on the south side of SR-22 some 4.2 miles (6.8 km) west of the bridges over the Willamette as you leave Salem.

SALEM CAMPGROUND AND RVs *(Open All Year)*

Reservations:	(800) 826-9605
Information:	(503) 581-6736, www.salemrv.com
Location:	Salem, *N 44° 54' 44", W 122° 59' 07"*, 200 Ft

220 Sites – This has long been the most popular of the campgrounds in Salem. It's a little old now, with few pretensions, but it's still a good reliable park with a handy location. There are tent sites here with tents pitched on grass in a treed area and also RV sites of various types including pull-thrus to 65 feet. Take Exit 253 from I-5 and head east on the North Santiam Hwy (SR-22). Take the Lancaster Dr. SE offramp in just .2 mile (.3 km) and go south on Lancaster for 100 yards. Turn right into Hagers Grove Rd. SE, the campground is at the end of the road in .3 mile (.5 km).

PHOENIX RV PARK *(Open All Year)*

Reservations:	(800) 237-2497
Information:	(503) 581-2497
Location:	Salem, *N 44° 58' 09", W 122° 58' 50"*, 100 Ft

107 Sites – This is a new big-rig campground with back-ins and pull-thrus to 70 feet. Take Exit 256 from I-5 and drive east on Market St. NE to Lancaster Dr. NE, about 5 blocks or .3 mile (.5 km). Turn north on Lancaster and drive 1.2 miles (1.9 km) to Silverton Road NE. Turn right and you'll see the campground entrance on the right in .1 mile (.2 km).

SILVER FALLS STATE PARK *(Open All Year)*

Reservations:	(800) 452-5687, www.reserveamerica.com
Information:	(503) 873-8681, (800) 551-6949, www.oregonstateparks.org
Location:	22 Miles (35 Km) E of Salem, *N 44° 52' 19", W 122° 38' 58"*, 1,300 Ft

100 Sites – This is Oregon's largest state park – by area. It has ten waterfalls, lots of trails, and a large campground. Many sites here are back-ins over 50 feet long, some stretch to 80 feet. To reach the campground drive east on SR-22 about 6 miles (10 km) to the junction with SR-214, then follow SR- 214 some 16 miles (26 km) to the park.

JOHN NEAL MEMORIAL PARK *(Open April 15 to Oct 15 - Varies)*

Res. and Info.:	(541) 967-3917, www.co.linn.or.us, www.co.linn.or.us/parks,
Location:	22 Miles (35 Km) E of Salem, *N 44° 46' 58", W 122° 36' 30"*, 700 Ft

40 Sites – John Neal is a small Linn County park in the town of Lyons. The park is on the bank of the North Santiam River and has a boat ramp. Some sites overlook the river, the longer ones are about 30 feet. From Salem drive east on SR-22 about 21 miles (34 km). Turn right and follow SR-226 into Lyons. In 1.1 mile (1.8 km) follow the main street left until you reach North 13th Street. Turn left and the park is about three blocks ahead.

TILLAMOOK AND THE THREE CAPES LOOP

Most people probably know **Tillamook** for its cheese, and cheese factories are a big part of the draw here. The **Tillamook Cheese Visitors Center** is north of town along US-101 at Mile 63.9. There is another factory nearby, the **Blue Heron French Cheese Company**, at Mile 65. Our favorite attraction in Tillamook is the **Tillamook Naval Air Station Museum**. It is located south of town near Mile 68.1. The museum is housed in a huge blimp hanger, you really can't miss it. Inside is a collection of World War II fighters and bombers along with other interesting aircraft.

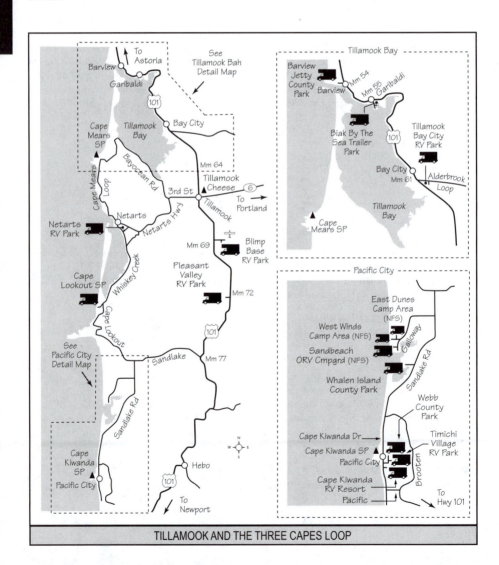

TILLAMOOK AND THE THREE CAPES LOOP

As you drive between Tillamook and Lincoln City you may want to leave US-101 and follow the **Three Capes Loop**. The north junction is in Tillamook at the west end of Third Street, the south junction is at Mile 90.4. The 28-mile (45 km) loop will lead you past **Netarts, Cape Lookout, Cape Kiwanda, and Pacific City.** A side trip from near Netarts will take you to **Oceanside** and **Cape Mears**.

▣ BARVIEW JETTY COUNTY PARK *(Open All Year)*

Res. and Info.: (503) 322-3522, parks@co.tillamook.or.us, www.co.tillamook.or.us/gov/parks
Location: 12 Miles (19 Km) N of Tillamook, *N 45° 34' 08", W 123° 56' 43"*, Near Sea Level

245 Sites – This county campground rivals the state campgrounds along the coast in size and facilities. It occupies the peninsula at the base of the north jetty protecting the entrance to Tillamook Bay. There are back-in and pull-thru full-hookup spaces to 70 feet and lots more RV and tent camping spaces with no hookups. The campground entrance is located 2.3 miles (3.7 km) south of Rockaway Beach and 1.8 miles (2.9 km) west of Garibaldi off US-101.

▣ BIAK BY THE SEA TRAILER PARK *(Open All Year)*

Res. and Info.: (503) 322-2111
Location: 9 Miles (15 Km) N of Tillamook, *N 45° 33' 26", W 123° 54' 51"*, Near Sea Level

64 Sites – This is one of several RV parks dedicated to fisherman near the marina at Garibaldi. Biak seems to be better taken care of than the others but is pretty basic. Sites are back-ins and pull-thrus on gravel to 40 feet. In Garibaldi follow S 7th Street out to the marina, the campground is the one on the left about .1 mile (.2 km) from where you left US-101.

▣ TILLAMOOK BAY CITY RV PARK *(Open All Year)*

Reservations: (800) 200-2075
Information: (503) 377-2124
Location: 4 Miles (6 Km) N of Tillamook, *N 45° 30' 40", W 123° 52' 31"*, Near Sea Level

46 Sites – The Tillamook Bay City RV Park is one of the nicer and better maintained campgrounds along the highway north of Tillamook. The RV and tent sites are in a grassy well-clipped field. The RV sites are back-ins and pull-thrus to 60 feet. Although the campground is located along US-101 the entrance is off Alderbrook Loop Road which leaves US-101 just .5 mile (1 km) south of Bay City and 4.3 miles (6.9 km) north of Tillamook.

▣ NETARTS RV PARK *(Open All Year)*

Res. and Info.: (503) 842-7774, www.netartsbay.com
Location: 6 Miles (10 Km) W of Tillamook, *N 45° 25' 35", W 123° 56' 18"*, Near Sea Level

83 Sites – This is a nice upscale resort overlooking the ocean at Netarts Bay which is on the ocean west of Tillamook. Sites are in two areas. An older section of the park has sites overlooking the water and also behind the main resort buildings along a canal. Some of these sites will take RVs to 45 feet but many restrict slide-outs. There is also a newer area of the park inland which has long back-in sites that can easily handle large modern RVs with slides. Amenities include boat rentals. To reach the RV park follow SR-6 west from Tillamook. Follow signs for Netarts and as you approach the town you'll see the campground signs pointing to your left. If you miss the sign just continue to Netarts, turn south along the coast, you'll see the RV park on your left in just .5 mile (1 km) from the turn.

CAPE LOOKOUT STATE PARK *(Open All Year)*

Reservations: (800) 452-5687, www.reserveamerica.com
Information: (503) 842-4981, (800) 551-6949, www.oregonstateparks.org
Location: 10 Miles (16 Km) SW of Tillamook, *N 45° 21' 46", W 123° 58' 09"*, Near Sea Level

212 Sites – This is one of the nicer Oregon State coastal campgrounds because the camping area is right next to the wide sandy beach. There are a limited number of hookup sites, only 38 of them. Many sites here exceed 40 feet, some reach 55. There are no pull-thrus and many sites are difficult to access with longer RVs because leave the driveway at a 90-degree angle. To reach the campground follow signs west from Tillamook on 3rd Street which becomes SR-6 or Netarts Highway West. In 4.4 miles (7.1 km) take the left fork at the Y, the road becomes Whiskey Creek Road. Ten miles (16 Km) from Tillamook you'll see the entrance on the right.

SANDBEACH ORV CAMPGROUND *(Open May 1 to Oct 15 - Varies)*

Reservations: (877) 444-6777, www.reserveusa.com
Information: (541) 750-7127
Location: 18 Miles (29 km) W of Tillamook, *N 45° 17' 03", W 123° 57' 18"*, Near Sea Level

101 Sites – Sand Beach is a Siuslaw National Forest campground. It's primarily an ORV (off road vehicle) campground with access to large areas of sandy dunes. This is the northernmost of these ORV campgrounds along the Oregon coast. You'll find several more listed under *Reedsport and the Oregon Dunes* below. There are actually three camping areas in the immediate vicinity. The main campground, Sand Beach, is a normal Forest Service type campground with separated back-in sites to about 45 feet. Many are extra large to allow parking for ATV trailers. There are also two large paved lots called the East Dunes Camp Area and the West Winds Camp Area where overnight camping is allowed in RVs. These two parking-lot style campgrounds cost less

THE TILLAMOOK CHEESE FACTORY

($10 per night) and reservations are not available in them. All three areas have handicapped-accessible restrooms with flush toilets but no hookups. Some of the sites in the main camping area overlook the beach along Sandlake estuary. Access is easiest from US-101 south of Tillamook. Follow Sandlake Road west from its junction with US-101 some 10.5 miles (17 km) south of Tillamook. After 4.4 miles (7.1 km) Sandlake makes a 90-degree turn, the Cape Lookout Road continues straight. Turn left and in 1 mile (2 km) turn right on Galloway Rd. Follow Galloway 2.3 miles (3.7 km) to the campground.

WHALEN ISLAND COUNTY PARK *(Open May 15 to Oct 15 - Varies)*

Res. and Info.: (503) 965-6085
Location: 18 Miles (29 Km) SW of Tillamook, *N 45° 16' 22", W 123° 56' 58"*, Near Sea Level

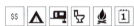

30 Sites – This is a small Coos County campground located along the east side of the Sandlake estuary. Sites are near the water in an open area bordered by trees. Sites are not clearly laid out, people park where you can level the RV or where there is a level spot for the tent. Picnic tables and fire pits are provided. Access is easiest from US-101 south of Tillamook. Follow Sandlake Road west from its junction with US-101 some 10.5 miles (17 km) south of Tillamook. After 4.4 miles (7.1 km) Sandlake makes a 90-degree turn, the Cape Lookout Road continues straight. Turn left and in 3.5 miles (5.6 km) you'll see the campground on the right.

WEBB COUNTY PARK *(Open All Year)*

Res. and Info.: (503) 965-5001, parks@co.tillamook.or.us, www.co.tillamook.or.us/gov/parks
Location: 27 Miles (44 Km) SW of Tillamook, *N 45° 12' 59", W 123° 58' 07"*, Near Sea Level

40 Sites – There is a small cluster of campgrounds located just south of Cape Kiwanda in the town of Pacific City. They are inland from the beach but really just across the highway. This county park is the smallest of them. The sites are back-ins on grass. Some will take RVs to 35 feet although most are shorter and better for smaller RVs and tents. It's a nice little campground. Easiest access is from US-101. From the junction with Brooten Road about 24 miles (39 km) south of Tillamook drive northwest about 2.7 miles (4.4 km) to the center of Pacific City. Jog toward the beach on Pacific Ave and then turn north on Cape Kiwanda Dr. for 1 mile (2 km) to the cluster of campgrounds on your right. This campground is the farthest north of the group.

TIMICHI VILLAGE RV PARK *(Open All Year)*

Res. and Info.: (503) 965-7006, tomichivillagervpark@earthlink.net
Location: 24 Miles (39 Km) SW of Tillamook, *N 45° 12' 57", W 123° 58' 08"*, Near Sea Level

40 Sites – This campground is the second from the north in the cluster of campgrounds north of Pacific City. It's located behind the convenience store. There are large back-in and pull-thru sites that start at 56 feet long, many are much longer. From the junction of US-101 with Brooten Road about 24 miles (39 km) south of Tillamook drive northwest about 2.7 miles (4.4 km) to the center of Pacific City. Jog toward the beach on Pacific Ave and then turn north on Cape Kiwanda Dr for 1 mile (2 km) to the cluster of campgrounds on your right.

CAPE KIWANDA RV RESORT *(Open All Year)*

Res. and Info.: (503) 965-6230, capekiwanda@oregoncoast.com
Location: 24 Miles (39 Km) SW of Tillamook, *N 45° 12' 53", W 123° 58' 07"*, Near Sea Level

155 Sites – The final campground in the cluster at Cape Kiwanda is the largest. It has nice amenities including an indoor pool. There are tent sites here, as well as back-ins and pull-thrus, a few of the latter reach 60 feet. From the junction of US-101 with Brooten Road about 24 miles (39 km) south of Tillamook drive northwest about 2.7 miles (4.4 km) to the center of Pacific City. Jog toward the beach on Pacific Ave and then turn north on Cape Kiwanda Dr for 1 mile (2 km) to the cluster of campgrounds on your right.

BLIMP BASE RV PARK (PORT OF TILLAMOOK CAMPGROUND) *(Open March 15 to Oct 31 - Varies)*

Information: (503) 842-7152, (503) 842-2413, www.potb.org
Location: 2 Miles (3 Km) S of Tillamook, *N 45° 25' 08", W 123° 49' 13"*, Near Sea Level

52 Sites – This is a campground located on the west side of the Tillamook airport. The best-known feature of this airport is the air museum which is located in a huge World War II blimp hanger on the far side of the field – hence the name of the RV park. The campground is gravel roads and sites in an open field. There are picnic tables and fire pits. Not a lot of work was done in constructing the sites or making them useable. Most parking areas are higher than the surrounding ground and pretty narrow but they are as long as 50 feet. Amenities are limited to a restroom building over by the airport gate, several hundred yards away. Still, the price is good, and sites are usually available. There is no access across the airport to the museum, you must drive around to reach it. The campground is located on the east side of US-101 about 2.3 miles (3.7 km) south of Tillamook.

PLEASANT VALLEY RV PARK *(Open All Year)*

Res. and Info.:   (503) 842-4779, www.pleasantvalleyrvpark.com
Location: 6 Miles (10 Km) S of Tillamook, *N 45° 22' 14", W 123° 48' 19"*, 100 Ft

76 Sites – This commercial RV park is one of the nicest in the area. Sites are back-ins and pull-thrus to 60 feet under shade trees. Facilities are in good condition and the park is well run. It's located on the west side of US-101 about 6.3 miles (10.2 km) south of Tillamook.

WALDPORT AND FLORENCE

Waldport (population 2,100) is about 14 miles (23 km) south of Newport. The highway crosses the new Alsea Bay Bridge here, and at the south end of the bridge is the **Alsea Bay Interpretive Center** with displays covering transportation along the coast.

South of Waldport the twenty miles (32 km) between Yachats at Mile 165 and Mile 186 are very scenic. They're in the Siuslaw National Forest. You may want to stop at the **Cape Perpetua Interpretive Center** at Mile 167.3. The center, run by the Forest Service, has exhibits covering the forest and coastline in this area. Nature trails and tide pools are accessible from the center. This is also another popular whale-watching site. There is adequate parking for larger RVs.

Heceta Head Lighthouse is one of the most scenic of the eight along the Oregon coast. You can walk to the lighthouse using a trail that leads from **Heceta Head Lighthouse State Scenic Viewpoint** at Mile 178.3. There is also a bed and breakfast here in the former assistant lighthouse keeper's house, **Heceta House**.

Sea Lion Caves, at Mile 179.3, have long been a do-not-miss stop for travelers along the coast. This is a commercial operation. An elevator drops through the cliff to a lookout window which lets visitors watch a colony of undisturbed Stellar sea lions in a large natural sea cave. In the distance you can also see the Heceta Head Lighthouse to the north. Parking is limited for

RVs, it's best to visit the caves in a tow car or smaller RV. Just north of the caves is a pull-off where you can sometimes see sea lions on the rocks and in the water below. This is also an excellent spot to get a photo of the Heceta Head Lighthouse to the north and to watch for whales.

Florence (population 6,700), originally a lumber mill town, is located near the mouth of the Siuslaw River. It has become an attractive tourist destination, particularly in the **Old Town** area along the waterfront. Like the old towns in several other cities along the coast this one has interesting shops and restaurants, Florence is not a flashy as some. There's also a marina and an RV park run by the port.

The Siuslaw River is navigable for 20 miles (32 km) upstream and fishing for a variety of species is popular.

Golfers will probably appreciate the Sand Pines Golf Course and the Ocean Dunes Golf Links, both take advantage of the rolling dunes in the area.

Florence has a **Rhododendron Festival** during the third week of May.

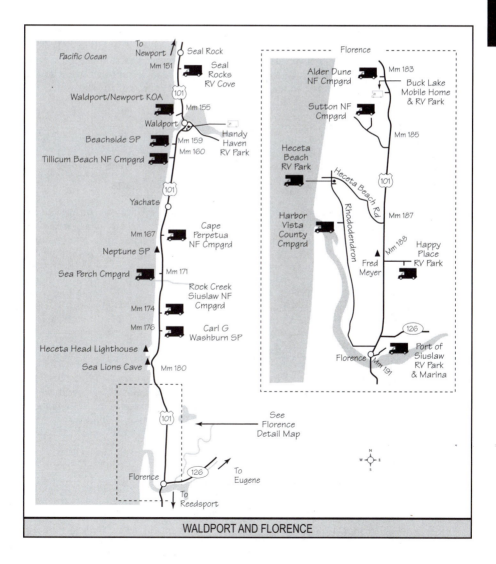

WALDPORT AND FLORENCE

OREGON

⛺ SEAL ROCKS RV COVE *(Open All Year)*

Res. and Info.:   (541) 563-3955, info@sealrocksrv.com, www.sealrocksrv.com
Location: 5 Miles (8 Km) N of Waldport, *N 44° 29' 33", W 124° 04' 57"*, Near Sea Level

44 Sites – This small RV park sits above the highway with ocean views. No two sites are alike. They include tents sites, partial hookup sites, a few pull-thrus, and some long back-ins with full-hookups that will take 45 foot RVs. The RV Park is located on the east side of US-101 near Mile 151 about 9 miles (15 km) south of Newport and 5 miles (8 km) north of Waldport.

⛺ WALDPORT/NEWPORT KOA *(Open All Year)*

Reservations: (800) KOA-3443
Information: (541) 563-2250, orcstkoa@casco.net
Location: 1 Mile (2 Km) N of Waldport, *N 44° 26' 08", W124° 04' 31"*, 100 Ft

91 Sites – The Waldport KOA has a location with fantastic views of Waldport's Alsea Bay bridge just to the south. It's a popular place, reservations are essential all summer long. There is a trail to the beach. Sites here run the usual KOA gamut with cabins, tent sites, back-ins and pull-thrus. Some sites reach 65 feet in length. The campground is on the west side of US-101 just north of Waldport's bridge.

⛺ BEACHSIDE STATE PARK CAMPGROUND *(Open March 1 to Oct 30)*

Reservations: (800) 452-5687, www.reserveamerica.com
Information: (541)563-3220, (800) 551-6949, www.oregonstateparks.org
Location: 3 Miles (5 Km) S of Waldport, *N 44° 22' 56", W 124° 05' 19"*, Near Sea Level

76 Sites – As the name suggests this small state campground is located right next to the beach. Most sites are 40 feet long but maneuvering room is limited so care is required when parking and many sites restrict use of slide-outs. There are no sewer connections and no dump station at this campground. The entrance is on the west side of US-101 near Mile 159. That's 3 miles (4.8 km) south of Waldport.

⛺ TILLICUM BEACH NATIONAL FOREST CAMPGROUND *(Open All Year)*

Reservations: (877) 444-6777, www.reserveusa
Information: (541) 563-3211
Location: 4 Miles (6 Km) S of Waldport, *N 44° 21' 59", W 124° 05' 29"*, Near Sea Level

60 Sites – Tillicum Beach is one of the few national forest campgrounds in this part of the US with electrical hookups, seven of these sites have them. The campground is set just above the beach, access is easy. Sites are back-ins and pull-thrus, many reach 40 feet. The campground is on the west side of US-101 at Mile 160.5. It is 4 miles (6.5 km) south of Waldport.

⛺ CAPE PERPETUA CAMPGROUND *(Open May 20 to Oct 3 - Varies)*

Reservations: (877) 444-6777, www.reserveusa
Information: (541) 563-3211
Location: 11 Miles (18 Km) S of Waldport, *N 44° 16' 56", W 124° 06' 26"*, 100 Ft

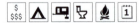

38 Sites – This national forest campground occupies an inland valley south of the Cape

Perpetua and north of Captain Cook Point and the coastal Neptune State Park. Hiking trails run throughout the cape area giving access from the campground to the interpretive center, overlooks, inland trails, and also trails to the ocean. Sites are shorter back-ins for small RVs to about 25 feet. They're all off one long access road that follows Cape Creek up the valley. The campground entrance is near Mile 167, about 11 miles (17.7 km) south of Waldport.

■ SEA PERCH CAMPGROUND (Open All Year)

Res. and Info.:	(541) 547-3505, seaperch@peak.org, www.seaperchrvpark.com
Location:	14 Miles (23 Km) S of Waldport, N 44° 13' 49", W 124° 06' 34", Near Sea Level

38 Sites – The Sea Perch, as you would expect, perches above the ocean. It's a nice little commercial park with good views from almost all the sites and easy access to the beach. Sites are back-ins and pull-thrus to 65 feet. The campground is on the west side of US-101 near Mile 171.

■ ROCK CREEK CAMPGROUND (Open May 20 to Sept 5 - Varies)

Reservations:	(877) 444-6777, www.reserveusa
Information:	(541) 563-3211
Location:	18 Miles S of Waldport, N 44° 11' 05", W 124° 06' 54", Near Sea Level

15 Sites – This little Siuslaw National Forest campground is on the east side of US-101. The sites are all back-ins to 25 feet arranged off a road which runs inland along Rock Creek. Watch for the entrance near Mile 174.

■ CARL G. WASHBURNE STATE PARK (Open May 20 to Sept 5 - Varies)

Information:	(541) 547-3416, (800) 551-6949, www.oregonstateparks.org
Location:	14 Miles (23 Km) N of Florence, N 44° 09' 36", W 124° 06' 47", Near Sea Level

56 Sites – The campground in this smaller state park is on the east side of the highway, there is a day use area and dump station on the beach side. The campground has access to a good trail system including trails north to Cape Perpetua. Sites here are all back-ins and stretch to 57 feet, most are over 40 feet long. The campground is near Mile 176 of US-101 just north of Heceta Head. It's about 20 miles (32 km) south of Waldport and 14 miles (23 km) north of Florence.

■ ALDER DUNE CAMPGROUND (Open May 1 to Sept 30)

Information:	(541) 902-8526
Location:	7 Miles (11 Km) N of Florence, N 44° 04' 10", W 124° 06' 01", Near Sea Level

39 Sites – This Siuslaw National Forest campground is located just east of US-101 between Alder and Dune Lakes. There is a trail around Alder Lake. The dunes nearby can we walked, off-road vehicles are not allowed. Sites are back-ins to 30 feet, many will not accept RVs with slide-outs. The campground is located at Mile 183.5.

■ SUTTON CAMPGROUND (Open All Year)

Information:	(541) 902-8526
Location:	3 Miles (5 Km) N of Florence, N 44° 03' 15", W 124° 06' 27", Near Sea Level

80 Sites – Sutton is another modern Forest Service campground with electrical hookups. There are big sites here, some to 60 feet and many in the 34 to 40 foot range. Trails leave from

the campground to follow Cottonwood Creek, cross Alder Dune to Alder Dune Campground, and also to go to Cottonwood Lake. The campground is located off Sutton Beach Road which goes west from US-101 at Mile 185.5, about 3 miles (5 km) north of Florence. The campground is on the right .7 mile (1.1 km) from the highway.

HARBOR VISTA COUNTY CAMPGROUND *(Open All Year)*

Reservations: (541) 997-5987
Information: (541) 682-2000, www.lanecounty.org/parks
Location: 4 Miles (6 Km) NW of Florence, *N 44° 00' 55", W 124° 07' 30"*, 100 Ft

38 Sites – This is a well-kept county campground with paved sites and electrical hookups. There are vistas from the campground of the coast, but not from the sites. Sites are all back-ins, some as long as 55 feet. To drive to the campground turn west from US-101 on Heceta Beach Road from Heceta Junction, about a mile north of Florence. Follow the road northwest for 1.9 mile (3.1 km) and turn left on North Rhododendron Drive just after passing Heceta Beach RV Park. Now drive 1.2 miles (1.9 km) south on N. Rhododendron and turn right on Jetty Road North, you'll see the campground entrance on the left almost immediately.

HECETA BEACH RV PARK *(Open All Year)*

Res. and Info.:   (541) 997-7664, hecetabeachrvpark@yahoo.com, www.hecetabeachrvpark.net
Location: 3 Miles NW of Florence, *N 44° 01' 58", W 124° 07' 43"*, Near Sea Level

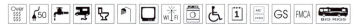

56 Sites – This campground is not on the beach, but you can walk there in about five minutes through a residential neighborhood. The RV park has grassy tent sites. The RV sites here are back-ins and pull-thrus from 50 to 60 feet. They are separated by hedges. A good-size mini-mart is out front, as well as a laundry and a recreation room. To drive to the campground turn west from US-101 on Heceta Beach Road from Heceta Junction, about a mile (2 km) north of Florence. Follow the road northwest for 1.9 miles (3.1 km) and you'll see the campground on the left.

HAPPY PLACE RV PARK *(Open All Year)*

Res. and Info.:   (541) 997-1434, happyplacerv@aol.com,
                    www.touroregon.com/happyplacervpark/index.html
Location: Florence, *N 44° 00' 08", W 124° 05' 59"*, Near Sea Level

64 Sites – Happy Place is a newer RV park designed for big RVs. It's located next to a storage locker facility. Sites are back-ins and pull-thrus, mostly about 55 feet long and separated by strips of grass and shrubs. Watch for the sign on the east side of US-101 on the northern approaches to town.

PORT OF SIUSLAW RV PARK AND MARINA *(Open All Year)*

Res. and Info.:   (541) 997-3040
Location: Florence, *N 43° 58' 08", W 124° 06' 04"*, Near Sea Level

92 Sites – The Port of Siuslaw (Florence) operates this RV park next to their marina. It has a nice location inland from the Old Town, within easy walking distance of the shops and

restaurants there. The restrooms are a little grim but the sites themselves are fine. Tenters have grass and trees away from the water or grass along the bank of the estuary. RV sites are all back-ins and reach 50 feet. Some back up to the water and do not have sewer, some are back-ins on an open area, and others are back-ins in trees. For easiest access follow Nopal Street southeast from US-101 from a point about .3 mile (.5 km) north of the bridge, the turn is marked with a campground sign. In two blocks turn left on 1ˢᵗ and the campground is at the end of the street.

WALLOWA LAKE REGION

The Wallowa Lake Region is located in the far northeast corner of Oregon. Easiest access is from I-84 at La Grande. Take Exit 261 which is marked for Elgin.

Head out of La Grande on Highway 82, this highway takes a few unexpected turns but you will have no problem following it if you just watch for signs for Elgin and then Enterprise. If you zero your odometer when you leave the freeway you'll reach Elgin at 19 miles (31 km), Enterprise at 63 miles (102 km), and Joseph at 70 miles (113 km).

You may want to make two stops in Enterprise before going on to Joseph. Just before you arrive in town you'll pass **the Wallowa Mountains Visitor Center**. A stop here will bring you up to speed on the area's attractions. Then, in Enterprise you'll find the last large supermarket in this neck of the woods, you might stop and pick up groceries for the next few nights.

The small town of Joseph and nearby Wallowa Lake make a very attractive destination. Almost anyone can find something of interest in this area.

Joseph itself is a small town with a population of some 1,300 people. It has become a bit of an art colony in the last few years. The town is known for its bronze foundries that produce bronze statues of all sizes, most with western themes. There are showrooms and you can tour a couple of the foundries, just ask at the showrooms.

The Wallowa Lake area was the traditional summer home of the Nez Percé Indians. You can visit the **Wallowa County Museum** in Joseph to learn more about them. South of town and overlooking the lake you'll find **Chief Joseph's grave**. This is the grave of old Chief Joseph, father of the Chief Joseph who led his people on the "Trail of Tears" toward Canada in 1877.

Wallowa Lake is a 4-mile-long jewel extending from near Joseph back into high mountains. At the south end of the lake is a tourist area with the state park, a couple of private RV campgrounds, miscellaneous attractions for the tourist hordes, and some trail heads for hikes into the Wallowa Mountains. The lake is very popular for water sports of all kinds including water skiing and fishing. The top tourist attraction here must be the **Mount Howard Tram** which lifts visitors to 8,200 feet for several miles of hiking trails and great views in all directions.

Joseph celebrates **Chief Joseph Days** in late July and **Alpenfest** on the third weekend after Labor Day.

MINAM STATE RECREATION AREA *(Open March 1 to Nov 30 - Varies)*
Information: (541) 547-3416, (800) 551-6949, www.oregonstateparks.org
Location: 36 Miles (58 KM) NW of Joseph, *N 45° 38' 13", W 117° 43' 43"*, 2,400 Ft

12 Sites – This is a small campground with a minimum of facilities, more like a traditional national forest campground than most Oregon state parks. It is located next to the Wallowa River, a really beautiful location. You can fish the river for rainbows or use this as an access point for floating the Wallowa and Grande Ronde. Sites a are very large, some to 60 feet, and can take any RV. The 1.5-mile (2.4 km) gravel entrance road leaves SR-82 some 13 miles (21 km) east of Elgin and 20 miles (32 km) west of Lostine.

OREGON

WALLOWA LION'S RV PARK *(Open April 15 to Sept 30 - Varies)*

Location: In Wallowa, 25 Miles (40 Km) NW of Joseph, *N 45° 34' 37", W 117° 32' 09"*, 2,800 Ft

20 Sites – This camping area is little more than a grassy park but the price is right, it's free. There are no hookups but any size RV can park on the grass here and there are port-a-potties. There is also a nearby dump station, also free and also run by the Lions. Donations are accepted. The campground is located toward the northern edge of the small town of Wallowa. You'll see the sign pointing east as you enter town.

WALLOWA RIVER RV PARK *(Open April 15 to Oct 15 - Varies)*

Information: (541) 886-7002, (866) 886-7002, wrrv@uci.net
Location: In Wallowa, 24 Miles (39 Km) NW of Joseph, *N 45° 34' 13", W 117° 31' 21"*, 2,100 Ft

31 Sites – This is a handy small campground at the southern edge of Wallowa. It has 50-foot pull-thru sites and full hookups. At the southern edge of Wallowa where the highway curves to meet 1st Street follow 1st to the east, the campground is on the left in .1 mile.

OUTPOST RV PARK *(Open All Year)*

Res. and Info.:   (541) 426-4027
Location: Enterprise, 7 Miles (11 Km) N of Joseph, *N 45° 26' 16", W 117° 17' 10"*, 3,700 Ft

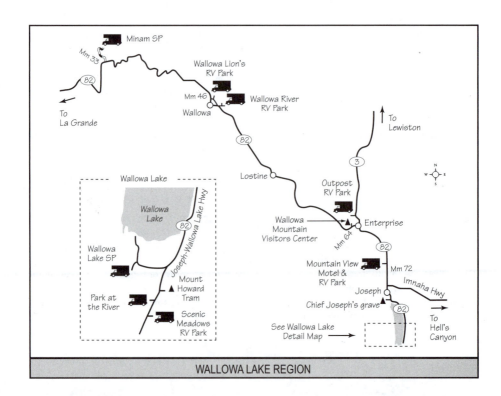

WALLOWA LAKE REGION

30 sites – This park is located on the northern approaches to Enterprise. It has a Western theme and big sites with pull-thrus to 60 feet. From central Enterprise follow SR-3 north toward Lewiston for .9 mile (1.5 km) to the campground, it's on the left overlooking town.

Mountain View Motel and RV Park *(Open All Year)*

Reservations: (866) 262-9891
Information: (541) 432-2982, montainviewmotel@yahoo.com, www.rvmotel.com
Location: 1 Mile N of Joseph, *N 45° 22' 51", W 117° 13' 49"*, 3,900 Ft

30 Sites – The Mountain View is a motel with a good campground in the rear. It's away from the crowds down at the southern end of Wallowa Lake and is the handiest campground for visits to Joseph. Sites are long back-ins that will take RVs to 45 feet with lots of room to park a tow car. Watch for the motel and campground on the west side of the highway about a mile north of central Joseph.

Wallowa Lake State Park *(Open All Year)*

Reservations: (800) 452-5687, www.reserveamerica.com
Information: (541) 432-4185, (800) 551-6949, www.oregonstateparks.org
Location: 6 Miles (10 Km) S of Joseph, *N 45° 16' 51", W 117° 12' 46"*, 4,400 Ft

210 Sites – This state park is actually world famous, National Geographic once chose it as one of the six best state parks in the west. There is lots to do here and the setting is magnificent. There is a boat launch and swimming area along the lake shore. Within walking distance you'll find restaurants, mini-golf, the tram to the top of Mount Howard, horse rides, and go-karts. Sites are very large with many longer than 50 feet. To reach the campground just follow Highway 82 south 6 miles (10 km) from Joseph. The road reaches the lake at 2 miles (3 km), then follows the eastern lake shore for 4 miles (6 km) to the south end. At a Y there go right to the park entrance. This is a very popular park, even during the week you should have reservations or arrive very early in the day.

Park at the River *(Open All Year)*

Res. and Info.: (541) 432-4704, (541) 432-8800, info@eaglecapchalets.com, www.eaglecapchalets.com
Location: 6 Miles (10 Km) S of Joseph, *N 45° 16' 35", W 117° 12' 33"*, 4,400 Ft

59 Sites – This medium-sized RV park is quiet and will take RVs to 50 feet and longer in its well-separated back-in sites. It is affiliated with Eagle Cap Chalets across the street, they have a swimming pool, hot tub, and snack bar available to the folks at the RV park. At the Y at the south end of Wallowa Lake go left, the campground is on the right in .3 mile (.5 km).

Scenic Meadows RV Park *(Open May 1 to Oct 1 - Varies)*

Res. and Info.: (541) 432-9285
Location: 6 Miles (10 Km) S of Joseph, *N 45° 16' 28", W 117° 12' 35"*, 4,400 Ft

19 Sites – A nice little well-run RV park with amenities some will like and others hate including a go-kart track (right next to the camping sites), mini-golf, and horses. Kids love it. Sites are mostly back-ins but there are 4 pull-thrus that will take RVs to 45 feet. Located in the south Wallowa Lake tourist area. From the Y at the south end of Wallowa Lake go left, the campground is on the left in .4 mile (.6 km).

OREGON

Warm Springs and Madras

Ninety-five miles (153 km) after leaving US-205 in Portland and heading southeast across the shoulder of Mt Hood you will reach the town of Warm Springs in the 600,000-acre **Warm Springs Indian Reservation**. You may want to take a break and tour **The Museum at Warm Springs**. It documents the heritage of the tribes that make up the Confederated Tribes of Warm Springs: the Wasco, Paiute and Warm Springs (Walla Walla) Tribes. If you decide to stay a while you can drive north on Hwy 3 to **Kah-Nee-Ta Vacation Resort** which boasts an RV park and a golf course as well as the **Indian Head Gaming Center**, a casino.

In another 14 miles (23 km) along US-26 you will reach Madras and US-97, the east-of-the-Cascades north-south highway. Nearby are several reservoirs that make great camping destinations.

The largest of these is **Lake Billy Chinook**. This reservoir fills a stunning canyon behind Round Butte Dam. The canyon is formed by three rivers: the Deschutes, the Metolius, and the Crooked Rivers. The reservoir has 72 miles (116 km) of shoreline and 4,000 surface acres. Watersports of all kinds are popular in the reservoir and there is fishing for Kokanee, trout, and bass.

Kah Nee Ta High Desert Resort and Casino *(Open All Year)*

Res. and Info.: (541) 553-1112, www.Kahneeta.com
Location: Warm Springs, *N 44° 51' 42", W 121° 12' 01"*, 1,400 Ft

51 Sites – Kah Nee Ta is a very upscale resort with a large RV park adjoining a very nice swimming pool that is fed by hot springs. It's located on the Warm Springs Reservation. There are a number of very colorful teepees that can be rented for camping but other tents are not allowed. The casino is within walking distance and the area has hiking trails too. The campground is very popular with vacationing families since there's so much to do. This is a destination in itself which is good since it's remote from other attractions. Sites in the RV park are large with pull-thrus, the longest site is a little over 70 feet. To reach the campground drive north from Warm Springs on BIA-3 for 11.5 miles (18.5 km). The route is well signed.

Pelton Park *(Open April 20 to Sept 25 - Varies)*

Res. and Info.: (541) 475-0517, peltonpark@pgn.com, www.portlandgeneral.com/parks
Location: 13 Miles (21 Km) NW of Madras, *N 44° 41' 14", W 121° 14' 02"*, 1,500 Ft

70 Sites – This campground is operated by Portland General Electric and the Confederated Tribes of Warm Springs. It is situated on the shore of Lake Simtustus, the reservoir behind Pelton Dam. While some sites here reach 50 feet the maneuvering room is limited and the campground is recommended only for RVs to 40 feet. Amenities include a marina with groceries and a small restaurant as well as a covered cooking area with electric burners that is very handy for tent campers. The campground can be reached from US-26 (the Warm Springs Highway) at a point 4 miles (6 km) southeast of Warm Springs. Turn south on NW Pelton Dam Road and follow it 3.4 miles (5.5 km) to the campground.

Lake Simtustus Park *(Open All Year)*

Res. and Info.: (541) 475-1085, www.lakesimtustusrvresort.com
Location: 15 Miles (24 Km) NW of Madras, *N 44° 40' 27", W 121° 13' 56"*, 1,600 Ft

90 Sites – This campground spills down the steep cliff on the east side of Lake Simtutus. The good access road makes it possible for large RVs to easily reach the terraces and lakeside where there are back-in sites to 40 feet near the lake. This campground also has a dock and boat ramp. Best access for large RVs is from the north. From US-26 (the Warm Springs Highway) at a point 4 miles (6 km) southeast of Warm Springs turn south on NW Pelton Dam Road and follow it 5.0 miles (8.1 km) to the campground.

CROOKED RIVER CAMPGROUND (COVE PALISADES STATE PARK) *(Open All Year)*

Reservations: (800) 452-5687, www.reserveamerica.com
Information: (541) 546-3412, (800) 551-6949, www.oregonstateparks.org
Location: 14 Miles (23 Km) SW of Madras, *N 44° 32' 32", W 121° 15' 20"*, 2,300 Ft

91 Sites – Cove Palisades has two campgrounds and they are so different that we have listed them separately here. This one is located on the east side of the reservoir and is not near the water. It is on a bench well above the lake. Sites are all back-ins in a large grassy field. Many sites

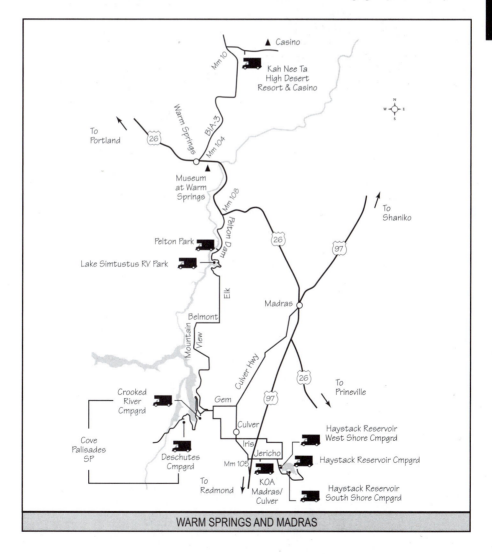

WARM SPRINGS AND MADRAS

OREGON

CAMP IN A TEPEE AT THE KAH NEE TA HIGH DESERT RESORT

are over 40 feet long, some are over 50 feet. The campground is most easily accessed from US-97 some 7 miles (11 km) south of Madras and 15 miles (24 km) north of Redmond. Turn west on SW Iris Lane and drive 2.3 miles (3.7 km). Turn right on SW Feather Drive and drive north for 1.2 miles (1.9 km). Now turn left on SW Fisch Lane for .5 miles (.8 km) and follow it as it turns 90° to the north and becomes SW Frazier Dr. In .5 mile (.8 km) take the left on SW Jordan Rd and follow it another .9 miles (1.5 km) to the park entrance, which is on the left.

DESCHUTES CAMPGROUND (COVE PALISADES STATE PARK) *(Open April 30 to Oct 1 - Varies)*

Reservations:	(800) 452-5687, www.reserveamerica.com
Information:	(541) 546-3412, (800) 551-6949, www.oregonstateparks.org
Location:	19 Miles (31 Km) SW of Madras, *N 44° 32' 20", W 121° 16' 41"*, 2,100 Ft

178 Sites – Deschutes Campground is a little harder to reach than Crooked River but is still accessible to big RVs. It is located down in the canyon on a peninsula between the Deschutes and Crooked River Arms. Sites are back-ins to 60 feet. There is no dump station down there, but some sites do have full hookups. There is a good trail system from the campground. To reach the campground follow the instructions given above for the Crooked River Campground. Drive right by that campground entrance and follow the road for another 4.7 miles (7.6 km) as it winds down into the canyon, follows Crooked Arm south and crosses a bridge to the peninsula and then climbs to the Deschutes Campground entrance.

KOA MADRAS/CULVER *(Open March 1 to Nov 15)*

Reservations:	(800) 562-1992, www.koa.com
Information:	(541) 546-3046, info@madras-koa.com
Location:	11 Miles (18 Km) S of Madras, *N 44° 30' 04", W 121° 10' 42"*, 2,700 Ft

83 Sites – This is a typical KOA with full facilities including a swimming pool. The location is somewhat out of the way for a campground that isn't a destination in itself (for most people anyway) but it's close to the Haystack Reservoir for those folks wanting more than the federal campgrounds there have to offer. Sites here will take big RVs, many are 70-foot pull-thrus. To reach the campground turn east from US-97 some 9 miles (15 km) south of Madras and 15 miles (24 km) north of Redmond on SW Jericho Lane. You'll see the campground on the right in .6 mile (1 km).

🚐 **HAYSTACK RESERVOIR CAMPGROUND** *(Open May 15 to Sept 30 - Varies)*
  Information: (541) 475-9272
  Location: 14 Miles (23 Km) S of Madras, *N 44° 29' 26". W 121° 08' 23"*, 2,800 Ft

24 Sites – This is a Crooked River National Grasslands campground. National grasslands are run by the same folks who run national forests, the USDA Forest Service. The campgrounds here are much like you would expect a national forest campground to be. This campground is set on the shore of a small reservoir known as Haystack Reservoir. There are no hookups but the sites are nice back-ins. The reservoir is popular for both fishing and water sports. This is an open sunny campground with fairly long sites, many to 45 feet. To reach the campground turn east from US-97 some 9 miles (15 km) south of Madras and 15 miles (24 km) north of Redmond on Jericho Lane. Follow the road east for 1.3 miles (2.1 km). Turn right on SW Haystack Drive and follow it for 2.3 miles (3.7 km) as it curves around the south side of the reservoir to the campground entrance which is on the east side of the lake.

🚐 **HAYSTACK RESERVOIR SOUTH SHORE CAMPGROUND** *(Open May 15 to Sept 30 - Varies)*
  Information: (541) 475-9272
  Location: 13 Miles (21 Km) S of Madras, *N 44° 29' 30", W 121° 09' 08"*, 2,800 Ft

40 Sites – The South Shore Campground has poorly defined campsites scattered next to the south shore of Haystack Reservoir. The only amenities are vault toilets. Rings of rocks contain campfires and there are no picnic tables. Any size RV can find a place to boondock here, it's excellent for tent campers. To reach the campground turn east from US-97 some 9 miles (15 km) south of Madras and 15 miles (24 km) north of Redmond on Jericho Lane. Follow the road east for 1.3 miles (2.1 km). Turn right on SW Haystack Drive and follow it for 1.2 miles (1.9 km) as it curves around the south side of the reservoir to the campground entrance.

🚐 **HAYSTACK RESERVOIR WEST SHORE CAMPGROUND** *(Open May 15 to Sept 30)*
  Information: (541) 475-9272
  Location: 12 Miles (19 Km) S of Madras, *N 44° 29' 37", W 121° 09' 36"*, 2,800 Ft

10 Sites – While you could pitch a tent here this is really an RV camping area. RVs park parallel along the shore of the reservoir in a large gravel lot. There's a boat ramp and dock here as well as rings of rocks for fires and a vault toilet. To reach the campground turn east from US-97 some 9 miles (15 km) south of Madras and 15 miles (24 km) north of Redmond on Jericho Lane. Follow the road east for 1.3 miles (2.1 km). Turn right on SW Haystack Drive and follow it for .4 mile (.6 km) as it curves around the west side of the reservoir to the campground entrance.

Information Resources

See out Internet site at www.rollinghomes.com for Internet information links.

Ashland

Ashland Chamber of Commerce, 110 East Main Street (PO Box 1360), Ashland, OR 97520; (541) 482-3486; marypat@ashlandchamber.com

Applegate Trail Interpretive Center, 500 Sunny Valley Loop, Sunny Valley, OR 97497; (541) 472-8545

Grants Pass-Josephine County Chamber of Commerce, 1995 W Vine St (PO Box 970), Grants Pass, OR 97528; (541) 476-7717 or (800) 547-5927; vcb@visitgrantspass.org

Harry and David Country Village, 1314 Center Drive, Suite A, Medford, OR 97501; (541) 864-2278

Oregon Shakespeare Festival, 15 S Pioneer Street, Ashland, OR 97520; (541) 482-2111 for brochure, (541) 482-4331; for tickets, boxoffice@osfashland.org

Wolf Creek Inn, 100 Front St (PO Box 6), Wolf Creek, OR 97497; 541 866-2474

Astoria, Seaside and Cannon Beach

Astoria Visitors Center, 111 W Marine Dr (PO Box 176), Astoria, OR 97103; (503) 325-6311; awacc@seasurf.com

Astoria-Warrenton Highway 101 Visitor Center, 143 S Highway 101, Warrenton, OR 97146; (503) 861-1031

Cannon Beach Information Center, 207 N Spruce St (PO Box 64), Cannon Beach, OR 97110; (503) 436-2623; chamber@cannonbeach.org

Columbia River Maritime Museum, 1972 Marine Drive, Astoria, OR 97103; (503) 325-2323

Flavel House, 441 8th St, Astoria, OR 97103; (503) 325-2203; cchs@seasurf.net

Fort Clatsop National Memorial, 92343 Fort Clatsop Rd, Astoria, OR 97103-9197; (503) 861-2471; focl_superintendent@nps.gov

Seaside Aquarium, 200 N Promenade, Seaside, OR 97138; (503) 373-86211

Seaside Museum and Historical Society, 570 Necanicum Dr, Seaside, OR 97138; (503) 738-7065

Seaside Visitors Bureau, 7 N Roosevelt Drive (PO Box 7), Seaside, OR 97138-6825; (503) 738-6825 or (800) 444-6740; visit@seaside-oregon.com

Baker City and Sumpter

Baker County Visitors and Convention Bureau, 490 Campbell St. Baker, OR 97814; (541) 523-3356; bakervc@oregontrail.net

Greater Sumpter Chamber of Commerce, PO Box 250, Sumpter, OR 97877; (541) 894-2362 or (541) 894-2290

National Historic Oregon Trail Interpretive Center, PO Box 987, Baker City, Oregon 97814-0987; (541) 523-1843; Nhotic_Mail@or.blm.gov

Sumpter Valley Railroad, PO Box 389, Baker City, OR 97814-0389; (541) 894-2268; svrydepot-staff@eoni.com

Bandon

Bandon Chamber of Commerce, 300 SE Second Street (PO Box 1515), Bandon, OR 97411; (541) 347-9616; bandoncc@harborside.com

West Coast Game Park Safari, 46914 Hwy 101, Bandon, OR 97411; (541) 347-3106

Bend and La Pine

Deschutes National Forest, 1001 SW Emkay Drive, Bend, OR 97702; (541) 383-5300

Central Oregon Welcome Center, 63085 N US-97, Bend, OR 97701; (541) 389-8799 or (800) 800-8334

High Desert Museum, 59800 South Hwy 97, Bend, OR 97702; (541) 382-4754

La Pine Chamber of Commerce, 51425 Hwy 97, Suite A (PO Box 616) LaPine, OR 97739; (541) 536-9771; director@lapine.org

Sunriver Area Chamber of Commerce, Sunriver Village, Bldg 0 (PO Box 3246), Sunriver, OR 97707; (541) 593-8149

OREGON

Brookings

Brookings-Harbor Chamber of Commerce, 16330 Lower Harbor Rd (PO Box 940), Brookings, OR 97415; (541) 469-3181; chamber@wave.net

Oregon State Welcome Center, 1650 US-101, Brookings, OR 97415; (541) 469-4117

Camp Sherman and the Metolius River

Deschutes National Forest, 1001 SW Emkay Drive, Bend, OR 97702; (541) 383-5300

Metolius Recreation Association, PO Box 64, Camp Sherman, OR 97730; (541) 595-6117

Cascade Lakes Scenic Byway Loop

Deschutes National Forest, 1001 SW Emkay Drive, Bend, OR 97702; (541) 383-5300

Cave Junction

Illinois Valley Chamber of Commerce Visitor Information Center, 201 Caves Hwy (PO Box 33), Cave Junction, OR 97523; (541) 592-2631 or (541) 592-3326

Oregon Caves Information Station, Oregon Caves National Monument, 19000 Caves Hwy, Cave Junction, OR 97523; (541) 592-2100

Charleston

Bay Area C of C, 50 E Central Ave (PO Box 210), Coos Bay, OR 97420; (541) 269-0215; bacc@ucinet.com

Charleston Information Center, Boat Basin Dr & Cape Arago Hwy (PO Box 5735), Charleston, OR 97420; (541) 888-2311 or (800) 824-8486

South Slough National Estuarine Reserve, PO Box 5417, Charleston, OR 97420; (541) 888-5558

Columbia Gorge

Bonneville Dam Visitor Center, US Corps of Engineers, Cascade Locks, OR 97014-0150; (541) 374-8820

Columbia River Gorge National Scenic Area, USDA Forest Service, 902 Wasco, Suite 200, Hood River, OR 97031; (541) 386-2333

Columbia Gorge Discovery Center, 5000 Discovery Drive, The Dalles, OR 97058; (541) 296-8600

Hood River Chamber of Commerce, 405 Portway Ave, Hood River, OR 97031; (541) 386-2000 or (800) 366-3530

Mount Hood Railroad, 110 Railroad Ave, Hood River Oregon 97031; (541) 386-3556 or (800) 872-4661

Port of Cascade Locks Visitors Center, 355 Wapana St (PO Box 307), Cascade Locks, OR 97014; (541) 374-8619

The Dalles Chamber of Commerce, 404 W 2nd St, The Dalles, OR 97058; (541) 296-2231 or (800) 255-3385; tdacc@gorge.net

Crater Lake National Park

Crater Lake National Park, PO Box 7, Crater Lake, OR 97604; (541) 594-2211

Umpqua National Forest, PO Box 1008, 2900 NW Stewart Parkway, Roseburg, OR 97470; (541) 672-6601

Eugene

Eugene and Lane County Convention and Visitors Association, 115 W 8th, Suite 190 (PO Box 10286), Eugene, OR 97441; (541) 484-5307 or (800) 547-5445; or@cvalco.org

Gold Beach

Gold Beach Visitors Center, 29279 Ellensburg Ave, Gold Beach, OR 97444; (541) 247-7526 or (800) 525-2334; visit@goldbeach.org

Jerry's Rogue Jets, PO Box 1011, Gold Beach, OR 97444; (800) 451-3645 or (541) 247-4571; jerrys@roguejets.com

Mail Boat Hydro-Jet Trips, PO Box 1165, Gold Beach, OR 97444; (800) 458-3511 or (541) 247-7033

Hells Canyon

Snake River Campground Information, Idaho Power Company, PO Box 169, Oxbow, OR 97834; (541) 785-3323

John Day Country

Grant County Chamber of Commerce, 281 Main, John Day, OR 97845; (541) 575-0547 (800) 769-5664; grant@grantcounty.cc

John Day Fossil Beds National Monument, 32651 Hwy 19, Kimberly, OR 97848; (541) 987-2333

Klamath Falls

Favell Museum of Western Art and Indian Artifacts, 125 W Main, Klamath Falls, OR 97601; (541) 882-9996

Klamath Basin National Wildlife Refuge, 4009 Hill Rd, Tulelake, CA 96134; (530) 667-2231

Klamath County Tourism, 507 Main St, Klamath Falls, OR 97601; (800) 445-6728 or (541) 884-0666; tourism@co.klamath.or.us

Kla-Mo-Ya Casino, 34333 Hwy 97 N, Chiloquin, OR 97624; (541) 793-7529

Lava Beds National Monument, PO Box 867, Tulelake, CA 96134; (530) 667-2282

Lakeview and the Outback Scenic Byway

Lake County Chamber of Commerce, 126 North E Street, Lakeview, OR 97630; (541) 947-6040 or (877) 947-6040; info@lakecountrychamber.org

Lincoln City to Newport

Depoe Bay Chamber of Commerce, 630 SE Hwy 101 (PO Box 21), Depoe Bay, OR 97341; (541) 765-2889

Greater Newport Chamber of Commerce, 555 SW Coast Hwy, Newport, OR 97365; (541)265-8801 or (800) 262-7844; chamber@newportnet.com

Lincoln City Visitor & Convention Bureau, 801 SW Hwy 101, Suite 1, Lincoln City, OR 97367; (541) 994-8378 or (800) 452-2151; lcvcbadmin@harborside.com

Maryhill Region

Klickitat County Tourism, Maryhill Hwy, Goldendale, WA 98620; (509) 773-3466

Maryhill Museum of Art, 35 Maryhill Museum Drive, Goldendale, WA 98620; (509) 773-3733; maryhill@maryhillmuseum.org

Nehalem Bay and Manzanita

Nehalem Bay Area Chamber of Commerce, 8th and Tohl St (PO Box 159), Nehalem, OR 97131; (503) 368-5100

Newberry National Volcanic Monument

Lava Lands Visitor Center, 58201 South Hwy 97, Bend, OR 97707; (541) 593-2421

Pendleton

Pendleton Chamber of Commerce, 501 S Main, Pendleton, OR 97801; (541) 276-7411 or (800) 547-8911; Pendleton@pendleton-oregon.org

Pendleton Round-Up, 1205 SW Court (PO Box 609), Pendleton, OR 97801; (800) 457-6336 (541) 276-2553

Wildhorse Casino and Resort, 72777 Hwy 331, Pendleton, OR 97801; (541) 278-2274

Port Orford

Port Orford Chamber of Commerce, 520 Jefferson (PO Box 637), Port Orford, OR 97465; (541) 332-8055; pochamb@harborside.com

Portland

International Rose Test Garden, 400 SW Kingston, Ave, Portland, OR 97201; (503) 823-3636

Oregon City Chamber of Commerce, PO Box 226, Oregon City, OR 97045; (503) 656-1619; ochamber@easystreet.com

Oregon's Mt Hood Territory, 619 High Street, Oregon City, OR 97045; (503) 655-5511

Oregon Museum of Science and Industry, 1945 SE Water Ave, Portland, OR 97214-3354; (503) 797- 4000 or (800) 955-6674

Portland Oregon Visitors Association Visitor Center, 701 SW 6th Ave #1, Portland, OR 97204; (503) 275-8355

Washington Park Zoo, 4001 SW Canyon Rd, Portland, OR 97221; (503) 226-7627

Oregon Museum of Science and Industry, 1945 SE Water Ave, Portland, OR 97214-3354; (503) 797- 4000 or (800) 955-6674

Prineville

Ochoco National Forest, 3160 NE 3rd St, Prineville, OR 97754; (541) 416-6500

Prineville-Crook County Chamber of Commerce, 390 Fairview, Prineville, OR 97754; (541) 447-6304

Redmond and Sisters

Redmond Chamber of Commerce, 446 SW 7th, Redmond, OR 97756; (541) 923-5191; rcc@empnet.com

Sisters Area Visitor Information Center, 164 N Elm Street (PO Box 430), Sisters, OR 97759; (541) 549-0251; chamber@outlawnet.com

Reedsport and the Oregon Dunes

Oregon Dunes National Recreation Area Visitor Center, 855 Highway 101 S, Reedsport, OR 97467; (541) 271-3611

Reedsport/Winchester Bay Chamber of Commerce, 855 Hwy Ave (PO Box 11), Reedsport, OR 97467; (541) 271-3495 or (800) 247-2155; reewbycc@harborside.com

Siuslaw National Forest, 4077 SW Research Way (PO Box 1148), Corvallis, Oregon 97339; (541) 750-7000

Roseburg and the Umpqua Valley

Colliding Rivers Information Center, 18782 N Umpqua Hwy, Glide, OR 97443; (541) 496-0157

Douglas County Museum of History and Natural History, PO Box 1550, Roseburg, OR 97470; (541) 957-7007

Roseburg Visitors and Convention Bureau, 410 SE Spruce (PO Box 1262), Roseburg, OR 97470; (541) 672-9731 and (800) 444-9584

Wildlife Safari, 1790 Safari Road, Winston, OR 97496: (541) 679-6761

Salem

Enchanted Forest, 8462 Enchanted Way SE, Turner, OR 97392; (503) 363-3060 or (503) 371-4242

Salem Convention & Visitors Association, 1313 Mill St SE, Salem, OR 97301; (800) 874-7012 or (503) 581-4325; information@travelsalem.com

Visitor Services, Oregon State Capitol, Salem, OR 97310; (503) 986-1388

Tillamook and the Three Capes Loop

Pacific City Chamber of Commerce, PO Box 331, Pacific City, OR 97135; (503) 965-6161

Tillamook Chamber of Commerce, 3705 Hwy 101 N, Tillamook, OR 97141; (503) 842-7525; till-chamber@wcn.net

Waldport and Florence

Florence Area Chamber of Commerce, 270 Hwy 101 (PO Box 26000), Florence, OR 97439; (541) 997-3128 or (800) 524-4864

Waldport Chamber of Commerce, 620 NW Spring St, Waldport, OR 97394; (541) 563-2133

Yachats Area Chamber of Commerce and Visitor Center, 241 Hwy 101 (PO Box 728); Yachats, OR 97498; (541) 547-3530 or (800) 929-0477; info@yachats.org

Wallowa Lake Region

Wallowa County Chamber of Commerce, 107 SW 1st, Enterprise, OR 97828; (541) 426-4622 (800) 585-4121; wallowa@eoni.com

Wallowa Mountains Visitor Center (National Forest Service), 88401 Hwy 82, Enterprise, OR 97828; (541) 426-5546

Warm Springs and Madras

Crooked River National Grassland, 813 SW Hwy 97, Madras, OR 97741; (541) 475-9272

Museum at Warm Springs, 2189 Hwy 26, Warm Springs, OR 97761; (541) 553-3331

Jefferson County Chamber of Commerce, 274 SW 4th St (PO Box 770); Madras, OR 97741; (541) 475-2350 or (800) 967-3564; coc@madras.n

WASHINGTON

British Columbia

WASHINGTON

IDAHO

Sandpoint and Lake Pend Orielle
Pg 251

Coeur d'Alene
Pg 194

Spokane
Pg 272

Moscow, Pullman and the Palouse
Pg 227

WASHINGTON
IDAHO

Grand Coulee
Pg 203

Lake Pateros Region
Pg 221

Moses Lake and the Potholes
Pg 229

Winthrop and the Methow Valley
Pg 284

Chelan
Pg 188

Wenatchee
Pg 277

Yakima River Canyon
Pg 289

North Cascades National Park
Pg 240

Leavenworth
Pg 225

Ellensburg
Pg 196

Lake Wenatchee and Fish Lake Recreation Area
Pg 224

Cle Elum and Roslyn
Pg 191

Yakima and the Yakima Valley
Pg 267

Maryhill Region (OR)
Pg 128

Bellingham
Pg 186

Skagit Valley
Pg 269

Whidbey Island
Pg 281

Lake Easton and Lake Kachees
Pg 219

Mt Rainier National Park
Pg 232

WASHINGTON
OREGON

Columbia Gorge (OR)
Pg 94

Seattle
Pg 261

Tacoma
Pg 275

Mt St Helens National Volcanic Monument
Pg 237

Port Townsend
Pg 256

Sequim
Pg 267

Kitsap Peninsula and Bainbridge Island
Pg 216

Olympia
Pg 247

Port Angeles and the North Olympic Park
Pg 248

Hood Canal
Pg 208

Westport
Pg 279

Ilwaco and Long Beach
Pg 213

British Columbia
WASHINGTON

Forks and the Western Sections of Olympic National Park
Pg 197

Ocean Shores and the North Beaches Area
Pg 243

WASHINGTON
OREGON

Chapter 5 - Washington

Like the rest of the Pacific Northwest Washington State has a mild but wet west and a dry eastern half. The Cascade Mountains make the difference as they isolate the eastern half of the state from the influence of the Pacific Ocean.

Washington state has three National Parks. These are the Olympic National Park, the North Cascades National Park, and Mt Rainier National Park. At first glance these all seem to be parks celebrating mountains, but that's not entirely true. The Olympic National Park has a section that encompasses a great deal of the Pacific coast of the state.

While this chapter is titled *Washington* we have also included a few northern Idaho destinations. We just couldn't bring ourselves to leave them out.

REGIONS AND THEIR CAMPGROUND RESOURCES

Olympic Peninsula

The dominating feature of the Olympic Peninsula is the Olympic Mountains that occupy the center. These mountains make up the largest portion of Olympic National Park. The mountainous interior is circled by a mostly two-lane highway. It's a good road so there's decent access to the entire peninsula.

The Olympic Peninsula is remote, it's also pretty wet. Those two characteristics make the area a great camping destination. It's important to know that the amount of rainfall varies a lot depending upon where you are in relation to the mountains. Along the western front of the range it's so wet that the area is considered a rain forest. On the east and northeast side of the mountains there's a lot less rain. The town of Sequim is known for the fact that it sits in the "rain shadow" of the Olympic Mountains.

The Olympic Peninsula destinations in this book ring the mountains. Traveling counterclockwise they are as follows: • *Port Townsend,* • *Sequim,* • *Port Angeles and the North Olympic National Park,* • *Forks and the West Border of Olympic National Park.*

Pacific Coast

Washington's Pacific coast isn't nearly as well known as Oregon's. That means it's usually not nearly so crowded. There are good campgrounds along the coast, including some great state parks. The water's a little cooler than farther south but the coast is wilder and just as much fun to visit. Here are the coastal destinations from north to south: • *Ocean Shores and the North Beaches Area,* • *Westport,* • *Ilwaco and Long Beach,* • *Forks and the West Border of Olympic National Park.*

Puget Sound

The most populous area of Washington State is the Puget Sound region. That doesn't mean that you can't camp here. You'll find lots of spots in the many less dense areas, many near a saltwater beach. And don't forget that you can camp when you visit the cities too. From north to south here are the destinations in this chapter in the Puget Sound area and along the I-5 corridor: • *Bellingham,* • *Skagit Valley,* • *Whidbey Island,* • *Kitsap Peninsula and Bainbridge Island,* • *Hood Canal,* • *Seattle,* • *Tacoma,* • *Olympia.*

Cascade Mountains

Just as they do in Oregon to the south, Washington's Cascade mountains measure about 80 miles (130 km) from west to east. Those in Washington are even more rugged and impenetrable that those farther south. There are only four east-west highway crossings (five counting along the Columbia River). One of these, the North Cascades Highway, is closed by snow in winter. Major mountains in the Washington Cascades include Mt Baker (10,778 ft.), Mt Rainier (14,408 ft.), Mt Adams (12,307 ft.) and Mt St Helens (8,364 ft.). Two of the state's three national parks are also located in the Cascades. These are the Cascade Mountains destinations in this book listed from north to south: • *North Cascades National Park,* • *Winthrop and the Methow Valley,* • *Chelan,* • *Lake Wenatchee and Fish Lake Recreation Area,* • *Leavenworth,* • *Lake Easton and Lake Kachess,* • *Cle Elum and Roslyn,* • *Mt Rainier National Park,* • *Mt St Helens National Volcanic Monument.*

East of the Cascades

Eastern Washington is a popular summer destination because the weather is reliably good and the Columbia River and its reservoirs provide a way to keep cool. Most of eastern Washington is in the Columbia Basin, the huge area drained by the Columbia River. Many of the destinations listed in this book are actually located along the river, or at least close by. The Columbia is dammed along almost its entire length, it's really a series of big lakes. Destinations in Washington state east of the Cascades are the following: • *Winthrop and the Methow Valley;* • *Lake Pateros Region;* • *Chelan;* • *Wenatchee;* • *Grand Coulee;* • *Ellensburg,* • *Moses Lake and the Potholes;* • *Spokane;* • *Yakima and the Yakima Valley;* • *Yakima River Canyon;* • *Moscow, ID, Pullman, WA, and the Palouse.*

Northern Idaho

We've included a few destinations in this book that are really in Idaho, not Washington. They're great places to visit, it would be a shame to leave them out just because they're in Idaho. These destinations are: • *Coeur d'Alene;* • *Sandpoint and Lake Pend Oreille;* • *Moscow, ID, Pullman, WA, and the Palouse.*

GOVERNMENT LANDS AND THEIR CAMPGROUNDS

Washington State Campgrounds

Washington state has one of the best campground systems in the country. Like those in Oregon, most Washington campgrounds offer hookups as well as restrooms with flush toilets and hot showers. Many campgrounds can handle big rigs. These state campgrounds are the best choice for a place to spend the night in many destination areas. In addition to individual campsites many parks offer group areas, cabins, platform tents, or yurts.

WASHINGTON

Washington state campgrounds always charge for showers, they use coin boxes that take quarters. The campgrounds only accept credit cards if there is a manned entry booth. If a self-pay system is in effect credit cards are not accepted.

The website for Washington state parks is at www.parks.wa.gov. It's a nice website with descriptions of the campgrounds. You can also get information about the state campgrounds by calling the overall information number of (360) 902-8844. Each park can also be called although these numbers are not always monitored, the telephone numbers are listed in our individual campground descriptions.

Reservations for state parks can be made by calling (888) CAMPOUT ((888) 226-7688) or by using the state reservation website (www.camis.com/wa). A fee of $7.00 is charged for each reservation no matter how many days it covers. Only 48 of the 79 state campgrounds that have individual campsites accept reservations, we tell you which ones do in the individual entries in this chapter. At most campgrounds reservations are only accepted for individual campsite camping during the period from May 15 to September 15, reservations are not considered necessary during the remainder of the year. Only Deception Pass, Cape Disappointment, Grayland Beach, Ocean City, Pacific Beach, Steamboat Rock and Fort Worden accept year-round reservations. Pearrygin Lake accepts individual campsite reservations from April 15 to October 31 and Dosewallips accepts them from May 1 to September 30. Reservations can be made as much as 9 months in advance or as little as 1 day before arrival date.

There are a few state campsites that do accept reservations but that are not included in the overall reservation system. The only one listed in this book is Fort Worden which accepts reservations for the Lower Campground year-round and for the Upper Campground from February 14 to November 30. This state park does not accept telephone reservations, only reservations by mail, email, or fax. See the individual Fort Worden listing in this chapter for details about this park.

Washington State offers state campground discounts for state residents who have reached the age of 62 years. This Off-Season Senior Citizen Pass costs $50 and gives free camping from October 1 to March 31 and from Sunday through Thursday in April. You'll still have to pay $6 for electricity.

Federal Campgrounds

Washington state has a lot of federal land and many federal campgrounds. They fall into the categories of national park campgrounds, national forest campgrounds, and BLM campgrounds.

The three national parks in Washington are the Olympic National Park, the North Cascades National Park, and Rainier National Park. Campgrounds in these parks are listed under *Port Angeles and North Olympic National Park, Forks and West Olympic National Park, Hood Canal, North Cascades National Park, and Mt Rainier National Park.* The park service also administers the Roosevelt National Recreation Area above Grand Coulee Dam, you'll find a campground in this area listed in the *Grand Coulee* section.

Washington has many national forests including Wenatchee, Olympic, Gifford Pinchot, Mt Baker-Snoqualmie, and Okanogan. You'll find national forest campgrounds listed in the following destination sections: *Cle Elum and Roslyn, Forks and the Western Sections of Olympic National Park, Hood Canal, Lake Easton and Lake Kachess, Lake Wenatchee and Fish Lake Recreation Area, Leavenworth, Port Angeles and Northern Olympic National Park, Rainier National Park, Winthrop and the Methow Valley.*

Northern Idaho national forests include the Kaniksu National Forest, see the *Sandpoint and Lake Pend Oreille* section for a campground in this forest.

BLM campgrounds described in this chapter are all located in the *Yakima River Canyon* section.

See the Oregon chapter for general information about reservations in federal campgrounds. Each individual campground description in this chapter tells whether reservations are available and gives you the information necessary to make them.

WASHINGTON

DESTINATIONS AND THEIR CAMPGROUNDS

BELLINGHAM

Whatcom County's largest town and the farthest north major city along the I-5 corridor is Bellingham (population 67,000). Founded in 1852 as a sawmill town Bellingham has gone through phases as a coal town, a gold stampede supply town, a railroad town, and a fishing and salmon-packing town. Today it's the home of Western Washington University and also the southern terminus of the Alaska Marine Highway System.

The center for tourist activities in Bellingham is **Fairhaven** on the south side of the city. It's also the port for the Alaska ferries. Fairhaven is most easily reached from I-5 by taking Exit 250 and heading west on the Old Fairhaven Parkway. From June to September there is a farmer's market in Fairhaven on Wednesdays.

North from Fairhaven along the waterfront there is quite a bit of recent tourist development to replace the older industries that are disappearing from the city. There are waterfront trails, a new luxury hotel, a marina, restaurants, and waterfront parks.

South from the Fairhaven district is **Chuckanut Drive**. This narrow highway along a steep hillside overlooking Samish Bay was opened in 1896. It was the main route for travelers from the south and was famous as a very scenic road. Today it's too narrow for big RVs, anything over 18,000 pounds GVW is not allowed and drivers of wide-bodied RVs will be uncomfortable when they meet traffic. The scenic, narrow section only extends 10 miles (16 km) south of Bellingham, then you're in the flats of the Skagit Valley.

Bellingham has an interesting museum, the regional **Whatcom Museum of History and Art** which in addition to historical displays also has some natural history exhibits. Bellingham is a good place to take **water tours**. Perhaps you could catch the Alaska State Ferry up the Inside Passage as a deck passenger. If you don't have time for that you might instead try a day-long boat

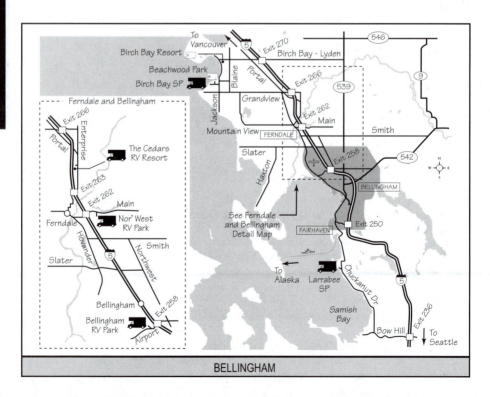

BELLINGHAM

tour through the San Juan Islands to Victoria, B.C. and back.

Tent campers will find Bellingham a bit of a challenge with the two nearest state parks pretty far from the center of things. Larrabee State Park is probably the best bet but The Cedars is a possibility with easy access even if it's pretty far north of town. Big rig campers are well taken care of by the commercial campgrounds, all are good for them. The state parks, however, don't service big rigs very well in this area.

BIRCH BAY STATE PARK *(Open All Year)*

Reservations: (888) 226-7688, www.camis.com/wa
Information: (360) 371-2800, (360) 902-8844, www.parks.wa.gov
Location: 20 Miles (32 Km) N of Bellingham, *N 48° 54' 11", W 122° 45' 38"*, Near Sea Level

167 Sites – This state park campground occupies a ridge overlooking the beach at the south side of Birch Bay. Along the beach is a day-use area where it is possible to swim and a boat launch. Most sites here are non-hookup but there is an area with 15 hookup sites (a few with sewer) in the North Campground for RVs to about 30 feet. There are larger sites, including some pull-thrus but no hookups, for RVs to 35 feet in the South Campground. Some sites reach 55 feet but maneuvering room limits accessibility. From I-5 take Exit 266 and follow Grandview Road (SR-548) westward for 5.8 miles (9.4 km). Turn right onto Jackson Road and then in .8 mile (1.3 km) turn left into Helweg Road. The campground entrance is just ahead.

THE CEDARS RV RESORT *(Open All Year)*

Res. and Info.: (360) 384-2622
Location: 9 Miles (15 Km) N of Bellingham, *N 48° 52' 14", W 122° 35' 07"*, Near Sea Level

170 Sites – The Cedars is a very nice resort for tents and RVs conveniently located just north of Ferndale with easy freeway access. Most sites are pull-thrus of about 50 feet in length. Amenities include seasonal swimming pool, instant-on telephone at the sites, and Wi-Fi. From I-5 take Exit 263 and drive north on Portal Way. The campground will be on your left in .9 mile (1.5 km).

NOR'WEST RV PARK *(Open All Year)*

Res. and Info.: (360) 384-5038, nwrvferndale@aol.com
Location: 7 Miles (11 Km) N of Bellingham, *N 48° 50' 45", W 122° 34' 11"*, Near Sea Level

27 Sites – This modern, small and tidy RV park is very popular. Reservations are necessary all through the summer months. Sites are paved back-ins and pull-thrus, mostly about 50 feet long. From I-5 take Exit 262 and follow Main Street east for .3 mile (.5 km). The campground entrance is on the right.

BELLINGHAM RV PARK *(Open All Year)*

Reservations: (888) 372-1224
Information: (360) 752-1224, bellrvpark@msn.com, www.BellinghamRVPark.com
Location: Bellingham, *N 48° 47' 15", W 122° 31' 12"*, 100 Ft

56 Sites – The most convenient park to Bellingham is this new big-rig park just off the free-way. All of the sites here are 65-foot pull-thrus. Restrooms are exceptionally nice. Take Exit 258 from I-5 as it passes through Bellingham. You'll spot the park on the south side of the freeway.

🚐 LARRABEE STATE PARK *(Open All Year)*

Reservations:	(888) 226-7688, www.camis.com/wa
Information:	(360) 676-2093, (360) 902-8844, www.parks.wa.gov
Location:	5 Miles (8 Km) S of Bellingham, *N 48° 39' 13", W 122° 29' 25"*, 100 Ft

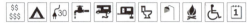

85 Sites – This state campground is located south of Bellingham at the north end of Chuckanut Drive. It's a venerable campground, in fact it was the first Washington state park. Sites here are arranged off a narrow loop. Although there are some pull-thrus here to 70 feet they are narrow and sloping. Limited maneuvering room makes this campground only suitable for RVs to 30 feet. The campground must be approached from the north if you are in an RV because Chuckanut Drive to the south is very narrow and long rigs are restricted. From I-5 take Exit 250. Drive west on Old Fairhaven Parkway for 1.2 miles (1.9 km) until you reach Chuckanut Drive North. Turn south and you'll reach the campground in 5.1 miles (8.2 km).

CHELAN

The town of Chelan (population 3,500) occupies a moraine at the south end of 55-mile-long (89 km) **Lake Chelan**. Chelan is mostly known for two things in Washington state, its apples and the lake which is a popular recreation destination for folks from far around. In fact, most weekends during the summer find Chelan packed with visitors, many from west of the mountains.

During spring, summer, and fall the area's **apple orchards** are hard to miss. There are about 10,000 acres planted in Red Delicious, Golden Delicious, and other varieties. One of the best things about Chelan is that popular as it is with tourists, the orchards remain an important part of the economy and the atmosphere here. Chelan apples are thought to be better than those grown in many other locations because the lake tends to moderate the temperatures in the valley.

LAKE CHELAN IS POPULAR FOR ALL WATER SPORTS

WASHINGTON

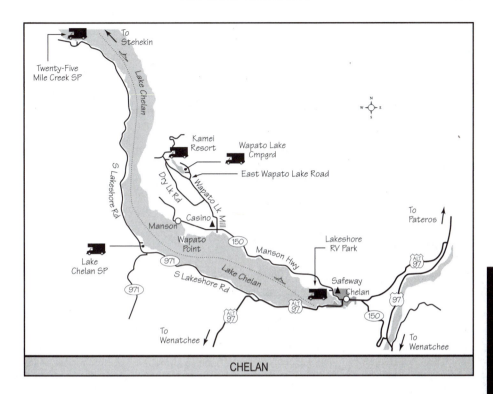

CHELAN

One of the best places to see apples is on the slopes above **Manson**, located about 8 miles (13 km) up the east shore of the lake from Chelan. The town promotes a 16-mile (26 km) **scenic driving loop** that offers views of the lake, orchards, and surrounding area. It's also an excellent bicycle route. Manson hosts two apple-related festivals during the year: the **Manson Apple Blossom Festival** is in early May and the **Manson Harvest Festival** is in the middle of October. There's also a **casino** nearby.

The deep and narrow lake winds its way back into the Cascades, the far north end is actually inside the North Cascades National Park Service Complex. One of the popular things to do in Chelan is to take a ferry ride to **Stehekin** which is at the north end of the lake. These ferries do not carry vehicles. At least one boat each day leaves in the morning and returns in the afternoon, in summer more boats operate and there is even a high-speed catamaran making two trips each day. A one-way trip on the cat takes only an hour and 15 minutes. In Stehekin you can wander around the isolated little town or take one of several tours offered to visitors. Stehekin is an important access point to the North Cascades National Park, there is a park information center and a shuttle bus to help you access nearby campgrounds and trails.

Chelan itself has a full plate of both sports and cultural related attractions. During the year the town hosts events related to arts and crafts, hang gliding, music, mountain biking, fine arts, hydro racing, running and fishing. There should be something for everyone.

At the south end of the lake near Chelan the main focus on the lake is water sports. You have a choice of personal water craft, water skiing, even sailing. The water is a little chilly, even in the middle of the summer, but the air is warm so no one seems to mind.

Chelan in the summer is a very busy place. Reservations are highly recommended. The Lakeshore and Lake Chelan State Park are the big campgrounds in the area. Both are good for tent camping although the state park is best. For big rigs the Lakeshore is the most popular choice. Sometimes during the week there is room up above Manson at the Kamei and Wapato Lake campgrounds when everything else is full. They're also much quieter and more pleasant when things are busy, but they're not near Lake Chelan either.

LAKESHORE RV PARK *(Open All Year)*

Res. and Info.:   (509) 682-8023, www.chelancityparks.com
Location: Chelan, *N 47° 50' 41", W 120° 01' 28"*, 1,200 Ft

163 sites – The largest and most convenient of the Chelan campgrounds is located right in town on the shore of the lake. This is a city campground, it's very nice. The park has restrooms with hot showers, a swimming beach, tennis courts and a playground. Best of all, it's just a short stroll to the center of town as well as a nearby Safeway. Sites are back-ins and pull-thrus, some will take rigs to 60 feet. Rates are considerably less expensive during shoulder and off seasons. The campground is on the lakeshore near where the road heads out to Manson. If you follow signs for Manson from any of the entrances to Chelan you'll see it on your left as you start out of town.

KAMEI RESORT *(Open Late April to Labor Day - Varies)*

Res. and Info.:   (509) 687-3690
Location: 10 Miles (16 Km) N of Chelan, *N 47° 55' 17", W 120° 10' 31"*, 1,300 Ft

50 sites – Kamei is a small private campground located alongside Wapato Lake in the hills above Lake Chelan. It's good for RVs to about 35 feet. The campground is located in a beautiful area full of apple orchards and fishing in the small lake can be pretty good. There's a boat ramp and boat rentals. To reach Kamei Resort head out of Chelan along the lakeshore toward Manson. Turn right in 5.8 miles (9.4 km) on Wapato Lake Road at what would be about Mile 1.5 on the mileposts. You'll pass the Mill Bay Casino and in 3.6 miles (5.8 km) see the campground on your right.

WAPATO LAKE CAMPGROUND *(Open April 15 to Sept 15)*

Res. and Info.:   (509) 687-6037, Manson_parks@manson.org, www.lakechelan.com/mansonparks
Location: 9 Miles (15 Km) N of Chelan, *N 47° 54' 48", W 120° 09' 13"*, 1,300 Ft

50 sites – This is a small lakeside City of Manson park located at the southeast end of little Wapato Lake, the same lake that Kamei Resort borders. Some spaces here will take RVs to 35 feet. Pets are limited, none are allowed on major holidays and only one pet per site is allowed at other times. Some of these sites are waterfront, it's a nice little park with decent facilities. A boat ramp is next door and there is a swimming beach at the park. To reach Wapato Lake Campground head out of Chelan along the lakeshore toward Manson. Turn right in 5.8 miles (9.4 km) km) on Wapato Lake Road at what would be about Mile 1.5. You'll pass the Mill Bay Casino and in 2.3 miles (3.7 km) see East Wapato Lake Road going right. Turn right and in another .2 miles (.3 km) you'll see the campground on your left.

LAKE CHELAN STATE PARK *(Open All Year)*

Reservations: (888) 226-7688, www.parks.wa.gov
Information: (509) 884-8702, (360) 902-8844, www.parks.wa.gov
Location: 9 Miles (15 Km) W of Chelan, *N 47° 52' 26", W 120° 11' 59"*, 1,200 Ft.

144 sites – The maximum RV size that will comfortably fit in this very popular state park is about 30 feet. There's a swimming beach and a boat launch, the campground is located 9 miles (15 km) from Chelan up the western shore of the lake. In is an extremely popular campground, reservations are a must all summer long.

🚐 TWENTY-FIVE MILE CREEK STATE CAMPGROUND *(Open March 31 to Oct 9 - Varies)*

Reservations: (888) 226-7688, www.camis.com/wa
Information: (509) 687-3710, (360) 902-8844, www.parks.wa.gov
Location: 20 Miles (32 Km) NW of Chelan, *N 47° 59' 33", W 120° 15' 34"*, 1,200 Ft

68 sites – This state campground is at the end of the road that goes up the west side of Lake Chelan. There is a small boat harbor here with a boat ramp as well as a small store alongside the ramp. The entrance road is steep but paved and some sites will take RVs to 35 feet although most people using this campground are in smaller rigs or tents. To reach the campground just drive SR-971 up the west side of the lake, the campground is at about Mile 10, some 9.7 miles (15.6 km) beyond Lake Chelan State Park.

CLE ELUM AND ROSLYN

Little Cle Elum (population 1,800), is located where I-90 departs the Cascade Mountains as it heads east. This is Ponderosa pine country, with a much sunnier and dryer climate than just a few miles to the west. Just 2 miles (3 km) northwest of Cle Elum is little Roslyn (population 1,000), close enough that they are really almost one community. The main service center is Cle Elum which is near the freeway and has shopping and restaurants including a supermarket.

These towns began at the end of the 19th century as coal-mining communities. Even today you can see evidence of this, particularly in Roslyn where the immigrant cemetary dating from its mining days is one of the attractions.

Today this area is actually beginning to be a bit of a bedroom community for Seattle, 80 miles (130 km) away across Snoqualmie Pass. It's a 1.5 hour drive, assuming that snow doesn't slow you to a stop in the pass during the winter. Some folks can live with that, the trade-off is

WASHINGTON

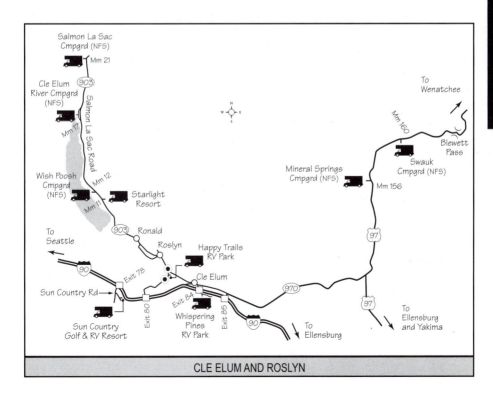

CLE ELUM AND ROSLYN

more winter sunshine. For other Seattle-area residents this is a great place for a weekend get-a-way.

Rosalyn is probably best known today as the setting for the television series Northern Exposure. Although the town of Cicily was supposed to be in Alaska the show was actually filmed here. You'll probably recognize several of the shooting locations.

From Cle Elum the Wenatchee National Forest is very accessible. SR-903 goes north through Roslyn and then Ronald for many miles. It's known as the Salmon La Sac Road and three of the forest service campgrounds listed below are located along the road. From Cle Elum it's 25 miles (40 km) northeast to Blewett Pass on US-97. This busy highway connects with the Wenatchee Valley and passes through the national forest. Two forest service campgrounds along this highway as it climbs to the pass are listed below, there are many dirt roads allowing access to back country from US-97.

Tent campers here will be attracted by the Wenatchee National Forest campgrounds, all a bit out of town but in attractive settings in the woods. None of the forest service campgrounds are good for really big rigs. If you have one of them the place to go is the Whispering Pines, it's conveniently located just off the freeway. If you're a golfer, however, you'll probably want to stay at the Sun Country Golf and RV Resort. The best big rigs forest service sites are at Salmon La Sac, but exercise caution.

WHISPERING PINES RV PARK *(Open All Year)*

Res. and Info.: (509) 674-7278, whisperingpines@cjb.net, www.whisperingpines.cjb.net
Location: Cle Elum, *N 47° 11' 21", W 120° 56' 12"*, 2,000 Ft

35 sites – The Whispering Pines is a new campground set up for modern big rigs with both full hookup and partial hookup sites. Nearby is a RV parts store and service facility run by the same owners, very convenient. The campground is located on the south side of Interstate 90. Westbound on I-90 take Exit 84 and then turn left and go south .2 miles (.3 km) to the campground. Eastbound on I-90 there is no Exit 84 so you should continue on to Exit 85. A U-turn is difficult so just drive into Cle Elum and in 2.3 miles (3.7 km) from the exit turn left at the stoplight onto Oaks Avenue and follow it across the railroad tracks and freeway to the campground, a distance of .6 miles (1 km) from the stoplight.

SUN COUNTRY GOLF AND RV RESORT *(Open April 15 to Oct 15 - Varies)*

Res. and Info.: (509) 674-2226
Location: 5 Miles (8 Km) W of Cle Elum, *N 47° 11' 15", W 121° 03' 02"*, 1,900 Ft

25 sites – This small 9-hole golf resort also has RV sites. While there are 25 back-in sites with parking on grass only about four are suitable for longer coaches because the front of the sites drop off making leveling very difficult. To reach the campground take Exit 78 from I-15, about 5 miles (8 km) west of Cle Elum. Drive south .1 mile (.2 km) to Sun Country Road (also called Nelson Siding Road). Turn left and follow the road .4 miles (.6 km) up and over a hill to the golf resort.

HAPPY TRAILS RV PARK *(Open All Year)*

Res. and Info.: (509) 649-2937
Location: 2 Miles (3 Km) W of Cle Elum, *N 47° 12' 22", W 120° 58' 52"*, 2,100 Ft

16 Sites – This small campground is conveniently located between Cle Elum and Roslyn. It's only suitable for self-contained rigs because there are no facilities other than the very large paved back-in sites. Easiest access to the campground is from Exit 80 of I-90. Turn north toward

Roslyn and in 2.5 miles (4 km) you'll see the campground on the right.

STARLIGHT RESORT *(Open All Year)*
  Res. and Info.: (509) 649-2222
  Location: 9 Miles (15 Km) NW of Cle Elum, *N 47° 16' 27", W 121° 04' 27"*, 2,300 Ft.

15 Sites – The Starlight Resort is a restaurant and convenience store with a few RV sites on the hillside at the rear. Although some sites have full hookups the ones available for traveler use are usually electricity-only back-in sites. The only restrooms are in the convenience store and are not available when it is closed, there are no showers. The campground is on the east side of the Salmon La Sac Road near Mile 11 about 5 miles (8 km) north of Roslyn.

WISH POOSH CAMPGROUND *(Open May 1 to Sept 30 - Varies)*
  Information: (509) 674-4411
  Location: 10 Miles (16 Km) NW of Cle Elum, *N 47° 16' 47", W 121° 05' 10"*, 2,100 Ft

39 sites – This Wenatchee National Forest campground is located on the shore of Cle Elum Lake. The campground has a large boat ramp area and a swimming beach. Some sites have room for RVs to 40 feet but maneuvering room is limited and access for really big rigs is difficult so the campground is best for RVs to 30 feet. The campground is located on the west side of the Salmon La Sac Road near Mile 12 about 5 miles (8 km) north of Roslyn.

CLE ELUM RIVER CAMPGROUND *(Open May 1 to Sept 30 - Varies)*
  Information: (509) 674-4411
  Location: 15 Miles (24 Km) NW of Cle Elum, N *47° 21' 02", W 121° 06' 19"*, 2,300 Ft

19 sites – This is a smaller campground with the sites all back-ins off one road that runs parallel to the Salmon La Sac Road about 100 yards away. Sites overlook the flood plain of the Cle Elum River but it is too far in the distance to enjoy and not visible from the sites. The campground is located on the west side of the Salmon La Sac Road near Mile 17 about 10 miles (16 km) north of Roslyn.

SALMON LA SAC CAMPGROUND *(Open May 1 to Sept 30 - Varies)*
  Reservations: (877) 444-6777, www.reserveusa.com
  Information: (509) 674-4411
  Location: 18 Miles (29 Km) N of Cle Elum, *N 47° 24' 14", W 121° 05' 52"*, 2,300 Ft

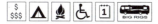

112 Sites – Salmon La Sac is a very large campground with sites that can be reserved so it is a poplar place. One of the loops has some large pull-thru sites suitable for RVs to 40 feet. The campground is located on the west side of the Salmon La Sac Road near Mile 21 about 14 miles (23 km) north of Roslyn.

SWAUK CAMPGROUND *(Open May 1 to Sept 30 - Varies)*
  Information: (509) 674-4411
  Location: 21 Miles (34 Km) NE of Cle Elum, *N 47° 19' 44", W 120° 39' 27"*, 3,000 Ft

25 Sites – This small Forest Service campground is located along US-97, the Blewett Pass highway between Cle Elum and the Wenatchee Valley. Road noise is a definite problem here. The sites are located off a small loop beyond a rest area, they are suitable for RVs to 25 feet. The

campground is located near Mile 160, about 21 miles (34 km) northeast of Cle Elum.

 MINERAL SPRINGS CAMPGROUND *(Open May 1 to Sept 30 - Varies)*

Information: (509) 674-4411
Location: 17 Miles (27 Km) NE of Cle Elum, *N 47° 17' 24", W 120° 41' 58"*, 2,700 Ft

$$$ ▲ ♨

7 Sites – Another very small Forest Service campground right next to US-97, the Blewett Pass highway between Cle Elum and the Wenatchee Valley. It's very near the highway so road noise is a problem. Sites are small and suitable for RVs to 25 feet. The campground is located near Mile 156, about 17 miles (27 km) northeast of Cle Elum.

COEUR D'ALENE, IDAHO

Coeur d'Alene (population 38,000), located on the north shore of Lake Coeur d'Alene, is a friendly-sized city in a beautiful lakeside setting. It has long been a tourist destination and offers a good selection of restaurants and shopping. Coeur d'Alene is only 30 miles (48 km) east of Spokane, Washington on Interstate 5.

Beginning with the construction of the 18-story **Coeur d'Alene Resort** on the lakeshore in town in 1986 local businessman Duane Hagadone has almost single-handedly developed the town into an international destination. A related development is the **Coeur d'Alene Resort Golf Course** just east of town. Don't miss a walk through the resort and along the waterfront.

Another golf attraction in the area is the **Circling Raven Golf Club** in Worley, about 26 miles (42 km) south of Coeur d'Alene on US-95.

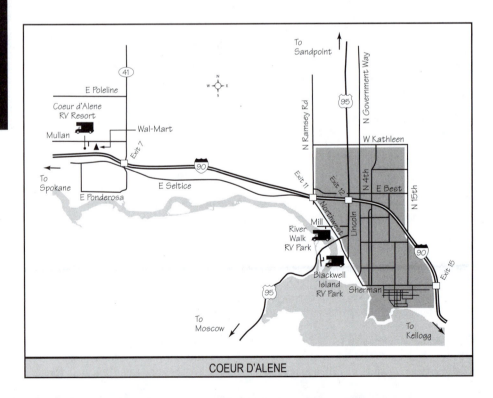

COEUR D'ALENE

The big attraction, though, must be the lake. **Lake Coeur d'Alene** is a huge alpine lake extending 25 miles (40 km) from north to south. It's popular for all sorts of waters sports, from houseboats to kayaking. You'll see an amazing collection of watercraft on the lake on any warm summer day.

The drive around the lake is popular too. Take I-5 east 7 miles (11 km) to Exit 22. Turn south on little two-lane SR-97. This road follows the eastern shoreline south for 36 miles (58 km) to join SR-3 before reaching St Maries. **St Maries** is known for the wild-rice grown in the neighborhood. You better stop and pick some up before heading east on SR-5 along the short south shore and then north on US-95 back to Coeur d'Alene. US-97 doesn't follow the lake shore so it's not very scenic. A much longer but more scenic alternate to get back to town would be to follow SR-3 southeast from St Maries to meet SR-6. Drive southwest through Harvard, Princeton, and Potlatch to catch US-95 north again to Coeur d'Alene. All together this route is 175 miles (282 km), it makes a long day. An alternate would be to spend the night at one of the RV parks listed in this book under *Moscow, Pullman and the Palouse.*

RIVER WALK RV PARK *(Open All Year)*

Reservations:	(888) 567-8700	
Information:	(208) 765-5943	
Location:	Coeur d'Alene, *N 47° 41' 26", W 116° 48' 05",* 2,100 Ft	

43 Sites – This is the smallest of the Coeur d'Alene parks listed in this book and also the closest to the lakefront in town. It's small but well run and maintained. Sites here can handle only a few RVs to 40 feet but most will take 36 footers. Reservations are recommended. From I-90 take Exit 11 and head south toward the center of town. In .7 mile (1.1 km) turn right onto W. Mill Ave., the campground entrance will be on your left almost immediately.

BLACKWELL ISLAND RV PARK *(Open April 15 to Oct 15)*

Reservations:	(888) 571-2900	
Information:	(208) 665-1300	
Location:	1 Mile (1.6 Km) W of Coeur d"Alene, *N 47° 40' 50", W 116° 48' 09",* 2,100 Ft	

172 Sites – This is a new big-rig campground with big sites to 70 feet and lots of maneuvering room located just across the Spokane River from central Coeur d'Alene. This is a riverfront campground and amenities include a beach, a boat dock, a boat ramp, and a meeting room. Easiest access from I-90 is to take Exit 12 and head south on Lincoln Way which is also US-95. In .7 mile (1.1 km) turn right on West Walnut Avenue (also US-95) and follow it for .7 mile (1.1 km) across the river. Just beyond the river you'll see the big RV park on your left and the entrance road.

COEUR D'ALENE RV RESORT *(Open All Year)*

Res. and Info.:	(208) 773-3527	
Location:	7 Miles (11 Km) W of Coeur d'Alene, *N 47° 42' 50", W 116° 54' 45",* 2,100 Ft	

189 Sites – Despite the name this huge RV park is in Post Falls, about 6 miles (10 km) east of Coeur d'Alene. This is a big-rig park with lots of large pull-thrus and back-ins. The stand-out amenity is the building which houses the offices, restrooms, lounge area and indoor swimming pool. Also nice is the nearby Wal-Mart. To reach the park take Exit 7 from I-90 and drive north on SR-41 for .2 miles (.3 km). Turn left on East Mullan Avenue and drive .8 miles (1.3 km), past the Wal-Mart, to the campground entrance which is on the left.

ELLENSBURG

Ellensburg (population 16,500) is probably best known for its Labor Day celebration, the Ellensburg Rodeo. It's in the center of the ranching area in western Washington. It's also a college town, home of the Central Washington University.

Ellensburg, once you get downtown away from the freeway, is a nice little town. You'll want to visit the **Clymer Western Art Museum** and take a look at the **Ellensburg Bull** statue on 4th and Perl. There's also a cowboy one block up on fifth. The **university campus** is just at the northeast edge of the central district and offers a **Japanese garden** and an **art gallery**.

On Labor day there's the **Ellensburg Rodeo**, but at the same time there's the **Kittitas County Fair**. Both are held in the fairgrounds just east of downtown and stretching northward. Another popular event is the **Ellensburg National Art Show and Auction** in late May.

All of the campgrounds listed below are fairly near town but the only one that lets you easily wander around the center in the evening is the fairgrounds. That's where we stay.

🚐 DAYS INN (E&J RV RESORT) *(Open All Year)*

Reservations: (888) 889-9870
Information: (509) 933-1500, www.randrresort.com
Location: Ellensburg, *N 46° 58' 14", W 120° 32' 08"*, 1,500 Ft

79 Sites – This campground behind a Day's Inn is a very large paved lot with long sites, many are pull-thrus. It has lots of amenities including instant-on telephone hookups at the sites. Take Exit 109 from I-10. Drive south for .2 mile (.3 km) and turn left onto Berry Road just beyond the Flying J truck stop. In another .1 mile (.2 km) you'll see the hotel and campground on the left.

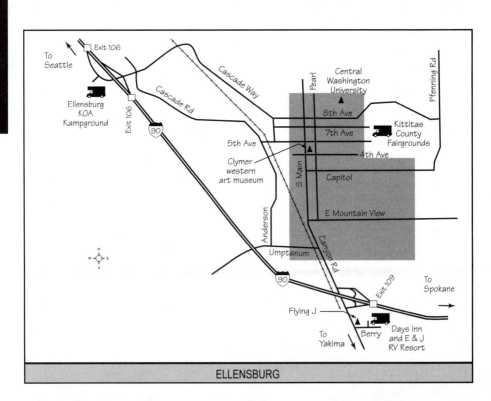

ELLENSBURG

ELLENSBURG KOA KAMPGROUND *(Open All Year)*

Res. and Info.: (509) 925-9319, ellensburgkoa@hotmail.com, cwww.koa.com
Location: Ellensburg, *N 47° 00' 20", W 120° 35' 40"*, 1,500 Ft

140 Sites – This is an older KOA but it has a very nice location next to the Yakima River. Take Exit 106 from I-90. Turn south and immediately you'll see the KOA entrance on your left.

KITTITAS COUNTY FAIRGROUNDS *(Open All Year)*

Reservations: (800) 426-5340
Information: (509) 962-7639, fairgrounds@co.kittitas.wa.us, www.co.kittitas.wa.us/fairgrounds
Location: Ellensburg, *N 46° 59' 52", W 120° 32' 01"*, 1,600 Ft

200 Sites – This is a great place to stay if there are no events in progress. Call to find out. The fairgrounds has lots of hookup sites with electricity and water in many locations, but the ones used by travelers are back-in sites with parking on grass. Restroom facilities including showers are nearby. The fairgrounds are within easy walking distance of the center of town. Easiest access is from Main Street in the center of downtown. Drive east on 7th Ave. At the east end you'll find a big paved parking lot, park here and go find the office to check in. The office is at the west edge of the fairgrounds between 5th and 6th and is open until 5 p.m. If the office is closed folks generally just park and pay in the morning.

FORKS AND THE WESTERN SECTIONS OF OLYMPIC NATIONAL PARK

When logging was going full blast Forks (population 3,200) was known as the logging capital of the Olympic Peninsula. It probably still is the capital but the tourist industry is getting more and more important to the local economy. This might seem surprising since Forks is the rainiest town in the state with an annual rainfall of over 100 inches. Forks is the center of an interesting region on the western border of the Olympic National Park. From Forks there is good access to an otherwise isolated coastal section of the park as well as the rain forests on the western slope of the Olympic Mountains.

The town of **Forks** lines both sides of US-101. You'll find several restaurants as well as a good-sized supermarket, the best places to get supplies on the northwest side of the peninsula. There is also a **National Park Information Center**. South of town is the **Forks Visitor's Center** and next door the **Forks Timber Museum**. Forks holds an annual celebration during the week ending with the **Fourth of July**, it has traditional logging contests as well as a fun run and other activities.

From US-101 just north of Forks a 14-mile (23 km) paved road runs west to the coast. At the end of the road is the Quileute Indian town of **La Push**. Just before reaching La Push you'll see parking areas for the National Park's **Third Beach** and **Second Beach**. You must hike to these beaches, 1.3 miles (2 km) to Third and .5 miles (.8 km) to Second. **First Beach** is accessible from La Push itself.

About 11 miles (18 km) along the road from Forks to La Push you'll reach **Mora Junction**. If you turn north here you'll be able to follow a road leading past the big national park campground called Mora to **Rialto Beach**. Rialto Beach is located just across the Quillayute River outlet from La Push, it is one of the most scenic of all Washington State beaches and is known for its accumulation of driftwood.

If you travel north from Forks and then west along the Strait of Juan de Fuca you'll reach the Makah Indian fishing town of **Neah Bay**. This is the home of the **Makah Cultural and**

Research Center, one of the best such museums in the U.S. You can drive on past Neah Bay to the **Cape Flattery Lookout** which offers impressive views of the rocky coast at the most northwesterly point in the Lower 48. From the road out to Neah Bay another road goes south to **Ozette Lake**. There's a small National Park Service campground at the end of the road and a parking lot. From there you can walk on boardwalks 3 miles (5 km) out to the coast and then, if you're ambitious, north or south for many miles.

Also easily accessible from Forks is the Olympic National Park's **Hoh Rain Forest**. Drive south from Forks for 12 miles (19 km), then turn east on the Upper Hoh Road. This 18-mile (29 km) paved road leads to the Olympic National Park's Hoh Rain Forest Visitor Center. There is a large national park campground near the visitor center and there are several very good hiking trails allowing you to wander through one of the very few temperate rain forests in the world.

South from the Hoh River Valley Cut-off US-101 soon curves west to the coast. For about 12 miles (19 km) it runs along the ocean with frequent parking areas and trails leading short distances down the hill to the beach. **Ruby Beach**, the farthest north, is a good place to stop and walk down to the beach. Those red pebbles on the beach are not rubies, they're garnets. The island offshore is Destruction Island, it has its own lighthouse.

Watch for the **Kalaloch Lodge** above the beach just off the road, the Kalaloch Campground is nearby, so is **Kalaloch Visitor Information Center**. Consider taking a break here and looking around, you might decide to stay. The highway soon turns inland and passes through Queets. The gravel **Queets River Road** leads inland for 14 miles (23 km) from an intersection about 8 miles (13 km) east of Queets on US-101 giving access to trails and also a primitive campground inside the park.

The Lake Quinault area provides visitors with very accessible rain forest access. The lake itself is actually part of the Quinault Indian Reservation but south of the lake is Olympic National Forest land and the north is Rainier National Park land. There are several campgrounds along the south shore of the lake. A **trail system** on the hillside above provides an excellent way to get out in the rain forest among the tall trees on trails that are fun but not too challenging. The **world's largest Sitka Spruce** is just east of the Lake Quinault Rain Forest Village. The south shore is also home to the venerable Lake Quinault Lodge, built in 1926 and certainly worth a look-through.

There's quite a selection of campgrounds in this region. Where you stay will probably depend upon your interests. Tent campers will enjoy all of the national park campgrounds. Many of these will also take RVs but have no hookups. For those who don't need hookups and whose rigs aren't too large the Washington Department of Natural Resources campgrounds are priced right. Commercial parks in the area are a good alternative for RVers who must have hookups, several will take the largest rigs.

🚐 **FORKS 101 RV PARK** *(Open April 15 to Oct 15 - Varies)*

    Reservations: (800) 962-9964
    Information: rzornes@centurytel.net, www.forks-101-rv-park.com
    Location: Forks, *N 47° 56' 31", W 124° 23' 06"*, 300 Ft

36 Sites – This is a commercial campground right in Forks. If you want to be in town, this is the place. There are back-ins and pull-thrus to over 60 feet. A large grocery store is right across the road. Watch for the campground on the east side of the highway near the south end of town.

🚐 **MORA CAMPGROUND** *(Open All Year)*

    Information: (360) 565-3130
    Location: 13 Miles (21 Km) W of Forks, *N 47° 55' 00", W 124° 36' 24"*, Near Sea Level

PILES OF DRFITWOOD ON RIALTO BEACH

94 Sites – This large Olympic National Park campground sits in a grove of huge hemlocks and Sitka spruces along the Quillayute River some two miles (3 km) from the coast at Rialto Beach. A few sites in the campground will take RVs to 35 feet with careful maneuvering. Most sites, however, are best for RVs to 25 feet. Give up the hook-ups for a night to appreciate the big trees and lush vegetation of this part of the state. It is located right off the road to Rialto Beach, you can't miss it.

THREE RIVERS RESORT *(Open All Year)*

Res. and Info.: (360) 374-5300, threerivers@centurytel.net, www.forks-web.com/threerivers
Location: 9 Miles (15 Km) W of Forks, *N 47° 54' 47", W 124° 32' 03"*, 100 Ft

19 Sites – This little resort has rental cabins, gas sales, a convenience store and a restaurant. It is located at the confluence of the Quillayute, Sol Duc, and Bogachiel Rivers and is popular with fishermen, guided fishing trips are offered. There are RV and tent camping sites in a grove of trees to the rear. Some sites have electricity and water hookups, a few have sewer, others have no hookups. They vary in size but some will take RVs to 40 feet. To reach the campground head west on the La Push Road (SR-110). It leaves US-101 about 1 mile (2 km) north of Forks. The campground is located right where Mora Road to Rialto Beach goes right 7.8 miles (12.6 km) from US-101.

LONESOME CREEK STORE AND RV PARK *(Open All Year)*

Res. and Info.: (360) 374-5267, (800) 487-1267, www.ocean-park.org
Location: La Push, *N 47° 54' 13", W 124° 37' 48"*, Near Sea Level

42 Sites – This is a full-hookup big-rig campground that is right on the beach in La Push. This is an open beach, popular with surfers. Two nearby beaches are accessible via good hiking

WASHINGTON

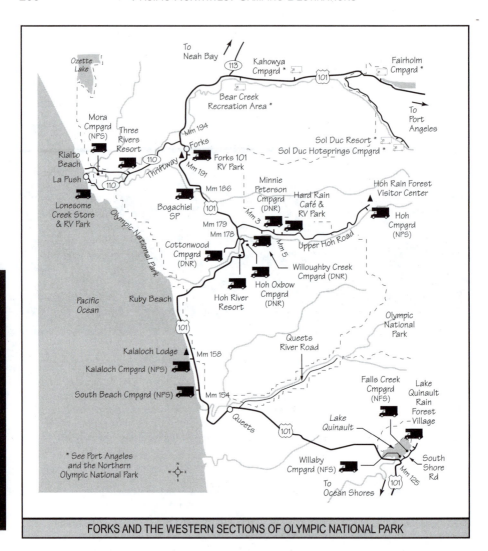

FORKS AND THE WESTERN SECTIONS OF OLYMPIC NATIONAL PARK

trails. Sites are back-ins to 45 feet. Restrooms are located at the back of the store, a long walk from the sites. Their use is not limited to campground residents and they were dirty when we visited. To reach the campground head west on the La Push Road (SR-110). It leaves US-101 about 1 mile (1.6 km) north of Forks. The campground is located near the entrance to La Push, 13.6 miles (21.9 km) from US-101.

BOGACHIEL STATE PARK *(Open All Year)*

Information: (360) 374-6356, (360) 902-8844, www.parks.wa.gov
Location: 5 Miles (8 Km) S of Forks, *N 47° 53' 39", W 124° 21' 51"*, 200 Ft

42 Sites – Many of the campgrounds nearby, including those out along the upper Hoh Road, do not have dump stations or showers. Bogachiel is where those campers come for both of those services. The campground has tent and RV sites although only six have hookups. Although some of the sites exceed 40 feet in length, the lack of maneuvering room limits users

of this campground to rigs of about 35 feet. The dump station is accessible to larger rigs. The campground is located off US-101 about 5 miles (8 km) south of Forks and 7.5 miles (12 km) north of the cutoff to the Upper Hoh Road.

WILLOUGHBY CREEK WASHINGTON STATE DEPARTMENT OF NATURAL RESOURCES CAMPGROUND *(Open All Year)*

Information: (800) 264-0890
Location: 16 Miles (26 Km) SE of Forks, *N 47° 49' 20", W 124° 11' 48"*, 200 Ft

3 Sites – This is a very small campground with only three sites. It's right next to the Upper Hoh Road on the bank of the Hoh River. There is no drinking water at the campground. Sites will take RVs to 30 feet although you'll probably have to back in the short distance from the highway. Watch for the campground on the south side of the Upper Hoh Road 3.6 miles (5.8 km) from US-101.

MINNIE PETERSON WASHINGTON STATE DEPARTMENT OF NATURAL RESOURCES CAMPGROUND *(Open All Year)*

Information: (800) 264-0890
Location: 17 Miles (27 Km) SE of Forks, *N 47° 49' 08", W 124° 10' 28"*, 200 Ft

8 Sites – The eight sites in this campground are off a loop road. It's a nice tent-camping campground and will also take RVs to about 30 feet. There is no drinking water at the campground. The campground is on the north side of the Upper Hoh Road 4.7 miles (7.6 km) from US-101.

HARD RAIN CAFÉ AND RV PARK *(Open All Year)*

Res. and Info.: (360) 374-9288, hardraincafe@olypen.com
Location: 18 Miles (29 Km) SE of Forks, *N 47° 49' 01", W 124° 09' 14"*, 200 Ft

20 Sites – The Hard Rain is a small rural store and restaurant with a few tent and 13 RV sites in the rear. These are back-ins that will take any size rig, half have electric and water and the remainder are full hookups. There is also a restroom with shower. The campground is located on the north side of the Upper Hoh Road 5.8 miles (9.4 km) from US-101 and 12.1 miles (19.5 km) from the end of the road at the Hoh Rain Forest Visitor Center.

HOH CAMPGROUND *(Open All Year)*

Information: (360) 565-3130, www.nps.gov/olym/
Location: 31 Miles (50 Km) SE of Forks, *N 47° 51' 34", W 123° 56' 10"*, 500 Ft

88 Sites – This campground is adjacent to the Hoh Rain Forest Visitor Center and trails. It's a great place to stay and enjoy the area. Expect rain! Sites are off three loops and there are back-ins and pull-thrus that will accept RVs to 35 feet. The campground is 18 miles (29 km) from US-101.

COTTONWOOD WASHINGTON STATE DEPARTMENT OF NATURAL RESOURCES CAMPGROUND *(Open All Year)*

Information: (800) 264-0890
Location: 17 Miles (27 Km) S of Forks, *N 47° 46' 48", W 124° 17' 28"*, 100 Ft

9 sites – This campground is located some distance from US-101 and requires driving on a little gravel but it's really pretty convenient. The nine sites are off two loops. No potable water is provided. Although some sites are as long as 55 feet a lack of maneuvering room makes 35 feet the practical maximum. The campground is located off the Lower Hoh Road. This road leaves US-101 13.7 miles (22.1 km) south of Forks, about 1.2 miles (1.9 km) south of the junction for the Upper Hoh Road. Follow the paved road southwest for 2.1 miles (3.4 km). Then turn left on a gravel road and follow it .8 mile (1.3 km) to the campground.

HOH OXBOW WASHINGTON STATE DEPARTMENT OF NATURAL RESOURCES CAMPGROUND *(Open All Year)*

Information:	(800) 264-0890
Location:	14 Miles (23 Km) S of Forks, *N 47° 48' 34", W 124° 14' 58"*, 200 Ft

7 Sites – This campground is located inside an oxbow turn of the Hoh River and right next to US-101. There is no drinking water at the campground. Sites are located off a loop, a few of the back-ins will take RVs to 35 feet and there is one pull-thru of about the same length. Some sites are along the river. The campground entrance is on the east side of the highway about 14.4 miles (23.2 km) south of Forks.

HOH RIVER RESORT *(Open All Year)*

Res. and Info.:	(360) 374-5566, www.hohriverresort.com
Location:	16 Miles (26 Km) S of Forks, *N 47° 47' 23", W 124° 15' 02"*, 100 Ft

23 Sites – This is an older campground behind a country convenience store with gas pumps. It's very popular with fishermen. Sites are in an open area. They are back-ins that will take RVs to 40 feet. The resort is on the west side of US-101 some 15.6 miles (25.2 km) south of Forks.

KALALOCH OLYMPIC NATIONAL PARK CAMPGROUND *(Open All Year)*

Reservations:	(800) 365-2267, http://reservations.nps.gov
Information:	(360) 565-3130, www.nps.gov/olym
Location:	33 Miles (53 Km) S of Forks, *N 47° 36' 46", W 124° 22' 30"*, 100 Ft

170 Sites – This Olympic National Park campground has a desirable location above a wild beach. It has tent and RV sites suitable for RVs to 35 feet and is very convenient to the highway. The campground is located within walking distance of the Kalaloch Inn and Park Service Information Center. Note that although you can drive through this part of the park without paying the national park entrance fee, if you stay at the campground you'll have to pay it. The campground is near Mile 158 of US-101, about 33 miles (53 km) south of Forks and 61 miles (98 km) north of Hoquiam.

SOUTH BEACH OLYMPIC NATIONAL PARK CAMPGROUND *(Open May 15 to Sept 30 - Varies)*

Information:	(360) 565-3130, www.nps.gov/olym
Location:	36 Miles (58 Km) S of Forks, *N 47° 33' 56", W 124° 21' 35"*, Near Sea Level

Approx. 100 Sites – South Beach serves as a sort of overflow to nearby Kalaloch campground. We actually like it better. It's a large open bench above the beach. Parking is on grass and gravel. Since sites are not delineated any size rig will fit. There are picnic tables and fire pits as well as a restroom building with flush toilets. The campground is located 3.4 miles (5.5 km) south of Kalaloch Campground and is just a short distance off US-101 overlooking a great beach.

LAKE QUINAULT RAIN FOREST VILLAGE *(Open All Year)*
Res. and Info.: (800) 255-6936, (360) 288-2535, mail@rfv.com, www.rainforestresort.com
Location: 69 Miles (111 Km) S of Forks, *N 47° 28' 31", W 123° 49' 52"*, 200 Ft

31 Sites – This resort has been here on the south shore of beautiful Lake Quinault for many years. It is located just down the road from famous Lake Quinault Lodge. All spaces are back-in ones with room for big rigs. A word of warning about winter camping at this campground. The sites sit very near the lake and in winter the lake level sometimes rises to cover them. It is hard for them to forecast when this might happen, if the lake is up the campground is closed. It is best to call ahead to check. To reach the campground just follow the South Shore Road from Mile 125.5 of US-101. The resort is about 3.2 miles (5.2 km) from the highway.

FALLS CREEK CAMPGROUND *(Open Memorial Day to Labor Day - Varies)*
Information: (360) 288-2525
Location: 68 Miles (110 Km) S of Forks, *N 47° 28' 10", W 123° 50' 42"*, 200 Ft

31 Sites – This is a small Olympic National Forest campground just .2 miles (.3 km) east of Lake Quinault Lodge. Vehicle access is very cramped, sites here are best for tent campers and rigs to 16 feet. There are walk-in tent sites in addition to the vehicle sites. To reach the campground follow South Shore Road from Mile 125.5 of US-101 for 2.4 miles (3.9 km) to the entrance.

WILLABY CAMPGROUND *(Open Memorial Day to Sept 30 - Varies)*
Information: (360) 288-2525
Location: 67 Miles (108 Km) S of Forks, *N 47° 27' 44", W 123° 51' 27"*, 200 Ft

34 Sites – Like Falls Creek this is an Olympic National Forest campground for tents and smaller rigs to 21 feet. Access is better than at Falls Creek because sites are located along a paved loop road. There's a boat ramp here. To find the campground follow South Shore Road from Mile 125.5 of US-101 for 1.6 (2.6 km) miles to the entrance.

GRAND COULEE

As you drive into the town of Coulee Dam from the north you couldn't possibly miss the massive dam spanning the river valley ahead. **Grand Coulee Dam** was one of the big government programs of the 1930's. It was a huge project with several aims. It was to provide work for thousands of men. It was to provide irrigation water for an extensive area. And it was to provide lots of electricity. Today there are 11 dams on the Columbia south of the Canadian border. This is the largest of them and by far the most impressive. It also provides a benefit that may not have been deemed to be very important by its planners and builders, the dam has created two huge lakes that are recreation areas in a region that almost always has beautiful weather during the summer.

The large lake behind the dam is known as **Roosevelt Lake**. Access to this lake from the Grand Coulee Dam area is limited. There is one federal campground on the lake near the dam with road access, but road access to the remainder of Roosevelt Lake requires that your travel eastward and detour away from the lake.

There is a second more convenient lake, however. **Banks Lake**, created as part of the Grand Coulee irrigation scheme, dominates recreation in the area. It stretches some 30 miles (48 km) south from Grand Coulee's towns, and is shallow enough to become quite warm in summer. Banks Lake attracts water sports lovers from all over the state.

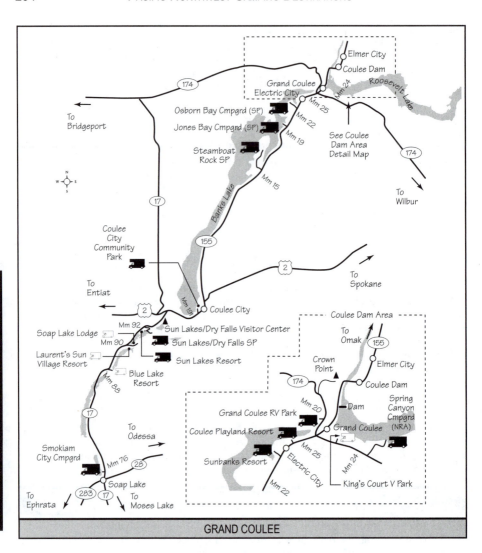

GRAND COULEE

There are actually four towns surrounding the dam. **Coulee Dam** (population 1,000) is sit-uated below the dam, **Elmer City** (population 300) is downstream along the Columbia (north). **Grand Coulee** (population 900) and **Electric City** (population 1,000) are just above the dam along the shore of Banks Lake (south).

The dam provides the focus for many tourist activities in the area. The first stop is the U.S. Bureau of Reclamation's **Visitor Arrival Center**. It is located just below the dam on the left bank (as you face downstream). Stop here to find out about the tours and evening laser light show. Tours are generally available but not always, it depends upon the security level in effect when you visit.

During the summer there is a nightly **laser light show** projected on the face of the dam. It's a fun evening activity and takes about 35 minutes. The time of the show varies during the year from 10 p.m. to 8:30 p.m. depending upon when it gets dark. A good place to park and watch is **Crown Point**, located far above the dam about 2 miles (3.2 km) outside Grand Coulee off SR-174 in the direction of Bridgeport.

There's more to this area than the dam and lakes however. The **Grand Coulee** is actually a valley that stretches south from the dam as far as Soap Lake, about 45 miles (73 km). It is said to have been formed during the Ice Age Floods. These huge floods inundated western Washington periodically during the last ice age. A huge lake, Lake Missoula, was repeatedly formed when the ice blocked the Clark Fork River in Montana. The lake would periodically break through the ice dam causing tremendous floods which would rush through western Washington and out through the Columbia Gorge. The whole thing is explained with exhibits at the **Sun Lakes-Dry Falls Visitor Center** which overlooks the Dry Falls Cliffs on SR-17 south of Coulee City. Exhibits there say that the floods would crash over the 350-foot cliffs with a water depth of 400 feet, and a width that was 5 times what Niagara Falls is today.

SMOKIAM CITY CAMPGROUND *(Open April 15 to Oct 15 - Varies)*

Information: (509) 246-1211
Location: Soap Lake, *N 47° 23' 32", W 119° 29' 02"*, 1,000 Ft

43 Sites – This is a Soap Lake municipal campground. It's located on the south shore of Soap Lake, convenient for taking a dip in the lake. Some sites are large back-ins suitable for RVs to 45 feet with full hookups. You'll see the campground on the lakeshore as you leave Soap Lake driving north on SR-17.

SUN LAKES DRY FALLS STATE CAMPGROUND *(Open All Year)*

Reservations: (888) 226-7688, www.camis.com/wa
Information: (509) 632-5583, (360) 902-8844
Location: 5 Miles (8 Km) S of Coulee City, *N 47° 35' 22", W 119° 23' 26"*, 1,100 Ft

180 Sites – This state campground shares an idyllic location at the foot of Dry Falls with

GRAND COULEE DAM

a commercial camping resort and a golf course. Park Lake is excellent for swimming and water sports and there is a small marina and a good boat launch available. The campground sits away from the lake and is actually two different campgrounds now that a new full-hookup big-rig campground has been completed at a location about a quarter-mile (.4 km) east and above the older camping area. Sites in the new campground are 60 feet long, the older sites are crowded together and best for smaller rigs although some have hookups. The entrance road to the campground is toward the bottom of the Dry Falls grade on SR-17. It's 5 miles (8 km) southwest of Coulee City.

➤ SUN LAKES RESORT *(Open All Year)*

Res. and Info.: (509) 632-5291, www.sunlakesparkresort.com
Location: 5 Miles (8 Km) S of Coulee City, *N 47° 35' 27", W 119° 23' 43"*, 1,100 Ft

121 Sites – This resort is located in the same area as Sun Lakes Dry Falls State Campground. Its run by a concessionaire on state park land. Sites here are in an area back from the lake and will take RVs to 45 feet. Amenities include a swimming pool, grocery store, kiosk food takeout, swimming beach, nearby golf course, and a boat launch and marina shared with the state park. The entrance road to the campground is toward the bottom of the Dry Falls Grade on SR-17. It's 5 miles (8 km) southwest of Coulee City. After turning on the state park entrance road you'll see this resort on the right just after the dump station and before you reach the state park camping area.

➤ COULEE CITY COMMUNITY PARK *(Open April 1 to Oct 31)*

Information: (509) 632-5043, (509) 632-5331, www.couleecity.com
Location: Coulee City, *N 47° 37' 00", W 119° 17' 34"*, 1,500 Ft

55 Sites – This city park has lots of room for campers, both in tents and RVs. It's on the south shore of Banks Lake. Tents are pitched on grass, RV sites are both back-ins and pull-thrus and some will take rigs of any size. The park is in the middle of town on the shore of the lake, the main highway runs right along here so it's hard to miss.

➤ STEAMBOAT ROCK STATE PARK *(Open All Year)*

Reservations: (888) 226-7688, www.camis.com/wa
Information: (509) 633-1304, (360) 902-8844, www.parks.wa.gov
Location: 8 Miles (13 Km) S of Electric City, *N 47° 51' 11", W 119° 07' 55"*, 1,500 Ft

126 Sites – This is a very popular state campground located along Banks Lake on a peninsula formed by Steamboat Rock, the formation looms over the campground. It's great for water sports. The long back-in sites here reach 50 feet. The campground entrance is on SR-155 some 8 miles (13 km) south of Electric City and 17 miles (27 km) north of Coulee City.

➤ JONES BAY AND OSBORNE BAY CAMPGROUNDS *(Open All Year)*

Location: (Jones) 3 Miles (5 Km) S of Electric City, *N 47° 53' 26", W 119° 04' 38"*, 1,500 Ft
(Osborne) 2 Miles (3 Km) S of Electric City, *N 47° 55' 24", W 119° 03' 35"*, 1,500 Ft

44 Sites (Jones) and 25 Sites (Osborne) – These two smaller campsites are really part of Steamboat Rock State Park. They're remote from the rest of the park and the campsites have no hookups and no potable water. Both are waterside campgrounds. The sites at Jones Bay are spread over a large area with each site having access to the water, those in Osborne Bay are along

the edge of a large parking lot. Both locations have boat ramps. From the entrance to Steamboat Rock State Park drive north 7.5 miles (12.1 km) to Jones Bay, 10.2 miles (16.5 km) to Osborne Bay.

SUNBANKS RESORT *(Open All Year)*

Reservations: (888) 822-7195, info@sunbanksresort.com
Information: (509) 633-3786, www.sunbanksresort.com
Location: Electric City, N 47° 55' 40", W 119° 03' 21", 1,500 Ft

205 Sites – This large resort-style RV park occupies a peninsula projecting into Banks Lake just south of Electric City. This means that it is away from the highway, a fortunate circumstance. There are a variety of site types at this campground, you'll want to choose the right one for your camping lifestyle. There are a line of large sites designed for big rigs located just in front of the huge log main building. These have full hookups with 50 amp-power and are the only real choice if you have a big rig (to 45 feet). They're good sites with views across a lawn to the lake. The rest of the RV sites in the resort have only electricity and water hookups, there is a dump station however. Many sites are on grass along the lake, you can tie your boat up in front of your camp. There are also quieter sites on the hill overlooking everything, choose one of these for a little more seclusion. The resort has a large main lodge built of logs. It houses the reception office, a small store, and a good restaurant. There's a sandy beach, a boat launch, and a dock area with rental boats of various kinds. To reach the resort head south just a short distance along the east shore of Banks Lake from Electric City. The campground is on the right just before the highway starts across a levee.

COULEE PLAYLAND RESORT *(Open All Year)*

Res. and Info.: (509) 633-2671, www.couleeplayland.com
Location: Electric City, *N 47° 56' 04", W 119° 01' 47"*, 1,500 Ft

65 Sites – This waterside campground at the north end of Electric City offers long sites suitable for any length rig. It's an older campground, the location is the draw. There's a grocery store and a boat launch. This is the only place on the lake to get fuel for your boat.

SPRING CANYON CAMPGROUND *(Open All Year)*

Reservations: (877) 444-6777, www.reserveamerica.com
Information: (509) 633-9188
Location: 3 Miles (5 Km) E of Electric City, *N 47° 55' 59", W 118° 56' 22"*, 1,400 Ft

78 Sites – A handy Lake Roosevelt National Recreation Area campground with room for RVs to about 30 feet overlooking Roosevelt Lake. The campground is located about 3 miles (5 km) east of Grand Coulee on the south shore of the lake. There are no hookups but there is a boat launch and a very popular beach at the day use area below the campground. Many sites have great views. Some sites are under sun shelters which limit height to between 9 and 11 feet, each one has the clearance marked on the front.

GRAND COULEE RV PARK *(Open All Year)*

Res. and Info.: (509) 633-0750, (800) 633-0750, www.grandcouleedam.com/gcrv/
Location: Grand Coulee, N 47° 57' 01", W 119° 00' 05", 1,621 Ft

40 Sites – Grand Coulee RV Park is a small commercial campground offering full hookups. It's a good base for exploring the area if you aren't interested in a waterside location. The park is

very convenient to the lookout point at Crown Point, a good place to watch the laser light show on the face of the dam in the evening. Sites here reach 45 feet and larger, particularly in the new area above the more established entrance area. The campground is located off SR-174 which leaves Grand Coulee toward Bridgport. It's .9 miles (1.5 km) from the junction of SR-174 with SR-155 in Grand Coulee.

HOOD CANAL

The word canal is really not an accurate description of the **Hood Canal**. Actually, this canal is really is a 70-mile-long (115 km) inlet. On a map the canal appears to be a giant hook which forms the western boundary of the Kitsap Peninsula. Because the canal is so long and shallow its waters are fairly warm. It is quite popular with water sports enthusiasts. Oysters grow here, you will probably see them if you walk the beaches. Many folks from the more populous regions of Puget Sound have summer cabins along the shore of the canal. In winter the water is clear and scuba divers love it.

Belfair is located at the very end of the long warm-water Hood Canal, and also at the base of the Kitsap Peninsula. From there SR-106 leads westward along the south edge of the canal for 20 miles (32 km). Where the canal turns north SR-106 intersects with US-101. US-101 follows the west side of the canal northward for 40 miles (65 km) through the small communities of Hoodsport, Lilliwaup, and Brinnon to Quilcene. Just west of the canal are the Olympic Mountains and Olympic National Park. Several small roads climb to give access to this forest area.

Many of the campgrounds listed below are located at or near sea level along or near these two highways. However, five of them are located along a two-lane paved road that rises from Hoodsport on the west shore of the canal. These five include an Olympic National Park campground as well as an Olympic National Forest campground, a state Department of Natural Resources campground, and two commercial campgrounds (one of these is a former state campground).

⌲ BELFAIR STATE PARK *(Open All Year)*

Reservations:	(888) 226-7688, www.camis.com/wa
Information:	(360) 275-0668, (360) 902-8844
Location:	3 Miles (5 Km) NW of Belfair, *N 47° 25' 50", W 122° 52' 38", Near Sea Level*

184 Sites – This large state park campground at the end of Hood Canal offers many sites including large RV sites near the water. These RV sites are back-ins and pull-thrus to 60 feet and since they're set in an open grass field there is no problem with slide-outs. Many more sites are forest-type back-ins for tent-campers and smaller rigs. Swimming is in a small salt water lake at the beach. The campground is near Belfair. From the center of town west of the Safeway follow Clifton Lane north. Clifton becomes SR-300 and 3.5 miles (5.6 km) from the Safeway you'll reach the park entrance.

⌲ TWANOH STATE PARK *(Open All Year)*

Information:	(360) 275-2222, (360) 902-8844
Location:	8 Miles (13 Km) W of Belfair, *N 47° 22' 39", W 122° 58' 22", Near Sea Level*

47 Sites – This state campground is situated on the south shore of Hood Canal. There is a day use area with swimming in Hood Canal and boat ramp on the canal side of the highway. The small camping area is on the opposite side. This is an older forest-type campground with cramped entry roads. There are back-in and pull-thru sites, a few to 45 feet long, but lack of maneuvering room limits use to RVs of about 35 feet. The campground is located on SR-106 some 8.5 miles (13.7 km) west of Belfair.

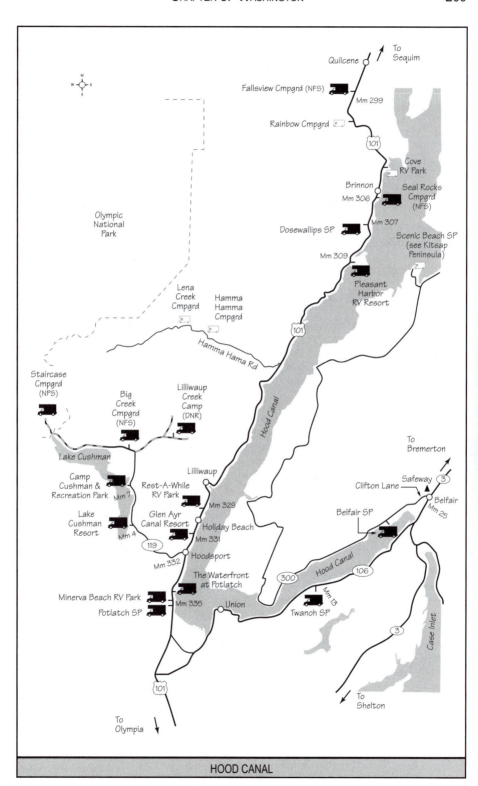

To Sequim

Quilcene

Fallsview Cmpgrd (NFS)

Mm 299

Rainbow Cmpgrd

101

Cove RV Park

Brinnon

Mm 306

Seal Rocks Cmpgrd (NFS)

Mm 307

Olympic National Park

Dosewallips SP

Scenic Beach SP (see Kitsap Peninsula)

Mm 309

Pleasant Harbor RV Resort

Lena Creek Cmpgrd

Hamma Hamma Cmpgrd

101

Hamma Hama Rd

Hood Canal

Staircase Cmpgrd (NPS)

Big Creek Cmpgrd (NFS)

Lilliwaup Creek Camp (DNR)

To Bremerton

Safeway

Lake Cushman

Clifton Lane

3

Camp Cushman & Recreation Park

Mm 7

Lilliwaup

Rest-A-While RV Park

Mm 329

Belfair

Mm 25

Belfair SP

Lake Cushman Resort

Mm 4

Glen Ayr Canal Resort

Holiday Beach

Mm 331

119

Hoodsport

Mm 332

The Waterfront at Potlatch

300

Hood Canal

106

Minerva Beach RV Park

Mm 335

Union

Mm 13

Potlatch SP

Twanoh SP

3

Case Inlet

101

To Shelton

To Olympia

WASHINGTON

HOOD CANAL

POTLATCH STATE PARK *(Open All Year)*

Information: (360) 877-5361, (360) 902-8844
Location: 2 Miles (3 Km) N of the Intersection of US-101 and SR-106,
N 47° 21' 43", W 123° 09' 29", Near Sea Level

37 Sites – This campground too is located on Hood Canal, but it is on the west side where the canal cuts north along the eastern edge of Olympic National Park. This campground has a day use area along the water but the campground is on the mountain side of the highway. It's a forest-type campground and like Twanoh is old and has limited maneuvering room. Although there are a few back-in and pull-through sites to 60 feet in length the practical size limit here is RVs to only 35 feet. The campground is located on the west side of Hood Canal off US-101 some 2 miles (3.2 km) north of its intersection with SR-106.

MINERVA BEACH RV PARK *(Open All Year)*

Res. and Info.: (360) 877-5145, (866) 500-5145, minervabeach101@hotmail.com,
http://home.att.net/~minervabeach/
Location: 2 Miles (3 Km) N of the Intersection of US-101 and SR-106,
N 47° 21' 49", W 123° 09' 31", Near Sea Level

51 Sites – This commercial campground occupies two sides of the highway just north of Potlatch State Park. The main traveler park is away from the water above a large gravel lot surrounding a building housing an older laundry room and restrooms. There are tent sites in a grassy field and back-in RV sites with full hookups that extend to 35 feet and allow slide-outs. The campground is along US-101 some 2.1 miles (3.4 km) north of its intersection with SR-106.

THE WATERFRONT AT POTLATCH *(Open All Year)*

Res. and Info.: (360) 877-9422, canal@hctc.com, www.thewaterfrontatpotlatch.com
Location: 3 Miles (5 Km) N of the Intersection of US-101 and SR-106,
N 47° 22' 13", W 123° 09' 32", Near Sea Level

14 Sites – These are brand-new premium RV sites set alongside and in front of a hotel on the shore of Hood Canal. There are pull-thrus to 60 feet and back-ins to 45. All sites overlook the canal, this is a prime location. The hotel is along US-101 some 2.6 miles (4.2 km) north of its intersection with SR-106.

BIG CREEK CAMPGROUND *(Open May 15 to Sept 15 - Varies)*

Information: (360) 877-5254
Location: 9 Miles (15 Km) W of Hoodsport, N 47° 29' 33", W 123° 12' 36", 900 Ft

25 Sites – Big Creek is an Olympic National Forest Campground. Sites here are forest-type with back-ins to about 30 feet. Access is via the SR-119 that climbs from Hoodsport about 5.3 miles (8.5 km) north of the intersection of US-101 and SR-106. In 9.3 miles (15 km), after passing Lake Cushman, you will come to a T. Turn left here and in just .1 mile (.2 km) you'll see the campground on your right.

STAIRCASE NATIONAL PARK CAMPGROUND *(Open All Year - Sometimes Snows In)*
Information: (360) 565-3130
Location: 16 Miles (26 Km) W of Hoodsport, *N 47° 30 055", W 123° 19' 46"*, 700 Ft

56 Sites – Staircase is an Olympic National Park campground. It's a forest-type campground located just beyond the far west end of Lake Cushman along the North Fork of the Skokomish River. Sites here are almost all back-ins, limited maneuvering room limits use to RVs to 30 feet. Access is via the SR-119 that climbs from Hoodsport about 5.3 miles (8.5 km) north of the intersection of US-101 and SR-106. In 9.3 miles (15 km), after passing Lake Cushman, you will come to a T. Turn left here and follow the road to the end, about 6.4 more miles (10.3 km). Just before coming into the park you'll have about 3.8 mile (6.1 km) of gravel, the rest is paved.

LILLIWAUP CREEK CAMP *(Open May 15 to Sept 15 - Varies)*
Information: (800) 264-0890
Location: 11 Miles (18 Km) W of Hoodsport, *N 47° 30' 13", W 123° 10' 35"*, 1,100 Ft

11 Sites – Lilliwaup is a small forest-style Washington Department of Natural Resources campground with a loop access road and sites to about 30 feet. It's a good tent-camping and small RV campground with no amenities other than vault toilets and nearby trails. There is no potable water. Access is via the SR-119 that climbs from Hoodsport about 5.3 miles (8.5 km) north of the intersection of US-101 and SR-106. In 9.3 miles (15 km), after passing Lake Cushman, you will come to a T. Turn right here, the road becomes gravel. In 1.5 mile (2.4 km) at the junction take the right fork, the campground is on the left in another .3 mile (.5 km).

CAMP CUSHMAN AND RECREATION PARK *(Open April 15 to Oct 31 - weekends only in April and Oct)*
Res. and Info.:   (360) 877-6770, (866) 259-2900, camp@lakecushman.com, www.lakecushman.com
Location: 7 Miles (12 Km) W of Hoodsport, *N 47° 27' 45", W 123° 12' 59"*, 700 Ft

82 Sites – Camp Cushman is located on the north shore of Lake Cushman. It is a former state campground now operated by the same folks who own Lake Cushman Resort. There are back-ins to 45 feet and pull-thrus to 60 feet off two loops, also walk-in tent sites as well as smaller vehicle sites. The campground has swimming at the lake shore, a boat ramp, a small grocery, and hiking trails. Access is via the SR-119 that climbs from Hoodsport about 5.3 miles (8.5 km) north of the intersection of US-101 and SR-106. You'll reach the campground in 7.0 miles (12 km).

LAKE CUSHMAN RESORT *(Open All Year)*
Res. and Info.:   (360) 877-9630, (800) 588-9630, resort@lakecushman.com, www.lakecushman.com
Location: 5 Miles (8 Km) W of Hoodsport, *N 47° 25' 45", W 123° 13' 08"*, 700 Ft

74 Sites – This resort on the shore of Lake Cushman has a small store and restaurant overlooking the lake. It also has 22 water and electric hookup sites, all back-ins, and many more no-hookup smaller sites. Most of the large sites will accept slide-outs. While there is no dump station there is one a few miles down the road at Camp Cushman. Other amenities include a boat ramp and docks. Access is via SR-119 that climbs from Hoodsport about 5.3 miles (8.5 km) north of the intersection of US-101 and SR-106. You'll reach the campground in 4.8 miles (7.7 km).

WASHINGTON

GLEN-AYR CANAL RESORT *(Open All Year)*

Res. and Info.: (360) 877-9522, (866) 877-9522, glenayr@hctc.com, www.glenayr.com
Location: 1 Mile (1.6 Km) N of Hoodsport, *N 47° 25' 13", W 123° 07' 51"*, Near Sea Level

38 Sites – The Glen-Ayr is located across the road from the shore of Hood Canal. There are 8 pull-thrus to 45 feet and many back-ins, some to 40 feet. Slide-outs are OK. This is a fairly upscale place. Their pride is a large indoor hot tub situated to overlook the canal. The resort is located north of Hoodsport, 5.3 miles (8.5 km) north of the intersection of US-101 and SR-106.

REST-A-WHILE RV PARK *(Open All Year)*

Res. and Info.: (360) 877-9474, (866) 637-9474, www.restawhile.com
Location: 2 Miles (3 Km) N of Hoodsport, N 47° 26' 27", W 123° 07' 08", Near Sea Level

87 Sites – The campground office here is a small country convenience store. Sites are located near the canal and also across the road. There are both pull-thrus and back-ins to 45 feet with full hookups. Slide-outs are OK. There is also a small restaurant on site and others nearby. The campground is located north of Hoodsport, 8.1 miles (13.1 km) north of the intersection of US-101 and SR-106.

PLEASANT HARBOR RV RESORT *(Open All Year)*

Res. and Info.: (360) 796-9970, www.pleasantharborrv.com
Location: 22 Miles (35 Km) N of Hoodsport, *N 47° 39' 24", W 122° 55' 23"*, Near Sea Level

63 Sites – Pleasant Harbor RV Resort is a large parcel of land along northern Hood Canal. There is a marina and RV park. Sites are pull-thrus and back-ins to 50 feet. Amenities include a swimming pool and shellfish beach. The campground is located 27.7 miles (44.7 km) north of the intersection of US-101 and SR-106.

DOSEWALLIPS STATE PARK *(Open All Year)*

Reservations: (888) 226-7688, www.camis.com/wa
Information: (360) 796-4415, (360) 902-8844
Location: 25 Miles (40 Km) N of Hoodsport, *N 47° 41' 07", W 122° 54' 03"*, Near Sea Level

140 Sites – The largest part of the campsites in this park are pinwheel-style back-ins off 8 circles. Some reach 40 feet, full hookup sites are available. There are also a few back-in sites on the east side of the highway. These are accessed by driving under a bridge from the park on the west side of the highway and have no hookups. The park has shoreline along Hood Canal and also along the Dosewallips River. There is swimming in the river. The campground is located 30 miles (48 Km) north of the intersection of US-101 and SR-106, about two miles (3 km) south of Brinnon.

SEAL ROCKS CAMPGROUND

Information: (360) 765-2200
Location: 26 Miles (40 Km) N of Hoodsport, *N 47° 42' 28", W 122° 53' 36"*, Near Sea Level

42 Sites – This older Olympic National Forest campground is one of the few in the state

WASHINGTON

located along the ocean. The roads are cramped here and although there are some longer sites we recommend it for RVs no longer than 30 feet. The campground is located near the northern end of the stretch of US-101 along Hood Canal. It is 32 miles (52 km) north of the intersection of US-101 and SR-106.

 FALLSVIEW CAMPGROUND *(Open May 10 to Sept 25 - Varies)*

Information:	(360) 765-2200
Location:	33 Miles (53 Km) N of Hoodsport, *N 47° 47' 26", W 122° 55' 30"*, 500 Ft

$$\boxed{\$\$} \quad \boxed{\triangle} \quad \boxed{\spadesuit}$$

30 Sites – This Olympic National Forest campground is located in Walker Pass and offers a trail to a waterfall near the campground. Sites are off two loops. Many are long pull-thrus and back-ins but sites and roads are narrow so we recommend the campground for RVs to 35 feet, many sites will not take slide-outs. The campground is located 39 miles (63 km) north of the intersection of US-101 and SR-106 and just 3 miles (5 km) south of Quilcene.

ILWACO AND LONG BEACH

During the late 1800s the Long Beach Peninsula, like Seaside in Oregon to the south, was a beach resort frequented by folks from Portland. During the middle 1900s the peninsula was almost forgotten, but lately it has begun to be noticed again.

There are actually two centers of interest here. First there's the area near the mouth of the Columbia near Ilwaco. Second is the Long Beach Peninsula itself which starts just a few miles north of Ilwaco and runs northward for 28 miles (45 km). The peninsula forms the western border of Willapa Bay, famous for its oysters.

Ilwaco (population 1,000) is a fishing town. It is located a few miles east of the mouth of the Columbia on the north shore. In addition to serving fishermen, the town also hosts the Cape Disappointment Coast Guard Station. This is the Coast Guard's lifeboat school, it is located

ONE OF CAPE DISAPPOINTMENT'S TWO LIGHTHOUSES

here because there are lots of opportunities to practice in the wild surf of the Columbia bar. The Coast Guard station is actually right next to one of the nicest Washington state parks, **Cape Disappointment**. This park, in addition to a fine campground, has **two lighthouses**, a nice beach, miles of trails, and the excellent **Lewis and Clark Interpretive Center**. There's also a great view of the mouth of the Columbia, complete with ships crossing the bar, from the interpretive center or the nearby lighthouse.

Historically the **Long Beach Peninsula** (also sometimes called the North Beach Peninsula) was connected to the river port at Ilwaco by a narrow-gauge railroad. Today the rail lines have been replaced by a road, SR-103. As you drive up the peninsula you'll find a number of small towns: Seaview, Long Beach, Klipsan Beach, Ocean Park, Surfside, Nahcotta, and Oysterville. Most of the tourist activities center around the town of Long Beach, that's where you'll find the majority of the restaurants and shops. The real attraction is out of sight to the west, it's the longest beach in the continental U.S. The peninsula finally ends at Leadbetter Point State Park, an excellent birding location. As you return (and if you are an oyster fan) stop in Nahcotta to

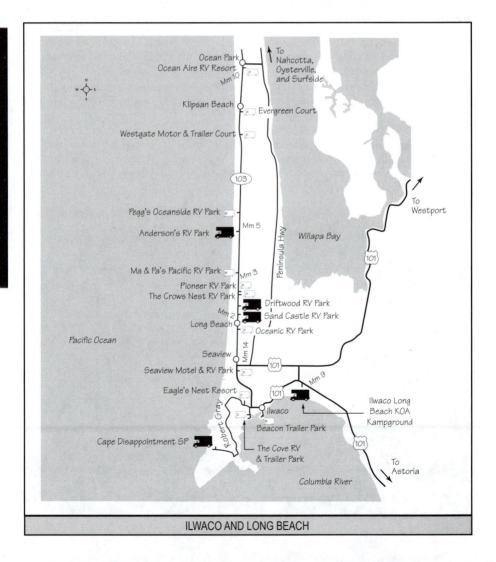

ILWACO AND LONG BEACH

visit the **Willapa Bay Oysterhouse Interpretive Center** and perhaps to buy oysters and other seafood at the wharf (in season).

Long Beach (population 1,400) is definitely a tourist town, it hosts several annual events. Early in the season, in April, there's the **Ragtime Rhodie Dixieland Jazz Festival**. There's also a Fourth of July event called **Fireworks on the Beach**. Biggest of all it the **Washington State International Kite Festival** the third week of August.

CAPE DISAPPOINTMENT STATE PARK *(Open All Year)*

Reservations:	(888) 226-7688, www.camis.com/wa
Information:	(360) 642-3078, (360) 902-8844
Location:	3 Miles (5 Km) SW of Ilwaco, *N 46° 17' 00", W 124° 03' 21"*, Near Sea Level

232 Sites – Formerly called Fort Canby, this is one of the most popular parks in the state. The attraction is the great beaches, two scenic lighthouses, and a Lewis and Clark museum. The park occupies the point on the north side of the mouth of the Columbia River. RV sites are back-ins off circles, they reach 50 feet in length. From central Ilwaco follow the signs west for the park. The entrance is 3.3 miles (5 Km) from the intersection in town.

ILWACO LONG BEACH KOA KAMPGROUND *(Open May 15 to Oct 15)*

Reservations:	800 562-3258, www.koa.com
Information:	(360) 642-3292, ilwacokoa@hotmail.com
Location:	2 Miles (3 Km) E of Ilwaco, *N 46° 19' 17", W 124° 00' 19"*, Near Sea Level

122 Sites – Probably because it's located a bit east of Ilwaco the KOA usually has room when other nearby campgrounds are full, a good thing to know in this popular area. It's at the intersection of US-101 and SR-401.

SAND CASTLE RV PARK *(Open All Year)*

Res. and Info.:	(360) 642-2174, www.sandcastlerv.com
Location:	Long Beach, *N 46° 21' 32", W 124° 03' 13"*, Near Sea Level

48 Sites – This is a small RV park convenient to the attractions of central Long Beach. It's located on the east side of SR-103 near Mile 2.

DRIFTWOOD RV PARK *(Open All Year)*

Res. and Info.:	(360) 642-2711, (888) 567-1902, www.driftwood-rvpark.com
Location:	Long Beach, *N 46° 21' 42", W 124° 03' 14"*, Near Sea Level

56 Sites – This is one of the larger Long Beach campgrounds with some of the best facilities. There is room for big rigs to park with careful maneuvering. It is at the northern edge of town near Mile 2 of State Route 103.

ANDERSON'S RV PARK *(Open All Year)*

Res. and Info.:	(360) 642-2231, (800) 645-6795, info@andersensrv.com, www.andersensrv.com
Location:	1 Mile (2 Km) N of Long Beach, *N 46° 24' 08", W 124° 03' 14"*, Near Sea Level

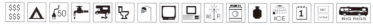

60 Sites – This campground is located next to the beach about 2 miles (3 km) north of cen-

tral Long Beach. Two long lines of long back-in sites stretch from the office and other buildings out toward the shore. It's a well-run friendly park and very popular. The campground is on the west side of SR-103 at Mile 5 north of Long Beach.

KITSAP PENINSULA AND BAINBRIDGE ISLAND

West of the Seattle/Tacoma metro area, across Puget Sound, is a rural region known as the Kitsap Peninsula. Access for many to this area is by Washington State Ferry. In fact, the ferries make access so easy that this area, the Kitsap Peninsula and the connected Bainbridge Island, are a bedroom community for Seattle.

Another access route, and this one is better for RVs of any size larger than a van, is the suspension bridge linking Tacoma with the west side of the sound. Almost immediately you will find yourself in another world, you pass from the crowded Seattle-Tacoma metropolis to the green countryside of rural western Puget Sound and the Kitsap Peninsula. You might want to stop and take a look at **Gig Harbor**, sometimes called the Northwest's Sausalito. The little

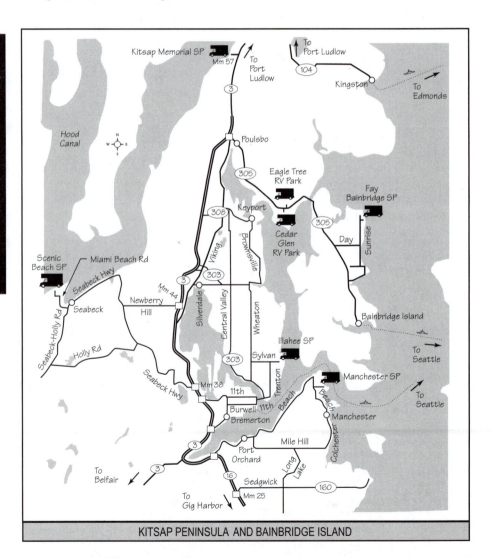

KITSAP PENINSULA AND BAINBRIDGE ISLAND

waterfront town is filled with small shops and has a nice nautical flavor. It's so close to Tacoma that we've included its campground under the *Tacoma* heading elsewhere in the chapter, but it's a good base for exploring the Kitsap Peninsula.

Stay on SR-16 as it leads north to Bremerton. Just short of that city the highway will meet SR-3. You can turn left here and in 8 miles (13 km) be in Belfair. Belfair has a nice state park campground along Hood Canal, we've listed it in the *Hood Canal* section. It too can make a nice base for exploring the Kitsap Peninsula

If you decide to head north and explore the peninsula you might want to make your first stop **Port Orchard**. This little harbor town is a good place to shop for antiques, arts, or just plain knickknacks.

Port Orchard is directly across Sinclair Inlet from much larger **Bremerton**, known as the home of the Puget Sound Naval Shipyard. You'll have to drive around the west end of Sinclair Inlet to get there if you want to take your car. The alternative is a passenger-only ferry running across the inlet. The waterfront in Bremerton is the center of interest. There you'll find a boardwalk and shipyard-related sights including the destroyer **Turner Joy** which is open to self-guided tours, and the **Bremerton Naval Museum**. There are a number of moth-balled ships in Bremerton, you can take a commercial harbor tour to see them but you are not allowed on board the ships.

If you find that you enjoy the Bremerton Naval Museum you may want to drive a few miles north on SR-3 through Silverdale and then turn east on SR-308 to Keyport. There you'll find the **Naval Underwater Museum**. The Kitsap Peninsula plays an important part in supporting the U.S. submarine fleet. Along the west coast of the peninsula on Hood Canal is the **Bangor Trident Nuclear Submarine Base** and Keyport is home to the **Naval Undersea Warfare Center**, neither is open for tours, however.

Since you've come so far north already you might as well visit **Poulsbo**, it's only about three miles (5 km) farther north. Poulsbo is another cute harbor town offering antiques and shops. The difference here is that Poulsbo is proud of its Norwegian heritage and shows it off with Scandinavian-theme architecture and products.

Beyond Poulsbo SR-305 connects with Bainbridge Island. Bainbridge has one of the ferry ports for Seattle arrivals and departures as well as many homes. It also has a nice state park campground.

You will see that when visiting the Kitsap Peninsula you have a wide choice of state campgrounds. For tent campers in smaller vehicles or on bicycles these are easily accessible from Seattle by ferry and make good weekend destinations, particularly when reservations are available.

In addition to the campgrounds listed below several others are located nearby and allow easy access to the area. Gig Harbor (listed under *Tacoma* in this book) has a nice commercial campground. There's also a nice state park campground near Belfair (that will take big rigs and offers hookups and reservations). It's listed in the *Hood Canal* section of this book.

If you are visiting the Northwest and would like to visit Seattle in a unique way you might consider camping on the Kitsap Peninsula or Bainbridge Island and using the ferry to visit the city. Leave your vehicle and walk on. The ferries dock right downtown and you can walk or use public transportation to get around Seattle.

⛺ MANCHESTER STATE PARK *(Open All Year)*

Reservations:	(888) 226-7688, www.camis.com/wa
Information:	(360) 871-4065, (360) 902-8844, www.parks.wa.gov
Location:	6 Miles (10 Km) E of Port Orchard, *N 47° 34' 36", W 122° 33' 17"*, Near Sea Level

50 Sites – This state campground is located on the Puget Sound shoreline to the east of Port Orchard. The camping area is away from the water. Campsites are forest-type and include some pull-thrus. Narrow roads and sites limit RV size to about 35 feet. Access to this park involves driving on narrow back roads. One route would be to head east along the waterfront from Port

Orchard on Beach Drive East. The road follows the waterfront to the northeast and then turns south to head inland. Five miles (8 km) from Port Orchard you'll see the sign for the park on the left.

ILLAHEE STATE PARK *(Open All Year)*

Information: (360) 478-6460, (360) 902-8844, www.parks.wa.gov
Location: Bremerton, *N 47° 35' 44", W 122° 35' 56"*, Near Sea Level

25 Sites – This state park is located just northeast of Bremerton along the shore of Puget Sound. The small forest-type campground is away from the water and is located on a hillside with narrow access roads. Practical RV size here is about 30 feet. The park also has a small boat ramp and a wide, gently-sloping beach. To reach the campground most easily follow SR-303 some 6.7 miles (10.8 km) southeast from its intersection with SR-3 near Silverdale. SR-303 starts as NW Waaga Way, then becomes Wheaton Way after it turns south toward Bremerton. Turn east on Sylvan Way (SR-306) and follow it 1.5 miles (2.4 km) to the campground entrance.

CEDAR GLEN RV PARK *(Open All Year)*

Res. and Info.: (360) 779-4305
Location: 2 Miles (3 Km) E of Poulsbo, *N 47° 42' 20", W 122° 35' 49"*, 100 Ft

28 Sites – This small commercial campground south of the highway is associated with a much larger mobile home park on the north side. Most sites are occupied by long-term RVs but there are often sites for travelers. Sites are long back-ins to 100 feet off a straight gravel access road. Slide-outs are not a problem. The check-in office and laundry are at the mobile home park. Follow SR-305 southeast from its intersection with SR-3 near Poulsbo. The campground is on the right in 4.9 miles (7.9 km). If you are coming the other way from Bainbridge Island the campground is 1.5 miles (2.4 km) from the bridge.

EAGLE TREE RV PARK *(Open All Year)*

Res. and Info.: (360) 598-5988, info@eagletreerv.com, www.eagletreerv.com
Location: 3 Miles (5 Km) E of Poulsbo, *N 47° 42' 22", W 122° 35' 25"*, 200 Ft

87 Sites – The Eagle Tree is a newer big-rig park. There are full-hookup back-in and pull-thru sites from 40 to 80 feet in length which will accommodate slide-outs. Follow SR-305 southeast from its intersection with SR-3 near Poulsbo. The campground is on the left in 5.3 miles (8.5 km). If you are coming the other way from Bainbridge Island the campground is 1.1 miles (1.8 km) from the bridge.

FAY BAINBRIDGE STATE PARK *(Open All Year)*

Information: (206) 842-3931, (360) 902-8844, www.parks.wa.gov
Location: 8 Miles (13 Km) N of Bainbridge Island Ferry Terminal,
N 47° 42' 10", W 122° 30' 28", Near Sea Level

36 Sites – This campground has both tent sites in a forest setting and RV and tent sites near the beach with views across the Sound. The RV sites are all back-ins and a few will accept RVs to 40 feet. These sites are not separated by trees so slide-outs present no problems. This campground is on Bainbridge Island and is the closest state campground to the ferry. From the bridge onto the island follow SR-305 south and turn left on NE Day Road W. Coming the other way this intersection is 4.3 miles (6.9 km) from the ferry terminal. Follow Day Road east for 1.3 miles (2.1 km) until you reach Sunrise Dr. NE. Follow Sunrise north for 1.6 miles (2.6 km) to

the campground entrance which is on the right.

KITSAP MEMORIAL STATE PARK *(Open All Year)*

Information:	(360) 779-3205, (360) 902-8844, www.parks.wa.gov
Location:	4 Miles (6.4 Km) S of the Hood Canal Bridge,
	N 47° 49' 04", W 122° 39' 00", Near Sea Level

40 Sites – Kitsap Memorial is on the east side of the peninsula on the shore of Hood Canal. The camping sites here are back-ins to 40 feet in an open area. The restroom building is brand-new and one of the nicest in the state with individual shower rooms, you'll think you're in an Oregon state park except that you have to feed them with quarters here. There are also new rental cabins. Campsites do not have a water view but are just across a grassy field from the small and narrow beach. The entrance road to the park is off SR-3 just 2.9 miles (4.7 km) south of the Hood Canal Floating Bridge.

SCENIC BEACH STATE PARK *(Open All Year)*

Reservations:	(888) 226-7688, www.camis.com/wa
Information:	(360) 830-5079, (360) 902-8844, www.parks.wa.gov;
Location:	9 Miles (15 Km) SW of Silverdale, *N 47° 38' 50", W 122° 50' 48"*, Near Sea Level

49 Sites – Scenic Beach is another state campground on Hood Canal. The beach here is small and narrow. Campsites are all forest-type off paved roads on two loops. There are back-ins to 50 feet and pull-thrus that are even longer but access roads are narrow making the campground only suitable for RVs to 35 feet. The campground is somewhat isolated since it is located away from the main thoroughfares on the island. From SR-3 near Silverdale drive east on NW Newberry Hill Road. In 2.8 miles (4.5 km), at the T turn right on Seabeck Hwy. NW and follow this road as it goes north and then turns west to follow the shoreline. In 5.1 miles (8.2 km) turn right on Miami Beach Road and follow it to the campground, another 1.4 miles (2.3 km).

LAKE EASTON AND LAKE KACHESS

For Seattle area residents the Lake Easton and Lake Kachess region is a convenient wilderness destination. Exit 62, the epicenter of the campgrounds in the area, is (of course), 62 miles (100 km) from the beginning of I-90 in Seattle. It's an easy drive in the summer with at least four lanes all the way.

This area is the headwaters of the Yakima River. Both Lakes Easton and Kachess are dammed reservoirs offering water sport activities. Kachess is much larger and more remote. It's 5 miles (8 km) north of the highway and covers 6,535 acres. Fishing is possible for kokanee, rainbows and cutthroats. Lake Easton is much smaller and good for small unpowered boats. It's really more of a wide spot in the river than a lake. While 10 horsepower engines are allowed the many stumps in the lake make it easy to have an accident with a powered boat.

This area is in the Wenatchee National Forest and back country can be accessed using trails and logging roads. It is also crossed by the **John Wayne Trail and Iron Horse Trail State Park**. This trail extends from Cedar Falls on the west side of the Cascades across the state to the Idaho border. It follows an abandoned railroad right-a-way and can be used by hikers, bikers, and horseback riders.

The Lake Easton area is also a popular winter sports destination with miles of cross country ski trails, nearby snow machine country, and even overnight parking at the state park.

This area has camping opportunities for everyone. Tenters will enjoy any of the government campgrounds although only the state park offers showers. Most RVers seem to favor the state campground. When it's full the commercial campgrounds provide overflow room for those desiring hookups.

LAKE KACHESS CAMPGROUND *(Open May 1 to Sept 30 - Varies)*

Reservations: (877) 444-6777, www.reserveusa.com
Information: (509) 674-4411
Location: 5 Miles (8 Km) NE of I-90 Exit 62, *N 47° 21' 19", W 121° 14' 59"*, 2,200 Ft

183 Sites – This is a very large Wenatchee National Forest campground on the shores of Kachess Lake. Most sites here are only suitable for RVs to 30 feet but there are some pull-thru sites along one loop that will take RVs to 40 feet. To reach the campground take Exit 62 from I-90 and drive 5 miles (8 km) northeast on the paved Kachess Lake Road.

CRYSTAL SPRINGS CAMPGROUND *(Open May 1 to Sept 30 - Varies)*

Information: (509) 674-4411
Location: I-90 Exit 62, *N 47° 18' 31", W 121° 18' 47"*, 2,300 Ft

183 Sites – This small Wenatchee National Forest campground is conveniently located near the highway but road noise isn't bad. Sites are off loops and a few will take larger rigs but very narrow roads mean RV size should be limited to 35 feet and even then caution is necessary. To reach the campground take Exit 62 from I-90 and go south, the campground is on the right in .3 mile (.5 km).

RV TOWN *(Open May 1 to Oct 30 - Varies)*

Res. and Info.: (509) 656-2360
Location: I-90 Exit 62, *N 47° 14' 49", W 121° 11' 02"*, 2,300 Ft

70 Sites – This commercial campground has a gas station and restaurant out front. It's an older place but has parking on gravel and grass under trees with room for larger rigs. Take Exit 70 from I-90, go east along the road that parallels the north side of the freeway for just a short distance to the campground.

LAKE EASTON RESORT *(Open All Year)*

Information: (509) 656-2255
Location: I-90 Exit 62, *N 47° 14' 49", W 121° 11' 14"*, 2,300 Ft

123 Sites – This is an older membership campground but travelers are accepted if the campground has room. It does often fill up during summer weekends and no reservations are accepted. Take Exit 70 from I-90. Go east along the road that parallels the south side of the freeway for a short distance, the entrance is on the right.

LAKE EASTON STATE PARK *(Open March 24 to Oct 23 - Varies, Snow Park all Winter)*

Reservations: (888) 226-7688, www.camis.com/wa
Information: (509) 656-2586, (360) 902-8844, www.parks.wa.gov
Location: I-90 Exit 62, *N 47° 14' 40", W 121° 11' 09"*, 2,200 Ft

135 Sites – This is a popular lakeside campground. It has swimming and a boat ramp as well as offering easy access to the John Wayne Pioneer Trail. In winter it is used as a Sno-Park offering overnight parking in a large cleared lot for the large number of people who come to this area for

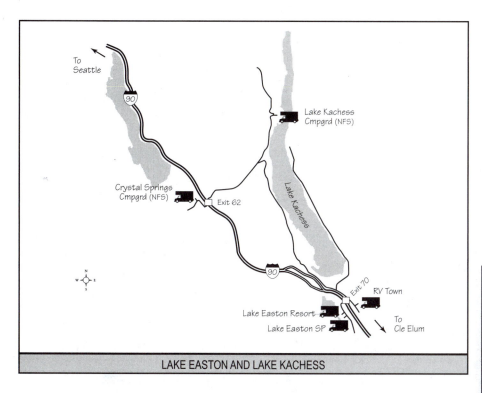

LAKE EASTON AND LAKE KACHESS

winter activities. Take Exit 70 from I-90 and travel east on the road that parallels the freeway on the south side, you'll see the campground entrance on the right in just .4 mile (.6 km).

LAKE PATEROS REGION

Lake Pateros fills the Columbia River valley behind Wells Dam at Mile 515.8 of the Columbia River. The upper end of the 30-mile (48 km) lake is near Chief Joseph Dam at Mile 545.1 of the Columbia. The valley at this point turns to the east toward the Grand Coulee and the massive dam there.

This section of the river doesn't get a lot of tourist attention, but maybe it should. Lake Pateros, and also Lake Rufus Wood behind Chief Joseph Dam, offer hot weather, watersports, and fishing.

Pateros (population 600) is the town farthest downriver on the lake. This is a fruit growing region and fruit processing is clearly the town's main business. There's a municipal park along the waterfront for walking and camping. There are also two large tanks on the hillside above town that you'll probably notice, they've been beautified with a reflector art installation by eastern Washington artist Richard Elliot. The three annual celebrations in Pateros are the **Apple Pie Jamboree** about the middle of July, the **Pateros Fun Run** (a motorcycle rally) at the end of July, and **hydroplane races** on Lake Pateros at the end of August.

Other towns in the area are **Brewster** (population 2,200) and **Bridgeport** (population 2,000). Both have city campgrounds.

East of Brewster an interesting stop is **Fort Okanogan**. The access road goes south from SR-17 just east of its intersection with US-97. Here you'll find a state information center which overlooks the confluence of the Columbia and Okanogan Rivers. Fort Okanogan was a fur-trading station located near the confluence during the 1800s. The actual sites (there were two of them) of the forts are far below near the rivers, you can look through a couple of sighting contraptions at the center to see where they once stood.

Fishing is popular in both lakes. Lake Pateros has salmon, steelhead, walleye and bass while Lake Rufus Woods in known for its big rainbows as well as walleye and kokanee. On Lake Rufus Woods if you are shore fishing outside the state park you need a Coleville Tribe fishing license in addition to your Washington state license.

For both tent campers and RVers the best campgrounds in this region are the state campgrounds. Unfortunately, neither of them take reservations. For RVers the Marina Park in Bridgeport is a great alternate, and they do take reservations!

BRIDGEPORT STATE PARK *(Open March 24 to Oct 31 - Varies)*

Information: (509) 686-7231, (360) 902-8844, www.parks.wa.gov
Location: 3 Miles (5 Km) NE of Bridgeport, *N 48 ° 00' 52", W 119° 36' 03"*, 900 Ft

34 Sites – Bridgeport State Park is on the north side of Rufus Woods Lake behind Chief Joseph Dam on the Columbia River. This is a beautiful campground, nice and green because there's lots of water available. Amenities include a swimming beach, boat launch, and a very green 18-hole golf course. Fishing, wind-surfing, and warm-water boating are popular activities here. There are long pull-through sites here which will take 45 foot RVs. To reach the campground follow the access road north for 2 miles (3 Km) from a junction with SR-17 just across the bridge from Bridgeport.

MARINA PARK *(Open April 1 to Oct 31 - Varies)*

Res. and Info.: (509) 686-4747 (April - Oct) or (509) 686-4041 (Nov - March), clerk@nwi.net
Location: Bridgeport, *N 48° 00' 51", W 119° 40' 39"*, 700 Ft

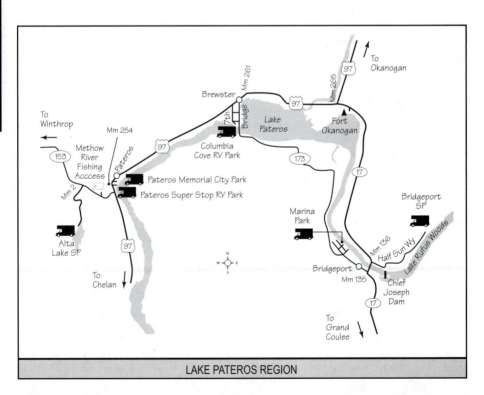

LAKE PATEROS REGION

22 Sites – This riverside campground in Bridgeport is a little gem and also a real value. It's a municipal campground. Back-in and pull-through sites will take rigs to 45 feet and there is a boat ramp. The small campground even has a host. The park is located toward the western end of the town of Bridgeport, follow Columbia Ave. west and then turn north toward the river on 7th Street to the campground.

COLUMBIA COVE RV PARK *(Open May 1 to Oct 31 - Varies)*

Res. and Info.: (509) 689-4050
Location: Brewster, *N 48° 05' 28", W 119° 47' 02"*, 700 Ft

23 Sites – This is another city campground near the river. Not quite as nice as the one in Bridgeport this campground offers similar amenities. There's a nearby boat launch and even a swimming pool next door. Restrooms are open to the general public as well as campground residents and are located across the road. Some sites are 45 feet long. To reach the campground follow 7th Street to the water from US-97 in central Brewster.

PATEROS SUPER STOP RV PARK *(Open All Year)*

Res. and Info.: (509) 923-2200 ext. 181, www.paterossuperstop.com
Location: Pateros, *N 48° 03' 05", W 119° 54' 05"*, 700 Ft

13 Sites – This convenience store, restaurant, and RV park is located right along the Columbia River in downtown Pateros adjoining the city park. The park offers restrooms with showers. These back-in sites will take rigs to 45 feet or longer and have full hookups. They back up to a grassy area on the bank of the river near a boat launch. As you enter town from the south on US-97 watch for the Chevron station on the right. The camping sites are directly behind it.

PATEROS MEMORIAL CITY PARK *(Open All Year)*

Information: (509) 923-2571
Location: Pateros, *N 48° 03' 05", W 119° 54' 05"*, 700 Ft

13 Sites – It is possible to park along the street at the waterfront city park in Pateros for a small fee. The park has restrooms with flush toilets and showers as well as an outdoor kitchen area, horseshoe pits and docks. There is a stand with payment envelopes near the kitchen area.

ALTA LAKE STATE PARK *(Open March 24 to Oct 31 - Varies)*

Information: (509) 923-2473, (360) 902-8844, www.parks.wa.gov
Location: 4 Miles (6 Km) SW of Pateros, *N 48° 01' 46", W 119° 56' 10"*, 1,200 Ft

200 Sites – Alta Lake is an alpine lake accessible by road. It's a unique place for a large state campground and very popular. There are a variety of site types. A large open grassy field is used by both tenters and RVers not needing hookups. Additional back-in sites off loops are small but some have water and electric hookups to about 25 feet. Finally, one loop has a paved parking lot-style area with hookups sites to 45 feet. There are swimming and watersports possibilities in the lake (including personal watercraft) with docks and launch ramps although launching is difficult when water levels are down. There are also hiking trails from the campground and a nearby 18-hole golf course. A small grocery operates in the park. The road to the campground leaves SR-153 about 1.7 miles (2.7 km) west of Pateros. It climbs to the south, it's 1.8 miles (2.9 km) to the campground from the intersection.

LAKE WENATCHEE AND FISH LAKE RECREATION AREA

About 20 miles (32 km) north of Leavenworth in the Wenatchee National Forest the Wenatchee River valley holds two interesting lakes and miles of hiking trails.

The largest of the lakes is Lake Wenatchee. This is a large glacial lake. Near the south shore are two campgrounds. One is a large state park with two separate campgrounds (the park is bisected by the Wenatchee River, the outlet of the lake), the other is a modern national forest campground. Lake Wenatchee offers swimming and boating as well as fishing. The lake has salmon, trout, perch and whitefish.

Nearby is the much smaller Fish Lake. This is a popular fishing lake with at least two commercial fishing lodges offering campsites along the shore. It's a 500 acre lake offering stocked rainbows, German browns, perch, and bass.

This area is a popular winter destination too. There are miles of cross country ski trails and you can ice fish in Fish Lake. The day-use area of the state park remains open in winter as a camping area.

LAKE WENATCHEE STATE PARK *(Open May 1 to October 31 - Varies, in winter a plowed lot is open for camping)*

Reservations: (888) 226-7688, www.camis.com/wa
Information: (509) 763-3101, (360) 902-8844, www.parks.wa.gov
Location: 19 Miles (31 Km) N of Leavenworth, *N 47° 48' 45", W 120° 43' 16"* and *N 47° 48' 11", W 120° 43' 05"*, 1,900 Ft

197 Sites – This is a very large state campground in two different sections separated by a mile or so. The two areas are called the North and South campgrounds. The nearby lake is

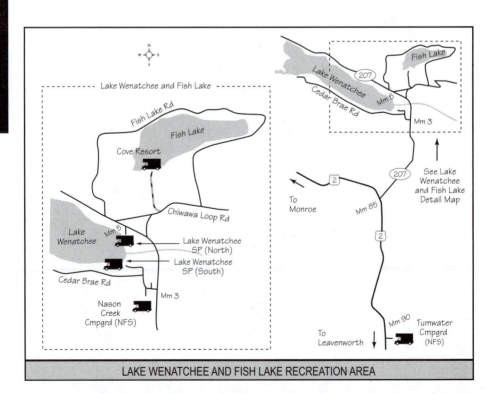

LAKE WENATCHEE AND FISH LAKE RECREATION AREA

the attraction here, there's a popular swimming beach near the south campground. The South Campground is older, has no hookups, and is suitable for RVs to about 30 feet. The North Campground has the hookups and some sites are suitable for RVs to 45 feet. It's about a quarter-mile (.4 km) from the lake. To reach the campgrounds drive north from Leavenworth on US-2 for 16 miles (26 km), then turn north on SR-207. The entrance to the South Campground is in 3.5 miles (5.6 km), the North is another mile (1.6 km).

NASON CREEK CAMPGROUND *(Open May 1 to Sept 30 - Varies)*

Information: (509) 763-3103
Location: 19 Miles (31 Km) N of Leavenworth, *N 47° 48' 03", W 120° 42' 54"*, 1,900 Ft

73 Sites – This large Wenatchee National Forest campground is located just outside the gates of the south section of Lake Wenatchee State Park. Most of the campground is a modern Forest Service campground with paved interior roads and large sites (some pull-thrus) suitable for large rigs of any size. To reach the campgrounds drive north from Leavenworth on US-2 for 16 miles (26 km), then turn north on SR-207. The entrance to the campground is in 3.5 miles (5.6 km) on the left.

COVE RESORT *(Open May 1 to Sept 30 - Varies)*

Information: (509) 763-3130, www.coveresortatfishlake.com
Location: 20 Miles (32 Km) N of Leavenworth, *N 47° 49' 44", W 120° 42' 49"*, 1,900 Ft

110 Sites – This north woods style fishing resort has a dock for fishing as well as rental row-boats and a boat ramp. Fishing tackle and advice are offered in the office. In the woods behind are lots of campsites, some with hookups and others without. Most sites will only take rigs to 30 feet but a few near the main buildings will take RVs to about 35 feet. To reach the resort drive north from Leavenworth on US-2 for 16 miles (26 km), then turn north on SR-207. In 4.2 miles (6.8 km) turn right on Chiwawa Loop Road and you'll see the resort entrance road on the left in .5 mile (.8 km). There is a .8 mile (1.3 km) gravel driveway.

TUMWATER CAMPGROUND *(Open May 1 to Oct 31 - Varies)*

Information: (509) 548-6977
Location: 10 Miles (16 Km) N of Leavenworth, *N 47° 40' 42", W 120° 44' 04"*, 1,700 Ft

84 Sites – Conveniently located right off US-2 Tumwater Wenatchee Forest Campground has paved sites suitable for RVs to about 35 feet and is set in pine trees and situated next to Chiwaukum Creek. To reach the campground drive north on US-2 for 10 miles (16 km) from Leavenworth. The entrance is between Mileposts 90 and 91.

LEAVENWORTH

Leavenworth (population 2,200) is a small out of the way town that has recreated itself as a tourist destination. Beginning in the early 60s Leavenworth's business community began to build and rebuild using a Bavarian theme. Today the buildings, together with a stunning location surrounded by mountains, actually does look somewhat Bavarian.

Best of all, at least in the view of the businesses in town, some 1.5 million people each year visit Leavenworth to shop, dine, and enjoy the events scheduled throughout the year. It would be hard to drive through town on US-2 and not stop for at least a quick look around. A better plan is to stay at one of the nearby campgrounds and spend at least an evening.

Leavenworth is full of shops, restaurants, and art galleries. They provide a lot to keep you

THE BAVARIAN VILLAGE OF LEAVENWORTH

busy any day of the year. But the town also hosts special events. These include **Fasching** in early February, **Maifest** in early May, **Leavenworth Summer Craft Fair** in early June, **Kindrfest** at the middle of June, a **Summer Theater** in July, August and September, a **Chamber Music Festival** in July, **Wenatchee River Salmon Festival** in the middle of September, an **Autumn Leaf Festival** in late September, **Oktoberfest** in the first half of October, **Christkindlmarkt** in late November, and lots more. Check with the Chamber of Commerce for exact dates and information about additional events.

Pine Village KOA Kampground *(Open March 20 to Nov 1 - Varies)*

Reservations	(800) 562-5709, www.koa.com
Information:	(509) 548-7709
Location:	1 Mile (2 Km) NE of Leavenworth, *N 47° 35' 55", W 120° 38' 22"*, 1,100 Ft

135 Sites – This is the handiest place to stay if you are interested in visiting the village for shopping or to visit a restaurant. The large campground sits in tall evergreens above the Wenatchee River. There's a shuttle bus to take you in to town, the distance is less than a mile. This is a large KOA with a full list of amenities. Sites are mostly back-ins although there are a few pull-thrus. The campground is located on the east side of town. From US-2 you'll see signs pointing north just east of the bridge next to the Safeway, the campground is .6 mile (1 km) up the road, the entrance is on the right.

Icicle River RV Park *(Open May 1 to Sept 30 - Varies)*

Res. and Info.:	(509) 548-5420, info@icicleriverrv.com, www.icicleriverrv.com
Location:	3 Miles (5 Km) SW of Leavenworth, *N 47° 32' 58", W 120° 41' 13"*, 1,200 Ft

114 Sites – Farther from town than the KOA, this campground has beautiful sites, some

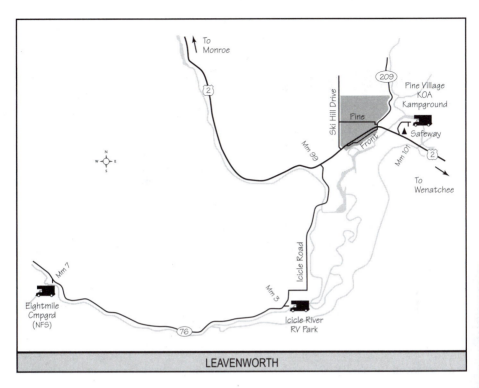

LEAVENWORTH

along the river. To reach the campground drive 1 mile (1.6 km) west on US-2 to Icicle Road from central Leavenworth. Turn left here and drive 3 miles (5 km) to the campground which is on the left.

EIGHTMILE CAMPGROUND *(Open May 1 to Oct 15 - Varies)*

Information: (509)548-6977
Location: 7 Miles (11 Km) SW of Leavenworth, *N 47° 33' 03", W 120° 45' 53"*, 1,900 Ft

45 Sites – Eightmile Wenatchee National Forest campground is in a very scenic location in the canyon of Icicle Creek. There are many hiking trails in the area. Sites here are suitable for RVs to 30 feet. To reach the campground drive 1 mile (1.6 km) west on US-2 to Icicle Road from central Leavenworth. Turn left here and drive 6.7 miles to the campground which is on the left.

MOSCOW, ID, PULLMAN, WA, AND THE PALOUSE

These two college towns are located just a few miles from each other on opposite sides of the Washington-Idaho state line. The climate here is ideal for summer visits with clear bright sunny days and comfortable evenings.

Moscow (population 21,000) is the home of the **University of Idaho**. The campus (with an enrolment of about 14,000) overlooks the town from the southwest. In addition to the campus, attractions in Moscow include the old-fashioned and active **central business district**, the **Appaloosa Museum and Heritage Center**, the **Idaho Forest Fire Museum**, and the **Latah County Historical Museum**. Bikers and walkers appreciate the 9-mile (14.5 km) bike trail connecting Moscow with Pullman.

A major attraction for RVers in the Moscow area is the annual **Life on Wheels** RV Confer-

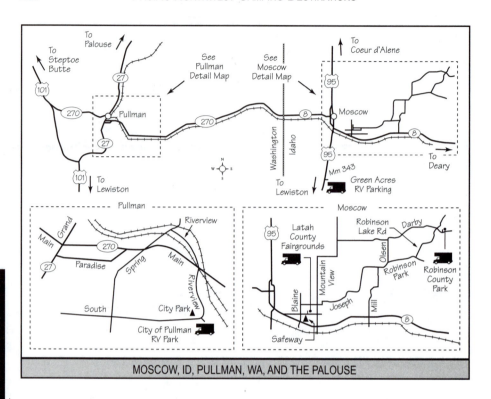

MOSCOW, ID, PULLMAN, WA, AND THE PALOUSE

ence held on the University of Idaho campus each July. The school attracts hundreds of rigs for classroom instruction in all aspects of the RV lifestyle.

Pullman (population 27,000) is home to **Washington State University**. The university has 22,000 students so it considerably augments the town's population and social life. Pullman is similar to Moscow with a pleasant downtown area and an attractive campus. The school here runs its own creamery. You wouldn't want to visit this area and not purchase some of their famous **Cougar Cheese**, particularly the Cougar Gold!

Moscow and Pullman are surrounded by an area of rolling cropland known as the **Palouse**. This scenic area produces dry peas, lentils, and wheat. In fact, the Palouse is the dry pea and lentil capital of the nation. Pullman hosts the **National Lentil Festival** during the second half of August. For a view of the Palouse your best bet is **Steptoe Butte**. The 3,612-foot-tall quartzite outcrop is a Washington state park. It is located about 30 miles (48 km) north of Pullman beyond Colfax. Unfortunately there is no campground.

🚐 **CITY OF PULLMAN RV PARK** *(Open April 1 to November 30)*
Res and Info: (509) 334-4555, (509) 338-3227
Location: Pullman, *N 46° 43' 32", W 117° 10' 15", 2,400 Ft*

23 Sites – This is a small city campground. Some sites will take coaches to 45 feet. Restroom facilities are limited to port-a-potties. From SR-270 between Pullman and Moscow you want to drive north on NE Spring Street. This is the first street west of the railroad overpass which is about a half-mile east of Main in downtown Pullman. Follow NE Spring and then NE Riverview around to the right and under the highway for .4 mile (.6 km) to the campground entrance.

LATAH COUNTY FAIRGROUNDS *(Open All Year)*

Information: (208) 883-5722
Location: Moscow, *N 46° 43' 25", W 116° 59' 03"*, 2,600 Ft

30 Sites – This fairgrounds in Moscow has a variety of sites. There are 5 full-hookup back-ins, 10 sites with electricity only, and more with no hookups. The sites will take RVs to 45 feet. The fairgrounds are conveniently located near the Safeway on the east side of town. There are frequent weekend events at this small fairgrounds, often the camping areas are occupied. It is always a good idea to call ahead to check availability. From central Moscow head east on SR-8. Turn north on South Blaine Street, the street just west of the Tesoro and Safeway. Go one block, turn right, and you'll soon see the fairgrounds entrance on your left.

GREEN ACRES RV PARKING *(Open All Year)*

Information: (208) 882-7487
Location: 1 Mile (2 Km) S of Moscow, *N 46° 41' 47", W 117° 00' 27"*, 2,700 Ft

6 Sites – Although facilities are minimal this is a convenient place for self-contained rigs. Sites are back-ins and pull-thrus and some will take RVs to 45 feet. The RV park is located just off the east side of US-95 some 1.5 miles (2.4 km) south of Moscow.

ROBINSON COUNTY PARK *(Open All Year)*

Res. and Info.: (208) 883-5709
Location: 5 Miles (8 Km) E of Moscow, *N 46° 45' 16", W 116° 54' 30"*, 2,700 Ft

5 Sites – This little county park is located in the countryside just east of Moscow. There are five back-in RV sites that will take RVs to 45 feet. There is also a separate tent-camping area. From Moscow drive east on SR-8. About .2 miles (.3 km) past the Safeway turn left on Mountain View Road. There is a sign at this turn and at the other turns on the route to the park. In .5 miles (.8 km) turn right on Joseph Street and follow the signs for 4.4 miles (7.1 km) to the park.

MOSES LAKE AND THE POTHOLES

Moses Lake (population 16,500) is located at the center of Washington state in a region with hot dry summers and cold, but clear, winters. If fact, the weather here is clear so predictably that the local airport is a beehive of flying activity. Much of the country's large aircraft flight training takes place out of the Moses Lake airport because it's so big, so remote, and has such decent weather. Of course it's also conveniently close to the Boeing factories in Seattle. Moses Lake has even been designated an alternate landing site for the space shuttle.

Recreational activities are centered around two large lakes. **Moses Lake** itself practically surrounds the town and to the south is the large **Potholes Reservoir**. Water sports of all types are popular. Even the fishing is good with warm water species like walleye, trout, bass, perch, crappie, and catfish.

There are other attractions. In town there's the **Moses Lake Museum and Art Center** with an extensive collection of native American artifacts as well as changing art exhibits. For physical fun try the **Family Aquatic Center**, a large water park with 200-foot slides, a beach area, and other attractions.

Just south of Moses Lake is the **Grand County Off Road Vehicle Area**. It's located in an area of sand dunes and has no facilities, but camping is allowed. Follow Division Street south or

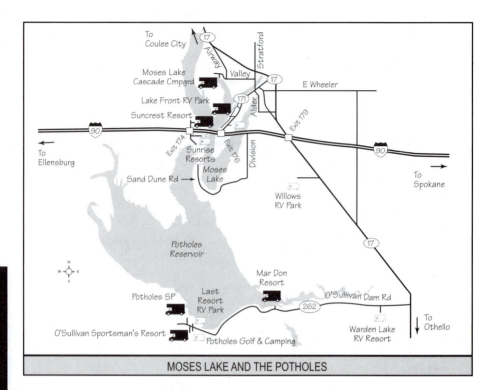

MOSES LAKE AND THE POTHOLES

take Exit 174 and drive south. Both enter the off-road area.

Moses Lake is also a well known birding area. Hotspots are south of town and include the northern border of Potholes Reservoir as well as the **Seep Lakes Wildlife Area** and **Columbia National Wildlife Refuge** south of the reservoir.

MOSES LAKE CASCADE CAMPGROUND *(Open April 15 to October 15 - Varies)*

Res. and Info.: (509) 766-9240
Location: 2 Miles (3 Km) W of Moses Lake, *N 47° 08' 22", W 119° 18' 40"*, 1,000 Ft

75 Sites – This is a municipal campground set on the shore of Moses Lake to the west of the central part of the town of Moses Lake. Parking here is on grass and many sites are suitable for RVs to about 25 feet but since sites are not really delineated a few rigs to 35 feet manage to park if things aren't too crowded. To reach the campground leave I-90 at Exit 176. Drive north on SR-171 for 2.8 miles (4.5 km) and turn left on S. Alder Street. Drive .4 mile (.6 km) across the bridge and turn left on West Valley Road. Follow West Valley for 1.6 miles (2.6 km) until it curves to the right and descends the hillside, you'll see the campground along the shore of the lake below. Turn left into the entrance and then immediately left again to access the campground.

LAKE FRONT RV PARK *(Open All Year)*

Res. and Info.: (509) 765-8294
Location: Moses Lake, *N 47° 06' 36", W 119° 18' 26"*, 1,000 Ft

42 Sites – This is a small campground that is located on the lakeshore near downtown Moses Lake. It was formerly called the Big Sun Resort. It's an older place but is being renovated,

sites have been enlarged and some are now over 55 feet long. These have pull-in access directly off the city street. Exit I-90 at Exit 176 and drive north on SR-171. At .6 mile (.9 km) you'll see the sign for the campground, turn left and drive a block to the campground. Park on the street, there's always lots of room, and walk into the park to check in.

♨ SUNCREST RESORT *(Open All Year)*

Res. and Info.:	(509) 765-0355, infor@suncrestresort.com, www.suncrestresort.com
Location:	5 Miles (8 Km) SW of Moses Lake, *N 47° 06' 29", W 119° 20' 34"*, 1,000 Ft

82 Sites – Suncrest is a modern big-rig resort located just off I-90 just outside and to the west of Moses Lake. Although it's not on the lakeshore there's a beautiful pool and huge hot tub (60-person capacity!). Access is via Exit 174 of I-90. Drive north a short distance and you'll see the entrance.

♨ POTHOLES STATE PARK *(Open All Year)*

Reservations:	(888) 226-7688, www.camis.com/wa
Information:	(509) 346-2759, (360) 371-2800, www.parks.wa.gov
Location:	22 Miles (35 Km) S of Moses Lake, *N 46° 58' 25", W 119° 20' 51"*, 1,000 Ft

126 Sites – This campground is located on the shores of the Potholes Reservoir to the south of Moses Lake. This reservoir and the area to the south, known as the Seep Lakes, are very popular with birders. It's also an important part of the Columbia River irrigation scheme. The state park is a large one and sites can take any size rig since they are back-ins off large circles that are paved in the middle. The park is water oriented with a boat ramp and swimming area. Water levels in the reservoir fluctuate quite a bit from spring to fall. There are also large grassy areas that are great for kids. Take Exit 179 from I-90 and drive south on SR-17 for 9.9 miles (16 km). Turn right on the O'Sullivan Dam Road which is also known as SR- 262. It will lead you 12.3 miles (19.8 km) to the campground entrance; you'll cross the large earth dam en route.

♨ O'SULLIVAN SPORTSMAN'S RESORT *(Open All Year)*

Reservations:	(888) 346-2447
Information:	(509) 346-2447, osullivan@nwi.net, www.osullivansportsmanresort.com
Location:	21 Miles (34 Km) S of Moses Lake, *N 46° 58' 12", W 119° 20' 43"*, 1,000 Ft

200 Sites – This is a membership campground located near the state park. It usually has room for non-members. The campground is not located next to the water but has large sites for RVs to 45 feet and good amenities including a seasonal swimming pool and cable TV. Take Exit 179 from I-90 and drive south on SR-17 for 9.9 miles (16 km). Turn right on the O'Sullivan Dam Road which is also known as SR-262. It will lead you 11.2 miles (18.1 km) to the campground entrance; you'll cross the large earth dam en route.

♨ MAR DON RESORT *(Open All Year)*

Reservations:	(800) 416-2736	**Information:**	(509) 346-2651, www.mardonresort.com
Location:	20 Miles (32 Km) S of Moses Lake, *N 46° 57' 57", W 119° 19' 12"*, 1,000 Ft		

184 Sites – This is a large and venerable resort located on the shore of Potholes Reservoir. Sites here vary, there are many long-term residents and also many tent and RV sites for travelers. Some of these RV sites will take RVs to 45 feet with careful maneuvering. Amenities include a grocery store, restaurant, and swimming beach. Take Exit 179 from I-90 and drive south on SR-17 for 9.9 miles (16 km). Turn right on the O'Sullivan Dam Road which is also known as SR- 262. It will lead you 10 miles (16.1 km) to the campground entrance; you'll cross the large earth dam en route.

MT RAINIER NATIONAL PARK

The centerpiece of this national park is 14,411 ft. Mt Rainier. It's the tallest mountain in the Cascades, the tallest along the west coast until you reach Mt Whitney in California. This was an early national park, it was created in 1899 and many of the structures in the park were built by the CCC during the 1930s.

Think of the park as having two centers of interest for vehicle-based visitors. One centers around the visitor center at **Paradise** on the south side of the mountain, the other centers around the visitor center at **Sunrise** on the northeast side of the mountain. Of course, if you are a hiker the entire park is open to you.

Paradise sits at the 5,400-foot level of the mountain. Most people who climb the mountain start from the huge Paradise parking lot. There is a year-round visitor center here. You'll also want to visit the old Paradise Inn. If the weather allows you can follow trails through the surrounding meadows and enjoy the wildflowers and the views.

There may be two centers of interest but there are three entrance to the park. Campgrounds tend to be near these entrances, both inside and outside the park. It's best not to take large RVs (say over 25 feet) up onto the mountain since roads are steep and narrow. Instead park them at one of the campgrounds near the entrances and use a tow car to access Paradise or Sunshine. Note that no fuel is available inside the park. Also note that both the Stevens Canyon Road (from the Ohanepecosh Entrance) and the Sunrise Road are closed by snow in winter.

The **Nisqually Entrance** is located at the far southwest corner of the park. This is often thought of as the main entrance. It provides the shortest access route to the Paradise area on the south side of the mountain. Campgrounds near this entrance are the first ones listed below: Cougar Rock Campground, Sunshine Point Campground, Mounthaven Resort, and Big Creek Campground. Not far inside the entrance is Longmire, which has the only hotel in the park that is open year-round. At Longmire take a look at the **National Park Inn** and the **Longmire Museum**. The short and easy **Trail of the Shadows** lets you explore the immediate area. The highway distance to Paradise from the Nisqually Entrance is 17 miles (27 km).

Also giving access to Paradise, but with a much longer access route, is **Ohanapecosh Entrance**. It's near the southeast corner of the park. Near this entrance are Ohanapecosh Campground, La Wis Wis Campground, and the Packwood RV Park. The Stevens Canyon Road leads from this entrance to Paradise, a distance of 21 miles (34 km). From Ohanapecosh the highway climbs over Backbone Ridge, descends to cross the Muddy Fork of the Cowlitze River at Box Canyon, and then climbs through Stevens Canyon to reach the high country at Paradise. The lower elevations crossed by the highway are largely covered with old-growth evergreen forest. An excellent way to enjoy the trees is to hike the 1.5 mile (2.4 km) **Grove of the Patriarchs interpretive trail**. It's located near the entrance. Another good stop is the one at **Reflection Lakes** for a photo of the mountain.

On the eastern border of the park but outside the park entrances SR-410 and then SR-123 cross Cayuse Pass at 4,694 feet. This highway connects Enumclaw to the north with US-12 which crosses south of the park. SR-410 is also the location of the third entrance to the park, the White River Entrance. Campgrounds handy to this entrance are White River Campground, The Dalles Campground, and Silver Springs Campground. It's 15 miles (24 km) from SR-410 up to Sunrise. The road passes White River Campground, the Frying Pan Creek Trailhead, and then loops its way up the side of the mountain to the meadows around Sunrise. You'll find a visitor's center here, also the **Sunrise Lodge**, and lots of trails. Sunrise is as high as you can get on the mountain in your car, 6,400 feet, and is only accessible and open from July to early September.

Near the White River Entrance but toward the east away from the park SR-410 climbs to cross Chinook Pass. You might want to take a short side trip up to Lake Tipsoo just below the pass for great views back westward to the mountain (assuming good weather).

The campgrounds along US-12 south of the mountain aren't quite as convenient to Mt Rainier as the ones near the entrances but they have an additional benefit. From the area of Randle you can easily access the eastern viewpoints of **Mt St Helens National Monument**. Campgrounds listed below that are in this area are Cascade Peaks Resort and Campground, Maple Grove Resort and Golf Course, and Iron Creek Campground.

To access the Windy Ridge Viewpoint, which has great views of the caldera blowout on Mt St Helens, you drive south from Randle on forest service roads a distance of 36 miles (58 km). The route is well signed, the road is paved, and the view is spectacular. It's also a lot less crowded than the main viewpoints accessible from farther west. See the *Mt St Helens* section for information about access and campgrounds on that side.

COUGAR ROCK CAMPGROUND *(Open May 25 to October 15 - Varies)*

Reservations:	(800) 365-2267, http://reservations.nps.gov
Information:	(360) 569-2211
Location:	9 Miles (15 Km) Inside Nisqually Entrance,
	N 46° 46' 03", W 121° 47' 32", 3,200 Ft

200 Sites – Cougar Rock is the main Mt Rainier National Park Campground for the southwest part of the park. It is convenient for visits to the Paradise Visitor Center. Some sites here can take RVs to 35 feet although the campground is set on uneven ground so sites are irregular and many are much shorter. Reservations are available only from late June to Labor day. The campground is 8.6 miles (14 km) inside the Nisqually Entrance, 8.9 miles (14.4 km) km) from Paradise Visitor Center.

RAINIER SEEN FROM THE SUNRISE VISITOR CENTER

WASHINGTON

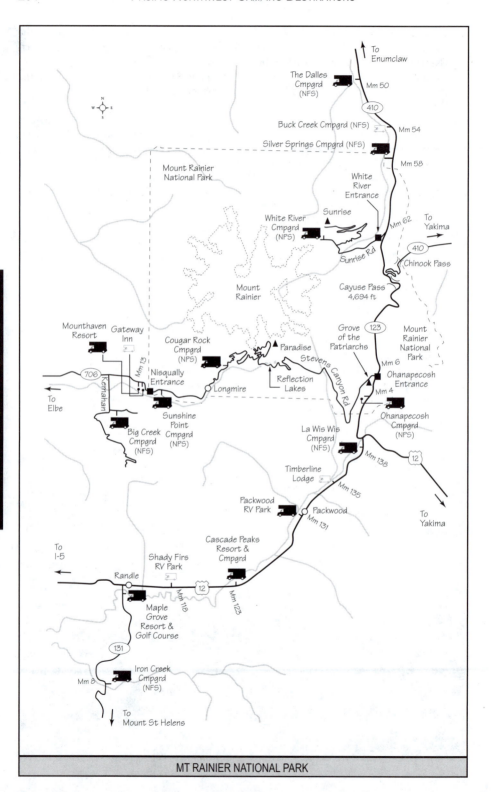

SUNSHINE POINT CAMPGROUND *(Open All Year)*

Information: (360) 569-2211
Location: Nisqually Entrance, *N 46° 44' 16", W 121° 54' 35"*, 2,000 Ft

18 Sites – This is a small national park campground just .4 mile (.6 km) inside the Nisqually entrance. It sits on a flat next to the Nisqually River so maneuvering is easy, several sites will take RVs to 35 feet. It's an open, light campground, very pleasant.

MOUNTHAVEN RESORT *(Open All Year)*

Reservations: (800) 456-9380
Information: (360) 569-2594, info@mounthaven.com, www.mounthaven.com
Location: 1 Mile (2 Km) Outside Nisqually Entrance,
                    N 46° 44' 55", W 121° 55' 39", 2,000 Ft

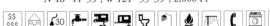

16 Sites – This resort is located very near the southwest entrance to the park and is a good base if you like more amenities than the park campgrounds offer. It has cabins and good long RV sites to 60 feet with full hookups under big trees. The campground is known for it's quiet and is well-managed, amenities include a hot tub. The resort is located on the south side of the highway .8 mile (1.3 km) outside the Nisqually entrance to the park.

BIG CREEK CAMPGROUND *(Open Memorial Day to Sept 15 - Varies)*

Reservations: (877) 444-6777, reserveusa.com   **Information:**   (360) 497-1100
Location: 5 Miles (8 Km) From Nisqually Entrance, *N 46° 44' 09", W 121° 58' 15"*, 1,800 Ft

29 Sites – This is a Gifford Pinchot National Forest campground convenient to the southeast entrance to Rainier Park. Some sites here will take coaches to 35 feet but access roads are narrow so exercise caution. From a point on SR-706 some 3.5 miles (5.6 km) west of the Nisqually entrance to the park drive south on Kemahan Rd. In 1.4 miles (2.3 km) the road makes a 90° left and in another .5 mile (.8 km) you'll see the entrance on your right.

OHANAPECOSH CAMPGROUND *(Open May 25 to Oct 10 - Varies)*

Reservations: (800) 365-2267, http://reservations.nps.gov   **Information:**   (360) 569-2211
Location: 2 Miles (3 Km) S of Ohanapecosh Entrance, *N 46° 43' 58", W 121° 34' 09"*, 2,000 Ft

190 Sites – Ohanapecosh is an older national park campground that serves the southeastern portion of the park. It is set in huge evergreens and tends to be a little dark. Sites were laid out in the days of much smaller rigs, the park recommends a size limit of 27 feet for trailers (and 5th wheels) and 32 feet for motorhomes. The limits are due to both site size and access road complications. Reservations are available only from late June to Labor Day. The campground entrance is actually outside the park entrance station. It's 1.8 miles (2.9 km) south on SR-123 from the entrance road.

LA WIS WIS CAMPGROUND *(Open May 15 to September 30 - Varies)*

Reservations: (877) 444-6777, www.reserveusa.com   **Information:**   (360) 494-0600
Location: 6 Miles (10 Km) E of Packwood, *N 46° 40' 40", W 121° 34' 39"*, 1,400 Ft

115 Sites – This Gifford Pinchot National Forest campground is convenient to the southeast entrance to the park. It's an older campground with small sites suitable for RVs to about

25 feet. It borders the Clear Fork of the Cowlitz River, trout fishing is possible. There are short trails to the Blue Hole on the Ohanapecosh River and to Purcell Falls. The entrance to the campground is on the north side of the highway .6 miles (1 km) south of the intersection of US-12 and SR-123. It's 6 miles (10 km) east of Packwood and 6.1 (9.8 km) miles from the Ohanapecosh Entrance to the Park.

PACKWOOD RV PARK *(Open All Year)*

Res. and Info.:	(360) 494-5145
Location:	Packwood, *N 46° 36' 22", W 121° 40' 21"*, 1,000 Ft

89 Sites – Located in the middle of Packwood, this old RV park is a relaxed place in a relaxed town. You can stroll across the street to a restaurant or the grocery store, things couldn't be more convenient. The campground is set under large trees providing lots of shade. Parking is on grass with room for any size rig. Full hookups are available, as are sites with electricity and water only. Some sites are pull-thrus suitable for RVs to 45 feet. The campground sits near the center of town, it is well-signed and hard to miss.

WHITE RIVER CAMPGROUND *(Open June 15 to Sept 15 - Varies)*

Information:	(360) 569-2211
Location:	43 Miles (69 Km) SE of Enumclaw, *N 46° 54' 08", W 121° 38' 20"*, 4,200 Ft

112 Sites – White River is the Mt Rainier National Park campground that services the northeast portion of the park. The entrance to this area is called the White River entrance and one road leads up to the Sunrise Visitor Center. This campground is off that road. It sits in a valley with the mountain looming at the top. Climbers often start here to head up this side of the mountain. There are several trails including one that climbs steeply to Sunrise and another that leads to an overlook of Emmons Glacier. Sites here are remarkably short, most would not accommodate a 25-foot RV comfortably, but there are a few that will take very carefully driven 30-footers. The campground entrance is on the left 5.3 miles (8.6 km) from the White River Entrance and 10 miles (16 km) from Sunrise.

THE DALLES CAMPGROUND *(Open Memorial Day to Labor Day - Varies)*

Reservations:	(877) 444-6777, reserveusa.com	**Information:**	(360) 825-6585
Location:	26 Miles (42 Km) SE of Enumclaw, *N 47° 04' 06", W 121° 34' 37"*, 2,100 Ft		

44 Sites – The Dalles Mt Baker-Snoqualmie National Forest campground is situated next to the White River along the SR-410, the Mather Parkway, as it climbs toward Chinook and Cayuse Passes. Sites here vary a great deal in size from back-ins suitable only for RVs to 22 feet to a few large back-in sites that will just barely take a 45-footer. The campground is located 26 miles (42 km) southeast of Enumclaw and 12 miles (19 km) north of the cutoff to Sunrise.

SILVER SPRINGS CAMPGROUND *(Open Memorial Day to Labor Day - Varies)*

Reservations:	(877) 444-6777, reserveusa.com	**Information:**	(360) 825-6585
Location:	32 Miles (52 Km) SE of Enumclaw, *N 46° 59' 36", W 121° 31' 56"*, 2,700 Ft		

56 Sites – This is a second national forest campground located along SR-410, the Mather Parkway, as it climbs toward the passes. This one too is along the White River. There are a few more large sites in this campground but it is very similar to The Dalles, described above. The campground is located 32 miles (52 km) southeast of Enumclaw and 6 miles (10 km) north of the cutoff to Sunrise.

WASHINGTON

CASCADE PEAKS RESORT AND CAMPGROUND *(Open All Year)*

Reservations: (866) 255-2931
Information: (360) 494-9202, (360) 494-7931, www.cascadervresort.com
Location: 7 Miles (11 Km) W of Packwood, *N 46° 32' 03", W 121° 46' 39"*, 900 Ft

Over 1,000 Sites – This is a very large campground. It has a lot of amenities and sells memberships and individual sites. Travelers are welcome, however. Amenities include two swimming pools, a hot tub and sauna. Sites are varied with tent areas, full-hookups for RVs to 45 feet, and many electric and water sites set in trees. The campground is located north of US-12 some 8 miles (13 km) east of Randle and 7 miles (11 km) west of Packwood.

MAPLE GROVE RESORT AND GOLF COURSE *(Open All Year)*

Information: (360) 497-2742
Location: Randle, *N 46° 31' 47", W 121° 57' 15"*, 800 Ft

165 Sites – This is another membership resort. It does not take reservations for non-members but often has room for travelers during the week in the summer and all week the rest of the year. Amenities include a nine-hole golf course and an indoor swimming pool and hot tub. The campground is in two areas. There's a big-rig park with pull-thrus suitable for 45 footers in a big open field. There's also a shaded area with smaller sites much like a forest service campground but with electrical hookups in about half of the 78 sites. The campground is located just south of the intersection of US-12 and SR-131 in Randle.

IRON CREEK CAMPGROUND *(Open May 15 to Sept 30 - Varies)*

Reservations: (877) 444-6777, www.reserveusa.com
Information: (360) 497-1100
Location: 9 Miles (15 Km) S of Randle, *N 46° 25' 42", W 121° 59' 07"*, 1,100 Ft

98 Sites – This campground in the Gifford Pinchot National Forest makes a great base for exploring both Rainier and the east side of Mt St Helens. For a national forest campground it's a big place with almost 100 sites and it can accommodate big rigs with sites to 45 feet and adequate maneuvering room. It sits on the Cispus River, fishing is possible. From Randle drive south on SR-131. At the fork at .9 miles (1.5 km) stay right, you'll reach the campground 9.2 miles (14.8 km) south of Randle.

MT ST HELENS NATIONAL VOLCANIC MONUMENT

When Mt St Helens blew on May 18, 1980 it created a unique tourist attraction. The thousands of square miles of devastated landscape make an impressive destination, and a lot of effort and money have been spent to make the mountain accessible. The area is now known as **Mount St Helens National Volcanic Monument**. Easiest access for motorized travelers is from the west and that's what we'll talk about in this sections. See the *Mt Rainier National Park* section for information about approaching the mountain from the east.

A parkway, the **Spirit Lake Memorial Highway**, leads from Exit 49 of I-5 some 51 miles (82 km) eastward toward the mountain. Most of the parkway was built after the eruption. It is wide and beautiful, suitable for any rig. The only problem is that after the Hoffstadt Bluffs Visi-

WASHINGTON

OUTSIDE THE JOHNSTON RIDGE OBSERVATORY AT MT ST HELENS

tor Center at Mile 27 the road climbs rather steeply, sometimes with seven percent grades. You can leave trailers or big rigs at the visitor center and use the tow car to drive on up.

Along the road there are now no less than 5 information centers. This must be the highest concentration of such places in the world and a trip to the mountain for most people is largely a drive from one center to the next. If you do want to get off the road and explore however, you can do so. There are a number of hiking trails accessible from the parkway.

The first stop is **Mount St Helens Visitor Center**. It is about 5 miles (8 km) from I-5 and run by the Forest Service. It has exhibits that make a great introduction to your drive up to the mountain with background information about the eruption. The mountain is not visible from this center.

Stop number two is **Hoffstadt Bluffs Visitor Center** at Mile 27. This center is the most commercial of the five, it seems to be dedicated mostly to selling souvenirs and services. From here you can take a helicopter tour, have a meal in a large restaurant, or buy a souvenir.

The third center is called **The Charles W. Bingham Forest Learning Center** and is at Mile 33. This one is a Weyerhaeuser operation and explores the timber and logging aspects of the eruption. A huge amount of timber was blown down, much was destroyed but a lot was salvaged. Weyerhaeuser is now doing a lot of replanting. Don't miss this stop, we find it the most interesting of all the centers, it is very well done.

At Mile 43 is **Coldwater Ridge Visitor Center**. This Forest Service facility has a great view of the mountain and exhibits about the impact of the eruption on the plants and animals in the surrounding area. There's also a cafeteria and a souvenir store.

Finally, at Mile 51, is **Johnston Ridge Observatory**. This new center is very close to the mountain, just 5 miles (8 km) from the crater. You can actually see the new swelling lava dome inside the crater because the crater walls on this side were blown out during the eruption. The observatory is so close to the mountain that it is sometimes closed when geologists report that the mountain is active. Johnston Ridge overlooks the devastated Sprit Lake and gives you the best idea of the massive devastation caused by the eruption.

☎ MT ST HELENS RV PARK *(Open All Year)*

Res. and Info.: (360) 274-8522, MSHRVP@msn.com
Location: 2 Miles (3 Km) E of I-5 Exit 49, *N 46° 18' 22", W 122° 52' 36"*, 400 Ft

88 Sites – This modern RV park, not far from I-5 Exit 49, makes an excellent base for your visit to Mt St Helens. The sites are arranged on a terraced hillside. You'll find a variety of site types, the largest rigs will fit although sites do not have a lot of separation. Full hookups including cable are available. The campground can provide information and advice about a trip up the mountain. Amenities include a laundry, recreation hall, and playground. Down the hill is an Imax theater offering a film about the eruption. To find the campground take Exit 49 from I-5. Drive east on SR-504 for 2 miles (3 km). Turn left on Tower Road, you'll see the campground entrance on the right soon after the turn.

☎ SEAQUEST STATE PARK *(Open All Year)*

Reservations: (888) 226-7688, www.camis.com/wa
Information: (360) 274-8633, (360) 371-2800, www.parks.wa.gov
Location: 6 Miles (10 Km) E of I-5 Exit 49, *N 46° 17' 45", W 122° 49' 04"*, 400 Ft

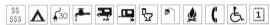

92 Sites – This state park offers sites set in huge evergreens. Most sites are suitable for RVs to about 35 feet but the full-hookup area has open side-by-side sites suitable for RVs to 35 feet. The campground is just off SR-504 and a convenient location for a visit to the monument. From Exit 49 on I-5 follow SR-504 east toward the mountain for 6 miles (10 km), the entrance is on the left.

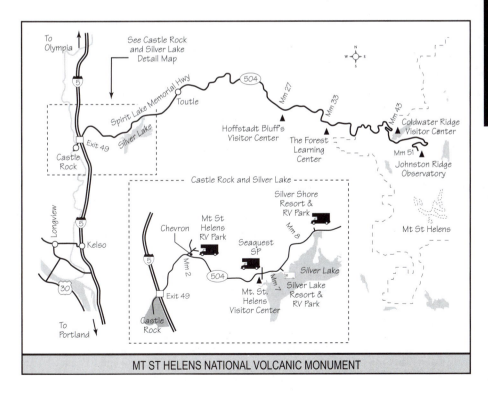

MT ST HELENS NATIONAL VOLCANIC MONUMENT

SILVER SHORES RESORT AND RV PARK *(Open All Year)*
Res. and Info.:   (360) 274-0400
Location: 8 Miles (13 Km) E of I-5, Exit 49, *N 46° 19' 11", W 122° 46' 29"*, 400 Ft

40 Sites – This is a roadside fishing resort with a dock and rental boats. The restaurant and bar here seem to be very popular with the motorcycle crowd. On the hillside behind the restaurant are RV sites, nice tents sites are located below and to the right at the edge of the trees. From Exit 49 on I-5 follow SR-504 east toward the mountain for 8.2 miles (13.2 km), the entrance is on the left.

NORTH CASCADES NATIONAL PARK

You may be surprised at the nature of this national park. Although we sometimes call it a national park in this book it is technically a national park complex. The **North Cascades National Park Service Complex** is actually composed of three parts: **North Cascades National Park**, **Ross Lake National Recreation Area**, and **Lake Chelan National Recreation Area**. SR-20 actually never enters the national park itself, instead the park is split by the Ross Lake N.R.A., and the road passes through this N.R.A.

The reason for this is that long before the park was established three dams were built here by Seattle City Light to provide Seattle with power. They form three lakes: little Gorge Lake, larger Diablo Lake, and huge Ross Lake. There are also two Seattle City Light company towns inside the N.R.A.: Newhalem and Diablo. The park itself lies to the north and south and has little in the way of man-made intrusions. Only trails and boats provide access.

Newhalem itself presents a very neat and well-tended appearance. Seattle City Light employees who work at the dams live here. Seattle City Light maintains a **visitor center** in Newhalem, it's a good place to check for information about local sights and hikes since most short ones are related to City Light facilities. Just a few miles further along, on a side road from near Mile 126, is another Seattle City Light town, **Diablo**.

There are a wealth of **hiking opportunities** in this park. Passenger boats ply both Diablo and Ross Lake, you can catch a ride to the beginning points for many wilderness hikes. Register with the back-country ranger station in Marblemount or at the ranger stations in Sedro-Woolley or Winthrop (if you are coming the other way) before your hike if you plan to camp overnight. Also, you should be aware that if you park at a trailhead in the national forests to the west and east (not the park complex though) you need a Northwest Forest Pass available at forest service offices.

Shorter hikes from the road that do not require registration include the River Loop Trail, Newhalem Rockshelter Trail, To Know a Tree Trail, Trail of the Cedars, and Ladder Creek Falls Trail, all in the Newhalem area. There's also the Thunder Woods trail at Mile 131, the Ross Dam Trail (Mile 134), Happy Creek Forest Walk (Mile 135), and Ruby Creek Trail (Mile 138).

For us, however, the main attraction is the road. It has long reached as far as the town of Diablo. In 1972 a new portion opened that continued on over the Cascades. The road is spectacular because it travels through true wilderness. There are no towns, just mountains everywhere. This new road is only open in the summer, during the winter it is closed from Mile 134 to Mile 171. Open dates depend upon the snow, usually the road is open from mid April to some time in November. Highlights of this new portion of road are the **overlooks** at **Diablo Lake** (Mile 131) and **Ross Lake** (Mile 135), and **Rainy Pass** (4,855 feet at Mile 157) and **Washington Pass** (5,277 feet at Mile 162).

If you are approaching the park from the west you'll want to make a stop at the **North Cascades National Park Service Complex Headquarters** in Sedro-Woolley. It's at about Mile 64 and located right next to the road. They can give you information about activities in the park ahead. They can also give you the status of campgrounds in the park and tell you whether any sites remain available. This information is invaluable in making your plans for the evening stop.

Driving east from Sedro-Woolley you will be following the Skagit River Valley and pass through the towns of Concrete, Rockport, and Marblemount. Near Rockport SR-530, which forms a loop from the south that starts near Arlington, joins the highway. If you want hookups when you stop for the night the commercial campground in Marblemount or one of the two campgrounds near Rockport make a good place to stop. They are listed under campgrounds below. These campgrounds are outside the national recreation area.

The stretch of road eastward to Marblemount closely follows the **Skagit River**. The Skagit has been designated a **Wild and Scenic River** and during the winter hosts one of the largest gatherings of **bald eagles** in the lower 48 states. The section of river between Rockport and Newhalem is a prime viewing area from mid-December through February. About 500 bald eagles gather in the area during this time. There is a two-day **Upper Skagit Bald Eagle Festival** held in the area at the beginning of February each year. People come to see eagles perch in trees overlooking the river or munch on decaying salmon along the gravel bars.

The town of Marblemount, at Mile 106, is your last chance for gas on this side of the mountains. Don't forget to check your gauge. Marblemount is also home to the park's **Wilderness Information Center** where you get back-country permits for the park.

At about Mile 111 you actually enter the park. Before you know it you will be entering the Seattle City Light company town of Newhalem. Before you really reach the town, at about Mile 120, you'll see the sign for the right turn into the **North Cascades Visitor Center** and Newhalem Campground. The visitor center is well worth a stop, It is the most important Park Service facility in the park, there are exhibits and a very well done slide show.

Gorge Lake, behind **Gorge Dam**, is the smallest of the three dam-created lakes. It covers 210 acres. The dam here was built in the 1920s. You can see most of Gorge Lake from the highway which passes along its northern shore.

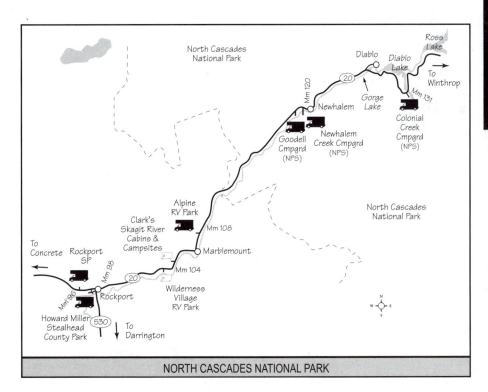

NORTH CASCADES NATIONAL PARK

At the east end of Gorge Lake the road crosses to the south side of the Skagit River. The original road goes on in to **Diablo**, the new road passes south of **Diablo Lake** which is the second largest of the lakes and covers an area of 910 acres. The road dips down to the shore of the lake at Colonial Creek at Mile 130. There is a large campground here as well as a boat launch. There is an excellent view of this lake from the **overlook** at Mile 131, just up the hill past the campground.

Ross Lake behind **Ross Dam** is the largest of the lakes. There is no road access to Ross Lake, the best view is from the **Ross Lake Overlook** at Mile 135.

Before you know it you will be past the lake area and climbing toward Rainy Pass. Once you leave the lakes you also leave the N.R.A., you're now in the Okanogan National Forest. **Rainy Pass** is 4,860 feet high (Mile 157). There's a picnic area and trails there. In fact, the Pacific Crest National Scenic Trail crosses the road at the pass.

Five miles farther along is **Washington Pass**, 5,477 feet (Mile 162). A stop here is essential, the view from the overlook is spectacular. You look across the valley at Liberty Bell and the Early Winter Spires, also straight down at the highway climbing from the east side of the pass.

From Washington Pass the road descends steeply for a few miles, then follows the Methow Valley on in to Winthrop.

The campgrounds listed below are arranged from west to east. There are other campgrounds listed in this book convenient to the area. To the west see the *Skagit Valley* section for more campgrounds, to the east see *Winthrop*.

ROCKPORT STATE PARK *(Open April 1 to Oct 31 - Varies)*

Information: (360) 853-8461, (360) 902-8844, www.parks.wa.gov
Location: 1 Mile (2 Km) W of Rockport, N 48° 29' 15", W 121° 36' 55", 400 Ft

50 Sites – This state park campground is set in a grove of 300-year-old Douglas firs and cedars. The dense canopy makes the campground pretty dark and you probably wouldn't want your rig parked here during a windstorm. It's an older campground and a sign at the entrance limits rigs to 38 feet. We recommend rigs no longer than 35 feet due to the limited maneuvering room. An 11-mile (18 km) trail leads from the campground up 5,400 ft. Mt Sauk. Parking for hikers is not at the campground. Rockport State Park is located just a mile (1.6 km) west of Rockport on the north side of SR-20.

HOWARD MILLER STEELHEAD COUNTY PARK *(Open All Year)*

Res. and Info.: (360) 853-8808, parksrec@co.skagit.wa.us
Location: Rockport, N 48° 29' 04", W 121° 35' 47", 200 Ft

59 Sites – This campground is in the town of Rockport. Our guess is that when the campground is full Rockport's population doubles. There's a small store and a tavern above the campground for limited supplies. This is a large open grassy campground right next to the Skagit River. Sites are large, some to 60 feet long, and there are no trees to block your slide-out. You might not even notice Rockport from the main road. It is near Mile 98 and inside the angle formed by the intersection of SR-20 and SR-530. There are two entrances to the campground, one signed off SR-20 which brings you down through the village, the other off 530 just north of the bridge.

ALPINE RV PARK *(Open All Year)*

Res. and Info.: (360) 873-9002, jra@cnw.com, alpinervpark@hotmail.com
Location: Marblemount, N 48° 33' 03", W 121° 25' 27", 300 Ft

32 Sites - This reasonably-priced commercial campground is a good alternative to the state and federal campgrounds in the area. It's a basic campground but has the facilities you need. Big rigs will find that the back-in sites will take RVs to 45 feet and longer and there's plenty of room to maneuver. The campground is located on the north side of the highway just east of Marblemount and 12 miles (19 km) west of Newhalem.

GOODELL CAMPGROUND *(Open May 15 to Oct 15 - Varies)*

Information:	(360) 856-5700
Location:	Newhelem, *N 48° 40' 19", W 121° 16' 15"*, 400 Ft

21 Sites – This is a small national park campground located just down the highway from the Newhalem Creek Campground. It's on the north side of the river and a popular put-in point for the rafting companies. It's an older campground suitable only for RVs to about 30 feet. The campground entrance road is .5 miles (.8 km) west of Newhalem.

NEWHALEM CREEK CAMPGROUND *(Open All Year)*

Reservations:	(877) 444-6777, www.reserveusa.com
Information:	(360) 856-5700
Location:	Newhalem, *N 48° 40' 15", W 121° 15' 39"*, 400 Ft

116 Sites – Newhalem is the most civilized and probably the busiest of the park's campgrounds. Although it is left open in the winter the water is turned off about the middle of October and on again about May 1. Sites here are off paved loop roads with some sites to 45 feet and even longer. The campground is at the western approaches to Newhalem. The main visitor center for the park is located in the same area.

COLONIAL CREEK CAMPGROUND *(Open All Year)*

Information:	(360) 856-5700
Location:	9 Miles (15 Km) E of Newhalem, *N 48° 41' 18", W 121° 05' 42"*, 1,200 Ft

98 Sites – This large North Cascades National Park campground is located just west of the point where the highway is barricaded during the winter. It's right where the highway crosses an arm of Diablo Lake. The campground is an older one, it's not designed for big rigs. The largest practical size for RVs here is 30 feet and most sites just don't have room for slide-outs. While the campground is theoretically open all year the snow isn't usually cleared and there is no water in winter. The campground is located 9.5 miles (15.3 km) east of Newhalem and 63 miles (102 km) west of Winthrop.

OCEAN SHORES AND THE NORTH BEACHES AREA

The **North Beaches Area** stretches from Ocean Shores on the north point of the entrance to Grays Harbor for about 30 miles (48 km) north to the Quinault Indian Reservation. The name North Beaches refers to the fact that these beaches are north of the mouth of Grays Harbor. There are also fine beaches south of Grays Harbor, see the *Westport* section for more about this area. The North Beaches are the closest Pacific beaches to Seattle, they can be reached in about 3 hours by freeway, so you will find much more activity here than on the more remote beaches to the north in the Olympic National Park.

There are a number of small towns along the coast. From south to north they are **Ocean Shores, Ocean City, Copalis Beach, Pacific Beach, Moclips,** and finally, inside the Quinault Indian Reservation, **Taholah**. The towns north of Ocean Shores are small, most have little more than a few motels, campgrounds, and restaurants. The beaches out front are wide and solid, driving is allowed on many of them. One of the big attractions is the razor clams, there are beds of clams in front of the towns, when the tide is particularly low and the season open you'll usually find hundreds of folks digging clams on the beach. The beaches are great when there are no clams too, you can ride a bicycle, fly a kite, surf fish, or just comb the tide line.

Ocean Shores (population 4,400) is a different story. This town was developed during the 1960s as a resort and retirement haven. It has big beachside motels, a golf course, restaurants and shops, a casino, and even a lake and canals that offer decent fishing. Ocean Shores has a marina just inside the mouth of Grays Harbor, the somewhat down-at-the-heels commercial campground is located at the marina. You can arrange a fishing charter here or, during the summer, catch a small walk-on only passenger ferry across the mouth of Grays Harbor to Westport.

Ocean Shores hosts a large number of events. These include the **Beachcombers Fun Fair** in early March, the **Festival of Colors** in May, the **Ocean Shores International Kite Challenge** in June, and the **Dixieland Jazz Festival** in November.

Two larger towns, **Hoquiam** (population 9,000) and **Aberdeen** (population 16,400), are about 20 miles (32 km) east of Ocean Shores. These larger towns make a good place to pick up supplies. They also have their own attractions. The **Grays Harbor Historical Seaport** in Aberdeen is the home port for the **Lady Washington**. This is a full-sized sailing replica of one of the ships in which an expedition led by Captain Gray discovered both the Columbia River and Grays Harbor in 1788. Although the Lady Washington is usually at sea visiting other areas, there is an interpretive center and museum.

A little west of Hoquiam you'll find the entrance road for **Bowerman Basin**. This is a wildlife refuge, during late April and early May it is a wonderful place to view thousands of shorebirds.

The campgrounds below are listed from north to south. Along this coast the state parks are without a doubt the nicest sites for both tents and RVs. The commercial campgrounds provide a decent back-up, many of them also accept tents. The last place to fill is usually Quinault Mari-

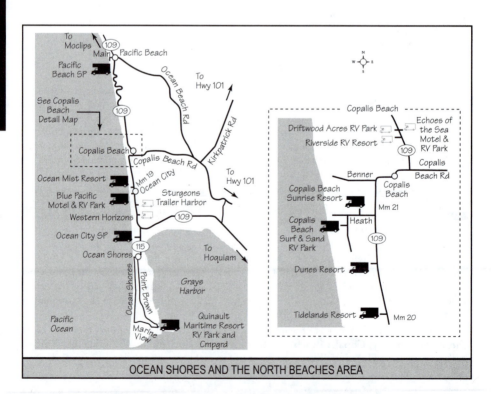

OCEAN SHORES AND THE NORTH BEACHES AREA

time Resort RV Park and Campground.

⛺ PACIFIC BEACH STATE PARK *(Open All Year)*

Reservations: (888) 226-7688, www.camis.com/wa
Information: (360) 276-4297, (360) 902-8844, www.parks.wa.gov;
Location: 15 Miles (24 Km) N of Ocean Shores, *N 47° 12' 21", W 124° 12' 10"*, Near Sea Level

64 Sites – RV sites here are in an open area next to the beach with no trees. Views are great and the beach very accessible. This is a very popular campground, particularly during open clam tides. Sites are back-ins, some extend to 50 feet and nearly all will accept 45-footers. About two-thirds have electrical and water hookups and there is a dump station. The campground located right in the town of Pacific Beach and is well signed from the entrance road to town.

⛺ COPALIS BEACH SUNRISE RESORT *(Open All Year)*

Res. and Info.: (360) 289-4278
Location: 7 Miles (11 Km) N of Ocean Shores, *N 47° 06' 41", W 124° 10' 34"*, Near Sea Level

78 Sites – The Sunrise is a membership club resort but will allow non-members to stay if it is not full. It has large sites with about half of them being pull-thrus to 60 feet. Restroom are older but serviceable. It's a big place, the main attraction is the beachside location. The resort is located right in Copalis, follow the signs on Heath Road from SR-109 which passes just inland of the town.

⛺ COPALIS BEACH SURF AND SAND RV PARK *(Open All Year)*

Res. and Info.: (866) 787-2751, (360) 289-2707
Location: 7 Miles (11 Km) N of Ocean Shores, N *47° 06' 39", W 124° 10' 39"*, Near Sea Level

50 Sites – This older campground is located right along the beach in Copalis. Restrooms are useable but not anything special. Unlike the campgrounds to the south it is not separated from the ocean by Connor Creek. To find the campground follow the road toward the beach as the coastal road passes inland from Copalis. There's a big sign on SR-109 at Heath Road. The campground is on the left after two blocks and is just south of the Sunrise Resort.

⛺ DUNES RESORT *(Open All Year)*

Res. and Info.: (360) 289-3873, (877) 386-3778, thedunesresort@aol.com, www.olympicbeaches.com
Location: 6 Miles (10 Km) N of Ocean Shores, *N 47° 06' 25", W 124° 10' 34"*, Near Sea Level

34 Sites – This is the first of a string of campgrounds stretching south from Copalis Beach. All of these campgrounds face the ocean but are separated from the beach by small but diffi-cult-to-cross Connor Creek. This campground has a rowboat (the Titanic) that can sometimes be pulled across the water using a hand line. There are six tent sites and 28 back-in RV sites to 40 feet which occasionally take 45 footers. The facilities are old but were well-maintained and in good shape when we visited. The entrance road is off SR-109 a few hundred yards south of Copalis.

⛺ TIDELANDS RESORT *(Open All Year)*

Res. and Info.: (360) 289-8963, Tidelandsresort@aol.com, www.TidelandsResort.com
Location: 6 Miles (10 Km) N of Ocean Shores, *N 47° 06' 10", W 124° 10' 32"*, Near Sea Level

WASHINGTON

80 Sites – Sites in this park are in large grassy fields next to the beach dunes. The campground is separated from the ocean by Connor Creek. There is lots of room for tent campers and 42 RV sites in two areas. Nine are pull-thrus with full hookups and cable for rigs to about 35 feet. The remainder of the RV sites are back-ins with water and electric hookups for rigs of any size. Facilities here are old but serviceable. The resort is located about .4 miles (.6 km) south of Copalis with the access road off SR-109.

▨ OCEAN MIST RESORT *(Open All Year)*

Information:	(360) 289-3659, www.kmresorts.com/1-oceanmist.shtml
Location:	5 Miles (8 Km) N of Ocean Shores, *N 47° 05' 02", W 124° 10' 07"*, Near Sea Level

121 Sites – The Ocean Mist is a membership campground. Non-members are allowed to stay here if there is room. This campground too is near the ocean but has a bridge over Conner Creek so there is ocean access. Facilities here are well maintained and in good shape. All sites are full-hookup with cable TV. Many are pull-thrus and will take RVs to 40 feet. The resort is located about 1.8 miles (2.9 km) south of Copalis with the access road off SR-109.

▨ BLUE PACIFIC MOTEL AND RV PARK *(Open All Year)*

Res. and Info.:	(360) 289-2262, www.bluepacificmotel.com
Location:	5 Miles (8 Km) N of Ocean Shores, *N 47° 04' 37", W 124° 10' 05"*, Near Sea Level

19 Sties – This is a small but well-run and well-maintained campground and motel. It too is separated from the ocean by Connor Creek. They plan to bridge the creek to allow ocean access within the near future. The bridge has been acquired but had not yet been installed when we visited. The grassy camping area has back-in sites, some with full hookups and some with electricity and water only. They will accept RVs to 38 feet. The RV park is located about 2 miles (3 km) south of Copalis with the access road off SR-109.

▨ OCEAN CITY STATE PARK *(Open All Year)*

Reservations:	(888) 226-7688, www.camis.com/wa
Information:	(360) 289-3553, (360) 902-8844, www.parks.wa.gov
Location:	1 Mile (2 Km) N of Ocean Shores, *N 47° 01' 54", W 124° 09' 31"*, Near Sea Level

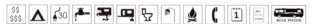

178 Sites – This is a very large state campground located next to the beach. Only a small number (29) have hookups, but many of the sites are large with room for big rigs and good maneuvering room. The entrance to the campground is a half mile (.8 km) south of the intersection of SR-109 and SR-115 (on the Ocean Shores access highway).

▨ QUINAULT MARITIME RESORT RV PARK AND CAMPGROUND *(Open March 1 to Oct 31 - Varies)*

Information:	(360) 276-8215, ext 239
Location:	Ocean Shores, *N 46° 56' 53", W 124° 07' 52"*, Near Sea Level

100 Sites – This campground is located next to the marina where the ferry to Westport docks. That means that it is quite a distance south of the central business district but convenient to both Damon Point State Park and the Oyhut State Game Refuge at the far south end of the peninsula. The facilities here are old and poorly maintained. Still, the large pull-thru sites with full hookups attract a good number of campers, particularly when everything else in the area is full. To reach the campground follow signs to the marina. As you arrive in Ocean Shores on US-115 take Point Brown Avenue (to the left after the sharp right turn as you arrive in town) and follow it south for 5.5 miles (8.9 km).

OLYMPIA

Olympia (population 43,000) is located along I-5 at the southern end of Puget Sound. The city is the capital of Washington State and the attractions for a tourist mostly relate to that fact. Together with nearby Tumwater and Lacey the area has a population of about 90,000 people. In addition to the government activities Olympia is home to Evergreen State College. This is a strategic location for travelers because it's where US-101 and SR-8, the roads to the Olympic Peninsula and coast, intersect I-5.

There is a visitor center at 14th and Capitol Way. Most of the interesting government buildings can be visited including the domed **Legislative Building**, the **Temple of Justice**, the **Capitol Conservatory**, and the **Governor's Mansion**. There is also a **State Capitol Museum** and a **Vietnam Memorial**.

If you're more interested in outdoor activities you should try visits to **Percival Landing Park** (Olympia's waterfront) on Budd Inlet or the **Olympia Farmer's Market**. The market is in operation from Thursday to Sunday in summer and is located on Capitol Way to the north of the central area.

➤ MILLERSYLVANIA STATE PARK *(Open All Year)*

Reservations: (888) 226-7688, www.parks.wa.gov
Information: (360) 753-1519, (360) 902-8844, www.parks.wa.gov
Location: 15 Miles (24 Km) Southeast of Olympia, *N 46° 54' 35", W 122° 54' 25"*, 200 Ft

177 Sites – Millersylvania sits on the shore of Deep Lake, about 7 miles (11 Km) as the crow flies southeast of Olympia. Campsites here are of two types. There are hookup sites in a large open field with back-in sites (and two pull-thrus) to 70 feet and lots of slide-out room. There are also back-in forest-type sites that are great for tents and smaller rigs. Campsites are

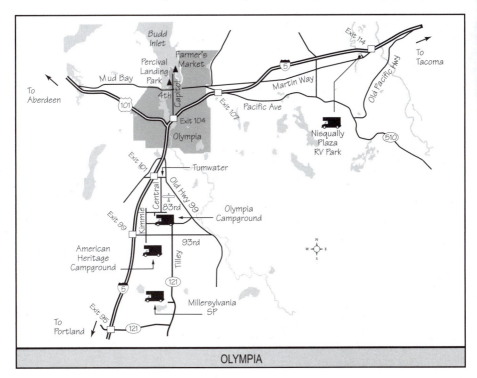

OLYMPIA

WASHINGTON

away from the lake but it's an easy stroll and there are two buoyed swimming beaches. Take Exit 99 from I-5 about 11 miles (18 km) south of Olympia. Drive east on SR-121 (93rd Ave. SE) for 1.5 miles (2.4 km) and turn right on Tilley Rd. S. Drive 3 miles (5 km) south, the campground entrance is on the right.

AMERICAN HERITAGE CAMPGROUND *(Open All Year)*

Res. and Info.: (360) 943-8778, olycamp@comcast.net, www.americanheritagecampground.com
Location: 7 Miles (12 Km) S of Olympia, *N 46° 56' 55", W 122° 55' 41"*, 200 Ft

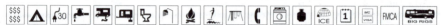

95 Sites – This commercial campground has the feel of a state park with forest-type back-in sites to 60 feet under tall Douglas-firs. Full-hookup, partial-hookup, and no-hookup sites are available. Amenities include a swimming pool in the summer months. The campground is owned and managed by the same people who own the Olympia Campground, listed below. During the winter (from Labor Day to Memorial Day) you must go to that campground first to check in. To go directly to the campground take Exit 99 from I-5 about 11 miles (18 km) south of Olympia. Drive east on SR-121 (93rd Ave. SE) for .4 mile (.6 km) and turn south on Kimmie St. SW. The campground is just ahead on the left.

OLYMPIA CAMPGROUND *(Open All Year)*

Res. and Info.: (360) 352-2551, olycamp@comcast.net, www.olympiacampground.com
Location: 10 Miles (16 Km) SE of Olympia, *N 46° 58' 01", W 122° 55'18"*, 100 Ft

99 Sites – This family-run campground sits behind a Texaco service station and quick-stop convenience store. The sites at the front of the park are long pull-thrus to 65 feet with hookups and room for slides, those at the rear are forest-type back-ins. Amenities include a swimming pool. Take Exit 101 from I-5 about 9 miles (15 km) south of Olympia. Drive east on Tumwater Blvd. SW for .5 miles (.8 km) and turn south on Central St. SW. Drive .5 miles (.8 km) south on Central and at the T turn right on 83rd Ave. You'll see the Texaco just ahead on the left, the campground entrance is on the east side.

NISQUALLY PLAZA RV PARK *(Open All Year)*

Res. and Info.: (360) 491-3831
Location: 7 Miles (11 Km) N of Olympia, *N 47° 04' 00", W 122° 43' 22"*, Near Sea Level

50 Sites – Nisqually Plaza is conveniently located next to I-5. It's primarily a long-term campground, not a traveler place, but we list it because there are generally a few sites available for travelers and it is convenient for an overnight stop. There is a swimming pool but it is un-heated, even in summer. Sites are all back-ins, most reach 60 feet and have room for slide-outs. Take Exit 114 from I-5. This is about 7 miles (11 km) north of central Olympia. You'll see the campground on the east side of the highway.

PORT ANGELES AND THE NORTH OLYMPIC PARK

With a natural harbor in a very convenient location at the mouth of Puget Sound it is no wonder that Port Angeles (population 19,000) is a fishing and ferry port. You can join a fishing charter for salmon or bottom fish or take a ferry across the Strait of Juan de Fuca to Victoria for a day trip. For a view of the city and the mountains in the park to the south drive out **Ediz Hook**, the sand spit which forms the harbor. Port Angeles hosts the **Clallam County Fair** the third weekend of August.

WASHINGTON

THERE IS NOTHING BETTER THAN A DIP IN THE SOL DUC HOT POOLS

WASHINGTON

The big attraction of Port Angeles is, of course, access to the northern reaches of **Olympic National Park**. The 17-mile (27 km) road up to **Hurricane Ridge** actually begins in Port Angeles. This is an excellent drive for those desiring views of the park's high country without much hiking. Thirty miles (48 km) east from Port Angeles on US-101 the **Sol Duc Road** also gives access to the park and hot springs there. You'll find hiking trails from both roads.

The presence of the park might make you forget the southern coastline of the Strait of Juan de Fuca. Don't let it, there are many coastal destinations in the region. Some are listed in the sections of this book covering Sequim (to the east) and Forks (to the west). Closer to Port Angeles are the sites along the Straight of Juan de Fuca accessible from SR-112 to the west of Port Angeles. These include Salt Creek County Park and Crescent Beach. Both offer camping sites.

It is possible to travel to Canada from Port Angeles by ferry. You can go over to Victoria as a day trip on foot or in a vehicle, or you can cross on the ferry in your RV to explore the region. See the *Victoria* section in the British Columbia chapter for more information about that area.

Campgrounds below are listed from east to west. For hookups near Port Angeles we prefer the Elwha Dam RV Park. Tent campers have lots of choices, particularly in the park. Families with children will like the KOA. Farther west the Sol Duc Hot Springs area is a favorite for both tent and RV camping, there are even hookups. Along the coast the Salt Creek County Park is great, it will be even better when the planned hookups are installed.

🚐 CONESTOGA QUARTERS RV PARK *(Open All Year)*

Res. and Info.: (360) 452-4637, (800) 808-4637, reservations@conestogaquarters.com, www.conestogaquarters.com
Location: 6 Miles (10 Km) E of Port Angeles, *N 48° 05' 46", W 123° 17' 27"*, 300 Ft

38 Sites – This is an older RV park with simple facilities. Parking is on grass or gravel, there are back-in and pull-thru sites to 50 feet. The RV park is on the north side of US-101 about 7 miles (11 km) west of Sequim and 6 miles (10 km) east of Port Angeles.

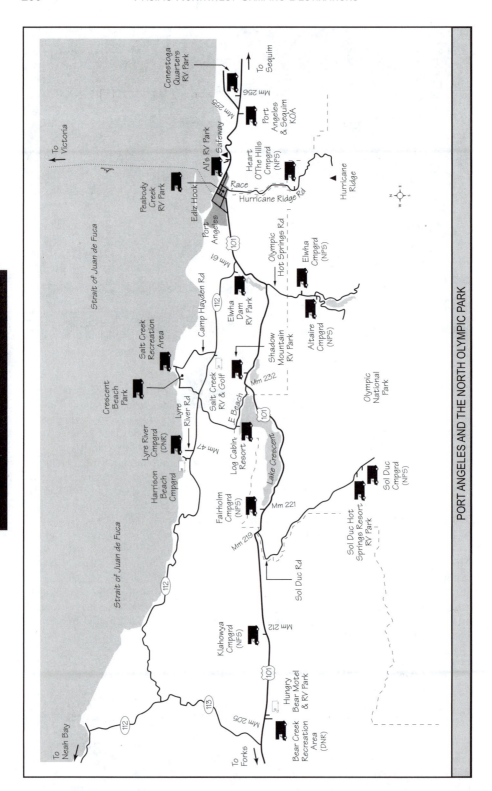

PORT ANGELES AND SEQUIM KOA *(Open All Year)*

Reservations: (800) 562-7558, www.koa.com
Information: (360) 457-5916, portangeleskoa@olypen.com, www.portangeleskoa.com
Location: 5 Miles (8 Km) E of Port Angeles, *N 48° 05' 41", W 123° 18' 19"*, 300 Ft

120 Sites – Located mid-way between Sequim and Port Angeles this KOA has all of the normal KOA amenities including both big sites and tent sites, swimming pool, mini golf, bike rentals, and movies. Sites include pull-thrus to 60 feet. The campground is located on the south side of US-101 about 8 miles (13 km) west of Sequim and 5 miles (8 km) east of Port Angeles

AL'S RV PARK *(Open All Year)*

Res. and Info.:   (360) 457-9844
Location: Port Angeles, *N 48° 06' 32", W 123° 23' 04"*, 100 Ft

31 Sites – Al's is a basic but well-managed and maintained small park. There are lots of long-term residents but also several spaces for travelers. The park has back-in spaces to 35 feet although the room can usually be found for rigs to 45 feet. A small lawn area provides tent campers with a place to pitch their tent. The campground is located at the eastern edge of Port Angeles. A sign on US-101 points you north on North Brook Ave. Almost immediately jog left onto N. Lees Creek and the campground is on the right in .3 miles (.5 km).

PEABODY CREEK RV PARK *(Open All Year)*

Res. and Info.:   (360) 457-7092, (800) 392-2361, patm@tenforward.com, www.peabodyrv.com
Location: Port Angeles, *N 48° 06' 57", W 123° 25' 53"*, Near Sea Level

36 Sites – The Peabody Creek is an older RV park located in a ravine in central Port Angeles. It's a unique place due to its central location which lets you walk anywhere in town. There are quite a few long-term residents but also traveler sites. Most sites here are small (to about 30 feet), maneuvering room is limited. The managers say they can accommodate RVs to 45 feet however. Tenters often use the small grassy area set aside for them. The campground is located off Lincoln Street which is the route US-101 takes going through town. It is on the east side of the street, opposite 2nd Ave.

HEART O'THE HILLS CAMPGROUND *(Open All Year)*

Information: (360) 565-3130
Location: 5 miles (8 Km) S of Port Angeles, *N 48° 02' 09", W 123° 25' 40"*, 1,800 Ft

105 Sites – This federal campground, like most of those in Olympic National Park, is best for tent campers and those with smaller RVs. The managers recommend rigs to 21 feet although they note that there are some sites to 35 feet. With caution rigs to 35 feet can use this campground although most sites would not allow the use of slide-outs. The campground is located off the Hurricane Ridge Road. From central Port Angeles drive south on S. Race Street. This becomes Hurricane Ridge Road. You'll soon pass the park visitor center and in another 5.1 miles (8.2 km) will reach the campground entrance.

ELWHA DAM RV PARK *(Open All Year)*

Res. and Info.:   (360) 452-7054, (877) 435-9421, paradise@elwhadamrvpark.com,
                      www.elwhadamrvpark.com

Location: 5 Miles (8 Km) W of Port Angeles, *N 48° 05' 51", W 123° 33' 11"*, 300 Ft

39 Sites – Although it is some distance outside town this is our favorite park when we visit Port Angeles. There is a large grassy area with shade if you want it for tent campers. The park has some long term residents but they are along the border of the park and separate from the traveler sites. Some traveler sites are pull-thrus to 60 feet. There is a hiking trail to the Lower Elwha Dam. To reach the campground turn north on SR-112 which leaves US-101 about 4 miles (6.5 km) west of Port Angeles. Follow SR-112 for .7 mile (1.1 km), turn left into Lower Dam Road, then turn left again immediately into the campground entrance.

ALTAIRE CAMPGROUND *(Open May 15 to Oct 15 - Varies)*

Information: (360) 565-3130

Location: 12 Miles (19 Km) W of Port Angeles, *N 48° 00' 35", W 123° 35' 28"*, 400 Ft

30 Sites – This Olympic National Park campground is at a pretty little place along the Elwha River. Sites are back-ins and pull-thrus off one loop. It's a narrow road but RVs to 35 feet can manage to use the campground if they are extremely cautious. It's better for tent campers and smaller rigs. To reach the campground turn south on Olympic Hot Springs Road from US-101 about 7 miles (11 km) west of Port Angeles. You'll pass through a park entrance booth and then see the campground on your right just after crossing the Elwha at 4.7 miles (7.6 km).

ELWHA CAMPGROUND *(Open All Year)*

Information: (360) 565-3130

Location: 10 Miles (16 Km) W of Port Angeles, *N 48° 01' 41", W 123° 35' 20"*, 300 Ft

41 Sites – This Olympic National Park campground is located in a dense stand of Douglas-Fir and Hemlocks. It's a little dark but a nice campground anyway. There are back-in and pull-thru sites to 40 feet but an extremely narrow access loop road closely bordered by big trees makes 25 feet the maximum practical RV size for this park. To reach the campground turn south on Olympic Hot Springs Road from US-101 about 7 miles (11 km) west of Port Angeles. You'll pass through a park entrance booth and then see the campground on your right just after crossing the Elwa at 2.9 miles (4.7 km).

SALT CREEK RECREATION AREA *(Open All Year)*

Information: (360) 928-3441, www.clallam.net/CountyParks/html/parks_saltcreek.htm

Location: 15 Miles (24 Km) W of Port Angeles, *N 48° 09' 42", W 123° 41' 56"*, 100 Ft

93 Sites – This is a Clallum County Campground. Plans are afoot to add electrical hookups to the campground but at the time of publication only dry camping is available. Camping is in two areas. There is a forest-type campground with back-in sites to 40 feet. There is also a large grassy area overlooking the water that will take any size rig, this is where the electrical hookups (and paved sites) will be added. This site was a military base until after WWII. Now it offers beach access (from a point to the west), and a marine life sanctuary with tide pools. About 4 miles (6.4 km) west of Port Angeles turn north on SR-112. Follow SR-112 for 7.2 miles (11.6 km) and turn north on Camp Hayden Road. You'll reach the campground in another 3.5 miles (5.6 km).

⊞ CRESCENT BEACH PARK *(Open All Year)*

Reservations: (866) 690-3344
Information: (360) 928-3344, crescent@olypen.com, www.olypen.com/crescent
Location: 15 Miles (24 Km) W of Port Angeles, *N 48° 09' 33", W 123° 42' 41"*, Near Sea Level

36 Sites – Crescent Beach Park is very unique, it has its own beach. The beach is about a half-mile long, in summer the water gets warm enough for swimming and when the weather is right this can be a surfing destination too. The highway runs about 100 yards back from the beach and the campground is on the south side of it. Parking is on grass, any size rig will fit just fine and it's also good tent camping. About 4 miles (6 km) west of Port Angeles turn north on SR-112. Follow SR-112 for 7.2 miles (11.6 km) and turn north on Camp Hayden Road. You'll reach the campground in another 4.2 miles (6.8 km).

⊞ LYRE RIVER WASHINGTON DEPARTMENT OF NATURAL RESOURCES
CAMPGROUND *(Open All Year)*

Information: (360) 374-6131
Location: 19 Miles (31 Km) W of Port Angeles, *N 48° 09' 00", W 123° 49' 59"*, 100 Ft

9 Sites – Lyre River is a very small and dark forest-type campground in dense trees. Sites are small and there is little or no maneuvering room, it's OK for RVs to about 25 feet but even rigs this small will have to struggle to turn around. Fishing for steelhead and salmon is possible in the Lyre River. About 4 miles (6.4 km) west of Port Angeles turn north on SR-112. Follow SR-112 15 miles (24 km) and turn north on E. Lyre River Rd. at the campground sign. The campground entrance is about .5 miles (.8 km) from the highway.

⊞ SHADOW MOUNTAIN RV PARK *(Open All Year)*

Reservations: (877) 928-3043
Information: (360) 928-3043, mountain@olypen.com, www.shadowmt.com
Location: 13 Miles (21 Km) W of Port Angeles, *N 48° 05' 07", W 123° 42' 36"*, 600 Ft

50 Sites – This campground occupies terraces on the hillside behind a Texaco station and convenience store along the highway west of Port Angeles. Sites are full-hookup back-ins to 40 feet with good maneuvering room. There are also tent sites in a separate meadow. From Port Angeles travel west 13 miles (21 km) along US-101 to the campground.

⊞ LOG CABIN RESORT *(Open May 1 to Oct 31 - Varies)*

Res. and Info.: (360) 928-3325, logcabin@tenforward.com
Location: 14 Miles (23 Km) W of Port Angeles, *N 48° 05' 44", W 123° 47' 25"*, 500 Ft

42 Sites – About 15 miles (24 km) west of Port Angeles is beautiful Lake Crescent. On the north shore is an old resort, originally established in 1895. There is a small lodge with a restaurant and cabins, swimming and fishing out front, and a fine but rustic little RV park. To reach the resort start at the junction of US-101 and SR-112 which is about 3 miles (5 km) west of Port Angeles. Drive west 10.8 miles (17.4 km) on US-101 Just before you reach the east end of the lake East Beach Rd., a well-marked little paved road, goes right. Follow the road behind cabins along the lake shore for about three miles (5 km) to the resort.

WASHINGTON

WASHINGTON

FAIRHOLM CAMPGROUND *(Open May 15 to Oct 15 - Varies)*

Information: (360) 565-3130
Location: 25 Miles (40 Km) W of Port Angeles, *N 48° 04' 12", W 123° 55' 06"*, 600 Ft

88 Sites – Fairholm is an older Olympic National Park campground located right off the highway at the west end of Crescent Lake. It's best for tent campers, the Park Service recommends that RVs no longer than 21 feet use this campground. From Port Angeles drive west on US-101 for 25 miles (40 km) to the campground.

SOL DUC HOT SPRINGS RESORT RV PARK *(Open March 15 to Oct 15 - Varies)*

Reservations: (866) 4-SOL-DUC
Information: (360) 327-3583, pamsdr@aol.com, www.visitsolduc.com;
Location: 38 Miles (61 Km) W of Port Angeles, *N 47° 58' 08", W 123° 51' 41"*, 1,700 Ft

17 Sites – This hot springs resort has occupied the same location since the early part of the last century. There are rental cottages, a restaurant, a snack bar, and several hot pools. There is also an RV campground. It has 17 back-in sites around a large gravel lot, there is room for any rig. Only electricity and water are available, there is a dump station a little farther up the road. Behind the sites are picnic tables and fire pits. The resort is a short walk away, the restrooms are located there. To reach the resort head west from Port Angeles for 26 miles (42 km). Turn south on the Sol Duc Road, the campground is on the right in 12.5 miles (20.2 km). The RV park entrance is separate from the one for the resort, it is just beyond the main entrance.

SOL DUC OLYMPIC NATIONAL PARK CAMPGROUND *(Open All Year)*

Information: (360) 565-3130
Location: 39 Miles (63 Km) W of Port Angeles, *N 47° 57' 58", W 123° 51' 25"*, 1,700 Ft

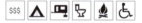

79 Sites – About .2 mile (.3 km) beyond the Sol Duc resort is a park campground. The sites are located off two loops. A few of the sites will take RVs to 35 feet, narrow roads and sites require cautious driving. Many sites do not have room for slide-outs. Loop A is better for RVs than loop B. To reach the resort head west from Port Angeles for 26 miles (42 km). Turn south on the Sol Duc Road, the campground is on the right in 12.7 miles (20.5 km). The entrances for loops A and B are separate, they are located just beyond the dump station.

KLAHOWYA NATIONAL FOREST CAMPGROUND *(Open May 15 to Sept 15 - Varies)*

Information: (360) 374-6522
Location: 34 Miles (55 Km) W of Port Angeles, *N 48° 03' 48", W 124° 06' 38"*, 700 Ft

57 Sites – This Olympic National Forest campground is good for tents and RVs to 40 feet. The campground sits alongside the Sol Duc River. There are hiking trails from the campground and fishing for salmon and steelhead is possible. There's also a boat ramp for drift boats. From Port Angeles drive west for 34 miles (55 km) on US-101, the campground entrance is on the right.

BEAR CREEK DEPARTMENT OF NATURAL RESOURCES RECREATION AREA *(Open All Year)*

Information: (360) 374-6131
Location: 40 Miles (65 Km) W of Port Angeles, *N 48° 03' 58", W 124° 14' 23"*, 500 Ft

15 Sites – This small campground is located right next to the highway and is a good place to overnight. Sites are back-ins and pull-thrus off a loop road. Limited maneuvering room limits use to RVs to 35 feet. From Port Angeles drive west for 40 miles (65 km) on US-101, the campground is on the south side of the highway.

PORT TOWNSEND

Port Townsend (population 8,800) is not particularly large or economically important today, but at one time this was the major metropolis on Puget Sound. The city was established in 1851. It had an extremely handy location at the entrance to Puget Sound so in the days of sailing ships it was the logical place for a port to serve the area. The town is filled with historic Victorian buildings dating from this era when Port Townsend ruled the sound. Unfortunately for Port Townsend, railroads eventually reached the northwest, and they led to Tacoma and Seattle, not Port Townsend.

The resulting economic bust in Port Townsend was very beneficial to today's tourist trade. The movers and shakers eventually moved out but left the town pretty much as it was at the end of the nineteenth century. Over 70 commercial buildings and homes in the town date from the era and have been preserved.

Port Townsend actually has two old business areas and one new one. As you come into town from the south you will be in the newest one. Behind the Safeway on the left is a parking lot where you can leave your rig and ride a shuttle in to town, parking for big rigs is very limited downtown. Just past the Safeway you will see the Visitor Information Center. They can give you a map of the town with directions for finding some of the more interesting older buildings.

Continuing straight ahead you will soon find yourself in the **historic waterfront district** of town along Water Street. The handsome old buildings in this part of town are filled with shops and restaurants, this is the place to do some poking around.

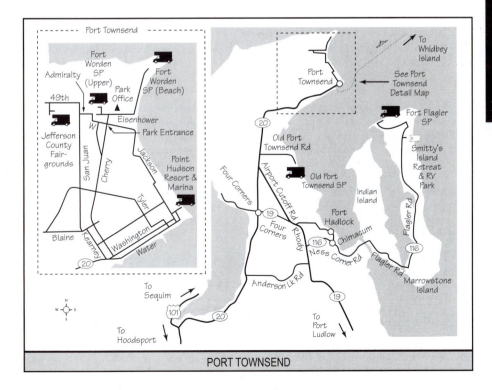

PORT TOWNSEND

The third business area in Port Townsend is up on the bluff overlooking the waterfront. This was once the "sophisticated" shopping area, a place to shop for ladies who didn't want to have to visit the rowdy waterfront area below. To get there you'll probably drive. While you are doing that take the time to wend your way to the north and take a look at **Fort Worden**. The fort occupies a commanding position near Point Wilson. Now a state-owned conference center (with two campgrounds), the fort was once one of three that guarded the entrance to the sound. The **Coast Artillery Museum** at the fort will show you how it all worked.

Port Townsend celebrates a **Rhododendron Festival** in May and a **Wooden Boat Festival** in September.

You will notice that there is a ferry dock in Port Townsend. Using it you can make the short crossing to Whidbey Island. Whidbey has many campgrounds, see the *Whidbey Island* section of this guide. It is also possible to take a passenger ferry (no vehicles) from Port Townsend to either Victoria, B.C. or to Seattle.

OLD FORT TOWNSEND STATE PARK *(April 1 to Oct 15 - Varies)*

Information: (360) 385-3595, (360) 902-8844, www.parks.wa.gov
Location: 3 Miles (5 Km) S of Port Townsend, *N 48° 04' 28", W 122° 47' 20"*, 100 Ft

40 Sites – This state park encompasses the former Fort Townsend which dated from 1856. An interpretive trail with 13 stations helps you explore the site. While this is a waterfront state park the campsite are in two locations away from the water. Sites 1 to 27 are forest-type sites in a loop with narrow roads, a sign at the entryway limits use to vehicles under 21 feet. Sites 28 to 40 are narrow pull-thru sites to 38 feet. They will not accommodate slide-outs and the turn to exit the area is very tight, big rigs would need to back out. We recommend that RVs no longer than 30 feet use this area. The campground is located south of Port Townsend along Port Townsend Bay. The Old Fort Townsend Road leaves SR-20 about 2 miles (3 km) south of Port Townsend, it leads east for 1.3 miles (2.1 km) to the park.

JEFFERSON COUNTY FAIRGROUNDS *(Open All Year)*

Information: (360) 385-1013, jeffcofairgrounds@olypen.com, www.jeffcofairgrounds.com
Location: Port Townsend, *N 48° 07' 56", W 122° 47' 02"*, Near Sea Level

81 Sites – The fairgrounds are located just west of Port Townsend and make a good inexpensive place to stay while visiting the town. Parking is in a very large grassy field with full, partial, and no hookup sites suitable for any size rig. There's a self check-in system so the site is unattended. There are dedicated restrooms for the campground and they are generally kept in decent shape. From SR-20 as you enter Fort Townsend from the west you will see both the fairgrounds and Fort Worden (see below) signed to the left on Kearney Street. Turn left here and drive .3 mile (.5 km) on Kerney. At the T turn left on Blaine and then take the first right onto San Juan Ave. Now follow San Juan north for 1.5 miles (2.4 km). You'll see the fairgrounds on your left. To enter follow the road as it makes a turn left onto 49th Street and you'll find the camping entrance on the south side off 49th.

FORT WORDEN STATE PARK *(Open All Year)*

Reservations: www.fortworden.org/camping.html, fwcamping@parks.wa.gov
Information: (360) 344-4431, (360) 344-4400, (360) 902-8844, www.fortworden.org
Location: Port Townsend, N 48° 08' 02", W 122° 45' 53", Near Sea Level

80 Sites – Camping at Fort Worden is in two areas known as the Beach and Upper campgrounds. The beach sites are near Point Wilson and really are not on the beach, but they're near

it. These are long paved back-in and pull-thru sites to 70 feet in an open area of grass. The upper campground sites are about a mile (1.6 km) away. These are all back-ins to about 55 feet on gravel. This state park has its own reservation system and does not use the system used by the other Washington state parks. Reservations are accepted by mail, fax, or email. Take a look at the website referenced above for information about how to do this or call to have a form mailed to you. From SR-20 as you enter Fort Townsend from the west you will see both the fairgrounds and Fort Worden (see below) signed to the left on Kearney Street. Turn left here and drive .3 mile (.5 km) on Kerney. At the T turn left on Blain and then take the first right onto San Juan Ave. Now follow San Juan north for 1.4 miles (2.3 km). Turn right on Admiralty Street and follow it as it turns right and then left, you'll reach the state park entrance in .5 mile (.8 km). Turn left into the park, proceed ahead for two blocks to Eisenhower Ave, turn right and you'll soon see the reception office on the left. Park and go inside to check in.

➥ Point Hudson Resort and Marina *(Open All Year)*

Reservations:	(800) 228-2803
Information:	(360) 385-2828, info@portofpt.com
Location:	Port Townsend, *N 48° 07' 06", W 122° 45' 02"*, Near Sea Level

44 Sites – For convenience it is hard to beat this little campground. It is located right on Point Hudson which is at the north end of Port Townsend's waterside business area. From this campground you can easily stroll to the center of town to shop or visit a restaurant in the evening. The resort was once a Coast Guard station and the tidy white-painted buildings maintain the atmosphere. So does the location on the point where you can keep an eye on all the passing ships, ferries, and yachts. Sites here are back-ins and pull-thrus to 70 feet. The campground is not difficult to find. The main drag along the waterfront is known as Water Street. As you approach the end of the street you will see the RVs directly ahead. You must jog left on Monroe Street for two blocks to Jefferson St. to enter the campground.

➥ Fort Flagler State Park *(Open March 1 to Nov 1 - Varies)*

Reservations:	(888) 226-7688, www.camis.com/wa
Information:	(360) 385-1259, (360) 902-8844, www.parks.wa.gov
Location:	17 miles (27 Km) SE of Port Townsend, *N 48° 05' 39", W 122° 41' 51"*, Near Sea Level

116 Sites – Fort Flagler is located just 2.5 miles (4 km) from Port Townsend across Port Townsend Bay. You can easily see the town from the campground area, but getting there in your rig is a little more involved. Campsites at Fort Flagler are in two areas, an upper campground and the beachside campground. Sites are paved and are both long pull-thrus and back-ins to 45 feet. All of the 15 electrical sites are back-ins in the beachside campground. Some of the no-hookup sites in the beach campground have spectacular locations along the water. On a clear day Mt Baker is clearly visible. The roundabout route to the campground is as follows. From the Four Corners intersection on SR-20 drive east on SR-19. Four Corners is 4 miles (6.5 km) south of Fort Townsend and 6 miles (9.7 km) north of the intersection of US-101 and SR-20 at the foot of Discovery Bay. Follow Four Corners Road 1.3 miles (2.1 km) east to the intersection with Rhody Drive and then follow Rhody south 1.2 miles (1.9 km) to Ness Corner Road. Follow Ness Corner Road (SR-116) east for 10.5 miles (16.9 km) as it crosses onto Indian Island and then Marrowstone Island and leads you directly to the park entrance. The road changes names along the way but the route is well signed.

SANDPOINT AND LAKE PEND OREILLE, IDAHO

Sandpoint (population 7,600) is located on the northwest shore of beautiful Lake Pend Oreille. This is an attractive little lakeshore town with plenty of shopping and restaurants. The town also has a number of art galleries. The **Bonner County Historical Museum** offers local history and Native American artifacts. Sandpoint has walking and bicycle trails and a number of nearby golf courses. The city hosts quite a few events during the year. Among them are the **Northern Idaho Timberfest** in early June, **Sandpoint Wooden Boat Festival** in July, the **Festival at Sandpoint** music festival in early August, and the **Bonner County Fair and Rodeo** in late August.

A major attraction near Sandpoint is **Schweitzer Mountain Resort**. This regional ski area offers both winter and summer attractions. There's skiing from late November to early April. In summer the chairlifts are used for sightseeing and there are hiking trails, mountain biking, and horseback riding. It's only 11 miles (18 km) up to the slopes from Sandpoint.

Lake Pend Oreille is the largest lake in Idaho. It has a surface area of 180 square miles and over 100 miles of shoreline. It's also a deep lake with depths in some places of over 1,100 feet. That means it has excellent fishing for cold water fish like rainbows and lake trout.

Only one campground below is near Sandpoint. The others are scattered around the lake

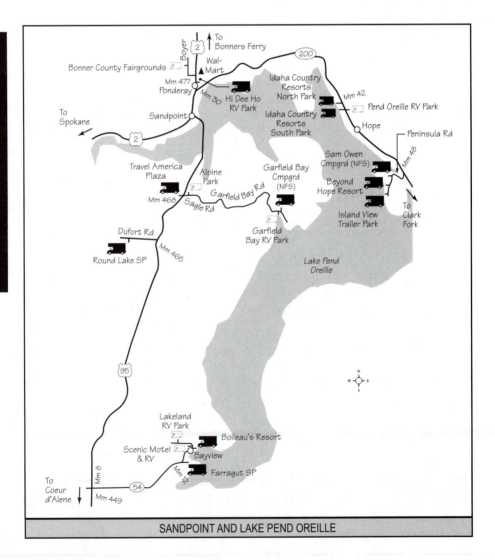

SANDPOINT AND LAKE PEND OREILLE

or along the highway south of Sandpoint. There's a good selection with forest service, state, and commercial campgrounds all represented.

HI DEE HO RV PARK *(Open All Year)*

Reservations: (800) 763-3922
Information: (208) 263-3922, sharon@lakerv.com, www.lakerv.com
Location: 2 Miles (3 Km) N of Sandpoint, *N 48° 17' 51", W 116° 32' 43"*, 2,100 Ft

31 Sites – This is a modern big-rig campground with large pull-thru sites suitable for rigs longer than 45 feet and 50-amp power. It is operated in conjunction with a RV service center and parts store and has an excellent new restroom and laundry building. It's located in an industrial park but is the closest park in this guide to the town of Sandpoint. From the intersection of SR-200 and US-2 in Ponderay just north of Sandpoint drive .5 miles (8 km) north on US-2, the entrance is on the right.

IDAHO COUNTRY RESORTS *(Open All Year)*

Reservations: (800) 307-3050
Information: (208) 264-5505, idahoresorts@nidlink.com, www.idahoresorts.com
Location: 13 Miles (21 Km) E of Sandpoint, *N 48° 16' 43", W 116° 21' 10"*, 2,000 Ft

160 Sites – This resort is actually two waterfront campgrounds located near each other on the east shore of Lake Pend Oreille. The offices are in the southern resort which has 93 sites, most are large full-hookup sites suitable for RVs to 45 feet. Amenities are more upscale at the southern park than at the northern one but both have marinas, swimming beaches, and boat launches. The southern park also has internet access. The northern park is usually less crowded and better for tent campers. There are a variety of sites here and any size rig can be accommodated. Both campgrounds are located on the east shore of Lake Pend Oreille off SR-200 some 13 miles (21 km) east of Sandpoint and 12 miles (19 km) north of Clark Fork.

ISLAND VIEW TRAILER PARK *(Open May 1 to Oct 1)*

Res. and Info.: (208) 264-5509
Location: 21 Miles (34 Km) E of Sandpoint, *N 48° 12' 32", W 116° 17' 16"*, 2,000 Ft

60 Sites – This is a smaller RV resort located on the Hope Peninsula on the east shore of Lake Pend Oreille. This peninsula is a game reserve, deer are very plentiful. Because the location is a little off the beaten path most residents here stay for several months but there are usually some spaces for travelers and it's a very pleasant RV park. Sites vary in size and are back-ins, some will take RVs to 45 feet. Amenities include a boat launch and marina. The Hope Peninsula road leaves SR-200 some 18 miles (29 km) east of Sandpoint and 7 miles (11 km) north of Clark Fork. It's 1.9 miles (3.1 km) from the cutoff to the resort.

BEYOND HOPE RESORT *(Open May 1 to Oct 1)*

Reservations: (877) 270-HOPE
Information: (208) 264-5251, www.beyondhoperesort.com
Location: 21 Miles (34 Km) E of Sandpoint, *N 48° 12' 55", W 116° 17' 07"*, 2,000 Ft

95 Sites – This campground is located near the Island View but much larger. Amenities include a boat launch, marina, and restaurant. Parking is on grass, sites will take large rigs. The

Hope Peninsula road leaves SR-200 some 18 miles (29 km) east of Sandpoint and 7 miles (11 km) north of Clark Fork. It's 1.4 miles (2.3 km) from the cutoff to the resort.

⊞ SAM OWEN CAMPGROUND *(Open May 20 to Sept 15 - Varies)*

Reservations: (877) 444-6777, www.reserveusa.com
Information: (208) 263-5111
Location: 20 Miles (32 Km) E of Sandpoint, *N 48° 13' 10", W 116° 17' 06"*, 2,000 Ft

81 Sites – This is a large Kaniksu National Forest campground located on the Hope Peninsula on the east side of Lake Pend Oreille. There is a beach area for swimming, campsites are located in the trees behind. Some of these sites will take RVs to 45 feet but maneuvering room is tight. The Hope Peninsula road leaves SR-200 some 18 miles (29 km) east of Sandpoint and 7 miles (11 km) north of Clark Fork. It's 1.1 miles (1.7 km) from the cutoff to the campground entrance.

⊞ GARFIELD BAY CAMPGROUND *(Open May 1 to Sept 30)*

Information: (208) 265-1438
Location: 14 Miles (23 Km) S of Sandpoint, *N 48° 11' 24", W 116° 26' 04"*, 2,200 Ft

24 Sites – This is a small forest service-type campground run by Bonner County that climbs a hillside behind Garfield Bay on the west shore of Lake Pend Oreille. It's quite a climb to the campground from the lakeshore, about a quarter mile. Sites here are small, a couple are suitable for RVs to about 30 feet. On the shore of the lake down the hill is a park with wheelchair-accessible flush toilets, swimming beach, boat launch, and dump station but the restrooms in the campground are outhouses. From US-95 some 5 miles (8 km) south of Sandpoint follow Sagle Road and then Garfield Road east 8.7 miles (14.0 km) to the campground entrance.

⊞ TRAVEL AMERICA PLAZA *(Open All Year)*

Res. and Info.: (208) 263-6522, (208) 263-7511
Location: 5 Miles (8 Km) S of Sandpoint, *N 48° 12' 11", W 116° 34' 01"*, 2,200 Ft

76 Sites – This campground occupies a large field behind a gas station, restaurant, and quick-stop grocery along the highway south of Sandpoint. Sites are large and will accommodate large rigs. Restrooms and the laundry are in an old mobile home, it's best to be self-contained here. Sign in at the grocery store out front. The campground is on the west side of the highway 5 miles (8 km) south of Sandpoint.

⊞ ROUND LAKE STATE PARK *(Open All Year)*

Reservations: (866) 634-3246, www.idahoparks.org
Information: (208) 263-3489, rou@idpr.state.id.us, www.idahoparks.org
Location: 10 Miles (16 Km) S of Sandpoint, *N 48° 10' 00", W 116° 38' 13"*, 2,200 Ft

52 Sites – This campground is on a lake to the west of Lake Pend Oreille and south of Sandpoint. Some sites will take RVs to 30 feet. There is a swimming beach, a boat launch, and a two-mile (.3 km) nature trail around the lake. Only electric motors are allowed on Round Lake. To reach the campground follow US-95 south from Sandpoint for 8 miles (12.9 km). Turn west on Dufort Road, the campground entrance is on the left in 1.9 miles (3.1 km).

FARRAGUT STATE PARK *(Open All Year)*

Reservations: (866) 634-3246, www.idahoparks.org
Information: (208) 683-2425, far@idpr.state.id.us, www.idahoparks.org
Location: 30 Miles (48 Km) S of Sandpoint, *N 47° 56' 59", W 116° 36' 22"*, 2,100 Ft

183 Sites – This, the most popular state park in Idaho, occupies a huge area that was formerly the Farragut Naval Station. There are three campgrounds here with a total of 183 sites. Amenities include a swimming beach, bicycle trails, a museum and two disk golf courses. Some sites will take RVs to 45 feet. The access road is the four-lane SR-54 which heads east from US-95 some 25 miles (40 km) south of Sandpoint. In 4.3 miles (6.9 km) you'll see the exit on the right for the campground headquarters and sign-in station.

BOILEAU'S RESORT *(Open All Year)*

Res. and Info.:   (208) 683-2213, tina@bayviewmarinas.com, www.bayviewmarinas.com
Location: 33 Miles (53 Km) S of Sandpoint, *N 47° 58' 52", W 116° 33' 30"*, 2,000 Ft

29 Sites – Located in the town of Bayview, this big-rig marina-side campground has full-hookup spaces with room for RVs to 45 feet. There are pull-thrus and back-ins. Access is easiest via SR 54 through Farragut State Park. Follow four-lane SR 54 east from US-95 some 25 miles (40 km) south of Sandpoint. In 6.7 miles (10.8 km) follow the sign for Bayview left and in another 1 mile (1.6 km) you'll arrive in the small town and see the rigs parked on your right.

SEATTLE

The Seattle Metropolitan Area is the Northwest's giant with an area population (including Everett, Tacoma, and the Eastside) of almost 1,500,000 people. Access to Seattle is easy. Seattle-Tacoma International Airport (locally called Sea-Tac) provides connections to national and international flights. If you happen to be arriving in your own vehicle the city is conveniently located at the intersection of the west coast's I-5 and east-west I-90 which connects this part of the Northwest with points east. Seattle makes an extremely interesting tourist destination. It is a very popular with visitors from both the U.S. and other countries.

Driving in Seattle can be confusing and the roads congested. Roads must detour around lakes and hills. A major highway, I-5, runs north and south right through the middle of the city, sometimes it is as much of a barrier as the hills, lakes, and canals. A ring-road freeway, I-405 circles east of Lake Washington, others were planned but never built. Two major freeways connect I-5 and I-405 across Lake Washington on floating bridges. One of those sank several years ago, but it has been replaced. Even with all this concrete there is not nearly enough highway for the number of cars, so be sure to avoid the extended rush hours.

The city has no light rail or subway system, but it does have a pretty good bus system. Most of the campgrounds listed below have decent bus transportation available that can get you to downtown Seattle. Unfortunately it is more difficult to use the busses from the campgrounds to reach the outlying neighborhoods and suburbs since the lines tend to radiate from the center rather than circle it. That means that you will probably want to use the bus to go downtown because both traffic and parking are difficult there. When bound for destinations away from the city center you will probably want to use your tow car or smaller RV.

Seattle has two other transportation options, both are tourist destinations in their own right. The state's ferry fleet serves the far shore of Puget Sound from a terminal in downtown Seattle. No visit to Seattle would be complete without a ferry outing. Also, Seattle still has its monorail, originally built for the 1964 World's Fair. The monorail's usefulness is limited but it does provide a good way to visit the Space Needle and Seattle Center from downtown.

WASHINGTON

Seattle's **central downtown area** is fairly compact, about 9 blocks deep from the water up to the I-5 freeway and 13 wide from Jefferson to Olive. The streets in this section don't run north and south like they do in most of the rest of Seattle, they are cocked at a 45-degree angle to parallel the waterfront. The area is compact, but walking it can be tiring because the streets climb steeply uphill from the water. It is good to know that bus service in the central area is free, just climb on and ride.

When you arrive in town you will probably alight near the uptown shopping district centered around **Westlake Center** at 4th and Pine at the north end of the downtown area. There are a cluster of large stores here including the flagship Nordstrom department store. Westlake is also the terminal for the monorail, more on that later.

Directly toward the water from Westlake is one of Seattle's most famous attractions. **Pike Place Market**, at 1st and Pike, is an actual operating farmer's market, but much more. In addition to produce you'll find fish, exotic foods of all kinds, arts and crafts, and even restaurants. It's set in several funky buildings dating from 1907, although there are lots of upscale additions in the vicinity.

Just down 1st Avenue from the market is the new **Seattle Art Museum**. It offers permanent displays of Asian and Northwest Indian art as well as temporary traveling exhibits. You can find the museum by watching for the **Hammer Man** sculpture out front, you really can't miss it.

From the market or museum you can descend to the waterfront using either stairs or a handy elevator. The **downtown Seattle waterfront** stretches for over a mile from Pier 70 next to Myrtle Edwards Park in the northwest to the Colman Dock ferry terminal (Pier 52) in the southeast. The piers between the two offer restaurants, stores, a marina, and even public parks. The area draws crowds on any sunny day. Don't miss the **Seattle Aquarium** on Pier 59. You can easily travel the length of the waterfront on a streetcar running on the far side of the road, the streetcar line turns inland at the south end of the waterfront and runs east through Pioneer Square to the International District.

THE BOEING MUSEUM IN SEATTLE

At the south end of the waterfront is Colman Dock, the terminal for the **Washington State Ferry System**. Walk onto a ferry for an inexpensive two-hour round trip ride to the far side of the sound. You'll find commercial tour-boat operators along the waterfront, they'll take you on a **sightseeing tour** of Elliott Bay or through the ship canal. You can also travel to **Tillicum Island** for a traditional-style salmon bake.

To the south of the central downtown are is the **Pioneer Square Historical District**. This is the original Seattle. The whole swampy mess burned down in 1893 and handsome brick buildings were built as replacements. Later, fill from projects to flatten Seattle's hills (called the Regrade) was used to raise the street levels and fill the tidelands to the south. Today you'll see two huge sports arenas built on the fill, one for baseball and one for football. The center of the action in this part of town is tiny **Pioneer Square.** It is located at the foot of Yesler, the original "**Skid Road**" and near the location of Seattle's first large employer, the steam-powered Yesler's Mill. The mill is long gone but the square and surrounding streets do offer lots of shops and restaurants. Here you can take a tour of Seattle's "**underground**". The underground is actually the first floors of the nearby buildings. When the streets were raised during the Regrade the first floors of these buildings were abandoned, entrances were moved up to the second floors.

East of the Pioneer Square area is Seattle's **International District**. One easy way to reach it is to ride the trolley from the waterfront or Pioneer Square area. Covering about 30 blocks the district is filled with Chinese, Japanese, Korean, Filipino, and Southeast Asian shops and restaurants. Worth a walk-through is the large Uwajimaya Asian supermarket.

Back at the central shopping district you have one more thing to do. Hop on the monorail and ride to the **Seattle Center**. This was the site of the 1964 World's Fair and continues to offer a number of attractions including the **Space Needle**, Seattle's professional basketball arena, the **Pacific Science Center**, and even an amusement park. You can ride the elevator to the top of the Space Needle for the view or tour the child-friendly exhibits of the Science Center.

North of the downtown Seattle area and probably most easily reached using your own set of wheels is another of Seattle's popular attractions. The **Hiram M. Chittenden Locks** mark the beginning of the canal that connects the salt water Puget Sound with Lake Washington. You can watch work boats and yachts as they float up and down and also take a peek through **viewing windows** at the fish ladder that lets salmon and steelhead bypass the locks.

If you drive eastward near the north shore of the canal you'll pass through Ballard, Fremont, and Wallingford and find yourself in the **University District**. Most of the stores and restaurants here are along the north-south 45th Avenue, usually just called the "Ave". The campus lies just a block east of the Ave and is huge, 35,000 students attend class here. The University grounds are very attractive, you'll enjoy a walk on the campus.

Because Seattle used to be home to Boeing it is known for aviation, and there are two interesting aviation-oriented destinations. The first is the **Museum of Flight**, which is located south of downtown along the west side of Boeing Field. The museum has a collection of more than 40 aircraft including the first Air Force 1 (a Boeing 707), a B-17, a B-29, a Concorde, and a Blackbird supersonic spy plane. North of Seattle at Paine Field near Everett is the **Boeing 747, 767, 777 Production Facility**. Tours of this huge hanger are very popular, call first to inquire about the best time to arrive. You reach it by driving west from Exit 189 off I-5 near Everett and then following the signs.

None of Seattle's campgrounds are near the center of town. For RVers the best choice probably depends upon which direction you arrive from. Tenters are not well served. Most campgrounds, even if they would accept tenters, do not have proper sites for tents. The best tent campgrounds are Vasa Park, the KOA, and the Lakeside. Also, campers, even tent campers if they have the necessary transportation to get to the ferry terminal, might consider camping on the Kitsap Peninsula or Bainbridge Island and using the ferries to access Seattle.

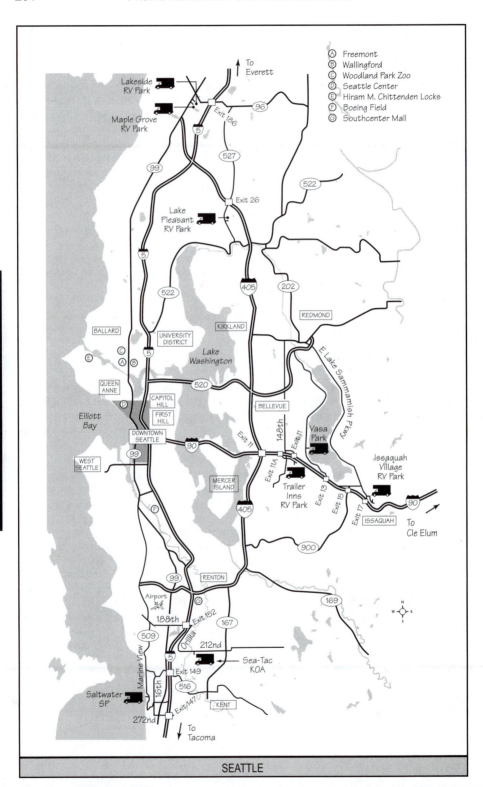

LAKESIDE RV PARK *(Open All Year)*

Reservations: (800) 468-7275
Information: (425) 347-2970, (425) 742-7333
Location: 20 Miles (32 Km) N of Downtown Seattle, *N 47° 53' 09", W 122° 15' 39"*, 500 Ft

200 Sites – The Lakeside is a large big-rig park with pull-thrus to 55 feet, there are also some grassy tent sites. Most of the campground is paved but the crowding is somewhat offset by the small adjoining lake and walking trail. Facilities are modern and there is bus service available nearby to both Seattle and Everett. This campground is north of Seattle off Interstate 5, actually in southern Everett. Take Exit 186, drive west on 128 St. SW for 1.5 miles (2.4 kilometers), turn left on US-99 and you'll see the campground on the left in .2 miles (.3 km)

MAPLE GROVE RV PARK *(Open All Year)*

Reservations: (866) 793-2200
Information: (425) 423-9608, info@maplegroverv.com, www.maplegroverv.com
Location: 20 Miles (32 Km) N of Downtown Seattle, *N 47° 53' 05", W 122° 15' 37"*, 500 Ft

87 Sites – The Maple Grove is located just south of the Lakeside RV Park in southern Everett. It is also a big-rig park with sites to 55 feet. They have excellent restrooms and like the Lakeside above also have good bus service. Take Exit 186 from I-5, drive west on 128 St. SW for 1.5 miles (2.4 kilometers), turn left on US-99 and you'll see the campground on the left in .2 miles (.3 km)

LAKE PLEASANT RV PARK *(Open All Year)*

Reservations: (800) 742-0386
Information: (425) 487-1785
Location: 20 Miles (32 Km) NE of Downtown Seattle, *N 47° 46' 48", W 122° 13' 00"*, 100 Ft

200 Sites – This is a very unusual park for Seattle. Sites are set around a small lake, a great location. Most sites are back-ins around the lake, some are parallel-type parking. There are also some pull-thrus away from the lakeshore but large rigs will find that they are really back-ins due to lack of maneuvering room. Sites vary from 30 to 70 feet in length. Take Exit 26 from I-405 and head south on SR-527 (Bothell Everett Hwy.). In 1.2 miles (1.9 km), as you descend a hill, slow and watch for the entrance on your left. Exercise caution as the traffic moves right along through here.

TRAILER INNS RV PARK *(Open All Year)*

Reservations: (800) 659-4684
Information: (425) 747-9181, www.trailerinnsrv.com
Location: 10 Miles (16 Km) E of Downtown Seattle, *N 47° 34' 35", W 122° 07' 59"*, 300 Ft

100 Sites – The closest campground to downtown Seattle, this one is located near the Eastgate interchange right next to I-90 on the east side of Lake Washington. The campground is an older one, really a large paved lot with the RVs parked very close together. Many rigs are long-term. There are pull-thru spaces to 55 feet for carefully driven big rigs. Amenities include a good indoor swimming pool. There is a lot of traffic noise due to the location. The entrance roads are somewhat confusing because Eastgate has lots of freeway on- and off-ramps. From the east take Exit 11 marked Eastgate. Drive south across the freeway, then turn left at the frontage road (signed) and drive about a half mile (.8 km) to the entrance. From the west on I-90 take

Exit 11A (which is east of the intersection of I-405 and I-90). You'll come to a stop sign at the top of the ramp, proceed directly ahead onto the frontage road and you'll see the campground on the right in about a half-mile (.8 km).

ISSAQUAH VILLAGE RV PARK *(Open All Year)*

Reservations:	(800) 258-9233
Information:	(425) 392-9233, issaquahrv@earthlink.net, http://home.earthlink.net/~issaquahrv
Location:	16 Miles (26 Km) E of Downtown Seattle, *N 47° 32' 12", W 122° 01' 52"*, 100 Ft

56 Sites – Issaquah, which is 20 miles (32 km) east of Seattle, may seem a long way from the city. Just remember that thousands of commuters make the trip every day. The campground is modern and has mostly back-in sites, some to about 50 feet. To reach the park take Exit 17 from I-90 and drive north on East Lake Sammamish Parkway SE. In just 250 yards turn right into 229th Ave. SE. Go just one block and turn right on SE 66th, the park will be on your left in another .5 mile (.8 km).

VASA PARK *(Open All Year)*

Res. and Info.:	(425) 746-3260, www.vasaparkresort.com
Location:	13 Miles (21 Km) E of Downtown Seattle, *N 47° 34' 35", W 122° 06' 48"*, Near Sea Level

22 Sites – Vasa Park is a small swimming resort on the shore of Lake Sammamish to the east of Seattle. It's a popular place for the local kids during the summer and also an unusual camping destination. At the north end of the resort is an area set aside for camping. There are back-in RV sites with full hookups as well as back-in grass-covered sites for tent campers and RVs with partial hookups. Full-hookup sites are about 50 feet in length while the partials are longer, about 80 feet. Amenities include a bath house with laundry, food service kiosk in summer, swimming beach, and boat ramp. The main downside to this park is that there is no convenient bus service, you'll have to walk about a mile to catch one. From May 1 to October 16 this is a daily camping area, the rest of the year only monthly rates are available. Take Exit 13 from I-90 between Eastgate and Issaquah. Drive north on West Lake Sammamish Parkway for 1 mile (1.6 km), the campground entrance is on the right just at the end of the curve. Watch you speed, the police monitor this section of road constantly.

SEA-TAC KOA *(Open All Year)*

Reservations:	(800) 562-1892, www.koa.com
Information:	(253) 872-8652, seattlekoa@aol.com, www.seattlekoa.com
Location:	15 Miles (24 Km) S of Downtown Seattle, *N 47° 24' 43", W 122° 15' 45"*, Near Sea Level

157 Sites – This KOA is a nice one and if you are approaching Seattle from the south it's about your only choice for a campground unless you want to travel to those on the northern or eastern approaches to the city. Even though it's called the Seattle Tacoma KOA it's quite a distance from Tacoma. Sites are back-ins and pull-thrus to 80 feet. There are also grassy tent sites. Amenities include a seasonal outdoor swimming pool, pancake breakfasts in summer, nearby bike trails, and a bus to Seattle within 6 blocks. Take Exit 152 from I-5, this is 12 miles (19 km) from central Seattle and 19 miles (31 km) north of central Tacoma. Follow Orilla Road south on the east side of the freeway as it descends into the valley. In 2.4 miles (3.9 km) you'll see the campground on your right.

SALTWATER STATE PARK *(Open All Year)*

Information: (253) 661-4956, (360) 902-8844, www.parks.wa.gov
Location: 20 Miles (32 Km) S of Downtown Seattle,
                  N 47° 22' 22", W 122° 19' 21", Near Sea Level

50 Sites – Saltwater is a little off the beaten path to be convenient for visitors to Seattle. On the other hand, if you are looking for a non-commercial campground near the city this is one of the few possibilities. The beach area has a food kiosk and is a popular scuba-diving destination. The campground is in a valley inland. Near the entry are large back-ins to 55 feet as well as a few pull-thrus. Farther back is an area only suitable for tent campers, both car campers and hiker/ bikers. The campground is located quite a distance from I-5 and it is necessary to pick your way through the commercial and residential areas of Des Moines to reach it. Take Exit 149 from I-5 and head west on the Kent Des Moines Road (SR-516). In 2 miles (3 km) you'll reach Marine View Drive (SR-509). Follow Marine View 1.5 miles (2.4 km) south to the park.

SEQUIM

Between Port Townsend and Port Angeles you'll find yourself driving though the town of **Sequim**, a popular retirement town due to a well-publicized annual rainfall that is far less than that of most of western Washington due to the "rain-shadow effect" of the Olympic Mountains to the southwest.

The **Dungeness Spit** is directly north of town, this is a national wildlife refuge. The 5.5-mile (8.9 km) spit is the longest natural one in the world and an excellent place to see seabirds. There is also a campground at the base of the spit in Clallam County's Dungeness Recreation Area. In town you might want to visit the **Museum and Arts Center** which houses exhibits re-

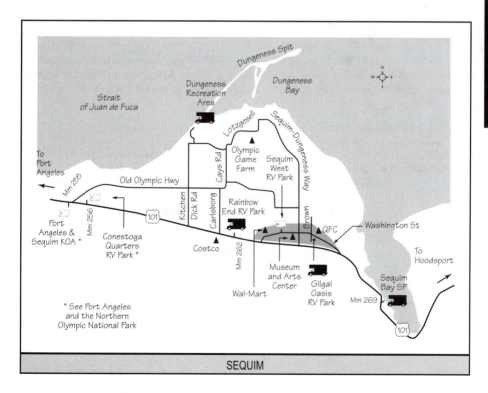

SEQUIM

lated to mastodons dug up nearby. The find was unusual because there was a spear point found between the ribs of one of the beasts, evidence that they were hunted by early Americans. For more active animals there is the **Olympic Game Farm** located north of town, it is home to many animals that starred in TV and movies and has a large collection of endangered and unusual animals as well as a petting farm and aquarium. There are also some wineries in the area, the 7 **Cedars Casino**, and a golf course.

Outdoor-oriented tent and RV campers will find the Dungeness Recreation Area campground to be their best bet in this area. Big rig RVers will probably enjoy the small but modern and well-done Gilgal Oasis.

SEQUIM BAY STATE PARK *(Open All Year)*

Reservations:	(888) 226-7688, www.camis.com/wa
Information:	(360) 683-4235, (360) 371-2800, www.parks.wa.gov
Location:	4 Miles (6 Km) E of Sequim, *N 48° 02' 26", W 123° 01' 47"*, 100 Ft

89 Sites – Sequim Bay State Park is a shoreline park with a boat ramp. Campsites are away from the water and there is no real beach. The sites are small here and off three loops. One loop is to the right as you enter and has back-in full hookup sites in an open area that are long enough for RVs to about 30 feet. The Upper Loop is to the left as you enter and has forest-type sites, a sign restricts rig length here to 25 feet due to the narrow roads. Straight ahead when you enter is the lower loop. These sites are forest-type sites on a hillside, RVs to about 30 feet should be able to use this area. A trail leads under the highway to tennis courts and a softball field. The campground is on the north side of US-101 about 4 miles (6.4 km) east of Sequim.

GILGAL OASIS RV PARK *(Open All Year)*

Reservations:	(888) 445-4251
Information:	(360) 452-1324, info@gilgaloasisrvpark.com, www.gilgaloasisrvpark.com
Location:	Sequim, *N 48° 04' 38", W 123° 05' 26"*, 100 Ft

29 Sites – Gilgal Oasis is a new but small big-rig RV park located near the center of Sequim. There are back-in sites to 35 feet and pull-thru sites to 50 feet. From Washington Street in central Sequim turn south on South Brown Road (opposite the QFC store) for just a block to the park.

RAINBOW END RV PARK *(Open All Year)*

Reservations:	(877) 638-3863
Information:	(360) 683-3863, office@rainbowsendrvpark.com, www.rainbowsendrvpark.com
Location:	1 Mile (2 Km) W of Sequim, *N 48° 04' 40", W 123° 09' 37"*, 200 Ft

38 Sites – The Rainbow End is a popular commercial park located just west of Sequim. It's an older park and sites here vary a lot in size, there are just three pull-thrus. Some sites will squeeze in 45-footers but the campground is more comfortable for 35 to 40-footers. The park is on the north side of US-101 about 1 mile (2 km) west of Sequim.

DUNGENESS RECREATION AREA *(Open Feb 1 to Sept 30)*

Information:	(360) 683-5847, ccpdu@olypen.com, www.clallam.net/countyparks
Location:	6 Miles (10 Km) N of Sequim, *N 48° 08' 18", W 123° 11' 45"*, 100 Ft

66 Sites – This is a Clallam County Recreation Area located at the foot of the Dungeness Spit which is a National Wildlife Refuge. Hiking in the area, particularly on the spit, is excellent. Sites here are back-ins to 40 feet but lack of maneuvering room makes 35 foot RVs the practical maximum. The campground is located north of Sequim near the coast. Easiest access is by using Kitchen Dick Road. Kitchen Dick goes north from US-101 about 3 miles (5 km) west of Sequim. Follow Kitchen Dick for 3.2 miles (5.2 km) to the north, then jog right and then left to enter the park.

SKAGIT VALLEY

This area is a popular day trip or weekend destination for folks from the Seattle area. There are quite a cluster of attractions easily accessible from the campgrounds below. A tow car or small RV is a real advantage for visiting them.

Deception Pass is the narrow channel that separates the north end of Whidbey Island from Fidalgo Island. Two soaring bridges span the gap, they provide opportunities for some great pictures. The water in the passage below runs pretty fast, it is fun to watch boats fighting the current. The pass is within Deception Pass State Park, you can walk beaches within the park on both Whidbey Island and Fidalgo Island. See the *Whidby Island* section for more about Deception Pass State Park and the other Whidbey Island Campgrounds.

Ferries run from the town of **Anacortes** on Fidalgo Island into the **San Juan Islands**. It can be hard to get a vehicle onto these ferries (auto service is chronically inadequate to the San Juans) but there is usually plenty of room for walk-on passengers. The islands are very scenic, we suggest the ride out to Friday Harbor on San Juan Island. You can easily explore Friday Harbor on foot, have a nice meal, and then catch another ferry back to Anacortes. This is definitely a day-long trip.

The little town of **La Conner** attracts hordes of visitors from Seattle on any sunny weekend. It sits next to the Swinomish Channel separating Fidalgo Island from the mainland and has lots

THE BRIDGE ACROSS DECEPTION PASS

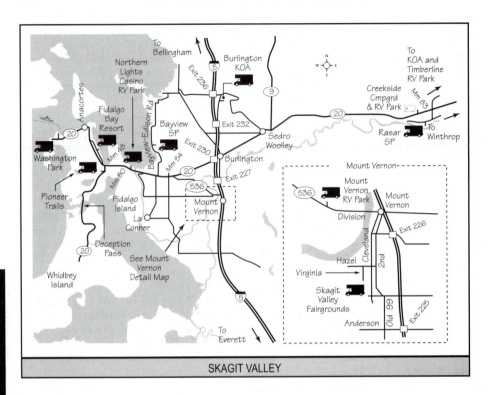

SKAGIT VALLEY

of little shops and restaurants. This is a particularly popular destination during the **Skagit Valley Tulip Festival** during the first half of April each year. Acres and acres of tulips and daffodils fill the fields of the Skagit delta between La Conner and Mount Vernon.

RASAR STATE PARK *(Open All Year)*

Reservations:	(888) 226-7688, www.camis.com/wa
Information:	(360) 826-3942, (360) 371-2800, www.parks.wa.gov
Location:	25 Miles (40 Km) NE of Mt Vernon, *N 48° 31' 07", W 121° 54' 06"*, 100 Ft

38 Sites – Rasar is one of the newer parks in the Washington state park system. It is near the Skagit River, a trail leads from the campground to the river. Over 500 bald eagles winter on the river and this is a popular bird-watching campground. Facilities are excellent. Sites will take RVs to 40 feet. To reach the campground drive east from Sedro Woolley for 16 miles (26 km). Turn south on Russell Road and drive .7 miles (1.1 km). At the intersection turn right and you'll reach the campground in another 1.2 miles (1.9 km).

MT VERNON RV PARK *(Open All Year)*

Reservations:	(800) 385-9895
Information:	(360) 428-8787
Location:	Mt Vernon, *N 48° 25' 23", W 122° 21' 05"*, Near Sea Level

82 Sites – This is an meticulously groomed, excellent urban campground in a pleasant little town. It's very popular and reservations are recommended. Sites include large pull-thrus to 65 feet, it's a good big-rig campground. From central Mt Vernon SR-536 goes west toward

Anacortes. If you zero your odometer as you leave the bridge over the Skagit River you'll see the campground on your right in .5 miles (.8 km).

SKAGIT VALLEY FAIRGROUNDS *(Open All Year)*

Res. and Info.:	(360) 336-9453, audreys@co.skagit.wa.us, www.skagitcounty.net/fairgrounds
Location:	Mt Vernon, *N 48° 24' 37", W 122° 20' 29"*, Near Sea Level

80 Sites – The fairgrounds are at the southern edge of Mt Vernon. The camping area is inside the fairgrounds. It is a large gravel area and the nearby lawn with electrical and water hookups is good for tents or any size RV. It's easy to check in. Unless the fair is in progress (early August) just pull in and use the self-payment system to pay. The restrooms are near the parking area and easy to spot. There is a caretaker who will no doubt come by and answer any questions you may have. During the time that the fair is scheduled call ahead and you may be able to make reservations even then. From I-5 take Exit 225. Go west just a short distance to Old Highway 99. Drive north for .9 mile (1.5 km) making sure to take the left fork as 99 becomes S. Second St. Turn left on W. Hazel Street. Drive 3 blocks west on Hazel and turn left on Virginia Street. Virginia ends at the fairgrounds gate, drive straight in to the camping area which is signed.

BAY VIEW STATE PARK *(Open All Year)*

Reservations:	(888) 226-7688, www.camis.com/wa
Information:	(360) 757-0227, (360) 371-2800, www.parks.wa.gov
Location:	11 Miles (18 Km) W of Mt Vernon, *N 48° 29' 19", W 122° 28' 45"*, Near Sea Level

76 Sites – Bay View has sites in three locations. There are a few back-in sites with electricity and water outside the entry kiosk. These sites are the most suitable for RVs and some will take RVs to 35 feet. Another group of electrical and water hookup sites surround a grassy field inside the park, they handle RVs to about 30 feet. Finally, many sites with no hookups are in an area of trees, some will take RVs to 30 feet. There is a new restroom building now, a big improvement. This is a good campground for birders. Just down the road is the 2.2-mile (3.5 km) Padilla Bay Shore Trail which runs along a dike overlooking a tidal estuary. Also nearby is the Breazeale Padilla Bay Interpretive Center. To reach the campground turn north from SR-20 on the Bayview-Edison Road, the intersection is 6.3 miles (10.2 km) west of I-5 Exit 230 or 2.1 miles (3.4 km) east of the Swinomish Channel bridge. Drive north 3.7 miles (6 km) to the campground.

FIDALGO BAY RESORT *(Open All Year)*

Res. and Info.:	(800) 727-5478, reserve@fidalgobay.com, www.fidalgobay.com
Location:	13 Miles (21 Km) W of Mt Vernon, *N 48° 28' 55", W 122° 35' 35"*, Near Sea Level

187 Sites – A nice big-rig RV park next to Fidalgo Bay just outside Anacortes. It has a great view of the March Point refinery across the bay. There are back-in and pull-thru sites to 70 feet. Some sites are beachfront. To find it drive .3 mile (.5 km) northwest on the SR-20W spur toward Anacortes from its intersection with SR-20 as it comes north from Oak Harbor and Deception Pass. Turn north onto Fidalgo Bay Road and follow it 1.2 miles (1.9 km) to the resort.

NORTHERN LIGHTS CASINO RV PARK *(Open All Year)*

Res. and Info.:	(360) 299-1672, www.swinomishcasino.com
Location:	9 Miles (15 Km) W of Mt Vernon, *N 48° 27' 33", W 122° 31' 10"*, Near Sea Level

36 Sites – This casino has a new RV park located behind it just across the railroad tracks from Padilla Bay. This is a big-rig park with back-ins and pull-thrus to 55 feet. It's good only for

self-contained campers since there are no restroom facilities other than those in the casino itself. The casino is located Off SR-20 just west of the bridge over the Swinomish Channel. This is 8.6 miles (13.9 km) west of Exit 230 on I-5 and 5 miles (8 km) east of Anacortes.

PIONEER TRAILS *(Open All Year)*

Reservations:	(888) 777-5355
Information:	(360) 293-5355, www.pioneertrails.com
Location:	13 Miles (21 Km) W of Mt Vernon, *N 48° 27' 19", W 122° 35' 13"*, 200 Ft

94 Sites – This is a big-rig campground in a grove of large evergreens. Even with the trees, though, it's not dark. Sites vary a lot but there are back-ins and a few long pull-thrus. Eleven and six-tenths miles (18.7 km) west of Exit 230 off I-5 and 2 miles east of Anacortes highway SR-20 cuts south toward Whidbey Island. The campground is .5 mile (.8 km) south of this intersection on the west side of the highway.

WASHINGTON PARK *(Open All Year)*

Information:	(360) 293-1927
Location:	3 Miles (5 Km) W of Anacortes, *N 48° 29' 56", W 122° 41' 34"*, Near Sea Level

68 Sites – Washington Park is a city campground with back-in and pull-thru sites in a forested area. It's a dark campground but there is a great beach area nearby as well as good hiking trails. For tent campers it is excellent, it's also OK for RVs to about 30 feet. Rig size is limited by narrow roads and lack of maneuvering room more than site size, a few of the sites actually reach over 40 feet. Facilities are older and useable but not great. The campground occupies a point of land just west of the San Juan Islands ferry terminal in Anacortes. From central Anacortes follow the ferry terminal signs west on 12th Street and then Oakes Ave. After 3.1 miles (5 km) the road forks with the ferry to the right. Go straight ahead on Sunset Ave. instead and you'll reach the campground in another .8 mile (1.3 km).

BURLINGTON KOA *(Open All Year)*

Reservations:	(800) 562-9154, www.koa.com
Information:	(360) 724-5511
Location:	11 Miles (18 Km) N of Mt Vernon, *N 48° 33' 08", W 122° 20' 02"*, Near Sea Level

100 Sites – Facilities are normal KOA standard, like all of them it's a good place if you have kids along. Amenities include an indoor pool and hot tub. Sites vary but there are both tent sites and big-rig sites to 65 feet. The campground is located not far off I-5 north of Burlington and Mt Vernon. Take Exit 236 and head east and down the hill. At the intersection with old US-99 in .8 mile (1.3 km) turn right. In just .2 mile (.3 km) turn left into N. Green Road and the campground will be in your left almost immediately.

SPOKANE

Spokane (population 196,000) is Washington's largest city east of the Cascades. The city sits astride I-90 just 18 miles (29 km) from the Idaho border. It serves as a business center for eastern Washington and also northern Idaho and western Montana.

The centerpiece of the town has to be **Riverfront Park** (not to be confused with Riverside

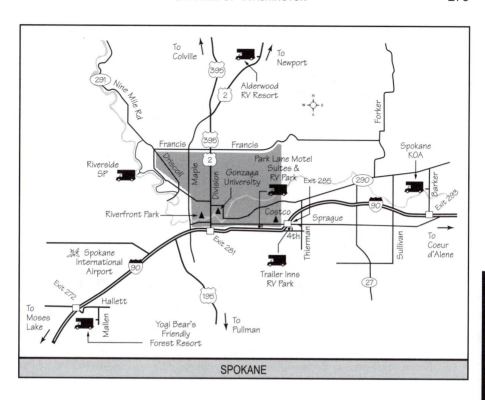

State Park). This 100 acre area around **Spokane Falls** was turned into a beautiful park in preparation for the 1974 World's Fair and Exposition. You'll find a gondola offering great views of the falls as well as an amusement park and IMAX theater.

Spokane has an impressive museum, the **Northwest Museum of Arts and Cultures**. It overlooks the Spokane River on the west side of town. It has a very large collection of indigenous artifacts as well as exhibits on Northwest history and art.

Spokane is also home to **Gonzaga University**. The campus is located north of the river east of the city center. Attractions here include the Bing Crosby Memorabilia Room (he was an alumnus) and the **Jundt Art Muesum**.

One of our favorite Spokane attractions is the 37-mile (60 km) **Spokane Centennial Trail**. This paved bike trail follow the Spokane River all the way from the Idaho Border, through the city, and then through Riverside State Park on the west side as far as Nine Mile Falls.

PARK LANE MOTEL SUITES AND RV PARK *(Open All Year)*

Res. and Info.:   (509) 535-1626, reservations@parklanemotel.com, www.parklanemotel.com
Location: 2 Miles (3 Km) E of Downtown Spokane, *N 47° 39' 25", W 117° 20' 42"*, 1,900 Ft

19 Sites – This is a popular RV park located behind a small motel in the big-box store area along Sprague Ave. east of central Spokane. The back-in sites will accept RVs to 45 feet. Only self-contained rigs are accepted because there are no restrooms for the RV park. Sites have instant-on telephone (you get a phone and phone book when you check in) as well as free Wi-Fi which is useable from your rig in the park. Take Exit 285 from I-90 and drive west for 1.1 miles (1.8 km), the motel is on the left.

WASHINGTON

WASHINGTON (vertical, left margin)

▦ TRAILER INNS RV PARK *(Open All Year)*

Reservations: (800) 659-4864
Information: (509) 535-1811, www.trailerinnsrv.com
Location: 3 Miles (5 Km) E of Downtown Spokane, *N 47° 39' 16", W 117° 19' 22"*, 1,900 Ft

97 Sites – Trailer Inns has large parks like this one in Spokane, Yakima, and Seattle. All are older paved parks with closely spaced rigs and many long-term tenants, but all can accept large rigs (with careful maneuvering). This one is conveniently located near I-90 east of central Spokane. To reach the park take Exit 285 and drive east for about .3 miles (.5 km). Turn right on S. Thieman St. and drive 3 blocks, then turn right on E. 4th Ave. and you'll see the campground entrance on the right in another .3 mile (.5 km).

▦ RIVERSIDE STATE PARK *(Open All Year)*

Information: (509) 465-5064, (360) 371-2800, www.camis.com/wa
Location: 4 Miles (6 Km) E of Downtown Spokane, *N 47° 41' 45", W 117° 29' 40"*, 1,800 Ft

33 Sites – West of central Spokane along the Spokane River is a large state park. It has a small campground. Sites are in two closely located areas. An older area near the entrance booth is best for tents and smaller RVs. Two of these sites have full hookups. Below is a new area near the river with 14 large sites with electricity and water that are suitable for RVs to 45 feet and longer. Swimming here is in the river. Access to this campground is a little roundabout. From I-90 take Exit 298 and drive north on Division Street (US-2). In 4.2 miles (6.8 km) turn left on E. Francis Ave. Follow Frances and then W. Nine Mile Rd. west for 3.8 miles (6.1 km). Turn left following signs to the park and wind through the trees along the river for another 2.1 miles (3.4 km) to the campground entrance.

▦ ALDERWOOD RV RESORT *(Open All Year)*

Reservations: (888) 847-0500
Information: (509) 467-5320, alderwood@air-pipe.com, www.alderwoodrv.com
Location: 9 Miles (15 Km) N of Downtown Spokane, *N 47° 47' 07", W 117° 21' 17"*, 1,900 Ft

108 Sites - This is a new modern big-rig campground on the north side of Spokane. Facilities are excellent including landscaped sites, an indoor swimming pool, and free Wi-Fi at the sites. The campground is located off US-2 on the north side of Spokane. This is 10.3 miles (16.6 km) north of Exit 298 off I-90 and involves driving through central Spokane so this campground is best if you are approaching town from the north.

▦ SPOKANE KOA *(Open All Year)*

Reservations: (800) 562-3309, www.koa.com   **Information:** (509) 924-4722
Location: 14 Miles (23 Km) E of Downtown Spokane, *N 47° 41' 05", W 117° 09' 17"*, 2,000 Ft

149 Sites – This is a fairly standard KOA with an seasonal outdoor pool. It's easy to access from the interstate and it's a large flat open lot so it's a good big-rig park. To reach the campground from I-90 take Exit 293 east of Spokane and drive north on North Barker Road for 1.2

miles (1.9 km), the campground is on your left.

YOGI BEAR'S FRIENDLY FOREST RESORT *(Open All Year)*

Res. and Info.:   (509) 747-9415, yogi@jellystonewa.com, www.jellystonewa.com
Location: 11 Miles (18 Km) W of Downtown Spokane, *N 47° 34' 57", W 117° 32' 35"*, 2,500 Ft

178 Sites – This is a membership campground located quite a distance west of Spokane. It's also a Yogi Bear campground, there are other Yogi Bear resorts around the country but few in the Pacific Northwest. Not all are membership resorts like this one. Sites here can take RVs to 45 feet and larger, they're set in trees. Amenities include instant-on telephones, an indoor pool and lots of playgrounds and sports equipment including mini-golf. Non-members are welcome. From Exit 272 of I-90 about 6 miles (10 km) west of Spokane drive east on West Hallett Road for about 2 miles (3.2 km) following signs for the park. Turn right on Thomas Mallen Road and the park entrance will be on your right in .7 mile (1.1 km).

TACOMA

Tacoma (population 198,000) is located about 35 miles (56 km) south of Seattle along I-5. This second-largest city on Puget Sound has long been known for its smell, even today you'll be aware of the pulp mills as you drive by. Fortunately the campgrounds are some distance from the city.

That smell, however, means that Tacoma is one of the least expensive places to live in the area. As the region grows Tacoma is starting to improve itself. There has been a lot of redevelopment in the old downtown area and Tacoma has become an interesting town to visit.

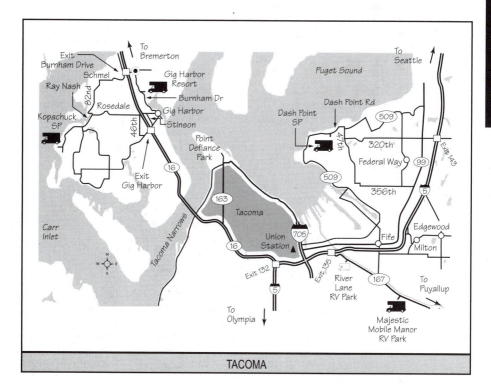

TACOMA

The centerpiece of rebuilding Tacoma's downtown is the restored **Union Station**. This railroad station was built in 1911, it had actually been boarded up when it was chosen to be redone as the federal courthouse. Near the station you'll find two good museums. One is the excellent **Washington State History Museum**. The second is a new museum, the **Tacoma Art Museum**. Not far away, and linked to these museums by the **Chihuly Bridge of Glass**, is the new **Museum of Glass**. Together these museums will keep you busy all day long.

Tacoma also has a great park. **Point Defiance Park** to the west of the city covers 700 waterfront acres. It has gardens and a zoo and aquarium.

In addition to the three campgrounds listed below you might note that the Nisqually Campground listed under *Olympia* is also a possibility for Tacoma.

DASH POINT STATE PARK *(Open All Year)*

Reservations:	(888) 226-7688, www.camis.com/wa
Information:	(253) 661-4955, (360) 371-2800, www.parks.wa.gov
Location:	16 Miles (26 Km) N of Downtown Tacoma, *N 47° 19' 02", W 122° 24' 24"*, 300 Ft

138 Sites – This campground along the shore of Puget Sound is not far north of Tacoma. However, in order to reach it you must find your way through the commercial and residential areas of Federal Way. The park has a very popular beach area good for beachcombing and even swimming since the tide bares a lot of sand which the sun warms. The campground itself is away from the water and off two loops. Only 27 of the sites have utilities, these will take RVs to 30 feet. A few no hookup sites will take RVs to 40 feet. One way to reach the park is to leave I-5 at Exit 143. Follow SW 320th westward for 4.5 miles (7.3 km). Turn right on 47th Ave. SW and drive north for .4 mile (.6 km). Now, at the T, turn left on SW Dash Point Road and you'll reach the campground entrance in .8 mile (1.3 km).

MAJESTIC MOBILE MANOR RV PARK *(Open All Year)*

Reservations:	(800) 348-3144
Information:	(253) 845-3144, majesticrvpark@juno.com
Location:	5 Miles (8 Km) E of Downtown Tacoma, *N 47° 12' 34", W 122° 20' 15"*, Near Sea Level

118 Sites – Majestic Mobile Manor is just what the name suggests. This is a mobile home park with a campground adjacent to it. The campground has a lot of long-term rigs closely packed on gravel. Sites are back-ins, they reach 40 or even 45 feet in a pinch. This is not a vacation park but if you are visiting Tacoma it's a place to base yourself. There is a swimming pool in summer. From I-5 just east of Tacoma take Exit 135 and head southeast on SR-167 toward Puyallup. The campground will be in your right in 3.7 miles (6.0 km).

GIG HARBOR RV RESORT *(Open All Year)*

Reservations:	(800) 526-8311
Information:	(253) 858-8138
Location:	11 Miles (18 Km) NW of Downtown Tacoma, *N 47° 20' 41", W 122° 35' 55"*, 100 Ft

93 Sites – Gig Harbor is the nicest of the campgrounds serving the Tacoma area. It is located on the far side of the Tacoma Narrows which is a problem if you are a commuter but not if you're a visiting tourist and can avoid rush hour traffic. Besides, central Gig Harbor is just down the road and has plenty of restaurants, shops, and harbor-side ambiance. The campground is located on a hillside which makes for an attractive park, but makes some sites a little difficult to get into with a big rig. This is a big-rig park, however, with large back-in and pull-thru sites to

65 feet. There's also a dedicated tent-camping area. Amenities include a summer-only swimming pool. To reach the campground from the Tacoma area take Exit 132 from I-5. Drive west and across the Narrows Bridge for 12 miles (19 km) and take the Burnham Drive NW exit. From the roundabout on the east side of the highway take the first exit (Burnham Dr. NW), which is signed for the campground, and follow Burnham Dr. for 1.2 miles (1.9 km) to the campground. It's on the left.

KOPACHUCK STATE PARK *(Open All Year)*

Information:	(253) 661-4955, (360) 371-2800, www.parks.wa.gov
Location:	16 Miles (26 Km) W of Tacoma, *N 47° 18' 30", W 122° 40' 54"*, 200 Ft

41 Sites – Kopachuck is a small state park located on the coast south of Gig Harbor. Many folks who live in the area call this their favorite local state park which is something considering there are so many similar waterside state parks on the Kitsap Peninsula. The attraction is the wide sandy beach, suitable for swimming, seafood gathering, and sunning. We've listed this one under Tacoma since it is technically not really on the Kitsap Peninsula and is relatively handy to Tacoma. Sites here are back-ins in a dark forest setting high above the beach. Narrow roads and narrow back-in sites limit RV size to about 30 feet. To reach the campground from the Tacoma area take Exit 132 from I-5. Drive west and across the Narrows Bridge for 9 miles (14.5 km) and take the Gig Harbor exit. Follow Stinson Ave. north for .8 mile (1.3 km) and turn left on Rosedale St. NW. Follow Rosedale east for 2.9 miles (4.7 km) and turn left on Ray Nash Dr. NW. Follow Nash, which becomes Kopachuck Dr. NW for 2.3 miles (3.7 km), the entrance is on the right.

WENATCHEE

Wenatchee (population 29,000) is located just below the point where the Wenatchee River joins the Columbia. The city is probably best known as the center of the apple-growing industry in Washington State.

Apples are featured at the **Washington Apple Commission Visitor's Center** at the north end of town, you'll see it on the right if you're driving to Wenatchee Confluence State Park. The **Wenatchee Valley Museum and Culture Center**, located downtown, has more about apples, but also about the history of the town.

A wonderful outdoor attraction in Wenatchee is the **Riverfront Park**. It features a paved 10-mile (16 km) loop trail that follows the river on both banks, with bridges at each end. It's great for bikes, walking, jogging, or even rollerblades.

Perched above the town to the south is the **Ohme Gardens**. The gardens, set in dry rocky terrain, are great. So is the view.

Wenatchee's big celebration is the **Washington State Apple Blossom Festival**. It features parades, dances, a carnival, a run, and an Apple Queen. The festival takes place at the end of April and beginning of May.

WENATCHEE CONFLUENCE STATE PARK *(Open All Year)*

Reservations:	(888) 226-7688, www.parks.wa.gov
Information:	(509) 664-6373, (360) 371-2800, www.parks.wa.gov
Location:	Wenatchee, *N 47° 27' 37", W 120° 19' 49"*, 600 Ft

59 Sites – This park is conveniently located at the confluence of the Wenatchee and Columbia Rivers in the town of Wenatchee. A great trail system runs right by the park, it forms a loop with trails on both sides of the river and provides easy walking access to central Wenatchee, about 2 miles (3 km) away. Sites here are paved and up to 45 feet long. They are widely separated

WASHINGTON

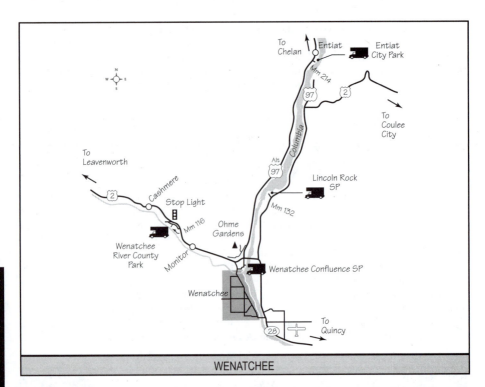

WENATCHEE

by beautiful lawns. From the intersection of US-97 and US-2 on the west side of the bridge over the Columbia north of Wenatchee turn south. In .4 mile (.6 km) turn left on Euclid Ave. following signs to the park. In another .4 miles (.6 km) turn left into the park entrance road, you'll reach the gate in another .2 miles (.3 km).

ENTIAT CITY PARK *(Open April 15 to Sept 30 - Varies)*

Reservations:	(800) 736-8428
Information:	(509) 664-6373
Location:	14 Miles(23 Km) N of Wenatchee, *N 47° 40' 04", W 120° 13' 08",* 700 Ft

31 Sites – This medium-sized city park and campground has back-in sites to 45 feet. Tenters camp on grass nearby. The park is on the bank of the Columbia River, a great location. There is also a boat launch here and extensive lawns. This campground is easy to spot from Alt US-97 and occupies most of the waterfront in the town of Entiat. This is about 14 miles (23 km) upstream from Wenatchee on the west bank.

LINCOLN ROCK STATE PARK *(Open All Year)*

Reservations:	(888) 226-7688, www.camis.com/wa
Information:	(509) 884-8702, (360) 371-2800, www.parks.wa.gov
Location:	5 Miles (8 Km) NE of Wenatchee, *N 47° 32' 06", W 120° 17' 00",* 700 Ft

94 Sites – This very large state park is also upstream from Wenatchee, this time on the east bank about 5 miles (8 Km) from Wenatchee. Sites here are widely spaced and separated by well-watered and manicured grass. They are big paved sites suitable for any rig, many are pull-thrus. A very park-like setting. In addition to the many campsites in the park there is a boat launch, tennis courts, and sports fields.

🚐 **WENATCHEE RIVER COUNTY PARK** *(Open All Year)*

Res. and Info.:   (509) 667-7503, www.co.chelan.wa.us
Location: 4 Miles (6 Km) W of Wenatchee, *N 47° 29' 06", W 120° 24' 34"*, 700 Ft

43 Sites – This very pleasant county park is located up the Wenatchee Valley from the town of Wenatchee. Noise is a bit of a problem in this park with the train tracks on one side and US-2 on the other, but it's not serious, you quickly become accustomed to the occasional train. Sites are large paved back-ins to 45 feet and are arranged in pinwheels off circular drives. Drive west from Wenatchee on US-2 for 4 miles (6.4 km), the campground is on the south side of the highway at about Mile 115.5.

WESTPORT

Although Westport (population 2,300) is just across the entrance of Grays Harbor from Ocean Shores the atmosphere is entirely different. Westport is very devoted to fishing, both charter and commercial. During the off season it seems almost derelict, but when the fish are running it is another story. The thing to do in Westport is take a charter fishing trip to catch salmon, halibut, tuna, or bottom fish. Also popular these days are boat trips out to the "whale hole" to watch the gray whales as they pause during their spring migration to Alaska during March, April, and May.

When you aren't out on the ocean there are other things to do in Westport. Along the waterfront next to the harbor there are a number of tourist shops and restaurants. Tourist sights include the **Westport Maritime Museum** and the privately owned **Westport Aquarium**. There is also a boat during the summer that ferries walking passengers across to Ocean Shores.

Westport hosts its share of events, there's something almost every weekend during the sum-

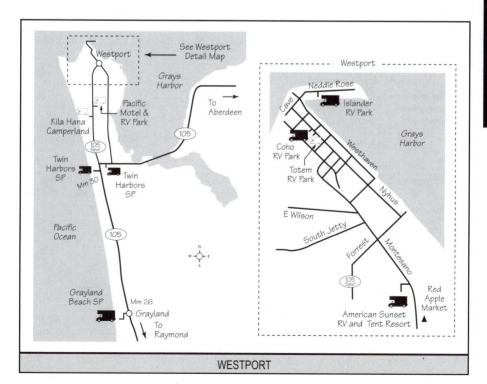

WESTPORT

mer months. Among them are the **Rusty Scupper Pirate Daze** the last weekend in June, a **Kite Festival** in early July, the **International Nautical Chainsaw Carving Competition** in early August, the **Westport Art Festival** about the middle of August, and the **Westport Seafood Festival and Craft Day** on Labor Day. Check with the Chamber of Commerce for more events and exact dates.

▨ AMERICAN SUNSET RV AND TENT RESORT *(Open All Year)*

Reservations:	(800) 569-2267
Information:	(360) 268-0207, www.AmericanSunsetRV.com
Location:	Westport, *N 46° 53' 58", W 124° 06' 22"*, Near Sea Level

120 Sites – This is a nice large park located about .7 miles (1.1 km) from the dock area in Westport. The location means that the temperature here is warmer. The campground has less of a fisherman's camp atmosphere than those closer to the docks. In addition to the RV area (long back-ins) there is a large tent camping area and also a seasonal swimming pool. From the dock area in Westport proceed south on SR-105 for about a mile (1.6 km), the entrance will be on your right.

▨ COHO RV PARK *(Open All Year)*

Reservations:	(800) 572-0177
Information:	(360) 268-0111, coho@techline.com, westportwa.com/coho
Location:	Westport, *N 46° 54' 33", W 124° 06' 57"*, Near Sea Level

76 Sites – This older park is conveniently located about a block from the Westport docks and marina. It's also a motel. Fishing charters can be arranged, they run two boats. It's easy to walk to the marina, shops and restaurants. Sites are all back-ins, RVs to 45 feet will fit although they'll project a bit into the driveway. The Coho is on Nyhus between Coast Rd. and Harbor Ave.

▨ ISLANDER RV PARK *(Open All Year)*

Reservations:	(800) 322-1740
Information:	(360) 268-9166, info@westport-islander.com, www.westport-islander.com
Location:	Westport, *N 46° 54' 43", W 124° 06' 55"*, Near Sea Level

57 sites – This campground sits next to the associated hotel. While the hotel is one of the nicer in town the RV park is a step down, although it is located overlooking the boat harbor. The hotel and RV park are located at the northwest corner of the boat harbor, right where the road heads out along the northern breakwater.

▨ TWIN HARBORS STATE PARK *(Open All Year)*

Reservations:	(888) 226-7688, www.camis.com/wa
Information:	(360) 268-9717, (360) 371-2800, www.parks.wa.gov
Location:	1 Mile (1.6 Km) S of Westport, *N 46° 51' 28", W 124° 06' 23"*, Near Sea Level

302 Sites – This is a very large state campground just south of Westport. It is in two parts, one near the beach and the other across the highway. Only 49 sites have hookups and these are all closely grouped back-ins, some are 60 feet long. These hookup sites are away from the ocean on the east side of the highway. The smaller sites with no hookups are much nicer and occupy

WASHINGTON

the beach side of the park. The campground is located right at the junction where the stub road north to Westport meets SR-105. The entrance is on the road toward Aberdeen.

GRAYLAND BEACH STATE PARK *(Open All Year)*

Reservations: (888) 226-7688, www.camis.com/wa
Information: (360) 268-9717, (360) 371-2800, www.parks.wa.gov
Location: 5 Miles (8 Km) S of Westport, *N 46° 47' 34", W 124° 05' 29",* Near Sea Level

113 Sites – This state park is farther south than Twin Harbors but nicer with the sites arranged off 6 rings. The campground has 60 campsites with full hookups, some are 70 feet long. There is a nature trail through the dunes to the beach. From the intersection south of Westport where SR-105 from the south and SR-105 from Aberdeen meet, drive south 4.5 miles (7.3 km) to the entrance which is just south of the small town of Grayland.

WHIDBEY ISLAND

Whidbey Island stretches for 40 miles (65 km) from just north of Seattle to just south of Anacortes. It's a rural destination just a few miles from the Seattle metro area. However, the island isn't as crowded as you might expect, largely because access for Seattle residents requires a long drive or a ferry ride.

There are actually three ways to bring a vehicle onto the island. The only bridge is at the far north end across Deception Pass. The main ferry access is at the south end of the island from Mukilteo. This is only 25 miles (40 km) north of the Seattle business district and ferries are frequent, but they're expensive and during some tides access is difficult for big rigs. Finally, there's also a small ferry that operated from Port Townsend. This route doesn't bring nearly as many people onto the island as the other two.

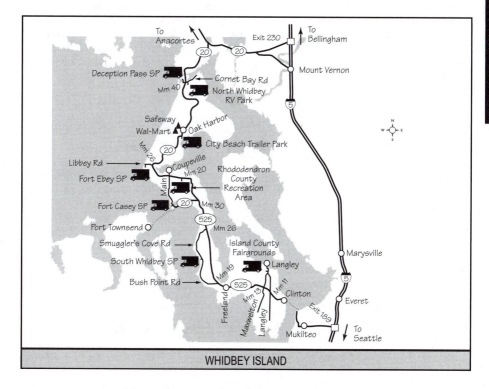

WHIDBEY ISLAND

WASHINGTON

With four state parks as well as commercial and local government campgrounds Whidbey has a lot to offer campers. An added bonus is that many of these campgrounds are near the beach.

DECEPTION PASS STATE PARK *(Open All Year)*

Reservations:	(888) 226-7688, www.camis.com/wa
Information:	(360) 675-2417, (360) 371-2800, www.parks.wa.gov
Location:	8 Miles (13 Km) N of Oak Harbor, *N 48° 23' 30", W 122° 38' 50",* Near Sea Level

250 Sites – This large state park has a very impressive location offering views of Deception Pass, trails, fishing and swimming in a nearby lake, and excellent ocean beaches on Puget Sound. The camping areas are set in dense evergreens and do not have views. Some of the hookup sites will take RVs to 35 feet although leveling may be difficult, the park is better for smaller rigs. Driving north on SR-20 on Whidbey Island watch for the Mile 40 marker. Turn left at the stoplight which is .8 miles (1.3 km) from the marker. From the Deception Pass bridge just drive south on SR-20 for a mile (1.6 km) to the stop light, the campground entrance will be on the right.

NORTH WHIDBEY RV PARK *(Open All Year)*

Reservations:	(888) 462-2674
Information:	(360) 675-9597, managers@northwhidbeyrvpark.com, www.northwhidbeyrvpark.com
Location:	8 Miles (13 Km) N of Oak Harbor, *N 48° 23' 26", W 122° 38' 44",* 100 Ft

99 Sites – Located just a mile (1.6 km) from Deception Pass and right across from the entrance to Deception Pass State Park this campground is a nice commercial alternative to the state campground. Driving north on SR-20 on Whidbey Island watch for the Mile 40 marker. Turn right on Cornet Bay Road at the stop light which is .8 miles (1.3 km) from the marker, the campground will be in the right immediately after the turn. From the Deception Pass bridge just drive south on Highway 20 for a mile (1.6 km), turn left on Cornet Bay Road, the campground will be on the right.

OAK HARBOR CITY BEACH TRAILER PARK *(Open All Year)*

Information:	(360) 679-5551, www.oakharbor.org
Location:	Oak Harbor, *N 48° 17' 08", W 122° 39' 26",* Near Sea Level

56 Sites – This is one of the most popular and least expensive campgrounds for big rigs on the Island. Sites are long back-ins set next to the large grassy waterfront park, there are 30-amp outlets. Tents are allowed but the gravel RV sites don't make a great campsite for a tent. SR-20 makes an almost 90-degree bend in Oak Harbor. From the north continue straight at the turn, the road becomes South Beeksma Drive, and you'll reach the park in a block. From the south turn right at the bend.

FORT EBEY STATE PARK *(Open All Year)*

Reservations:	(888) 226-7688, www.camis.com/wa
Information:	(360) 678-4636, (360) 371-2800, www.parks.wa.gov
Location:	8 Miles (13 Km) SW of Oak Harbor, *N 48° 13' 20", W 122° 45' 46",* 100 Ft

54 Sites – Fort Ebey is one of 2 state parks on the Island that are former wartime gun bat-

teries built to protect the approaches to Puget Sound. The campground here is in trees without views, sites are large enough for big RVs but maneuvering room is limited so very careful driving is required. Most sites are standard no-hookup sites, but there are 10 electricity-water sites. This park has extensive walking/bike trails and a long beach. A small lake offers fishing for small-mouth bass. It's a popular hang gliding location too. To reach the campground leave SR-20 at about Mile 25 just north of Coupeville on Libby Road and follow signs for 1.2 miles (1.9 km) to the park entrance.

⊞ RHODODENDRON COUNTY RECREATION AREA *(Open April 1 to Oct 31)*

Information: (360) 679-7373
Location: 12 Miles (19 Km) S of Oak Harbor, *N 48° 12' 24", W 122° 39' 12"*, 200 Ft

10 Sites – This small county park is an inexpensive campground for tents and smaller RVs to about 25 feet. It's set in a dense grove of Douglas Fir and cedars. The campground is located just off SR-20 south of Coupeville. Turn west at the sign near Mile 20.

⊞ FORT CASEY STATE PARK *(Open All Year)*

Information: (360) 678-4519, (360) 371-2800, www.parks.wa.gov
Location: 13 Miles (21 Km) S of Oak Harbor, *N 48° 09' 26", W 122° 40' 26"*, Near Sea Level

35 Sites – Fort Casey is the second park located on the grounds of one of the former naval batteries set up to protect Puget Sound. Unlike Fort Ebey, the campsites here are set next to the water with great views, the ferry to Port Townsend docks right next to the campground. The sites have no hookups but many are long back-ins. Easiest access is from the outskirts of Coupeville. Head south on South Main Street from SR-20 (near the pedestrian overpass), you'll reach the park entrance in 3.4 miles (5.5 km).

⊞ SOUTH WHIDBEY STATE PARK *(Open All Year)*

Reservations: (888) 226-7688, www.camis.com/wa
Information: (360) 331-4559, (360) 371-2800, www.parks.wa.gov
Location: 23 Miles (37 Km) S of Oak Harbor, *N 48° 03' 36", W 122° 35' 39"*, 200 Ft

56 Sites – Sites in this campground are set in a grove of trees with no views. Most sites are suitable for RVs to 30 feet although a few of the utility sites will take 35 footers. To reach the campground head west from SR-525 on Bush Point Road at about Mile 19, just west of Freeland. The park entrance is on the left after 4 miles (6.4 km).

⊞ ISLAND COUNTY FAIRGROUNDS *(Open May 1 to Sept 30)*

Information: (360) 221-4677
Location: 35 Miles (56 Km) S of Oak Harbor, *N 48° 01' 50", W 122° 24' 11"*, 200 Ft

60 Sites – If they have no major activities scheduled the fairgrounds in Langley offer a good place to spend the night at the south end of the island. You can call ahead to check. Parking here is on grass with utility posts (electricity and water) scattered across the field. There is a self-service payment kiosk, the office here is open irregular hours. Restroom are available near the office, they have showers. There are no sewer drains at the sites and there is no dump station. From SR-525 near Mile 11 drive north on Langley Road, the fairgrounds entrance is on the left in 2.6 miles (4.2 km).

WINTHROP AND THE METHOW VALLEY

Since the opening of the North Cascades Highway the little town of **Winthrop** (population 400) has become a four-season tourist Mecca. The town rebuilt itself as a western town by building false fronts on the buildings and covering the sidewalks with boardwalks. In the winter this is one of the top cross-country skiing areas in the state, and the surrounding hills are filled with summer hiking trails. There are a number of annual events celebrated in Winthrop including **49ers Days** during the second weekend of May, **Winthrop Rodeo Days** on Memorial Day weekend, **Winthrop Rhythm and Blues Festival** in mid-July, the **Labor Day Rodeo** and the **Methow Valley Mountain Bike Festival** in the first part of October.

Two miles (3 km) north of town is **Pearrygin Lake**. In the summer the lake offers a welcome respite from the relatively hot and dry countryside. There is a very popular state campground at the lake.

If you have a smaller vehicle you might want to drive the 19-mile (31 km) road up to **Harts Pass** and Slate Peak which at 7,448 feet is the highest point that can be driven to in Washington State. Consider yourself warned that much of this road is gravel and some sections have steep drop-offs and no guard rails. Trailers are not allowed on the latter portion of the drive beyond Ballard Campground. The road leaves SR-20 at Mazama which is about 14 miles (23 km) west of Winthrop.

Winthrop can get very crowded, particularly on weekends in the summer. The best way to handle it is to play along and enjoy it. There are many restaurants and small shops and the weather is usually great here on the dry side of the Cascades. There are a fine selection of nearby campgrounds to use as a base.

The surrounding countryside is mostly within the **Okanogan National Forest**. There is a ranger station on SR-20 just west of town where you can pick up information about interesting destinations and hikes in the national forest.

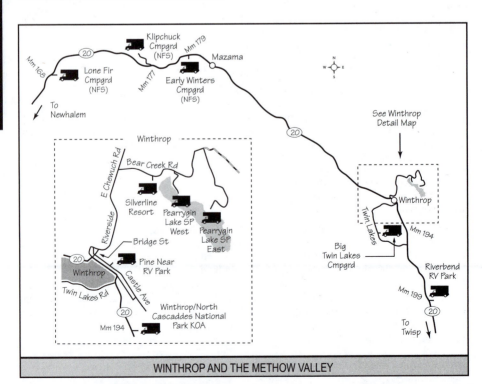

WINTHROP AND THE METHOW VALLEY

🚐 RIVERBEND RV PARK *(Open All Year)*

Reservations: (800) 686-4498, reservations@riverbendrv.com
Information: (509) 997-3500, www.riverbendrv.com
Location: 6 Miles (10 Km) S of Winthrop, *N 48° 23' 28", W 120° 08' 07"*, 1,600 Ft

87 Sites – If you want to put some distance between yourself and the crowds in Winthrop but still want to be able to visit the town this is a good choice. The campground has a variety of site types including pull-thrus to 60 feet. It's located on the bank of the Methow River just north of Twisp, about 6 miles (10 km) down the valley from Winthrop.

🚐 BIG TWIN LAKES CAMPGROUND *(Open April 25 to Oct 31 - Varies)*

Res. and Info.: (509) 996-2650, bigtwinlake@comcast.net
Location: 4 Miles (6 Km) SW of Winthrop, *N 48° 26' 51", W 120° 11' 55"*, 1,800 Ft

79 Sites – This is another campground located away from the madness of Winthrop. It occupies an open valley with a small lake. Parking is on grass with trees providing some shade, very pleasant. Sites are very long allowing rigs of any size to park here. This is a stocked lake so fishing is possible, only electric motors are allowed. There is swimming in the lake and you can rent paddle boats and rowboats. The campground is located off Twin Lakes Road. To reach it from Winthrop drive south 2.5 miles (4.0 km), or 5 miles (8 km) north from Twisp, and turn west on Big Twin Lake Road. In another 2 mile (3.2 km) you'll see the campground entrance on the right.

🚐 WINTHROP/NORTH CASCADES NATIONAL PARK KOA *(Open April 15 to Nov 1)*

Reservations: (800) 562-2158, www.koa.com
Information: (509) 996-2258, campkoa@mymethow.com, www.methownet.com/koa
Location: 1 Mile (1.6 Km) S of Winthrop, *N 48° 27' 45", W 120° 10' 13"*, 1,700 Ft

100 Sites – This is a well-run KOA, without a doubt the most popular commercial campground in the Winthrop area. Sites vary a great deal. Parking is on grass, and some pull-through sites will take 45-footers and larger. The campground has a seasonal swimming pool. Because it is not actually in Winthrop the campground provides a shuttle bus. Watch for the entrance on the east side of the highway 1 mile (1.6 km) south of Winthrop and 7 miles (11.2 km) north of Twisp.

🚐 PINE NEAR RV PARK *(Open All Year)*

Res. and Info.: (509) 996-2391, pinenear@mymethow.com, www.pinenear.com
Location: Winthrop, *N 48° 28' 36", W 120° 10' 47"*, 1,800 Ft

46 Sites – This is the only campground right in Winthrop. It would be much more crowded if more people knew it was here. It's a good campground with room to park large rigs on grass in pull-thru sites with full hookups. It's in a quiet neighborhood back from the main highway and across the street from the Shafer Museum, but you can walk the two blocks to the main drag in as many minutes. One route to the campground is to drive up the hill to the east (Bridge Street) from where SR-20 makes the 90-degree turn in central Winthrop. Take the first right onto Castle Ave., the campground is on the left in another block. The office is somewhat hidden

WASHINGTON

on the back side of the mobile home next to the road.

SILVERLINE RESORT *(Open April 20 to Oct 20 - Varies)*

Res. and Info.:	(509) 996-2448, www.silverlineresort.com
Location:	2 Miles (3 Km) NE of Winthrop, *N 48° 29' 37" W 120° 09' 51"*, 1,900 Ft

70 Sites – This is a very nice lakeside resort. They offer swimming in the lake, boat rentals, and mini golf. A great family vacation destination. Sites vary from full hookup pull-thrus that will take 45-footers to small tent sites with everything in between. From the point where SR-20 makes a 90-degree turn in central Winthrop drive north on Riverside Ave. which curves around and eventually turns into E. Chewuch Road. At 1.6 miles (2.6 km) from the 90-degree turn take the right onto Bear Creek Road. In .5 mile (.8 km) you'll see the entrance road on the right.

PEARRYGIN LAKE STATE PARK *(Open March 31 to Oct 31 - Varies)*

Reservations:	(888) 226-7688, www.camis.com/wa
Information:	(509) 996-1370, (360) 371-2800, www.parks.wa.gov
Location:	2 Miles (3 Km) NE of Winthrop, *N 48° 29' 34", W 120° 09' 31"*, 1,900 Ft

165 Sites – There are now two sections to this very popular state campground. The original state campground (east campground) has 85 sites and the layout is normal for a state campground with mostly back-in sites off paved loops. Many sites are pull-thrus to 60 feet. Everything is set on beautiful lawns. The second section (west campground) is a former commercial campground next door. It is accessed by a separate road, you'll reach it before you reach the original campground entrance. The west campground appears to be in transition. When we visited it had 80 sites including back-in side-by-side hookup sites and no-hookup sites along the lake. Sites here also reach 60 feet. There was even a laundry, it will be interesting to see how long that lasts. From the point where SR-20 makes a 90-degree turn in central Winthrop drive north on Riverside Ave. which curves around and eventually turns into E. Chewuch Road. At 1.6 miles (2.6 km) from the 90-degree turn take the right onto Bear Creek Road. In .9 mile (1.5 km) from the turn you'll reach the entrance to the west campground, at 1.7 miles (2.7 km) the entrance to the east campground.

EARLY WINTERS CAMPGROUND *(Open June 1 to Sept 30 - Varies)*

Information:	(509) 996-4000
Location:	15 Miles (24 Km) W of Winthrop; *N 48° 35' 48", W 120° 26' 46"*, 2,200 Ft

6 Sites – This very small Okanogan National Forest campground is near the highway so it's not really very popular. Actually though, the highway isn't that busy and the nearby stream helps provide white noise so that traffic isn't so noticeable. We like this campground, it's economical and convenient. Sites are small and will take RVs to about 25 feet. Lots of people not staying in the campground stop to use the restrooms since it's so handy. The campground is on the south side of SR-20 some 15 miles (27 km) west of Winthrop.

KLIPCHUCK CAMPGROUND *(Open June 1 to Sept 30 - Varies)*

Information:	(509) 996-4000
Location:	18 Miles (29 Km) W of Winthrop, *N 48° 35' 51", W 120° 30' 51"*, 2,100 Ft

46 Sites – Klipchuck is a larger Okanogan National Forest campground that is away from the highway yet easily accessible on a paved road. Paved loops run through the campground which has some sites that will take carefully driven 40-footers. There's good hiking from this

campground. The entrance road leaves SR-20 some 17 miles (27 km) west of Winthrop, then it's another 1.3 miles (2.1 km) to the campground.

LONE FIR CAMPGROUND *(June 1 to Sept 15 - Varies)*

Information:	(509) 996-4000
Location:	24 Miles (39 Km) W of Winthrop, *N 48° 34' 52", W 120° 37' 26"*, 3,600 Ft

27 Sites – Lone Fir is near the highway and quite a bit higher than the other two Okanogan National Forest campgrounds west of Winthrop. Some sites here will take 35 foot rigs if they are very carefully driven, the access road is paved but narrow with trees that could cause problems for larger RVs. The Lone Fir Loop Trail makes a nice walk. The campground is on the south side of SR-20 some 25 miles (40 km) west of Winthrop and 49 miles (79 km) east of Newhalem.

YAKIMA AND THE YAKIMA VALLEY

You'll probably be amazed by the many things to do and see in the Yakima area. The valley, stretching southeast from Yakima itself, includes the towns of Union Gap, Wapato, Toppenish, Zilah, Granger, Grandview, Sunnyside and Prosser. The Yakima Valley can be hot in the middle of the summer, spring and summer visits are great. Here are just a few of the offerings.

In Yakima (population 72,000) the **Yakima Valley Museum** is excellent, it has displays covering the Oregon Trail, Yakama Indians, Chief Justice William O. Douglas, and horse-drawn vehicles. Another good area museum is in Union Gap, this is the **Central Washington Agricultural Museum**. It does a good job on the agricultural aspect of the area's history. It's big with farm machinery, a tool museum, and 18 display buildings.

The irrigated Yakima Valley has long been an important fruit-growing center and in recent years has also become the wine center of Washington state. There are many **wineries with wine tasting rooms** and gift shops throughout the valley. The best way to visit is in your own vehicle, pick up a wine tour pamphlet and map at any visitor center or commercial campground. An added bonus is that throughout the valley you'll find stands offering fresh fruits and vegetables. Offerings vary, it just depends upon what is in season.

There's a large Latin population in the Yakima valley making this a great place for **Mexican food and specialties**. One favorite seems to be the El Ranchito complex just south of Zilah. They have inexpensive food, a bakery, Mexican groceries and crafts, and even a tortilla factory. There's good parking for big rigs across the street.

The huge 1.4 million-acre **Yakama Nation Reservation** stretches westward from the Yakima Valley all the way to Mt Adams. Near Toppenish you'll find a cluster of Yakima Nation-owned attractions including the **Yakama Nation Cultural Center** and restaurant, the **Yakama Nation Legends Casino**, and the **Yakama Nation Resort RV Park**.

The town of **Toppenish** (population 9,200) is the commercial center for the reservation. It is known for the outdoor murals painted on the buildings around town, some fifty of them in all. There's also the **American Hop Museum** with everything you ever wanted to know about hops.

The most popular annual event in the valley is probably the **Central Washington State Fair** in the latter part of September and first of October, it offers a rodeo and the other things you would expect of a large state fair.

CIRCLE H RV RANCH *(Open All Year)*

Res. and Info.:	(509) 457-3683, Circlehrvranch@msn.com, www.Circlehrvranch.com
Location:	Yakima, *N 46° 35' 25", W 120° 28' 39"*, 1,100 Ft

64 Sites - This older but well-run RV park makes a good place to stay while visiting Ya-

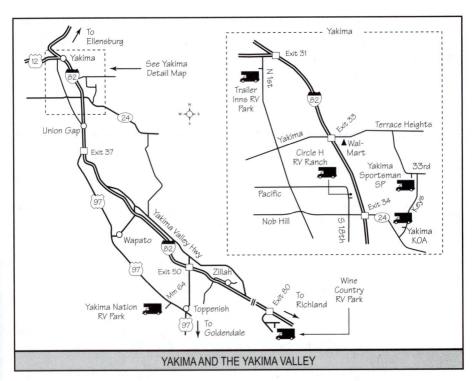

YAKIMA AND THE YAKIMA VALLEY

kima. It has a restaurant, a seasonal pool, mini-golf, and even free Wi-Fi. What more could you want? Back-in and pull-thru sites will take RVs to 45 feet. To reach the campground take Exit 34 from I-82. Drive west on E. Nob Hill Blvd. and take the first right onto S. 18th Street. The campground is on the right in .3 mile (.5 km).

▣ YAKIMA SPORTSMAN STATE PARK *(Open All Year)*

Reservations:	(888) 226-7688, www.parks.wa.gov
Information:	(509) 575-2774, (360) 371-2800, www.parks.wa.gov
Location:	1 Mile (2 Km) E of Yakima, *N 46° 35' 32", W 120° 27' 18"*, 1,000 Ft

64 Sites – This is a heavily used campground due to its location near the city. The park offers the normal excellent state campground amenities in a convenient location. There are long sites to at least 50 feet, both back-ins off circles and pull-through side-by-side sites. From I-84 in Yakima take Exit 33B southbound, Exit 33 northbound. Drive east on Terrace Heights Way for 1.3 miles (2.1 km), passing the Wal-Mart. Then turn right on Keys Road and in 1.2 miles (1.9 km) you'll see the park entrance on the right.

▣ YAKIMA KOA KAMPGROUND *(Open All Year)*

Reservations:	(800) 562-5773, www.koa.com
Information:	(509) 248-5882
Location:	1 Mile (2 Km) E of Yakima, *N 46° 34' 56", W 120° 27' 29"*, 1,000 Ft

174 Sites – Located very near Yakima Sportsman State Park, this campground has a pleasant out of town ambiance yet is near central Yakima. It offers 50-amp power and the normal

KOA amenities. Take Exit 34 from I-84, drive east .7 mile (1.1 km), turn north on Keys Road (also now called Dike Road). You'll see the campground on your left immediately.

YAKIMA TRAILER INNS RV PARK *(Open All Year)*

Reservations:	(800) 659-4784
Information:	(509) 452-9561, www.trailerinnsrv.com
Location:	Yakima, *N 46° 37' 20", W 120° 30' 43"*, 1,000 Ft

154 Sites – This commercial campground has an urban Yakima location with bus service and convenient access to the Yakima green belt bike trail nearby. There's an indoor pool with a spa and sauna room. Sites are back-ins and pull-thrus to 45 feet. Take Exit 31 from I-82 and drive .2 miles (.3 km) south on First Street, the entrance is on the right.

YAKAMA NATION RV PARK *(Open All Year)*

Reservations:	(800) 874-3087 **Information:** (509) 865-2000, www.yakamanation.com
Location:	19 Miles (31 Km) S of Yakima, *N 46° 22' 41", W 120° 20' 41"*, 800 Ft

125 Sites – This large modern big-rig campground is conveniently located for visiting the wine tasting rooms in the Zilah area. A bonus is that both the Yakama Nation Cultural Center and Legends Casino are in the immediate area. The spacious campground has 95 full-hookup RV spaces, tent sites, and even rental teepees. Parking is on long paved back-in and pull-through sites surrounded by well-clipped grass. Facilities include swimming pool and spa, a weight room, basketball and volleyball courts, and a very popular one-mile walking and jogging track around the campground. Just next door is the Yakima Nation Cultural Center. It has a restaurant offering buffets and cultural favorites like salmon, buffalo, and fry bread. There is also a theater, a museum, a library, and a gift shop. The Legends Casino is about a half-mile from the campground. The campground is about 17 miles (27 km) south of Yakima. Driving south on I-82 from Yakima take the US-97 exit (Exit 37) and watch for the cultural center on the right in 14 miles (23 km) just north of Toppenish. It is well signed and located just west of the highway with excellent access.

WINE COUNTRY RV PARK *(Open All Year)*

Res. and Info.:	(509) 786-5192, (800) 726-4969, winecountry@winecountryrvpark.com,
	www.winecountryrvpark.com
Location:	1 Mile (2 Km) N of Prosser, N 46° 13' 11", W 119° 47' 07", 700 Ft

136 Sites – Wine Country is a good big rig park just off I-82 near Prosser. As the name says, this is the heart of Washington's wine country. There's a pool as well as large pull-thru sites to 60 feet, even a few tent sites. From I-82 about 45 miles (73 km) southeast of Yakima take Exit 80. Drive south to the first left, turn and drive eastward past the rest area for .3 mile (.5 km), the campground entrance is on the right.

YAKIMA RIVER CANYON

The **Yakima River Canyon** is extremely scenic between Yakima and Ellensburg. Its worth your time to get off the freeway and take a look. SR-821 leaves the I-82 freeway about four miles

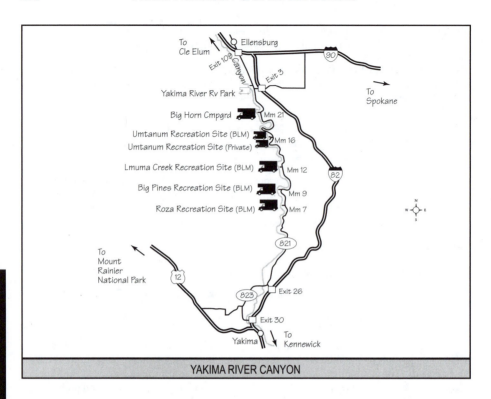

YAKIMA RIVER CANYON

(6 km) north of Yakima and follows the river for 27 miles (44 km) north to Ellensburg. The river is a favorite of fly fishermen and summer river rafters. A note of caution, keep your speed down, the authorities watch this road carefully.

The canyon is managed by the BLM and virtually all camping is at BLM sites. There are no hookups – but it's a beautiful place. The campgrounds below are listed from the Ellensburg end toward Yakima, from north to south, driving downstream. Note that things are in a state of flux here. Facilities are being improved and rates and opening dates are changing

⛟ BIG HORN CAMPGROUND *(Open All Year)*
Location: 32 Miles (52 Km) N of Yakima, *N 46° 53' 39", W 120° 30' 00"*, 1,400 Ft

16 Sites – This is an important launch site for folks floating the Yakima River Canyon. A private company owns the land. Camping is allowed, there are many spots to set up camp upstream from the launch site in the trees. Port-a-potties are on-site in summer but not winter although camping is allowed all year. Some sites are suitable for RVs to about 30 feet, access roads are poor. The BLM, which manages this area, may acquire this site in the near future along with a similar piece described below under Umtanum Recreation Site. The campground is located near Mile 21.5, about 6 miles (9.7 km) south of Ellensburg.

⛟ UMTANUM RECREATION SITE *(Open All Year)*
Location: 21 Miles (34 Km) N of Yakima, *N 46° 51' 16", W 120° 28' 46"*, 1,400 Ft

7 Sites – There are actually two campground at this location. One is the BLM site which has a large gravel parking lot as well as seven back-in sites suitable for RVs to 35 feet. They have

picnic tables and fire pits and handicapped-accessible vault toilets. There's also a footbridge across the river. The use (camping) fee is $2. The other campground is a privately-owned camping area next to the river (to the left as you enter). The fee here is $10 per night like at Big Horn (described above) and the facilities are similar including port-a-potties in summer. It is possible that the BLM will acquire the private area in the near future. The campground is located near Mile 16.

LMUMA CREEK BLM RECREATION SITE *(Closed In Winter)*

Location: 17 Miles (27 Km) N of Yakima, *N 46° 48' 50", W 120° 27' 01"*, 1,300 Ft

7 Sites – This recreation site next to the river has a launch ramp and seven campsites. It's a large gravel parking lot with the sites arranged around the perimeter, some right next to the river. Picnic tables and fire pits are provided and there are modern vault toilets. The two dollar use fee here only applies from May 15 to Sept. 15, the camping is free the rest of the year if the campground is open. The campground is near Mile 12.

BIG PINES BLM RECREATION SITE *(Open All Year)*

Location: 14 Miles (23 Km) N of Yakima, *N 46° 47' 36", W 120° 27' 21"*, 1,300 Ft

10 Sites – This site has not been improved like Lmuma Creek, Roza, and Umtanum but tables, fire pits, and port-a-potties are provided. There is also a launch site. It will probably be improved to the standard of the other sites in the near future. Until then it's a good place for larger rigs because parking slots are big and not clearly defined. This site is near Mile 9.

ROZA RECREATION SITE *(Closed In Winter)*

Location: 12 Miles (19 Km) N of Yakima, *N 46° 45' 50", W 120° 27' 18"*, 1,200 Ft

5 Sites – This site is a large paved lot with a paved boat ramp and restrooms (vault toilets). It has the highest level of improvements of the BLM sites along the river but not necessarily the best campsites. The emphasis here is on the boat ramp. Camping is allowed in five sites arranged around the perimeter of the lot, sites have picnic tables and vault toilets. This site is near Mile 7.

Information Resources

See our internet site at www.rollinghomes.com for internet information links.

Bellingham

Bellingham Visitor Information Center, 904 Potter St, Bellingham, WA 98229; (360) 671-3990

Chelan

Lady of the Lake, 1418 W Woodin Ave, Chelan, WA 98816; (509) 682-4584

Lake Chelan Chamber of Commerce and Visitor Information Center, 102 East Johnson Ave., Chelan, WA 98816; (509) 682-3503 or (800) 424-3526; info@lakechelan.com

Mill Bay Casino, Mill Bay, WA; (509) 687-2102

Wenatchee National Forest, Chelan Ranger District, 428 W Woodin Ave, Chelan, WA 98816; (509) 682-2576

Cle Elum and Roslyn

Cle Elum Chamber of Commerce, 401 W 1st St, Ele Elum, WA 98922; (509) 674-5958

Coeur d'Alene, Idaho

Coeur D'Alene Post Falls Convention and Visitor Bureau, 1621 N 3rd St, Suite 100 (PO Box 850) Coeur D'Alene, ID 83816-0850; (208) 665-2350

Ellensburg

Ellensburg Chamber of Commerce and Visitor Information, 436 N Sprague St, Ellensburg, WA 98926; (509) 925-3137

Forks and Western Sections of Olympic National Park

Forks Chamber of Commerce, Visitor's Center, 1411 S Forks Ave, Forks, WA 98331; (360) 374-2531 and (800) 443-6757

Olympic National Forest Information Center, 551 S Forks Ave, Forks, WA 98331; (360) 374-7566

Grand Coulee

Coulee City Chamber of Commerce, 220 E Chelan St, Coulee City, WA 99115; (509) 632-5043

Grand Coulee Dam Area Chamber of Commerce, 306 Midway St, Grand Coulee, WA 99133; (509) 633-3074

Grand Coulee Dam, Visitor Arrival Center, Grand Coulee Power Office, PO Box 620, Grand Coulee, WA 99133; (509) 633-9265

Soap Lake Chamber of Commerce, 515 Main Ave E, Soap Lake, WA 98851; (509) 246-1821

Hood Canal

North Mason Visitors Info Center, 22871 NE State Route 3, Belfair, WA 98528; (360) 275-5548

Ilwaco and Long Beach

Lewis and Clark Interpretive Center, Ilwaco, WA ; (360) 642-3029

Long Beach Peninsula Visitor Information, 3914 Pacific Hwy, Seaview, WA 98644; (360) 642-2400

Willapa National Wildlife Refuge, 3888 State Route 101, Ilwaco, WA 98624; (360) 484-3482

Kitsap Peninsula and Bainbridge Island

Bainbridge Isle Chamber of Commerce, 590 Winslow Way E, Bainbridge Isle, Wa 98110; (206) 842-3700

Kitsap Peninsula Visitor and Convention Bureau (North Visitor Center), 32220 Rainier Ave NE (PO Box 270), Port Gamble, WA 98364; (360) 297-8200

Kitsap Peninsula Visitor and Convention Bureau (South Visitor Center), Day's Inn Parking Lot, Hwy 16, Sedgwick Exit, Port Orchard, WA; (360) 297-8200

Lake Easton and Lake Kachess

US Forest Service Visitor Information Center, 69805 State Route 906, Snoqualmie Pass, WA 98068; (425) 434- 6111

Lake Pateros Region

Brewster Chamber of Commerce, 109 S Bridge St, Brewster, WA 98812; (509) 689-0189

Leavenworth

Leavenworth Chamber of Commerce, 940 Hwy 2 (PO Box 327), Leavenworth, WA 98826; (509) 548-5807; info@leavenworth.org

Wenatchee National Forest, Leavenworth Ranger District, 600 Sherbourne, Leavenworth, WA 98826; (509) 548-6977

Moscow, Idaho and Pullman, WA and the Palouse

Life on Wheels; (866) 569-4646; www.lifeonwheels.com

Moscow Chamber of Commerce, 411 South Main Street, Moscow, ID 83843; (208) 882-1800 (800) 380-1801; staff@moscowchamber.com

Pullman Chamber of Commerce, 415 North Grand Ave, Pullman, WA 99163; (509) 334-3565 or (800) 365-6948

Moses Lake and the Potholes

Moses Lake Chamber of Commerce, 324 S Pioneer Way, Moses Lake, WA 98837; (509) 765-7888

Mt Rainier National Park

Gifford Pinchot National Forest, Packwood Information Center, 13068 US 12, Packwood, WA 98361; (360) 494-00600

Mt Rainier National Park, Star Route, Tahoma Woods, Ashford, WA 98304; (360) 569-2177

Mt St Helens National Volcanic Monument

Castle Rock Visitor Information Center, 147 Front Ave NW, Castle Rock, WA 98611; (360) 274-6603

Mt St Helens Cinedome Theater, 1239 Mt St Helens Way NE, Castle Rock, WA 98611; (360) 274-8000

Mt St Helens National Monument Visitor Center, 3029 Spirit Lake Hwy, Castle Rock, WA 98611; (360) 274-2100

North Cascades National Park

North Cascade Chamber of Commerce, 59831 State Route 20, Marblemount, WA 98267; (360) 873-2106

North Cascades NPS Complex, 810 State Route 20, Sedro Woolley, WA 98284; (360) 856-5700

North Cascades Visitor Center, State Route 20, Mile 120, Newhalem, WA; (206) 386-4495

North Cascades Wilderness Information Center, 7280 Ranger Station Rd, Marblemount, WA 98267; (360) 873-4500

Ocean Shores and the North Beaches Area

Ocean Shores Visitor Information Center, 120 W Chance a La Mer NW, Ocean Shores, WA 98569; (360) 289-9586

Washington Coast Chamber of Commerce, 2616 A State Route 109, Ocean City, WA 98569; (360) 289-4552

Olympia

Olympia and Thurston County Convention Bureau, 1600 4th Ave E, Olympia, WA 98506; (360) 704-7544 or (877) 704-7500

Washington State Capitol Campus Visitor Information; (360) 586-3460

Victoria Express, 115 E Railroad Ave #108, Port Angeles, WA 98362; (360) 452-8088

Port Angeles and the Northern Olympic National Park

North Olympic Peninsula Visitor and Convention Bureau, 338 W 1st St, #104, Port Angeles, WA 98362; (360) 452-8552

Olympic National Park, 600 East Park Ave, Port Angeles, WA 98362-6798; (360) 565-3130

Port Angeles Chamber of Commerce, 121 E Railroad Ave, Port Angeles, WA 98362; (360) 452-2363

US Government Information Center, Port Angeles, WA 98362; (360) 565-3130

WASHINGTON

Port Townsend

Port Townsend Chamber of Commerce Visitor Center, 2437 E Sims Way, Port Townsend, WA; (360) 385-2722

Seattle

Argosy Cruises, Pier 55, Seattle, WA 98101; (206) 623-1445

Boeing Everett Tours; (206) 544-1264

King County Transit, (206) 553-3000

Museum of Flight, 9404 E Marginal Way S, Tukwila, WA 98108; (206) 764-5720

Seattle Aquarium, 1483 Alaskan Way #59, Seattle, WA 98101, (206) 386-4320

Seattle Art Museum, 100 University Street, Seattle, WA 89101-2902; (206) 654-3100

Seattle Chamber of Commerce, 1301 5th Ave #2500, Seattle, WA 98101; (206) 389-7200

Seattle's Convention and Visitor Bureau, Visitors Information at Washington State Convention and Trade Center, 8th and Pike St, Seattle, WA 98101; (206) 461-5840

Simply Seattle Visitor Info, 201 Pine St, Seattle, WA 98101; (206) 223-0480

Underground Tours, 608 1st Ave, Seattle, WA 98104, (206) 682-4646

Sequim

Dungeness National Wildlife Refuge, 33 S Barr Rd, Port Angeles, WA 98362; (360) 457-8451

Olympic Game Farm, 1423 Ward Rd, Sequim, WA 98382; (360) 683-4295

Seven Cedars Casino, 270756 Hwy 101, Sequim, WA 98382; (360) 683-7777

Sequim Chamber of Commerce, 1192 E Washington St, Sequim, WA 98382; (360) 683-6197

Skagit Valley

Anacortes Chamber of Commerce, 819 Commercial Ave #F, Anacortes, WA 98221; (360) 293-3832

La Conner Chamber of Commerce, 606 Morris St, La Conner, WA 98257; (360) 466-4778

Mt Vernon Chamber of Commerce, 105 E Kincaid St #101, Mt Vernon, WA 98273; (360) 428-8547

Spokane

Spokane Visitor Information, 201 W Main Ave, Spokane, WA 99201; (509) 747-3230

Tacoma

Point Defiance Zoo and Aquarium, 5400 Pearl St, Ruston, WA 98407; (253) 591-5337

Tacoma Art Museum, 1701 Pacific Ave, Tacoma, WA 98402; (253) 272-4258

Tacoma Regional Convention & Visitor Bureau, 1119 Pacific Ave #5, Tacoma, WA 98402; (253) 627-2836

Wenatchee

Ohme Gardens County Park, 3327 Ohme Rd, Wenatchee, WA 98801; (509) 662-5785

Wenatchee Valley Convention & Visitors Bureau, 25 N Wenatchee Ave #C111, Wenatchee, WA 98801; (509) 663-3723

Westport

Grayland Beach Visitor Information, 2071 Cranberry Rd, Grayland, WA 98547; (360) 267-2003

Westport/Grayland Chamber of Commerce, 2985 S Montesano St, Westport, WA 98595; (360) 268-9422

Westport Aquarium, 321 E Harbor St, Westport, WA 98595; (360) 268-0471

Westport Maritime Museum, 2201 Westhaven Dr, Westport, WA 98595; (360) 268-0078

Whidbey Island

Central Whidbey Chamber of Commerce, 107 S Main St, Coupeville, WA 98239; (360) 678-5434

Deception Pass Visitors Center, 40751 State Route 20, Oak Harbor, WA 98277; (360) 675-9438

Oak Harbor Chamber of Commerce, 32630 State Route 20, Oak Harbor, WA 98277; (360) 675-3755

WASHINGTON

Winthrop and the Methow Valley

Winthrop Chamber of Commerce and Methow Valley Information Center, 202 Hwy 20, Winthrop, WA 98862; (509) 996-2125

Wenatchee National Forest Winthrop Visitor Information Center, 49 Highway 20, Winthrop, WA 98862; (509) 996-4000

Yakima and the Yakima Valley

American Hop Museum, 22 S B Street, Toppenish, WA 98948; (509) 865-4677

Central Washington Agricultural Museum, 4508 Main Street, Union Gap, WA 98903; (509) 457-8735

Cultural Heritage Center, Hwy 97, Toppenish, WA 98948; (509) 865-2800

Prosser Chamber of Commerce, 1230 Bennett Ave, Prosser, WA 99350; (509) 786-3177

Yakima Valley Museum, 2105 Tieton Dr, Yakima, WA 98902; (509) 248-0747

Yakima Valley Visitors Bureau, 110 N 9th St, Yakima, WA 98901; (509) 248-2021

Yakima Valley Visitors and Convention Bureau, 10 N 8th St, Yakima, WA 98901; (509) 575-3010

Yakima River Canyon

BLM Wenatchee Field Office, 915 Walla Walla, Wenatchee, WA 98801; (509) 665-2100

WASHINGTON

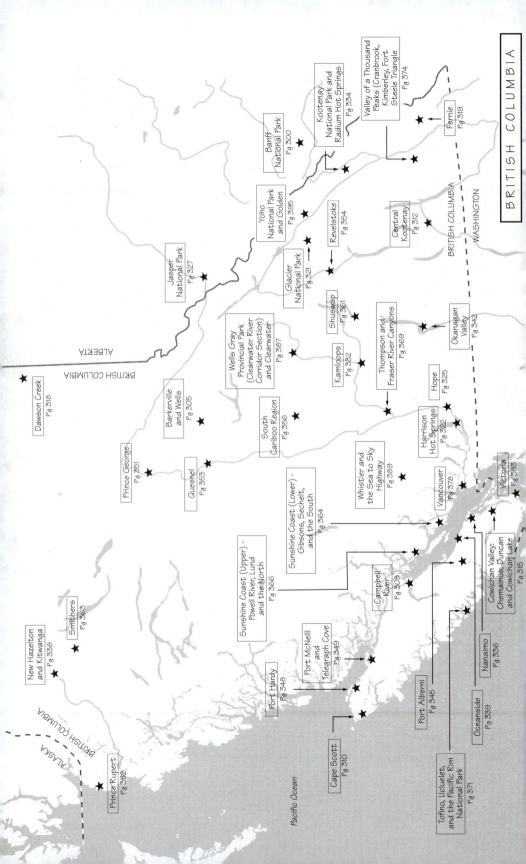

ALBERTA

BRITISH COLUMBIA

ALASKA

BRITISH COLUMBIA

BRITISH COLUMBIA

WASHINGTON

Pacific Ocean

Chapter 6 - British Columbia

It's easy to make the argument that British Columbia is the ultimate camping destination. The province offers both rugged and civilized seacoasts, islands, sophisticated cities, wilderness, and some of the most varied mountain terrain in the world.

Of course, unlike Washington and Oregon, British Columbia is in Canada, not the U.S. Fortunately, crossing the border is not very difficult. We've included a section about crossing the border, going both north and south, in the *Introduction* chapter of the book.

For most of us British Columbia is a spring, summer and fall destination. Vancouver Island, the Sunshine Coast, and Vancouver and the lower Fraser Valley have a marine climate. That means winter temperatures are generally above freezing but wet. The remainder of the province is much less temperate with higher elevations that mean cool winter temperatures and snow.

Although we have titled this chapter British Columbia it actually covers part of Alberta too. Some of the Rocky Mountain National Parks covered here; Jasper and Banff; are in that Province.

REGIONS AND THEIR CAMPGROUND RESOURCES

Vancouver Island

This large 250 kilometer (275 mile) long island offers Victoria, the sophisticated capital of the province, as well as remote beaches, northwest Indian culture (called First Nations in Canada), some of the best salmon fishing in the world, and pristine evergreen forests. Victoria is in the far south with a chain of mountains occupying the center ridge of the island. The east coast is relatively accessible with a good highway running all the way from Victoria up to Port Hardy in the far north. The rugged west coast of the island can only be reached in a few places using roads running east across the mountain spine.

Vancouver Island is easily accessible using frequent ferries from near Vancouver on the mainland. There are also ferry connections from Port Angeles and Anacortes in Washington and from Powell River at the upper end of the Sunshine Coast. There's even ferry service from Prince Rupert south to Port Hardy. All of these runs are described in our *Introduction* chapter.

From south to north the destinations covered in this chapter are: • *Victoria,* • *the Cowichan Valley,* • *Nanaimo,* • *Oceanside,* • *Port Alberni,* • *Tofino, Ucluelet and the Pacific Rim National Park,* • *Campbell River,* • *Port McNeil and Telegraph Cove,* • *Port Hardy,* • *Cape Scott.*

Sunshine Coast

Stretching 100 kilometers (62 miles) north from the city of Vancouver along the mainland this region offers surprisingly good weather and warm water because it is in the rain shadow of Vancouver Island's mountains. The weather is very similar to that just to the west on the eastern side of Vancouver Island.

The Sunshine Coast is isolated. In the south a long inlet separates the region from Vancouver. It is necessary to use a ferry from Horseshoe Bay just north of Vancouver to Langdale. Then, after 81 km (50 miles) of two-lane paved road, you must take another ferry ride between Earl's Cove and Saltery Bay to reach the upper Sunshine Coast. From there you can backtrack or continue on by ferry from Powell River to Vancouver Island. There's no problem taking RVs on any of these ferries, see our *Introduction* chapter for more information.

Two sections of this chapter cover the Sunshine coast: • *Sunshine Coast – Lower* and • *Sunshine Coast – Upper.*

Vancouver and the Lower Fraser Valley

British Columbia's largest city is cosmopolitan and fun. Lots of people live downtown so there's always a lot going on. It's a pretty good-sized city with heavy traffic. Fortunately there are a good selection of campgrounds spaced around the perimeter, some with decent public transportation options.

The lower Fraser Valley is a fairly flat plain extending to the east from Vancouver. There are two destinations in this region described in this book: • *Harrison Hot Springs* and • *Hope.*

Interior

Much of the interior of British Columbia is mountainous. In the south the mountains run north and south and there are temperate valleys, often filled with lakes, between them. In the north there are mountainous areas as well as wide fairly flat plateaus. From north to south the interior destinations in this book are: • *Dawson Creek,* • *Prince Rupert,* • *New Hazelton and Kitwanga,* • *Smithers,* • *Prince George,* • *Barkerville and Wells,* • *Quesnel,* • *South Cariboo Region,* • *Wells Gray Provincial Park and Clearwater,* • *Kamloops,* • *Shuswap,* • *Revelstoke,* • *Glacier National Park,* • *Whistler and the Sea to Sky Highway,* • *Thompson and Fraser Canyons,* • *Okanagan Valley,* • *Central Kootenay,* • *Valley of a Thousand Peaks,* • *Fernie.*

Canadian Rockies

Along the border between British Columbia and Alberta the Rocky Mountains have peaks to 12,000 feet. While not perhaps as high as some Rocky Mountain peaks in Colorado these are some of the most rugged and impressive peaks in the entire chain. A large part of the border area is set aside as national parks. Destinations in this area in this book are: • *Jasper National Park,* • *Banff National Park,* • *Yoho National Park and Golden,* • *Kootenay National Park.*

GOVERNMENT LANDS AND THEIR CAMPGROUNDS

Provincial Park Campgrounds

British Columbia has an excellent system of provincial campgrounds. Prices are generally lower than commercial campgrounds in the areas where they are found. These provincial campgrounds do not have hookups.

There is a reservation system that includes most campgrounds. Our campground descriptions tell whether the individual campground being described takes reservations. Generally, some

THE BEACH AT MIRACLE BEACH PROVINCIAL PARK NEAR CAMPBELL RIVER

sites in a campground are reserveable and some are not. Also, most campgrounds have a period at the beginning and end of the season when they are not busy and reservations are not available or required. Reservations are made through Discover Camping, you can use the internet (www.discovercamping.ca) or call (800) 689-9025, in the Vancouver area only call (604) 689-9025. The reservation service is in effect from April 1 to September 15, telephone operators are only available from 7 am to 7 pm weekdays, 9 am to 5 pm on weekends and holidays. Reservations can be made up to three weeks in advance and must be made at least two days prior to your arrival. There is a reservation fee of $6.42 Canadian per site per night for the first three nights at a site, reservations exceeding three days pay a reservation fee for only the first three days as long as you do not change sites. There is a 14 day stay limit at most parks. Discounts of ½ off are available for B.C. residents over 65 years old before June 15 and after Labour Day.

There is often a host at the larger provincial campgrounds. Provincial campgrounds no longer provide firewood for free although it is almost always available for purchase unless a fire ban is in effect. Sites in provincial campgrounds usually are separated by areas of undeveloped forest, sites vary in length, often with each one being different. Many provincial campgrounds will take larger rigs. See the individual campground write-ups for information about this.

You can always use a credit card to pay for sites that you reserve by phone or on the internet. Some campgrounds will accept credit cards at the campground for payment, many will not. If we indicate that a provincial campground accepts credit cards that means that they are accepted at the campground itself, but usually only if the campground entrance station is in use when you enter.

National Park Campgrounds

The national park campgrounds vary a great deal. Some have full hookups, some have none. Almost all are great for tent campers and a few have been optimized for large RVs. See the individual campground write-ups for more information.

Beginning in 2006 all of the National Park campgrounds in this chapter except Kootenay have been incorporated into a new reservation system. Not all campgrounds in the parks accept

BRITISH COLUMBIA

reservations, see the individual campground write-ups for more information. To make a reservation call (866) 787-6221 in Canada or (905) 426-4648 from outside the country. You can also make reservations on the Internet at www.pccamping.ca. Reservations can be made up to midnight of the day before you will arrive. There is an $11 Canadian fee per reservation.

Many larger national park campgrounds have entrance kiosks, but not all. If they do they will usually accept credit cards (Visa and Master Card).

One downside of the national parks is that there can be a number of fees. There is almost always an entrance fee to the national park. Of course there is also a camping fee. There's a fee for campfires and also a fee to use the sani-station. If you make a reservation there is a fee for that too.

Forest Service Recreation Sites

The BC Ministry of Forests has developed hundreds of small campgrounds throughout the province. For the most part these are sites with minimal facilities, usually just picnic tables and outhouses. These sites fall into three categories: Managed With Fees, Managed Without Fees, and User Maintained. There are no reservations for these sites and there is a 14-day stay limit. All of the Forest Service sites listed in this book are the User Maintained type. That means that it is important that you carry out your trash and leave the sites in at least as good condition as you found them. This type site is free. You'll find Forest Service Recreation Sites listed in the *Cape Scott* and *Sea To Sky Highway* sections of this Chapter.

DESTINATIONS AND THEIR CAMPGROUNDS

BANFF NATIONAL PARK

Banff was Canada's first National Park. The section of the park in the Bow Valley, roughly from Lake Louise to the townsite of Banff, is the most frequented part of the park and offers plenty to keep a visitor busy for a long time. It is also truly beautiful because it is ringed by some of the highest and most spectacularly rugged peaks in the world. A second and much smaller road, the **Bow Parkway**, offers a scenic and quiet alternative to the four-lane highway, and follows pretty much the same route except that it is on the east side of the Bow River instead of the west. You'll want to traverse the Bow Parkway at least once so you can stop occasionally and enjoy the valley. The distance between Banff and Lake Louise along the Bow Parkway and a short section of Hwy 1 near Banff is 56.6 kilometers (35.1 miles).

If you arrive on the Trans-Canada (Hwy 1) from the west you'll almost immediately see the exit for **Lake Louise**. This is the smaller of the two population centers of the park. Just off the highway to the west is what is known as the village of Lake Louise, it is really little more than a shopping center offering a tourist info centre, small stores, tourist services, and gasoline. Just past the village is a turn to the left for the giant Lake Louise Campground. If you go straight instead you will wind up the hillside for about 4 kilometers (2.5 miles) to beautiful Lake Louise. There are big parking lots here but it is best not to try to take a very large rig or a trailer, the lots are big but still crowded. At the foot of the lake you'll see a huge hotel, the **Chateau Lake Louise**, it has been there in one form or another since 1890. You'll no doubt be part of a throng of visitors. You can walk through the hotel lobby and take some pictures from the lawn of the spectacular view featuring the emerald-colored lake and the glacier at the far end. Then you can explore part of the trail network along and above the lake, there are even a couple of teahouses where you can stop for refreshments.

At the lower end of the valley is the town of **Banff** with a population of about 7,500. We'll call it the Banff townsite to distinguish it from the park in general. This is the major population, business, and tourist center of the park. In addition to many park-type wonders in the area you'll find a wealth of shops and restaurants that rival any resort town. You'll also find a supermarket and other services required by RVers including some very big government-owned campgrounds. Banff is the largest town to be found inside any national park in either Canada or the U.S.

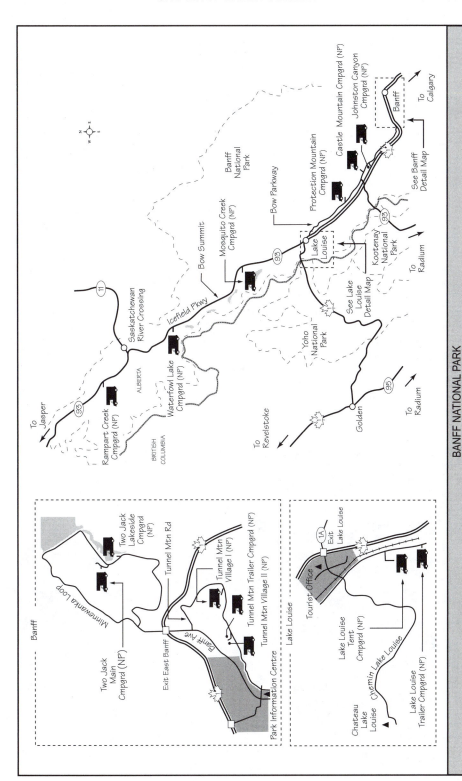

BANFF NATIONAL PARK

BRITISH COLUMBIA

There are several interesting sights in the townsite area. It would be a good idea to make your first stop at the downtown **Park Information Centre** for local maps and information. The **Banff Springs Hotel** is one of the early Canadian Pacific Railways resort hotels and remains a fascinating place to visit. Just off the entrance road to the hotel is the road to the golf course, it leads past **Bow Falls** to a loop route through the golf course and can be a good place to see **elk**, they favor the course as a place to graze and relax. The original reason Banff was established was hot springs, you can visit the **Cave and Basin Centennial Center** built at the site of the original hot springs. You can't swim there any more but you will find lots to see. The Sundance **Canyon Trail** starts at the center and takes you along the Bow River to Sundance Canyon, about 7 kilometers (4.4 miles) round trip. If you do want to swim you can do so at **Upper Hot Springs**. Near Upper Hot Springs is the **Sulphur Mountain Gondola Lift** which takes you up to an observatory and restaurant high on Sulphur Mountain. There are two worthwhile museums in Banff townsite, the **Whyte Museum of the Canadian Rockies** and the **Park Museum**.

There are several good drives in the Banff townsite area in addition to the one up to the Sulphur Mountain Gondola Lift. You can drive to an excellent viewpoint overlooking the townsite by following **Mt. Norquay Drive**. It is on the far side of Highway 1 at the West Banff Exit and climbs about 300 meters in 5.8 kilometers (3.6 miles). From the East Banff Exit you can follow **Lake Minnewanka Road** to visit the ghost town of **Bankhead,** view **Lake Minnewanka** or take a commercial boat tour, then return on a loop drive past **Two Jack Lake** and **Johnson Lake.**

The **Icefields Parkway** enters Banff National Park from Jasper National Park to the north. See the *Jasper National Park* section of this chapter for information about the parkway north of the border between the two parks. The information below continues the description in that section and progresses from north to south.

The two parks meet at **Sunwapta Pass**. Thirty-two kilometers (29 miles) south of the pass the road crosses the North Saskatchewan River. To the west is the Howse Valley. The North Saskatchewan River and the Howse Valley were one of the early passes used by explorers and fur traders to cross the Rocky Mountains. Highway 11 heads east from here to Rocky Mountain House and Red Deer.

BEAUTIFUL LAKE LOUISE

Thirty-five kilometers (22 miles) from the crossing the road crosses another pass. This is the Bow Summit and is even higher than Sunwapta Pass. At 2,067 meters (6,787 feet) this is the highest point on the parkway.

Bow Lake is one of the scenic highlights of the highway, you'll reach it in another 6 km (4 miles). Viewpoints along the highway let you look across the bright blue lake at the peaks beyond, don't forget to take some pictures.

The southern end of the parkway meets Hwy 1 some 35 kilometers (21 miles) south of Bow Lake.

The campground descriptions below are arranged from the north end of the park to the south near Banff townsite. Every one of these campgrounds is a national park campsite.

RAMPART CREEK CAMPGROUND – BANFF NATIONAL PARK *(Open June 23 to Sept 5 - Varies)*
Information: (403) 762-1550
Location: 92 Km (57 Miles) N of Lake Louise, *N 52° 02' 31", W 116° 52' 03"*, 4,700 Ft

50 Sites – This is an older campground with rough and narrow interior roads. Some sites will take RVs to 35 feet, the others are smaller. This is the farthest-north Banff campground. It is 92 km (57 miles) north of Lake Louise and 37 km (23 miles) south of the Icefield Centre in Jasper National Park.

WATERFOWL LAKE CAMPGROUND – BANFF NATIONAL PARK *(Open June 23 to Sept 11 - Varies)*
Information: (403) 762-1550
Location: 60 Km (37 Miles) N of Lake Louise, *N 51° 50' 33", W 116° 37' 15"*, 5,500 Ft

114 Sites – The campground is located on the south shore of Waterfowl Lake where the Mistaya River flows into the lake. Trails lead to Cirque and Chephren Lakes. This is another older campground with narrow access roads, some sites will take carefully-driven 35-foot RVs. The campground is 60 km (37 miles) north of Lake Louise and 69 km (43 miles) south of Icefield Centre.

MOSQUITO CREEK CAMPGROUND – BANFF NATIONAL PARK *(Open All Year)*
Information: (403) 762-1550
Location: 27 Km (17 Miles) N of Lake Louise, *N 51° 37' 49", W 116° 19' 49"*, 6,000 Ft

32 Sites – Sites here are in trees on either side of a large open lot, and also in the lot. This open area can be cleared of snow, that's why this campground can stay open all year long. The sites themselves will take RVs to 30 feet while the open area will take any size. The campground is 27 Km (17 miles) north of Lake Louise and 102 km (63 miles) south of Icefield Centre.

LAKE LOUISE CAMPGROUNDS – BANFF NATIONAL PARK *(Open All Year)*
Reservations: (877) 737-3783, www.pccamping.ca
Information: (403) 762-1550
Location: Lake Louise, *N 51° 25' 06", W 116° 10' 25"*, 5,000 Ft

399 Sites – The Lake Louise Campground is really two campgrounds sharing a common entrance station. One is an RV campground (called the trailer campground) with long pull-thru sites with electric and water hookups as well as a dump station. The other is for tenters (called the tent campground) and those in soft-sided RVs, the sites have vehicle parking at the site, not remote parking. The tent campground is completely surrounded by an electric fence to keep

out bears, soft sided rigs (like tent trailers) are not allowed in the RV campground because it has no such fence. There is also a nearby overflow campground with no hookups. Campfires are only permitted in the tent campground. The trailer campground is open all year long, the tent campground only from May 8 to September 2 (Varies). Trails lead from the camping areas to the Lake Louise business area and to the lake. It's about .9 km (.5 mile) to the business area, 5 km (3 miles) to the lake.

PROTECTION MOUNTAIN CAMPGROUND – BANFF NATIONAL PARK *(Open June 23 to Sept 5 - Varies)*

Information: (403) 762-1550
Location: 16 Km (10 Miles) S of Lake Louise, *N 51° 19' 38", W 116° 02' 15"*, 4,900 Ft

89 Sites – Protection Mountain Campground has two camping areas, one marked for RVs and one for tents. The RV area has some large sites suitable for RVs to 40 feet but caution is necessary since access roads are narrow and rough. Parking sites in the tent campground are very small. The campground is located off the Bow Parkway 16 km (10 miles) south of Lake Louise and 40 km (25 miles) north off Banff.

CASTLE MOUNTAIN CAMPGROUND – BANFF NATIONAL PARK *(Open May 19 to Sept 4 - Varies)*

Information: (403) 762-1550
Location: 27 Km (17 Miles) S of Lake Louise, *N 51° 16' 06", W 115° 54' 43"*, 4,700 Ft

43 Sites – This is a more commodious campground than Protection Mountain with wider driveways. Still it's most suitable for RVs only up to 35 feet, just a site or two will take a 40-footer. A restaurant and small store are nearby. The campground is located off the Bow Parkway 27 km (17 miles) south of Lake Louise and 37 km (23 miles) north of Banff.

JOHNSTON CANYON CAMPGROUND – BANFF NATIONAL PARK *(Open June 2 to Sept 18 - Varies)*

Information: (403) 762-1550
Location: 23 Km (14 Miles) N of Banff, *N 51° 14' 32", W 115° 50' 15"*, 4,700 Ft

132 Sites – This campground is large enough to warrant a manned entrance station. Sites here are off three loops, a limited number of sites large enough for 40-foot RVs are available. You can walk up Johnston Canyon to take a look at two waterfalls. The campground is located off the Bow Parkway 34 km (21 miles) south of Lake Louise and 23 km (14 miles) north of Banff.

TUNNEL MOUNTAIN VILLAGE I – BANFF NATIONAL PARK *(Open May 5 to Oct 2 - Varies)*

Reservations: (877) 737-3783, www.pccamping.ca
Information: (403) 762-1550
Location: 3 Km (2 Miles) E of Banff, *N 51° 11' 28", W 115° 31' 12"*, 4,700 Ft

618 Sites – Tunnel Mountain Village I is a huge place, sites here have no hookups. It's the main Banff-area no-hookup park and has good facilities. If you don't need hookups this is the place to stay, some sites will take RVs to 40 feet. The campground is located on the Tunnel Mountain Loop slightly farther from town than the Tunnel Mountain II and Tunnel Mountain Trailer campgrounds. Easiest access is from the eastern-most Banff offramp of Hwy 1. From the exit drive south on Banff Avenue for .8 km (.5 mile) and turn left on Tunnel Mountain Road. Follow the road as it winds up the hill, you'll see the campground entrance on your right in 3 km (2 miles). This access route lets you avoid downtown Banff which is congested. There is bus service into town from the campground. The distance to town is about 3 km (2 miles).

TUNNEL MOUNTAIN VILLAGE II AND TUNNEL MOUNTAIN TRAILER CAMPGROUND – BANFF NATIONAL PARK *(Open All Year)*

Reservations: (877) 737-3783, www.pccamping.ca   **Information:** (403) 762-1550
Location: 2 Km (1 Mile) E of Banff, *N 51° 11' 18", W 115° 32' 24"*, 4,800 Ft

509 Sites – These two campgrounds share a common entrance with a manned entrance booth. After passing the booth you turn left for Tunnel Village II and right for Tunnel Mountain Trailer Campground. Both of these campgrounds are hookup campgrounds that have sites exceeding 60 feet but they are different. Tunnel Mountain II is the all-year campground here. There are wide paved access roads with sites set along the side, rigs parallel park. The campground is arranged this way to facilitate removal of snow in the winter. Sites have electrical hookups but no water or sewer, instead there is a sani-dump. The Tunnel Mountain Trailer Campground, on the other hand, has full hookups. The 321 sites here are long pull-thrus arranged off gravel drives. This campground is only open from about May 6 - September 19 (Varies). Easiest access to these campgrounds is from the eastern-most Banff offramp of Hwy 1. From the exit drive south on Banff Avenue for .8 km (.5 mile) and turn left on Tunnel Mountain Road. Follow the road as it winds up the hill, you'll see the campground entrance on your right in 5 km (3 miles). This access route lets you avoid downtown Banff which is congested. There is bus service into town from the campground. The distance to town is about 2 km (1 mile). Note that the Banff area also has an overflow area (in addition to the Two Jack campgrounds) with no hookups that is available when the other campgrounds are full.

TWO JACK MAIN CAMPGROUND – BANFF NATIONAL PARK *(Open May 19 to Sept 4 - Varies)*

Information: (403) 762-1550
Location: 10 Km (6 Miles) N of Banff, *N 51° 13' 40", W 115° 30' 20"*, 4,800 Ft

380 Sites – This is a much less convenient place to stay than Tunnel Mountain, it tends to serve as the overflow camping area for Tunnel Mountain. The staff here recommends RVs no larger than 30 feet because sites are located off very tight loop roads. There are only two sites that will take RVs to 40 feet. To reach the campground drive north from the easternmost Banff entrance offramp from Hwy 1. Turn right in .8 km (.5 miles) at the sign for Two Jack Campground and drive for 5.5 km (3.4 miles) to the entrance on your left. You'll pass the entrance to Two Jack Lakeside Campground before you reach the entrance to this campground. There is no bus service into Banff.

TWO JACK LAKESIDE – BANFF NATIONAL PARK *(Open May 19 to Sept 4 - Varies)*

Information: (403) 762-1550
Location: 8 Km (5 Miles) N of Banff, *N 51° 13' 04", W 115° 30' 01"*, 4,600 Ft

74 Sites – Although they share a name this is a separate campground from Two Jack Main. It is usually considered to be more desirable because it has showers and will take slightly larger rigs. It's also quite a bit smaller and does not have a dump station, you have to go over to Two Jack Main and use theirs. Some sites are along the lake. To reach the campground drive north from the easternmost Banff entrance offramp from Hwy 1. Turn right in .8 km (.5 miles) at the sign for Two Jack Campground and drive for 4.2 km (2.6 miles) to the entrance on your right. There is no bus service into Banff.

BARKERVILLE AND WELLS

From a junction 3 km (2 miles) north of Quesnel Hwy 26 leads west to Wells and Barkerville. It's a paved highway suitable for RVs. Wells is 76 km (47 miles) from the junction and Barkerville another 6 km (4 miles) beyond.

Wells (population 300) is an active town with a year-round population. It was formerly the company town for the Cariboo Gold Quartz Mine but today makes its living off the tourists attracted by nearby Barkerville, winter sports, gambling, and the Bowron Lake Provincial Park to the east. Wells offers stores, a gas station, galleries, a museum and the Jack O'Clubs 1930s Casino and Music Hall. In winter the Troll Resort offers downhill skiing and both cross-country skiing and snowmobiling are popular. The first three campgrounds listed below are located in Wells.

Barkerville Historic Town started life as a gold rush town that was founded after Billy Barker made one of the most important strikes of the Cariboo gold rush here in 1862. The town was restored by the provincial government in 1958 and since that time Barkerville has been a popular tourist destination. The town itself is open year round, but most activities are available only during the summer season from mid-May to the beginning of September. During the season you'll be entertained by tours being led by costumed guides, gold-panning, shopping, and presentations at the Theatre Royal.

The Barkerville Provincial Park encompasses the old town and the last three campgrounds listed below are all provincial park campsites.

WHITE CAP INN *(Open All Year)*
  Res. and Info.:   (250) 994-3489, (800) 377-2028, whitecap@goldcity.net, www.whitecapinn.com
  Location: Wells, *N 53° 06' 02", W 121° 34' 01"*, 4,000 Ft

22 Sites – The White Cap is a decent campground affiliated with the motel across the street. Sites vary from tent and no-hookups to full-hookups that will take 40-footers. Restrooms are in

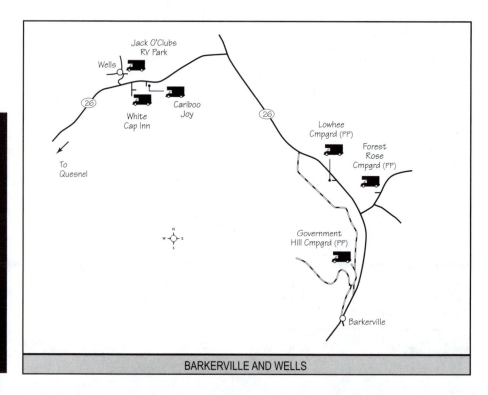

BARKERVILLE AND WELLS

the motel and there are hot showers available for an extra charge. There's also a hot tub. As you enter Wells from the west continue straight ahead (don't turn up the hill into the town), you'll soon see the White Cap sign pointing up the hill to the right.

JACK O'CLUBS RV PARK *(Open June 30 to Sept 5 - Varies)*
  Res. and Info.:   (250) 904-3222, (866) 994-3222, www.jackoclubs.com
  Location: Wells, *N 53° 06' 12.5", W 121° 34' 04"*, 3,900 Ft

32 Sites – This new campground is affiliated with the casino next door. There are both pull-thru and back-in sites that will accommodate RVs to 40 feet. Some sites are dry, others have water and electrical hookups. As you enter Wells take the left turn to go up into the town, you'll see signs for the RV park.

CARIBOO JOY *(Open May 1 to Sept 30 - Varies)*
  Res. and Info.:   (250) 994-3463, www.cariboojoy.com
  Location: Wells, *N 53° 06' 08", W 121° 33' 50"*, 3,900 Ft

24 Sites – This small campground is located in Wells so you can walk to the local attractions. Sites vary but a few can take RVs to 40 feet and there are pull-thrus and full hookups. Watch for the campground on the right as you leave Wells heading east.

BARKERVILLE PROVINCIAL PARK – LOWHEE CAMPGROUND *(Open June 1 to Sept 30)*
  Reservations: (800) 689-9025, www.discovercamping.ca   **Information:** (604) 398-4414
  Location: Barkerville, *N 53° 05' 16", W 121° 31' 02"*, 4,000 Ft

90 Sites – Lowhee is the main campground in this provincial park. Sites here are back-ins, they will take RVs to 45 feet. This campground has showers and a dump station near the entrance. Follow Hwy 26 east from an intersection just north of Quesnel. In 73 km (45 miles) you'll enter Wells. Continue straight and in another 6 km (3.5 miles) you'll reach the campground entrance which will be on your right. The Barkerville historic town is another 2 km (1 mile) beyond the campground entrance.

BARKERVILLE PROVINCIAL PARK – GOVERNMENT HILL CAMPGROUND *(Open June 15 to Sept 15)*
  Information: (604) 398-4414
  Location: Barkerville, *N 53° 04' 32", W 121° 30' 44"*, 4,300 Ft

25 Sites – Government Hill is the closest of the provincial park campgrounds to historic Barkerville. The campground sits just above the parking lot and is for tenting and small rigs, some sites are suitable for RVs to 25 feet. Follow Hwy 26 east from an intersection just north of Quesnel. In 73 km (45 miles) you'll enter Wells. Continue straight and in another 4.9 km (3 miles) turn right at the sign onto a gravel road. The campground will appear in another 2.3 km (1.4 miles).

BARKERVILLE PROVINCIAL PARK – FOREST ROSE CAMPGROUND *(Open July 1 to Sept 2)*
  Information: (604) 398-4414
  Location: Barkerville, *N 53° 05' 11", W 121° 30' 25"*, 4,100 Ft

56 Sites – The third of the campgrounds in the provincial park is the only one with pull-

thru sites. Some will take 45-foot RVs. This campground is just a little farther from the historic town than Lowlee Campground, but still convenient if you have a tow car or don't mind a little hike. Follow Hwy 26 east from an intersection just north of Quesnel. In 73 km (45 miles) you'll enter Wells. Continue straight and in another 6.5 km (4 miles) turn left. The campground is a short distance ahead on your left.

CAMPBELL RIVER

Campbell River (population 30,000) is probably best known as a fishing destination. The town is located on the east side of Vancouver Island at the south end of Discovery Passage, a place where there are extraordinary numbers of bait fish. The bait fish attract salmon year-round. The huge Tyee (large king) salmon are the most-desired prize, but you can also fish for sockeye (red), coho (silver), chum (dog) and pink salmon.

Because Campbell River is a fishing resort town you will find a wide variety of tourist facilities including RV parks, restaurants, and fishing charter operators.

One of the most interesting places to visit in Campbell River is the **Discovery Pier** (a saltwater fishing pier. It is located right next to the downtown boat harbor and juts out into Discovery Passage. Lots of fish are caught here, it's great fun to watch the action.

From Campbell River you can catch a small ferry across Discovery Passage to **Quadra Island**. You'll need to take a vehicle for transportation on the island, it is quite large. There's an excellent First Nations museum here called **Kwagiulth Museum** in Cape Mudge Village south of the ferry landing. There are also **petroglyphs** on display that have been moved here from nearby locations for protection from vandals.

Highway 28 leads westward from Campbell River through **Strathcona Provincial Park** to Gold River and the west coast of Vancouver Island. There are two large campgrounds in this largest of Vancouver Island's parks that are suitable for RVs. The park also has a number

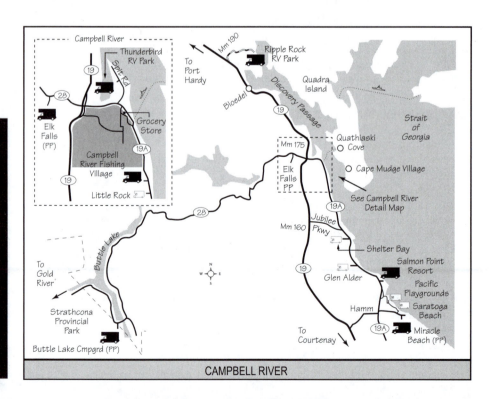

CAMPBELL RIVER

of hiking trails, particularly along the side road that leaves Highway 28 near the Buttle Lake Bridge and heads south along the east shore of Buttle Lake. Ninety-two kilometers (57 miles) from Campbell River the road reaches Gold River, a factory town for a pulp mill, and then continues another 14 kilometers (9 miles) to tidewater. From there you can ride the converted minesweeper MV Uchuck III which carries supplies to remote communities along the west coast of the island.

The campgrounds listed below run from south to north with the last one west of Campbell River in Strathcona Provincial Park. The provincial park campgrounds are great for both tenters and RVers while the waterfront sites at the Ripple Rock RV Park are some of the most outstanding in North America, well worth the short drive on gravel to reach them.

➤ MIRACLE BEACH PROVINCIAL PARK *(Open All Year)*

Reservations: (800) 689-9025, www.discovercamping.ca **Information:** (250) 248-9460
Location: 16 Km (10 Mile) S of Campbell River, *N 49° 50' 58", W 125° 5' 45"*, Near Sea Level

201 Sites – This is a large and very popular sea-side campground. It is one of the Provincial Parks with an entry gatehouse, a sign of how popular the park really is. The draw here is the beach, families love to spend their vacations camping in this park. Sites here are large enough to handle RVs to 45 feet. There are reduced services and fees from October 1 to April 30. The campground is located off Hwy 19A about 10 miles south of Campbell River.

➤ SALMON POINT RESORT *(Open All Year)*

Res. and Info.: (250) 923-6605, (866) 246-6605, sales@salmonpoint.com, www.salmonpoint.com
Location: 10 Km (6 Miles) S of Campbell River, *N 49° 53' 23", W 125° 07' 40"*, Near Sea Level

150 Sites – A large commercial RV resort on the coast south of Campbell River. It offers large sites alongside a first-class marina. Some sites are beachside, some are inland from the marina under trees. There is a fine swimming pool with an indoor hot tub as well as an excellent restaurant. There is also a boat ramp. The campground is well-signed from Hwy 19A about six miles south of Campbell River.

➤ CAMPBELL RIVER FISHING VILLAGE *(Open All Year)*

Res. and Info.: (250) 287-3630, fishvil@oberon.ark.com, www.fishingvillage.bc.ca
Location: Campbell River, *N 50° 00' 08", W 125° 13' 54"*, Near Sea Level

47 Sites – One of three small RV parks along Hwy 19A across the highway from the ocean just south of downtown Campbell River. This is an older campground but it's handy for access to central Campbell River. A bike trail runs along the beach across the street and you can easily walk in to town. A few of the sites here will take RVs to 40 feet, most sites are good for RVs to 25 or 30 feet. From central Campbell River drive south, the campground is 1.2 miles south of the Discovery Pier fishing dock.

➤ THUNDERBIRD RV PARK *(Open All Year)*

Res. and Info.: (250) 286-3344, samalone@oberon.ark.com, www.thunderbirdrvpark.com
Location: Campbell River, *N 50° 02' 34", W 125° 15' 00"*, Near Sea Level

55 Sites – This RV park is located just outside Campbell River to the north on the Tyee Spit. It's located across the road from the beach, a large ship loading pier is just to the south. This

is a decent big-rig park but outside the central area. To reach the campground drive out the Spit Road from Hwy 19A in northeast Campbell River near the shopping centers. The campground is on the left about 1.1 km (.7 miles) from the cutoff from 19A.

ELK FALLS PROVINCIAL PARK *(Open All Year)*

Reservations:	(800) 689-9025, www.discovercamping.ca
Information:	(250) 248-9460
Location:	2 Km (1 Mile) W of Campbell River, *N 50° 2' 11", W 125° 17' 44"*, 100 Ft

122 Sites – This large provincial park campground along the Quinsam and Campbell Rivers is handy because it is very near the city of Campbell River, just 1.5 km (.9 miles) to the west off Hwy 28 to Strathcona Provincial Park. Many sites are right along the river which has runs of salmon. The 75-foot Elk Falls of the Campbell River is nearby. These are back-in sites, some will take RVs to 45 feet. There are good hiking trails from the campground. From October 1 to April 30 no services are available but the campground is open, fees are reduced.

RIPPLE ROCK RV PARK *(Open April 1 to Oct 31)*

Res. and Info.:	(250) 287-7108, ripplerockrvpark@telus.net, www3.telus.net/ripplerockrvpark
Location:	23 Km (14 Miles) N of Campbell River, *N 50° 9' 34", W 125° 22' 21"*, Near Sea Level

60 Sites – This is a first class campground overlooking the sea north of Campbell River. It's nice enough that it wins lots of awards. Huge pull-in sites have great views and full hookups. Amenities include a boat ramp, hot tub, very upscale game room, and of course, the view. Within a short walk is an associated marina with a restaurant and store known as Brown's Bay. We're told that soon this campground will be probably be renamed Brown's Bay RV Park. The access road leaves Hwy 19 some 18 km (11 miles) north of Campbell River near Km 189. It's a 5.0 km (3.1 mile) gravel road.

BUTTLE LAKE CAMPGROUND – STRATHCONA PROVINCIAL PARK *(Open April 1 to Oct 31)*

Reservations:	(800) 689-9025, www.discovercamping.ca
Information:	(250) 248-9460
Location:	48 Km (30 Miles) W of Campbell River, *N 49° 49' 59", W 125° 37' 40"*, 700 Ft

85 Sites – A provincial park campground in a quiet location along the shore of Buttle Lake in Strathcona Provincial Park. Fishing is good in the lake and there are a number of hiking trails in the vicinity. The park has a sandy beach for sunning and swimming, canoeing and kayaking are popular on the lake, so is wind surfing when the weather is right. Large back-in sites will take rigs to 45 feet. The campground is located about 48 kilometers (30 miles) west of Campbell River along Hwy 28 to Gold River.

CAPE SCOTT

Cape Scott Provincial Park occupies the far remote northwest corner of Vancouver Island. The park is difficult to get to and doesn't get throngs of visitors. That make it a great destination if you like to hike wild country and enjoy sometimes fighting the elements.

The park encompasses over 100 kilometers (62 miles) of coastline and 22,131 hectares (85 square miles) of rain-swept headlands and marshes. Expect inclement weather with rain and wind. The park is well-known for muddy hiking conditions so come prepared.

The short 2.5-kilometer (1.5-mile) trail to the beach at San Josef Bay is the most popular with visitors because it's easy and the trail well-maintained. Tent camping is allowed at San Josef Bay. Much longer hikes lead to remote Cape Scott (23.6 km), beaches at Experiment Bight (18.9

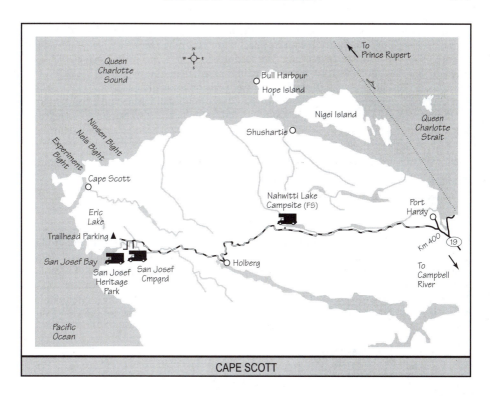

CAPE SCOTT

km), Nels Bight (16.8 km) and Nissen Bight (15 km), the abandoned Cape Scott settlement (12 km), and Eric Lake (3 km). Tent camping is allowed at Experiment Bight, Nels Bight, Nissen Bight, and Eric Lake.

The road to the park heads west from a junction near Port Hardy. From the highway to the park is a distance of 65 kilometers (40 miles), all except 2.4 km (1.5 miles) is gravel. Much of the distance you're on active logging roads requiring careful driving.

The road ends at a small parking lot. Trails begin here and lead to various destinations including several places suitable for tent camping. The lot is a tough place to maneuver in anything longer than about 25 feet. Longer vehicles should go to San Josef Heritage Park or San Josef Campground for parking. See the driving directions below under San Josef Heritage Park for more information.

None of the campgrounds below offer hookups. Due to the sometimes narrow and rough gravel road these campgrounds are only suitable for smaller rigs, see the campground descriptions for specifics.

SAN JOSEF HERITAGE PARK *(Open All Year)*

Res. and Info.: (250) 288-3682
Location: 65 Km (40 Miles) W of Port Hardy, *N 50° 41' 00", W 128° 15' 02"*, Near Sea Level

$$$ ▲   ♨   1

12 Sites – This old homestead is the closest camping area to the provincial park parking area. The manager lives on-site so it makes a good place to leave your car if you are worried about break-ins at the lot while you're hiking in the park. It also makes a good place to camp for day hikes into the park. The area has been cleared and is a mowed lawn. Sites are set in the trees along the edge. There are picnic tables and fire pits, also an outhouse. Kayaks and canoes can be launched in the San Josef River at the campground. While the campground can take any

size rig the access roads make about 30 feet the practical maximum size for RVs to this area. To reach the campground leave Hwy 19 some 1.9 km (1.2 miles) west of where the road goes north to the Port Hardy ferry terminal. The road is signed for Cape Scott Provincial Park and Holberg. For the first 2.4 km (1.5 miles) the road is paved, then it turns to gravel. At 43 km (27 miles) from the highway you'll reach Holberg. Continue on through town following Cape Scott signs. As you approach the park the road narrows to the point that bushes will brush the side of motorhomes. You'll come to a Y at 63 km (39 miles) from the highway, San Josef Campground is left (see below), take the right fork. There's another fork in just .5 km (.3 mile), the small provincial park parking lot is straight ahead .3 km (.2 miles). For San Josef Heritage Park turn left at the fork and you'll reach the campground in another .5 km (.3 mile).

SAN JOSEF CAMPGROUND *(Open All Year)*

Location: 63 Km (39 Miles) W of Port Hardy, *N 50° 40' 54", W 128° 14' 16"*, Near Sea Level

13 Sites – This is a small wilderness campground provided by Western Forest Products, the local logging company. It is on the bank of the San Josef River, canoes and kayaks can be launched from this campground. There are back-in sites suitable for rigs to about 35 feet however the access roads make 30 feet the practical maximum size for this area. There are also outhouses, picnic tables, fire pits, and firewood, but no potable water. To find the campground just follow the instructions given for San Josef Heritage Park, the entrance road for this campground is just before the one for San Josef Heritage Park.

NAHWITTI LAKE CAMPSITE *(Open All Year)*

Location: 23 Km (14 Miles) W of Port Hardy, *N 50° 42' 15", W 127° 51' 45"*, 700 Ft

8 Sites – This is a small forest service campground located near (about 100 feet from the shoreline) Nahwitti Lake. The back-in sites here are suitable for RVs to about 25 feet. There are picnic tables, fire pits, and outhouses but no water except the lake. There is good trout fishing in the lake during June and July. The campground is on the north side of the highway to Holberg and Cape Scott some 23.4 km (14.5 miles) from the intersection near Port Hardy.

CENTRAL KOOTENAY

The Central Kootenay region just north of the U.S border and south of Kootenay Lake is a little remote but fun to visit. The campgrounds below make it easy to visit four major towns there: Nelson, Castlegar, Trail and Rossland.

Nelson (population 9,500) is the farthest north of the four. It occupies a beautiful site on the south shore of the west arm of Kootenay Lake. Originally a mining, and then an agricultural and timber town, Nelson has preserved its **historical buildings**. A pamphlet from the info centre will lead you around town and teach you a bit about Victorian architecture. When you've tired of that it's time to head down to **Lakeside Park** and relax on the beach or under the shade trees. Nelson has a city museum (the **Nelson Museum, Archives and Art Gallery**) and is home to the **Nelson Brewing Company** which give tours. During the summer Nelson hosts **Artwalk**. Downtown businesses set themselves up as galleries and there are grand opening days toward the beginning of August and September

Castlegar (population 7,000) is the crossroads of the area. It sits at the confluence of the Kootenay and Columbia Rivers and the intersection of Highways 3 and 3A. Probably the most interesting thing about Castlegar is that is was the place selected by a group of Russian **Doukhobors** when they left Russia due to religious persecution and settled here in the early 1900s. Two sites are interesting to visit, **Zuckerberg Island Heritage Park** and its Russian Orthodox Chapel House and the **Doukhobor Village Museum**.

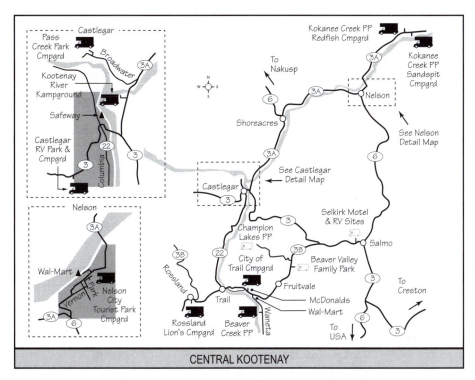

CENTRAL KOOTENAY

Downstream from Castlegar is **Trail** (population 8,000). Trail is home to the Teck Cominco smelter, it dominates the downtown area. The town is home to many Italian immigrants and is well known for both its **Italian restaurants** and its **Fiesta Italiao** in September. The other major holiday in Trail is **Silver City Days** in May.

Up the mountain behind Trail is the former mining town of **Rossland** (population 3,500). The **Le Roy Mine** is no longer in operation but you can still visit, it is one of the top attractions in town. Actually, though, Rossland is known today as an outdoor sports town and home to the Red Mountain Ski Resort and miles and miles of mountain bike trails.

NELSON CITY TOURIST PARK CAMPGROUND *(Open April 15 to Sept 15 - Varies)*

Information: (250) 352-7618
Location: Nelson, *N 49° 29' 51", W 117° 17' 10"*, 1,900 Ft

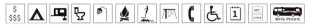

37 Sites – This small municipal campground occupies a sloping site in a residential neighborhood. It is possible for just a few RVs as large as 35 feet to get into the campground and park but maneuvering is very difficult. The campground is best for tenters and RVs to about 30 feet or smaller. The location is very convenient, the central area of town is less than a half-mile distant on city sidewalks. Easiest access is by turning east on Vernon or Baker Streets in central Nelson from Hwy 3A as it passes though town. In a few blocks the main route turns left to curve around the hillside. There are campground signs so you shouldn't miss the turn. You'll soon see the campground sign on the right, watch closely since if you drive past turning around is difficult.

KOKANEE CREEK PROVINCIAL PARK *(Open May 1 to Sept 30 - Varies)*

Reservations: (800) 689-9025, www.discovercamping.ca   **Information:**   (250) 825-4212
Location: 18 Km (11 Miles) NE of Nelson, *N 49° 36' 19", W 117° 07' 17"*, 1,700 Ft

168 Sites – There are actually two campgrounds in this park. Coming from the direction of Nelson you'll first see Redfish Campground on the left. This is the smaller campground and sites are suitable only for tents and RVs to about 25 feet. Just beyond, on the right, is Sandspit Campground. This is a large campground with an entry booth and sites suitable for RVs to 45 feet. It's on the lake side of the highway and there is a swimming beach as well as a boat ramp. During the off season it is possible for self-contained rigs to overnight in a parking lot. From Nelson head northeast on Hwy 3A for about 18 km (11 miles) to the campground.

PASS CREEK PARK CAMPGROUND *(Open April 15 to Sept 30 - Varies)*

Res. and Info.: (250) 304-2062, passcreekpark@hotmail.com
Location: 5 Km (3 Miles) N of Castlegar, *N 49° 20' 18", W 117° 39' 42"*, 1,400 Ft

30 Sites – This campground is in a small regional park. It's a government campground with an on-site manager. When sufficient water is available in the nearby creek a large pond is filled for swimming but some years this is not possible. When there's water this is a popular place, when there's not, it is not. Sites are back-ins suitable for any rig, the manager can run electrical lines for a few rigs but otherwise there are no hookups. You'll see this campground signed off Hwy 3A just north of Castlegar and north of the bridge over the Kootenay. Follow signs 3 km (2 miles) east, the entrance road is on the right.

KOOTENAY RIVER KAMPGROUND *(Open All Year)*

Res. and Info.: (250) 365-5604, www.kootenayriverrv.com
Location: 3 Km (2 Miles) NE of Castlegar, *N 49° 18' 51", W 117° 38' 12"*, 1,300 Ft

43 Sites - This is an older residential RV park with a few sites for travelers. Sites can take RVs to 40 feet and have full hookups. From Hwy 3A just north of Castlegar and south of the Kootenay River crossing follow the entrance road west for a short distance to the campground.

CASTLEGAR RV PARK AND CAMPGROUND *(Open April 1 to Oct 31 - Varies)*

Res. and Info.: (250) 365-2337, (866) 687-7275, info@castlegarRV Park.com,
        www.castlegarRVpark.com
Location: 3 Km (2 Miles) SW of Castlegar, *N 49° 16' 16", W 117° 40' 42"*, Ft

42 Sites – An excellent little campground located southwest of Castlegar with good camping for tents or RVs. RV sites are back-ins suitable for any size RV with parking on grass. The park is located on the south side of the Crowsnest Highway (Hwy 3) about 3.7 km (2.3 miles) to the southwest of Castlegar.

CITY OF TRAIL CAMPGROUND *(Open May 15 to Sept 15 - Varies)*

Res. and Info.: (250) 368-3144, tcoc@netidea.com
Location: 5 Km (3 Miles) E of Trail, *N 49° 05' 29", W 117° 38' 21"*, 1,400 Ft

31 Sites – Trail's municipal campground has nicely landscaped tent and RV sites with water and electric hookups. Some hookup sites are pull-thrus, some but not all will take RVs to 45 feet. The McDonalds right next door is handy but not intrusive. This is an easy campground to miss since there is no sign other than a generic pictogram across the road. Watch for it just west of the McDonalds some 5.3 km (3.3 miles) east of the bridge in Trail on Hwy 3B.

🚐 **ROSSLAND LION'S CAMPGROUND** *(Open May 1 to Canadian Thanksgiving - 2nd Monday in Oct)*
Location: Rossland, *N 49° 04' 39", W 117° 49' 06"*, 3,400 Ft

19 Sites – A nice little campground located just west of Rossland next to the local ballpark. It has tent and RV sites suitable for RVs to 30 feet. Restrooms here are outstanding and modern with four rooms, each with sink, toilet, and shower. From Rossland drive east. The campground is on the south side of Hwy 22 just .5 km (.3 mile) west of the intersection of Highways 22 and 3B on the western edge of town.

🚐 **BEAVER CREEK PROVINCIAL PARK** *(Open All Year As Weather Allows)*
Reservations: (800) 689-9025, www.discovercamping.ca
Information: (250) 367-9165
Location: 5 Miles E of Trail, *49° 04' 01", W 117° 36' 17"*, 1,300 Ft

19 Sites – This small campground overlooks the Columbia River. Sites vary, some will take RVs to 45 feet although the narrow access roads require careful driving. This is a Provincial campground managed by the local Kiwanis, a building with showers and flush toilets has been constructed near the entrance, several hundred meters from the campsites. There is also a ball field and boat ramp. Services are available only during the peak season from May to September but the gates remain open for use without services. From the bridge over the Columbia in Trail head east on Hwy 3B for 6.3 km (3.9 miles) and turn south on Waneta Road (Hwy 22A). Coming from the east on Hwy 3B the turn is just past the Wal-Mart. Follow Waneta Road for 3.1 km (1.9 miles), the campground entrance is on the right.

COWICHAN VALLEY: CHEMAINUS, DUNCAN, AND COWICHAN LAKE

Chemainus (population 4,000) has become famous for the murals painted on the small town's buildings. It seems like everyone stops to take a look around, you might as well too. You'll see the sign taking you east to Chemainus from the highway about 29 kilometers (18 miles) south of Nanaimo. There is quite a bit of parking, even for RVs. Footprints painted on the ground lead you from one mural to the next, and many shops have sprung up to sell you food and souvenirs.

Nearby Duncan (population 22,000) has yellow footsteps painted on the sidewalks, just like Chemainus. These, however, lead to totem poles, not murals. There are about 60 of them. Duncan also is home to the well-known **Cowichan Native Village**. There you'll find a gift shop featuring Cowichan sweaters, the Khowutzun Gallery, and the Longhouse Story Center with a multimedia show of the history of the Cowichan people. There's also a large totem carving shed and the Bighouse from Expo 86 in Vancouver, it's a replica of a traditional long house. Duncan is also home to the **BC Forest Museum**. The museum has 100 acres of logging displays and a narrow-gauge railway. It is located off Highway 1 just north of Duncan.

Duncan is situated right next to the **Cowichan River** which runs from Cowichan Lake to tidewater. This is an excellent fishing river, much of it open only to fly fishing. It has steelhead, brown trout and rainbow trout.

There is an paved highway (Highway 18) to **Cowichan Lake** leading west from a point north of Duncan on Highway 1. Twenty-six kilometers (16 miles) up this road you will reach the small community of Lake Cowichan. From here roads follow the north and south shores of the lake, they lead to a web of unpaved logging roads that can take you to Bamfield, Port Renfrew, Carmanah Walbran Provincial Park and Nitinat Lake. These are gravel logging roads with lots of logging truck traffic, before using them check with local information centers to see if they are passable in your rig and to see how much logging traffic you are likely to meet.

Cowichan Lake is one of the largest on Vancouver Island. The southern shore is unusual

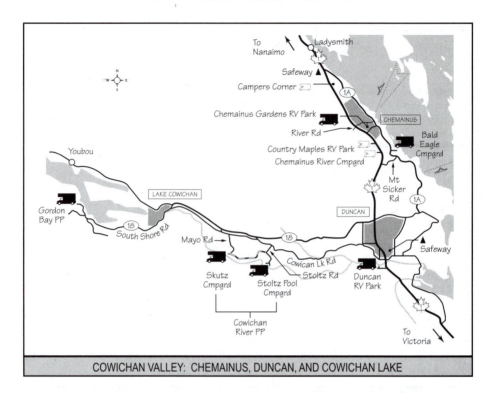

COWICHAN VALLEY: CHEMAINUS, DUNCAN, AND COWICHAN LAKE

in that it has much warmer weather than the surrounding region, it has an average maximum temperature of about 75 degrees Fahrenheit. Gordon Bay Provincial Park, the last campground described below, is a large campground perfectly positioned to take advantage of this fact.

CHEMAINUS GARDENS RV PARK *(Open All Year)*

Res. and Info.: (250) 246-3569, www.chemainusrvpark.com
Location: Chemainus, *N 48° 55' 3", W 123° 43' 38"*, 200 Ft

63 Sites – This is a very unusual campground. Campsites are set in extensive formal gardens complete with ponds full of Koi. Individual sites are well separated, almost like a provincial park. Even better, this campground is within walking distance of Chemainus, you can walk to the center of town in about 10 minutes. Sites here vary a great deal in size, a few will take RVs to 45 feet. From Chemainus drive south on Hwy 1A. Just outside town turn right on River Road. The campground entrance will be on your left in 1 km (.6 mile). From Hwy 1 you can take the River Road Exit for Chemainus, the campground will be on your right in 1.3 km (.8 miles).

BALD EAGLE CAMPGROUND *(Open All Year)*

Res. and Info.: (250) 246-9457, becamp@cow-net.com
Location: 6 Km (4 Miles) S of Chemainus, *N 48° 53' 17", W 123° 41' 16"*, 100 Ft

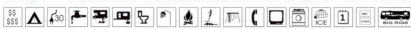

60 Sites – Another campground convenient to Chemainus, this one is next to the Chemainus River and offers swimming in the river. Back-in sites at the center of the campground will take RVs to 45 feet. Easiest access is from Chemainus. Just drive south on the Chemainus Road, Hwy 1A, for 6 kilometers (4 miles). The campground is on the left.

BRITISH COLUMBIA

DUNCAN RV PARK *(Open All Year)*

Res. and Info.: (250) 748-8511
Location: Duncan, *N 48° 46' 14", W 123° 42' 04"*, 200 Ft

85 sites – This older commercial campground is conveniently located within walking distance of downtown Duncan and the Cowichan Native Village. For travelers there are pull-thru sites that will take RVs to 40 feet, also a lot of no-hookup tent sites near the river. Heading south from Duncan on Hwy 1 cross the bridge and take the first right onto Boys Road. Take another right in one block and the campground will be straight ahead.

STOLTZ POOL CAMPGROUND – COWICHAN RIVER PROVINCIAL PARK *(Open All Year)*

Reservations: (800) 689-9025, www.discovercamping.ca
Information: (250) 474-1336
Location: 20 Km (12 Miles) W of Duncan, *N 48° 46' 23", W 123° 53' 19"*, 400 Ft

43 Sites – Cowichan River Provincial park is located on the Cowichan River between Duncan and Cowichan Lake. This is one of two campgrounds in the park, the other is Skutz Campground described below. From the campgrounds there is access to hiking trails along the river, not to mention the river itself which is popular for fishing and for swimming and tubing in the summer. The campground is fairly new with back-in sites suitable for RVs to about 35 feet. Access is from Hwy 18. Watch for the sign for the campground 15 kilometers (9.5 miles) from the Hwy 18 intersection with Hwy 1. Then drive another 5.0 km (3.1 miles) south to the campground entrance.

SKUTZ CAMPGROUND – COWICHAN RIVER PROVINCIAL PARK *(Open May 15 to Sept 10)*

Information: (250) 474-1336
Location: 21 Km (13 Miles) W of Duncan, *N 48° 46' 56", W 123° 57' 02"*, 400 Ft

33 Sites – This second of the two Cowichan River Provincial Park campgrounds is upstream from the first. It's a good place to start for a river float. This is a smaller campground than Stoltz Pool with parking on grass in two fields. Sites aren't large, a couple will take an RV to 35 feet, most sites are good for RVs to 25 feet. It's a very nice campground for tenters. To reach the campground take the signed cutoff from Hwy 18 which is 18.1 km (11.2 miles) from the intersection with Hwy 1 near Duncan. It's 3.4 km (2.1 miles) in to the campground. There's also a gravel road paralleling the river from the Stoltz Pool campground.

GORDON BAY PROVINCIAL PARK *(Open All Year)*

Reservations: (800) 689-9025, www.discovercamping.ca
Information: (250) 474-1336
Location: 40 Km (25 Miles) W of Duncan, *N 48° 50' 06", W 124° 11' 47"*, 600 Ft

134 Sites – This large lakeside provincial campground is on the warm south side of Cowichan Lake and features a swimming beach and boat launch. The campground is open with full services from March 15 to October 31. During the rest of the year self-contained RVs can overnight in the boat launch area for a reduced fee. To reach it take Hwy 18 west from a point just north of Duncan, drive 26 kilometers (16 miles) to the town of Lake Cowichan, then another 14 kilometers (9 miles) on South Shore Road.

DAWSON CREEK

Dawson Creek (population 13,000) is the kick-off point for a drive to Alaska up the Alaska Highway. Don't confuse this town with Dawson City, the gold rush town located on the Yukon River north of Whitehorse. Don't be deceived by the small population figure above, Dawson Creek really serves as an important services town in the agricultural Peace River Block with a population of over 50,000 people.

The **Dawson Creek Visitor Information Centre** has brochures and pamphlets covering sights and campgrounds north along the highway. It is located near the intersection of Highway 49 and Highway 2 near the center of town. They can also give you information about road conditions farther north. It is in a complex called the **NAR (Northern Alberta Railway) Park** which also houses the **Dawson Creek Station Museum** which concentrates on the agricultural history of the area and the Alaska Highway. They have an excellent film of the building of the Alcan, a good introduction. In the same complex is the Dawson Creek Art Gallery. In the parking lot is the Mile Zero Cairn, claimed to be the true Mile 0 of the Alaska Highway. There's also a second Mile 0 Marker in town, it's a short two-block stroll away.

Another Dawson Creek attraction is the **Walter Wright Pioneer Village** at the Mile 0 Rotary Park, there are historic buildings from before the highway was constructed. The park is located near the intersection of the Hart (highway from Prince George) and Alaska Highways.

Dawson Creek hosts the Fall Fair Exhibition and Pro Rodeo about the middle of August.

All of the campgrounds described below are located near the junction of Hwy 97 from Prince George and the Alaska Highway at the northern edge of Dawson Creek. You'll find them full of Alaska-bound travelers.

⊞ MILE 0 RV CAMPSITE *(Open May 1 to Sept 30)*

Information: (250) 782-2590, mile0campground@aol.com, www.citydirect.ca/mile0
Location: 2 Km (1 Mile) N of Dawson Creek, *N 55° 46' 12", W 120° 15' 39"*, 2,200 Ft

100 Sites – This municipal campground is the nicest of the Dawson Creek campgrounds with widely spaced sites separated by grass. There are back-ins and pull-thrus to 80 feet as well as tent sites. From the intersection of Hwy 97 from Prince George and the Alaska Highway just north of Dawson Creek travel north for just a short distance, the campground is on the left.

⊞ NORTHERN LIGHTS RV PARK *(Open April 1 to Nov 1)*

Res. and Info.:   (250) 782-9433, (888) 414-9433, nlrv@pris.bc.ca, www.pris.bc.ca/rvpark
Location: 3 Km (2 Miles) W of Dawson Creek, *N 55° 45' 59", W 120° 17' 27"*, 2,200 Ft

70 Sites – The Northern Lights is located west of town. It overlooks Dawson Creek from a low hill. There are tent sites as well as back-ins and pull-thrus to 50 feet. From the intersection of Hwy 97 from Prince George and the Alaska Highway just north of Dawson Creek travel west on Hwy 97 for 2.4 km (1.5 mile) to the campground.

⊞ TUBBY'S RV PARK *(Open May 1 to Oct 31)*

Res. and Info.:   (250) 782-2584
Location: Dawson Creek, *N 55° 45' 60", W 120° 15' 37"*, 2,200 Ft

100 Sites – Tubby's RV Park has large pull-thrus to about 60 feet, some with full hookups. For some reason this park seems to get less traffic than other parks in town, often caravans use it. There is a large 3-bay RV wash out front. From the intersection of Hwy 97 from Prince George

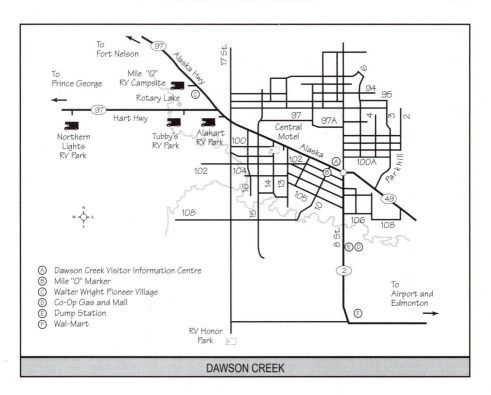

DAWSON CREEK

and the Alaska Highway just north of Dawson Creek travel west on Hwy 97 for .5 km (.3 mile) to the campground.

ALAHART RV PARK *(Open All Year)*

Res. and Info.: (250) 782-4702, alahart@pris.ca, www.alahartrvpark.com
Location: Dawson Creek, *N 55° 45' 57", W 120° 15' 09"*, 2,200 Ft

75 Sites – The Alahart is a motel and RV park with a restaurant out front along the highway. There are back-in sites to 40 feet around a loop in a grassy field as well as some longer pull-thru sites to about 55 feet. From the intersection of Hwy 97 from Prince George and the Alaska Highway just north of Dawson Creek travel south toward the city for just a short distance to the campground, it's on the right.

FERNIE

Fernie (population 5,000) is the center of commerce in the Elk River Valley. This valley extends to the north and Crowsnest Pass, the pass used by both Hwy 3 and the old Canadian Pacific Railroad to cross the Rockies. Part of Fernie's charm is its brick buildings, required by law after the town burned down in 1908. A favorite is the Fernie Courthouse. There is a free booklet available at the info centre that outlines a downtown walking tour and points out the most interesting buildings. Fernie is a ski town, the **Fernie Alpine Resort** is a few miles south of town. In summer it's open for mountain bikes and also has a camping area.

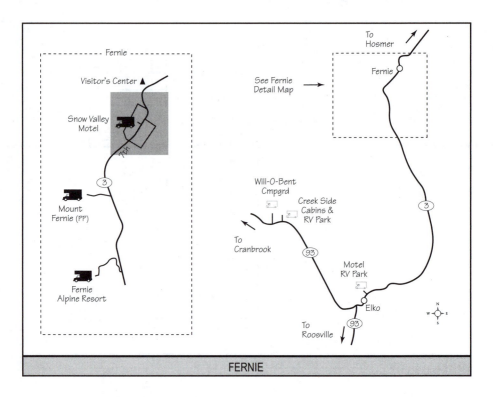

FERNIE

SNOW VALLEY MOTEL *(Open May 1 to Oct 31)*

Res. and Info.:	(250) 423-4421, (877) 696-7669, info@fernieaccomodations.com, www.snowvalleymotel.com
Location:	Fernie, *N 49° 30' 35", W 115° 03' 47"*, 3,300 Ft

10 Sites – In winter this motel rents sites only on a monthly basis but in the summer it caters to travelers and it's the closest campground to the center of town. Amenities include an indoors hot tub. While the sites are really suitable for RVs to 30 feet, some 40 footers squeeze into the parking area. Only two of the ten sites have sewer connections, the rest have electricity and water only. The hotel is located on the north side of the Crowsnest Hwy 3 (7th Ave.) as it passes through town between 10th and 11th Streets.

MOUNT FERNIE PROVINCIAL PARK *(Open June 1 to Sept 30)*

Reservations:	(800) 689-9025, www.discovercamping.ca
Information:	(250) 422-3003
Location:	3 Km (2 Miles) S of Fernie, *N 49° 29' 13", W 115° 05' 26"*, 3,400 Ft

38 Sites – This handy campground is located just south of town. The campground is situated on flat ground and sites are good size with several that will take RVs to 45 feet. The top loop may be useable outside the open dates depending upon weather, there is no fee for use outside the open dates. From Fernie drive south about 2.4 km (1.5 miles) and turn west on an .8 km (.5 mile) access road to the campground.

FERNIE ALPINE RESORT *(Open All Year)*
Res. and Info.:   (250) 423-4655, info@skifernie.com, www.skifernie.com
Location: 6 Km (4 Miles) S of Fernie, *N 49° 27' 32", W 115° 05' 09"*, 3,600 Ft

39 Sites – Fernie Alpine Resort is Fernie's downhill ski resort. It's located not far south of town and has a gravel-surfaced all-year camping area near one of the chairlifts. Sites have electricity but no sewer or water. It's about a 300-yard walk to the restaurant and main resort buildings. Showers and washroom are available in a maintenance building. From Fernie drive south about 6 km (3 miles) and then turn west on the access road to the resort. In 1 km (.6 miles) you'll come to a Y, you want to turn left here. The campground office is in the bottom floor of the building straight ahead which also houses a gas station and small store. You can stop and check in and then drive up the hill to the campground area or use the deposit box at the camping area.

GLACIER NATIONAL PARK

Between Revelstoke and Golden the Trans-Canada Highway crosses 1,330 meter (4,365 foot) Rogers Pass. The pass is surrounded by Glacier National Park. Since the Trans-Canada is the main east-west highway in Canada there is no charge for driving through the park – as long as you don't stop. Fee collection stations are located at the park boundaries to the west and east of the park.

This region receives a great deal of precipitation, almost every day it either rains or snows. That means that a great deal of snow accumulates in the winter. Campgrounds here open late and backcountry travel permits are required because of the avalanche danger. When the weather is clear, though, this is a beautiful place.

Right at the top of the pass is the **Rogers Pass Centre** where you can stop to see films and

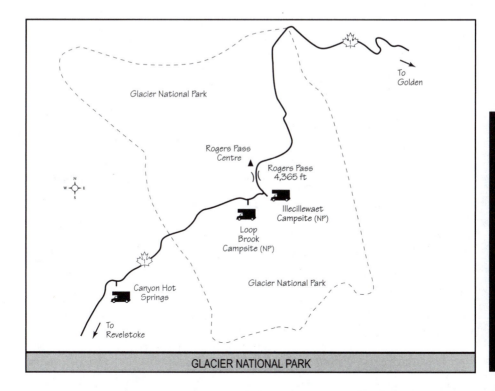

GLACIER NATIONAL PARK

exhibits about the park. You can also get information about the park's hiking trails. There's a motel next door with a coffee shop.

Two of the campgrounds listed below are national park campgrounds located inside the park. As in most Canadian national parks you have to pay a park entrance fee to stay in them, in addition to the campground fee. Here it's $7 Canadian.

CANYON HOT SPRINGS *(Open May 15 to Sept 30 - Varies)*

Res. and Info.:	(250) 837-2420, www.canyonhotsprings.com
Location:	35 Km (22 Miles) W of Rodgers Pass Visitor Center,
	N 51° 08' 18", W 117° 51' 26", 2,300 Ft

200 Sites – If you want to visit Glacier National Park but don't want to give up your hook-ups, this is the place. In addition to the hookups the campground has two hot spring swimming pools. There are good tent sites in trees and also large back-in RV sites suitable for RVs to 45 feet with electric and water hookups. The campground is on the south side of Hwy 1 midway between Revelstoke and the Rodgers Pass Visitor Center in the park, it's 35 km (22 miles) from each.

LOOP BROOK CAMPSITE – GLACIER NATIONAL PARK *(Open June 15 to Sept 30 - Varies)*

Information:	(250) 837-7500
Location:	6 Km (4 Miles) W of Rodgers Pass Visitor Center,
	N 51° 15' 31", W 117° 32' 23", 3,700 Ft

20 Sites – This is a small national park campground with back-in sites suitable for RVs to about 25 feet. It's excellent for tent campers since it has a shelter cabin with a woodstove and restrooms with flush toilets and even a dish-washing sink with hot water. There's an interesting railroad history-related trail from the campground. Normally in the Spring the nearby Illecillewaet campsite opens a week or so earlier than this one. The campground is just a short distance off the highway on the south side some 6 km (4 miles) west of the Rodgers Pass Visitor Center.

ILLECILLEWAET CAMPSITE – GLACIER NATIONAL PARK *(Open June 10 to Sept 30 - Varies)*

Information:	(250) 837-7500
Location:	3 Km (2 Miles) W of Rodgers Pass Visitor Center,
	N 51° 16' 15", W 117° 30' 10" 4,024 Ft

60 Sites – This is the main Glacier National Park Campground. It wasn't designed for today's big rigs, maneuvering room and short sites limit use to RVs to about 30 feet. Some sites are along the river. The campground is located on the south side of the highway about 3 km (2 miles) west of the Rodgers Pass Visitor Center.

HARRISON HOT SPRINGS

Harrison Hot Springs (Population 1,300) makes a great camping destination just 100 km (60 miles) east of Vancouver. The resort town sits at the south shore of Harrison Lake. This 40-mile long lake is very shallow out as far as Echo Island which you can see just offshore, but then the bottom drops to depths of up to 900 feet. Today it's a popular boating destination but in early days it was a steamboat route to the Cariboo gold fields.

Harrison's **beach** is one of its best features. It's wide and sandy. There's a swimming lagoon, lawns, even a boat launch. Actually, though, this is not a natural beach, a great deal of money has been spent to make it so nice. If you would like water a little warmer than that in the lake or the lagoon, you might try the **Public Pool** near the beach. A hot springs rises just west of town and water is piped to the pool. During the trip the water is cooled to a perfect soaking temperature of 38° C (100° F).

Like any resort town Harrison tries its best to keep you occupied. There are lots of restaurants and shops, even a 9-hole golf course. There are also many trails near the town. Another way to attract visitors is annual festivals and events and Harrison has its share. Probably the best known is the **World Championship of Sand Sculpture** held on the beach during early September. Harrison is also a great place to see bald eagles, they congregate on the Harrison River south of town and can most easily bee seen from the Morris Valley Road on the west side of the river north of its confluence with the Fraser at Harrison Mills. There's even a bald eagle festival at Harrison Mills at the end of November.

SASQUATCH SPRINGS RV PARK *(Open April 1 to Oct 15)*
Res. and Info.:   (604) 796-9228, camping@harrisonhotsprings.org, www.harrisonhotsprings.org
Location: Harrison Hot Springs, *N 49° 18' 02", W 121° 47' 11"*, 100 Ft

113 Sites – This well-run and nicely laid-out campground is located conveniently near central Harrison Hot Springs, the beach is well within walking distance. It is set along the Miama Slough and has a canoe dock. The campground has tent sites as well as RV sites of various sizes, some will take RVs to 45 feet. The campground entrance is off Hot Springs Avenue, just .3 km (.2 mile) from the lake.

GLENCOE RV PARK *(Open All Year)*
Res. and Info.:   (604) 796-2574
Location: Harrison Hot Springs, *N 49° 18' 05", W 121° 47' 05"*, 100 Ft

19 Sites – The campground here is in a lot behind a small hotel. There is tent camping on grass and a sink for tenters to do their dishes. RV sites are on grass or are paved, most will take RVs to about 35 feet although there are 3 long pull-thrus that will take 45-footers with careful maneuvering. Watch for the Glencoe on the east side of Hot Springs Avenue as you drive into the central area of Harrison Hot Springs. It's about two blocks from the Lake.

HOT-SPRING RV CAMPING PARK *(Open All Year)*
Res. and Info.:   (604) 796-3467, (866) 345-2225
Location: Harrison Hot Springs, *N 49° 18' 08", W 121° 47' 01"*, 100 Ft

21 Sites – The Hot-Spring RV Camping Park is a small RV park right in central Harrison Hot Springs and across the street from the public swimming pool. Sites here are not huge but some will take 40-footers with slide-outs. The campground is located on the south side of Lillooet Ave. just east of Hot Springs Ave. Lillooet is the street that parallels the lake shore but one block back from the beach.

HICKS LAKE CAMPGROUND – SASQUATCH PROVINCIAL PARK *(Open March 18 to Oct 11 - Varies)*
Reservations: (800) 689-9025, www.discovercamping.ca
Information: (604) 795-6169
Location: 10 Km (6 Miles) NE of Harrison Hot Springs, *N 49° 20' 46", W 121° 42' 37"*, 800 Ft

71 Sites – This is one of those campgrounds located east of Harrison Hot Springs in Sas-

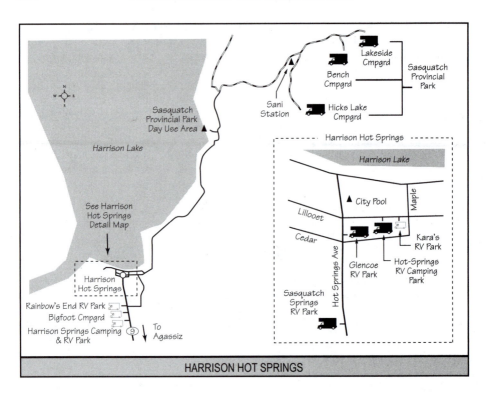

HARRISON HOT SPRINGS

quatch Provincial Park. It's the nearest to town. Sites here are all back-ins off a large loop. A few sites reach 40 feet but most are shorter. A few are on the shore of Hicks Lake. There are no hookups but there is a dump station on the entrance road to the park which serves campers in all three campgrounds in the park. There is a boat ramp near the campground, Hicks lake has a 10 horsepower restriction. In Harrison Hot Springs drive east on Lillooet Ave. It soon turns north and follows the shore of Harrison Lake for 5 km (3.1 miles) to a Y. Turn right and in another 1.1 km (.7 miles) you'll come to another Y. Turn right and the road becomes gravel, you'll see a sani-station 2.9 km (1.8 miles) from the Y and in another 3 km (.2 mile) the campground entrance is on the right.

▄ BENCH CAMPGROUND – SASQUATCH PROVINCIAL PARK *(Open May 13 to Sept 6 - Varies)*

Reservations:	(800) 689-9025, www.discovercamping.ca
Information:	(604) 795-6169
Location:	11 Km (7 Miles) NE of Harrison Hot Springs, *N 49° 21' 57", W 121° 41' 29"*, 800 Ft

64 Sites – This campground is near but not on Deer Lake, the Lakeside Campground is nearby. Sites here are all back-ins but tend to be larger than in Hicks Lake campground with many 50-foot sites. Follow the directions for reaching Hicks Lake Campground above, then continue on another 1.3 km (.8 miles) to the entrance for the campground which will be on your right.

▄ LAKESIDE CAMPGROUND – SASQUATCH PROVINCIAL PARK *(Open All Year)*

Reservations:	(800) 689-9025, www.discovercamping.ca
Information:	(604) 795-6169
Location:	11 Km (7 Miles) E of Harrison Hot Springs, *N 49° 22' 04", W 121° 41' 03"*, 700 Ft

42 Sites – Lakeside Campground is on the shore of Deer Lake. There is a boat launch, only electric motors are allowed on the lake. Sites here are back-ins and reach 45 feet but many have a good slope making RV parking difficult. The campground has full services only from March 18 to October 11, outside that time period camping is free but no services are available. To reach the campground follow the directions to Bench Campground above and then continue straight when you reach the Bench Campground entrance road.

HOPE

Hope (population 6,000) is probably best known as the setting for the filming of the cult movie classic *First Blood*, the first of the Rambo movies. The peaceful little town couldn't be more unlike the one shown in the movie, but you can still see some evocative scenery that may remind you of the movie. If you visit the info centre they can tell you where to see locations that are shown in the movie. Probably the best-known are various locations near the five **Othello Tunnels** in the Coquihalla Canyon Provincial Park to the east of town. There's a hiking trail through the tunnels.

Another attraction here are the two-dozen or so **chainsaw sculptures** scattered around town. They were created by local artist Pet Ryan and have turned Hope into the Chainsaw Carving Capital of British Columbia.

If you travel east of Hope you're beyond Hope. Get it? You'll probably hear this old joke several time when you visit but you might take it a little more seriously if you visit the **Hope Slide Viewpoint** located 16 kilometers (10 miles) east of Hope on Hwy 3. You'll see that the entire face of the mountain to the north has slid into the valley. This happened fairly recently, on January 9, 1965. Four people were killed by the slide.

The highways near Hope can be a little confusing. The Trans-Canada Highway (Hwy 1) becomes Hwy 3 right at Hope and then east of town the main route goes north as Hwy 5 (the Coquihalla Highway) while Hwy 3 continues east. When traveling eastward to stay on Hwy

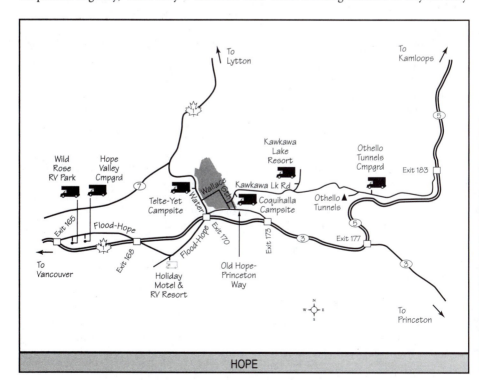

HOPE

1 you actually have to exit the freeway at Exit 170 and drive north through Hope and up the Fraser River Valley. Through the Fraser River Valley Hwy 1 is a winding two-lane highway. Most modern eastbound through traffic follows the Coquihalla Highway (a toll road) and rejoins Hwy 1 in Kamloops.

◼ TELTE YET CAMPSITE *(Open May 15 to Oct 15 - Varies)*

Res. and Info.:   (604) 869-9994, chawath@uniserve.com
Location: Hope, *N 49° 22' 54", W 121° 26' 51"*, 100 Ft

30 Sites – This campground is located right in Hope on the bank of the Fraser River. It's the most convenient place to stay if you want to explore the town on foot. The campground is operated by the Chawathil First Nation band, the campground name means "Up-River People" Campsite. Sites here vary in size and configuration and most are large enough only for RVs to 35 feet but there are two very long 60-foot pull-thrus. The restrooms are old but better than they look from the outside. The entrance to the campground is off Water Avenue, the road that runs along the river on the west side of the central area of the town. Easiest access is from Exit 170 where Hwy 1 exits the freeway when it becomes Hwy 3.

◼ COQUIHALLA CAMPSITE *(Open March 1 to Oct 31 - Varies)*

Res. and Info.:   (604) 869-7119, (888) 869-7118, hopecamp@uniserve.com
Location: 1 Km (.5 Mile) E of Central Hope, *N 49° 22' 48", W 121° 25' 35"*, 300 Ft

122 Sites – This campground is set in thick trees on the east side of Hope. Sites vary in configuration but some will take RVs to 45 feet. The largest part of the campground is non-hookup sites but there are some with electricity and water and ten long back-in sites with full hookups including TV. The campground is located along the Coquihalla River and some sites are next to a dike and walking trail along the river. To reach the campground take Exit 170 from Hwy 3. Follow old Hope-Princeton Way eastward along the north side of the highway for 1 km (.6 mile). Turn left on Seventh Avenue and in .2 km (.1 mile) turn right on Kawkawa Lake Road. You'll see the campground on the right in another .3 km (.2 mile).

◼ KAWKAWA LAKE RESORT *(Open April 1 to Sept 30)*

Res. and Info.:   (604) 869-9930, www.kawkawalake.net
Location: 5 Km (3 Miles) E of Hope, *N 49° 23' 02", W 121° 23' 35"*, 300 Ft

63 Sites – Little Kawkawa Lake is located east of Hope. This campground is a fishing and family holiday resort with a boat ramp and swimming beach. Some of the sites will take RVs to 35 feet although most are smaller. To reach the campground follow the instructions given for the Coquihalla Campsite above. Continue east past the entrance to the Coquihalla Campsite, cross the river, and in another 2.3 km (1.4 miles) take the left at the Y and drive north along the east shore of the lake for another .5 km (.3 mile) to the campground.

◼ OTHELLO TUNNELS CAMPGROUND *(Open All Year)*

Res. and Info.:   (604) 869-9448, (877) 869-0543, othellocamp@uniserve.com, www.othellotunnels.com
Locations: 6.5 Km (4 Miles) E of Hope, *N 49° 22' 51", W 121° 21' 13"*, 700 Ft

35 Sites – This park is just a 10 minute walk from the famous Quintette Tunnels walking trail. It's a great campground for tent campers and RVs to about 30 feet. The park has a rainy day shelter with a fireplace, a large barbeque for groups, a rainbow trout pond, a basketball hoop, and a game room. You can reach the campground by following the instructions given above

for the Kawkawa Lake Resort and then taking the right fork of the Y at 2.3 km (1.4 miles) to continue another 3.4 km (2.1 miles) to the campground. Alternately, take Exit 183 from Hwy 5 (the Coquihalla Hwy) and travel south and west on the northwest side of the freeway for 3.2 km (2 miles) to the campground.

HOPE VALLEY CAMPGROUND *(Open All Year)*

Res. and Info.: (604) 869-9857, (866) 869-6660
Location: 5 Km (3 Miles) W of Hope, *N 49° 21' 59", W 121° 30' 25"*, 100 Ft

150 Sites – This former KOA is conveniently located west of Hope just off Hwy 1. Sites are set in evergreens and range from tent sites to pull-thrus to about 65 feet. There is also a seasonal outdoor swimming pool. To reach the campground take Exit 165 from Hwy 1 and travel eastward on the Flood-Hope road on the north side of the freeway for .7 mile to the campground entrance.

WILD ROSE RV PARK *(Open April 1 to Sept 30)*

Res. and Info.: (604) 869-9842, (800) 463-7999, wildrose@uniserve.com, www.wildrosecamp.com
Location: 6 Km (3.5 Miles) W of Hope, *N 49° 21' 57", W 121° 30' 49"*, 100 Ft

58 Sites – The Wild Rose is just down the highway from the Hope Valley Campground. It's more open with fewer trees and has tent sits as well as RV sites including pull-thrus to 60 feet. Take Exit 165 from Hwy 1 and travel eastward on the Flood-Hope road for .5 km (.3) mile to the campground entrance.

JASPER NATIONAL PARK

Highway 16 crosses the Rockies through Yellowhead Pass. Jasper National Park encompasses most of this crossing of the Rockies. Right in the middle of the crossing you'll find the town of **Jasper** (population 5,500) which serves as the service and administration center of Jasper National Park just as Banff townsite does for Banff National Park. Many of the attractions of the park are near the town, so are several very large campgrounds.

Jasper definitely reflects its roots as a division town on the Grand Trunk Pacific and Canadian Northern Railways. The town has a number of worthwhile sites to visit. The Park Visitor Centre is near the center of town. There's also a museum, the **Jasper-Yellowhead Museum**, with exhibits about the history of the park.

The Jasper area has its own mountain tram. The **Jasper Tramway** climbs the Whistlers Mountain to a terminal at 2,285 meters (7,516 feet). From there you can climb a trail to the summit at 2,464 meters (8,085 feet). Jasper also has its own old hotel, the **Jasper Park Lodge**, located east of the townsite on Lac Beauvert and accessible off Maligne Lake Road. The lodge also has an 18-hole golf course.

There are some interesting drives in the Jasper region. **Maligne Lake Road** leads eastward from the Jasper townsite area for 44 kilometers (28 miles) to the very scenic **Maligne Lake**. Along the way you can take a look at **Maligne Canyon** and **Medicine Lake**. At Maligne Lake you can either rent your own canoe or take a commercial boat cruise on this 22-kilometer-long mountain lake.

Another good drive is to follow Hwy 16 to the north as it follows the Athabasca River on its descent to the eastern plains. Along the way the highway passes between two large lakes: Jasper and Talbot. Forty-four kilometers (27 miles) from Jasper townsite is the junction with Miette Hot Spring Road. Turn right here, and in just 1.3 kilometers (.8 miles) stop at the **Punchbowl Falls** pull-off and take the short walk to the overlook for the very scenic falls. If you continue along the road you will reach **Miette Hot Springs** some 17 kilometers (10.5 miles) from the highway, Parks Canada operates a swimming pool complex here.

If you drive west you can follow Hwy 16 across **Yellowhead Pass** (1,131 meters, 3,711 feet), and into Mt. Robson Provincial Park. You'll be driving along the upper Fraser River Valley and pass Yellowhead and Moose Lakes. **Mt. Robson** is the highest mountain in the Canadian Rockies (3,954 meters, 12,972 feet). You can stop at the visitor center near the western border of the park some 62 kilometers (39 miles) west of Yellowhead Pass. From the visitor center you have a spectacular view of the mountain. The reason it is so impressive is that the visitor center sits at an altitude of only about 850 meters (2,800 feet) and is only 11 kilometers from the mountain, you definitely get the full effect

Running north and south between Jasper National Park and Banff National Park is the 230 kilometer (143 mile) **Icefields Parkway**. It's one of the most scenic roads in North America and not to be missed. The north junction is right at Jasper townsite. Don't try to hurry along this highway, there is plenty of magnificent scenery and many places to stop, enjoy the view, and even take some hikes.

Like most Canadian national parks there is a day fee for the use of Banff and Jasper National Parks. It is possible to drive through Jasper on Hwy 16 without paying the fee, but not the Icefield Parkway. There are kiosks on both ends of the Parkway where the fee is collected.

As you travel south you'll soon come to the cutoff for **Highway 93A**. This loop road was formerly the main highway but has been bypassed by new construction. It's a little narrow and not in great condition so people driving large RVs probably won't like it. The old highway runs south along the western side of the valley parallel to today's road for about 25 kilometers and rejoins the Parkway near Athabasca Falls.

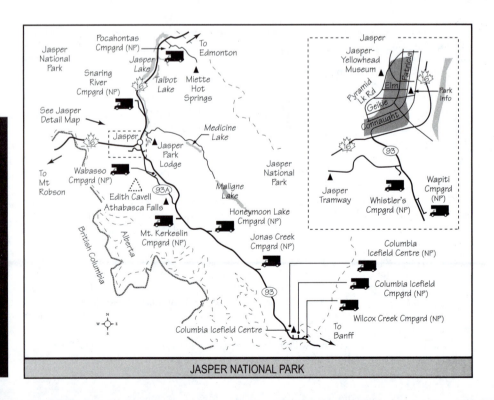

JASPER NATIONAL PARK

The old highway provides access to some interesting sights and locations. One is **Mt. Edith Cavell Road**. This narrow road climbs 14.5 kilometers (9 miles) to the foot of Mount Edith Cavell and the Angel Glacier. Trailers are not allowed on the road so if you have one you'll probably want to make this drive as a side trip from the Jasper area. Also worth a look is the **Athabasca Trail Exhibit** at the picnic area at the mouth of the Whirlpool River. The Athabasca Trail was another one of those cross-Rockies routes used by explorers and fur traders, it ascended the Athabasca River to this point from the east, then climbed the Whirlpool River through Athabasca Pass before descending to the Columbia River Valley.

Even if you don't take the Hwy 93A loop it's well worth the time to stop at **Athabasca Falls** at the southern end. The turn for Athabasca Falls from the Icefields Parkway is well marked, it is 31 kilometers (19 miles) south of Jasper town site. The Athabasca River drops over a ledge and tumbles through a narrow canyon. Overlooks and a pedestrian bridge offer excellent views, a great place for pictures.

Sunwapta Pass (2,035 meters, 6,675 feet) marks the boundary between Jasper National Park and Banff National park. A few kilometers north of the pass is the huge **Columbia Icefield Center**. This is an observatory with great views across the valley to the Athabasca Glacier and the Columbia Icefield. It also serves as the embarkation point for bus tours onto the glacier. Busses leave the Center and drive to edge of the glacier, there passengers change to special busses with huge tires called snocoaches to actually drive out onto the glacier. As an alternative you can drive to the foot of the glacier yourself and take a short hike for a close look. The Icefield Center also houses a Parks Canada Visitor Centre.

For more about the Icefields Parkway south of the border of Jasper National Park see the section of this chapter covering Banff National Park.

POCAHONTAS CAMPGROUND – JASPER NATIONAL PARK *(Open Victoria Day Holiday in late May to Canadian Thanksgiving - 2nd Monday in Oct)*

Reservations:	(877) RESERVE, www.pccamping.ca
Information:	(780) 852-6176
Location:	40 Km (25 Miles) W of Jasper, *N 53° 11' 50", W 117° 54' 33"*, 3,600 Ft

140 Sites – This large campground is located near the far east entrance to the park and away from the center of things. Many sites here are suitable for RVs up to 30 feet but a few will take 40-footers, the people at the entrance station know which ones they are. The campground is located off Hwy 16 some 40 km (25 miles) east of Jasper and 8 km (5 miles) from the eastern entrance to the park.

SNARING RIVER CAMPGROUND – JASPER NATIONAL PARK *(Open May 20 to Sept 18 - Varies)*

Information:	(780) 852-6176
Location:	15 Km (9 Miles) E of Jasper, *N 53° 00' 38", W 118° 05' 16"*, 3,300 Ft

66 Sites – This is another campground east of Jasper off Hwy 16. Sites are back-ins and some will take RVs to about 40 feet but access roads are narrow so the practical rig size limit here is about 35 feet. The entrance road is located 10 km (6 miles) east of Jasper and 39 km (24 miles) from the eastern entrance to the park. From the turnoff it's another 5 km (3 miles) on a paved road to the campground entrance.

WHISTLER'S CAMPGROUND – JASPER NATIONAL PARK *(Open May 6 to Oct 9 - Varies)*

Reservations:	(877) RESERVE, www.pccamping.ca
Information:	(780) 852-6176
Location:	2 Km (1 Mile) S of Jasper, *N 52° 51' 03", W 118° 04' 35"*, 3,400 Ft

781 Sites – This is Jasper's largest campground. Sites are arranged off circular drive which are in turn located off a huge one-mile loop drive. Sites are well-separated, some will take 45-footers. Elk often graze in the park, particularly in the sites on the western border. The location is convenient with Jasper just a short drive away. From Jasper drive south on Hwy 93, the campground entrance is on the right in 2 km (1 mile).

WAPATI CAMPGROUND – JASPER NATIONAL PARK *(Open May 20 to 22, June 17 to Sept 4, and Oct 10 to May 6 - Varies)*

Reservations:	(877) 737-3783, www.pccamping.ca
Information:	(780) 852-6176
Location:	3 Km (2 Miles) S of Jasper, *N 52° 51′ 03″, W 118° 04′ 35″*, 3,500 Ft

364 Sites – This is the second largest campground in the park and it too is near Jasper, just a short distance from the huge Whistler's Campground. Note the strange opening schedule, the campground serves as the winter campground for the park and also as a supplement to Whistler's Campground during busy times in the summer. Wapati puts its hookup rigs in a large paved lot that is also used as the winter campground. This lot will take RVs to 45 feet. From Jasper drive south on Hwy 93, the campground entrance is on the left in 3 km (2 miles).

WABASSO CAMPGROUND – JASPER NATIONAL PARK *(Open June 23 to Sept 4 - Varies)*

Reservations:	(877) 737-3783, www.pccamping.ca
Information:	(780) 852-6176
Location:	15 Km (9 Miles) S of Jasper, *N 52° 45′ 48″, W 117° 59′ 17″*, 3,500 Ft

200 Sites – Wabasso is off a paved loop road called Hwy 93A that runs from 6 km (4 miles) south of Jasper on Hwy 93 to the cutoff on Hwy 93 near Athabascan Falls, 19 miles south of Jasper. Some sites will take RVs to 45 feet and longer. The campground is 8.7 km (5.4) miles

RVS PARKING AT THE ICEFIELDS PARKWAY VISITORS CENTRE

from the north end of the loop road, 15 km (9 miles) from the south end. The road is much better in the north, we recommend access from that direction.

MT. KERKESLIN CAMPGROUND – JASPER NATIONAL PARK *(Open June 23 to Sept 4 - Varies)*

Information: (780) 852-6176
Location: 32 Km (20 Miles) S of Jasper, *N 52° 38' 04", W 117° 51' 59"*, 4,000 Ft

42 Sites – This is a smaller self-registration campground away from the Jasper area but convenient to Athabasca Falls. While some sites would take 40 foot RVs the access roads are narrow making the practical limit for this campground about 30 feet. It is 32 km (20 miles) south of Jasper and 65 km (40 miles) north of the Icefield Center.

HONEYMOON LAKE CAMPGROUND – JASPER NATIONAL PARK *(Open June 17 to Sept 4 - Varies)*

Information: (780) 852-6176
Location: 52 Km (32 Miles) S of Jasper, *N 52° 33' 24", W 117° 40' 50"*, 4,600 Ft

35 Sites – This campground is next to Honeymoon Lake, several sites are along the lakeshore. Some sites will take RVs to 35 feet but most are smaller. It is 50 km (31 miles) south of Jasper and 47 km (29 miles) north of Icefield Center.

JONAS CREEK CAMPGROUND – JASPER NATIONAL PARK *(Open June 17 to Sept 4 - Varies)*

Information: (780) 852-6176
Location: 76 Km (47 Miles) S of Jasper, *N 52° 25' 01", W 117° 23' 44"*, 5,200 Ft

25 Sites – Jonas Creek is another small campground just off the road. There are two long pull-thrus only suitable for RVs to about 35 feet due to limited maneuvering room. Other sites are good for RVs to about 30 feet. There are some nice walk-in tent sites on a small ridge a short distance above the campground but your car will be parked at the bottom of the hill. There is also a cooking shelter at the bottom of the campground near the highway. Jonas Creek is located 76 km (47 miles) south of Jasper and 21 km (13 miles) north of Icefield Center.

COLUMBIA ICEFIELD CENTRE – JASPER NATIONAL PARK *(Open April 15 to Oct 15)*

Information: (780) 852-6176
Location: 97 Km (60 Miles) S of Jasper, *N 52° 13' 14", W 117° 13' 44"*, 6,500 Ft

At least 100 Sites – The Icefield Center has a large paved lot which can be used for camping. This is called an overflow camping area but it's kept open all of the time during the season and used for parking by RVs visiting the center. It's available even if the nearby campgrounds (a very limited number, particularly for big rigs) are open. It may seem like boondocking but it's not free and there are vault toilets next to the campground for evening use when the flush toilets at the center are not available. The Icefield Center is about 97 km (60 miles) south of Jasper and 129 km (80 miles) north of Lake Louise.

COLUMBIA ICEFIELD CAMPGROUND – JASPER NATIONAL PARK *(Open June 20 to Sept 10 - Varies)*

Information: (780) 852-6176
Location: 98 Km (61 Miles) S of Jasper, *N 52° 13' 11", W 117° 12' 15"*, 6,600 Ft

32 Sites – This is a campground for tents and vans only. There's really not even room for

most pickup campers. Amenities include cook shelters and a great view across the valley to the west. This campground is just 2 km (1 mile) south of the Icefield Center.

WILCOX CREEK CAMPGROUND – JASPER NATIONAL PARK *(Open June 10 to Nov 9 - Varies)*

Information: (780) 852-6176
Location: 100 Km (62 Miles) S of Jasper, *N 52° 13' 04", W 117° 10' 47"*, 6,700 Ft

46 Sites – Wilcox Creek is set on the side of a mountain. There isn't enough room for back-in sites so everyone gets a pull-thru. Actually you park parallel next to your picnic table and fire pit and there are trees between sites. It's a nice arrangement and allows RVs to 35 feet to use what would otherwise be a cramped campground. Wilcox Creek is located 3 km (2 miles) south of Icefield Centre and 126 km (78 miles) north of Lake Louise.

KAMLOOPS

Kamloops (population 80,000) is so perfectly situated astride so many transportation corridors that it is inevitably an important crossroads and supply center. The town sits at the confluence of the North Thomson, the South Thompson, and the Thompson Rivers. It also is on both the Trans-Canada Highway (and at the northern junction of the Coquihalla) and the route of the Canadian Pacific Railway.

Because this is a large city it has a lot to offer. The central area hosts shopping and restaurants and the **Riverside Park** overlooks the place where the rivers meet. Probably the most interesting offering in Kamloops is the **Secwepemc Museum and Heritage Park**, owned and operated by the local First Nations people. This is an indoor and outdoor museum showing the history and culture of the original inhabitants of the area. Additionally, Kamloops has a mu-

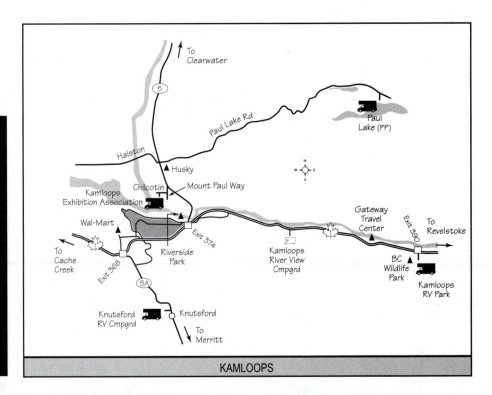

KAMLOOPS

BRITISH COLUMBIA

seum, the **Kamloops Museum**, which relates the region's more recent history. In addition to the museums you can take a ride on the river in the restored **Wanda Sue**, a paddlewheel riverboat, or ride the rails behind a steam engine on the **Kamloops Heritage Railway**. Sixteen km (10 miles) east of Kamloops at Exit 390/391 you'll find the **BC Wildlife Park**, it features native BC wildlife including bears, wolves, mountain lions, and moose in natural-looking areas, it's great for kids.

KNUTSFORD RV PARK *(Open May 15 to Nov 1)*

Res. and Info: (250) 372-5380, (866) 777-1954, knutsfordcamp@hotmail.com
Location: 6 Km (4 Miles) S of Kamloops, *N 50° 37' 01", W 120° 19' 18"*, 2,500 Ft

125 Sites – This is the most convenient commercial campground to Kamloops. It's a neat modern campground that sits in a protected valley on the hillside south of the city. There are good tents sites as well as good back-in RV sites that will take RVs up to 45 feet. The big-box stores including Wal-Mart are just 6 km (4 miles) down the hill. To reach the campground take Exit 368 from Hwy 1. Drive south up the hill for 5 km (3.4 miles), the campground entrance is on the right.

PAUL LAKE PROVINCIAL PARK *(Open May 1 to Oct 30)*

Information: (250) 578-7376
Location: 24 Km (15 Miles) NE of Kamloops, *N 50° 45' 00", W 120° 06' 31"*, 2,700 Ft

90 Sites – Paul Lake is a popular swimming lake for folks from Kamloops. The campground is on the hill about a quarter mile from the lake so it's away from most of the activity. Some sites will take RVs to well over 45 feet. In the off season self-contained units can camp in the day use area for free. There are some good hiking trails at this park. From Highway 1 take Exit 374 and drive north on Hwy 5 toward Clearwater. In 5.2 km (3.2 miles) turn right on Paul Lake Road at a Husky gas station and drive another 18 km (11 miles) to the campground.

KAMLOOPS EXHIBITION ASSOCIATION *(Open April 15 to Oct 15 - Varies)*

Res. and Info.: (250) 314-9645
Location: Kamloops, *N 50° 41' 18", W 120° 19' 43"*, 1,100 Ft

45 Sites – The closest place to camp to the center of town is the Kamloops Exhibition Center, a fairgrounds and horse racing track. You'll probably want to check ahead by telephone to make sure the campsites will be available because major events sometimes preempt or fill the campground. These are long back-in sites suitable for any size rig, some have full hookups. There are also tent sites. The facilities are best described as serviceable but rough, don't expect the standards of a normal RV park. From Highway 1 take Exit 374 and drive north on Hwy 5 toward Clearwater. In 3.2 km (2.0 miles) turn left on Mount Paul Way, in another .3 km (.2 mile) turn right on Chilcotin Road, you'll see the entrance to the fairgrounds on the left in .3 km (.2 mile). As you enter look straight ahead, the small yellow building peeking out from behind the larger building is the office. Check in here during normal business hours. If you're arriving when the office is closed turn left immediately after entering the fairgrounds and follow the road to the campground, someone will come around to collect or you may have to pay when the office opens.

KAMLOOPS RV PARK *(Open All Year - Reduced Facilities)*

Res. and Info.: (250) 573-3789, kamloopsrv@shaw.ca, rv-waterpark.kamloops.com
Location: 16 Km (10 Miles) E of Kamloops, *N 50° 39' 16", W 120° 04' 35"*, 1,100 Ft

110 Sites – This is a handy campground located next to a wildlife park east of Kamloops along Hwy 1. There are tent sites as well as RV sites for RVs to 45 feet. Take Exit 390 from Hwy 1 about 16 km (10 miles) east of Kamloops. The campground is on the south side of the highway.

KOOTENAY NATIONAL PARK AND RADIUM HOT SPRINGS

The Kootenay National Park is essentially a corridor that follows the Banff-Windermere Highway from its crossing of Vermillion Pass down into the Columbia River Valley at Radium Hot Springs. Kootenay is in British Columbia while Banff is in Alberta, the border is the Continental Divide. The distance from the border down to the Radium Hot Springs is 95 km (58 miles). Of course Kootenay is one of a whole complex of connected national parks in the Canadian Rockies and this highway makes a good entry route if you happen to be coming from the right direction.

Most of the attractions in Kootenay lie along the highway. There are three summer campgrounds in the park. These are Marble Canyon, McLeod Meadows, and Redstreak Campground. All are described below. Marble Canyon and McLeod Meadows are accessible from the Banff-Windermere Highway, Redstreak has an entrance from Radium Hot Springs. In winter these campgrounds are closed but there is another parking area known as Dolly Varden with vault toilets that serves as a campground. Dolly Varden is 34 km (21 miles) from Radium Hot Springs and is not described below since it is really not much more than a parking lot.

In addition to the campgrounds there are several good short trails along the highway. These include the Fireweed Trail at Vermillion Pass, Marble Canyon trail (88 km from Radium Hot Springs), the Paint Pots (88 km from Radium Hot Springs), and an interpretive trail at Olive Lake (13 km from Radium Hot Springs). There's also a visitor centre in the park (at Vermillion Crossing, 63 km from Radium).

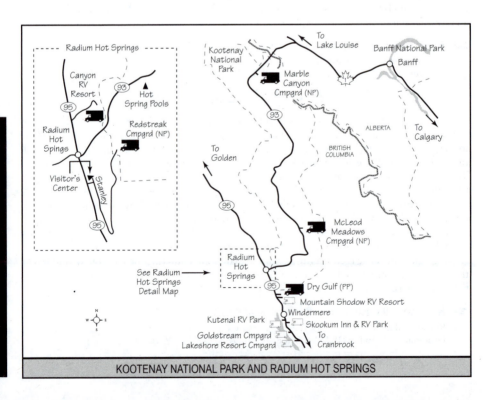

KOOTENAY NATIONAL PARK AND RADIUM HOT SPRINGS

The most popular attraction in the park, however, is actually very near the southern border. This is the Radium Hot Springs pools, a swimming area 3 kilometers from Radium. There are two pools here, a hot pool at 40° C (104° F). There is road access from the main park highway as well as a trail from Redstreak campground.

Radium Hot Springs (population 600) is located just outside the park. It's in the Columbia River Valley, also known as the Rocky Mountain Trench in this area. It is large enough to have restaurants and stores for supplies. One attraction here is a herd of bighorn sheep that often wander the streets of town. Below we list one campground in town and another a few miles to the south. The park's Redstreak Campground is also only accessible from a road that starts in town.

There is a campfire fee in these national park campsites.

MARBLE CANYON CAMPGROUND – KOOTENAY NATIONAL PARK *(Open June 24 to Sept 6 - Varies)*

| **Information:** | (250) 347-9361 |
| **Location:** | 87 Km (54 Miles) E of Radium Hot Springs, *N 51° 11' 06", W 116° 07' 12"*, 4,800 Ft |

60 Sites – This campground is best for tents and smaller rigs. While restrooms do not have showers they do have hot water in the sinks. Sites are arranged off small loops that make maneuvering tough for larger rigs. There is one loop called the big site loop that has a few very long sites but it too is a small-circumference loop limiting access to RVs about 35 feet long. The campground is the easternmost one in Kootenay National Park, it is 16 km (10 miles) from the intersection of Hwy 93 with Hwy 1 in Banff National Park and 87 km (54 miles) from Hwy 95 in Radium Hot Springs.

McLEOD MEADOWS CAMPGROUND – KOOTENAY NATIONAL PARK *(Open May 20 to Sept 6 - Varies)*

| **Information:** | (250) 347-9361 |
| **Location:** | 27 Km (17 Miles) E of Radium Hot Springs, *N 50° 46' 01", W 115° 56' 41"*, 3,600 Ft |

98 Sites – The sites here are back-ins off 10 different loops. Sites and access are suitable for RVs to 45 feet. This campground, like others in this park, has hot water in the restroom sinks. The campground is 77 km (48 miles) from the intersection of Hwy 93 with Hwy 1 in Banff National Park and 27 km (17 miles) from Hwy 95 in Radium Hot Springs.

CANYON RV RESORT *(Open April 15 to Oct 15)*

| **Res. and Info.:** | (250) 347-9564, www.canyonrv.com |
| **Location:** | Radium Hot Springs, *N 50° 37' 43", W 116° 04' 04"*, 2,800 Ft |

88 Sites – This well run and popular commercial campground sits in a canyon just outside Radium Hot Springs. Some sites can take RVs to 45 feet. During the camping season this is a busy place, reservations are recommended, especially for big rigs. At the northern edge of Radium Hot Springs follow the sign east to the campground.

REDSTREAK CAMPGROUND – KOOTENAY NATIONAL PARK *(Open May 6 to Oct 10 - Varies)*

Reservations:	(877) 737-3783, www.pccamping.ca
Information:	(250) 347-9361
Location:	3 Km (2 Miles) SE of Radium Hot Springs, *N 50° 37' 29", W 116° 03' 36"*, 3,300 Ft

242 Sites – This large national park campground is a good place to stay when visiting Radium Hot Springs, a trail leads to the pool from the campground. The hookup sites here are large and will take RVs to 45 feet. The campground is located inside the park but access is on a small road from the town of Radium Hot Springs. From the intersection of Hwy 93 from Banff and Hwy 95 in Radium Hot Springs go south .3 km (.2 miles). Turn left and then right and follow the campground access road for 2.4 km (1.5 miles) to the campground entrance.

 DRY GULCH PROVINCIAL PARK CAMPGROUND *(Open May 1 to Oct 11)*

| **Information:** | (250) 422-3003 |
| **Location:** | 3 Km (2 Miles) S of Radium Hot Springs, *N 50° 35' 13", W 116° 02' 18"*, 3,100 Ft |

26 Sites – Dry Gulch is a small provincial park set on a hillside. Most sites here are suitable for RVs to 30 feet although a couple would take rigs to 40 feet. The campground is located on the east side of Hwy 95 some 4.7 km (2.9 miles) south of the intersection of Highways 93 and 95 in Radium Hot Springs.

NANAIMO

Nanaimo (population 80,000) is the second largest city on Vancouver Island and British Columbia's third oldest incorporated town. The early reason for the town's existence was coal, big deposits close to tidewater were the economic driver. Today coal isn't mined here, there is little evidence that it ever was unless you know where to look. Nanaimo has three **ferry terminals**: north of the central area is Departure Bay with service to Horseshoe Bay on the mainland, south of town is Duke Point with service to Tsawwassen on the mainland, and there is also a

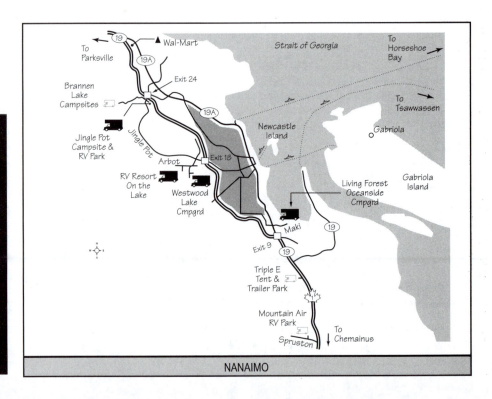

NANAIMO

small ferry to Gabriola Island. Actually, two even smaller ferries serve Newcastle Island Provincial Park and little Protection Island in the harbor.

The charm of Nanaimo is in its **waterfront**. There is a four-kilometer (2.5 mile) walking trail connecting a chain of parks. Look for **Swy-a-lana Lagoon Park** which is a man-made lagoon designed to attract marine life. Nearby is the pedestrian-only ferry out to **Newcastle Island**, a provincial marine park with a 7.5-kilometer (4.7-mile) trail that circles the island. At the southern end of the waterfront trail you are near the center of the city and several interesting sights. The **Bastion** is a blockhouse built by the Hudson's Bay Company in 1853, now it is the site of the Bastion Museum and a daily firing of cannons at noon during the summer. Nearby is the **Nanaimo Museum** with historical displays including a coal mine from the town's early days.

Nanaimo has a huge annual celebration known as the **Marine Festival** during the last half of July. The eagerly anticipated main event is the **World Championship Bathtub Race** between Nanaimo and Vancouver.

⊒ JINGLE POT CAMPSITE AND RV PARK *(Open All Year)*

Rese. and Info.: (250) 758-1614
Location: Nanaimo, *N 49° 12' 13", W 124° 1' 59"*, 300 Ft

120 Sites – This is a beautifully landscaped park with lots of flowers. Sites are terraced on a hillside with plantings between sites. There are pull-thru spaces suitable for RVs to 45 feet for travelers as well as lots of smaller sites. The access to the campground is from Exit 24 of Hwy 19 as it bypasses Nanaimo to the west. Turn southwest and almost immediately you'll see the sign for the campground entrance on your left.

⊒ RV RESORT ON THE LAKE *(Open All Year)*

Res. and Info.: (877) 826-9835, (250) 754-1975, admin@resortonthelake.com,
                www.resortonthelake.com
Location: Nanaimo, *N 49° 09' 53", W 124° 00' 12.5"*, 600 Ft

150 Sites – This is a large popular RV park that slopes down toward Westwood Lake. There's no beach on the lake, instead a walking trail follows the lake shore from a nearby day-use park. Facilities include a large swimming pool and an upscale clubhouse. It's great for big rigs with long back-ins suitable for RVs longer than 45 feet and lots of maneuvering room. The access to the campground is from Exit 18 of Hwy 19 as it bypasses Nanaimo to the west. Head west and in just .5 km (.3 mile) take the left turn marked for the campground. Drive up the hill and at the Y in .6 km (.4 mile) take the right fork. You'll see the campground entrance on the left in another .4 km (.3 mile).

⊒ WESTWOOD LAKE CAMPGROUND *(Open All Year)*

Res. and Info.: (250) 753-3922, westwoodlake@shaw.ca, www.westwoodlakecampgrounds.com
Location: Nanaimo, *N 49° 09' 51", W 123° 59' 46"*, 600 Ft

66 Sites – This is a smaller campground also located near Westwood Lake. The campground is just 100 yards or so down the lake from the day-use park, it's easy to walk over to the swimming beach. This campground has some excellent tent sites as well as RV sites, a few will take RVs to 40 feet. The access to the campground is from Exit 18 of Hwy 19 as it bypasses Nanaimo to the west. Head west and in just .5 km (.3 mile) take the left turn marked for the campground. Drive up the hill and at the Y in .6 km (.4 mile) take the left fork. You'll see the campground entrance on the left in another .3 km (.2 mile).

🚐 LIVING FOREST OCEANSIDE CAMPGROUND *(Open All Year)*

Res. and Info.:   (250) 755-1755, oceanrv@campingbc.com, www.campingbc.com
Location: Nanaimo, *N 49° 07' 49", W 123° 54' 46"*, 100 Ft

242 Sites – This is a large campground located about 5 kilometers (3 miles) south of central Nanaimo overlooking the outlet of the Nanaimo River. It's good if you want to be close to town. We prefer the sites overlooking the harbor. Swimming is on the river below the campground. To reach the campground from the north follow Hwy 19, the Nanaimo Parkway (bypass route) around the west side of town. At the south end of town take Exit 9 and head back toward Nanaimo on Hwy 1. Drive two blocks and turn right on Maki. The campground is just ahead.

NEW HAZELTON AND KITWANGA

The Cassiar Highway leaves the Yellowhead Highway some 481 kilometers (298 miles) west of Prince George and 243 kilometers (151 miles) east of Prince Rupert. It immediately crosses the Skeena River Bridge and in just .2 miles (.3 km) a road goes east to **Gitwangak** which is home to a fine collection of totem poles. If you find these interesting there's another group at **Gitanyow** along a short road from the highway about 21 km (13 miles) to the north.

Two miles north of Gitwangak you'll come to **Kitwanga**. This is the home of the **Kitwanga Fort National Historic Site** (Battle Hill) and has a modern RV park and a very small village campground.

Forty-four km (27 miles) east of the Cassiar Junction is the Hazelton area. There are actual-

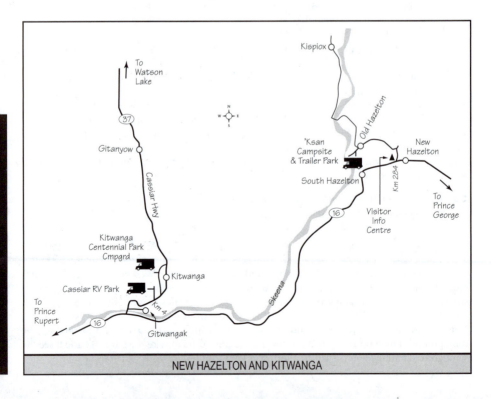

NEW HAZELTON AND KITWANGA

ly three towns called Hazelton. Both New and South Hazelton are along Hwy 16. Between them a road goes north to historic **Old Hazelton** which is the real attraction. Right at the junction there's a visitor info centre that is well worth a stop. Even the 5-mile road in to Old Hazelton is interesting since it crosses a **suspension bridge** across the Bulkley River. Old Hazelton itself is fun to visit mostly for the old buildings, many reconstructed and some still in use. Nearby is very popular **'Ksan Historical Village** which has seven very photogenic communal houses and a campground for RVs and tent campers. A good side trip is to continue north 13 km (8 miles) to **Kispiox** which has more totem poles.

🚐 **'KSAN CAMPSITE AND TRAILER PARK** *(Open May 1 to Oct 15)*

Information:	(250) 842-5940
Location:	Old Hazelton, *N 55° 14' 59", W 127° 40' 40"*, 700 Ft

50 Sites – This campground sits next to the river near historic Old Hazelton and right next to the Ksan Historical Village and Museum. There are small back-in sites without hookups for tenters and small boondocking RVs as well as large pull-thru sites with full hookups arranged in a large grassy field. To reach the campground leave Hwy 16 near Km 284, there is a visitor center with a sani-dump on the corner. Go north on the paved road. You'll cross an impressive suspension bridge at 1.6 km (1 mile), pass through a populated area, continue straight where the main road makes a 90-degree right at 6 km (3.7 miles) and at 7.4 km (4.6 miles) you'll see the campground entrance on your left.

🚐 **CASSIAR RV PARK** *(Open May 15 to Sept 30)*

Res. and Info.:	(250) 849-5799, cassiarrv@navigata.net
Location:	Kitwanga, *N 55° 06' 52", W 128° 02' 01"*, 800 Ft

60 Sites – This campground is the most southerly along the Cassiar Highway and is a popular stop for Alaska travelers. There are tent sites as well as back-in and pull-thru sites to 75 feet. To reach the campground drive west from Km 4 of the Cassiar Highway on Barcalow Road. The campground is on the left in .6 km (.4 mile).

🚐 **KITWANGA CENTENNIAL PARK CAMPGROUND** *(Open As Weather Allows)*

Location:	Kitwanga, *N 55° 07' 44", W 128° 01' 26"*, 700 Ft

11 Sites – This is a simple village-run campground in Kitwanga. Sites are small back-ins to about 25 feet in a grove of trees. The only amenity is an old outhouse. Stays are limited to three days. Easiest access is from Km 4.2 of the Cassiar Highway. Follow Kitwanga Valley Road left for .6 km (.4 mile) to the Tempo service station. The campground is across the street. Campground maintenance contributions are accepted at the service station.

OCEANSIDE

Oceanside is the tourist industry's name for one of the most popular family resort areas in Canada. The region is located on the east coast of Vancouver Island about 23 km (14 miles) northwest of Nanaimo. The two largest towns here are **Parksville** (population 10,000) and **Qualicum Beach** (population 7,000). Both are along the coast. The main north-south highway, Hwy 19, is inland here. A leisurely alternate route, Hwy 19A runs near the water. The beaches here are known for the shallow sandy stretches running far from shore that warm in the sun and make swimming in the ocean possible. In addition to the coast the area is overlooked by Mt. Arrowsmith and there are a number of inland parks that make great destinations. There's lots to do in the area with beaches, boating, and golf the top attractions. You'll also find good day-trip

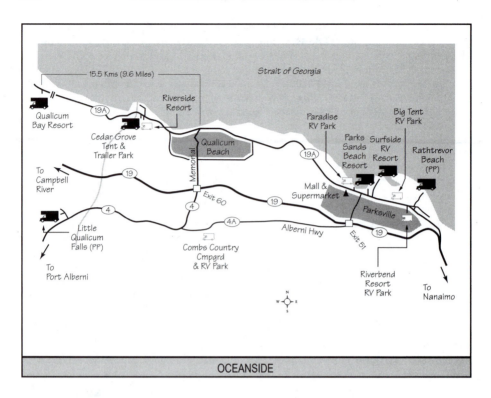

OCEANSIDE

destinations like the caves at Horne Lake Caves Provincial park, Butterfly World and Gardens, and Mt. Arrowsmith hikes.

 LITTLE QUALICUM FALLS PROVINCIAL PARK *(Open April 15 to Oct 15)*

Reservations:	(800) 689-9025, www.discovercamping.ca
Information:	(250) 248-9460
Location:	11 Km (7 miles) West of Qualicum Beach, *N 49° 18' 36", W 124° 32' 49"*, 500 Ft

105 Sites – The attraction at this park is the Little Qualicum River which runs near the campground. There are hiking trails with overlooks of the canyon and falls, also places upstream suitable for swimming. The park is located off the Alberni Highway (Hwy 4) some 9.0 km (5.6 miles) west of the intersection of the highway with Hwy 19, the Inland Island Highway.

QUALICUM BAY RESORT *(Open All Year)*

Res. and Info.:	(250) 757-2003, (800) 663-6899, info@resortbc.com, www.resortbc.com
Location:	13 Km (8 Miles) N of Qualicum Beach, *N 49° 24' 07", W 124° 37' 28"*, Near Sea Level

90 Sites – This is a campground set in trees with campsites around a pond. Swimming is in the pond and there is a hot tub. Sites include pull-thrus to 55 feet as well as partial-hookup sites, no-hookup sites, and tent sites. Zero your odometer at the point where Memorial Avenue in Qualicum Beach meets Highway 19A, the coastal highway. Memorial is the main north/south avenue through Qualicum Beach, it is an extension of the Port Alberni Highway Drive west

along the waterfront for 15.5 km (9.6 miles), the campground is on your left.

CEDAR GROVE TENT AND TRAILER PARK *(Open Easter to Canadian Thanksgiving -
2nd Monday in Oct)*

Res. and Info.:   (250) 752-2442
Location: 5 Km (3 Miles) NW of Qualicum Beach, *N 49° 21' 43", W 124° 29' 02"*, Near Sea Level

111 Sites – This campground is located northwest of Qualicum Beach. Although it's next to
the coastal highway the park is on the side of the road away from the beach. Swimming here is in
the river behind the park. Some back-in spaces will take RVs to 45 feet. Zero your odometer at
the point where Memorial Avenue in Qualicum Beach meets Highway 19A, the coastal highway.
Memorial is the main north/south avenue through Qualicum Beach, it is an extension of the
Port Alberni Highway. Drive west along the waterfront for 6.9 km (4.3 miles), the campground
is on your left.

PARK SANDS BEACH RESORT *(Open All Year)*

Res. and Info.:   (250) 248-3171, (877) 873-1600, www.parksands.com
Location: Parksville, *N 49° 19' 20", W 124° 18' 45"*, Near Sea Level

98 Sites – The Park Sands is a tradition in Parksville, long one of the most popular commercial campgrounds in the area. The campground is adjacent to the beach and within walking
distance of the malls and stores that line the highway along here. There are two sections of the
resort. Near the highway the sites are older with parking on gravel and grass. Farther from the
highway are larger sites with paved parking areas, many suitable for RVs to 40 feet. The campground is open all year but in winter takes self-contained rigs only as the restrooms are closed
up.

SURFSIDE RV RESORT *(Open All Year)*

Res. and Info.:   (250) 248-9713, relax@surfside.bc.ca, www.surfside.bc.ca
Location: Parksville, *N 49° 19' 41", W 124° 18' 2"*, Near Sea Level

230 Sites – The Surfside is an upscale ownership campground with some privately owned
sites put into a pool for rental. There are 230 sites in the park but about 50 are usually in the
rental pool. They're big sites suitable for 45 foot RVs. The campground is located on the beach
and has tennis courts, a pool, and a clubhouse. The campground entrance road, Corfield Street,
is about .6 km (.4 miles) east of the Parks Sands Beach Resort. Follow Corfield for .2 km (.1
mile) to the resort entrance.

RATHTREVOR BEACH PROVINCIAL PARK *(Open All Year)*

Reservations: (800) 689-9025, www.discovercamping.ca
Information: (250) 248-9460
Location: 1 Mile E of Parksville, *N 49° 19' 16", W 124° 16' 03"*, Near Sea Level

200 Sites – This is one of the most popular provincial parks in the system, the attraction
is the wide two-mile-long sandy beach. Twenty-five sites are walk-in tent sites. Many RV sites
are suitable for RVs larger than 45 feet, they are all back-ins. Reservations are required from the
last week of June to Labour Day in September. The campground is open all year long but from
October 16 to March 15 services are limited, there is a reduced fee during this period. The campground is located about 2 km (1 mile) east of Parksville on Highway 19A, the Island Highway.

OKANAGAN VALLEY

Canada's portion of the Okanagan River Valley stretches 200 kilometers (125 miles) north from the U.S. border. The outstanding feature here is probably the weather, the average rainfall is only 9 inches per year because the North Cascades shelter the valley from storms coming from the Pacific.

When you add the valley's water to the weather the Okanagan becomes a perfect playground. Several lakes dominate the valley, the largest by far is Okanagan Lake, it's 170 kilometers (105 miles) long. In summer they're plenty warm enough for swimming and have many very popular beaches. Boating of all kinds is extremely popular.

There are a number of small towns and three good-sized cities in the valley. Most are arranged off Highway 97 which runs up the center.

The most southern part of the region and stretching north to Penticton, is known for its fruit orchards and vineyards. Small towns line the road including **Osoyoos**, **Oliver**, and **Okanagan Falls**. There are also campgrounds along the lakes, not to mention fruit stands along the road and wineries to visit.

Farthest south of the three cities is **Penticton** (population 33,000). The town sits between two lakes: to the south is Skaha Lake and to the north is Okanagan Lake. There are excellent beach on both lakes, several RV parks are located on the Skaha Lake shore. Penticton attracts a lot of visitors and has all the facilities they require. You can't miss the **S.S. Sicamous**, an old sternwheeler beached on the shore of Okanagan Lake, it is now a museum and there are hopes of restoring it to operating condition. The town has an excellent museum covering all aspects of the town's history. The **Okanagan Game Farm** is located about eight kilometers south of town on Highway 97, it has a good selection of animals from around the world. You'll also find no shortage of golf courses, water slides, and vineyards offering tours. Penticton hosts several celebrations including a Peach Festival during the second week of August and the Okanagan Wine Festival in October.

RAFTERS ON THE CANAL AT PENTICTON

From Penticton Highway 97 follows the west side of Okanagan Lake to the north for 58 kilometers (36 miles). There are a number of small towns on this side of the lake, as well as a number of good campgrounds. Connecting the West Side to Kelowna is a long floating bridge similar to the ones used in Seattle.

Kelowna is the province's fourth largest city with a population of about 100,000 people. Like Penticton, Kelowna caters to visitors, there are many attractions devoted to them. Tours of vineyards and fruit-growing and packing operations are very popular, just check with the info centre to see what is available. The city is surprisingly pleasant with a number of excellent lake-side parks offering good beaches and an nice central downtown area. Kelowna hosts the Okanagan Wine Festival during the first week of October.

About 50 kilometers (36 miles) north of Kelowna is the region's third large city, Vernon, with a population in the neighborhood of 35,000. Along the way watch for the signs for **Ellison Provincial Park** about 16 kilometers (10 miles) south of Vernon, it is a fresh-water underwater park for snorkeling and scuba.

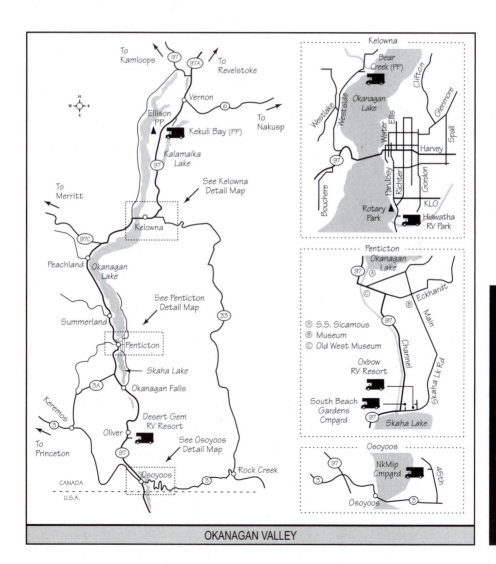

OKANAGAN VALLEY

BRITISH COLUMBIA

Vernon has fewer visitor attractions than the cities farther south. The **O'Keefe Ranch** is located 13 kilometers (8 miles) to the north on Hwy 97 toward Kamloops. It is an early cattle ranch and is open to the public as a non-profit historic site, there is a mansion and several other buildings. Also a restaurant.

NK'MIP CAMPGROUND *(Open All Year)*

Res. and Info.: (250) 495-7279, info@campingosoyoos.com, www.campingosoyoos.com
Location: 3 Km (2 Miles) NE of Osoyoos, *N 49° 02' 18", W 119° 26' 26"*, 900 Ft

320 Sites – This large campground is located on the east side of Osoyoos Lake. The large complex includes a 9-hole golf course, marina, Desert and Heritage Centre visitor center, and a winery. There's an indoor swimming pool a hot tub and a swimming beach. Sites here include tents sites as well as large back-ins to 60 feet. From the intersection in Osoyoos head east on Hwy 3. In 3.5 km (2.2 miles) turn north on 45th Street. You'll arrive at the campground entrance in about 1 km (.6 mile).

DESERT GEM RV RESORT *(Open All Year)*

Res. and Info: (888) 925-9966, (250) 498-5544, info@desertgemrv.com, www.desertgemrv.com
Location: Oliver, *N 49° 10' 21", W 119° 33' 15"*, 1,000 Ft

65 Sites – The Desert Gem is a modern big-rig park located right next to Hwy 97 as it passes through Oliver. All sites are full hookup, there are back-ins and pull-thrus to 60 feet. The park features instant-on phone connections. Watch for the campground at the southern edge of Oliver on the east side of the highway.

OXBOW RV RESORT *(Open March 15 to Oct 15)*

Res. and Info.: (250) 770-8147, info@oxbowrvresort.com, www.oxbowrvresort.com
Location: Penticton, *N 49° 27' 13", W 119° 35' 38"*, 1,200 Ft

75 Sites – The Oxbow is a small but well-run family park at the southern edge of Penticton. It's our favorite place to stay in the area. Skaha beach park is just across the road. Sites are back-ins to 35 feet, there is one long pull-thru. Traveling northbound on Hwy 97 continue strait onto Skaha Lake Road at the point where Hwy 97 turns inland to run along the channel. In .3 km (.2 mile) turn left into Skaha Place and then left again into the campground entrance.

SOUTH BEACH GARDENS CAMPGROUND *(Open May 1 to Sept 30)*

Res. and Info.: (250) 492-0628
Location: Penticton, *N 49° 27' 12", W 119° 35' 41"*, 1,200 Ft

270 Sites – This is a large holiday campground located right next to the Oxbow RV Resort. This one can be a little crazy when summer holidays are in full swing. There are tent sites as well as back-in and pull-thru RV sites to 48 feet. Traveling northbound on Hwy 97 continue strait onto Skaha Lake Road at the point where Hwy 97 turns inland to run along the channel. In .2 km (.1 mile) turn left into the campground entrance.

BEAR CREEK PROVINCIAL PARK *(Open March 30 to Oct 15)*

Reservations: (800) 689-9025, www.discovercamping.ca
Information: (250) 766-1835
Location: 6 Miles NW of Kelowna, *N 49° 55' 35", W 119° 30' 41"*, 1,100 Ft

122 Sites – This is a large lakeside provincial park. Sites will take RVs to 40 feet, all are back-ins. There is a swimming beach and a boat launch. To reach the park turn north on Westside Road off Hwy 97 from an intersection just 1.6 km (1 mile) west of the west end of the Okanagan Lake Floating Bridge. Follow Westside 8 km (5 miles) north to the park.

HIAWATHA RV PARK *(Open March 1 to Oct 15)*

Res. and Info.: (888) 784-7275
Location: Kelowna, *N 49° 50' 50", W 119° 29' 12"*, 1,100 Ft

85 Sites – The Hiawatha is one of the more popular campgrounds in Kelowna. It's located near the shore of Okanagan Lake but not on it. There are sites for tenters as well as back-ins and pull-thrus to 40 feet. From an intersection .6 km (.4 mile) east of the east end of the Okanagan Lake Floating Bridge turn south on Pandosy. Follow Pandosy south for 4.2 km (2.6 miles), along the way it will become Lakeshore Rd. The campground entrance is on the left.

KEKULI BAY PROVINCIAL PARK CAMPGROUND *(Open April 1 to Oct 31)*

Reservations: (800) 689-9025, www.discovercamping.ca
Information: (250) 545-8874
Location: 42 Km (26 Miles) N of Kelowna, *N 50° 10' 55", W 119° 20' 24"*, 1,400 Ft

69 Sites – This campground occupies a bench that overlooks the west shore of Kalamalka Lake. There is a boat launch and swimming in the lake. Two yurts are available for rental. Sites are open with no shade, most will take rigs to 45 feet and all are back-ins with gravel surfaces. From Kelowna travel north on Hwy 97 for 42 km (26 miles), the park entrance is on the east side of the highway. This is 10 km (6 miles) south of Vernon.

PORT ALBERNI

Port Alberni (population 18,000) is located at the eastern edge of the long narrow Port Alberni Inlet. That makes the town a west coast port although it's only 35 km (22 miles) from Qualicum Beach on the east coast of Vancouver Island. The main highway to the west coast's Pacific Rim region runs right through Port Alberni and there are good reasons to stop and spend some time.

Port Alberni is the home port for the **MV Lady Rose**. This little ship and another operated by the same company (the MV Frances Barkley) steam down Alberni Inlet and make deliveries to many little towns along the west coast. A day spent riding along is a popular trip. The ships depart from **Alberni Harbor Quay** which has additional attractions including shops, restaurants, and a maritime museum.

Another attraction in Port Alberni is **McLean Mill**. This is a designated national historical site and has an operating steam sawmill. You can get there by steam railroad from central Port Alberni or drive directly to the mill location north of town.

About 5 kilometers (3 miles) beyond Port Alberni watch for the sign for Sproat Lake Provincial Park. In addition to having a great campground, this lake is the home of two huge **Martin Mars flying boats**. They were built during World War II and today are used as water

SWIMMING IN THE SHADOW OF A MARTIN MARS FLYING BOAT AT SPROAT LAKE

bombers for fighting forest fires. If they're not in use you'll see them anchored just offshore from the park, really an unusual sight.

SPROAT LAKE PROVINCIAL PARK *(Open All Year)*

Reservations:	(800) 689-9025, www.discovercamping.ca
Information:	(250) 248-9460
Location:	6 Km (4 Miles) W of Port Alberni, *N 49° 17' 29", W 124° 55' 36"*, 200 Ft

59 Sites – Sproat Lake is a very large lake located just west of Port Alberni. Hwy 4 passes along its north shore. There are two camping areas in the provincial park. One is near the lake at the upper end of a day-use parking area. The second is on the far side of the highway. The lower campground is open all year but with no services available and a reduced fee from October 16 to March 21. The upper campground is open only from April 1 to October 15. The beach is popular for swimming, it also offers great views of two anchored WWII four-engine Martin Mars water bombers. Showers are available in the restroom buildings near the beach. We've seen black bears in this campground. The sites here will take RVs to 45 feet. To reach the campground drive west from Port Alberni on Hwy 4 for 6 km (4 miles). You'll first see the sign for the upper sites on the right, then the lower ones and beach on the left.

LAKESHORE CAMPGROUND AND COTTAGES *(Open All Year)*

Res. and Info.:	(250) 723-2030
Location:	8 Km (5 Miles) W of Port Alberni, *N 49° 17' 25", W 124° 56' 56"*, 200 Ft

36 Sites – This is primarily a family holiday campground with a beach and dock on Sproat Lake. The campground is a long narrow parcel of land leading from the road down to the lake. Most sites are pretty small but a couple will take big rigs with very careful maneuvering. We'd

make a telephone call to check site availability and make a reservation before visiting this camp-ground. The entrance road begins at the entrance to the Sproat Lake Provincial Park lakeside campground some 6 km (4 miles) east of Port Alberni. From there turn right and follow the road for 1.3 km (.8 miles) to the campground entrance which will be on your left.

▄▄ RIVERSIDE CAMPGROUND *(Open All Year)*

Res. and Info.:   (250) 723-7948, www.arrowvalecottages.com
Location: 2 Km (1 Mile) W of Port Alberni, *N 49° 16' 53", W 124° 51' 58"*, 100 Ft

30 Sites – This campground is in a country setting west of Port Alberni. This is a small farm with berry preserves and pies available for purchase. There are goats for the kids and swimming in the river below the campground. Parking is on grass, sites will take rigs to 45 feet. A few are pull-thrus. From Port Alberni head west on Hwy 4. Zero your odometer as you cross the Somass River bridge on the outskirts of town. In 3.4 km (2.1 miles) you'll see the campground sign pointing right. Turn here. In another .3 km (.2 mile) turn right following the campground sign. In another 1.6 km (1 mile) you'll come to a stop sign at a highway. The campground entrance is straight ahead across the highway.

▄▄ TIMBERLODGE AND RV CAMPGROUND *(Open All Year)*

Reservations: (800) 455-4496
Information: (250) 723-9415
Location: Port Alberni, *N 49° 15' 51", W 124° 45' 15"*, 400 Ft

25 Sites – This motel with a campground behind it is right on the main highway entering Port Alberni from the east, it's hard to miss. There are 25 back-in sites with full hookups. Some

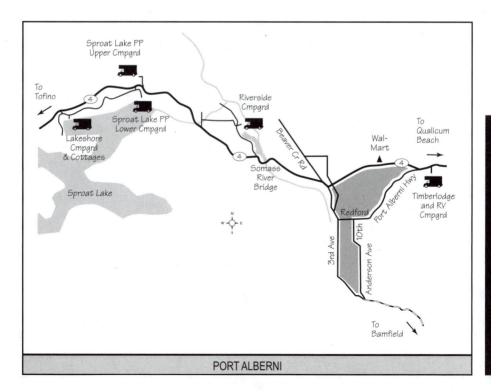

PORT ALBERNI

will take RVs to 45 and access is easy. Additional amenities include an indoor pool (open only in summer, however), a hot tub, and a restaurant.

PORT HARDY

Port Hardy (population 5,000) is the largest town at the north end of Vancouver Island. It's located at the end of the island's north-south Hwy 19. From Port Hardy the province operates ferries that travel even farther north, as far as Prince Rupert. As the commercial center of the northern island Port Hardy is the best place to pick up supplies. The town offers restaurants, gas stations, and shops with all the necessities.

QUATSE RIVER REGIONAL PARK & CAMPGROUND *(Open All Year)*

Res. and Info.: (250) 949-2395, (866) 949-2395, quatse@island.net, www.quatsecampground.com
Location: 3 Km (2 Miles) S of Port Hardy, *N 50° 41' 24", W 127° 29' 11"*, Near Sea Level

62 Sites – This campground is adjacent to the local fish hatchery and proceeds from the park help support the hatchery. Sites are wilderness-type with lots of trees and pretty good separation, many have hookups. The Quatse River runs next to the campground and many sites face it across the access loop road. Sites are back-ins and vary a great deal in size. A couple will take RVs to 40 feet but most are suitable for rigs to 30 or 25 feet. This is a good car-camping campground as some sites have grass and cars can park next to the tents. Restrooms are in the office building and are modern with flush toilets and showers. A nature trail runs through the campground and makes good walking in both directions. To reach the campground take the Coal Harbor Road to the south from a point 1.3 km (.8 miles) west (in the direction of Port Hardy) of the ferry access road. In just 1.0 km (.6 mile) turn left on Byng Road, the campground will be on your left in another .2 km (.1 mile).

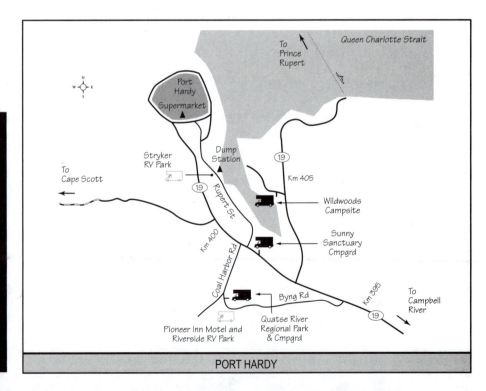

BRITISH COLUMBIA

SUNNY SANCTUARY CAMPGROUND *(Open All Year)*
Res. and Info.:   (250) 949-8111, sunnycam@island.net, www.island.net/~sunnycam
Location: 2 Km (1 Mile) SE of Port Hardy, *N 50° 41' 52", W 127° 28' 41"*, Near Sea Level

65 Sites – Sunny Sanctuary is a large campground with open unshaded sites, a pleasant campground good for rigs of any size. There's also good facilities for tent campers here with a grassy area to pitch tents and a room for cooking and washing dishes. This campground has the longest list of amenities in the Port Hardy area including Wi-Fi, TV hookups at some sites, large sites, a cooking area for tenters, mini-golf, and access to the community nature trail which also runs through this campground. This campground has dozens of rabbits hopping around the campground, some people like them and some don't. From the intersection of Hwy 19 and the ferry access road continue .8 km (.5 miles) toward Port Hardy, the campground entrance is on the north side of the highway.

WILDWOODS CAMPSITE *(Open May 1 to Oct 15 - Varies)*
Res. and Info.:   (250) 949-6753
Location: 5 Km (3 Miles) SE of Port Hardy, *N 50° 42' 30", W 127° 28 23"*, Near Sea Level

45 Sites – Wildwood is an older campground set in trees on uneven ground. There is limited maneuvering room and while a few sites will take RVs to 35 feet it's a challenging campground if you're over 30 feet long. The campground is off the ferry access road, 1.9 km (1.2 miles) from the junction with Hwy 19.

PORT McNEILL AND TELEGRAPH COVE

As you drive toward the north end of Vancouver Island from Campbell River there is a long stretch which is inland. Then, 185 km (115 miles) from Campbell River you reach the coast again. The main town here is Port McNeill, for travelers Telegraph Cover is also a popular destination.

Port McNeill (population 3,000) is the second largest town on the north shore of Vancouver Island, only Port Hardy is larger. This is a logging and fishing town, it offers stores, restaurants and service stations. The town is also the ferry terminal for trips to Alert Bay and Sointula. For visitors the town offers the **North Island Discovery Center** which is a logging museum. Port McNeill is also a good place to take marine tours to see orcas, there are lots of them in local waters of Johnstone Strait and Blackfish Sound.

Cluxewe Resort and Alder Bay Resort, the first two campgrounds listed below, are both oceanside campgrounds located respectively west and east of Port McNeill.

Telegraph Cove (population 6) is much smaller than Port McNeill but seem to get almost as many visitors. This is really a privately owned community dedicated to tourism. It's extremely photogenic, a dockside community clustered around a small rocky cove. Most people visit for the whale watching, fishing and kayaking. There are also restaurants, shops, a marina, and a campground. See the Telegraph Cove Resorts campground description below for information on how to get to Telegraph Cove and the campground.

CLUXEWE RESORT *(Open All Year)*
Res. and Info.:   (250) 949-0378, (250) 949-7030, relax@cluxewe.com, www.cluxewe.com
Location: 10 Km (6 Miles) W of Port McNeill, *N 50° 36' 45", W 127° 10' 21"*, Near Sea Level

127 Sites – A waterfront campground with sites in two areas. Some are in the main yard, mostly back from the water with no views. Others are on a spit of land to the west. May of these

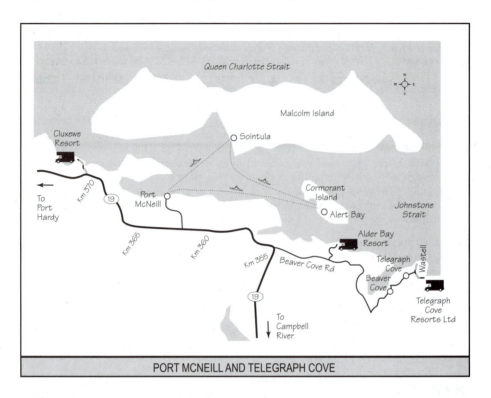

PORT MCNEILL AND TELEGRAPH COVE

sites have either ocean views or lagoon views of the estuary behind the spit. Some sites in this campground will take RVs to 45 feet. The campground is located west of Port McNeill, the .8 km (.5 mile) gravel access road goes north 8.9 km (5.5 miles) east of the Port McNeill cutoff.

ALDER BAY RESORT *(Open May 5 to Sept 30)*

Res. and Info.: (250) 956-4117, (888) 956-4117, abresort@island.net, www.Alderbayresort.com
Location: 15 Km (9 Miles) E of Port McNeill, *N 50° 33' 34", W 126° 54' 42", Near Sea Level*

95 Sites – This large sea-side resort offers great views across to Alert Bay. There's a marina and boat ramp here so it's a popular place for fishermen. It's a wide open campsite with no trees so you can take full advantage of the sun if it happens to be out when you visit. Some sites will take RVs to 45 feet. The campground is on the Telegraph Cove Road 4.2 km (2.6 miles) from its intersection with Hwy 19. You don't have to drive any gravel to get here.

TELEGRAPH COVE RESORTS LTD. *(Open May 1 to Canadian Thanksgiving - 2nd Monday in Oct - Varies)*

Res. and Info.: (250) 928-3131, (800) 200-4665, tcrltd@island.net, www.telegraphcoveresort.com
Location: 23 Km (14 Miles) E of Port McNeill, *N 50° 32' 24", W 126° 49 36", Near Sea Level*

125 Sites – The campground here is well away from the cove, it's a .6 km (.4 mile) walk or drive up the hill on a gravel road. The campground is set in trees in a small valley with no views. Some sites will take RVs to 45 feet, they are back-in sites. Another campground is set much closer to the lagoon, but these sites are now being sold as private campsites. The access road to Telegraph Cove when we last visited was long 14.8 km (9.2 miles), partially gravel, and convoluted. It involved driving through an active log-sorting yard. A new paved road is being

completed that will bypass the yard and give better access to the resort. The Telegraph Cove road leaves Hwy 19 near Km 355 which is 6.9 km (4.3 miles) east of the cutoff to Port McNeill. When you arrive at Telegraph Cove you must register for camping at the office at the cove. There is no area set aside for parking while you do this and there are no instruction signs. Don't pull into the pay parking lot with your rig as we saw several people do, it is very congested.

PRINCE GEORGE

Prince George (population 75,000) is by far the largest city of northern British Columbia. It's the commercial hub of the northern province and is large enough that it offers almost anything you could want in the way of supplies or services including a variety of big-box stores. For travelers Prince George is the last large city on the way north.

Visitor attractions in Prince George are limited but there are a few. For outdoor lovers there's **Forests of the World** on the University of British Columbia campus with several kilometers of nature trails featuring labels on local plants. Another walking area is **Cottonwood Island Nature Park**. The city has two good museums, the **Prince George Railway and Forest Industry Museum** and **Exploration Place**. Prince George is surrounded by pulp mills. One of them, **Canfor**, has good tours.

BLUE SPRUCE RV PARK AND CAMPGROUND *(Open April 1 to Oct 15)*

Res. and Info.: (250) 964-7272, bluesprucervpark@shaw.ca
Location: 4 Miles SE of Prince George, *N 53° 51' 33", W 122° 49 17"*, 2,300 Ft

28 Sites – The Blue Spruce is a great place to stop for the night if you're headed westward

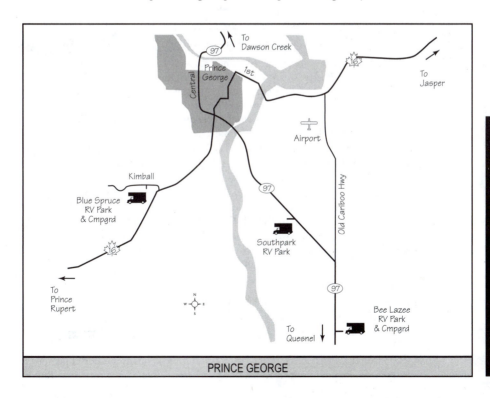

PRINCE GEORGE

toward Prince Rupert or if you just want to have a convenient place to stay while visiting Prince George. This campground has a swimming pool and mini golf. Sites include spaces for tents as well as pull-thrus to 70 feet. The campground is located southwest of Prince George on the highway toward Prince Rupert. If you zero your odometer at the junction of Hwy 16 with Hwy 97 and head south on Hwy 16 you'll see the sign for the campground in 6.1 km (3.8 miles). Turn right and you'll reach the campground entrance in just a short distance.

⛟ SOUTHPARK RV PARK *(Open All Year)*

Res. and Info.:   (250) 963-7577, (877) 963-7275, mail@southparkrv.com, www.southparkrv.com
Location: 8 Km (5 Miles) S of Prince George, *N 53° 50' 33", W 122° 41' 40"*, 2,200 Ft

53 Sites – Southpark is located at the southern approaches to Prince George. The campground can take tent campers and large rigs, there are pull-thrus to 100 feet. Also, this is a year-round campground. It's located right off Hwy 97 some 8 km (5 miles) south of town.

⛟ BEE LAZEE RV PARK AND CAMPGROUND *(Open May 1 to Sept 30)*

Res. and Info.:   (250) 963-7263, (866) 963-7263, drone@pgonline.com
Location: 15 Km (9 Miles) S of Prince George, *N 53° 46' 54", W 122° 39' 22"*, 2,200 Ft

40 Sites – The Bee Lazee is a good park for both tent campers and big rigs, as long as being near town isn't important. The campground also has honey bees, hence the name. There is a seasonal swimming pool and good facilities including a coin RV wash. The campground is right next to the highway and has tent sites and pull-thrus to 60 feet. This park is located on the east side of Hwy 97 some 15 km (9 miles) south of Prince George.

PRINCE RUPERT

The northwest British Columbian city of Prince Rupert (population 15,000) is the real gateway to Southeast Alaska. Prince Rupert is at the end of a good paved road and is much closer to Alaska than Bellingham, the most southerly port for the state ferries. Even Alaskans living in Southeast use the city as a gateway, many think it well worth the effort to drive 900 or so miles (1,450 km) through Canada to access the Lower 48. Incidentally, you can't get to Prince Rupert on the ferry from Bellingham, that boat doesn't stop here.

Prince Rupert is a very clean and well-organized little town with full services. It is the western terminus for one of Canada's few rail lines to the Pacific Ocean and dates from the early 1900s. Today the town continues to be an important port.

Probably the most interesting area of Prince Rupert for visitors is **Cow Bay**. This small waterfront area has historical buildings now housing restaurants, pubs, and gift shops. Also interesting is the **Museum of Northern British Columbia** at First and McBride overlooking the water. Other sights include the **Kwinitsa Railway Museum**, and our favorite, the **North Pacific Historic Fishing Village** in nearby Port Edward with displays about the salmon canning industry that was the lifeblood of this region for many years.

⛟ PARK AVENUE CAMPGROUND *(Open All Year)*

Res. and Info.:   (800) 624-5861, (250) 624-5861, campgrd@citytel.net
Location: Prince Rupert, *N 54° 17' 58", W 130° 20' 28"*, 100 Ft

120 Sites – This is a popular place to stay for folks waiting to board the ferries just down the road. There are tent sites and back-in RV sites to to 45 feet. When you enter Prince Rupert

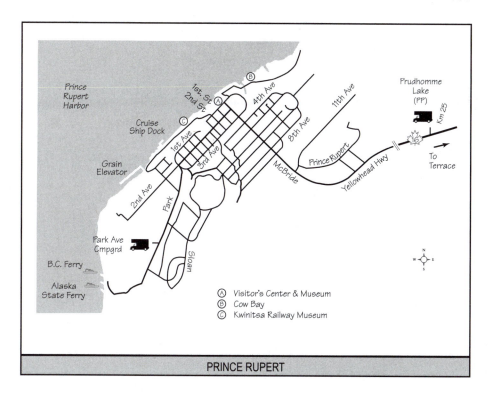

PRINCE RUPERT

just follow signs to the ferry docks. You'll find yourself on a wide highway called Park Avenue. The campground sign is on the right.

PRUDHOMME LAKE PROVINCIAL PARK *(Open May 15 to Sept 15)*

Information:	(250) 638-8490
Location:	20 Km (12 Miles) E of Prince Rupert, *N 54° 14' 27", W 130° 08' 05",* 200 Ft

24 Sites – This provincial campground has sites for tents and RVs to about 30 feet. It's right off Hwy 16 about 20 Km (12 Miles) east of Prince Rupert.

QUESNEL

Quesnel (population 10,000) is a pleasant little town on the banks of the Fraser River. Since there are campgrounds near the center it's a fun place to spend the night. The **Quesnel Museum**, right next to the visitor center, is probably the best in the Cariboo. Quesnel was originally a Hudson's Bay trading post, the site is in the park along the river. The town has a great **riverfront trail**. Pinnacle Provincial Park, just a few kilometers west of town has some great hoodoos. The big celebration in Quesnel is **Billy Barker Days**, held the third weekend in July.

FRASER BRIDGE INN AND CAMPSITE *(Open All Year)*

Reservations:	(800) 670-3366
Information:	(250) 992-5860, www.fraserbridgeinn.com
Location:	Quesnel, *N 52° 58' 31", W 122° 30' 11",* 1,500 Ft

10 Sites – This is a campground and motel very near the center of Quesnel. It's just across

BRITISH COLUMBIA

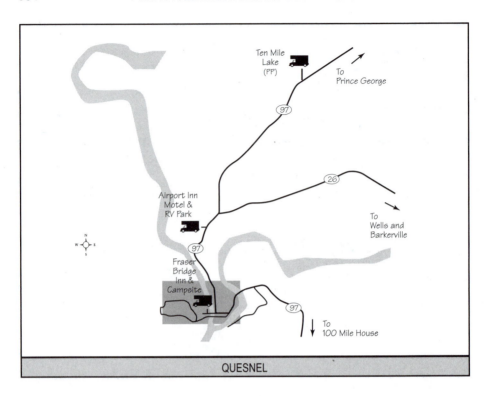

the Fraser River from the center of town. On Carson Avenue in Quesnel near the info centre follow signs for West Quesnel. They'll take you across the river, the motel is on your right just after the bridge.

AIRPORT INN MOTEL AND RV PARK *(Open All Year)*

Res. and Info.:   (250) 992-5942
Location: 2 Km (1 Mile) N of Quesnel, *N 53° 00' 31", W 122° 30' 23",* 1,600 Ft

54 Sites – The Airport Inn is located just north of Quesnel and has long pull-thrus to 70 feet. Watch for it on the west side of Hwy 97 about 1.6 km (1 mile) north of town and .8 km (.5 mile) south of the junction for Hwy 26 going east to Wells and Barkerville.

TEN MILE LAKE PROVINCIAL PARK *(Open May 15 to Sept 30)*

Reservations: (800) 689-9025, www.discovercamping.ca
Information: (250) 397-2523
Location: 10 Km (6 Miles) N of Quesnel, *N 53° 04' 04", W 122° 26' 35",* 2,400 Ft

144 Sites – Ten Mile Lake Provincial Park has two campgrounds: Lakeside and Touring. Some sites are pull-thrus, sites reach 50 feet. The Lakeside campground offers reservations, flush toilets, and coin-operated showers. The campground entrance is on the west side of Highway 97 some 10 km (6 miles) north of Quesnel.

REVELSTOKE

You'll probably be surprised at what this little town (population 6,500) on the Columbia

British Columbia

River has to offer. The historic downtown area is well preserved and pleasant with restaurants, shops and even frequent evening entertainment in **Grizzly Plaza**. The town has the excellent **Revelstoke Railway Museum** as well as a local historical museum called the **Revelstoke Museum**.

As you might expect of a town in such a spectacular mountainous location, several of the best attractions are in the surrounding area. **Mount Revelstoke National Park** is right outside town. You can drive the Meadows in the Sky Parkway which climbs steeply for 26 kilometers and about 1,100 meters. Near the end of the road there's a parking lot and a shuttle bus will carry you another kilometer to the top for spectacular views. Because the road is steep with switchbacks trailers are not permitted. There is a small parking lot where you can leave your trailer near the entrance at the bottom.

There are two dams on the Columbia River above Revelstoke. The nearest to Revelstoke is called **Revelstoke Dam**. It is located 8 kilometers (5 miles) north of town on Highway 23 and has a good self-guided tour of the facility including a trip to the top of the dam for the view.

If you are heading west on Highway 1 in the direction of the Shuswap through Eagle Valley you might want to keep an eye open for a few roadside attractions that have been developed with travelers in mind. One of these is **Craigellachie** where the last spike of the transcontinental rail line was driven. This is really just a rest stop with plenty of parking and restrooms as well as a display. There are also a bevy of commercial attractions including **Crazy Creek Waterfall**, **Beardale Castle Miniatureland**, **Enchanted Forest**, and the **Three Valley Gap Chateau and Heritage Ghost Town**.

CANADA WEST CAMPGROUND *(Open May 1 to Oct 4 - Varies)*

Res. and Info.: (250) 837-4420, canadawest@revelstoke.com, www.canadawest.revelstoke.com
Location: 3 Km (2 Miles) W of Revelstoke, *N 50° 59' 29", W 118° 15' 46"*, 1,700 Ft

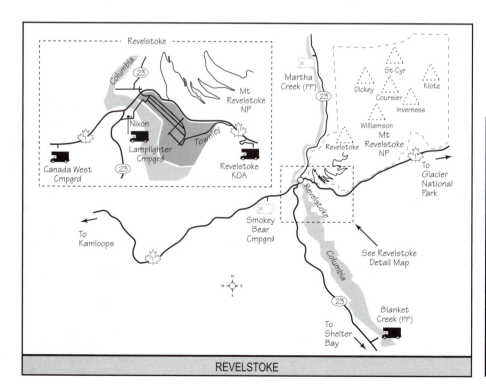

BRITISH COLUMBIA

100 Sites – This is an older campground that has been spruced up. Sites have older electrical hookups mounted in boxes between the sites. Parking is on grass with site long enough for 40 foot RVs but leveling is difficult for them. There is a swimming pool. Access is easy, the campground is on the south side of Hwy 1 some 3 km (2 miles) west of Revelstoke.

⛟ BLANKET CREEK PROVINCIAL PARK *(Open May 1 to Oct 15 - Varies)*

Reservations: (800) 689-9025, www.discovercamping.ca
Information: (250) 837-5734
Location: 24 Km (15 Miles) S of Revelstoke, *N 50° 49' 59", W 118° 04' 59"*, 1,400 Ft

63 Sites – This provincial park campground is set in a former farm next to the Arrow Lake Reservoir on the Columbia River. There is a large circular lagoon for swimming which is rimmed with a sandy beach. Most sites are suitable for RVs to 30 feet but a few will take 40 footers. To reach the campground drive south from Revelstoke on Hwy 23. Hwy 23 leaves Hwy 1 just west of the bridge over the Columbia just west of Revelstoke. It's 23.7 km (14.7 miles) to the campground entrance from the intersection.

⛟ LAMPLIGHTER CAMPGROUND *(Open April 15 to Oct 15 - Varies)*

Res. and Info.: (250) 837-3385, lampcamp@telus.net, www.revelstokecc.bc.ca/lamplighter
Location: Revelstoke, *N 51° 00' 04", W 118° 13' 07"*, 1,400 Ft

50 Sites – This is one of those campgrounds that makes us want to spend a few extra days. It's neat and tidy, has a convenient location within a short hike or bus ride of the center of town, and is a pleasant place to stay. Parking here is on grass with good tent sites as well as RV sites suitable for RVs to 45 feet. Easiest access is from Hwy 23 on the west side of the river. From the intersection of Hwy 1 and Hwy 23 drive south .3 km (.2 mile). Turn east on Nixon Road, in .3 km (.2 mile) you'll see the campground on the left.

⛟ REVELSTOKE KOA *(Open May 1 to Sept 30 - Varies)*

Reservations: (800) 562-8506, www.koa.com
Information: (250) 837-2085, revelstoke.koa@revelstoke.net, www.revelstokekoa.com
Location: 5 Km (3 Miles) E of Revelstoke, *N 50° 59' 29", W 118° 09' 14"*, 1,700 Ft

170 Sites – This is a very nice KOA located outside town along the highway to the east. Sites will take rigs to 45 feet. Swimming is in a pool. To reach the campground drive 5 km (3 miles) east from the main Revelstoke central exit, the campground is on the south side of the highway.

SOUTH CARIBOO REGION

This region is a large area stretching all the way from Cache Creek in the south to Lac La Hache in the north, a distance of about 160 km (100 miles). It's a high plateau region with hot dry summers and cold winters.

Highway 97 runs the length of this region. You'll notice that small towns along the way have names like 70 Mile House and 100 Mile House. That's because this was the access route to the Cariboo gold fields (see *Barkerville and Wells* in this section) and the mileages in the name reflect their distance from Lillooet.

Cache Creek (population 1,100) sits at the junction of Hwy 1, the Trans-Canada Highway, and Hwy 97. Cache Creek has grocery stores, restaurants, gas, a campground, and a dump station at the visitor centre. The **Hat Creek Ranch** is located about 11 kilometers north of Cache Creek and just west of Hwy 97 on Hwy 99. This historic ranch features a roadhouse and native

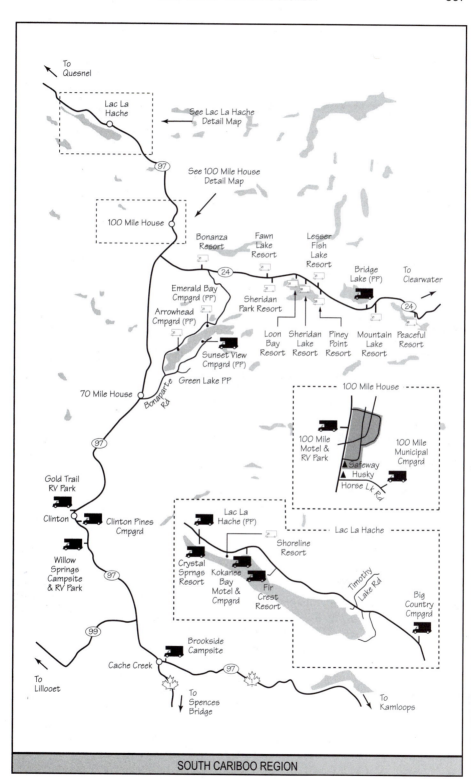

To Quesnel

Lac La Hache

See Lac La Hache Detail Map

97

See 100 Mile House Detail Map

100 Mile House

Bonanza Resort

Fawn Lake Resort

Lesser Fish Lake Resort

24

Bridge Lake (PP)

To Clearwater

Emerald Bay Cmpgrd (PP)

Sheridan Park Resort

Arrowhead Cmpgrd (PP)

24

Loon Bay Resort

Sheridan Lake Resort

Piney Point Resort

Mountain Lake Resort

Peaceful Resort

Sunset View Cmpgrd (PP)

Green Lake PP

70 Mile House

Bonaparte Rd

100 Mile House

100 Mile Motel & RV Park

Safeway
Husky

Horse Lk Rd

100 Mile Municipal Cmpgrd

Gold Trail RV Park

Clinton

Clinton Pines Cmpgrd

Lac La Hache (PP)

Shoreline Resort

Lac La Hache

97

Willow Springs Campsite & RV Park

Crystal Sprngs Resort

Kokanee Bay Motel & Cmpgrd

Fir Crest Resort

Timothy Lake Rd

Big Country Cmpgrd

99

Brookside Campsite

Cache Creek

97

To Lillooet

To Spences Bridge

To Kamloops

SOUTH CARIBOO REGION

village as well as a restaurant and gift shop. Cache Creek celebrates Grafitti Days with a Car Mania automobile rally in June.

Clinton (population 1,000) is not far north of Cache Creek, only 39 km (24 miles). Like Cache Creek Clinton offers stores, restaurants, and gas. Clinton has two campgrounds in town and another a few miles to the south. The town hosts a rodeo in May and the Clinton Jamboree in September.

100 Mile House (population 2,000) is the largest town along this section of highway. It has large supermarkets, services, restaurants, and fuel. We list two campgrounds in 100 Mile House.

The community of **Lac La Hache** (population 400) stretches about 18 km (11 miles) along the east shore of Lac La Hache. It's widely known as the longest town in the Cariboo but, truthfully, there are long distances between structures in this "town". Lac La Hache is good for boating and water sports. We list 5 campgrounds in the area and 3 of them are on the shore of the lake.

Near 100 Mile House Highway 24 branches off and heads east. This highway crosses an area of many lakes, a lot of them have lodges and campgrounds for fishermen. The nickname for this highway is the "Rainbow Road", it's known for the rainbow trout that inhabit many of the lakes. A lot of the lakes were stocked with trout in the 1940s and today the fish are thick. Bridge Lake Provincial Park, one of the campgrounds listed below, is along this highway and make a good fishing base.

BROOKSIDE CAMPSITE *(Open April 1 to Oct 31)*

Res. and Info.:   (250) 457-6633, brooksidecampsite@hotmail.com
Location: Cache Creek, *N 50° 48' 35", W 121° 18' 24"*, 1,600 Ft

97 Sites – A very good campground located just outside Cache Creek on Hwy 97 toward Kamloops. Amenities include pull-thrus suitable for RVs to 45 feet and a swimming pool.

WILLOW SPRINGS CAMPSITE AND RV PARK *(Open April 1 to Oct 31 - Varies)*

Res. and Info.:   (250) 459-2744
Location: 6 Km (4 Miles) S of Clinton, *N 51° 01' 56", W 121° 33' 01"*, 3,000 Ft

45 Sites – This is one of the prettier campsite you'll see along the highway with sites on grass sloping down to a small lake. Pull-thru sites will take RVs to 45 feet. Highway noise can be a problem here. It's located on the west side of Hwy 97 about 31 km (19 miles) north of Cache Creek and 6 km (4 miles) south of Clinton.

CLINTON PINES CAMPGROUND *(Open All Year)*

Res. and Info.:   (250) 459-0030, clintonpines@telus.net, www.clintonpines.com
Location: Clinton, *N 51° 05' 01", W 121° 35' 23"*, 3,000 Ft

16 Sites – This is a well-run newer family campground set in a landscaped former gravel pit. Sites include full-hookup pull-thrus for RVs to 45 feet. It is being gradually expanded each year. The campground is located on the southern border of Clinton on the east side of Hwy 97.

GOLD TRAIL RV PARK *(Open April 1 to Oct 31 - Varies)*
Information: (250) 459-2638
Location: Clinton, *N 51° 05' 40", W 121° 34' 53"*, 3,000 Ft

50 Sites – This campground is located in central Clinton giving you walking access to the town's shops and restaurants. It is known for its low rates. Sites are set on a grass lawn and will take RVs to 45 feet.

SUNSET VIEW CAMPGROUND – GREEN LAKE PROVINCIAL PARK *(Open May 15 to Sept 15)*
Reservations: (800) 689-9025, www.discovercamping.ca
Information: (250) 397-2523
Location: 19 Km (12 Miles) E of 70 Mile House, *N 51° 20' 42", W 121° 18' 23"*, 3,500 Ft

54 Sites – This is one of three campgrounds in Green Lake Provincial Park. The campground will take RVs to 45 feet. This is a popular boating and water sports lake and the campground has a boat launch. Sunset View is on the south side of the lake and is easily accessed from a cutoff at 70 Mile House. In 8 km (5 miles) you'll pass an information shelter and dump station and then reach the campground in another 11 km (6.9 miles).

100 MILE MUNICIPAL CAMPGROUND *(Open May 24 to Oct 1 - Varies)*
Information: (250) 395-2434
Location: 100 Mile House, *N 51° 38' 12", W 121° 17' 23"*, 2,000 Ft

11 Sites – This small municipal campground has back-in sites in a pleasant location at the edge of town. It's easily accessible. A few of the formal sites will take RVs to 40 feet and there is an overflow area for larger rigs but some leveling is required in this area. A short trail leads to a small waterfall. In 100 Mile House turn east at the Husky gas station on Horse Lake Road, the campground is on the left in .5 km (.3 mile).

100 MILE MOTEL AND RV PARK *(Open April 15 to Oct 1 - Varies)*
Res. and Info.: (250) 395-2234, (877) 466-6835, hunmotel@bcinternet.net
Location: 100 Mile House, *N 51° 38' 37", W 121° 17' 51"*, 2,000 Ft

48 Sites – This small motel in the town of 100 Mile House is handy for shopping or restaurants. It has pull-thru sites suitable for RVs to 45 feet. Watch for it on the west side of the highway .3 km (.2 mile) north of the Safeway supermarket.

BIG COUNTRY CAMPGROUND *(Open May 1 to Sept 30)*
Res. and Info.: (250) 396-4181
Location: 5 Km (3 Miles) S of Lac La Hache, *N 51° 47' 25", W 121° 24' 22"*, 2,800 Ft

41 Sites – This former KOA is the first Lac La Hache campground you'll reach if you're headed north. It's not on the lake. There are sites to 45 feet and the amenities you would expect in a KOA including a swimming pool. The campground is located 21 km (13 miles) north of 100 Mile House and 5 km (3 miles) south of the south end of Lac La Hache. It's on the east side of the road.

FIR CREST RESORT *(Open April 15 to Oct 15 - Varies)*

Res. and Info.:   (250) 396-7337, fircrestresort@bcinternet.net, fircrestresort.com
Location: Lac La Hache, *N 51° 50' 14", W 121° 33' 58"*, 2,700 Ft

90 Sites – This is one of the best big-rig campgrounds in the area. It has large pull-thru sites suitable for RVs to 45 feet overlooking the lake and good facilities. Swimming is in the lake and there are canoe and bicycle rentals. As you enter Lac La Hache from the south watch for the road to the right to Timothy Lake Resort Area (Timothy Lake Road). Continue straight, in 6.8 km (4.2 miles) turn left at the sign for the resort at Fircrest Road and drive .5 km (.3 mile) to the campground. From the north the right turn onto Fircrest Road is 6.6 km (4.1 mile) from the Lac La Hache Provincial Park entrance.

KOKANEE BAY MOTEL AND CAMPGROUND *(Open May 1 to Oct 15 - Varies)*

Res. and Info.:   (250) 396-7345, info@kokaneebaycariboo.com, www.kokaneebaycariboo.com
Location: Lac La Hache, *N 51° 50' 56", W 121° 35' 08"*, 2,700 Ft

50 Sites – Another shore-side Lac La Hache campground with waterfront sites and a pleasant atmosphere. Parking is on grass, there are large back-in sites suitable for RVs to 45 feet and longer. There's swimming in the lake and there is a boat ramp. As you enter Lac La Hache watch for the road to the right to Timothy Lake Resort Area (Timothy Lake Road). Don't turn, in another 9.4 km (5.8 miles) you'll see the motel and campground on the left. From the north the resort is 4.2 km (2.6 miles) from the Lac La Hache Provincial Park entrance.

CRYSTAL SPRINGS RESORT *(Open May 15 to Oct 15 - Varies)*

Res. and Info.:   (250) 396-4497, (888) 396-4497, crystalsprings@bcinternet.net,
   www.crystalspringsresort.net
Location: Lac La Hache, *N 51° 51' 31", W 121° 38' 26"*, 2,700 Ft

60 Sites – A smaller but very pleasant lakeside resort. Campsites are down the hill from the office building which is on the access road to the waterfront portion of Lac La Hache Provincial Park. Some back-in sites will take RVs to 45 feet. The park next door has a swimming beach and boat ramp. The resort is on the far side of the road from the Lac La Hache Provincial Park campground entrance.

LAC LA HACHE PROVINCIAL PARK *(Open May 15 to Sept 15)*

Reservations: (800) 689-9025, www.discovercamping.ca   **Information:**   (250) 397-2523
Location: Lac La Hache, *N 51° 51' 35", W 121° 38' 23"*, 2,700 Ft

83 Sites – This is a handy provincial park with facilities on two sides of the highway. Campsites are on the east side as is the dump station. There is also a swimming beach, picnic area, and boat ramp alongside the lake to the west. Camping sites will take RVs to 45 feet. The park is located at the north end of the strip of facilities that line the east side of Lac La Hache.

BRIDGE LAKE PROVINCIAL PARK *(Open May 15 to Sept 30)*

Information: (250) 397-2523
Location: 60 Km (37 Miles) E of 100 Mile House, *N 51° 29' 06", W 120° 41' 58"*, 3,700 Ft

13 Sites – This is a small and fairly remote provincial park. It's a handy place to stop if you are traveling the popular Hwy 24 between Hwy 97 and the Clearwater entrance to Wells Gray Provincial Park. The park has a boat ramp and is suitable for RVs to only 35 feet due to limited maneuvering room. It is located 52 km (32 miles) east of the 100 Mile House intersection with Hwy 97 some 8 km (5 miles) south of 100 Mile House.

SHUSWAP

Located north of the Okanagan, the Shuswap region is a popular summer family camping area. From early July to Labor Day the campgrounds are packed with vacationing families. The area is named after **Shuswap Lake** which is shaped a little like a big X. There are a few additional lakes too, most importantly Little Shuswap Lake, Adams Lake, and Mara Lake. The main towns are **Salmon Arm** (population 17,000), a good place for supplies, and **Sicamous** (population 3,000).

Water sports are the main attraction here, including **houseboating**. Sicamous is called the houseboat capital of Canada for good reason. It seems like hundreds of houseboats are cruising the lake during the summer season.

🚐 CHASE LION'S RV PARK *(Open May 1 to Sept 30 - Varies)*
Information: (250) 679-3690
Location: Chase, N 50° 49' 33", W 119° 41' 59", 1,100 Ft

12 Sites – This is a handy little campground if you aren't concerned about extra amenities. It has tent camping in a grassy field, back-in RV sites that will take RVs to 45 feet, full hookups, and restrooms with showers. It sits at the outlet of Little Shuswap Lake and has a boat ramp.

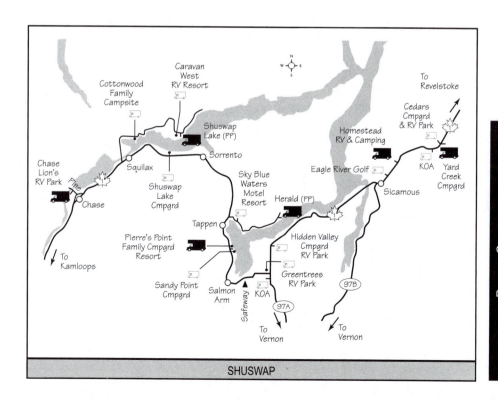

SHUSWAP

We've found this place practically empty when everything in the area is full. From Shuswap Ave. in central Chase turn north on Pine Avenue, the campground is on the left in 1 km (.6 mile), just before the bridge.

SHUSWAP LAKE PROVINCIAL PARK *(Open May 1 to Sept 30 - Varies)*

Reservations:	(800) 689-9025, www.discovercamping.ca
Information:	(250) 955-0861
Location:	26 Km (16 Miles) NE of Chase, *N 50° 54' 37", W 119° 26' 14"*, 1,100 Ft

272 Sites – This is a large and very popular campground in an ideal location on the north shore (more sun than the south shore) of the west arm of Shuswap Lake. While the location is a little remote, the facilities here are supplemented by the Shuswap Lake Camp Store just opposite the entrance which offers telephones, groceries and laundry and also by a restaurant next to the store. Some sites will accept RVs to 45 feet. In the off season it is possible for self-contained rigs to overnight in the day use area parking lot for no fee. The road out to the campground leaves Hwy 1 some 8 km (5 miles) east of Chase. The campground entrance is at 18 km (11.2 miles).

HERALD PROVINCIAL PARK *(Open May 1 to Sept 30 - Varies)*

Reservations:	(800) 689-9025, www.discovercamping.ca
Information:	(250) 955-0861
Location:	11 Km (7 Miles) E of Tappen, *N 50° 47' 14", W 119° 12' 19"*, 1,100 Ft

119 Sites – Like Shuswap Provincial Park, this campground is on the north shore of one of the arms of Shuswap Lake. This time it's Salmon Arm near Tappen. This campground also can take RVs to 45 feet but it's a little less convenient than Shuswap since there is no store at the gate. A short hike will take you to impressive Margaret Falls. There's a boat ramp at the park. To reach the campground leave Hwy 1 just north of Tappen. Follow the road along the north shore of the arm for 10.8 km (6.7 miles) to the entrance.

PIERRE'S POINT FAMILY CAMPGROUND RESORT *(Open May 15 to Sept 30 - Varies)*

Res. and Info.:	(250) 832-9588, pierres@sunwave.net, www.pierrespointcampground.bc.ca
Location:	Between Tappen and Salmon Arm, *N 50° 44' 17", W 119° 19' 02"*, 1,100 Ft

185 Sites – This is a good example of one of the family vacation resorts scattered around the shores of Shuswap Lake. Sites here tend to be small and the rigs really packed in. A few sites can take RVs to 35 feet but most limit campers to 25 or 30 feet. These campgrounds are full of smaller trailers and tents. Although there are many tenters there are no dedicated tent sites, tenters must pay for an electrical and water hookup. There's swimming in the lake, a small store, mini-golf, equipment rentals, and even a simple Thai restaurant. You'll find Pierre's well-signed between Tappen and Salmon Arm.

HOMESTEAD RV AND CAMPING *(Open All Year)*

Res. and Info.:	(250) 836-2583
Location:	5 Km (3 Miles) E of Sicamous, *N 50° 51' 57", W 118° 55' 42"*, 1,100 Ft

60 Sites – This is an older family-run campground on the banks of the Eagle River along Hwy 1 east of Shuswap Lake. All parking is on grass, many sites will take RVs to 45 feet and longer. Swimming is in a pool. Watch for the campground on the north side of the highway about 5 km (3 miles) east of Sicamous.

YARD CREEK CAMPGROUND *(Open May 1 to Sept 30 - Varies)*

Location: 15 Km (9 Miles) E of Sicamous. *N 50° 53' 52", W 118° 48' 45"*, 1,400 Ft

65 Sites – This is a small former provincial park now run by the local government. While some sites would take RVs as long as 45 feet sites are not level and the roads are narrow making maneuvering for large rigs very difficult. The practical length limit at this park is about 30 feet. The campground is on the south side of the Hwy 1 about 15 km (9 miles) east of Sicamous.

SMITHERS

Smithers (population 6,000) is situated on Hwy 16 some 371 km (230 miles) west of Prince George and 348 km (216 miles) east of Prince Rupert. The town is in the Bulkley Valley surrounded by mountains, a very scenic location.

To get out into those mountains you might drive up Kathlyn Glacier Road to a viewpoint overlooking **Twin Falls**. You can hike in to the **Kathlyn Glacier**. Another good nearby hiking destination is the **Babine Mountains Provincial Park** to the northeast of town. Along the way stop at the **Driftwood Canyon Provincial Park**, known for its fossil beds.

RIVERSIDE PARK *(Open May 15 to Oct 15 - Varies)*

Information: (250) 847-1600
Location: Smithers, *N 54° 47' 08", W 127° 08' 55"*, 1,500 Ft

80 Sites – This municipal campground is located below town on the bank of the Bulkey River. There are tent sites as well as back-in RV sites to 45 feet. Several hiking trails leave from

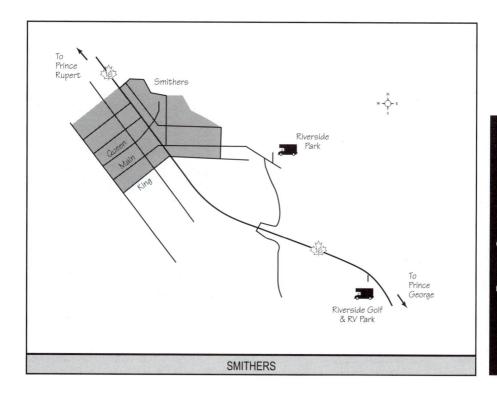

SMITHERS

the park. From central Smithers follow Main Street east to the park.

RIVERSIDE GOLF AND RV PARK *(Open April 15 to Oct 15)*

Res. and Info.:   (250) 847-3229
Location: 3 Km (2 Miles) E of Smithers, *N 54° 46' 01", W 127° 07' 32"*, 1,600 Ft

56 Sites – This campground is located right alongside a golf course. There are tent and back-in sites as well as pull-thrus to 50 feet. Restrooms are in the basement of the reception building. The campground is located on the south side of Hwy 16 about 3 km (2 miles) east of Smithers.

SUNSHINE COAST (LOWER) – GIBSONS, SECHELT, AND THE SOUTH

Access to the Sunshine Coast is a 45-minute ferry ride from Horseshoe Bay across Howe Sound to Langdale. There are frequent ferries from Horseshoe Bay (approximately every two hours) so you don't have to worry much about your schedule there. If you plan to continue on to the upper Sunshine Coast you should check when you buy your ticket to see when the Earls Cove to Saltery Bay ferry runs. Otherwise you might find yourself waiting for quite a long period at the dock in Earls Cove.

When you leave the boat in Langdale you are on the Sunshine Coast proper. Some folks call this area the Lower Coast. Highway 101 runs north near the coast for 79 kilometers (49 miles) through the communities of Gibsons, Roberts Creek, Sechelt, Halfmoon Bay, Madeira Park, and Pender Harbor to Earls Cove.

If you decide that you really love the lower Sunshine Coast you will find plenty of campgrounds along the way. There is a good provincial campground set in a cedar grove called Roberts Creek Provincial Park just 15 kilometers (9 miles) north of the Langdale ferry terminal and another larger one called Porpoise Bay Provincial Park about 23 kilometers (14 miles) north of the terminal. There are also a number of commercial campgrounds.

SUNSHINE COAST FERRY

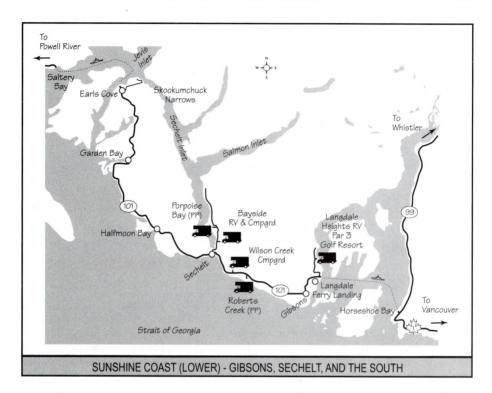

SUNSHINE COAST (LOWER) - GIBSONS, SECHELT, AND THE SOUTH

The **Skookumchuck Rapids** are famous world-wide. These are saltwater rapids, much like a river. In the narrows the salt water rushes both north and south, depending upon the tide. You'll want to be on hand when the tide changes at either high or low water so that you can see the flow change directions. You'll find that the best viewing times are easy to find in local papers, at the information centers, and even posted at the trailhead. To reach the narrows drive 6 kilometers (4 miles) east on Egmont Road from a point on Hwy 101 about 1 kilometer (.6 mile) south of the Earls Cove ferry landing. Park along the road in the parking lot and walk down an access road and then along a fine trail for a distance of 4 kilometers (2.5 miles) to the narrows.

LANGDALE HEIGHTS RV PAR 3 GOLF RESORT *(Open All Year)*

Res. and Info.:   (604) 886 2182, 800 234-7138, langdaleheights@uiserve.com,
                 www.langdaleheights.com
Location: 5 Km (3 Miles) N of Langdale Ferry Landing, *N 49° 27' 33", W 123° 29' 49"*, 400 Ft

54 Sites – This new campground and golf course sit on a hillside overlooking Howe Sound. Back-in sites will take RVs to 45 feet. There is also a grassy tent camping area. The green fee is included in the price of your campsite. From the ferry landing in Langdale head up the hill and in .8 km (.5 mile) take the first right onto the Port Mellon Highway. Take a left at the Y in 3.1 km (1.9 miles), the campground entrance is on the right 3.9 km (2.4 miles) from your turn onto the Port Mellon Highway.

ROBERT'S CREEK PROVINCIAL PARK *(Open May 15 to Sept 15)*

Information: (604) 885-3714, infor@sunshinecoastparks.com
Location: 18 Km (11 Miles) W of Langdale Ferry Landing,
                 N 49° 26' 26", W 123° 40' 17", Near Sea Level

21 Sites – This small provincial park campground has sites that will take any size rig and there is beach access a 1.4 km (.9 mile) hike from the campground. In the off season tent campers may walk in and use the park, there is no fee. The park is located along Hwy 101 some 13 km (8 miles) west of Gibsons and 8 km (5 miles) southeast of Sechelt.

WILSON CREEK CAMPGROUND *(Open All Year)*

Res. and Info.:	(604) 885-5937, (800) 565-9222
Location:	21 Km (13 Miles) W of Langdale Ferry Landing, *N 49° 26' 26", W 123° 42' 30"*, 100 Ft

38 Sites – This is a small commercial campground. It is located right along the highway in the small town of Wilson Creek, there is a small commercial mall next door. The campground has small sites but a few will take RVs to 35 feet. Amenities include a swimming pool. The campground is located 16 km (10 miles) north of Gibsons and 5 km (3 miles) south of Sechelt, 2.9 km (1.8 miles) north of the Robert's Creek Provincial Park.

PORPOISE BAY PROVINCIAL PARK *(Open All Year)*

Reservations	(800) 689-9025, www.discovercamping.ca	**Information:**	(604) 885-3714
Location:	31 Km (19 Miles) NW of Langdale Ferry Landing, *N 49° 30' 24", W 123° 44' 53"*, Near Sea Level		

94 Sites – This large provincial park campground is located east of Sechelt away from the main highway. It sits on Sechelt Inlet and has a swimming beach. Some of the sites here will take RVs to 45 feet. There is also a tent camping area suitable for about 10 tents. The campground gate is open from April 15 to October 15, services are provided, and there is a fee. Off season the family campground gate is closed but you can camp for free at the group site with no services. To reach the campground drive north on Wharf Road in central Sechelt. After just .5 km (.3 miles) turn right on Porpoise Bay Road, the campground is on the left in 3.4 km (2.1 miles).

BAYSIDE RV AND CAMPGROUND *(Open All Year)*

Res. and Info.:	(604) 885-7444
Location:	29 Km (18 Miles) NW of Langdale Ferry Landing, *N 49° 29' 29", W 123° 44' 50"*, 200 Ft

46 Sites – This new campground is built to provide lots of separation between sites, they aren't squeezed into a small area like in most commercial campgrounds. Some sites will take RVs to 45 feet. Despite the name this is not a waterside campground, but it's still a nice place. To reach the campground drive north on Wharf Road in central Sechelt. After just .5 km (.3 miles) turn right on Porpoise Bay Road, the campground is on the right in 1.5 km (.9 miles).

SUNSHINE COAST (UPPER) – POWELL RIVER, LUND AND THE NORTH

Powell River (population 20,000) was a forestry-dependant town for years, in fact it remains a forestry town since it is home to a huge Pacifica Papers pulp mill. Today, however, tourism is also an important force. Powell River occupies an area offering a full range of outdoor attractions including fishing, kayaking, scuba diving, canoeing, hiking, and golf. The town has all the amenities including good shopping for supplies, restaurants and public transit.

Powell River is actually made up of four communities. The farthest south is Westview. This is the first you will see when you arrive from the south, it has the ferry terminal and most of the services. North a few miles but south of the very short river that Powell River is named after is the original town site. It is actually called Townsite and is the site of the pulp mill as well as many residences. To the east of Townsite is a suburb built around Cranberry Lake, and north of the

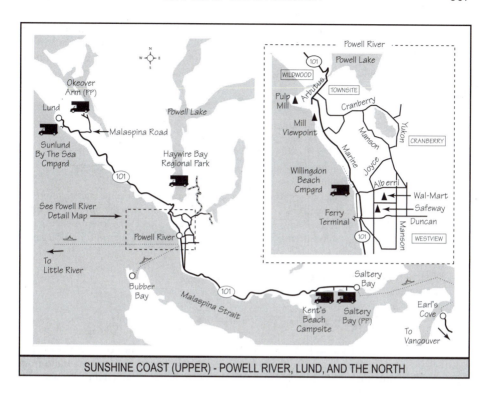

SUNSHINE COAST (UPPER) - POWELL RIVER, LUND, AND THE NORTH

mouth of the Powell River is Wildwood.

While you will probably spend most of your time in Westview, you will find a visit to **Townsite** interesting. It has actually been designated a Heritage Area by the Canadian government. From the Mill Viewpoint you can see the chain of 10 cargo ship hulks that make up the breakwater for the paper mill harbor. Tours of the mill are available during the summer and so are tours of the townsite. Check with the information centre about both.

There are a wide selection of hiking trails available in the Powell River area. Probably the easiest and most accessible is a short trail north from Willingdon Beach Park along the bed of an old beachfront railroad. You'll find signs identifying different trees and also vintage logging equipment on display from the nearby museum. Another interesting trail is the wheelchair accessible trail circling nearby Inland Lake. For a more challenging trail consider the 165-kilometer (102-mile) Sunshine Coast trail from Sarah Point in the north to Saltery Bay.

You should drive the final 30 kilometers (19 miles) along Highway 101 to Lund. This is the northern end of Highway 101 which is said to stretch all the way south to Chile. **Lund** is a jumping-off point for boating the waters to the north. The historic Lund Hotel makes a good place to catch a meal and there's a friendly little RV park in town too.

SALTERY BAY PROVINCIAL PARK *(Open All Year)*

Reservations:	(800) 689-9025, www.discovercamping.ca **Information:** (604) 885-3714
Location:	1.1 Km (.7 Mile) N of Saltery Bay Ferry Landing,
	N 49° 46' 57", W 124° 11' 34", Near Sea Level

42 Sites – This provincial park has two sections. From the south you'll first reach the campground, then there is a day use area with a boat ramp a mile or so north of the campground. The campground is well known for its rocky little cove which is a popular scuba destination with an

underwater statue. It's also a fun place to swim off the rocks and tiny beach. Camping sites are all back-ins, some will take RVs to 45 feet. The campground has services and a fee from May 13 to September 15, off season it is open with no services and there is no fee. The campground is located less than a mile north of the Saltery Bay ferry dock, 26 km (16 miles) south of Powell River.

▣ KENT'S BEACH CAMPSITE *(Open All Year)*

Res. and Info.: (604) 487-9386, kentsbch@prcn.org
Location: 3 Km (2 Miles) N of Saltery Bay Ferry Landing,
N 49° 46' 57", W 124° 12' 56", Near Sea Level

30 sites – This commercial campground has a sea-side location with some sites right on the beach. Others are in an open area back from the water and even more up the hill on gravel in a clearing. Big rigs will have no problems using the upper camping area, the lower areas are also accessible to big rigs with careful driving. The campground is located 3.1 km (1.9 miles) north of the ferry landing, 24 km (15 miles) south of Powell River.

▣ WILLINGDON BEACH CAMPGROUND *(Open All Year)*

Res. and Info.: (604) 485-2242, wbeach@prcn.org, www.willingdonbeach.ca
Location: Powell River, *N 49° 50' 51", W 125° 31' 50",* Near Sea Level

69 Sites – This is the most popular campground in the area. It's located on the beach just north of the ferry terminal. You can walk to some of the Powell River shops and restaurants from here. Sites are fairly small, most are suitable for RVs to about 30 feet although there are a few for RVs to 35 feet near the entry.

▣ HAYWIRE BAY REGIONAL PARK *(Open All Year)*

Information: (604) 483-3231, (604) 483-1097
Location: 6 Km (4 Miles) NE of Powell River, *N 49° 54' 20", W 124° 31' 02",* 300 Ft

41 Sites – This regional campground is located northeast of Powell River on the east shore of Powell Lake. Due to the narrow gravel access roads and small sites it is suitable for RVs to about 30 feet. The route to the campground is signed from Powell River. From the intersection of Alberni Street and Joyce in Powell River head north on Joyce. In .1.5 km (.9 miles) at the T turn left on Manson Avenue and you'll soon enter the Cranberry Lake area. In 2.3 km (1.4 miles) at another T turn right onto Cranberry. In 1.6 km (1 mile) the road to the campground goes left. You'll reach a Y at .6 km (.4 miles), go left. The road now turns to gravel and in another 5.2 km (3.2 miles) the entrance to the campground is on the left.

▣ SUNLUND BY THE SEA CAMPGROUND *(Open Easter to Canadian Thanksgiving -*
2nd Monday in October)

Res. and Info.: (604) 483-9220, info@sunlund.ca, www.sunlund.ca
Location: Lund, *N 49° 58 44", W 124° 45' 43",* Near Sea Level

35 Sites – Lund is a very small town clustered around a rocky cove. This great little campground is located within 100 yards of the bay but not within sight of it, there's a short trail to reach the boardwalk. As a jump-off point for boaters headed north into Desolation Sound the town is a virtual parking lot, not great for RVs. Fortunately this campground allows access to the village without having to deal with that. The campground has parking for RVs to 35 feet and access is no problem if you drive carefully. As you approach Lund (the road to Okeover Bay

Provincial Park will let you know you're getting close (it's about 2.4 km (1.5 miles) to the south) watch for the campground signs. They'll take you left onto Larson Rd., then almost immediately to the right and then to the right again and down into the campground.

OKEOVER ARM PROVINCIAL PARK *(Open May 15 to Sept 15)*

Location: 6 Km (4 Miles) E of Lund, *N 49° 59' 31", W 124° 42' 55",* Near Sea Level

18 Sites – This is a small provincial park located on Okeover Arm to the east of Lund. It's a popular put-in spot for kayakers and there's a well-known restaurant, the Laughing Oyster, next door. The campground is small but some sites will take RVs to 45 feet. In the off season it is possible to park outside the camping area with no services, there is no fee for this. Malaspina Road leaves the highway about 2.4 km (1.5 miles) south of Lund. This paved road will take you directly to the park, a distance of 3.7 km (2.3 miles).

THOMPSON AND FRASER RIVER CANYONS

On a map the Thompson and Fraser River Valleys appear to be the best route for a railroad or road from the coast at Vancouver to the interior of British Columbia. In fact, the rivers probably are the best route, but they certainly didn't prove to be easy routes. A trip through the canyons is interesting because it allows you to see the difficulties faced over the years by the people who needed to pass this way: first the Indians, then the fur traders, then the gold seekers, then the railroads, and finally the Trans-Canada Highway.

Leaving Cache Creek and heading south the highway crosses some high dry country and then descends to the level of the Thompson River. In many sections the road is built upon fill right in the river channel. At Spences Bridge the highway crosses over the river to the south shore.

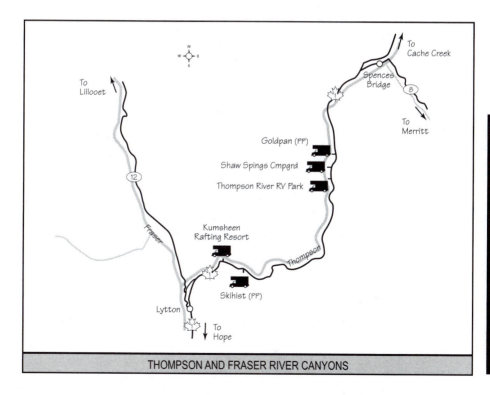

THOMPSON AND FRASER RIVER CANYONS

The Thompson and the Fraser come together at **Lytton** (population 400), you might want to drive through town to the mouth of the Thompson to see the muddy Fraser and the much clearer Thompson come together. A bridge crosses the Thompson here and you may be tempted to follow the small paved road 69 km (43 miles) north along the east shore of the Fraser River to Lillooet which is located in the *Whistler and the Sea to Sky Highway* section of this chapter.

From Lytton south the highway is in the Fraser River Canyon. Notice that there are two sets of railroad tracks in much of the canyon. Eight kilometers (5 miles) south of Lytton there are two railroad bridges where both sets of tracks cross to opposite sides. This seemingly useless exercise was necessary since the first set of tracks had been built along the easiest route by the Canadian Pacific Railroad. When the Canadian Northern built their set of tracks later there was only room on the other side of the river.

Fifty-four kilometers (33 miles) south of Lytton you will see the upper station of an aerial tram on the right side of the highway. You should at least stop and take a look. It is possible to walk down to the river here but the tram is much easier, it runs from April 1 to October 30. Below is **Hell's Gate**, a spot where the river flows so fast that the salmon have to use fishways to get through. Actually, before 1913 the fish could make it on their own, then railroad construction caused a slide that blocked the river to the fish much of the time. The fishways were constructed several years later to restore the run of salmon up the Fraser. The water level of the Fraser through here varies as much as 30 meters (100 feet) so at higher water levels you can't even see the top of the fishways. You may find it hard to believe but during the construction of the railroad a sternwheeler actually made it up the river through Hell's Gate.

Near Hell's Gate you will pass through 7 tunnels and cross a modern bridge across the river. This modern bridge replaced a much smaller suspension bridge, and that bridge remains, although it is only used by pedestrians. The walk from the highway down to the **Alexandra Bridge** is a nice short hike, the trail starts at Alexandra Bridge Provincial Park which is 10.3 kilometers (6.4 miles) south of the Hell's Gate tram station.

GOLD PAN PROVINCIAL PARK *(Open April 15 to Oct 10)*

Information: (250) 455-2708
Location: 29 Km (18 Miles) E of Lytton, *N 50° 20' 58", W 121° 23' 22"*, 700 Ft

14 Sites – This is a very popular little campground, probably because it is right on the river below the highway where everyone driving by sees it. The campground also attracts fishermen, gold panners, and river rafters. Maneuvering room is tight for big RVs, the campground is suitable for RVs to about 30 feet. There's a place to park temporarily next to the entrance road, take a look at the sites that are available before you commit yourself. The campground is right off the highway 8 km (5 miles) west of the bridge at Spences Bridge on Highway 1 and 29 km (18 miles) east of Lytton.

SHAW SPRINGS CAMPGROUND *(Open April to Oct - Varies)*

Information: (250) 458-2324
Location: 26 Km (16 Miles) E of Lytton, *N 50° 20' 21", W 121° 23' 48"*, 700 Ft

30 Sites – This is an old restaurant with a neglected campground and a few motel rooms. The sites here include pull-thrus that will take RVs to 40 feet. It's located 11 km (7 miles) west of the bridge at Spences Bridge and 26 km (16 miles) east of Lytton.

THOMPSON RIVER RV PARK *(Open All Year)*

Res. and Info.: (250) 458-2327
Location: 24 Km (15 Miles) E of Lytton, *N 50° 19' 51", W 121° 23' 52"*, 700 Ft

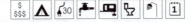

12 Sites – A very neat and well cared for older campground between the highway and the river. The RV sites are smaller back-ins suitable for RVs to 35 feet, there's also a large grass tenting area on the far side of the owner's house that is used by rafting companies. It's located 13 km (8 miles) west of the bridge at Spences Bridge and 23 km (15 miles) east of Lytton.

SKIHIST PROVINCIAL PARK *(Open April 14 to Oct 1 - Varies)*
Information: (250) 455-2708
Location: 8 Km (5 Miles) E of Lytton, *N 50° 15' 12", W 121° 30' 33"*, 900 Ft

58 Sites - A nice provincial park campground set in pines above the highway in a spectacular section of the Thompson River Canyon. Some sites are suitable for RVs to 35 feet. This can be a very warm campground in the middle of the summer, this is a hot and arid region. There's an 8 km trail from the campground that offers great views of the canyon. The old Cariboo Wagon Road ran through this park and there are sometimes elk around. The access road up to the campground is 27 km (17 miles) from the bridge at Spences Bridge on Highway 1 and 8 km (5 miles) east of Lytton.

KUMSHEEN RAFTING RESORT *(Open May 1 to Sept 6 - Varies)*
Res. and Info.:   (800) 663-6667, www.kumsheen.com
Location: 5 Km (3 Miles) E of Lytton, *N 50° 15' 35", W 121° 32' 07"*, 700 Ft

50 Sites – This place is primarily a river rafting resort. It offers many different rafting tours as well as rock climbing. Facilities include a good restaurant, swimming pool, and hot tub. Campsites are back-ins with a few suitable for RVs to 35 feet. No hookups are available. Camping fees are on a per person basis and include use of the very nice facilities as well as breakfast in the early season and breakfast and dinner in the main summer season between July 1 and September 6. Rates are $19 Canadian per person during the early and late season, $45 Canadian per person during the high season. It's located 31 km (19.5 miles) west of the bridge at Spences Bridge and 5.6 km (3.5 miles) east of Lytton.

TOFINO, UCLUELET, AND THE PACIFIC RIM NATIONAL PARK

As you drive east from Port Alberni toward the west coast of Vancouver Island you'll cross 574-meter Sutton Pass and then the road descends steeply and in another 10 kilometers (6 miles) you will reach a T intersection. Ucluelet is to the left (6 kilometers, 4 miles) and Tofino to the right (33 kilometers, 20 miles). Most of the Long Beach section of Pacific Rim National Park is also to the right. At this intersection there's a handy information centre. In the campground write-ups below we call this the Port Alberni road junction.

If you turn north you will almost immediately enter **Pacific Rim National Park Reserve**. There are actually three scattered sections to this park: Long Beach, the West Coast Trail, and the Broken Islands Group. This section, Long Beach, stretches along the coast almost as far as Tofino. Several short roads lead to beach parking lots, overlooks, and trails. There is a use fee for using this park, the parking lots have self-service machines allowing you to buy a ticket allowing you to park for several hours or all day long. The machines accept coins, currency, and credit cards. Note that you do not have to pay a fee to drive through the park, just to park in it. If it is late you may want to drive on to Tofino and then return to explore the following day.

Almost immediately after entering the park you'll see the turn for **Wickaninnish Centre** which offers museum-type displays and a restaurant as well as wheelchair-accessible views and trails. The center overlooks **Wickaninnish Beach**. As you continue to drive north toward Tofino you'll pass turn-offs for the **Rainforest Trail**, **Coombers Beach** and **Spruce Fringe Trail**, **Green Point Campground**, **Long Beach**, and **Radar Hill**.

BRITISH COLUMBIA

TOFINO HARBOR

The section of road through the park is 23 kilometers (14 miles) long. When you leave the park you'll start seeing the outskirts of Tofino. The road passes turnoffs to several resorts, restaurants, and campgrounds and then arrives in little Tofino, the end of the road.

The town of **Tofino** (population 1,100) is quite small and very tourist oriented. You'll find studios, stores, and restaurants in a compact area. Down the hill are three docks: the crab dock, Fisherman's Wharf, and the government wharf. Much of the activity of the town is oriented around **Clayoquot Sound**. There are popular charter trips for fishing, whale watching and sightseeing. One popular destination is **Hot Springs Cove** which offers the only hot springs on Vancouver Island. A much shorter hop is to **Meares Island** where you can follow hiking trails through the rain forest. These are also excellent kayaking waters.

The big event of the year in Tofino is the **Pacific Rim Whale Festival** held during the last half of March and first weekend of April. It celebrates the spring gray whale migration.

Ucluelet (population 1,500) is to the south. It's much like Tofino but less expensive and more focused on fishing. Natural destinations in the area include the 8.5 kilometer **Wild Pacific Trail** and **Big Beach**. The **Ucluelet Mini Aquarium** is great for both kids and adults. To the south in Barkley Sound is the **Broken Island Group** section of the Pacific Rim National Park, a wold-famous kayaking destination.

🚐 **SURF JUNCTION CAMPGROUND** *(Open Jan 15 to Oct 15)*

Res. and Info.:   (250) 726-7214, (877) 922-6722, www.surfjunction.com
Location: Just S of the Port Alberni Road Junction, *N 48° 59' 15", W 125° 35' 12"*, 200 Ft

49 Sites – This is the only campground listed in this section that is not located next to the water. The campground caters to the surfing crowd, they drive to whichever beach has the best surf on any particular day. Surprisingly, it's also a good place to stay for other tenters and RVers because it has large well-separated sites and a central location. When you arrive at the junction

where the road from Port Alberni meets the coastal road turn left toward Ucluelet. The campground entrance is on the left in .6 km (.4 mile).

UCLUELET CAMPGROUND *(Open April 1 to Sept 30)*

Res. and Info.:   (250) 726-4355, camp@uclueletcampground.com, www.uclueletcampground.com
Location: Ucluelet, *N 48° 56' 44", W 125° 33' 29",* Near Sea Level

106 Sites – Located on the north shore of the inner boat harbor in Ucluelet, some sites here have great views. The campground also has what may be the most scenically located dump site in B.C. Some sites, particularly back away from the water, are suitable for RVs to 45 feet. From the junction where the road from Port Alberni meets the coastal road turn left toward Ucluelet. The campground entrance is on the left in 6 km (3.7 miles).

ISLAND WEST RESORT *(Open All Year)*

Res. and Info.:   (250) 726-7515, fish@islandwest.com, islandwestresort.com
Location: Ucluelet, *N 48° 56' 44, W 125° 33' 29",* Near Sea Level

37 Sites – Like the Ucluelet Campground, under the same ownership, this campground is located next to the inner boat harbor in Ucluelet. Campsites are scattered around the grounds of this marina and restaurant, the main camping area is on a bluff above the marina. Some sites will take RVs to 45 feet. There is a boat ramp, the marina, and a restaurant on site. From the junction where the road from Port Alberni meets the coastal road turn left toward Ucluelet. In 6.5 km (4.0 miles) turn left on Bay Street and follow it down the hill to the resort entrance.

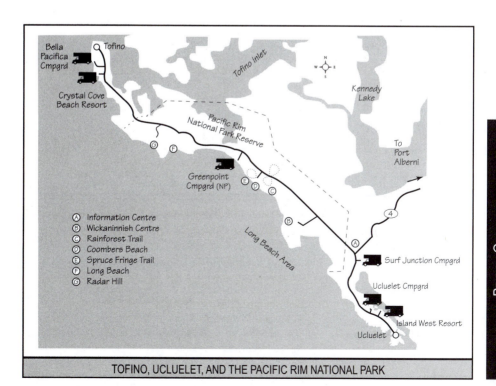

TOFINO, UCLUELET, AND THE PACIFIC RIM NATIONAL PARK

Ⓐ Information Centre
Ⓑ Wickaninnish Centre
Ⓒ Rainforest Trail
Ⓓ Coombers Beach
Ⓔ Spruce Fringe Trail
Ⓕ Long Beach
Ⓖ Radar Hill

BRITISH COLUMBIA

GREENPOINT CAMPGROUND – PACIFIC RIM NATIONAL PARK *(Open March 15 to Canadian Thanksgiving - 2nd Monday in Oct)*

Reservations	(877) 737-3783, www.pccamping.ca
Information:	(250) 726-7721
Location:	11 Km (7 Miles) N of Port Alberni Road Junction, *N 49° 03' 35", W 125° 43' 29", Near Sea Level*

114 Sites – The only national park campground in this park is usually booked solid, make reservations if you want to stay here. Some sites are suitable for RVs to 35 feet. From the junction where the road from Port Alberni meets the coastal road turn right toward Tofino. In 10.6 km (6.6 miles) you'll see the campground entrance on the left.

BELLA PACIFICA RESORT *(Open Feb 5 to Nov 14 - Varies)*

Res. and Info.:	(250) 725-3400, www.bellapacifica.com
Location:	27 Km (17 Miles) N of the Port Alberni Road Junction, *N 49° 07' 59", W 125° 54' 07", Near Sea Level*

176 Sites – This resort, like the Crystal Cove Beach Resort described below, is on Mackenzie Beach. It's a good beach for lying in the sun. Swimming is possible if you're tough. There are well-spaced sites with no hookups as well as more crowded sites with hookups overlooking the beach. A few sites will take RVs to 45 feet but most sites are much smaller. From the junction where the road from Port Alberni meets the coastal road turn right toward Tofino. In 27 km (16.9 miles) watch for the campground sign pointing west. This is about 2.9 km (1.8 miles) before you reach Tofino.

CRYSTAL COVE BEACH RESORT *(Open All Year)*

Res. and Info.:	(250) 725-4213, crystalc@alberni.net, www.crystalcovebeachresort.com
Location:	27 Km (17 Miles) N of the Port Alberni Road Junction, *N 49° 07' 38", W 125° 54' 05", Near Sea Level*

93 Sites – This resort is located about 2.4 km (1.5 miles) from Tofino next to MacKenzie Beach which is popular for sunning and even swimming. There are upscale rental cabins as well as the RV sites. The place is nicely landscaped. RV sites are a little crowded but 40 foot RVs do get in here. We think it's more suitable for RVs to 35 feet. All sites have full hookups. From the junction where the road from Port Alberni meets the coastal road turn right toward Tofino. In 27 km (16.6 miles) watch for the campground sign pointing west. This is about 3.4 km (2.1 miles) before you reach Tofino.

VALLEY OF A THOUSAND PEAKS (CRANBROOK, KIMBERLY, FORT STEELE TRIANGLE)

The Kootenay Rockies cover the entire southeast corner of British Columbia. The region runs east from the Okanagan Valley all the way to the true Rockies that form the border between British Columbia and Alberta. Just west of the high Rockies is a wide valley, sometimes called the Rocky Mountain Trench. It is said to run, in one form or another, all the way from Mexico. Within this trench, near the Canadian border with the U.S., is a region the publicists call the Valley of a Thousand Peaks. It's more commonly known as the Cranbrook, Kimberly, Fort Steele Triangle.

Cranbrook (population 19,000) is the largest town in this part of British Columbia and serves as the supply center for the region. Historically it's a railroad town, and the main reason to visit is to see the **Canadian Museum of Rail Travel** . This museum has a large collection of restored passenger rail cars and features seven from the famous Trans-Canada Limited dating from 1929. Cranbrook's summer festival is **Sam Steele Days** which is held the third weekend in June.

Fort Steele, of course, is named for the same Sam Steele. The fort is a restoration of early Fort Steele, which was a boom town during the East Kootenay gold rushes during the 1800s. The fort has over 60 restored buildings and townspeople dressed in costumes, a living museum. The fort is generally considered a top visitor attraction and a visit takes the better part of a day.

The final corner of the triangle is occupied by **Kimberly** (population 7,000). It's at 1,100 meters (3,600 feet) which makes it the highest town in British Columbia and second only to Banff in Canada. This is a former mining town, a company town for the Sullivan Mine which operated for 92 years and produced lead, zinc, and silver. Today the town has recreated itself with a Bavarian theme. The Bavarian center of the town is the **Platzl**, a central square with the largest cuckoo clock in Canada. Bavarian restaurants and shops complete the picture. The other big attraction in town is the old **Sullivan Mine** with an information center, the Bavarian City Mining Railway, the mine portal and a restored miners house. Kimberly is also a ski town with the **Kimberly Alpine Resort** just outside town. Kimberly hosts its share of events including the

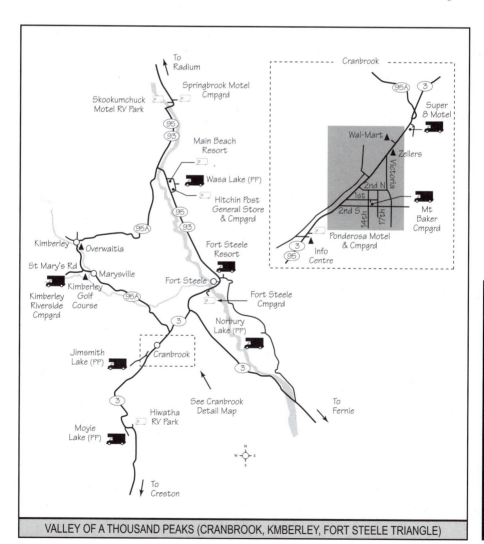

VALLEY OF A THOUSAND PEAKS (CRANBROOK, KMBERLEY, FORT STEELE TRIANGLE)

Kimberly Old Time Accordion Championships and **Julyfest** in in July. Of course there's also an **Octoberfest** in September.

The campgrounds in this section are arranged as if you were driving the Cranbrook, Kimberly, Fort Steele Triangle from the north in a counterclockwise direction. Wasa Lake Provincial Park is located near the junction of Hwy 95 and Hwy 95A about 37 km (23 miles) north of Cranbrook. From there you can drive 29 km (18 miles) southwest on 95A to Kimberly where the Kimberley Riverside Campground is located. From Kimberly it's another 37 km (18 miles) down to Cranbrook. The next four campgrounds listed give you a good choice for a stay although Moyie Lake Provincial Park is some distance to the south. Finally, it's 13 km (8miles) north to Forte Steele where two campgrounds provide a place to spend the night.

WASA LAKE PROVINCIAL PARK *(Open May 1 to Sept 15)*

Reservations:	(800) 689-9025, www.discovercamping.ca **Information:** (250) 422-3003
Location:	35 Km (22 Miles) N of Cranbrook, *N 49° 46' 52", W 115° 43' 42"*, 2,600 Ft

94 Sites – The campsites at Wasa Lake Provincial Park are near but not next to the lake. A highlight here is the paved walking or biking trail that runs all the way around the lake, a distance of 5 miles. There is also a swimming beach in the park on the lake. One hundred km (62 miles) south of Radium Hot Springs and 37 km (23 miles) north of Cranbrook Hwy 95 splits. Hwy 95A climbs to Kimberly in the west and Hwy 95 continues south to Fort Steele and Cranbrook. One and one-half miles south of this junction off Hwy 95 the road to Wasa Lake Provincial Park goes east to the campground. There is also access from another junction a short distance to the south.

KIMBERLEY RIVERSIDE CAMPGROUND *(Open April 15 to Oct 15)*

Res. and Info.:	(877) 999-2929, (250) 427-2929, www.kimberleycampground.com, info@kimberleycampground.com
Location:	6 Km (4 Miles) S of Kimberly, *N 49° 38' 05", W 115° 59' 50"*, 3,200 Ft

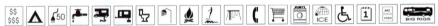

145 Sites – You'll be amazed by this unusual municipal campground. It's new, a huge place with nice big sites. It's laid out more like an upscale housing development than a campground. The wide campground road leads past the office down to sites in three different areas. The office houses a store and also has a large "resort" (shallow) swimming pool out back. This is a good big-rig campground with large pull-thru sites. There's also a tent area. Unfortunately the campground is about 5.6 km (3.5 miles) from Kimberly and there is no bus service so a vehicle is essential. The road to the campground, St. Mary's Road, leaves Hwy 95A some 2.9 km (1.8 miles) south of Kimberly on the northern edge of the town of Marysville. It climbs west for 2.7 km (1.7 miles), the campground is on the left.

MT. BAKER CAMPGROUND *(Open All Year)*

Reservations:	(877) 501-2288
Information:	(250) 489-0056, mtbaker.rv@shaw.ca
Location:	Cranbrook, *N 49° 30' 34", W 115° 45' 38"*, 3,000 Ft

70 Sites – Mt. Baker is Cranbrook's municipal campground. It's located just a few blocks east of the central area of town so it's extremely convenient for travelers. A Safeway is only two blocks away. An older campground, there are many smaller sites but a number will take RVs to 40 feet. There's also a large separate grassy tent area. Easiest access is by following Second Street east 11 blocks from Hwy 95 as it passes through central Cranbrook. The park entrance is off First Street just east of 14th Ave.

SUPER 8 MOTEL (REGENCY PARK RESORT RV PARK) *(Open May 15 to Sept 30 - Varies)*

Information: (250) 489-8028
Location: Cranbrook, *N 49° 32' 05", W 115° 44' 23",* 3,000 Ft

48 Sites – This is a very simple big-rig campground. Sites are set in a large field with almost no trees next to a Super 8 Motel. They're all long back-in sites suitable for RVs to 45 feet or larger with full hookups. The campground sits right on the east side of Hwy 95 at the north end of Cranbrook. Pull in to the campground entrance off 30th Ave. and walk over to the hotel to register because the hotel parking lot is too cramped for big rigs.

JIMSMITH LAKE PROVINCIAL PARK *(Open June 15 to Oct 11 - Varies)*

Information: (250) 422-3003
Location: 3 Km (2 Miles) S of Cranbrook, *N 49° 28' 57", W 115° 50' 24",* 3,600 Ft

35 Sites – This provincial park is located just outside Cranbrook to the south. It's a popular local swimming beach. The campground is behind the beach area on a hillside, some sites will take RVs to 45 feet. At the southern edge of Cranbrook on Hwy 3/95 there is an info centre on the east side of the highway. Opposite it is the road to the campground. Follow signs for 4 km (2.5 miles) to the entrance gate.

MOYIE LAKE PROVINCIAL PARK *(Open April 15 to Oct 30 - Varies)*

Reservations: (800) 689-9025, www.discovercamping.ca
Information: (250) 422-3003
Location: 18 Km (11 Miles) S of Cranbrook, *N 49° 22' 21", W 115° 50' 41",* 3,000 Ft

111 Sites – This park is on the north shore of large Moyie Lake. There are swimming beaches and a boat launch at the park. Sites will take RVs to 45 feet, they are all back-ins. From October 1 to October 30 the campground gate is open, no services are provided, and there is no fee. The park is located 18 km (11 miles) south of Cranbrook on the west side of Hwy 3.

FORT STEELE RESORT *(Open All Year)*

Res. and Info.: (250) 489-4268, resort@fortsteele.com, www.fortsteele.com
Location: 15 Km (9 Miles) N of Cranbrook, *N 49° 37' 17", W 115° 37' 28",* 2,600 Ft

176 Sites – This is the closest campground to the Ft. Steele park. It's a large campground sitting next to a gas station and store. Sites are large and will accept RVs to 45 feet in pull-thru sites. Swimming is in a pool. The campground is located about a quarter-mile north of Fort Steel just off Hwy 95.

NORBURY LAKE PROVINCIAL PARK *(Open All Year)*

Information: (250) 422-3003
Location: 29 Km (18 Miles) NE of Cranbrook, *N 49° 32' 13", W 115° 29' 11",* 2,700 Ft

46 Sites – Norbury Lake campground sits on the north shore of Norbury Lake. Peckham's Lake is nearby, a trail leads to that lake. There are rainbows in Peckham's lake, power boats are prohibited on both lakes. The park is near Fort Steele and sites will accept RVs to well over 45

feet, there's also good maneuvering room. This park has full services and a fee from May 15 to September 15, off season there are no services and no fee but the campground gate is open. From the junction just north of Ft Steele follow signs 15.6 km (9.7 miles) southeast to the campground.

Vancouver

Vancouver is by far the largest population center for western Canada. With about 1,500,000 people in the metropolitan area Vancouver is about the same size as Portland or Seattle. The city is probably best known for it's spectacular location. Mountains rise nearby both to the north and east. The ocean is not only to the west in the form of Howe Sound, but also, as Burrard Inlet and False Creek, to the north and south. To top it off there's the spectacular Lions Gate Suspension Bridge spanning the mouth of Burrard Inlet between Stanley Park and North Vancouver.

Highway access to Vancouver is decent by not great. Highway 1 from eastern Canada is a multi-lane freeway that enters the city from the east. Unfortunately, it does not connect with major highways from the U.S. so access from the south can be a little confusing. Most folks cross the border at the north end of the U.S. Hwy I-5 in Blaine, Washington. From there you can follow what appears to be the main road, Hwy 99, north into Vancouver. You will soon find yourself on boulevards and then cross into the downtown area, not the best place to be in a big RV. A better plan is to follow signs from the border that lead you up Hwy 15 (not a freeway but also not heavily trafficked) to connect with Hwy 1 to the east of Vancouver. From there you can use the freeway to get to Vancouver campgrounds to the north and east of downtown, travel north to Horseshoe Bay, or travel eastwards to the rest of the province.

Probably not too surprisingly, Vancouver got its start at about the same time as Portland and Seattle. The first European settlers to the area were fur trading companies that established forts along the Fraser River just to the east. Serious settlement of what is now Vancouver began in the 1850s. The large area now covered by Vancouver actually encompassed more than one small settlement. One of these was Granville, also called Gastown, today it is considered the place where Vancouver began.

In the beginning the city of Victoria, on Vancouver Island to the west, grew faster than Vancouver. Concern that Vancouver Island might be incorporated into the U.S. resulted in a concentrated British effort to develop the island, and gold discoveries up the Thompson and Fraser Rivers in the mountains east of Vancouver only gradually moved the center of population growth over to the mainland.

Other early events either precede or echo the histories of Portland and Seattle. Vancouver had its own serious fire in 1886, rebuilding resulted in many of the Gastown buildings you see today. The railroad reached Vancouver in the next year, and, just like Portland and Seattle, a direct and relatively easy to travel connection with the east really caused the city to take off.

As Canada's major West Coast port Vancouver grew rapidly and continues to do so today. More freight passes through Vancouver than any other Canadian port, and by some measures Vancouver too is called the largest port on the west coast of North America.

The original **Gastown** settlement is at the base of a peninsula and didn't have a great deal of area for growth because it is hemmed in by water. As a result the city has spread off the peninsula to the north and south and today continues to grow to the east up the wide Fraser Valley.

The downtown peninsula is bounded on the north by Burrard Inlet and on the south by False Bay. Just south of Gastown is the city's **Chinatown**. To the west of these is the modern downtown area and farther to the west a primarily residential area known as the West End and also Stanley Park. Visitors from the U.S. will be impressed with Vancouver's cosmopolitan air, and also with the number of people who live near the center of town.

North of the peninsula, across Burrard Inlet, is North Vancouver, you reach it via the scenic Lions Gate Bridge. South of the Peninsula is a large residential area known as Central Vancouver which is also the location of the University of British Columbia.

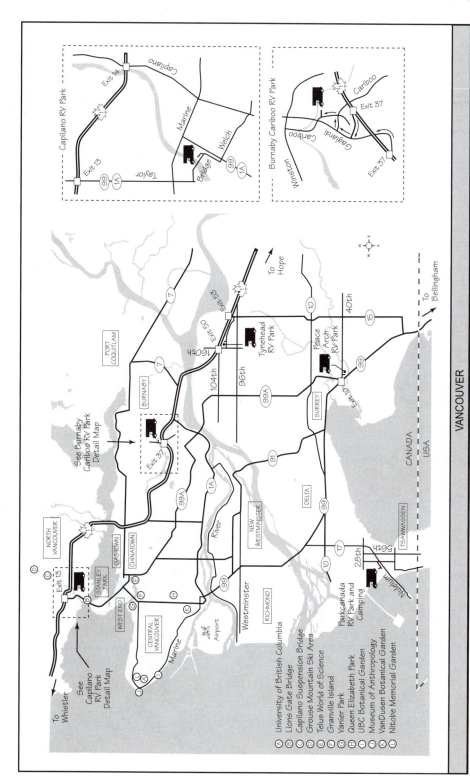

VANCOUVER

More remote suburbs include Richmond, to the south, New Westminster, to the southeast, and Burnaby and Port Coquitlam to the east. You can go even farther and still consider yourself in the Vancouver metropolitan area. Delta and Surrey are to the south toward the U.S. border and to the east up the Fraser Valley are Langley and Abbotsford.

Vancouver has an excellent public transportation system. The system's name has recently been changed from BC Transit to Translink. There are several different arms of this organization. Pamphlets with details about service are available at the many info centres in Vancouver and on approaches to the city. The Coast Mountain Bus Company is the bus arm. It provides excellent bus service throughout the greater Vancouver area. Vancouver has a light rail transportation system too. This is known as SkyTrain. There is one line, it is underground downtown and above ground elsewhere. It runs southeastward from downtown and provides service to Burnaby, New Westminster, and Surrey. Trains run every 5 minutes or so. SeaBus passenger ferries connect downtown Vancouver with North Vancouver. The Vancouver terminal is near Canada Place, the North Vancouver terminal is Lonsdale Quay. From the quay there is bus service to many North Vancouver destinations. There are also tiny passenger ferries that chug around False Creek and are appropriately known as the False Creek Ferries. There are docks at many tourist destinations including Granville Island, Vanier Park, and Telus World of Science.

When you arrive in Vancouver on public transportation you will probably find yourself in the central business district. The new center of attraction for visitors is **Canada Place**. Now a combination cruise ship dock, convention center, hotel, shopping center, and theater, the very modern soaring tent-like building on a pier was originally build as a pavilion for the Expo86 fair. Canada Place is served by the SkyTrain light rail system.

Up the hill from Canada Place Granville Street has been closed to most traffic to become a European-style pedestrian mall. Along or near Granville you'll find lots of shopping. From its intersection with Granville you can follow Robson Street northwestward toward the West End and Stanley Park. Robson is lined with restaurants and boutiques.

Stanley Park is Vancouver's jewel. This huge park covers the entire tip of the peninsula oc-

STANLEY PARK'S LITTLE MERIMAID

cupied by Vancouver. It is a big place, there are miles and miles of trails as well as roads allowing you to tour the park in an automobile. A Seaside Promenade runs along the entire coastline of the park. Stanley Park is also home to the excellent **Vancouver Aquarium**. The Golden Gate-like Lions Gate suspension bridge makes a scenic jump from Stanley Park to North Vancouver.

If you head eastward from Canada Place you'll soon find yourself in historic **Gastown**. Cobblestone streets and well-maintained 19th-century buildings make the neighborhood stand out, and because it is a designated historic district the shops are open on Sundays.

Just southeast of Gastown is **Chinatown**. This is the second largest such area on the West Coast, only San Francisco's Chinatown is larger. In addition to the usual shops and restaurants you might want to visit the Dr. Sun Yat-sen Classical Chinese Garden which is located on Carrall Street between W. Pender and Keefer.

You can easily visit **North Vancouver** as a pedestrian by taking a ferry across Burrard Inlet. The SeaBus terminal is just east of Canada Place, ferries dock in North Vancouver at Lonsdale Quay. There's a farmers market at the quay as well as restaurants and shops. Busses to the sights in North Vancouver also depart from the quay.

Two popular attractions lie up the mountain. The first is the **Capilano Suspension Bridge**. This dizzying suspension foot bridge crosses the Capilano River at a height of 70 meters (230 feet). Higher on the same road is **Grouse Mountain** ski area. You can ride the gondola up to the ski slope for magnificent views of the city and hiking trails.

There are a number of attractions south of downtown also. One of the closest and most easily accessible is **Telus World of Science**. This is a science/technology museum housed in a 17-story ball originally built for Expo86. There is also an Omnimax theater. It is served by SkyTrain and also by the False Creek Ferries.

From Telus World of Science you can use the ferry to hop over to **Granville Island**, also accessible by car or bus. Not long ago this was little more than an area of old warehouses but it has been completely redone. Now there's a visitor information centre, a public market, the Emily Carr Institute of Art and Design, a marina, shops, restaurants, and theaters.

The area on the south side of False Bay is known as Central Vancouver. Attractions there are mostly grouped in Vanier Park and on the University of BC campus although there are also two excellent gardens. The first of these is **Queen Elizabeth Park**, a 130-acre park located on Little Mountain which offers views of the city. The **Bloedel Floral Conservatory** in the park is a dome-style greenhouse housing tropical plants and birds. The **VanDusen Botanical Garden** is nearby and offers 55 acres of beautiful gardens.

Vanier Park is located on the south shore of English Bay just west of Granville Island. In the park you'll find two museums. The **Vancouver Museum** is a regional history museum much more interesting then most of this genre, probably because Vancouver's history includes the coastal Indian cultures and also the European exploration of the Northwest. There's much more of the latter at the nearby **Vancouver Maritime Museum**. The park also has a planetarium and an astronomical observatory.

West of Vanier Park and occupying 1,900 acres on Point Grey is the University of British Columbia. The **Museum of Anthropology** here is excellent and covers, of course, the Pacific Northwest Indian cultures. The university campus has miles of hiking trails and beaches. Also on campus are the **Nitobe Memorial Garden**, a traditional Japanese garden and the **UBC Botanical Garden**.

BURNABY CARIBOO RV PARK *(Open All Year)*

Res. and Info.: (604) 420-1722, camping@bcrvpark.com, www.bcrv.com, www.bcrvpark.com
Location: Burnaby, *N 49° 14' 55", W 122° 54' 44", Near Sea Level*

217 Sites – This is a convenient campground for folks approaching Vancouver from the

east. It is located just off Hwy 1 and is near Burnaby Lake Regional Park which has good hiking trails. There's an indoor swimming pool and Jacuzzi. The Lougheed Shopping Center is a short drive away. To find the campground take Exit 37 (Cariboo Rd.). You'll be on Gaglardi Way, drive north. Drive only a short distance and turn right at the Cariboo Rd sign. Again drive only a short distance and turn left on Cariboo Road. Now drive about .5 km (.3 miles) north and turn right on Cariboo Place, this is the entrance road to the campground. The route is signed so it is easier to drive than to read.

[handwritten: 295 TOMAHAWK Ave, North Vancouver, BC V7P 1C5]

CAPILANO RV PARK *(Open All Year)*

Res. and Info.:   (604) 987-4722, infor@capilanorvpark.com, www.capilanorvpark.com
Location: North Vancouver, N 49° 19' 26", W 123° 07' 53", Near Sea Level

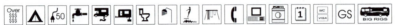

208 Sites – This campground is conveniently located in North Vancouver just north of the Lions Gate Bridge and near Hwy 1. It is also within easy walking distance of the Park Royal Shopping Centre. There is good bus service into Vancouver from near the campground. To most easily drive to the campground leave Hwy 1 at Exit 14. Drive south 1.8 km (1.1 miles). You will cross Marine Drive and continue south on Capilano Road, a paved two-lane road . Take a right on Welch Street, there is a sign for the RV park here. Follow Welch as it goes west and passes under the Lions Gate Bridge approach ramp, a distance of about .8 km (.5 mile). Turn right on Bridge Street and you'll see the park entrance on the right just as the road makes a 90° turn to the left.

PEACE ARCH RV PARK *(Open All Year)*

Res. and Info.:   (604) 594-7009, www.peacearchrvpark.com
Location: Surrey, N 49° 04' 29", W 122° 48' 50", Near Sea Level

215 Sites – If you're willing to stay a little farther from Vancouver when you visit you'll find that the parks are less expensive than those right near town. This campground has larger sites than those in town including pull-thrus suitable for RVs at least 45 feet long. Bus service to town is available and the site is very convenient to the crossing into the U.S. The campground is located just off Hwy 99 about 10 km (6 miles) north of the U.S. border crossing at Blaine. Take Exit 10 for the King George Highway (Hwy 99A) northbound. Almost immediately turn right on 40th Street, the campground entrance is on the right in .3 km (.2 miles).

PARKCANADA RV PARK AND CAMPING *(Open All Year)*

Reservations: (877) 943-0685
Information: (604) 943-5811, info@parkcanada.com, www.parkcanada.com
Location: Delta, N 49° 01' 57", W 123° 05' 32", Near Sea Level

124 Sites – This is an older park with many permanently parked rigs, but it's convenient to the Tsawwassen Ferry terminal for travel to Sidney near Victoria on Vancouver Island. Sites will accept rigs over 45 feet long. Bus access to Vancouver is from a stop about a mile from the campground. The campground is located right next to Hwy 17 (the Tsawwassen access route) and adjacent to a recreational water park with big slides so it's tough to miss. If you follow Hwy 17 south from its intersection with Hwy 99 you'll see the campground sign indicating the right turn in about 8.4 km (5.2 miles). From the ferry terminal the turn is about 4.0 km (2.5 miles). Turn north on 52nd Street and then immediately left to parallel the highway, you'll reach the water park entrance in .8 km (.5 mile). Proceed into the parking lot, the campground office and gated entrance are on the far side straight ahead.

TYNEHEAD RV PARK *(Open All Year)*

Res. and Info.: (604) 589-1161, tynehead@telus.net, www.tynehead.com
Location: Surrey, *N 49° 11' 18", W 122° 46' 18"*, 200 Ft

117 Sites – Tynehead is a park to the east of Vancouver. It's a little less expensive than some of the competition nearby and not hard to reach from the Trans-Canada (Hwy 1). Public transportation is not convenient from the park, however. In summer there's a swimming pool. Access is probably easiest from Exit 53. Head south on Hwy 15 but turn right almost immediately on Tynehead Drive. Tynehead Drive will carry you around the north side of Tynehead Regional Park for 3.7 km (2.3 miles), the campground entrance will be on your right.

VICTORIA

At the far south end of Vancouver Island the city of Victoria (population 335,000) has played many roles through the years. Originally the area was a popular First Peoples site, they harvested camas bulbs where Beacon Hill Park is today. In the 1840s the Hudson Bay Company selected a site on the excellent harbor for their western headquarters. Victoria soon became the capital city of the colonies of British Columbia and Vancouver Island. However, when Vancouver became the terminus for the transcontinental railroad Victoria remained the capital city, but slid into a long period of existence as a quiet tourist attraction and bastion of Britishness. Today the town is rapidly growing but still very pleasant. A great place to live or to visit.

The tourist business in Victoria probably can be dated to the construction of the huge Canadian Pacific Railway **Empress Hotel** in 1908. The hotel remains one of the most popular destinations for the millions of tourists that visit Victoria each year, quite a few on cruise boats

THE ACTIVE VICTORIA HARBOR IN FRONT OF THE PARLIAMENT BUILDING AND EMPRESS HOTEL

from Seattle. Many come for the formal afternoon tea at the hotel. The downtown area, particularly near the hotel, is full of sights and activities for these tourists.

In the immediate vicinity you'll find the following sights, and more. Red **double-decked busses** from London used for tours of the city and the area are popular. At the **docks** in front of the hotel you can sign up for whale-watching tours or catch one of the tiny harbor ferries. The **Parliament Buildings** face the hotel across grass lawns, they're lighted at night and tours are available. The excellent **Royal British Columbia Museum** should not be missed, it has full-sized displays of natural history, cultural history, and the art and culture of the area's First People populations. Other attractions devoted to the daily tourists including Miniature World, Ann Hathaway's Cottage, the Royal London Wax Museum, Helmcken House, Craigdarroch Castle, the Maritime Museum, the Crystal Gardens, and the Undersea Gardens.

There are several reasons to get out and away from Victoria. Probably the most popular attraction outside the city are the **Butchart Gardens**. They fill a former limestone quarry next to Tod Inlet on the east side of the Saanich Peninsula. The gardens are well worth a visit and cover over fifty acres. Nearby are the **Butterfly Gardens** where you'll find thousands of butterflies in an enclosed garden.

For a longer drive you might want to visit **Port Renfrew**. The town is located 104 kilometers (64 miles) from Victoria up the southwest shore of Vancouver Island, Highway 14 is paved for the entire distance. The highway travels past several provincial parks giving access to the beach and from China Beach Provincial Park to Port Renfrew the road is paralleled by the Juan de Fuca Marine Trail. Port Renfrew is known as the starting point for the 77-kilometer (48-mile) **West Coast Trail** which leads north along the wild coast to Bamfield. Botanical Beach in Port Renfrew is a great tide-pool area. It is possible to follow gravel logging roads north from Port Renfrew to Cowichan Lake and Port Alberni, check road conditions locally before attempting these drives.

⛺ GOLDSTREAM PROVINCIAL PARK *(Open All Year)*

Reservations:	(800) 689-9025, www.discovercamping.ca
Information:	(250) 474-1336
Location:	11 Km (7 Miles) W of Victoria, *N 48° 27' 38", W 123° 33' 30"*, 300 Ft

173 Sites – This is a large provincial park campground conveniently located very near Victoria. The fine hiking trails are a bonus. The campground itself is set in very tall old trees, it's very impressive but also a little dark. Many sites will take RVs to 45 feet. Although the campground is open all year long, from November 1 to March 14 there are reduced fees because no water, firewood, or sani-station are available. The campground is located right off Hwy 1 as you descend from Malahat Summit into town.

⛺ RV PARK AT FORT VICTORIA *(Open All Year)*

Res. and Info.:	(250) 479-8112, info@fortvictoria.ca, www.fortvictoria.ca
Location:	Vancouver, *N 48° 27' 36", W 123° 26' 33"*, 100 Ft

201 Sites – This is a very large and well-run campground conveniently located near the freeway where Highway 1 enters Victoria from the upper island. There is good bus service in to town. Sites here are large back-ins, it's an excellent big-rig campground. The park is easily visible from Hwy 1 as you approach Victoria from the north. Take Exit 8 marked Helmcken Road and follow the signs on a roundabout route about 1.8 kilometers (1.1 miles) to the campground.

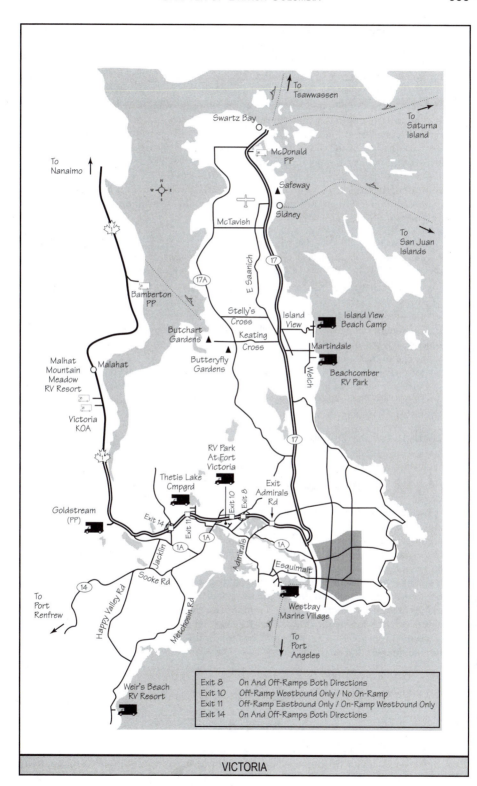

VICTORIA

WESTBAY MARINE VILLAGE *(Open All Year)*

Res. and Info.: (250) 385-1831, (866) 937-8229, info@westbay.bc.ca, www.westbay.bc.ca
Location: Vancouver, *N 48° 25' 32", W 123° 23' 43"*, Near Sea Level

61 Sites – This campground sits right on the shore of West Bay, there are views across Victoria's inner harbor of the city. It's a great place to watch the ships and floatplanes go by. You can also walk along waterfront bike paths right into town, a distance of about 4 kilometers (2.5 miles) or take the bus or the tiny harbor ferryboats. Sites are all back-ins, RVs to 45 feet will fit. This is a very popular campground, make reservations well in advance if you want to stay here. Follow signs from Highway 1 at the Admirals Road exit just west of Victoria. You'll drive south on Admirals Road for 4.5 kilometers (2.8 miles), turn left on Esquimalt Rd. and drive 1.4 kilometers (.9 miles), then turn right on Head and follow signs through the neighborhood to the campground.

WEIR'S BEACH RV RESORT *(Open All Year)*

Res. and Info.: (250) 478-3323, (866) 478-6888, office@weirsbeachrvresort.bc.ca
Location: 16 Km (10 Miles) W of Victoria, *N 48° 21' 07", W 123° 32' 45"*, Near Sea Level

60 Sites – Weir's Beach is located west of Vancouver on the beach on the south side of the island. It's a modern campground with excellent facilities, not to mention a row of campsites facing a quiet beach. It can take RVs to 45 feet with no problem. This campground is about a mile beyond the end of the bus route into town so it's not a great place to stay if you want to visit the city and don't have your own vehicle. One access route to the campground is to take Exit 8 from Hwy 1. Drive south for 1.2 km (.7 mile) to Hwy 1A, the Island Highway. Turn right and follow Hwy 1A for 5.8 km (3.6 miles) as it heads first west and then curves to the south. Turn left on Metchosin Road and follow it for 11 km (7 miles), you'll see the park entrance on the left.

THETIS LAKE CAMPGROUND *(Open Mid June to Mid Sept - Varies)*

Res. and Info.: (250) 478-3845, thetislake@home.com
Location: Victoria, *N 48° 27' 43", W 123° 28' 06"*, 200 Ft

139 Sites – This is a commercial campground located right next to Thetis Lake Regional Park. You can easily walk out a back gate to reach the swimming beach. The campground has many semi-permanent residents but about 30 hookup sites for travelers. It slopes up a steep hill so access and sites limit vehicle size to about 30 feet for these sites. There are lots more tent sites on the hillside with vehicle access for only automobiles (no RVs due to very steep roads in this section). Access is easy from up-island. Take Exit 11 from Hwy 1, turn north, and the entrance to the regional park parking lot will be on your left. Turn in and drive past the parking lot entrance to the campground entrance. From the east there is no exit possible at Exit 11 so it's easiest to take Exit 8 for Hemcken Road, go 1.1 km (.7 mile) south, turn right on Hwy 1A. In 1.6 km (1 mile) turn right on Six Mile road and follow it for 1 km (.6 mile) under the freeway and into the campground on the far side.

BEACHCOMBER RV PARK *(Open April 16 to Oct 15)*

Res. and Info.: (250) 652-3800, info@beachcomberrv.com, www.beachcomberrv.com
Location: 13 Km (8 Miles) N of Victoria, *N 48° 33' 28", W 123° 21' 48"*, Near Sea Level

59 Sites – The campground has a great location right on the beach on the east side of the Saanich Peninsula. It's for self-contained camping vehicles only because the only restroom facili-

ties are port-a-potties. Swimming is in the ocean. To find it follow Martindale Rd. east from Hwy 17 about 15.6 km (9.7 miles) south of the ferry docks in Schwartz Bay, 10.5 km (6.5 miles) north of the intersection of Hwy 1 and Hwy 17 near Victoria. Unfortunately there is no access to Martindale if you're southbound, you must exit 1.3 km (.8 miles) to the north on Island View Road, head east, and then turn right on Lochside Dr. to parallel the highway as you drive south to intercept Martindale. There's a long steep narrow access road down into the campground, but it is paved.

ISLAND VIEW BEACH CAMP *(Open April 1 to Oct 15)*

Res. and Info.:   (250) 652-0548, jrcountry@pocketmail.com
Location: 16 Km (10 Miles) N of Victoria, *N 48° 34' 29", W 123° 22' 05"*, Near Sea Level

87 Sites – Another campground right on the beach on the east shore of the Saanich Peninsula. Facilities are simple but the setting is nice. There are long back-in RV sites near the beach and very nice tent sites inland. Swimming is in the ocean. Note that there are no sewer drains or dump station at this campground. To reach the campground follow Island View Road from Hwy 17 about 14.4 km (8.9 miles) south of the ferry docks in Schwartz Bay, 11.8 km (7.3 miles) north of the intersection of Hwy 1 and Hwy 17 near Victoria. Drive 3 km (1.9 miles) east from Highway 17, then turn left when you reach the beach. The campground is at the north side of Island View Beach Regional Park parking lot.

WELLS GRAY PROVINCIAL PARK (CLEARWATER RIVER CORRIDOR SECTION) AND CLEARWATER

Clearwater (population 1,700) serves as the gateway to the Clearwater River Corridor section of Wells Gray Provincial Park. The small town stretches along the highway and offers a few

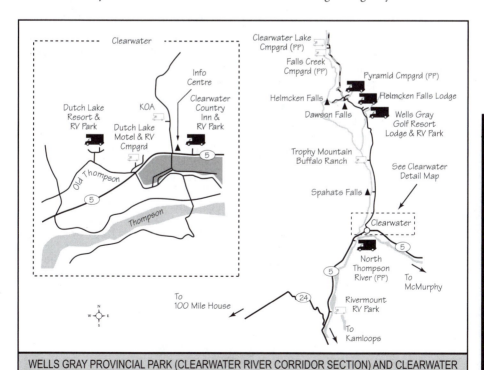

WELLS GRAY PROVINCIAL PARK (CLEARWATER RIVER CORRIDOR SECTION) AND CLEARWATER

restaurants, stores and campgrounds. There is also an info centre at the junction with Wells Gray Park Road, a good place to pick up information about facilities and conditions in the park.

Wells Gray Provincial Park is very large but much of it is pretty hard to reach. The southern portion of the park near Clearwater is the most accessible for RVers. This park is known for its waterfalls, you can see three of them by taking an easy three hour drive north from Clearwater. The road that leads from Clearwater into the park is not a major highway but also no particular challenge. It is paved all the way to Helmcken Falls, a distance of 47 kilometers (29 miles). From a junction just before you reach the falls an unpaved road continues on into the park to Clearwater Lake, another 28 kilometers (17 miles).

Spahats Falls is really in another park, Spahats Creek Provincial Park. It takes about 10 minutes to walk to the viewpoint where you see Spahats Creek fall about 60 meters out of an impressive gorge and then flow into Clearwater Creek. The falls are 10 kilometers (6 miles) from the junction in Clearwater.

Thirty-five kilometers (22 miles) from the junction in Clearwater you enter Wells Gray Provincial Park. In just another few kilometers you'll see the parking area for the **Dawson Falls** viewpoint on the left. A short walk takes you to a viewpoint where you can see the Murtle River flow over a 20 meter drop.

The most famous of the falls in the park is undoubtedly **Helmcken Falls**. This is the fourth highest waterfall in British Columbia and an unusually impressive sight due to the volume of water and the massive amounts of spray rising into the air. The water falls into a fairly restricted bowl causing strong updrafts and heavy mists. The falls are 47 kilometers (29 miles) from the junction in Clearwater.

CLEARWATER COUNTRY INN AND RV PARK *(Open All Year)*

    Res. and Info.:   (250) 674-3121, (888) 242-3533, park@clearwatercountryinnandrvpark.com,
                    www.clearwatercountryinnandrvpark.com
    Location: Clearwater, *N 51° 39' 06", W 120° 01' 55"*, 1,500 Ft

50 Sites – The easiest to find campground in Clearwater is probably this one. It is located behind a restaurant and motel on Hwy 5 just .2 km (.1 mile) east of the cutoff to Wells Gray Provincial Park. Sites here are huge, there are pull-thrus suitable for RVs to 45 feet as well as long back-ins on grass at least twice that long. There is also a swimming pool.

DUTCH LAKE RESORT AND RV PARK *(Open May to Nov 10 - Varies)*

    Res. and Info.:   (250) 674-3351, (888) 884-4424, admin@dutchlake.com, www.dutchlake.com
    Location: Clearwater, *N 51° 39' 06", W 120° 03 46"*, 1,300 Ft

71 Sites – This campground is away from the business strip along the highway but easy to find and access. It's quiet and good for tenters and big rigs too with full-hookup pull-thru sites for RVs to 45 feet. It's on a lake with a restaurant overlooking the water. From the info centre at the junction of the Wells Gray Park Road and Hwy 5 drive west on the highway for 1 km (.6 miles). Turn right on the Old Thompson Highway and drive 1.1 km (.7 miles) northwest to Dutch Lake Road. Turn right here and you'll soon see the campground entrance on your right.

NORTH THOMPSON RIVER PROVINCIAL PARK *(Open May 15 to Sept 30)*

    Information: (250) 674-2194
    Location: 5 Km (3 Miles) SE of Clearwater, *N 51° 37' 28", W 120° 05' 12"*, 1,400 Ft

61 Sites – This large provincial campground is near Clearwater just off the highway. The

Clearwater and Thompson Rivers meet here, a few sites are on the Thompson River. Some sites will take RVs to 45 feet, all are back-ins. From the junction of the Wells Gray Park Road and Hwy 5 drive southwest on Hwy 5 five km (3 miles), the campground entrance is on the left.

WELLS GRAY GOLF RESORT LODGE AND RV PARK *(Open April 15 to Oct 15 - Varies)*

Res. and Info.:   (250) 674-0072 or (877) 215-GOLF, wellsgraygolf@telus.net,
                     www.wellsgraygolf.bcresorts.com
Location: 34 Km (21 Miles) N of Clearwater, *N 51° 56' 21", W 120° 02' 55"*, 2,100 Ft

60 Sites – A wonderful place to stay that is convenient to the park, has good facilities, offers creek-side parking, and is also a 9-hole golf course. The Helmcken Falls Lodge with its restaurant is right next door and the campground offers great deals on camping/golfing packages. Sites are back-ins, they can take RVs longer than 45 feet and have easy access. From the intersection in Clearwater next to the info centre drive north on the park road for 34 km (21 miles), the entrance is on the right.

HELMCKEN FALLS LODGE *(Open April 15 to Oct 15 - Varies)*

Res. and Info.:   (250) 674-3657, info@helmckenfalls.com, www.helmckenfalls.com
Location: 34 Km (21 Miles) N of Clearwater, *N 51° 56' 13", W 120° 03' 27"*, 2,100 Ft

24 Sites – This lodge and restaurant offers camping in a quiet field behind and below the lodge. It is a very good tent camping location with grass for pitching your tent and restroom facilities with showers. There are also back-in RV sites suitable for RVs to 45 feet but there are no sewer or dump facilities. It's right next door to the Wells Gray Golf Resort Lodge and RV Park so the location is good for day trips into the park to see the waterfalls. From the intersection in Clearwater next to the info centre drive north on the park road for 34 km (21 miles), the entrance is on the right.

PYRAMID CAMPGROUND – WELLS GRAY PROVINCIAL PARK *(Open All Year)*

Information: (250) 674-2194, infor@explorewellsgray.com, www.explorewellsgray.com
Location: 43 Km (27 Miles) N of Clearwater, *N 51° 58' 16", W 120° 07' 10"*, 2,700 Ft

50 Sites – This campground is inside Wells Gray Provincial Park about 4 kilometers from Helmcken Falls. Sites are large back-ins with some suitable for RVs to 45 feet and there is a trail from the campground that leads 14 kilometers to Majerus and Horseshoe Falls on the Murtle River. The campground gates are open all year. From May 1 to September 30 there are fees, outside this period there are no services or fees. You can't miss this campground, the entrance is right at the junction of the paved road to Helmcken Falls and the gravel road to Clearwater Lake. It is 43 km (27 miles) north of Clearwater.

WHISTLER AND THE SEA TO SKY HIGHWAY

The Sea to Sky Highway is Hwy 99 as it climbs from Horseshoe Bay, just north of Vancouver, up into central British Columbia at Lillooet. Between Pemberton and Lillooet there are some steep hills. A few short sections reach a 15% grade, some longer sections are in the neighborhood of 10%. There are also switchbacks. Larger RVs do routinely travel this road but if you have reservations about the climbing or braking ability of your rig it is best to avoid the Pemberton to Lillooet section. The road is paved the entire distance.

Horseshoe Bay is just north of Vancouver, Hwy 1 leads directly to the ferry terminal there. Follow the signs for Whistler and Hwy 99 and you're on your way. The highway follows the shore of Howe Sound and in 44 km (27 miles) reaches Squamish.

Squamish (population 14,000) is the best supply center along the highway and a center for outdoor activity. Much of it revolves around the **Stawamus Chief** rock face and rock-climbing activities there, the mountain is just south of town. Squamish is also home to the **BC Museum of Mining** and the **West Coast Railway Heritage Park**.

Whistler (population 9,000) slated to be the site of the Winter Olympics in 2010, is the next town along the way. Whistler is spread over quite a large area with condos and golf courses visible through the trees but the center of the action is Whistler Village. Large parking lots are located behind the village, if it's not too busy there should be room for you. Whistler village has pedestrian-only streets, it is modeled after the ski villages in the alps. Even if you don't ski you'll want to take a look.

Whistler now has a commercial campground. If it's too crowded or not your style you can drive on another 27 km (17 miles) to Nairn Falls Provincial Park near Pemberton.

Just beyond Pemberton the highway climbs and the campgrounds get scarce. There are a number of BC Forest Service campgrounds along the road. They're small and most are suitable for only smaller rigs.

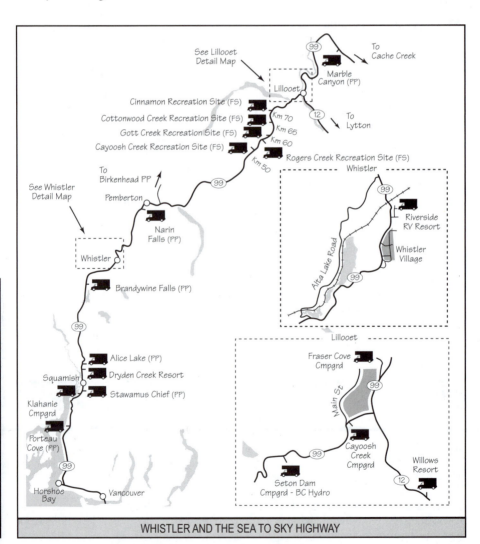

WHISTLER AND THE SEA TO SKY HIGHWAY

When you finally reach **Lillooet** you'll find that it is blessed with some very good campgrounds considering its remote location. Lillooet now has a population of 2,000 or so but for a very short time during the Cariboo Gold Rush in the early 1860's it was the second-largest town north of San Francisco. From here the Cariboo Wagon Road went north to the Cariboo Gold Fields. Lillooet sits at the bottom of the Fraser River Canyon and has a very hot (in summer) and dry climate. From here you can drive north to the Cariboo or south to Lytton and Highway 1 on paved roads.

PORTEAU COVE PROVINCIAL PARK *(Open All Year)*

Reservations: (800) 689-9025, www.discovercamping.ca   **Information:** (604) 986-9371
Location: 19 Km (12 Miles) S of Squamish, *N 49° 33' 31", W 123° 14' 04"*, Near Sea Level

60 Sites – This campground occupies a narrow piece of land between the highway and the ocean. It's one of the few provincial campgrounds that can't take really big rigs, the practical limit is about 35 feet here. The campground gate is open all year. From March 1 to October 31 there are full services. From November 1 to February 28 there are reduced services and a reduced fee. Some of the sites are walk-in tent sites. Porteau Cove is popular with scuba divers, it has an artificial reef out front. The campground is located off Hwy 99 some 15 miles north of Horseshoe Bay and 19 km (12 miles) south of Squamish.

KLAHANIE CAMPGROUND *(Open All Year)*

Res. and Info.: (604) 892-3435, klahaniecampground@telus.net, www3.telus.net/Klahanie
Location: 3 Km (2 Miles) S of Squamish, *N 49° 40' 19", W 123° 09' 45"*, 100 Ft

144 Sites – A commercial campground conveniently located just south of Squamish near the Stawamus Chief rock face. Sites here vary in size as they are scattered over a hillside among trees about 100 yards west of the highway. A few will take RVs to 45 feet. Facilities are older but OK and there's a restaurant out front along the highway. The campground is located off Hwy 99 some 39 km (24 miles) north of Horseshoe Bay and 3 km (2 miles) south of Squamish.

STAWAMUS CHIEF PROVINCIAL CAMPGROUND *(Open May 1 to Sept 30)*

Information: (604) 815-4299
Location: 3 Km (2 Miles) S of Squamish, *N 49° 40' 54", W 123° 09' 11"*, 200 Ft

62 Sites – This is primarily a tent camping park used by people who are climbing the Stawamus Chief granite face that looms above the campground. It is run jointly by the province and the Squamish Rock Climber's Association. Most sites are walk-ins, there is a cooking shelter. About 15 sites are accessible by vehicle, a few will take very small RVs to about 22 feet. Outside the open dates noted above the gates of the camping area are closed but tent campers can walk in and camp. The campground is located off Hwy 99 some 40 km (25 miles) north of Horseshoe Bay and 3 km (2 miles) south of Squamish. There is a rest stop along the highway here, a paved road runs about a quarter mile up the hill to the campground.

DRYDEN CREEK RESORT *(Open All Year)*

Res. and Info.: (604) 898-9726, dryden@uniserve.com, www.drydencreek.com
Location: 6 Km (4 Miles) N of Squamish, *N 49° 46' 02", W 123° 08' 13"*, 200 Ft

51 Sites – This is a very pleasant campground set east and well back from the highway so road noise is minimal. There is an excellent area for pitching tents on grass as well as an RV area which will take some 40 foot RVs and has full hookups. Reservations are very important here,

particularly for RVs, this is a very popular place. The campground is located off Hwy 99 some 6 km (4 miles) north of Squamish and 50 km (31 miles) south of Whistler.

ALICE LAKE PROVINCIAL PARK *(Open Mid March to Early Nov - Varies)*

Reservations:	(800) 689-9025, www.discovercamping.ca
Information:	(604) 986-9371
Location:	10 Km (6 Miles) N of Squamish, *N 49° 47' 31", W 123° 07' 34"*, 700 Ft

108 Sites – This large provincial park campground is another popular one due to its location near Vancouver and Whistler and the pleasant location. Sites will take RVs to 45 feet. There are trails around the lake and to three other nearby lakes and two swimming beaches on Alice Lake. Campground gates are closed when snow falls, weather determines the opening and closing dates. Tent camping is allowed when the gates are closed. The campground is located off Hwy 99 some 10 km (6 miles) north of Squamish and 48 km (30 miles) south of Whistler.

BRANDYWINE FALLS PROVINCIAL PARK *(Open May 15 to Oct 15)*

Information:	(250) 334-7559, www.seatoskyparks.com
Location:	40 Km (25 Miles) N of Squamish, *N 50° 02' 15", W 123° 07' 18"*, 1,600 Ft

15 Sites – This is a small provincial campground, a few sites next to a rest area where folks park to take a walk to Brandywine Falls. This is a spectacular 70 meter high waterfall. Sites are small and will take RVs to about 25 feet. Road noise is very noticeable here. During the off season the gate is closed but you can walk in and tent camp. The campground is located off Hwy 99 some 40 km (25 miles) north of Squamish and 16 km (10 miles) south of Whistler.

RIVERSIDE RV RESORT *(Open All Year)*

Res. and Info.:	(877) 905-5533, (604) 905-5533, info@whistlercamping.com, www.whistlercamping.com
Location:	Whistler, *N 50° 08' 11", W 122° 57' 08"*, 2,100 Ft

102 Sites – Whistler has only one RV park and this is it. It's a nice upscale campground with good-sized pull-thru and back-in sites as well as a pleasant tent camping area near the river. It's very important to reserve well ahead if you wish to stay here, Whistler needs more campgrounds. Amenities include an 18-hole putting course, a walking trail that runs past the park, and a shuttle to the village. There's also public bus service available. They have an overflow area (actually their parking lot) if you don't have reservations and can get by without hookups. Parking in the overflow area is pricey however. To reach the campground drive north from Whistler Village on Hwy 99. In 2 km (1.2 miles) turn right on Blackcomb Way and then immediately left to follow the access road to the campground.

NAIRN FALLS PROVINCIAL PARK *(Open April 29 to Oct 2)*

Reservations:	(800) 689-9025, www.discovercamping.ca
Information:	(604) 986-9371
Location:	27 Km (17 Miles) N of Whistler, *N 50° 17' 46", W 122° 49' 04"*, 800 Ft

94 Sites – Nairn Falls is a large provincial park that makes a good alternative in the Whistler area. Because it's some distance on the far side of Whistler from Vancouver it often has room for campers when other campgrounds within driving distance of Whistler are full. May sites are

large enough for RVs to 45 feet and longer. There are several good hiking trails. Although the gates to the campground are locked during the off season it is OK to walk in and tent camp, there is no fee for this. The campground is located off Hwy 99 some 27 km (17 miles) north of Whistler and 3 km (2 miles) south of Pemberton. You may find the dump station in Pemberton to be handy, it's at the visitor center.

CAYOOSH CREEK BC FOREST RECREATION SITE *(Open When Weather Allows)*
Location: 37 Km (23 Miles) SW of Lillooet, *N 50° 29' 55", W 122° 11' 06",* 3,200 Ft

7 Sites – This is a small forest service campground located along Cayoosh Creek, almost under a small bridge. Sites here are very small and the access road is short but narrow. All this makes the campground only suitable for vans, pickup campers, and car campers. The creek-side setting is pretty, there are picnic tables, fire rings, and pit toilets. The campground is on the west side of Hwy 99 near Km 55. This is 60 km (37 miles) from Pemberton and 37 km (23 miles) from Lillooet.

ROGER CREEK BC FOREST RECREATION SITE *(Open When Weather Allows)*
Location: 32 Km (20 Miles) SW of Lillooet, *N 50° 31' 53", W 122° 09' 17",* 3,000 Ft

7 Sites – Another forest service campground along Cayoosh Creek. This one is a little more spacious with room for RVs to 25 feet. There are picnic tables, fire rings, and pit toilets. The campground is on the east side of Hwy 99 near Km 59. This is 65 km (40 miles) from Pemberton and 32 km (20 miles) from Lillooet.

GOTT CREEK BC FOREST RECREATION SITE *(Open When Weather Allows)*
Location: 31 Km (19 Miles) SW of Lillooet, *N 50° 32' 07", W 122° 08' 10",* 2,700 Ft

3 Sites – This is a third forest service campground along Cayoosh Creek. It is a little farther from the road, maybe 100 yards. The three sites will take RVs to 25 feet, two of them are creek-side. There are picnic tables, fire rings, and pit toilets. The campground is on the west side of Hwy 99 near Km 60. This is 66 km (41 miles) from Pemberton and 31 km (19 miles) from Lillooet.

COTTONWOOD CREEK BC FOREST RECREATION SITE *(Open When Weather Allows)*
Location: 23 Km (14 Miles) SW of Lillooet, *N 50° 34' 59", W 122° 05' 30",* 2,200 Ft

12 Sites – A fourth forest service campground along Cayoosh Creek. Cottonwood will take carefully driving 30-foot RVs and there's a circular drive although the turns are tight for 30-footers. There are picnic tables, fire rings, and pit toilets. The campground is on the west side of Hwy 99 near Km 68. This is 74 km (46 miles) from Pemberton and 23 km (14 miles) from Lillooet.

CINNAMON BC FOREST RECREATION SITE *(Open When Weather Allows)*
Location: 19 Km (12 Miles) SW of Lillooet, *N 50° 36' 46", W 122° 06' 20",* 2,100 Ft

11 Sites – This is the one of the largest of the forest service recreation sites along Cayoosh Creek. It can take RVs to 35 feet, the sites are located off a circular drive. There are picnic tables, fire rings, and pit toilets. The campground is on the west side of Hwy 99 near Km 72. This is 79 km (49 miles) from Pemberton and 19 km (12 miles) from Lillooet.

SETON DAM CAMPGROUND – BC HYDRO *(Open When Weather Allows)*

Location: 5 Km (3 Miles) W of Lillooet, *N 50° 40' 04", W 121° 58' 35"*, 800 Ft

42 Sites – BC Hydro provides a very nice free campground just outside Lillooet near the Seton Lake Dam. Site are back-ins and will take RVs to 30 feet. There is a swimming beach nearby. From the intersection of Hwy 99 and Hwy 12 on the far side (east) of the Fraser River from Lillooet drive west across the river. Follow Hwy 99 for 5.5 km (3.4 miles), the campground entrance is on the left.

CAYOOSH CREEK CAMPGROUND *(Open April 15 to Oct 30 - Varies)*

Res. and Info.:   (877) 748-2628, www.cayooshcampground.com
Location: Lillooet, *N 50° 40' 52", W 121° 55' 44"*, 500 Ft

41 Sites – This tidy little campground just outside Lillooet is the best place in the area for big rigs and not bad for tenters either. Tents are pitched in a grassy field. There are pull-thru sites that will take 45 foot RVs with no problem, they have electric and water hookups and there is a dump station. From the intersection of Hwy 99 and Hwy 12 on the east side of the Fraser River from Lillooet drive west across the river. Follow Hwy 99 for .8 km (.5 mile), the campground entrance is on the left.

WILLOWS RESORT *(Open April 1 to Oct 31 - Varies)*

Res. and Info.:   (250) 256-0429, rivergirl@uniserve.com
Location: 6 Km (4 Miles) S of Lillooet, *N 50° 38' 59", W 121° 52' 53"*, 700 Ft

15 Sites – This is a very small older RV park that recently changed hands and is being re-furbished by its enthusiastic new owners. There are new restrooms with good showers and the hookups are gradually being updated. About a third of the sites have electric, water and sewer hookups. These are back-in sites, several can take RVs to 45 feet. Sites offer views of the Fraser River canyon across the small highway. From the intersection of Hwy 99 and Hwy 12 near Lillooet drive south toward Lytton for 5.3 km (3.3 miles), the campground entrance is on your left.

FRASER COVE CAMPGROUND *(Open April 15 to Oct 30 - Varies)*

Res. and Info.:   (250) 573-5869, camping@frasercove.com, www.frasercove.com
Location: 2 Km (1 Mile) NE of Lillooet, *N 50° 42' 31", W 121° 54' 40"*, 700 Ft

20 Sites – This campground has the most scenic location of all of the campgrounds in Lil-looet. It winds down the bluff to the river on the bank opposite Lillooet. The old walking bridge across the river is just upstream and provides a handy way to walk in to town. Some sites will take RVs to 40 feet but maneuvering room is limited and there is a switchback, disconnect your tow car before entering. You might even walk in and take a quick look before committing your-self. This is usually a self-service campground with no attendant on site. From the intersection of Hwy 12 and Hwy 99 near Lillooet drive north on Hwy 12 toward Cache Creek and Clinton for 2.1 km (1.3 miles), the entrance is on the left.

MARBLE CANYON PROVINCIAL PARK *(Open All Year)*

Information: (250) 378-5334
Location: 48 Km (30 Miles) NE of Lillooet, *N 50° 50' 1", W 121° 41' 35"*, 2,600 Ft

26 Sites – This small lakeside campground can only take tent campers and RVs to 25 feet. There's swimming in the lakes. The campground gate is open all year. From April 28 to October 1 there are services and a fee, outside that time services are limited and there is no fee. The campground is on Hwy 12 northeast of Lillooet. It's 48 km (30 miles) from Lillooet, 27 km (17 miles) from the intersection with Hwy 97 between Cache Creek and Clinton.

YOHO NATIONAL PARK AND GOLDEN

Yoho National Park is one of the many parks clustered in Canada's Rocky Mountains. It encompasses the region in which Hwy 1 and the Canadian Pacific Railroad make the steep climb up into the Rockies toward Kicking Horse Pass.

The park visitor center is just off Hwy 1 in the small town of Field. There are two campgrounds near each other and not far off the highway a few miles to the northeast. The park has another campground, Hoodoo Creek, off Hwy 1 near the western entrance to the park.

One of the more popular attractions in the park is **Lake O'hara**. You can only access the lake and its trail system using a shuttle bus or by hiking the 12 km (7.5 miles) to the lake. Reservations are a necessity if you want to ride the bus, this is a popular destination and the number of visitors is limited. No reservation is necessary, however, if you walk. The lake us usually icebound until mid July.

Easier to reach is beautiful **Emerald Lake**, a 10 km (6 mile) drive north of the highway. There's a trail system here, the most popular is the 5 km (3 mile) trail around the lake.

Golden (population 4,000) is actually outside the park but is the main population and service center in the area. The town is on the banks of the Columbia River which is flowing north at this point. This is an attractive little town, known for its whitewater rafting and hang-gliding.

Remember that if you decide to stay in the campgrounds inside Yoho National Park you will have to pay the park fee in addition to the campground fee listed below.

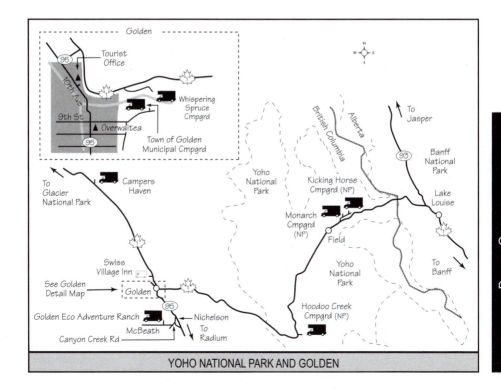

YOHO NATIONAL PARK AND GOLDEN

BRITISH COLUMBIA

CAMPERS HAVEN *(Open May 1 to Nov 15)*

Res. and Info.: (800) 563-6122, (250) 340-8482, www.campershaven.ca
Location: 26 Km (16 Miles) W of Golden, *N 51° 29' 22", W 117° 09' 43"*, 2,600 Ft

76 Sites – If you're looking for a quiet place to pull off the road with big sites and easy access Campers Haven fills the bill. The campground has big sites to 75 feet with full hookups. Parking is on grass. The entrance road intersects Hwy 1 some 26 km (16 miles) west of Golden, the campground is .5 km (.3 mile) from the highway so road noise is no problem.

TOWN OF GOLDEN MUNICIPAL CAMPGROUND *(Open May 15 to Oct 15 - Varies)*

Res. and Info.: (250) 344-5412
Location: Golden, *N 51° 17' 50", W 116° 57' 05"*, 2,600 Ft

70 Sites – An excellent place to stay if you want to explore the town of Golden. This is a riverside campground but you're more likely to think of it as a railroad-side campground since the river is hidden from view by a dike but the railroad can still be easily heard as trains pass on the far side of the river. There are sites in a wooded area that are good for tents as well as sites suitable for RVs to 45 feet, both with and without hookups. To reach the campground from Hwy 1 head south on Golden's main street, 10th Ave. You'll cross the bridge over the river, then in two blocks turn left on 9th Ave and follow it .8 km (.5 mile) to the campground.

GOLDEN ECO ADVENTURE RANCH *(Open April 15 to Oct 30 - Varies)*

Res. and Info.: (250) 344-6825, gear@cablerocket.com, www.goldenadventurepark.com
Location: 6 Km (4 Miles) S of Golden, *N 51° 14' 34", W 116° 55' 22"*, 2,600 Ft

69 Sites - There are two separate campgrounds set in trees sharing a very upscale and brand-new restroom and services building. One of the campgrounds is for tent campers (with vehicle parking at the sites) and the other has big RV sites. Most are pull-thrus with water and electric hookups, that will take RVs over 45 feet long. Sites are separated by vegetation so you're not competing with your neighbor for space to extend your awning. There's also a hang-gliding landing zone out in front of the campground, free entertainment! Drive south from Golden on Hwy 95 for 6 km (4 miles) from the bridge over the Columbia in town. Turn right on Nickelson road and after another .8 km (.5 mile) turn right on Canyon Creek Road. Drive another .5 km (.3 mile), turn right on McBeath Road and you'll soon see the long entrance driveway on your right stretching across a field to the offices and then beyond to the campgrounds in the trees.

WHISPERING SPRUCE CAMPGROUND *(Open April 15 to Oct 15)*

Res. and Info.: (250) 344-6680, www.whisperingspruce.net
Location: 2 Km (1 Mile) E of Golden, *N 51° 18' 02", W 116° 56' 51"*, 2,900 Ft

123 Sites – This is an older campground that was obviously a KOA at one time. It's located just off the highway to the east of town in a subdivision with motels and other businesses. Watch for a herd of urban bighorn sheep in the neighborhood, they're usually around. There are a variety of site types including tent sites on grass and long pull-thrus suitable for RVs to 45 feet. Follow Hwy 1 east from the main Golden exit for .8 miles, turn right and follow the access road for .3 miles to the campground.

HOODOO CREEK CAMPGROUND – YOHO NATIONAL PARK *(Open July 15 to Sept 15 - Varies)*

Information: (250) 343-6783
Location: 21 Km (13 Miles) W of Field, *N 51° 13' 35", W 116° 34' 26"*, 3,600 Ft

106 Sites – This campground is the lowest in the park and easy to access off Hwy 1. Watch for the entrance on the east side of the highway just 3.5 km (2.2 miles) after you enter the park from the west, 21 km (13 miles) east of Field.

MONARCH CAMPGROUND – YOHO NATIONAL PARK *(Open All Year)*

Information: (250) 343-6783
Location: 5 Km (3 Miles) E of Field, *N 51° 25' 15", W 116° 26' 31"*, 4,200 Ft

36 Sites – Monarch is a smaller campground that seems to act as an overflow area for the nearby Kicking Horse Campground. Actually, this is a very nice campground in its own right, better than Kicking Horse in some ways, including convenience. Some sites here are walk-in tent sites and the rest are back-in sites suitable for RVs to about 30 feet although there are a couple sites that will take RVs to 40 or perhaps even 45 feet. In winter the campground entrance area is kept plowed and the vault toilets open so that it serves as a winter campsite. The campground is located along the Yoho Valley Road which goes north off Hwy 1 some 3.1 km (1.9 miles) east of the Field Visitor Center. After turning you'll see a sani-dump on the left in .5 km (.3 miles) and the campground entrance on the left in .8 km (.5 miles).

KICKING HORSE CAMPGROUND – YOHO NATIONAL PARK *(Open June 1 to Oct 10)*

Information: (250) 343-6783
Location: 3 Km (2 Miles) E of Field, *N 51° 25' 23", W 116° 26' 06"*, 4,200 Ft

92 Sites – A large campground with a variety of sites including both tent sites and long pull-thrus in an open field suitable for RVs longer than 45 feet. The campground is located along the Yoho Valley Road which goes north off Hwy 1 some 3.1 km (1.9 miles) east of the Field Visitor Center. After turning you'll see a sani-dump on the left in .5 km (.3 miles), the Monarch Campground entrance on the left in .8 km (.5 miles), and the Kicking Horse Campground is to the left in 1.1 km (.7 miles).

Information Resources

See our Internet site at www.rollinghomes.com for Internet information links.

All British Columbia

BC Ferries, 1112 Fort Street, Victoria, BC V8V 4V2; (250) 386-3431 or (888) 223-3779

Banff National Park

Banff National Park, Box 900, Banff, AB T1L 1K2; (403) 762-1550

Banff Information Centre, 225 Banff Avenue, Banff, AB T1L 1K2; Parks Canada (403) 762-1550, Banff/Lake Louise Tourism Bureau (403) 762-8421

Banff Park Museum, Banff Avenue Next To Bow Bridge; (403) 762-1558

Lake Louise Visitor Centre, By the Sampson Mall, Lake Louise; (403) 522-3833

Whyte Museum of the Canadian Rockies, 111 Bear Street, Banff, AB; (403) 762-2291

Barkerville and Wells

Wells Visitor Info Centre, 4120 Pooley St (Box 123), Wells, BC V0K 2R0; (250) 994-2323; vic@wellsbc.com

Campbell River

Campbell River Visitor Info Centre, Shopper's Row (Box 400), Campbell River, BC V9W 5B6; (250) 287-4636

MV Uchuck III, PO Box 57, Gold River, BC V0P 1G0; (250) 283-2515; info@mvuchuck.com

Cape Scott

Information at (250) 949-6538

Central Kootenay

Castlegar Visitor Info Centre, 1995 – 6th Ave, Castlegar, BC V1N 4B7; (250) 365-6313; cdcoc@shawbiz.ca

Rossland Visitor Info Centre, Junction of Hwys 3B and 22 (Box 26), Rossland, BC V0G 1Y0; (250) 362-7722; museum@rossland.com

Trail Visitor Info Centre, 200 – 1199 Bay Ave, Trail, BC V1R 4A4; (250) 368-3144; tcoc@netidea.com

Cowichan Valley

Chemainus Visitor Info Centre, 9796 Willow St (Box 575), Chemainus, BC V0R 1K0; (250) 246-3944; ccoc@islandnet.com

Cowichan Native Village, 200 Cowichan Way, Duncan, BC V9L 6P4; (250) 746-8119 or (877) 746-8119

Duncan Visitor Info Centre, 381A Trans Canada Hwy, Duncan, BC V9L 3R5; (250) 746-4636; visitorinfo@duncancc.bc.ca

Ladysmith Tourist/Visitor Info Booth, 132C Roberts St (Box 598), Ladysmith, BC V9G 1A4; (250) 245-2112; info@ladysmithcofc.com

Lake Cowichan Tourist/Visitor Info Booth, 125 C South Shore Rd (Box 860) Lake Cowichan, BC V0R 2G0; (250) 749-3244; info@lakecowichan.ca

Dawson Creek

Dawson Creek Visitor Info Centre, 900 Alaska Ave, Dawson Creek, BC V1G 4T6; (250) 782-9595; info@tourismdawsoncreek.com

Fernie

Fernie Visitor Info Centre, 102 Commerce Rd, Fernie, BC V0B 1M5; (250) 423-6868; info@ferniechamber.com

Glacier National Park

Mt Revelstoke and Glacier National Park, Box 350, Revelstoke, BC V0E 2S0; (250) 837-7500

Rogers Pass Discovery Centre; Hwy 1, 69 Km (43 Miles) East of Revelstoke; (250) 837-7500

Harrison Hot Springs

Harrison Hot Springs Tourist/Visitor Info Booth, 499 Hot Springs Rd (Box 255), Harrison Hot Springs, BC V0M 1K0; (604) 796-5581; harrisoninfo@shaw.ca

BRITISH COLUMBIA

Hope

Hope Visitor Info Centre, 919 Water Ave (Box 370), Hope, BC V0X 1L0; (604) 869-2021; destinationhope@telus.net

Jasper National Park

Jasper National Park, Box 10, Jasper, AB T0E 1E0; (780) 852-6176

Icefield Centre (Info Desk), 103 Km (64 Miles) South of Jasper on Icefield Parkway; (780) 852-6288

Jasper Information Centre, 500 Connaught Drive, Jasper, AB; Parks Canada (780) 852-6176, Jasper Tourism and Commerce (780) 852-6176

Jasper-Yellowhead Museum, 400 Pyramid Lake Rd, Jasper, AB; (780) 852-3013

Kamloops

Kamloops Visitor Info Centre, 1290 West Trans Canada Hwy, Kamloops, BC V2C 6R3; (250) 374-3377; tourism@kamloopschamber.bc.ca

Kootenay National Park and Radium Hot Springs

Kootenay National Park, Box 220, Radium Hot Springs, BC V0A 1M0; (250) 347-9331

Kootenay Park Lodge Visitor Centre, Hwy 93, 63 Km (39 Miles) East of Radium Hot Springs

Radium Hot Springs Pools, Hwy 93, 3 Km (2 Miles) East of Radium Hot Springs; (250) 347-2100

Radium Hot Springs Visitor Info Centre, 7556 Main St E (Box 225), Radium Hot Springs, BC V0A 1M0; Parks Canada: (250) 347-9331, Chamber of Commerce: (250) 347-9331; info@radiumhotspringschamber.ca

Nanaimo

Nanaimo Visitor Info Centre, Beban House 2290 Bowen Rd, Nanaimo, BC V9T 3K7; (250) 756-0106; info@tourismnanaimo.com

New Hazelton and Kitwanga

Hazelton Visitor Info Centre, Junction of Hwys 16 and 62, 4070 – 9th Ave (Box 340), New Hazelton, BC V0J 2J0; (250) 842-6071; nhazel@uniserve.com

Oceanside

Parksville Visitor Info Centre, 1275 East Island Hwy (Box 99), Parksville, BC V9P 2G3; (250) 248-3613; info@chamber.parksville.bc.ca

Qualicum Beach Visitor Info Centre, 2711 West Island Hwy, Qualicum Beach, BC V9K 2C4; (250) 752-9532; info@qualicum,bc.ca

Okanagan Valley

Kelowna Visitor Info Centre, 544 Harvey Ave, Kelowna, BC V1Y 6C9; (250) 861-1515; info@tourismkelowna.com

Keremeos Tourist/Visitor Info Booth, 427 – 7 Ave (Box 490), Keremos, BC V0X 1N0; (250) 499-5225; siminfo@nethop.net

Oliver Visitor Info Centre, 36250 – 93rd St (CPR Station) (Box 460), Oliver, BC V0H 1T0; (250) 498-6321; info@oliverchamber.bc.ca

Osoyoos Visitor Info Centre, Junction of Hwys 3 and 97 (Box 500), Osoyoos, BC V0H 1V0; (250) 495-5070; tourism@osoyoos.ca

Peachland Tourist/Visitor Info Booth, 5812 Beach Ave, Peachland, BC V0H 1X7; (250) 767-2455; peachlandinfo@shawcable.com

Penticton Visitor Info Centre, 553 Railway St, Penticton; BC (250) 493-4055; visitors@penticton.org

Summerland Visitor Info Centre, 15600 Hwy 97 (Box 130), Summerland, BC V0H 1Z0; (250) 494-2686; summerlandchamber@shawbiz.ca

Vernon Visitor Info Centre, 701 Hwy 97S, Vernon, BC; (250) 542-1415; info@vernontourism.com

Westbank Visitor Info Centre, 4 – 2375 Pamela Rd, Westbank, BC V4T 2H9; (250) 768-3378; chamber@westbankchamber.com

Port Alberni

Alberni Valley Visitor Info Centre, 2533 Redford St, RR 2, Site 215, Com 10, Port Alberni, BC V9Y 7L6; (250) 724-6535 or (866) 576-3662; avcoc@alberni.net

MV Lady Rose, Lady Rose Marine Services, 5425 Argyle Street (PO Box 188), Port Alberni, BC V9Y 7M7; (250) 723-8313 or (800) 663-7192

Port Hardy

Port Hardy Visitor Info Centre, 7250 Market St (Box 249), Port Hardy, BC V0N 2P0; (250) 949-7622; phcc@cablerocket.com

Port McNeill and Telegraph Cove

Port McNeill Visitor Info Centre, 351 Shelley Crescent (PO Box 129), Port McNeill, BC V0N 2R0; (250) 956-3131; pmcc@island.net

Prince George

Prince George Visitor Info Centre, 1300 – 1st Ave, Suite 201, Prince George, BC V2L 2Y3; (250) 562-3700; tourism@initiativespg.com

Prince Rupert

Prince Rupert Visitor Info Centre, Suite 100, 215 Cow Bay Rd, Prince Rupert, BC V8J 1A2; (250) 624-5637; prinfo@citytel.net

Quesnel

Quesnel Visitor Info Centre, 703 Carson Ave, Quesnel, BC V2J 2B6; (250) 992-8716; qvisitor@quesnelbc.com

Revelstoke

Revelstoke Visitor Info Centre, 204 Campbell Ave (Box 490), Revelstoke, BC V0E 2S0; (250) 837-4223; revinfo@telus.net

South Cariboo Region

Cache Creek Tourist/Visitor Info Booth, Junction of Hwy 97 & 99 (Box 878), Cache Creek, BC V0K 1H0; (250) 457-9722; hhcr@goldtrail.com

South Cariboo Visitor Info Centre, 422 Cariboo Hwy 97 (Box 340), 100 Mile House, BC V0K 2E0; (250) 395-5353; visitors@dist100milehouse.bc.ca

Shuswap

Salmon Arm Visitor Info Centre, 200 Trans Canada Hwy SW (Box 999), Salmon Arm, BC V1E 4P2; (250) 832-2230; info@visitsalmonarm.com

Sicamous Visitor Info Centre, 11-Finlayson St (Box 346), Sicamous, BC V0E 2V0; (250) 836-3313; sicamouschamber@cablelan.net

Sorrento Visitor Info Centre, 2405B Centennial Dr (Box 7), Sorrento, BC V0E 2W0; (250) 675-3515; sorrentochamber@telus.net

Smithers

Smithers Visitor Info Centre, 1411 Court St (Box 2379), Smithers, BC V0J 2N0; (250) 847-5072; info@tourismsmithers.com

Sunshine Coast (Lower)

Gibsons Visitor Info Centre, 900 Gibsons Way, Unit 21 (Box 1190) Gibsons, BC V0N 1V0; (604) 886-2325; gibsonsvic@dccnet.com

Sechelt Visitor Info Centre, 5790 Teredo St (PO Box 1069), Sechelt, BC V0N 3A0, (604) 885-1036; visitorinfo@dccnet.com

Sunshine Coast (Upper)

Powell River Visitor Info Centre, 4690 Marine Ave, Powell River, BC V8A 2L1; (604) 485-4701; info@discoverpowellriver.com

Thompson and Fraser Canyons

Hells' Gate Air Tram, 43111 Trans Canada Hwy (Box 129), Boston Bar, BC V0X 1L0; (604) 867-9277

Lytton Visitor Info Centre, 400 Fraser St (Box 460), Lytton, BC V0K 1Z0; (250) 455-2523; lyttoncc@goldtrail.com

BRITISH COLUMBIA

Tofino, Ucluelet and the Pacific Rim National Park

Tofino Visitor Info Centre, 1426 Pacific Rim Hwy (Box 249), Tofino, BC V0R 2Z0; (250) 725-3414; tofino@island.net

Ucluelet Visitor Info Centre, 2791 Pacific Rim Hwy (Box 428), Ucluelet, BC V0R 3A0; (250) 726-4600; info@uclueletinfo.com

Valley of a Thousand Peaks

Cranbrook Visitor Info Centre, 2279 Cranbrook St N (Box 84), Cranbrook, BC V1C 4H6; (250) 426-5914; cbkchamber@cyberlink.bc.ca

Kimberly Visitor Info Centre, 150 Spokane St, Kimberley, BC V1A 2E4; (250) 427-3666; info@kimberleychamber.ca

Vancouver

Delta Visitor Info Centre, 6201 60th Ave, Delta, BC V4K 4E2; (604) 946-4232; tourism@delta-chamber.com

Grouse Mountain Resorts Ltd., 6400 Nancy Greene Way, North Vancouver, BC V7R 4K9; (604) 984-06691; info@grousemountain.com

Langley Visitor Info Centre, 5761 Glover Rd, Langley, BC V3A 8M8; (604) 530-6656; chamber@langleychamber.com

North Vancouver Visitor Info Centre, 102-124 West 1st St, North Vancouver, BC V7N 3M3; (604) 987-4488; admin@nvchamber.bc.ca

Telus World of Science, 1455 Quebec Street, Vancouver, BC V6A 3Z7; (604) 443-7443; info@scienceworld.ca

Vancouver Maritime Museum, 1605 Ogden Ave, Vancouver, BC V6J 1A3; (604) 257-8300

Vancouver Museum, 1100 Chestnut Street, Vancouver, BC V6J 3J9; (604) 736-4431

Vancouver Visitor Info Centre, Plaza Level, 200 Burrard St, Vancouver, BC V6C 3L6; (604) 683-2000

Victoria

Saanich Peninsula Visitor Info Centre, 10382 Patricia Bay Hwy (Box 2014), Sidney, BC V8L 3S3; (250) 656-0525; spcoc2@telus.net

Victoria Visitor Info Centre, 812 Wharf Street, Victoria, BC V8W 1T3; (250) 953-2033; info@tourismvictoria.com

Wells Gray Provincial Park and Clearwater

Clearwater Visitor Info Centre, 425 E Yellowhead Hwy (Box 1988), RR 1, Clearwater, BC V0E 1N0; (250) 674-2646; cwchamber@mercuryspeed.com

Whistler and the Sea to Sky Highway

Pemberton Visitor Info Centre, Hwy 99 (Box 370), Pemberton, BC V0N 2L0; (604) 894-6477; info@pembertonchamber.com

Squamish Visitor Info Centre, 37950 Cleveland Ave (Box 1009), Squamish, BC V0N 3G0; (604) 892-9244; information@squamishchamber.com

Whistler Visitor Info Centre, 201- 4230 Gateway Dr, Whistler, BC V0N 1B4; (604) 932-5922; info@whistlerchamber.com

Lillooet Visitor Info Centre, 790 Main St (Box 441), Lillooet, BC V0K 1V0; (250) 256-4308; lillmuseum@cablelan.net

Yoho National Park and Golden

Yoho National Park, Box 99, Field, BC V0A 1G0; (250) 343-6783

Golden Visitor Info Centre, 100-10th Ave N (Box 1320), Golden, BC V0A 1H0, (250) 344-6688; info@goldenchamber.bc.ca

Yoho Visitor Centre, In Field, BC; (250) 343- 6783

MAP INDEX

TERRI AND MIKE IN VANCOUVER'S STANLEY PARK

ABOUT THE AUTHORS

For the last fourteen years Terri and Mike Church have traveled in the western U.S., Alaska, Canada, Mexico, and Europe. Most of this travel has been in RVs, a form of travel they love. It's affordable and comfortable; the perfect way to see interesting places.

Over the years they discovered that few guidebooks were available with the essential day-to-day information that camping travelers need when they are in unfamiliar surroundings. *Pacific Northwest Camping Destinations, Southwest Camping Destinations, Traveler's Guide To Alaskan Camping, Traveler's Guide to Mexican Camping, Traveler's Guide to Camping Mexico's Baja, Traveler's Guide to European Camping, RV* and *Car Camping Vacations in Europe,* are designed to be the guidebooks that the authors tried to find when they first traveled to these places.

Terri and Mike live full-time in an RV – traveling, writing new books, and working to keep these guidebooks as up-to-date as possible. The books are written and prepared for printing using laptop computers while on the road.

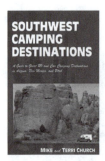

Southwest Camping Destinations
6" x 9" Paperback, 416 Pages, Over 100 Maps
ISBN 0-9749471-4-8

First Edition - Available September 2006

Bryce Canyon, Carlsbad Caverns, the Grand Canyon, and Mesa Verde are among the 100 destinations covered in this travel guide for RVers and car campers. Native American sites and desert habitats are also of interest in this region, making it a great vacation destination for families with children. Maps are provided for each destination along with descriptions of tourist attractions and listings for more than 500 traveler campgrounds.

For those who want to escape to a warm climate in the winter there is a special "snowbird" chapter which gives details on top snowbird destinations in the southwest. Over 350 campgrounds are compared in destination like Palm Springs, Las Vegas, Lake Havasu and Parker, Needles and Laughlin, Yuma, Quartzsite, Phoenix, Mesa, Apache Junction, Casa Grande, Tucson, and Benson. This analysis is accompanied by maps showing the exact locations of campgrounds in these favorite destinations.

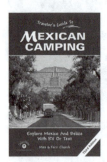

Traveler's Guide To Mexican Camping
6" x 9" Paperback, 480 Pages, Over 250 Maps
ISBN 0-9749471-2-1

Third Edition - Copyright 2005

Mexico, one of the world's most interesting and least expensive travel destinations, is just across the southern U.S. border. It offers warm sunny weather all winter long, beautiful beaches, colonial cities, and excellent food. Best of all, you can easily and economically visit Mexico in your own car or RV.

The third edition of *Traveler's Guide To Mexican Camping* is now even better! It has become the bible for Mexican campers. With this book you will cross the border and travel Mexico like a veteran. It is designed to make your trip as simple and trouble-free as possible. Maps show the exact location of campgrounds and the text gives written driving instructions as well as information regarding the size of RV suitable for each campground. In addition to camping and campground information the guide also includes information about cities, roads and driving, trip preparation, border crossing, vehicle care, shopping, and entertainment.

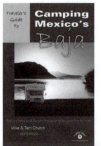

Traveler's Guide To Camping Mexico's Baja
6" x 9" Paperback, 256 Pages, Over 65 Maps
ISBN 0-9749471-5-6

Third Edition - Available August 2006

Sun, sand, and clear blue water are just three of the many reasons more and more RVers are choosing Mexico's Baja as a winter destination. The Baja is fun, easy, and the perfect RVing getaway. Only a few miles south of the border you'll find many great campsites, some on beaches where you'll camp just feet from the water.

Traveler's Guide To Camping Mexico's Baja starts by giving you the Baja-related information from our popular book *Traveler's Guide To Mexican Camping*. It then goes further. We've added more campgrounds, expanded the border crossing section, and given even more information about towns, roads, and recreational opportunities. Unlike the Mexico book, the Baja book is arranged geographically following Transpensinsular Highway 1 south. The book also covers nearby Puerto Peñasco. Like all our books, this one features easy-to-follow maps showing exactly how to find every campground listed.

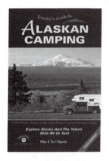

Traveler's Guide To Alaskan Camping
6" x 9" Paperback, 448 Pages, Over 100 Maps
ISBN 0-9749471-1-3

Third Edition - Copyright 2005

Alaska, the dream trip of a lifetime! Be prepared for something spectacular. Alaska is one fifth the size of the entire United States, it has 17 of the 20 highest peaks in the U.S., 33,904 miles of shoreline, and has more active glaciers and ice fields than the rest of the inhabited world. In addition to some of the most magnificent scenery the world has to offer, Alaska is chock full of an amazing variety of wildlife. Fishing, hiking, kayaking, rafting, hunting, and wildlife viewing are only a few of the many activities which will keep you outside during the long summer days.

Traveler's Guide To Alaskan Camping makes this dream trip to Alaska as easy as camping in the "Lower 48". It includes almost 500 campgrounds throughout Alaska and on the roads north in Canada with full campground descriptions, appropriate RV size for each campground, and maps showing exact locations. It also is filled with suggested things to do and see including fishing holes, hiking trails, canoe trips, wildlife viewing opportunities, and much more.

Traveler's Guide To European Camping
6" x 9" Paperback, 640 Pages, Over 400 Maps
ISBN 0-9652968-8-1

Third Edition - Copyright 2004

Over 350 campgrounds including the best choice in every important European city are described in detail and directions are given for finding them. In many cases information about convenient shopping, entertainment and sports opportunities is included.

This guide will tell you how to rent, lease, or buy a rig in Europe or ship your own from home. It contains the answers to questions about the myriad details of living, driving, and camping in Europe. In addition to camping and campground information *Traveler's Guide To European Camping* gives you invaluable details about the history and sights you will encounter. This information will help you plan your itinerary and enjoy yourself more when you are on the road. Use the information in this book to travel Europe like a native. Enjoy the food, sights, and people of Europe. Go for a week, a month, a year. Europe can fill your RV or camping vacation seasons for many years to come!

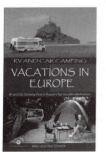

RV and Car Camping Vacations in Europe
6" x 9" Paperback, 320 Pages, Over 140 Maps
ISBN 0-9652968-9-X

First Edition - Copyright 2004

People from North America love to visit Europe on their vacations. One great way to travel in Europe is by RV or car, spending the night in convenient and inexpensive campgrounds. It's a way to travel inexpensively and get off the beaten tourist trail. It's also a great way to meet Europeans. Many of them travel the same way!

Most of us lead busy lives with little time to spend on planning an unusual vacation trip. With this book a camping vacation in Europe is easy. It tells how to arrange a rental RV or car from home, when to go and what to take with you. It explains the process of picking up the rental vehicle and turning it back in when you're ready to head for home. There's also information about shopping, driving, roads, and other things that you should know before you arrive. Then it describes a series of tours, each taking from a week to two weeks. The ten tours cover much of Western Europe and even the capitals of the Central European countries. The book has details about the routes and roads, the campgrounds to use, and what to do and see while you are there.

To order complete the following and send to:

Rolling Homes Press
161 Rainbow Dr., #6157
Livingston, TX 77399-1061

Name_____

Address_____

City_____State_____Zip_____

Telephone_____

Description	Qty	Price	Subtotal
Pacific Northwest Camping Destinations	_____	$19.95	_____
Southwest Camping Destinations	_____	$19.95	_____
Traveler's Guide To Alaskan Camping	_____	$21.95	_____
Traveler's Guide To Mexican Camping	_____	$21.95	_____
Traveler's Guide To Camping Mexico's Baja	_____	$14.95	_____
Traveler's Guide To European Camping	_____	$24.95	_____
RV and Car Camping Vacations in Europe	_____	$16.95	_____

Subtract - Multiple Title Discounts

3 Book Set (Any 3 Different Titles Shown Above)	**-10.00**	_____
4 Book Set (Any 4 Different Titles Shown Above)	**-15.00**	_____
5 Book Set (Any 5 Different Titles Shown Above)	**-20.00**	_____
6 Book Set (Any 6 Different Titles Shown Above)	**-25.00**	_____
7 Book Set (All 7 Titles)	**-30.00**	_____

Method of Payment
- ❏ Check
- ❏ Visa
- ❏ Mastercard

Order total _____
Shipping: 5.00 *
Total: _____

Credit Card #_____   Exp. date_____

Signature_____

To order by phone call (425) 822-7846
Have your VISA or MC ready
U.S. Dollars or MC/VISA only for non-U.S. orders
Rolling Homes Press is not responsible for taxes or duty on books shipped outside the U.S.

*$5 shipping regardless of quantity ordered for all orders sent to the same address in
the U.S. or Canada. Actual cost for multiple books shipped to other destinations.

Visit our web site at **www.rollinghomes.com**

For mail orders allow approximately 1 month for delivery, for phone orders allow 2 weeks for delivery